IMMIGRATION AND RACE RELATIONS IN BRITAIN, 1960–1967

The Institute of Race Relations is an unofficial and non-political body, founded in England in 1958 to encourage and facilitate the study of the relations between races everywhere. The Institute is precluded by the Memorandum and Articles of its incorporation from expressing a corporate view. The opinions expressed in this work are those of the authors.

Immigration and Race Relations in Britain 1960–1967

SHEILA PATTERSON

Published for the
Institute of Race Relations, London
OXFORD UNIVERSITY PRESS
LONDON NEW YORK
1969

Oxford University Press, Ely House, London W. 1
GLASGOW NEW YORK TORONTO MELBOURNE WELLINGTON
CAPE TOWN SALISBURY IBADAN NAIROBI LUSAKA ADDIS ABABA
BOMBAY CALCUTTA MADRAS KARACHI LAHORE DACCA
KUALA LUMPUR SINGAPORE HONG KONG TOKYO

PRINTED IN GREAT BRITAIN
BY EBENEZER BAYLIS AND SON, LTD.
THE TRINITY PRESS, WORCESTER, AND LONDON

FOREWORD

It has long been clear that an annual summary is needed of the main events and trends in race relations in Britain. The Institute's *Newsletter* does contain a monthly report on Britain, but this is based mainly on current press cuttings and, just because it is published monthly, it needs to be supplemented by a view in longer perspective. A year book of race relations in Britain was therefore something that we decided to produce.

But the first volume of a series of year books presents problems. It would be inadequate if it dealt only with the year immediately before the closing date to which it referred. How far back, then, ought it to go? And in what detail should it attempt to summarize the past? These are questions that do not admit of definite answers. It would be arbitrary to fix for the opening volume a period beyond which it could never stray. We decided therefore to produce a book that would provide the necessary data and baseline from which the year books might be developed. Sheila Patterson, as the editor of the *Newsletter* since 1961, was clearly the best person—perhaps the only person—to do this, and she has attempted to produce a book which will be at the same time a starting point or briefing for newcomers to the field, a useful work of reference in itself, and the introduction to an annual series.

The task of selection would in any case be a difficult one if the book was to be of a reasonable size. But it was made a good deal more difficult by the fact that race relations in Britain are clearly in a highly crucial stage of development. Until—to take a fairly arbitrary point in time—the autumn of 1964, the general public was only intermittently aware of the fact that Britain was becoming a multi-racial society, perhaps in serious danger of being split into two nations of first-class and second-class citizens. The first shock of this knowledge has been absorbed; it was succeeded by an uneasy and superficial consensus between the official views of the two larger parties, though in each there is a wide range and a divergent fringe at either end of the spectrum of opinion. In both parties, the leaders judge that they are themselves more ready to face the facts and needs of the situation than the rank and file of their constituents. In both parties there are dissident groups of the right and of the left. But the area of overlapping between the two is considerable. The party in power has taken some steps to amend the situation. We have a Race Relations Board, a Race Relations Act, and we have a National Committee for Commonwealth Immigrants. There is sharp criticism of all three, particularly of the inadequacy of the Act which is in force at the moment of writing, but which is shortly about to be amended. From both extremes, it is argued, from opposite points of view, that immigration policy exercises a more vigorous influence on race relations than attempts at conciliation. From one extreme it is argued that the immigration of coloured people should stop all together; from the other, that the present restrictions are in themselves discriminatory and vitiate the Act. It is apparent that public feeling can quickly be inflamed; it may be that it is also open to persuasion by enlightened leadership. Thus the situation is fluid, rapidly changing, open to many dangers. This has not made it easy to compile a summary. This volume carries the story to the summer of 1967 and will be succeeded by a series of year books.

The last four years have thus seen a transformation of the national scene. It would be contrary to all experience to suppose that the machinery now contemplated will be final; there are bound to be considerable modifications and these are likely to change the scope of the Institute's work. But there will surely continue to be a need for a body whose purpose is to stimulate and to some extent interpret research, to collect the fruits of research and to disseminate them, and to make information available in a detached and objective manner. It is ingenuous to suppose that, in any matter that concerns human beings, there is an ultimate truth which can be stated finally and for ever; it is perhaps even more ingenuous to suppose that to display unassailable fact will overcome irrational prejudice. But it is an implicit assumption behind the whole existence of the Institute of Race Relations that to display fact and to substitute informed and rational opinion for what is more emotional and less informed is to take a step towards a wiser general opinion. To this purpose, the present volume and the succeeding series of year books should make a contribution of importance.

April 1968 PHILIP MASON

AUTHOR'S PREFACE

In the two or more years since this survey was first projected, the subject of Commonwealth immigration and race relations in Britain has expanded well beyond the range of an individual writer.

Where time and opportunity allowed, advice and help have been sought from specialists in a number of fields, but inevitably the different sections must be marked by a certain unevenness of treatment and possibly there are some omissions. Moreover, it has not been possible to cover all relevant fields (for instance, such aspects as the mass media, the younger generation, students, and leisure must await a later volume). I hope that readers will forgive any shortcomings and themselves contribute to the accuracy and adequacy of the forthcoming series of year books by sending in detailed amendments and later reports. It is hoped that the first of the year books will cover the two-year period March 1967 (this report covers events up to that time) to March 1969 and will be more of a joint endeavour, with most chapters written by specialists in particular fields.

I should like to express my particular appreciation to the following individuals, who were kind enough to read and comment in detail upon particular chapters: Mr. E. J. B. Rose and Mr. Nicholas Deakin of the Survey of Race Relations; Miss Diana Cowan and Mr. David Spector; and Mr. Bob Hepple and Miss Elizabeth Burney, upon whose excellent studies the chapters on Employment and Housing lean so heavily. I am also grateful to a large number of people, who supplied specialized information and material with helpful promptness. They include the following: Mr. Edwin Barker of the Board of Social Responsibility, National Assembly of the Church of England; Mr. A. E. Bottoms of the Institute of Criminology, University of Cambridge; Mr. Eric Butterworth of the Department of Social Administration and Social Work, University of York; Mrs. Mary Dines of the Immigrants Advisory Committee, London Council of Social Service; Miss Julia Gaitskell, former secretary of C.A.R.D.; Miss Janet Henderson of the British Council of Churches; The Rev. Stanley Hollis of the Methodist Church Home Mission Department; Mrs. Shirley Joshi of C.A.R.D.; Mr. Daniel Lawrence of the Department of Sociology, University of Nottingham; Mrs. Joan Lawrence of the Council of Christians and Jews; Mr. Fred Moorhouse of the Student Movement House, International Centre of the Christian Movement; Miss Nadine Peppard of the National Committee for Commonwealth Immigrants; Mrs. Patty Thirlwell of the Westminster Overseas Committee; Mr. Douglas Tilbe of the Race Relations Committee of the Religious Society of Friends; Mr. Aubrey Weinberg of the Lanchester College of Technology, Coventry; Miss Dorothy Wood, until recently secretary of the Nottingham Commonwealth Citizens Consultative Committee; Mrs. Pamela Wylam of the Sikh Cultural Society.

I am also grateful to a number of national, local, and official agencies, particularly the Home Office and the Ministry of Labour, for their continued helpfulness and patience in the matter of statistics and other information;

the Ministries of Health and Social Welfare and the Department of Education and Science; the G.P.O. (Postal Order Department); the City of Birmingham Education Department and the City of Nottingham Education Committee; and the various High Commissions.

Finally, my thanks are also due to the Director and staff of the Institute of Race Relations, particularly Miss Hilary Arnott, for doing a very difficult editorial job with such success, and above all to my assistant, Miss Millie Yhap, without whose patience, cheerfulness, and fortitude over many months this book would never have been assembled in a coherent form.

September 1967 SHEILA PATTERSON

CONTENTS

PART IV OTHER ASPECTS

LIST OF TABLES

PART I

NATIONAL POLICIES AND PRACTICE

CHAPTER 1

Background to Recent Commonwealth Immigration

Small numbers of coloured people have been coming to Britain for centuries. There were slaves in the eighteenth century (many of whom were later absorbed in Victorian London's population); seamen have been in and out since the nineteenth century, and some of them have settled, often with local wives, in the port and dock areas of cities such as Cardiff, Liverpool, Tyneside, and London, to form small, isolated communities, visible only to a small minority of Britons. There have also been students from the Empire and Commonwealth, and a handful of professional men, mostly doctors, some restaurateurs, and even some itinerant Indian pedlars (mainly Sikhs). The war brought even more—for instance, some 7,000 West Indians served in the Royal Air Force and others came as volunteers to work in the war industries. Of these a number decided to stay on after the war.

Despite Britain's colonial history and links, the bulk of the general public was, thus, quite unaccustomed to contact with coloured people *en masse* in Britain itself before 1939. As recently as 1951 a national survey conducted by the Central Office of Information found that 50% of the population had never met a coloured person in their lives; of those who had, many had only done so while overseas in the armed forces, and of the remainder, comparatively few had ever had any real work or social contacts.

1. THE POST-1939 IMMIGRANTS

Since the Second World War, Britain has experienced the largest and most variegated influx of immigrants in her history, largely because of full employment and the country's chronic labour shortage. In addition to a new wave of Irish migrants, Britain has taken in at least a million immigrants from the European continent. These fall into two main categories: first, the East European political exiles and refugees, of whom the Poles form the largest single group, numbering today about

130,000–140,000, including British-born children. There are also communities of Ukrainians, Balts, Czechs, Rumanians, Yugoslavs, and Hungarians. The latter group received a reinforcement of some 16,000 in late 1956, after the abortive Budapest Rising. These political exile groups were characterized in general by a wide range of educational and occupational qualifications, by strong organizational links, and by resistance to assimilatory pressures. The majority were Catholics (or Orthodox) by religion, and few spoke English well. Another feature was the preponderance of men and the comparatively high age of many members.

The second category consisted of selected economic migrants from West and South Europe. These came mainly from Germany and Italy, followed by Austria and, more recently, Spain. They entered Britain under strict controls on Ministry of Labour permits, to fill jobs in the undermanned industries and services (particularly domestic) or to undertake specialized skilled work.[1]

For the most part these European migrants were widely dispersed through the British economy and formed no conspicuous settlements. An exception were those Italians who came in large batches to work in the brickfields and market gardens of Bedford and the Lea Valley, bought houses, imported their families, and set up a facsimile of Italian backstreet life.

The third and largest group of post-war arrivals consisted of unselected economic immigrants, mostly coloured, from the colonies and the new Commonwealth countries. Unlike the non-British immigrants, and like their forerunners, the Irish (who still have free entry), these newcomers were, until controls were introduced in July 1962, entitled as British subjects to enter Britain unconditionally and to settle and work wherever they could find lodging and a job (the latter is still the case). Apart from the reception and welfare arrangements set up by some governments, notably the West Indians, and augmented rather patchily by some local and voluntary organizations, no overall provision for reception, dispersal, placing, or general integration was made by the British authorities.

At first, these newcomers came mainly from the West Indies, with smaller contingents from West Africa, Aden and Somaliland, Cyprus and Malta. Later, just before controls were introduced, immigration from India and Pakistan began to accelerate, overtaking the West Indian movement in the first half of 1962.[2]

[1] The annual intake has varied between 20,000 and 50,000, a considerable proportion of whom return home after some years.

[2] For an analysis of the immigration at this period into Britain from these territories and others, see Kenneth Leech, 'Migration and the British Population, 1959–1962', *Race*, Vol. VII, no. 4, April 1966. See also p. 132, n. 1, below.

Table 1. *Estimated net inward movement of West Indians, Indians, and Pakistanis 1955-66*

	1955	1956	1957	1958	1959	1960	1961	1962 Jan-June	1962 July-Dec	1963	1964	1965	1966
West Indians	27,550	29,800	23,000	15,000	16,400	49,650	66,300	31,800	3,241	7,928	14,848	13,400	9,620
Indians	5,800	5,600	6,600	6,200	2,950	5,900	23,750	19,050	3,050	17,498	15,513	18,815	18,402
Pakistanis	1,850	2,050	5,200	4,700	850	2,500	25,100	25,080	−137	16,336	10,980	7,427	8,008
Total of West Indians Indians Pakistanis	35,200	37,450	34,800	25,900	20,200	58,050	115,150	75,930	6,154	41,762	41,341	39,642	36,030

Commonwealth Immigrants Act July 1st 1962

There are no accurate statistics for the first-generation immigrants, still less for their British-born children.[1] Towards the end of 1965, E. J. B. Rose, the Director of the Survey of Race Relations, estimated[2] that there were some 850,000 coloured Commonwealth immigrants in Britain, including some 200,000 children up to school-leaving age (of whom perhaps three-quarters were born in Britain and probably 100,000 were under the age of 5). Of the 850,000, about half came from the West Indies (at least 60% of them being Jamaican), about 180,000 from India, about 110,000 from Pakistan, and the remaining 110,000 mainly from East and West Africa, Hong Kong, and Malaysia. Another estimate at the end of 1965 was that made by the Economist Intelligence Unit: this gave the total number of Commonwealth immigrants (white and coloured but omitting those who are British by birth or descent) as 1,011,673, including 488,493 West Indians and 293,159 Indians and Pakistanis. The 'Dark Million' of *The Times* series of January–February 1965 was widely regarded as too high an estimate at that time, although it has been given by Ministers in the Commons in 1967.

Table 1 shows the general pattern of immigration into Britain by the three largest coloured Commonwealth groups, West Indians, Indians, and Pakistanis, in the years between 1955 and 1966.[3] The figures for the years before the Commonwealth Immigrants Act (1962) are estimates. The peak immigration year of the 1950s was 1956, but the numbers rose again in 1960 and 1961, at least partially as a beat-the-ban reaction to the looming threat of immigration controls.[4]

The main reason for the immigration was economic—the 'push' factors of over-population, under-employment, and poverty at home, combined with the restriction of West Indian immigration to the United States by the McCarran Act of 1952, and the additional political pressures of Partition and communal strife on millions in the Indian sub-continent.

Table 2 gives some idea of the volume of money remitted home by immigrants from the many countries of migration over the period 1960 to 1967.

Apart from a minority of professionals, white-collar, and skilled workers, the bulk of these new Commonwealth immigrants were not well equipped to enter a complex urban industrial society. So they followed the Irish into the lowest levels of the British economy.[5]

[1] An idea of the total number is given by D.E.S. statistics showing that there were 164,725 'immigrant children' in maintained schools in January 1967, including 73,605 West Indians, 32,122 Indians, and 11,862 Pakistanis.

[2] *Commonwealth Journal*, October 1965, p. 225.

[3] For other immigration statistics, see Appendix I.

[4] See C. Peach, 'West Indian Migration to Britain', *Race*, Vol. VII, July 1965 (1).

[5] For more details of their occupational background and status, see Ch. 5.

TABLE 2

*Statement of Money Orders advised and Postal Orders paid, 1960–7**
(Provided by the G.P.O.)

	Pakistan	India	Jamaica	West Indies (excluding Jamaica)	Irish Republic	Totals
1960–1	£'000	£'000	£'000	£'000	£'000	£'000
Money Orders	2,448	1,398	273	227	3,745	8,091
Postal Orders	291	1,476	4,567	1,444	1,904	9,682
Total	2,739	2,874	4,840	1,671	5,649	17,773
1961–2						
Money Orders	2,378	789	296	232	3,946	7,641
Postal Orders	358	1,193	6,027	1,749	1,905	11,232
Total	2,736	1,982	6,323	1,981	5,851	18,873
1962–3						
Money Orders	1,461	582	257	191	3,673	6,164
Postal Orders	279	946	6,038	1,764	1,978	11,005
Total	1,740	1,528	6,295	1,955	5,651	17,169
1963–4						
Money Orders	2,414	658	218	232	2,641	6,163
Postal Orders	223	1,187	5,837	2,508	2,132	11,887
Total	2,637	1,845	6,055	2,740	4,773	18,050
1964–5						
Money Orders	5,386	580	240	239	2,871	9,316
Postal Orders	65	1,007	5,936	2,512	2,436	11,956
Total	5,451	1,587	6,176	2,751	5,307	21,272
1965–6						
Money Orders	5,924	518	230	247	2,958	9,877
Postal Orders	41	619	5,931	2,659	2,200	11,450
Total	5,965	1,137	6,161	2,906	5,158	21,327
1966–7						
Money Orders	5,283	914	213	221	3,595	10,226
Postal Orders	30†	561	5,397	2,557	2,377	10,922
Total	5,313	1,475	5,610	2,778	5,972	21,148

* (a) The Post Office does not know—for obvious reasons—whether the senders of money orders and postal orders are immigrants or not. It can, however, be presumed that the majority are.

(b) The amounts shown under Postal Orders relate to the British postal orders cashed in the countries concerned (India, Pakistan, etc.). It is not known how many of these postal orders were sent from the U.K., and how many from other Commonwealth countries which also issue British postal orders. However, two samples taken of postal orders cashed in Jamaica show that of 2,000 £5 orders, 99% had been issued in the U.K., but of 1,000 £1 orders only 34% had been issued in the U.K.

† The actual figures for Pakistan for 1966–7 were not available and this figure is therefore an estimate.

2. SOCIO-CULTURAL BACKGROUND AND DIFFERENCES

There has been a misleading and meaningless tendency to lump these newcomers together under the description 'coloured immigrants'. In fact the various 'coloured' immigrant groups differ at least as much as the Irish do from the Jews, or the Poles from the Italians or Germans. They differ not only in demographic and occupational composition but in social organization, socio-economic and cultural background, and also in motives for migration and expectations of the host society.

A. THE WEST INDIANS

Most West Indians come from an English-speaking, Christian, British-oriented sub-culture, albeit an impoverished and rural one. Although they settle together in family and local groupings, they are mobile and individualistic, and resist the imposition of strong internal social controls. They also tend to have high expectations of full and immediate acceptance by the Mother Country. Such acceptance is at present slowed by real differences of values, cultural background, attitudes, and behaviour. It is also slowed by the British receiving society's general mild antipathy to and avoidance of outsiders, and by a set of historical preconceptions associating dark skin and Negroid features with alien and primitive cultures and with low socio-economic status.

The West Indians are nevertheless a potentially assimilating immigrant group, in type if not always in intention, although it is still too early for most of them to have passed through the initial phase of accommodation at work and perhaps in the neighbourhood. Quite a number do return home, but the high sex ratio, with virtual parity between men and women in the more established settlements, and the consolidation and enlargement of families, are both an indication of and an encouragement to permanent settlement.[1]

B. THE ASIANS

By contrast, the other two largest groups, the Indians and Pakistanis, are the least assimilating in type and intention of all recent immigrant

[1] For a more detailed account of West Indian characteristics see S. K. Ruck (ed.), *The West Indian Comes to England*, London, Routledge, 1960; S. Patterson, *Dark Strangers* (Tavistock) (p. 220f.); R. Davison, *West Indian Migrants*, O.U.P., 1962; K. Fitzherbert, *West Indian Children in London*, London, Bell, 1967, p. 218. A study of 'second-phase' settlement by successful West Indians moving from Brixton to Croydon in South London, is also being made by Iva Mildon for submission as a Ph.D. thesis at the University of Sussex; and a study of Dominican family structure and settlement in Britain by Teresa Spens at the University of Cambridge.

groups. They have their own entirely distinctive cultures (not always entirely compatible with that of the receiving society), their own religion and language, and a considerable degree of internal organization and control. Whereas many West Indians have made the decision to settle in this country, many Indians and Pakistanis are still at the stage when they intend to stay only a few years in Britain to accumulate savings or skills.[1] They avoid all contacts with the receiving society other than at work and are self-segregating to a degree that has hitherto been seen only among the Chinese. Their original intentions of avoidance and return are, however, being rendered increasingly difficult of fulfilment by the arrival of families and young children, who are exposed to the assimilatory pressures of the host society in the schools.

TABLE 3

Number of Dependants entering Britain between 1 July 1962 and December 1966

	Male	Female	Children	Total
West Indian	1,183	10,120	32,779	44,082
Indian	1,968	17,122	24,016	43,106
Pakistani	761	8,999	17,177	26,937
Total	3,912	36,241	73,972	114,125

The conflict between parental and home values and the values of the receiving society as purveyed in the schools is discussed in more detail in the section on education. Here we may note the approximate demographic position. Whereas the West Indians have virtually achieved parity between the sexes, there was until recently a great imbalance among Indians, still more among Pakistanis. This is now beginning to change, though more slowly than in the West Indian case, because it is not acceptable for most Indian and Pakistani women to go out to work, so that the expense of maintaining them here is greater.[2] Relatively more Indian women than Pakistanis seem to be joining their

[1] Statistics of re-migration or return migration were not available until the Commonwealth Immigrants Act of 1962 came into operation, and indeed, the statistics kept since then of numbers leaving Britain do not permit of precise distinctions between returning migrants, visitors, and others. In general, however, it has been estimated that the West Indians are the most settled of the three major groups, the Pakistanis by far the least settled and the Indians somewhere in between (see R. Hooper, *Colour in Britain*, London, B.B.C., 1965, p. 20).

[2] Table 3 gives a breakdown by national origin, sex, and age, which illustrates general trends; unfortunately, no separate figures are available for girls and boys within the category of 'children'.

husbands.[1] In 1965 one estimate gave the Indian ratio as one woman to two men and the Pakistani ratio as one woman to twenty-five men, but the imbalance is a good deal less than that today. Among the Pakistanis, there has however been more of a tendency to bring over teen-age boys to live with their fathers, leaving the mothers (for whom separate cooking and bathing facilities would have to be made) at home.

There are considerable cultural differences between the Indians and the Pakistanis, and between sub-groups within the two groups. While the village-kin group is basic to the great majority of immigrants from the Indian sub-continent,[2] there are important religious, linguistic, caste, class, and other divisions which persist in the migrant situation.

C. THE INDIANS

The vast majority of Indian immigrants to Britain come in fact from two traditional areas of emigration, 750 miles apart, the Punjab and Gujarat.[3] By religion, most Punjabis are Sikhs (a reformed Hindu sect), and speak only Punjabi (as do many immigrants from West Pakistan). They are generally supposed to constitute a majority of all immigrants from India, although estimates range between 60 and 80%. (In 1961–2, Desai estimated that of the 40,000 Indians then in Britain, only one-fifth were Gujaratis.) It has also been estimated that about 50% of the Sikh immigrants adhere to the beard, long hair, and turban, which are marks of their religion.

The abandonment of the distinctive long hair and turban is frowned upon by more orthodox Sikh temples, but several more liberal temples (Gurudwara) have apparently ruled that membership and office-holding are not conditional upon the retention of these diacritical religious marks (a recognition which is an index of partial accommodation). Like the Muslims but unlike the Hindus, the Sikhs have established religious associations wherever they have settled in Britain. Describing Sikhism as 'a religion of classic simplicity', Desai writes:

> The Sikhs are a minority in the territory in which they live. The Sikh temple provides an association which serves to express the solidarity of their com-

[1] Narindar Uberoi maintains that the Sikh migration to Southall has been a family one, with the women and children following the men; also that it is a permanent one, the migrants having no intention of returning to India ('The Singhs of Southall', unpublished manuscript, 1965).

[2] On the formation of one such Gujarati village-kin group in Birmingham, see R. Desai, *Indian Immigrants in Britain*, London, O.U.P. for I.R.R., 1963, pp. 109–16.

[3] For their educational and occupational background, see Desai, op. cit., Ch. 1, and below, Ch. 5, pp. 134–48. A social anthropological study of Sikh women and children in Southall is also being carried out by Anjali Patnaik for the Survey of Race Relations. See also Narindar Uberoi, 'Sikh Women in Southall', *Race*, Vol. VI, no. 1, July 1964.

munity in relation to the non-Sikhs around them and a centre for internal social activities.'[1]

Sikh religious and communal activities were stimulated by the arrival of their religious leader, Sant Fateh Singh, in 1966. He visited Sikh communities up and down the country, was received by the Archbishop of Canterbury, and had talks with Mr. Maurice Foley, then Minister in charge of immigrant affairs at the Home Office. He raised the matter of job discrimination and asked for Sikh representation on the N.C.C.I.[2] At the end of January 1967, the Sikhs celebrated the 300th anniversary of Guru Gobind Singh, tenth and last in the line of Sikh *gurus* or teachers. In London nearly 6,000 Sikhs celebrated the occasion by a gathering at the Albert Hall. Meanwhile, the recruitment of turbaned Sikhs had been accepted by Manchester's Transport Committee after a seven-year controversy.[3]

In early 1967, moves began to set up a Central Committee of Sikhs in Great Britain. Its aim is said to be the preservation of the Sikh religion and culture in Britain. Its membership is to consist of representatives from all the Sikh temples in the country. It will be concerned for the social welfare of Sikhs in Britain and act as a liaison body with other organizations, official and unofficial; and it will work in co-operation with other bodies to combat racial discrimination. Associated is the Sikh Cultural Society, whose function is to publish the *Sikh Courier* (published since 1960) and other Sikh publications of a religious or cultural nature.[4] Apart from its 'traditional' aims, this organization would also appear to have 'integrative' intentions. In its *Newsletter*, No. 5 (March 1967), Sikhs are informed about the activities of N.C.C.I. and asked to keep in touch with local Liaison Committees to promote action in cases of job discrimination ('especially those where the wearing of the turban appears to be at issue').

The other major Indian group, the Gujaratis, speak Gujarati and are mainly Hindu by religion, reportedly of the highest Brahmin caste. As with the Punjabis, migration does not involve any severance with the

[1] R. Desai, op. cit., pp. 93–4. He goes on to describe the establishment of the temple in Smethwick.

[2] For the immediate outcome, see I.R.R. *Newsletter*, March 1967, p. 107.

[3] See I.R.R. *Newsletter* of November 1966 and March 1967. For other activities by turbaned and unturbaned Sikhs in the employment sphere, see section on the Indian Workers' Association.

[4] The information in this paragraph was communicated by Mrs. P. M. Wylam (Manjeet Kaur), acting honorary secretary of the Central Committee. A slightly different communication from an I.W.A. (Southall) source reads: 'The Central Committee was formed to organise the celebrations of the tercentenary of Gobund Singh and has continued to exist. Because it does not raise any issues which are subjects of conflict within the Sikh community, no one objects. There is no central body representing the Sikhs and could not be because of factionalism among them.'

village-kin group and society at home. Desai's study of Indians in Birmingham is mainly concerned with Gujaratis, and readers are referred to it for fuller information about their background. Here, however, one should mention that since 1960, as a result of political developments in Africa, some Gujaratis have been entering Britain from Central and East Africa, where they or their parents originally went as immigrants. Most members of this sub-group speak English and may be better equipped educationally to enter the British economy than their compatriots from India.

D. THE PAKISTANIS

The Pakistani immigrants are all Muslims by religion, although the various regional groups do not identify with each other organizationally. Like the Sikhs, they establish mosques wherever the immigrant settlement can bear the cost.[1] Like most Indians, they come from only a few traditional areas of emigration or refuge areas. These are: in West Pakistan, the North-West Frontier area (often ex-servicemen), the Mirpur border area with Kashmir, and the area bordering on the Punjab; in East Pakistan (Bengal), the Sylhet border area with Assam, and the 'maritime' provinces of East Bengal.

Linguistically, the Punjabis and the immigrants from Mirpur can communicate since Punjabi and Kashmiri are similar. Otherwise, all the Pakistani immigrants speak totally different languages and can only communicate fragmentarily by using a form of Hindi-Urdu. There is no real mutual intelligibility between the Bengali-speaking East Pakistanis and the West Pakistanis from the Punjab. The latter can communicate freely only with the Punjabis from India, and, as Desai comments, these two Punjabi groups are also fortunate in that their language is nearest to the *lingua franca*.

Until recently, there has been very little published information about the recent Pakistani immigrants in Britain except for Hamza A. Alavi's report on 'Pakistanis in London'.[2] (This gives, *inter alia*, a brief note of some Pakistani organizations at that time.) In 1965, however, other material on Pakistanis and other Muslims in Britain[3] began to appear. Readers are referred to the following:

Zaynab Dahya, 'Pakistani Wives in Britain', *Race*, Vol. VI, no. 4, April 1965.

B. U. D. Dahya, 'Yemenis in Britain: an Arab Migrant Community', *Race*, Vol. VI, no. 3, January 1965.

[1] See the dispute in Bolton over the siting of a new mosque. (*The Times*, 21 February 1967; *Bolton Evening News*, 21 February 1967.)

[2] Published as a supplement to the I.R.R. *Newsletter*, July 1963, and also in *Immigrants in London*, N.C.S.S., 1963.

[3] Mostly Arabs from Aden, Somalia, and the Yemen.

'Muslims in Britain', report of one-day conference held by the Student Christian Movement in January 1965.

David Brewster, 'Muslims in Britain', *Crucible*, May 1965.

S. A. Khaliq, 'Pakistanis in Britain', *Plebs*, March 1966. (This compares the lot of Pakistanis in Britain with that of Turkish workers in Germany.)

Farrukh Hashmi, M.B., B.S., D.P.M., *The Pakistani Family in Britain*, pamphlet for the N.C.C.I., 1966 (a very useful background piece on Muslim customs, attitudes, family patterns, and religion).

Earlier established Muslim settlements are described in two published works by social anthropologists, Michael Banton, *The Coloured Quarter*, London, Cape, 1955, and Sydney Collins, *Coloured Minorities in Britain*, London, Lutterworth Press, 1957. There is also an unpublished report by Mary Dines on Pakistanis in London, produced in 1966; while an Urdu-speaking social anthropologist from East Africa has been studying a Pakistani settlement in a northern city.

3. GEOGRAPHICAL DISTRIBUTION IN BRITAIN

Both West Indians and Asians have generally gone where work was available, moving in the early years of settlement from areas of temporary recession to areas of continued labour shortage. This means that they have settled in industrial cities and large towns rather than in the dock and port areas of the earlier coloured settlements and are much more concentrated in urban areas than the native population as a whole.

According to the 1961 Census,[1] just under half the immigrants born in the West Indies, India, and Pakistan were resident in Britain's ten largest cities: London, Birmingham, Liverpool, Manchester, Bristol, Leeds, Coventry, Sheffield, Nottingham, and Bradford. Greater London itself has about twenty-eight of every hundred coloured immigrants, whilst Birmingham has the next largest group with seven out of every hundred.

Table 4 shows the estimated distribution of immigrants for these three groups in towns and cities in England, Scotland, and Wales with a coloured population of 3,000 or more.[2]

It is often claimed that coloured immigrants live concentrated in 'ghettoes' or 'little Harlems'. In fact, the 1961 Census showed that there were no boroughs in Britain in which more than 11% of the population were coloured immigrants and only ten with ratios of over 4%. It also

[1] But, for a comment on the Census, see p. 132, n. 1, below.

[2] See B.M.A.'s report 'Medical Examination of Immigrants', Appendix III, for 1965 estimates of Commonwealth citizens and aliens in twenty-six provincial areas.

TABLE 4

*Estimated distribution of West Indians, Indians, and Pakistanis in towns and cities in England, Scotland, and Wales**

	Total population	Coloured population	
1 *Greater London Conurbation*	8,186,830	350,000	⅔ West Indians, substantial numbers of Indians and smaller numbers of Pakistanis, Africans, and Chinese
2 *Birmingham*	1,106,040	70,000	⅔ West Indians, the rest Indians and Pakistanis
3 *Nottingham*	311,850	12,500	mostly West Indians, with smaller groups of Indians and Pakistanis
4 *Bradford*	298,220	12,500	nearly all Pakistanis
5 *Manchester*	644,500	10,000	mostly West Indians
6 *Liverpool*	729,140	10,000	very mixed, with substantial Chinese and West African colonies
7 *Wolverhampton*	150,200	7,500	nearly equal numbers of West Indians and Indians, with a few Pakistanis
8 *Leeds*	508,790	6,500	mostly West Indians, with smaller numbers of Indians, Pakistanis and Africans
9 *Coventry*	315,670	6,500	⅔ Indians, with equal numbers of Pakistanis and West Indians
10 *Huddersfield*	132,270	6,500	⅔ West Indians, the rest Indians and Pakistanis
11 *Bristol*	432,070	6,000	nearly all West Indians
12 *Leicester*	267,050	6,000	⅔ Indians and Pakistanis, ⅓ West Indians

* These figures do not include children born to immigrants in this country.

This is only a rough estimate, made up of figures collected by the Institute's 'Survey of Race Relations' from a number of sources in 1966–7.

In each case the first figure shows total population, second figure shows total coloured population.

13 *Sheffield*	490,930	6,000	$\frac{2}{3}$ West Indians, the rest mostly Pakistanis with some Arabs and Somalis
14 *West Bromwich*	97,600	5,700	equal numbers of West Indians and Indians, with a few Pakistanis
15 *Dudley*	63,890	5,250	mostly West Indians, with a few Pakistanis and fewer Indians
16 *Bedford*	66,430	5,000	mostly West Indians, with a few Pakistanis
17 *Newcastle*	260,750	5,000	very mixed
18 *High Wycombe*	54,060	4,500	nearly all West Indians
19 *Slough*	84,900	4,500	$\frac{1}{2}$ Indians, the rest mostly West Indians with a few Pakistanis
20 *Smethwick*	67,750	4,500	equal numbers of West Indians and Indians, with a few Pakistanis
21 *Glasgow*	1,036,321	4,000	$\frac{1}{2}$ Pakistanis, the rest mostly Indians and a few West Indians
22 *Northampton*	106,120	4,000	nearly all West Indians
23 *Walsall*	119,910	3,600	over $\frac{1}{2}$ West Indians, the rest Indians and Pakistanis
24 *Rowley Regis and Tipton*	87,120	3,400	over $\frac{1}{2}$ West Indians, the rest mostly Indians with a few Pakistanis
25 *Cardiff*	260,340	3,300	mainly West Indians, with some Pakistanis
26 *Reading*	123,310	3,300	nearly all West Indians, with a few Pakistanis
27 *Derby*	130,030	3,000	$\frac{2}{3}$ West Indians, $\frac{1}{3}$ Indians and Pakistanis
28 *Ipswich*	120,120	3,000	nearly all West Indians

showed that there were few Enumeration Districts (E.D.s) where Commonwealth immigrants constituted over 15% of the population. In London Lambeth had twenty such districts, Paddington thirteen, and Kensington eight, but there were only two in the whole country where West Indians formed between 30 and 40% of the population. Leaving aside certain historical connotations, including duress, the term 'ghetto' is not properly applied to districts with no more than a minority of immigrants.[1] Moreover, there was considerable statistical evidence of scatter, quite apart from the findings of researchers investigating particular situations. For instance, outward and upward residential mobility was well under way among Brixton's West Indians by 1960.[2] Moreover, the ground leases of at least one area of heavy settlement had been taken over by the Borough Council, thereby rendering the growth and consolidation of a genuine 'ghetto' less likely.[3]

4. THE LONG TERM

After Commonwealth immigration was curbed by the 1962 Act, the size of each major group is likely to be most influenced by the arrival of dependants and natural increase on the one side and return migration and mortality on the other. Little information is available on mortality, nor has much work as yet been done on the return migration figures.

In recent years considerable publicity has been given to quotations of very high immigrant birth-rates in a few towns or areas,[4] but the most substantial information is still that recorded for Birmingham in

[1] See Ruth Glass, articles in *The Times* (30 June 1965, 1 July 1965), and Kenneth Leech, 'Ghettoes in Britain?', I.R.R. *Newsletter*, July 1965.

[2] S. Patterson, *Dark Strangers*, Penguin, pp. 259–60.

[3] For further discussion of residential settlement and housing, see Ch. 6.

[4] In early 1965, there were several published reports which received wide publicity and were quoted in subsequent debates on immigration control. One was the 1963 report of Wolverhampton's Medical Officer of Health, which contained the following statement: 'Immigrants from the Commonwealth and Colonies who, according to the 1961 Census, were 3·9 per cent of the population, produced 22·7 per cent of all births.' The wife of the assistant M.O.H. was reported as saying that a white minority in parts of the Black Country could be a possibility in twenty-five years (*The Times*, 19 April 1965). Just before, Dr. John Lamb, secretary of the South Warwickshire B.M.A., was reported as saying that it was 'virtually impossible' for English women to have their first babies in hospital because the beds were full of immigrants who had been living in insanitary conditions. Later, *The Times* (25 June 1965) pointed out that a large proportion of the demand for maternity beds in some areas came from the Irish. See also I.R.R. *Newsletter* (May–June 1965, pp. 8–12). In May 1967, Mr. E. J. B. Rose, Director of the I.R.R. Survey, stressed in a letter to *The Times* (10 May) the need to bear in mind both the 'beat-the-ban' rush before the Commonwealth Immigrants Act and the age structure of the immigrant population before trying to draw conclusions about comparative birth-rates from these statistics. He pointed out that the immigrant population in the Wolverhampton area nearly doubled between 1961 and 1963 and that the age structure of immigrants is

1961, which suggested an average birth-rate among immigrants of 25 per thousand, as compared with the U.K. average of 16 per thousand.[1] The rate is likely to be higher in areas of West Indian settlement, because of the virtual sex parity, and lower in some areas of Asian and particularly Pakistani settlement, because of the disproportionate number of men.[2] As more Indian and Pakistani women arrive, the birth-rate in these groups can be expected to rise. In any case, a higher than average birth-rate should be expected among all these immigrant groups, because the majority are in the younger adult age-groups (according to a 1961 poll, 71% of the immigrants were between the ages of 18 and 34). Later, however, the immigrant birth-rate can be expected to decline, following the normal pattern of birth-rates in low-income groups under the influence of greater prosperity and of education.

In 1965 the *Economist* published a revised forecast up to the year 2015 of the numbers of U.K. residents in the three main immigrant groups—West Indians, Indians, and Pakistanis. This was based on an estimated total population of such immigrants, together with their British-born children, of nearly 700,000 by the end of 1964. As a basis for calculation, the forecast continued to assume the same birth-rate (25 per thousand), together with a notional death-rate of 5 per thousand to the year 1982 and 10 per thousand in subsequent years. The assumed future level of net immigration was revised upwards to an outside figure of 50,000, to allow for any years of exceptionally high inflow and for a possible further increase in the number of dependants arriving from India and Pakistan. Table 5 gives the details of the forecast:

---

quite different to that of a settled population in that immigrants fall overwhelmingly into child-bearing ranges. To get a true comparison of birth-rates the numbers of immigrants should therefore, he said, be expressed as a percentage of the citizens of Wolverhampton in the same age range. He mentioned that the latest figures for the birth-rate in Barbados were 26 per 1,000.

[1] This is, however, well below the birth-rate in many of the home countries: for example Jamaica 41 per thousand; India 42 per thousand. In November 1966, Birmingham reported a drop in the number of births to coloured or mixed coloured and white parents, and definite signs that the general growth in the size of coloured families in the area was coming to an end. (*Birmingham Post*, 28 November 1966.)

[2] Fertility tables based on the 1961 10% sample Census were published on 4 October 1966, H.M.S.O. The average number of children in a British family was given as 1·87. In the year before the Census, the following fertility rates were reported: for women from the Caribbean—73% above the British average; for Northern Ireland and the Irish Republic—22% and 35% above average respectively. The Indian rates may have been brought down by the fact that English mothers born in India would have been included in fertility rates. See also article by J. A. H. Waterhouse and D. H. Brabham, 'Enquiry into fertility of immigrants: preliminary report', *Eugenics Review*, Vol. 56, no. 1, April 1964.

TABLE 5

*West Indian, Indian, and Pakistani immigrants in the U.K., and the total forecast population, 1965–2015**

End of Year	Total Population of the U.K.	Population of West Indian, Indian, and Pakistani Origin	As a Per Cent of Total
	('000)	('000)	(%)
1965	54,820	759	1·4
1970	56,951	1,098	1·9
1975	58,904	1,473	2·5
1980	60,879	1,886	3·1
1985	63,017	2,309	3·7
1990	65,488	2,746	4·2
1995	68,363	3,216	4·7
2000	71,325	3,722	5·2
2005	74,442	4,267	5·7
2010	77,483	4,851	6·3
2015	80,523	5,484	6·8

* 'Commonwealth Immigrants and the Future of the U.K.', E.I.U. Report, May 1965, p. 2.

Forecasts of this sort are obviously hazardous, not only from a demographic viewpoint but because they can only be quantitative. They can lead to the sort of comment and assumptions made by Norman Pannell on the earlier E.I.U. forecast:

> The total population of the U.K. by the year 2000 is forecast at seventy million. If four million of that figure consists of people of African [*sic*] and Asian origin they will represent nearly 6% of the total. This compares with some 10% of coloured people in the U.S.A. The difficulties of that great humanitarian country in trying to solve the problems thus created should serve as a lesson and a warning to us.[1]

The assumption that the problems of all 'coloured' people are identical, the assumption that the problems of coloured immigrants in Britain are due only to colour at this juncture, the assumption that in thirty years' time the connotations of 'colour' will be the same, and that there will still be a single 'coloured' minority, unaffected by the processes of absorption, acculturation, acceptance, and intermarriage—all these are over-simplifications. As Richard Hooper comments (unpublished):

> Attitudes may change in the next forty years, and with them the readiness to use this kind of label. Fifty to seventy years ago, the immigration of Jews into this country was a burning issue, but how many Gentiles today—except for a minority—know or care how many Jews are living in England, or what their percentage is of the total indigenous population.

[1] N. Pannell and Fenner Brockway, *Immigration—What is the Answer?*, London, Routledge and Kegan Paul, 1965, p. 14.

CHAPTER 2

Immigration – Policies and Practices

1. FROM LAISSEZ-FAIRE TO RESTRICTION

Britain's 'open-door' policy towards Commonwealth immigration until 1962 was a legacy of two nineteenth-century traditions and policies —on the political side, the tradition of the Empire and the 'old' Dominions, with every Commonwealth citizen a British subject,[1] and thus assured free entry to the Mother Country—on the economic side, that of laissez-faire economic policies which required a free market in labour and disregarded long- and short-range planning of labour needs.

Owing to the persistence of virtually full employment in Britain in the last decade or so, the economic aspect presented fewer immediate problems than might have been anticipated. Most newcomers were absorbed without undue strain, though often in unskilled, low-paid or otherwise unattractive jobs unwanted by local workers.

From the socio-cultural, the administrative, and, ultimately, the political viewpoint, the problems raised by this large-scale, undirected migration appeared more long-term and complex. The relatively small numbers of immigrants from sparsely-populated old or 'white' Dominions had been easy to accept because of social and cultural similarities (including language) and compatibilities, reinforced by physical 'invisibility', and thus the principles of Commonwealth solidarity and free movement had undergone no strain. Nor had these principles been taxed by the small movement of Asian, African, and other 'visible' elites who had come to Britain for higher education, recreation, or professional or business purposes. It seemed, however, a very different matter, especially in the aftermath of Empire, to absorb a mass immigration of non-elites, mostly unskilled, rural, and poor, from the 'new' Commonwealth countries, most of whose members were 'visible' by reason of their colour, and in some cases by reason of their very different social and cultural backgrounds, including religion and language.

The strain on traditional pro-Commonwealth feelings in Britain, and also, among Labour supporters, on the traditional belief in the universal brotherhood of man, grew apace. This was particularly so among ordinary citizens in such labour-hungry industrial areas as the West Midlands, whose overstretched welfare services, schools, and neighbourhood

[1] The British Nationality Act of 1948 identifies the terms 'British subject' and 'Commonwealth citizen'.

amenities had borne the brunt of the influx[1] and who saw no official action at national and little at local levels to meet the real situations and problems that had arisen.

Despite occasional but increasing pressures for control of Commonwealth immigration the Conservative Government between 1954 and early 1961 consistently denied that Commonwealth immigration posed any special problems; it took the line that Commonwealth citizens were free to enter and would receive the same treatment as other citizens after entry, and did not make any special arrangements at national level for reception or long-term integration, or for extra provisions in areas of high immigrant settlement.[2]

Increasing demands for controls were, however, being heard, particularly from the rank and file of lower-middle- and working-class Tories and right-wing Labour in the areas most affected.[3] A strong rearguard action was fought in 1961–62 by the traditional Commonwealth-oriented Conservatives, the internationalist left of the Labour Party and the 'liberal centre' of all three major parties, but the rising statistics for immigrants from India and Pakistan (countries which, as was frequently pointed out, had between them a population of some 550,000,000, by contrast with three and a half million for the entire West Indies) made some controls appear essential, although much of the overall increase had certainly been triggered off by rumours of controls.

The Commonwealth Immigrants Bill was announced in the Queen's Speech on 31 October 1961. It was fought through both Houses of Parliament with a maximum of bitterness and recrimination[4] and finally

[1] For a statement on the need for planners to consider cultural rather than economic factors in setting the long-term limits to the rate of immigration into a particular country see W. D. Borrie, *The Cultural Integration of Immigrants*, U.N.E.S.C.O., 1959, Ch. V *passim*.

[2] In these early years, as those who were directly involved will remember, all suggestions for limitations and reception or integration measures were likely to be lumped together as discriminatory and racialist not only by liberal-minded Britons but also by the immigrants themselves (particularly West Indians) and their political leaders at home. In fact these interventions could usually be divided into 'control'- and 'integrative'-type statements, as Paul Foot points out (*Immigration and Race in British Politics*, Penguin, 1965, pp. 165–6). One of those who consistently stressed integration over the years was Mr. Marcus Lipton, Labour M.P. for Brixton. On 5 November 1954, for instance, he said: 'It [the immigration problem] cannot be left to the local authorities who are already over-burdened. . . . We cannot leave it to uncoordinated and sporadic private enterprise to solve the problem as best they can.' Ultimately, he, like most integrators, also came to support controls.

[3] See Foot, op. cit., pp. 128–35, pp. 161–4. A Gallup poll taken in June 1961 found 67% in favour of restrictions, 6% for a complete halt and only 21% in favour of continued free entry.

[4] For more detailed coverage of statements and viewpoints in Parliament, the press, and various Commonwealth countries see I.R.R. *Newsletter* supplements, 'Commonwealth Immigration to Britain', 4 November 1961—May 1962.

with the application of the guillotine in the committee stage, after the Bill had attracted 133 amendments from M.P.s of all parties. During the debates the then Home Secretary, Mr. R. A. Butler, was said to have laid himself and the Conservative Government open to charges of 'humbug', 'hypocrisy', and 'colour bar' legislation by stating that the controls section of the Bill would not apply to the Irish, because of the practical difficulties allegedly involved in applying such controls on the land frontier with Ulster or at British ports. A number of prominent Tories strongly objected to this exception of the Irish, as did *The Times* and many other influential national and provincial periodicals.[1] On the Labour side, the leader of the Opposition, Mr. Hugh Gaitskell, put up a categorical and uncompromising opposition to any closing of the Commonwealth door. This stand was later to expose his Party to charges of hypocrisy, expediency, and finally of a 'volte-face' from the Conservatives. These came, first, when the Labour Party's new leader, Mr. Harold Wilson, said that it no longer contested the need for control (when the Act first came up for renewal in November 1963), and later, when the new Labour Government not only went on renewing the Act in late 1964 and 1965, but also introduced further controls in the White Paper of August 1965. Among the Labour speakers whose statements were subsequently to be quoted against them were: Mr. Patrick Gordon Walker who, despite his advocacy of controls in 1954, had made a devastating speech against the Bill at Second Reading; and Labour's future Commonwealth Relations Secretary, Mr. Arthur Bottomley, who had said during a debate on 5 December 1958:

> The central principle on which our status rests is largely dependent on the 'open door' to all Commonwealth citizens. If we believe in the importance of our great Commonwealth we should do nothing in the slightest degree to undermine that principle.

During its passage in 1961–2 the Bill was, as a result of continued pressures, amended in a number of more or less minor points; but it went through substantially in its original form, with a rather low final vote of 277 for, 170 against (there were several Tory abstentions and an exceptionally poor Opposition vote). Apart from what many regarded as its racially discriminatory nature (*The Times*, 27 February 1962, 12 March 1962) it remained essentially a measure which used employment as the chief criterion of control when, although there was a temporary recession that winter, there was in fact little question of long-term major unemployment; the main arguments against continued

[1] Nevertheless, as a number of M.P.s and commentators pointed out, the Bill was introduced and passed at a time when both Britain and Ireland were involved in negotiations for entry into the European Economic Community, with provisions for increasingly free movement of labour between members.

unrestricted immigration were concerned with problems of housing shortage and overcrowding, welfare service inadequacies, and cultural frictions, all of which were greatest in the areas of industrial expansion and labour shortage into which the newcomers would continue to move, unchecked by any dispersal or registration procedures. Nor was the requirement of a health check, which was supported by many health authorities, explicitly incorporated in the Act.[1]

The Commonwealth Immigrants Act received the Royal Assent on 18 April 1962 and became law on 1 July of that year. Its main provisions are given below.

2. THE COMMONWEALTH IMMIGRANTS ACT (1962)—MAIN PROVISIONS

CHAPTER 21

An Act to make temporary[2] provision for controlling the immigration into the United Kingdom of Commonwealth citizens; to authorise the deportation from the United Kingdom of certain Commonwealth citizens convicted of offences and recommended by the court for deportation; to amend the qualifications required of Commonwealth citizens applying for citizenship under the British Nationality Act, 1948; to make corresponding provisions in respect of British protected persons and citizens of the Republic of Ireland; and for purposes connected with the matters aforesaid. (18th April, 1962.)

A. PART I—CONTROL OF IMMIGRATION

This provides for the control of the immigration into the United Kingdom of Commonwealth citizens and all other British subjects except for persons born in the U.K. or holding a U.K. passport and being citizens of the U.K. and Colonies, or holding such a passport issued in the U.K. or the Republic of Ireland; those persons ordinarily resident in the U.K. at the time of seeking entry or at any time during the previous two years; and the wife or children[3] under 16 of such residents or of those granted entry. (Control applies to citizens of the Irish Republic but is not imposed on persons travelling between Ireland and Britain.)

[1] Another issue that winter was the smallpox outbreak in early 1962 among newly-arrived Pakistanis (see E. Butterworth, 'The 1962 Smallpox Outbreak and the British Press', *Race*, Vol. VII, no. 4, April 1966).

[2] i.e., it was to operate for eighteen months from 1 July 1962 and thereafter come up for renewal annually.

[3] 'child' to include a step-child, an adopted child and, in relation to the mother, an illegitimate child.

Entry to be permitted to:

(a) holders of current employment vouchers issued by the Ministry of Labour (the explanatory memorandum of the original Bill states: 'The intention is that vouchers for this purpose will be issued to persons who can show that they have a job to come to, to those who possess training, skill or educational qualifications likely to be useful in this country, and to applicants outside these categories subject to any limit which the Government may from time to time consider necessary.'),

(b) students attending full-time or substantial part-time courses,

(c) entrants who can support themselves and their dependants without working in the U.K.,

(d) members of the home armed forces and those of other visiting forces who arrive in the U.K. to serve there in various recognized capacities.

Admission can be refused to:

(a) those apparently suffering from mental disorder or otherwise undesirable for medical reasons (on the advice of a medical inspector),

(b) persons convicted in any country of an extradition crime,

(c) persons whose admission would, in the opinion of the Secretary of State, be contrary to the interests of national security,

(d) persons in respect of whom a deportation order under Part II of the Act is in force.

The power to refuse or grant admission is exercised by immigration officers. It also applies to Commonwealth citizens who arrive in the U.K. as members of the crews of, or stowaways in, ships and aircraft.

The remainder of Part I contains supplementary provisions, including some dealing with offences in connexion with control of immigration, and ends with the proviso that this part of the Act shall continue in force until 31 December 1963 and shall then expire unless Parliament otherwise determines.

B. PART II—DEPORTATION

This applies to the same persons as Part I, and to citizens of the Republic of Ireland.[1]

Persons of 17 years and over convicted of an offence punishable by imprisonment[2] may be recommended for deportation. This provision does not apply to an offender who can satisfy the Court that:

[1] In practice the deportation provisions have been applied to the Irish, the controls not.

[2] This term includes an offence which would be so punishable apart from any enactment restricting the imprisonment of young offenders or of first offenders.

(*a*) he is or was ordinarily resident in the United Kingdom on the date of his conviction; and

(*b*) that he has been continuously so resident for a period of at least five years ending with that date:

Provided that for the purpose of calculating the period for which any person has been so resident (but not of determining whether he has been continuously so resident) no account shall be taken of any continuous period of six months or more during which he has been detained under a sentence or order passed or made by any court on a conviction of an offence.

No recommendation for deportation shall be made in respect of an offender unless a notice has been given to him at least seven days before the recommendation is made—

(*a*) describing the classes of persons in respect of whom such a recommendation may or may not be made; and

(*b*) containing a statement of the effect of subsection (4) of section six of this Act.

The remainder of Part II contains further notes on procedure and appeals, on deportation orders, and on offences in connexion with deportation orders. It is an offence for persons in respect of whom a deportation order has been made to return to the U.K., and for anyone knowingly to harbour them.

C. PART III—MISCELLANEOUS AND GENERAL

Other than persons recommended for deportation, Commonwealth citizens and citizens of the Republic of Ireland are qualified for registration, and British protected persons for naturalization, under section six (subsection 1) and section ten of the British Nationality Act, 1948, after they have satisfied the Secretary of State that they have been:

(*a*) ordinarily resident in the United Kingdom; or

(*b*) in Crown service under Her Majesty's Government in the United Kingdom; or

(*c*) partly the one and partly the other,

throughout the period of five years ending with the date of his application, or such shorter period so ending as the Secretary of State may in the special circumstances of any particular case accept.

A person guilty of an offence under the Act is liable on summary conviction to a fine not exceeding one hundred pounds or to imprisonment for a term not exceeding six months or both.

The remainder of Part III contains general provisions as to detained persons, Orders in Council, appointment and functioning of immigration officers and medical inspectors, etc.

Schedule I makes provisions for the examination by immigration officers of persons landing in the U.K.; for refusal of admission and admission subject to conditions; for the removal of immigrants refused admission on the same vessel on which they arrived (such directions must be given within two months of the date on which admission was refused); for the detention of immigrants pending further examination or removal; for landing and embarkation cards. There are also special provisions for the crews of ships and aircraft and for stowaways.

The second schedule contains supplementary provisions as to deportation, and the third schedule special provisions relating to action taken in the Channel Islands or the Isle of Man.

3. THE OPERATION OF THE ACT

A. EMPLOYMENT VOUCHERS

The Ministry of Labour's voucher scheme, as initially evolved,[1] provided for three categories of voucher:

Category 'A': Commonwealth citizens who have a specific job to come to in Britain.

Category 'B': Applicants who have a recognized skill or qualification which is in short supply in Britain.

Category 'C': All other applicants, priority treatment being given to those who have served in H.M. Government in war, and thereafter on a 'first come, first served' basis.

According to the provisions of the scheme, applications for Category 'A' vouchers are made on the initiative of the employer in Britain, who applies to the local employment exchanges.[2] The Manager has to satisfy himself that the vacancy is genuine and the wages and other conditions of employment are not less favourable than those currently applicable for similar work in the district concerned; but he does not take cognizance of unemployed already on his register as he would if the application were for an alien. 'A' vouchers are issued to the employer, who passes them on to the prospective immigrant. Category 'B' vouchers are applied for by the individuals concerned to the British High Commission Offices in their respective territories; the latter are responsible for verifying qualifications, after which the applicant is free to enter Britain to seek employment. Category 'C' vouchers are, or were, like 'B' vouchers, applied for and verified locally. All three categories of voucher must normally be presented within six months from the date of issue, and may not be used more than once.

[1] This scheme was not enshrined in the legislation and can therefore be changed by an administrative decision of the Ministry of Labour without reference to the House of Commons. (See R. B. Davison, *Commonwealth Immigrants*, Ch. 1, for more details.)

[2] In the spring of 1962 a leaflet explaining the procedure to employers was distributed to exchanges throughout Britain (Ministry of Labour leaflet E.D.L. 125).

The number of vouchers to be issued was left to the decision of a Council of Ministers which met fairly regularly. Their decisions were said to be based on a consideration of six main factors:[1]

(a) The general unemployment and employment situation.
(b) Housing.
(c) Health hazards (e.g. an outbreak of an epidemic abroad).
(d) Pressure on the educational system.
(e) Social tensions in the U.K. population arising from racial friction.
(f) The reactions of Commonwealth governments to the working of the Act.

A beneficial side-effect of the Act was that the Home Office (which controls actual immigration) and the Ministry of Labour (which issues employment vouchers) began to collect fuller and more accurate immigration statistics than ever before. There had been approximate estimates of net inward movement before mid-1962 but they were thought to be unreliable and probably under-estimated, particularly in the case of two out of the three largest coloured Commonwealth immigrant groups, the Indians and the Pakistanis.

In the case of the West Indians, the third and earliest group to start arriving in large numbers, estimates were much more reliable because of statistics kept since 1955, first by the British Caribbean Welfare Service, and then by the Migrant Services Division of the Federation of the West Indies. (These differentiated between men, women, and children, and the place of embarkation of West Indian immigrants, thereby providing an indication of changing trends and phases in the migration.) After the Act came into force, however, the improved statistics[2] provided similar indications for the other two groups, as well as for all other Commonwealth immigrants and visitors.

The overall estimates of net inward movement for the years after 1955 (see Table 1) show how West Indian immigration dominated the 1950s, with 1956 as its peak year; it rose again steeply in 1960, 1961, and the first half of 1962. Net immigration from India and Pakistan jumped proportionately much more steeply in 1961–2. While this could also be attributed in part to 'beat-the-ban' it seemed due at least as much to a 'snowball' effect, triggered off by 'push factors' in areas such as the

[1] Davison, *Commonwealth Immigrants*, p. 10, quoting a spokesman of the Ministry of Labour. The writer commented: 'Clearly (a) and (b) are immediately relevant, although it is not easy to see how a decision is reached if the employment situation calls for an increase in voucher issue while the housing situation (as it always will) indicates that immigration should be restricted.'

[2] See official 'control of immigration' statistics for 1962–3, 1964, 1965, and 1966, White Papers Cmnd 2151, Cmnd 2379, Cmnd 2658, Cmnd 2979, and Cmnd 3258, H.M.S.O., *et seq.*

Punjab, and assisted by the operations of currency speculators and agents selling forged passports, which circumvented attempts by the Indian and Pakistan Governments to control migration to Britain from their end.

Immediately after the introduction of controls the overall estimates showed, first a tremendous drop in net inward movement, and then a moderate but much more rapid recovery in the figures for Indians and Pakistanis. The West Indians, on the other hand, were slow off the mark in applying for vouchers and most of their new immigrants were dependants rejoining their menfolk.[1]

The statistics of applications for vouchers, applied for and issued, show very different patterns for different ethnic groups.[2] The Indians and Pakistanis were particularly quick off the mark in applying for all three categories of vouchers. Up to the end of 1963, for instance, about 4,700 from the two countries applied for, and 2,800 were issued with, 'A' vouchers (about two-fifths of the total issued); in the case of 'B' vouchers, there were over 6,200 applications and nearly 5,100 vouchers were issued out of a total of 8,670. It was, however, in the 'first come, first served' 'C' Category that the 'snowball' effect really became visible, with Indian and Pakistani applications of 53,893 and 76,125 respectively out of an overall total of 145,634. Of these Indian and Pakistani applications only 13,299 and 6,961 respectively had been issued by the end of June 1963 (a considerable minority to priority ex-service applicants); this was, however, over two-thirds of all 'C' vouchers issued and it became clear that enough 'C' applications were already in the pipe-line to last for several years, and that most of the new entrants in this category would be from India and Pakistan, if the 'first come, first served' principle continued to be applied. The time lag between the receipt of an application and its eventual issue inevitably increased, and was at least a year by mid-1963.

In July 1963, however, the 'first come, first served' principle was modified to ensure that no Commonwealth country received more than one-quarter of the available 'C' vouchers; this move meant that only 50% of the 'C' vouchers could go to the two countries. A further cut-back came on 5 June 1964, after which date Category 'C' applications were accepted from Indians and Pakistanis only if they were entitled to preference because of previous Forces service. The figures for 1964 therefore presented a very different picture from those of 1963. Of 26,153 'C' applications received from Indians only 550 were issued

[1] Of the net inward movement from the West Indies in the early years of 1963 and 1964, the percentage breakdowns into men, women, and children were, respectively, 2%, 46%, 52% and 10%, 37% and 53%, a strong contrast with the Pakistani and Indian breakdowns. (See Table 3.)

[2] See also pp. 142–4, below.

(477 to ex-servicemen), and of 19,292 Pakistani applications, only 537 were issued (428 with Forces service).

Moreover, Government thinking about Category 'C' vouchers as a whole was changing. In the first six months of controls (July 1962 to 28 December 1962) 17,494 'C' vouchers were issued, and 22,652 in 1963. The ceiling was, however, sharply lowered in 1964, in which only 2,221 'C' vouchers (1,284 to priority ex-servicemen applicants) were issued over the whole year, or rather up to September 1964, after which no more vouchers were issued.[1] This actual discontinuation was formalized in August 1965, when the Labour Government's White Paper on Commonwealth Immigration abolished Category 'C' altogether.[2]

The statistics for Category 'A' and 'B' vouchers between mid-1962 and 1965 showed consistently divergent patterns for different ethnic groups. The majority of applications and issues for Barbados, Cyprus, Hong Kong, and Malta fell into Category 'A'. In the case of Barbados most of this was due to the government-operated recruitment scheme started some years before controls, which supplied labour for London Transport, the catering trade, and other employers in Britain. On the other hand, most Cypriots, Maltese, and Hong Kong applicants were thought to be sponsored by compatriots, often relatives, with restaurants, grocery-stores, and other specialized work-establishments in Britain. A considerable minority of Pakistanis were also applied for under 'A' vouchers from the beginning (usually for restaurant work), and as the years went by there was an increase in applications for other West Indians (some as nurses but the majority as factory workers, mostly unskilled). This trend suggested that some West Indian workers already in Britain were sufficiently settled to recommend relatives and friends to their employers, or that some employers were beginning to resort to Barbadian-style recruitment schemes in other West Indian islands. Any such developments were however to be hamstrung by the introduction, after August 1965, of low fixed quotas for both Category 'A' and Category 'B' vouchers.

Category 'B' vouchers have gone to teachers, nurses, doctors, dentists, science and technology graduates, skilled craftsmen, and clerical workers (the two latter categories have been excluded since August 1965). Applications and issues have also tended to be concentrated among certain national groups, notably from India, with Pakistanis second, well behind but a long way ahead of all other groups, including Australians, Canadians, and Ceylonese. By contrast there were few West Indians and virtually no applicants from Cyprus, Hong Kong, or Malta in this category.

[1] This was arranged by Mr. Ray Gunter, the Minister of Labour, winding up the debate on the Expiry Laws Continuance Bill in November 1964.

[2] By mid-1965 the Category 'C' waiting list numbered over 300,000 (Cmnd 2739, p.3).

Between them, 'A' and 'B' vouchers appeared to be producing a flow of satisfactory immigrants for the British economy and British society. The tributes paid to the invaluable contribution of such immigrants to the health services,[1] and transport services in London and many provincial cities have become too numerous to list in detail. There were, however, certain other aspects of the scheme that evoked comment and sometimes criticism. From the angle of the exporting countries it was argued that to admit only such selected professional and skilled immigrants was to impose a 'brain drain' on developing countries which were a great deal shorter of such workers than was Britain. On the other hand, it was noted that the professional immigrants were far from filling the gap left by British professionals who emigrated to other parts of the world.[2] A third aspect concerned the matter of qualitative differences between the U.K. and various Commonwealth countries over skills and professional qualifications. This could lead to apparent discrimination, particularly against certain 'B' voucher-holders, e.g. certain teachers and engineering graduates from India and Pakistan who did not meet British professional requirements.[3]

(i) *Issue and Use of Employment Vouchers*

It has never been the case that all vouchers issued have been taken up. In 1962 and the first half of 1963 a considerable proportion was not taken up[4] and the rate of issue was therefore increased. Later it was found that a much higher proportion of vouchers were being used and the overall rate of issue was cut to 400 a week, of which about three-quarters were found to be taken up. This reduced rate of issue led to the discontinuation in practice of Category 'C' in September 1964, when the two priority categories 'A' and 'B' took up the whole issue and left nothing over for Category 'C' applicants.[5] The rate of 400 per week was maintained until the cut to 8,500 vouchers a year announced in the Government's White Paper of August 1965.

[1] For instance, on 10 March 1965 Lord Stonham told the House of Lords that 40% of all the junior hospital medical staff were from the new Commonwealth countries, and nearly 15% of all student nurses. Without that help some hospitals would have to close, just as without Commonwealth immigrants London Transport would be disrupted (Lords Hansard, 10 March 1965, Vol. 264, no. 49, col. 96).

[2] In 1963, for instance, immigrant teachers, nurses, professional engineers, and chemists numbered only about half as many as their British counterparts who left for other parts of the world. (David Ennals, M.P., Hansard, 23 March 1965, col. 393.)

[3] See pp. 279–83, below.

[4] Davison (*Commonwealth Immigrants*, p. 8) comments on the surprising variation in the speeds with which people from different countries were taking up their vouchers in the first year of the Act's operation. Barbados was fastest, with India and Pakistan at the other end of the scale.

[5] Cmnd 2739, August 1965, p. 3.

B. DEPENDANTS

From 1963 onwards the immigrants from *all* Commonwealth countries who entered Britain on employment vouchers after the imposition of immigration restrictions have constituted only a modest percentage of those who were admitted for settlement under other headings: 'long-term visitors' (over three months), students, dependants, and others (e.g. persons coming to marry and settle, persons of independent means coming for retirement). A similar relationship has applied in the case of the annual figures for net inward movement. These show that the number of voucher-holders, though higher than those of dependants in late 1962 and 1963, has declined or been cut, from 30,125 in 1963 to 5,461 in 1966, while the number of dependants has risen, from 26,234 in 1963 to 42,026 in 1966. It was the rising numbers[1] of such 'dependants', already visible in 1964, that was, along with 'evasions', to be a major topic of discussion and concern in 1965;[2] the outcome was the tightening up of immigration controls and procedure and the White Paper of August 1965.

The definition of 'dependant' in the 1962 Act included the 'wife or children under 16' of residents or those granted entry. In the 'Instructions to Immigration Officers' issued by the Home Office in May 1962,[3] the definition of a 'wife' was extended to a 'woman who has been living in permanent association with a man, even if not married to him'; and officers were instructed to bear in mind 'any local custom or tradition tending to establish the permanence of the association'.[4] The possibility of polygamous unions was not mentioned, but an answer given in November 1965, during the committee stage of the Expiring Laws Continuance Bill,[5] suggests that the situation in fact rarely, if ever, confronted immigration officers (although it was, in common with the

[1] Numbers were altogether a subject of preoccupation and fear. The title of the excellent *Times* series in January 1965, 'The Dark Million', reflected this more than its contents. See also I.R.R. *Newsletter*, May–June 1965, pp. 8–12.

[2] Two aspects of this were discussed: (a) the estimated natural increase in 'coloured' settlements in the decades to come; (b) speculation about the size of the 'dark cloud' of dependants still to join coloured immigrants already in the country. On the latter question, estimates varied from the 500,000 of Mr. Bowden, Lord President of the Council, on 23 March 1965 to the 250,000 of his Lords' colleague, Lord Stonham, on 10 March 1965.

[3] Cmnd 1716 H.M.S.O.

[4] Fiancés of either sex could also be admitted if the officer was satisfied (a) that the person would qualify for admission if the marriage had already taken place and (b) that the proposed marriage would take place within a reasonable time (three months).

[5] Mr. George Thomas, interjecting during a speech by Mr. Peter Thorneycroft (Hansard, 23 November 1965, Vol. 721, no. 11, col. 322). But see also *Daily Telegraph*, 9 July 1966 and 22 July 1966, for the suggestion that on occasion two wives have been allowed in.

existence of common law wives and their issue, to prove somewhat more of a complication for Inland Revenue offices dealing with immigrants' claims for allowances for families left behind).

The definition of 'child' was, as has already been noted, extended to 'stepchild', 'adopted child', and, in relation to the mother, 'illegitimate child', in the instructions to immigration officers. Children under 16 were entitled to admission if either parent was a Commonwealth citizen resident in the United Kingdom, and those coming to join relatives, other than parents, or the putative father, were also to be freely admitted provided that the immigration officer was satisfied about the arrangements made to look after them.

Children between 16 and 18 should, it was said, be freely admitted if they were joining a parent or parents. Persons over 18, on the other hand, should as a general rule qualify in their own right, as holders of vouchers or entry certificates, or as students. Exceptions might, however, be made to this rule: e.g. an unmarried daughter forming part of the family unit if the whole family was coming to settle, and unmarried sons under 21 who were still dependent on their parents.

Husbands should be treated as eligible for admission if the officer was satisfied that a man was coming to join his wife, that she was ordinarily resident in the U.K., and that she wished her husband to rejoin her. In the case of parents, widowed mothers, widowers above 60, and couples of whom one or both was above 60, should be admitted if their children were able and willing to support them. Other relatives of working age (below 60 for a man, below 55 for a woman) must qualify in their own right, but near relatives over working age (e.g. grandparents, brothers and sisters, aunts and uncles) could be admitted in certain circumstances if relatives here were able and willing to support them.

All these principles were to apply equally to Commonwealth citizens accompanying persons qualifying for admission and to those joining relatives already settled in the U.K.

(i) *Numbers of Dependants Admitted 1962–1966*

The overall number of Commonwealth dependants admitted between mid-1962 and the end of 1966 was as follows:

TABLE 6

Dependants admitted 1962–1966

Period	Men	Women	Children	Total
July 1962—end 1966	259	4,039	4,534	8,832
1963	833	11,331	14,070	26,234
1964	1,239	13,437	22,784	37,460
1965	1,485	14,992	24,737	41,214
1966	1,450	13,592	93,109	42,026
Totals	5,266	57,391	159,234	155,766

Several points should be noted about these statistics. First, the totals do not constitute a net inflow since there was an outflow of earlier arrivals and also of some of the newcomers themselves. Secondly, the term 'dependants' has a somewhat misleading annotation, since many of the newcomers have been women of working age who join the labour force, while the children are all potential members of the labour force after a shorter or longer period.

Another aspect of the 'dependants' question is that in recent years there has been an increasing tendency to equate in speech and print the terms 'Commonwealth', 'coloured', and 'immigrant'. In fact, the immigration control statistics published by the Home Office and the Ministry of Labour cover all Commonwealth immigrants, from Aden and Australia, through Canada, Hong Kong, India, Jamaica, and New Zealand, to Trinidad and Zambia. The overall figures are, however, often quoted as if they referred only to the 'new' Commonwealth countries or, more particularly, to the West Indies, India, and Pakistan, a confusion which has, of course, worked to the detriment of immigrants from the last-named three countries.

An examination of the detailed ethnic breakdown of the admission for settlement shows that the three largest 'new' Commonwealth immigrant groups contributed about 73% of all dependants in the four and a half years up to the end of 1966 (over 114,000 out of the total of about 156,000),[1] compared with a total of nearly 9,000 for the three 'old' Commonwealth countries (Canada, Australia, New Zealand). The latter countries, on the other hand, tended to figure in considerably larger numbers in such categories as 'long-term visitors' and 'other persons coming for settlement'.

(ii) *Evasion*

Evasion of controls became a burning topic in 1965. It was first mentioned by the then Home Secretary, Sir Frank Soskice, on 17 November 1964, and restressed on 4 February 1965 as an argument for stricter control of immigration.[2] It became one of the principal arguments for

[1] The totals for these three countries were: men, 3,912; women, 36,241; children, 73,972. See Table 3 for detailed breakdown.

[2] See I.R.R. *Newsletter*, December 1964, pp. 8–9, and March 1965, pp. 3–4. On 9 March the Prime Minister repeated the argument that evasion was almost fatally eroding the Act. Mentioned by various speakers as categories in which possible evasion might take place were dependants, students, long-term visitors, and ships' crews. The subject of 'evasion' and 'discrepancies' was again brought up by Mr. Peter Thorneycroft during the debate on the Expiring Laws Continuance Bill, 23 November 1965. By November 1966, the Home Secretary, Mr. Roy Jenkins, could discuss the matter of evasion in very much more moderate terms (Hansard, 8 November 1966, cols. 1229–3).

the imposition in the White Paper of more careful scrutiny of the intentions and *bona fides* of Commonwealth citizens seeking entrance, and a general power to impose conditions of admission on persons not appearing to have a clear right of entry, including registration with the police and repatriation of evaders. At the Labour Party Conference in September, the Prime Minister, defending the White Paper, added an additional gloss:

largely because of widespread evasion of the Act, in the concluding months of the Conservative Government . . . there are towns and cities in Britain which are being asked today to absorb a degree of immigration on a scale beyond their social capacity to absorb . . . (*Guardian*, 29 September 1965).

(iii) *An Analysis of Evasion Statistics*

The evidence for this 'evasion' was examined critically by Peter Norman in an article in the I.R.R. *Newsletter* of November 1965, under the title 'Who Is Guilty of Evasion?'

The figures from which estimates of 'evasion' are derived are collected in the operation of the Commonwealth Immigrants Act and published annually in the Home Office, *Control of Immigration, Statistics* (Cmnd 2151 for 1962–3 and Cmnd 2658 for 1964). Estimates derived from these annual figures were given by the Home Secretary in a written answer to Mr. E. Wainwright (Lab., Dearne Valley) on 22 March last; the Home Secretary's figures are reproduced in Table 7 below. The arithmetic by which the Home Secretary arrived at his results can be summarized as follows for 1963 and 1964 combined:

	Immigration from the 'New'* Commonwealth	Immigration from the 'Old'* Commonwealth
(*a*) Net overall gain	119,166	22,333
(*b*) Total admitted for settlement	108,911	6,795
(*c*) Difference, i.e. (*a*)−(*b*)	10,255	15,538

* The 'old' Commonwealth consists of Canada, Australia, and New Zealand; the 'new' Commonwealth includes all remaining Commonwealth countries.

Although in the written answer the result of these calculations is not called 'evasion' but presented as a statistical 'difference', exactly the same figures were given unequivocally by Lord Stonham on 10 March in the Lords: 'During the last two years the total evasion figure for the three older Commonwealth countries was 15,538 and for all the new Commonwealth countries it was 10,255.' (Official Report, 10 March, col. 94.)

TABLE 7

Evasion figures

	Immigration from Commonwealth countries other than Canada, Australia, and New Zealand		Immigration from Canada, Australia, and New Zealand	
	1963	1964	1963	1964
(1) Total number admitted	178,170	193,862	187,567	212,739
(2) Total number embarked	121,121	131,745	178,616	199,357
(3) Net balance (i.e. difference between (1) and (2))	+57,049*	+62,117*	+8,951*	+13,382*
(4) Number deliberately admitted for settlement:				
(*a*) with Ministry of Labour vouchers ...	28,678	13,888	1,447	817
(*b*) others (mainly dependants)	27,393	38,952	2,288	2,243
(*c*) Total number admitted for settlement ((*a*)+(*b*))	56,071	52,840	3,735	3,060
(5) Difference between (4)(*c*) and (3)	978	9,277	5,216	10,322†

* The net inward balance during the past two years is not necessarily an accurate measure of those admitted during that period who have settled permanently. No given period has a self-contained flow: some people who leave during the period will have arrived before it started, and some who arrive will not leave until after the period ends. Over a long time during which the flow had been relatively constant, the net balance should give a reasonable indication of the rate at which people were settling here.

† It is doubtful whether most of these have the intention of permanent settlement.

Source: Official Report Commons, 22 March 1965, written answers, col. 26.

The faulty logic of calling the 'difference' 'evasions' was clearly demonstrated by Lord Stonham in the same speech of 10 March: 'In the first four months that this Government were in office the evasion figures from the new Commonwealth countries was minus 5,133—that is, more out than in' [*sic*]. It is obvious that in any period when there is no net gain of Commonwealth citizens the calculations are bound to produce absurd results. There is only one situation in which there would be no evasion, either positive or negative, according to the method followed—if the total number of Commonwealth citizens admitted in any year, less those admitted specifically for permanent settlement, were exactly balanced by the number of embarkations in the same period. There is no reason why this should be expected to happen and even less reason for calling any surplus that might arise 'evasion'.

The first flaw in the Government's argument is the false assumption that there should be no net gains in any year in any category of Commonwealth immigrants except those specifically admitted for settlement. Obviously for persons entering the country as passengers in transit one would expect an exact balance, over the year, of arrivals and departures, since persons in this group are presumably staying only a few hours or days; in any other category of persons admitted on a temporary basis any fluctuation from year to year is likely to produce a net imbalance—plus or minus—over the period of one year.

Students are an obvious case in which one would *expect* more arrivals in 1964 than departures. Assuming that students following courses in this country stay an average of three years, then the number leaving in any year will be governed by the number arriving three years ago. British Council figures of 'new' Commonwealth students following courses in Britain rose from 37,430 in the academic year 1961–2 to 40,650 in 1963–4—an increase of 3,220. The increase in the number of Commonwealth students over the past three years is almost certain to have produced a net gain of students in 1964, since more arrived in that year than three years previously.

Unfortunately, no one is in a position to say precisely that there have been net gains or losses of a specified size in any category; the statistics of persons subject to control entering and leaving the U.K. are collected in such a way that no net calculations are possible. On entry to this country, all Commonwealth citizens subject to control are interrogated by the immigration officer and either refused entry or admitted in one of ten specified categories.[1] Commonwealth citizens leaving the U.K. are counted, but no check is made on the category, if any, under which they were originally admitted. Hence there is no way of deriving a figure of net gain or loss in any category. It is complete speculation for the Government to say, as they do, that the overall net balance consists of so many permanent settlers and so many 'others'. If the figures are available, they have certainly never been produced.

Having arrived at a figure of 'evasions' by a false process, the Government has presented its results misleadingly as a measure of behaviour which is not measurable. When on 9 March 1965 Mr. Wilson referred to the degree of evasion 'almost fatally eroding the Act', he went on to describe how 'this situation arises from the use of false passports, impersonation, false statements about the purpose of travel to this country, and so on'. (Official Report, Commons, 9 March 1965, col. 248.) If by 'evasions' the Government means those persons who gave false information to immigration officers, then there

[1] The complete list of the ten categories is: (1) visitors for three months or less; (2) visitors for more than three months; (3) students; (4) holders of Ministry of Labour vouchers; (5) dependants accompanying or coming to join the head of the household; (6) persons coming for settlement not included elsewhere; (7) diplomats and officials and their dependants; (8) passengers in transit; (9) persons joining crews of ships or aircraft; (10) persons returning to the U.K. from temporary absence abroad.

is no possible measure of the scale of evasion. Every Commonwealth citizen interrogated by the immigration officer is presumably refused admission if the officer can show that he or she is not telling the truth. Hence every Commonwealth citizen, like every alien, who is admitted to the country, must have satisfied the immigration officer that he or she is entitled to enter. There is no justification whatever for presenting figures of persons actually admitted by the immigration officer as evidence for evasion of the control.

Finally, the Government shows discrimination in presenting its 'evidence'. The figures given in the Home Secretary's written answer show a much larger unaccounted balance from the three 'old' Commonwealth countries than from the remainder. The table from Hansard reproduced here includes a footnote to the figures for the 'old' Commonwealth—Canada, Australia, and New Zealand—saying of the unaccounted difference for 'white' immigrants: 'it is doubtful whether most of these have the intention of permanent settlement.' In references to 'evasion' both before and since the Home Secretary's written answer, it is the 10,000 or so balance from the 'new' 'coloured' Commonwealth which is mentioned and not the 15,500 balance from the three 'white' Commonwealth countries (Official Report, Commons, 4 February, col. 1285; 23 March, cols. 446–447; 2 August, col. 1062. Official Report, Lords, 15 March, col. 94). The figures for both are from exactly the same source (and both equally misleading). But the so-called 'evidence' has been presented selectively to create public alarm about evasion by coloured immigrants alone. By constant repetition, the Government's estimates of 'evasions' have acquired the status of fact and are no longer questioned. Careful analysis shows how little their estimates are worth.

(iv) *Other Forms of Evasion*

Other forms of evasion include the traditional kind adopted by the stowaway. Between 1946 and 1958 the average annual number of colonial stowaways was 407. Thereafter it dropped to 305 in 1950, and ranged between 179 and 56 up to and including 1960.

A form of evasion that has almost certainly been numerically larger (although its extent is difficult to estimate accurately) is that concerned with forged or falsified passports, employment vouchers, and other documents often associated with the activities of travel and currency-smuggling agencies, particularly in Pakistan and India. Yet another is based on misrepresentation of an alleged dependant's age or relationship to an immigrant already here, e.g. kinship, marriage, or intention to marry.[1]

A possible route of evasion about which little is known, though dark rumours circulate from time to time, is via the Republic of Ireland. If

[1] For press and other references, see I.R.R. *Newsletter*, September 1963, p. 11, October 1963, pp. 4–5, February 1964, p. 6, March 1964, p. 3, May 1964, pp. 3–4, January 1965, p. 8, February 1965, p. 7, December 1965, pp. 3–5, April 1966 pp. 21–2.

used to any extent, this route has probably been more or less corked up by the tighter controls at ports of entry imposed in 1965.

4. AN UNFAVOURABLE CLIMATE OF OPINION

The Commonwealth Immigrants Act and the subsequent heavy drop in the net immigration figures had a lulling effect on public opinion in Britain for a while.[1] It had been widely assumed and stated that the Act (which made 'temporary provision' for controls) was intended to provide a 'breathing space' during which integration could proceed and be promoted. A laissez-faire situation nevertheless continued in which virtually no further provisions were made at national level for reception, briefing, placing, housing, dispersal, or any other procedures that are part of the machinery employed by most countries of immigration. The existing problem of housing and the associated problems of education, health services, and other local amenities were intensified in those industrial areas of chronic labour shortage, which were also areas of heavy immigrant settlement. Moreover, apart from the reports of the non-statutory Commonwealth Immigrants Advisory Council set up in 1962 by the then Home Secretary, R. A. Butler, there was little guidance and no official help to local authorities at national level.[2]

The housing situation was underlined by the first C.I.A.C. report in July 1963, by the simultaneous revelations about 'Rachmanism' in Paddington and North Kensington, and, in 1964, by the report of the Milner Holland Committee. The education issue hit the national press in October 1963, when the then Minister of Education, Sir Edward Boyle, dealt firmly with protesting Southall parents who demanded segregated schools by laying down the general principle of dispersal with a maximum quota of one-third per school.

The resurgence of an unfavourable climate of opinion in 1964–5 was basically and predictably the outcome of a near-decade of uncontrolled and unplanned[3] economic migration from the 'new' Commonwealth which had exacerbated, not caused, grave national and local shortages and problems, notably in the spheres of housing, schools, and the health and welfare services, and had set up certain additional frictions of

[1] Philip Mason, *Race and Religion*, C.I.I.R., 1964, p. 196.

[2] The gap was to some extent filled by the small voluntary committee of non-official persons nominated by the Commonwealth Immigrants Advisory Committee set up in April 1964 with Miss Nadine Peppard as its Advisory Officer. This was to evolve later into a much larger body, but at the time its functions were advisory and its resources small.

[3] With the exception of the small Barbadian schemes. (See R. B. Davison, 'West Indian Migration to Britain, 1955–61', *The West Indian Economist* 4, Pt. II, pp. 10–11.)

a social and cultural nature.[1] It was, however, more immediately attributable to the introduction of immigration and colour issues to the political scene in the 1964 general election (the year of Smethwick), some by-elections, and a number of local government elections.[2]

This adverse climate of opinion in relation to immigration and immigrants from the 'new' Commonwealth countries, found expression in, *inter alia*, demands for increased and rigid controls; in the emergence of what was frequently called a 'Dutch auction of illiberalism' between the two major parties, Labour (in power after October 1964) and Conservatives in opposition; in a continual and often highly coloured coverage of the 'colour problem' by most of the press and other mass media; and in an increasing and compensatory tendency for immigrants to organize themselves in defensive or protest associations.

A. SOME BIDS IN THE 'DUTCH AUCTION'[3]

In the prolonged parliamentary and extra-parliamentary dialogue between Labour and Conservatives from the opening of the new

[1] Cf. Julius Isaac, *The Economics of Migration*, London, Kegan Paul, 1947. In Ch. V he discusses 'the case against free immigration' and for 'planned immigration' ('symptoms which call for restrictions are likely to be produced by a much smaller influx of immigrants, if immigration is free, than under conditions of planned immigration'). In the U.N.E.S.C.O. series, 'Population and Culture', concerned with pre-war, post-war European immigrants, there was widespread acceptance of the fact that cultural rather than economic factors set the long-term limits to the rate of immigration, because cultural integration involves more changes in roles and institutions than economic absorption and therefore takes longer. According to W. D. Borrie (*The Cultural Integration of Immigrants*, U.N.E.S.C.O., 1959, Ch. V *passim*) the relative success of post-war migration planning appeared to be due, in considerable measure, to a much more realistic view of the interrelationships between economic and cultural factors in the processes of adjustment, to greater care in selection and placing, to greater inter-governmental and international co-operation, and to better understanding of the techniques of promoting economic growth.

[2] Nor can one overlook the steady drip of verbal and written anti-immigration propaganda that had been emanating for years not only from the neo-Nazi splinter-parties but, more important, from the new-style anti-immigration groupings in Birmingham, Smethwick, and the West Midlands generally. These helped to produce the Peter Griffiths victory, much of the backing for Sir Cyril Osborne's and similar petitions in favour of immigration control, and in general what may be called the 'Birmingham syndrome' in politics; it affected mainly the Conservatives (though by no means all) but also some Labour politicians and at least one Liberal. See Paul Foot, op. cit., and Nicholas Deakin (ed.), *Colour and the British Electorate*, London, Pall Mall Press for I.R.R., 1965, *passim*. See also Ch. 12, below.

[3] For this 'Dutch auction' period, including the Labour Government's moves and attitudes, see monthly *Newsletters* from November 1964 to September 1965; Paul Foot, op. cit., and Nicholas Deakin, op. cit. It should be remembered that until the 1966 election the Labour Government was operating on a slender majority of four.

Parliament in late 1964 it must be said that 'restrictionist' Conservative leaders and speakers consistently outbid the Government in calling for intensified and extended controls. Not only did their demands become increasingly restrictive but their numbers increased, while the numbers and voices of the 'liberal' and 'traditional' pro-Commonwealth Conservatives dwindled to a handful in the year between the debates on the renewal of the Commonwealth Immigrants Act in November 1964 and November 1965. The small group of back-benchers, led by Sir Cyril Osborne, who had waged a long and lonely campaign for control of coloured immigration since the early 1950s, was able to claim a second victory when the Conservative Party, instead of, as in the past, rejecting such initiatives, gave serious consideration to his proposal to bring in a bill restricting all immigration, except for those whose parents or grandparents were born here, until local authorities had dealt with the urgent problems arising from previous immigration.

Leave to introduce the modified Osborne Bill was refused by a majority of 261 votes to 162 or 99 votes on 1 March 1965. The *Economist* (March 1965) commented that the Conservative hierarchy had acted very stupidly over 'the Osborne affair':

> Sir Cyril's original draft was monstrously extremist. The party leaders should have let him and other right-wing emotionalists stew in their own prejudices, and sat aside while the Bill was negatived by a massive majority. Instead, they brainwashed Sir Cyril into making his Bill, while still pretty nasty in intention, not too grossly illiberal in actual wording; and then let it be known that, although no whips were being issued, Sir Alec Douglas-Home and Mr. Heath would lead the mass of the Conservative Party into the division lobby in Sir Cyril's support. The political calculations were, first, that this would avoid the embarrassment of a small number of Conservative M.P.s voting for the original enormity of intolerance; second, that it might reap electoral advantage by demonstrating that the Conservatives are still in essence more anti-immigrant than Labour. But the actual political effect would have been to make Sir Cyril appear as the official voice of the party on this issue, and thus have made it almost inevitable that an already dangerous trend in Conservative thinking would keep rolling further towards racialism in future.
>
> That danger has fortunately been mitigated by the fact that seven Conservative M.P.s had the courage to vote with Labour, thus appearing in the opposite lobby to Sir Alec; while another fifty or so Conservative M.P.s abstained or tactfully stayed away. Sir Cyril's Bill was therefore defeated by a thumping majority of 99. But—the prominent names in the roll-call of discredit on Tuesday need to be reiterated—Sir Alec Douglas-Home, Mr. Heath, Mr. Selwyn Lloyd, Mr. Thorneycroft, Mr. Sandys, Mr. Powell, Mr. Godber have shown themselves willing to vote beside Sir Cyril, on a matter and in a tactic which no truly liberal statesman should have been eager to touch.

On 4 February Sir Alec Douglas-Home had started the restrictionist ball rolling at shadow cabinet level with four new demands on immigration: (a) the repatriation of all immigrants entering illegally; (b) Government assistance for those who wanted to return; (c) dependants to be included in a limit set on the overall official numbers; and (d) a further reduction in the numbers allowed entry. The next day the Home Secretary, Sir Frank Soskice, announced tighter restrictions on immigration. Mr. Peter Griffiths, M.P. (who had escalated to some respectability within the Conservative Party, although some former supporters in Smethwick were disappointed by his new moderation), commented, correctly enough, that Sir Alec's demands were almost identical with the ten points that he had made to the Press at the General Election, and that the Labour Government was now adopting the very policies that he had been reviled for advocating at the election.

The official Conservative line on controls became increasingly tough after Mr. Peter Thorneycroft took over from Sir Edward Boyle as front-bench spokesman for Home Affairs on 16 February. Three days after the Osborne Bill debate, Mr. Thorneycroft called in the strongest terms yet for further legislation to control immigration, thereby raising the Home Secretary's bid to tighten controls by means of tougher instructions to immigration officers. Later in March he also rejected a bi-partisan policy.

Thereafter came a period of counter-attacks or rearguard actions by Conservative liberals and moderates, and all-party attempts to take the issue out of party politics, a reiteration of the 'tough line' in April and May, with a threat to make immigration a major electoral issue if the Government did not agree to a dramatic cut-back, and growing indications of a refocusing of attention by 'moderates' away from negative controls and towards possible measures of integration.

Meanwhile a small Conservative Party policy group on immigration had been meeting under the chairmanship of Mr. Selwyn Lloyd, since the beginning of 1965. It consisted of a few M.P.s, mostly 'moderates', and outside specialists. Its conclusions were not published, but over the months its proceedings followed the general trends reported above. In the 'Dutch auction' its chairman, Mr. Selwyn Lloyd, got in smartly ahead of the Labour Government (whose long-awaited White Paper was not published until early August); while his statement was described as representing his personal views and not forecasting the findings of the group, it was generally, though not necessarily with complete accuracy, taken as a pointer to the conclusions agreed on by all group members and also to likely official party policy after October.

Mr. Lloyd's proposals on controls were the application of a 'one in, one out' principle 'for at least a period of years'; proper health tests and conditions about jobs and accommodation; better methods of checking what happens to immigrants after they arrive; more stringent measures to deal with illegal immigrants; more assistance to those who want to go home; and more stringent measures for repatriation of those who obviously do not fit into the community. Positive integratory measures, which the group had worked out in detail, included special assistance for local authorities where special problems had arisen, hostels for unmarried immigrants, special staffing arrangements for schools and auxiliary maternity homes, a large increase of the Government grant to the co-ordinating National Committee for Commonwealth Immigrants, and no economic discrimination against and a fair chance of apprenticeships for the second generation. The 'drastic restrictions' were needed, said Mr. Lloyd, to produce the proper psychological atmosphere (i.e. by inducing a local sense of security in areas of heavy immigrant settlement), which would enable the problems of immigration to be solved. (*Sunday Times*, 4 July; *Glasgow Herald*, 5 July; *Daily Telegraph*, 5 July.)

This statement received a varied reception from the Press—the *Daily Mail* (5 July) called it 'a sane approach', while the *Guardian* (6 July) regarded it as a virtual admission that 'Britain, under the Conservatives, has failed to create a society or an environment which is adequate for the native British to live in, let alone our Commonwealth friends'. The *North Western Evening Mail* (6 July) called it the highest bid to date in the political auction, and condemned as socially undesirable the exclusion of wives and other dependants, which would result from the application of the 'one out, one in' formula. The *Oldham Evening Chronicle* (5 July), while agreeing that it was time to act, quoted the Liberal, Mr. Jeremy Thorpe, on this particular proposal as nonsensical if only in terms of the economy's need for skilled personnel. The *Economist* (10 July) spoke of the 'pernicious notion' inherent in the 'one out, one in' suggestion that dependants should be excluded and of the clear need for more workers, and added 'his speech is not yet, and never should be, official Conservative policy'. In the *New Statesman* (9 July), Gerald Kaufman, writing about the 'Dutch auction', maintained that there was little doubt that Mr. Lloyd's statement would get the support of most Tories—Mr. Christopher Chataway, for instance, who had been firm in his opposition to the original Commonwealth Immigrants Bill, found no difficulty in going along with these conclusions—partly because of the detailed integratory measures, partly because the actual 'one-for-one' policy was intended to apply roughly over a period of years, and was not so vicious as crude headlines might imply.

Within the Conservative Party immediate and outspoken opposition came only from Mr. Norman St. John-Stevas, who issued a statement of protest against the 'one-for-one' policy as 'arbitrary, inhuman, and unjust'. It would flatly contradict the pledge given by Mr. Thorneycroft in the Commons in March, that close dependants of Commonwealth citizens already here would be allowed to come in. To enforce the separation of families while talking about treating all citizens equally was 'humbug and hypocrisy'. It was time to end the 'Dutch auction in illiberalism' which Mr. Wilson, with the approach of 'a cynical opportunist', 'was clearly straining at the leash to join'. Mr. St. John-Stevas was subsequently reported to be under fire for his statement at a meeting of the 1922 Committee; he made it clear that he had no intention of making a personal attack on Mr. Lloyd, but pointed out that Mr. Lloyd's views had also been expressed publicly, with no prior discussion in the Home Affairs Committee of the Party (*Daily Telegraph*, 9 July). Several newspapers hoped editorially that it was Mr. St. John-Stevas and not Mr. Lloyd who spoke with the authentic voice of Conservatism on this matter. The Conservatives were simultaneously reported to be anxious to correct the interpretation that the 'one-for-one' principle would present dependants of immigrants joining them here (*Guardian*, 9 July). On 12 July, the 'one-for-one' policy was endorsed by a majority of those attending the Home Affairs Committee, and on 13 July, reviewing *Colour and the British Electorate 1964*, Mr. Selwyn Lloyd repeated his formula in a milder version, but suggested that the finding of decent accommodation was in practice likely to be a more limiting factor (*Sunday Telegraph*, 18 July). Meanwhile, in July, Sir Cyril Osborne twice called in the Commons for emergency legislation to ban all immigration, except for genuine students and professional people who would return after a limited stay.

Mr. St. John-Stevas was joined by Liberal spokesmen in his criticism of the Lloyd scheme, and the Liberal Party study group on immigration, apart from recommendations for integration, came to the conclusion that the country was quite capable of maintaining and absorbing the present net inward flow of up to 75,000. (Midland Liberals were, however, said to be likely to resist this view.) (*The Times*, 30 June; *Guardian*, 12 July.) Little or no comment on the Lloyd proposals came from the Labour side, the appropriate ministerial committee reportedly not having reached agreement over the new ceiling to be set on immigration (the *Guardian* [11 July] spoke of weeks of 'acrimonious disputes'). Even the most liberal Ministers were, however, said to be accepting the Mountbatten Committee's reported recommendation of 10,000 work vouchers, while a figure as low as 5,000 was being canvassed by restrictionists (*New Statesman*, 9 July; *Daily Express*, 9 July). Meanwhile, predictions about the Government scheme included comments on the need to remedy the lack of balance between the issue of work vouchers to Commonwealth citizens (14,705 in 1964) and of work permits to aliens (58,338 in 1964). (*Sunday Citizen*, 4 July; *Financial Times*, 12 July.)

Even after the publication of the White Paper on Immigration (Cmnd 2739) on 2 August (for details see below), the Conservatives were to continue the bidding with a proposal (not made by the policy group) in the 1966 Election manifesto that new immigrants should be admitted on a probationary basis, to be reviewed at the end of two or more years to determine whether they could become 'permanent'. They would also have to register the number of dependants they wished to bring with them. There had, however, been evidence at the 1965 Party Conference of a moderation of tone, with much of the debate focused on the more positive aspects of integration. Any encouragement that the 1966 manifesto might have given to more extreme elements in the Party was also sharply checked by the new leader, Mr. Edward Heath, and the chairman, Mr. Edward du Cann.

After the election, in which few candidates took a 'strong line' and there was no evidence to show that it helped the campaign of those who did, the atmosphere lightened still more with the disappearance from the House of Mr. Thorneycroft, Mr. Peter Griffiths and other advocates of a 'tough line'. By the time of the debate on the Expiring Laws Continuance Bill in November 1966, most Conservative speakers were still negative but subdued (with the exception of Mr. Norman St. John-Stevas and, to a lesser extent, Sir George Sinclair). Mr. Quintin Hogg, however, winding up the debate for the Opposition as Shadow Home Secretary, made it clear that he thought it inhumane and socially harmful to both societies involved if married men were not allowed to bring their families after them, and that any check on dependants should not be a condition of entry, but might be useful to enable a dependant's claims to be verified later. On the first point, he (like Lord Brooke a week earlier) expressed agreement with the Home Secretary (Mr. Roy Jenkins) on the principle that dependants must be allowed to come. On his side, Mr. Jenkins had pointed out that any future substantial reduction would mean going back on that principle, if not in relation to those already here, then to new immigrants, a distinction for which he saw no social, moral, or logical grounds.

The culminating point of this negative and restrictive trend on the Labour side was the Labour Government's White Paper of August 1965, which covered virtually the same ground as the Osborne Bill (see above). Whilst a legacy of bitterness and distrust remained from all this political auctioneering, one positive gain seemed likely, in that many politicians and others were beginning to face the realities of any migratory movement, including the need for some restrictions on entry, however selective, phased, and flexible, and for comprehensive planning of integratory measures at national and local levels, such as is found in most traditional countries of immigration. A swing of the pendulum away from intolerance and hostility seemed to be starting in the latter part of 1965, as back-bench protests against the Labour Government's White Paper grew and more concerted integrative action got under way. Such action had in fact been initiated before the White Paper, following the statement on 9 March 1965 by the Prime Minister, Mr. Harold Wilson, announcing a three-pronged attack on immigration problems.[1]

B. THE 1965 WHITE PAPER ON IMMIGRATION FROM THE COMMONWEALTH[2]

The Conservative Government in 1961 had met with considerable criticism on the grounds that the legislation to restrict immigration from the Commonwealth had been introduced without adequate 'consultation' with the Commonwealth. In the first half of 1965, the Labour Government's proposed high-level mission to discuss the problem of controls did the rounds of the Commonwealth countries most concerned.[3] These included Malta, India, Nigeria, Jamaica, Trinidad and Tobago, Cyprus, and Pakistan (where the mission's leader, Earl Mountbatten, was declared unwelcome by the local press and did not go personally).

The White Paper on Immigration finally came out on 2 August 1965, too late to be debated before October. The Government's proposals were outlined to the Commons by Mr. Herbert Bowden, Lord President of the Council; to quote the *Economist* (7 August 1965), he was the one person on the Labour benches who, having, as chief whip for nine years, made no speeches, 'could eat his Party's liberal words without also eating his own'.

[1] (a) that once they are here they should be treated for all purposes as U.K. citizens; to speed local integration Mr. Maurice Foley, Parliamentary Under-Secretary at the Department of Economic Affairs, would be responsible in a personal capacity for co-ordinating Government action and promoting, through the departments concerned, the efforts of local authorities and voluntary bodies; (b) vigorous measures must be taken to prevent racial discrimination; the Government would introduce a Bill to deal with racial discrimination in public places and the evil of incitement to racial hatred; (c) fresh examination of the whole problem of control, as evasion was almost fatally eroding the Act; the Government proposed to send a high-level mission to certain Commonwealth Governments to discuss this whole matter (*The Times*, 10 March). Sir Alec Douglas-Home welcomed and agreed with Mr. Wilson's statement, describing it as 'sensible and very fair'.

[2] Cmnd 2739, H.M.S.O., August 1965.

[3] The matter was not placed on the official agenda of the Commonwealth Prime Ministers' Conference, but Dr. Eric Williams, Prime Minister of Trinidad, and Mr. Donald Sangster, then Acting Prime Minister of Jamaica, managed to raise it both inside and outside the conference chamber.

Part I of the White Paper consisted of an introductory section outlining the pre-1962 and post-1962 situation and the policy adopted over the issue of vouchers. It also stressed (para. 11) that the Home Secretary had found evidence that evasion of controls was being practised on a considerable scale; that there would be more careful scrutiny of the intentions and *bona fides* of Commonwealth citizens seeking entry by immigration officers; that students would be admitted only for a specified period; and that staff in certain overseas ports dealing with applications for entry certificates would be reinforced.

The White Paper's new proposals on controls were contained in Part II:

(i) *Vouchers* Category 'C' (unskilled) to be discontinued. The annual issue of 'A' and 'B' vouchers to be cut to 8,500, this figure to include a special arrangement of 1,000 vouchers per annum for Malta[1] for at least two years. In category 'A' (workers with jobs to come to) no more than 15% of the vouchers issued would go to any one Commonwealth country. Separate attention would be paid to the need for immigrant workers for seasonal employment, and also the promotion of arrangements for industrial training for limited periods.
(ii) *Dependants, Students, and Visitors* No change in the statutory right of the wife and children under 16 to follow an immigrant; but stricter tests of eligibility, admission of children between 16 and 18 only in cases of hardship. Students to be allowed in freely for the duration of their course, but generally for a year in the first instance. Visitors to be admitted for an initial period of up to six months.
(iii) *Health Checks* A double check, in the country of origin and at the port of entry (at discretion) for any immigrant—but no question of refusing entry on medical grounds to entitled dependants.
(iv) *Repatriation* Powers to be given to the Home Secretary to deport at his discretion (without a court recommendation) immigrants with less than five years' residence whom he considers have flouted immigration controls.
(v) *Registration* The Government to seek powers to allow immigration officers to demand that entrants whom they suspect of evading restrictions must register with the police in the same way as aliens.

The measures proposed to assist integration into what was called 'already a multi-racial society', were outlined in Part III under the following headings:

[1] This special provision was widely interpreted as an extra turn of the colour-bar screw in favour, first of the white Irish, and then of the white Maltese. It was not on the whole seen as a breach of the official non-discriminatory principle, which could be repeated to give special treatment to other specially deserving cases such as the West Indian territories.

(vi) *Housing* It would be wrong to give special treatment to immigrants in housing matters; the solution must be in a determined attack on the housing shortage generally, and particularly on the shortage of accommodation to rent reasonably. Meanwhile, local authorities can use powers they already possess to relieve the immigrants' housing problems and assist integration (including the promotion of housing associations). Legislation to control multi-occupation may also be strengthened.
(vii) *Education* To be tackled on the basis of the Ministry of Education circular (7/65), issued on 4 June—see pp. 256–9.
(viii) *Employment* Employment exchanges have already been instructed not to help employers who practise discrimination and to persuade them to adopt a more co-operative line. The Government will encourage trade unions and managements to promote understanding between hosts and immigrants at the place of work.
(ix) *Health* Increased employment of immigrants to help communication; arrangements for the detection and prevention of T.B.; increased hospital provisions for all in areas of greatest medical need; arrangements for inspection and supervision of child-minding.
(x) *Financial Assistance* For local authorities who need extra staff to deal with problems of transition and adjustment.
(xi) *General* A new National Committee for Commonwealth Immigrants to replace the Commonwealth Immigrants Advisory Council set up in 1962; it will have sufficient finances and staff to expand existing services to the voluntary liaison committees and the regional organizations, to promote a wider sharing of experience, extend information work, organize conferences of workers in the field, arrange training courses, and stimulate research and the examination of particular problems.

C. SOME REACTIONS TO THE WHITE PAPER

National Press reactions to this document were not generally favourable. *The Times* (3 August) saw it as ironic that a Government which had laid such stress upon developing the Commonwealth should now propose to continue poaching from members their scarce skilled and professional manpower while keeping out their unskilled workers; the special provision for Malta also seemed invidious. It was now time for M.P.s to move to change public opinion and for some goodwill and common sense to be applied. The *Guardian* (3 August), commenting that the actual proposals for integrative action seemed minimal compared with the draconian immigration controls, said that though the control proposals might seem more progressive than those of Mr. Selwyn Lloyd, closer examination showed there might be a net decrease under the Labour scheme, allowing for those intending to return. The

Daily Telegraph (3 August) spoke of Commonwealth and other chickens coming home to roost and found the provisions for remedying material grievances unclear, in view of Labour's cut-back on local government expenditure. The *Daily Worker* (3 August) attacked the White Paper as thoroughly dishonest and dangerous, and as going 'further than the Tories ever did' in discriminating against coloured immigrants.

Most provincial papers that commented editorially found the proposals 'sensible', 'reasonable', 'realistic', 'distasteful, but necessary'. Some added that it afforded a breathing-space for positive action, and expressed relief that the issue now seemed to have been taken out of party politics, if only because a bipartisanship of strictness had been achieved. The *Northern Despatch* (3 August) called Labour's change of attitude 'a backward step'; the *Scotsman* (3 August) said that negative restrictions had gone far enough; and the *Oxford Mail* (3 August) considered that the pendulum might have swung too far, and asked whether the West Indies did not also have a claim to a special quota. The *Glasgow Herald* (3 August) added Gibraltar to the list for special provisions.

Under the heading 'Black Paper', the *Economist* (7 August) roundly castigated the Government for 'pinching the Tories' white trousers' and winning the approval of Sir Cyril Osborne. Commonwealth immigration was to be slashed while European and Irish immigration (30,000 net increase from Ireland in 1964) went on. The proposals would strain not only liberal consciences but the British economy. The proposals for integration were inadequate, especially on housing, and the proposal to deport with no recourse to the courts was 'utterly intolerable'. *New Society* (5 August), reviewing the proposals under the heading 'John Bean Naked', also found the positive proposals weak and unspecific, notably in relation to heavier general aid to the affected areas; it commented on the fact that the Australian Labour Party had on the same day dropped its call for a white Australia, thereby reaching the same position as British Labour today—that of allowing a trickle of coloured immigrants. 'Britain accepts the Colour Bar', wrote Mervyn Jones in the *New Statesman* (6 August), commenting on the continued absence of restrictions on the Irish, and the ease with which Australians and other 'old' Commonwealth citizens could arrive on visits and find jobs: 'Ironically, this utterly selfish White Paper appeared the day before Barbara Castle published her statement on aid to the poor nations of the world, whose predicament increases.' In the *Sunday Times* (8 August), Frank Giles also stressed the irony of Mrs. Castle's proposals to step up the supply of teachers for developing countries while the White Paper encouraged a further brain drain from them. The *Tribune* (6 August) called the plan 'as white as leprosy', and the *Spectator* (6 August) dubbed it a 'surrender to racial prejudice, vilely dressed up to appear reasonable' and a defeat for the 'liberal centre', largely self-inflicted.[1]

There was criticism of the White Paper from some Labour M.P.s, notably Dr. David Kerr (Wandsworth Central), who described it in the Commons as a 'grave and bitter disappointment', Mr. Reginald Freeson (Willesden East) and Mrs. Lena Jeger (Holborn and St. Pancras), who asked if it did not put Commonwealth citizens at a disadvantage as compared to aliens applying to come here (*Northern Echo*, 3 August). It was more than once reported that an emergency resolution criticizing Government intentions might be tabled at the Labour Party Conference in the autumn. In the *Tribune* (13 August), Lord Brockway said he wrote under a sense of shame as a member of the Labour Party. Dr. David Pitt, West Indian born, former Labour candidate, member of the Greater London Council and chairman of C.A.R.D., called the measures 'one big step back and some small steps forward'. He subsequently resigned from the executive of the London Labour Party and from the British Overseas Socialist Fellowship, calling the latter a farce and the Labour Government's policy 'pandering to what they believe are the prejudiced views of the electorate'. (*Guardian*, 3 August, 7 August; *The Times*, 7 August; *Observer*, 8 August.)

D. THE PARTY CONFERENCES—1965

Parts I and II of the White Paper in effect marked, for some time, the nadir of the negative debate on controls. Thereafter, imperceptibly, the debate was to be increasingly concerned with integration (Part III of the White Paper).

This was not, however, immediately apparent in the corridor and conference rooms of political power. Only the T.U.C. succeeded in avoiding a discussion on this subject (but see the *Guardian*, 10 September), thereby leaving the ultimate casting of the major unions' block votes at the Labour Party conference in Blackpool to surmise until the eve of the debate; then Dr. Jeremy Bray, M.P. (Middlesbrough West), speaking for the Transport and General Workers' Union, committed its million votes in support of the emergency motion asking the Government to withdraw the White Paper. This was the only large union to do so. As the *Economist* (12 October) commented: 'The representatives of the British working man faithfully reflected his aversion to any spirit of universal brotherhood which touched him too closely.' The *New Statesman's* political correspondent, Gerald Kaufman, in a rather critical

[1] Other published protests against various aspects of the White Paper included the following: Tony Coxon, *Second Class Citizens*, London, I.L.P.; *Prejudice or Principle*, London, N.C.C.L.; *A Spur to Racialism*, London, C.A.R.D.; *Strangers Within*, London, Young Fabian study group pamphlet; *The Victims Speak*, I.W.A. (Birmingham) pamphlet.

account of the rebels and the debate, maintained that the critics had thrown away much support by voting down a soberly-worded resolution from St. Albans and deciding to demand the withdrawal of the White Paper. In *Tribune* (1 October), Michael Foot said that the Labour Party had accepted the 'most pathetic and craven departure from principle on the issue which has world-wide implications'; the matter would, however, continue to be contested in the House of Commons and outside (Mr. Reg Freeson of Willesden had announced during the debate that forty-one M.P.s had now signed the appeal for a rational immigration policy and would continue the fight, and Mr. Silverman later stated that he would join the Liberals in voting against the Government's immigration policy).[1]

The actual debate at Blackpool did not always seem to live up to the words of the Prime Minister in his speech of the preceding day: 'I repudiate the libel that Government policy is based either on colour or racial prejudice. We repudiate, indeed I resent, the accusation of illiberality or of any desire . . . to act in an arbitrary manner.' Mr. Wilson also emphasized the problems caused by widespread evasions and the need for a positive attack on immigration problems; the Government's duty was to act to forestall 'a social explosion in this country of the kind we have seen abroad. We cannot take the risk of allowing the democracy of this country to become stained and tarnished with the taint of racialism or colour prejudice.' (*The Times*, 29 September; *Peace News*, 1 September.)

Press reactions included the *Guardian's* (30 September) comment on 'a colour bar camouflaged', as over half of the Commonwealth 'evaders' against whom the Government had claimed it was compelled to act were from the 'old' white Dominions. *The Times* (30 September), after criticizing the objectors for failing to attack the White Paper at the vital points, called the Government's record ambivalent, the Race Relations Bill a smokescreen, and expressed doubts about the workings of the positive machinery set up to promote integration.

At Scarborough the previous week, the Liberals had managed to continue on the path of principle, although the *Guardian* (25 September) commented that there had been a change of course towards the acceptance of some restraints on immigration. Mr. Jeremy Thorpe's motion asked for increased aid to Commonwealth countries and areas of acute

[1] The *Sunday Times* (26 September) listed the 'race rebels' (Labour and Conservative); Labour M.P.s ranging from John Mendelson, Frank Allaun and Michael Foot on the left, through middle-of-the-roaders like Shirley Williams, to Dick Taverne on the right. Reg Freeson's forthright attitude in marginal Willesden East was contrasted with those of two Birmingham Labour M.P.s who were said to have swung to the right on immigration recently. Some weeks earlier, *Mandrake* in the *Sunday Telegraph* (6 August) had noted the contrast between statements on immigration by certain Labour Ministers and M.P.s before 1962 and now.

housing shortage; facilities for teaching English and for health care for immigrants; the condemnation of the White Paper's restrictions on vouchers; the abolition of the present discrimination between Irish and Commonwealth citizens; more co-ordinating machinery; and the extension of the Racial Discrimination Bill to housing and employment. There were several liberalizing amendments and one asking for wider dispersal in jobs and residence (this came from Battersea and was supported by a Birmingham councillor—it was lost overwhelmingly). After a fervent debate (including a contribution by the Indian wife of a Liberal councillor), the motion was carried, only the proposal for restricting the Irish being thrown out. As one speaker said, a bad law is not made any better by applying it to the Irish (*Guardian*, 23–25 September).

The Conservatives, meeting in Brighton in mid-October, had the choice of allowing the more rabid anti-immigrationists to continue the 'Dutch auction in illiberalism' or concentrating on the more positive aspects of integration, while embarrassing the Government by stressing Labour's rapid conversion to restrictionist policies. On the whole, the latter course was followed in the debate: only a minority of delegates demonstrated definitely hostile feelings about colour, and they were roughly balanced by another minority with pronounced liberal sentiments. The real emotions were reserved for the emergency debate on Rhodesia the following day, when the range of Tory viewpoints emerged much more starkly and numerously, from 'kith and kin', economic interests, and post-colonial blues to 'multi-racialism' and internationalism. (A rare voice these days was that of a former colonial servant, who voiced the beliefs and principles of Commonwealth builders, in other non-settler parts of Africa, speaking in opposition to Lord Salisbury's amendment.) In the outcome, the head ruled the heart, as in the immigration debate moderation had dominated extremism.

E. THE LEGAL POSITION OF COMMONWEALTH IMMIGRANTS AND THE WHITE PAPER PROPOSALS

Certain features of the White Paper proposals drew comment from those concerned with the legal aspect of civil liberties. Cedric Thornberry summarized 'the legal position' of the six main categories of Commonwealth immigrants, the grounds for rejection and the proposed changes in the following table:[1]

[1] Taken from 'A Note on the Legal Position of Commonwealth Immigrants and the White Paper Proposals', *Race*, Vol. VII, no. 2, 1965.

TABLE 8

The 'legal position' of Commonwealth immigrants

Category	Controls under 1962 Act	Additional powers proposed in 'Immigration from the Commonwealth' White Paper
1. Returning residents.	May be rejected only where they are the subjects of deportation orders in force.	Liable on re-entry to conditions requiring registration with the police; limiting time of further stay; limiting possible employment. May be required to report to local medical officer of health.
2. Wives and Children (under 16) of already-resident Commonwealth citizens.	May be rejected only where they are the subjects of deportation orders in force.	Stricter application of the rules, i.e., as to legal formality of the relationship, and as to the evidence of relationship. Idea of 'entry certificate' establishing identity. Liable to conditions requiring registration; limiting time of stay; possible employment. May be required to report to local medical officer of health.
3. Commonwealth citizens coming for employment.	Must be in possession of 'A', 'B', or 'C' vouchers. 'C' vouchers discontinued September 1964. Rate of issue of all vouchers approximately 20,000 per annum until August 1965. May, even after issue of voucher, be rejected at port of entry on grounds of health, criminality, security, or if subject to deportation order in force.	Issue of 'A' and 'B' vouchers to be limited to 8,500 per annum. Liable to conditions requiring registration; limiting time of stay; possible employment. May be required to report to local medical officer of health.

TABLE 8 (*cont*)

4. Students.	May be rejected on grounds of health, criminality, security, or if subject to deportation order in force. May be admitted conditionally.	Uniform practice of attaching conditions to length of stay. To be limited in first instance to 12 months, subject to renewal. Registration; medical officer of health.
5. Temporary Visitors.	May be rejected on grounds of health, criminality, security, or if subject to deportation order in force. May be admitted conditionally.	Uniform practice of attaching conditions to length of stay. Initially 6 months, subject to renewal. Liable to registration; medical officer of health.
6. All others (except certain special categories, e.g. diplomatists).	May be refused at will or admitted absolutely or conditionally. Special consideration for various dependent relatives, e.g. children 16–18 in practice admitted in same circumstances as those in class 2.	'Concession' reference 16–18 years old children withdrawn. Must now qualify independently under categories 3, 4, or 5. Any admitted under this head liable to registration, residence, employment, medical officer of health provisions.

He pointed out that the Commonwealth Immigrants' Act had conferred wide powers on the Home Secretary, so that some of the changes could be given effect by new administrative directions (e.g. conditions for admission in the case of categories 4, 5, and 6). While the power to impose conditions seemed to have been used only rarely in the first years of the Act, it had been stepped up, especially in the case of students, since the Home Secretary's 'evasions' statement of 4 February 1965. On the other hand, the imposition of registration or 'reporting to the police' would require legislation, as would the provisions about eventual 'repatriation' of those who evaded controls, e.g. by gaining entry through misrepresentation or flouting the conditions on which they were omitted.

In this article and elsewhere Mr. Thornberry and others expressed concern at the intensified concentration of discretionary powers (with no legal limit) in the hands of the Home Secretary and his Department of Immigration and Nationality; at the exclusion of the court's powers of review; and at the failure to create an independent appeals system.

Mr. Thornberry pointed out that there was a narrow and a broad interpretation of the proposed repatriation powers (para. 25):

The *narrow* interpretation is that only those who obtain entry by misrepresentation, or who 'flout' the conditions on which they were admitted are liable to be deported under the new power. The *broad* interpretation is that the Home Secretary intends to assume, as in the case of aliens, power to deport any person in the deportable class where he 'deems it to be conducive to the public good'.

Although there may be reasons for believing that the Home Office might welcome the acquisition of the powers indicated under the broad interpretation, it will be supposed that the narrow is that intended. The terms of para. 25 more readily support this view. It will be seen that one's choice of interpretation is of little importance; however, it has already provoked some public controversy. It is always desirable to bear in mind, when examining the scope and likely incidence of a deportation power, that *the key to deportation lies in the system of admission control.* Where entry is, broadly speaking, conditional, and does not lead automatically to a right of permanent residence, a person whom the authorities no longer wish to remain will usually be removed without their needing to resort to deportation. For example, a student, subject to an initial 12-month residence limit may, on the expiration of that period, apply for renewal of his licence to reside. If the power to renew is wholly discretionary and subject to no limit, he may be told—for any reason that commends itself to the Department—that his application must be refused and that he must leave at once. Behind the refusal lies the sanction of deportation 'for flouting the conditions' on which he was admitted. The student may, for a variety of obvious and compelling reasons, wish to avoid the odium of deportation. He will therefore, predictably, leave, without his name or case figuring amongst the list of deported persons. If, at the same time, a power is taken to *vary* the conditions first imposed at the port of entry, the Department need not wait for the student to apply for renewal. It may, during the currency of a 12-month residence licence, shorten or terminate it quite arbitrarily—and if this discretion is unlimited, as it tends to be, for any reason, good or bad. It is in this sense, therefore, that the key to deportation lies in the form of admission control. This fact seems to be of the utmost importance in the context of this White Paper.

In the light of what has already been said of the proposed new power to attach conditions to the residence of Commonwealth citizens, and the fact that the White Paper asserts that the power is to be assumed to attach conditions to the residence of *any* Commonwealth citizen, it will be readily appreciated that the difference between the broad and the narrow interpretations of the White Paper's paragraph 25 becomes meaningless in practice. If the Home Secretary is to have the power to attach conditions in his absolute discretion, and to deport those who 'flout' them, then he will in fact have the power to deport anyone he sees fit.

The implications of the 'repatriation' provisions of the White Paper, in the context of the other powers proposed to be assumed, could scarcely be more grave. Most lawyers would probably agree that its terms are not greatly improved by the Chief Magistrate concession. This is not an appeal. A Commonwealth citizen referred to the Chief Magistrate will (if the aliens procedure is adopted) have no way of knowing what allegation he has to meet. If, for example, a Commonwealth citizen in class three (an employment voucher-holder) admitted initially for a year, is told by the Home Office that, though his employers are willing and anxious to retain his services, 'it is not in the public interest' that he be allowed to remain, his right of access to the Chief Magistrate is likely to be no great consolation. If the Home Office assert that his residence is being terminated on grounds of security, not even the minor solace of a trip to Bow Street will be offered him. Under the terms of the White Paper, this event is quite possible.

The key to the legal aspect of the White Paper lies in its paragraph 23—'The Government propose to seek a general power to impose conditions on the admission of any Commonwealth citizen who is subject to control.' In theory, and potentially at least in practice, this will, if enacted, place at risk every Commonwealth citizen who comes to Britain, who returns after temporary absence, or whose dependent relatives come here.

Unless such enactment breaks new ground (for Britain, though not for other countries) by its provisions being formulated in such a way as to meet the substantial legal objections advanced by Sir Elwyn Jones and others, the position of the Commonwealth citizen in this country will have been profoundly affected. A casual reading of the White Paper does not, perhaps, quite point to the gravity of some of its suggestions and their implications. If the enactment does not import the notion of 'due process', and limit the condition-imposing and reviewing power, it will create for the Commonwealth citizen many if not all of the undesirable legal conditions that have been allowed to develop in the case of the alien.

F. THE WILSON COMMITTEE

In September 1965, it was reported that the Lord Chancellor, Lord Gardiner, and other Government law officers, were studying Mr. Thornberry's criticisms of the White Paper as authoritarian and a fundamental encroachment on human rights. On 4 November the Prime Minister, asked by Mr. W. Hamilton, M.P. (Lab., Fife, West), whether he would withdraw the White Paper, answered: 'No, Sir.' In the Queen's Speech on 9 November, however, Mr. Wilson in effect backtracked on the proposals requiring legislation[1] (e.g. those concerning repatriation and registration). Instead he announced that a small independent committee would be appointed to decide whether immigrants and aliens refused admission or recommended for deportation should have any

[1] Those provisions in the White Paper for tighter controls that did not require legislation had for the most part been in force since the early part of the year. Some were subsequently to be modified, following the change of Home Secretaries in January 1966 and the subsequent transfer of Mr. Foley to the Home Office as Minister with special responsibility for Commonwealth immigrants.

right to appeal, and if so, how this should be arranged; only in the light of this committee's report would the legislation be prepared as soon as possible thereafter.

The legislation foreshadowed by the White Paper would, he said, be studied very carefully, particularly with regard to the view expressed in the House of Commons year after year, that fresh safeguards should be introduced for Commonwealth citizens and aliens refused admission or subsequently required to leave Britain.[1] The Government accepted this view:

> We think that the time is long overdue for placing on a permanent footing the law for the control of alien immigration which was first introduced as an emergency measure in the First World War and has been renewed every year since then.

Mr. Wilson announced that the committee would have the following terms of reference:

> To consider whether and if so what rights of appeal or any other remedies should be available to aliens and Commonwealth citizens who are refused admission to or are required to leave the country.[2]

Welcoming this decision, Cedric Thornberry (*The Times*, 17 November 1965) wrote:

> Many must hope that the new permanent legislation that should be drafted following the committee's report will be the last chapter of a mournful chronicle that has already lasted more than fifty years. In the week during which the First World War broke out the Aliens Restriction Bill was introduced, passed through all its stages, and became law on 5 August 1914. The Act conferred on the Crown the widest possible powers with regard to the admission, treatment, and deportation of aliens.
>
> The powers conferred were patently emergency powers and they were continued by an Act in 1919 for a period of one year. They have been prolonged ever since, on a year-to-year basis, by the annual Expiring Laws Continuance Acts.
>
> Their spirit, object, and effect were succinctly stated by Mr. Justice Stephenson during the Soblen saga. They are 'emergency powers conferred at a time, and only for a time, when the legislature considered that the

[1] See annual debates on the Expiring Laws Continuance Bill, which covers, *inter alia*, the Aliens Restriction (Amendment) Act of 1919 and the Commonwealth Immigrants Act, 1962. These were considered together for the first time in 1966 (Commons Hansard, 8 November 1966, col. 1167). The change may have reflected the growing feeling in many quarters, and on both sides of the House, that the present legislation should be consolidated and amended, so as to treat Commonwealth citizens and aliens on an equal footing.

[2] This brought the Government under attack for procrastination and running away from the White Paper: e.g. from Mr. Peter Thorneycroft and others on 23 November 1965 and Sir David Renton on 8 November 1966

executive, in its treatment of aliens, should be almost out of reach of the judiciary, and the judiciary was unwilling and unable to interfere with the executive's treatment of aliens.'

It was not only the virtually unlimited discretion that had been criticized, but also the absence of an appeal system, added the writer.

He went on to express satisfaction that the Committee's terms of reference would involve the reviewing of the law regarding both aliens[1] and Commonwealth immigrants:

> That relating to Commonwealth citizens is less unsatisfactory than the alien law. The Commonwealth Immigrants Act is less sweeping in the powers it confers; furthermore, the manner in which it was to be administered was laid down in published instructions to immigration officers. However, neither appeal nor judicial review is available. The Act was, unfortunately, conceived against the alien law background. . . . There is a belief that the present system might have continued for some while had not the paths of its critics and those of the Government's race relations policy converged last August. The cause of the alien and that of the Commonwealth citizen were at last identified as parts of a unitary whole. The announcement of the committee's appointment is unlikely to deflate the pressure which immediately preceded it.

The appointment of the Committee, under the chairmanship of Sir Roy Wilson, was finally announced on 26 February 1966. On 25 March, the secretary of the Committee wrote to *The Times* asking for evidence on the need for rights of appeal for immigrants refused admission to the U.K. or required to leave, and the forms these should take; the Committee had so far received no evidence from anyone outside the public service.

In subsequent months a considerable body of written evidence was received.[2] The Committee's members went to see the working of immigration controls at the points of entry, and the chairman and secretary went to North America to study at first hand the systems of control in the United States and Canada. According to Mr. Maurice Foley, speaking in the debate on the Expiring Laws Bill (Hansard, 8 November 1966, cols. 1177–1179), the Government wanted to get the legislation right. Thus no time limit had been set on the Committee's inquiry into a subject which had not been explored seriously outside the House and the framework of the Home Office for the past fifty years. It was hoped that the report would be received in the first half of 1967 and published as soon as possible thereafter. It would prepare the way for permanent legislation, which could not, however, be proceeded with during the current session of Parliament.

[1] For a more detailed pamphlet on the two sets of legislation, see C. Thornberry, *The Stranger at the Gate*, Fabian Research Series 243, August 1964. (This is based on a report by him, which became the policy of the Society of Labour Lawyers.)

[2] For details see below, pp. 60–2.

5. IMMIGRATION PROCEDURE AND PRACTICE

Evidence about the detailed, everyday application of the controls by immigration officers at the ports of entry before the 'evasion' statement made by the Home Secretary on 4 February 1965[1] is patchy and inadequate. Recorded complaints are relatively few, whether because there was less occasion for them or because they had not yet been assembled into a coherent body of evidence, or for both reasons. C.A.R.D.'s report to the Wilson Committee of inquiry into immigration controls contained the following comment:

> The introduction . . . in 1962 of controls on Commonwealth immigration . . . imposed a new and difficult task on immigration officers: namely, to take rapid decisions in the light of criteria of admission when decisive evidence . . . was often . . . lacking. Although we have always regarded these controls as intrinsically discriminatory, their application up to February 1965 was, as far as we have been able to judge, reasonably humane, in that there was a general practice of giving the would-be immigrant the benefit of the doubt. From February 1965, this policy was reversed; the eagerness of the then Home Secretary to check evasion quite evidently led to a practice of in all cases *denying* the prospective immigrant the benefit of any doubt.

The statistics for refusals given in Table 9 afford some evidence that the application of controls was generally tightened in 1965 (and relaxed in 1966 in relation to some groups). It is interesting to note that they hardly affected West Indian entrants, although this may be partly because West Indians were making greater use of the 'entry certificate' system than Indians and Pakistanis; thus rejections, when they happened, were more likely to occur at that stage, before the would-be entrant left home and presented himself at a British port of entry.

The reasons for refusal are not available, nor are there published details of refusals by categories of entrant. Other evidence suggests that among Indians and Pakistanis it was mainly dependants, followed by visitors and students, who were refused; among Australians it was mainly visitors. While refusals of Pakistanis, Nigerians, and Cypriots dropped in proportion to the numbers admitted after 1965, the proportion of Indians rejected rose sharply, for reasons which are not clear. The highest rates of refusals in 1965–1966 were for India, Pakistan, and Nigeria, all countries in which documentation of identity, age, family affiliation, and so on is frequently either lacking, inadequate, or inaccurate.

[1] It may be noted that this followed some weeks of detailed press disclosures of passport, work-voucher, and other rackets, operated mainly by Pakistanis or Indians, including a court case involving ten Pakistanis from four cities, one a former clerk in the High Commission. See I.R.R. *Newsletter*, for January and February 1965. See also 'The Dark Million—7' in *The Times*, 25 January 1965.

It is not, however, only the incidence of refusals that has been a subject of complaint, but the manner of such refusals, and indeed the general immigration procedure as it affects Commonwealth immigrants.

This section will concentrate on major aspects of procedure and practice after controls were tightened in February 1965, particularly in their application to the categories of dependants, visitors, and returning residents.

A. N.C.C.I. REPRESENTATIONS—1965–6

By late 1965, a certain body of evidence regarding the treatment of dependants had been assembled by the N.C.C.I., largely through the increasing network of voluntary liaison committees in Britain. This was reported upon by a N.C.C.I. deputation to the Home Secretary on 15 November 1965, led by Mr. Philip Mason.[1]

The following major points were raised by this deputation:

(i) *Existing Procedure* (*1965*)

There are three grounds on which entry is refused:

(a) Identity—the immigration officer is not satisfied that the person seeking entry is the person mentioned on the passport, or that his relationship with the sponsor is that which is alleged.
(b) Age—the immigration officer believes that he is over 16.
(c) The immigration officer is not satisfied that the type of accommodation offered is proper.

If the immigration officer has reason to question the identity or age of the alleged dependant, he arranges that he and his alleged parent or guardian should be questioned separately. If identity is in doubt, the boy (it is almost always a boy) is questioned as to the names of relations, the recent history of the family, the place of residence. If the answers are inconsistent with those of the guardian, he is sent back. If age is in dispute, the boy is questioned as to the time he spent at the various schools he has attended, as to any time since leaving school, the total being added up to see if it agrees with his age. He is usually not in possession of a birth certificate, and there is no type of documentary evidence which is prescribed as being normally accepted by the immigration officer as conclusive. If the alleged dependant expresses a wish to see a doctor he may see the port medical officer who will estimate his age; if he wishes to go further, he may be examined by X-rays of the teeth and wrist-bones.

[1] While the N.C.C.I.'s terms of reference were intended to be confined to integration, the Committee has from the start made it clear that it would be difficult, if not impossible, to dissociate the procedures of control from the problems of integration, since the former could be regarded by the immigrant communities as an explicit and official endorsement of racial discrimination, thereby adversely affecting the work of integration.

If the immigration officer is satisfied as to identity and age, he may inquire whether the accommodation offered is suitable. This he usually finds out by telephone from the police or other local authorities.

(ii) *Comment*

Most of these dependants have had their fares paid by sponsors in Britain; if they are rejected the sponsor has also to pay the return fare, in addition to possible disruption of family relationships. While some refusals are justified there is an impression that many could have been avoided if there was (a) more certain knowledge among sponsors and would-be immigrants about the conditions of entry; and (b) greater assistance to immigrants at the port of entry.

On the latter point it was stated that the cross-questioning of boys[1] who have probably just made their first long-distance flight by air and are in a strange country is obviously likely to produce confusion and hesitancy which might easily result in discrepancy in the answers given. The Home Office have given instructions to their immigration officers to carry out these interrogations sympathetically, and are satisfied that their immigration officers invariably follow these instructions. But officers would be more than human if they never misunderstood an answer and never received a wrong impression. What may be at stake is not merely the return fare, but family separation; so the issues are considerably more important to the persons involved than in many minor criminal cases. Yet it is established principle that in even minor criminal cases a person has the right to be represented by an adviser who can re-examine him so as to bring out the full intention of his replies.

On the bone-age X-ray check it was pointed out that general medical opinion holds that at the age of puberty only approximations of age can be given. The range of error is of the order of one to two years. It is suggested that there should be general instructions that the lowest age regarded as possible by a medical officer should be accepted when age is the only matter in doubt.[2]

Referring to the third ground for refusing entry, unsuitable accommodation, the deputation illustrated the type of difficulty that could arise by the following example:[3]

[1] Case of Ajit Singh, said to be the son of Mr. Thaker Singh of Wolverhampton, who gave pet names for brothers and sisters whereas his father used formal names. The Home Office gave lack of relationship as the reason of refusal but six months afterwards added another reason that the boy was over 16.

[2] This procedure was still being used a year later. A boy, Mohammed Khan, was deported on such evidence in December 1966. See C. Bagley, 'Bone Age Photograph and Immigration Procedure', I.R.R. *Newsletter*, February 1967, p. 21 f.

[3] Cf. also the case of Ghulam Shabir, a Pakistani boy aged 15, turned back on 19 July 1965 (raised by Mr. C. M. Woodhouse, M.P., in a written question to the Home Secretary on 29 July 1965 (official report col. 1651)).

A boy, about whose identity and age—about 12—there is no dispute, was to join his brother in England because his only surviving parent had recently died. The police reported that the house to which he proposed to go with his brother was occupied by male Pakistanis and was grossly over-crowded. (There has been dispute about the degree of over-crowding, but this seems irrelevant.) The brother (already resident in England) immediately offered to put the boy with an uncle who had a house of his own, and for whose respectability a British solicitor vouched. This offer however was refused on the grounds that there was no reason to believe that the boy would stay in the uncle's house and not subsequently move into the house where the brother was living. This raises two questions of principle. In the first place, since there can be no certainty that a person will stay in the accommodation to which he says he will go, is there really much point in making the stipulation that he must be provided with proper accommodation? But it may be felt to have some value, if not very much, and in that case surely the uncle's offer might have been accepted? No one would question the desirability of preventing over-crowding, but is it the right way to deal with this problem to prevent an orphan recently bereaved from joining his nearest relations?

It was further pointed out that the time allotted for investigation in Britain was very short: sometimes alleged dependants had arrived on a different flight and been sent back before sponsors or relations could take action. It was suggested that there should be arrangements for longer stops at ports of arrival in disputed cases.[1]

A further complication was that in some cases British authorities overseas issued entry certificates which were rejected at the port of arrival. The Home Office felt that it could not bind itself to accept these automatically but the remedy would be to improve the conditions upon which they were granted.

In general, the most satisfactory solution would be to have all inquiries carried out before departure, so that an immigrant or dependant could start his journey with the assurance that he would be accepted on arrival.

This latter course was officially said to present insurmountable practical difficulties but the N.C.C.I. deputation did not agree.

In February 1966 the N.C.C.I. made the following recommendations for interim measures to the Home Office.

Entry Certificates

It should be normal that any intending immigrant should have an Entry Certificate. This would entail special administrative arrangements with British Authorities in Commonwealth countries, particularly in India and Pakistan where long distances are involved, which may necessitate increased staffing in High Commission offices in these

[1] Case of Khadam Hussain, born in August 1945, son of Jalal Khan of Keighley, holder of a British passport issued in Liverpool in 1963. The boy arrived on a later 'plane; he was not met, and was returned because he gave an incorrect street address (Amberley for Emily Street) through bad English.

countries; these arrangements would have as their object both easier access for the intending immigrant and a more thorough investigation in the country of origin.

The Entry Certificate should normally be regarded as entitling the holder to enter. If an exception must be made H.M. Government should accept responsibility and should normally pay the fares both ways.

Airport Procedure

There should be at least three Reception Officers, of whom one should be a woman, at London Airport. Their functions would be to help the Immigration Officer as well as to act as advocate for the immigrant in doubtful cases. Executive instructions from the Home Office should make it obligatory for the Immigration Officer to inform the Reception Officer if he has any intention of refusing admission and to listen to the latter's submissions. The Reception Officers would be employed by the National Committee for Commonwealth Immigrants, who would be informed of any refusals of admission. Arrangements should be made so that disputed cases can remain for some days and in no case should they be returned until they have had the opportunity of communicating with relations in this country.

TABLE 9

Commonwealth citizens subject to control under the Act admitted and refused admission in 1964, 1965, and 1966*

Selected Territories that issued Passport	1964 Admitted	1964 Refused	1965 Admitted	1965 Refused	1966 Admitted	1966 Refused
Australia	71,458	48	81,334	79	82,398	74
Barbados	3,470	2	4,029	9	3,024	3
Canada	119,414	26	128,075	76	135,490	39
Cyprus	9,144	134	8,252	105	8,679	65
Guyana	4,381	3	4,226	14	4,042	5
India	44,468	61	50,829	173	53,469	315
Jamaica	18,697	9	18,020	22	17,016	13
Kenya	5,789	2	4,257	11	3,521	10
Leeward and Windward Islands	3,186	5	3,345	12	3,227	8
Malta	6,871	16	7,556	31	8,462	24
Nigeria	11,545	29	10,344	85	8,664	149
Pakistan	27,266	442	27,399	427	32,251	376
Trinidad and Tobago	5,938	7	5,830	16	3,692	12
Overall Total ...	406,601	907	433,573	1,335	442,742	1,339
Overall Net Balance...	+75,499		+63,819		+51,348	

* These are *gross* admission figures taken from the first table of the official annual statistics of immigration control under the Commonwealth Immigrants Act 1962, of successive annual statistics. This table also gives embarkation figures, from which the net balance over the year is calculated.

B. OTHER EVIDENCE OF PROCEDURAL DEFICIENCIES

Other evidence of or allegations about the deficiencies of the machinery of immigration control,[1] as well as recommendations for improvement, emerged in various submissions to the Wilson Committee (q.v.). C.A.R.D.'s evidence, published in November 1966, complained of 'a spate of hasty, harsh and unjust decisions . . . which, week by week, confirm Commonwealth people in their suspicions that they are not welcomed here and that British justice is being withheld from them'. The document went on to cite twenty fully documented cases of entry wrongfully refused, three of which had already been submitted to the Human Rights Commission at Strasbourg. Other concrete criticisms were:

(a) The total lack of instructional leaflets, other than those issued to immigration officers.
(b) The lack of official published explanation of the precise regulations and qualifications that would-be immigrants have to meet. Pamphlets giving relevant information of this nature are urgently required.
(c) The failure to provide written statements of the grounds on which any one immigrant has been refused entry, thus leaving an immigrant unable to understand why he has been rejected, unable to produce relevant documents (which in any case he may not have known were required) and unable to correct misunderstandings such as those caused by language difficulties. C.A.R.D. calls for more interpreters, and for detailed reasons for refusal to be given in writing on each occasion.
(d) Passports, birth certificates, and other similar documents are not being accepted as evidence. C.A.R.D. calls for all genuine documents to be accepted. At the moment, it suggests, these are rejected in favour of snap decisions by individual officers—often based on scanty and inappropriate interrogation.
(e) Entry certificates have become a gamble. Originally conceived as a means of simplifying entry, they no longer guarantee admission at all. Yet without them an airline or shipping line may refuse passengers. C.A.R.D. recommends automatic entry to all those with entry certificates.
(f) There are no appeals tribunals. These should be set up at all points of entry.
(g) At the moment those refused entry are detained or sent home. They

[1] From another angle, the report of the Estimates Committee for 1966 commented on the large number of extra staff required by the Home Office to administer relatively small changes in immigration laws. The new regulations introduced in 1965, requiring students and visitors to apply to the Immigration and Nationality Department if they wished to postpone their stay beyond the stated period, increased personal casework from about 24,000 cases in 1965 to 70,000 in 1966, and caused the Department to take on 152 additional staff.

should be admitted as visitors temporarily while their case is examined.

The National Council for Civil Liberties, in a Memorandum to the Wilson Committee of June 1966, stressed, *inter alia*, the following points:

(a) Any administrative decision should be subject to scrutiny and appeal before execution.
(b) All conditions of entry should be abolished and the only decision relating to immigrants should be whether or not they are in fact entitled to enter.
(c) Identification and documentation problems at the port of entry should be eased by the extension and improvement of the entry certificate system. Health certificates should also be issued before departure.
(d) Time should be allowed for those unable to prove their right of entry to have their case referred to the Home Office. Liaison officers should be available where needed and there should be an appeals system.

The N.C.C.I. also made far-reaching recommendations to the Wilson Committee in May 1966, along similar lines to those of its earlier representation to the Prime Minister but based on further evidence and more detailed investigations. Recommendations were as follows:[1]

(i) Liaison Officer at port of entry.
(ii) Visitor's permits to be issued in disputed cases.
(iii) Arrangements for issuing entry certificates to be improved: these to be honoured unless forged or based on blatant misrepresentation: burden of proof to rest on British authorities.
(iv) Reasons in writing for refusal to be given to intending immigrants.
(v) Conditions of entry to be dropped for returning residents and admitted immigrants.
(vi) No restrictions on work for students or visitors.
(vii) Appeals machinery to be provided.
(viii) Deportation not to be a double punishment.
(ix) Deportation not without judicial hearing.

Subsequently the N.C.C.I. drew attention to the following matters:

(a) The time lag in the issue of work vouchers—frequently about eight months. This meant that many vouchers were not being taken up because the applicant's circumstances had changed.
(b) The hardship entailed in the rigid definition of 'dependants' and 'children', which does not fully take into account the family structure

[1] These were followed up by a N.C.C.I. deputation at a hearing on 29 November 1966.

and obligations of, for instance, Asian families (e.g. in relation to unmarried women). The criterion for admitting children between 16 and 18 should be, not the exact age, but the degree of dependence on the father or guardian.

(c) The desirability of giving some priority in the issue of vouchers to those who have close relatives in Britain.

(d) The need to instruct immigration officers not to make assumptions as to the motives of persons seeking entry, but to confine themselves to factual verification.

Most of the reports and memoranda suggested that in practice restrictions were being applied more rigidly against citizens from 'new' Commonwealth or 'coloured' countries than against citizens from the 'old' or 'white' Commonwealth countries. That this view was not shared by all visitors or immigrants from the latter countries became clear when *The Times* (7 November 1966) published a report on 'Cool Greetings for "New" Foreigners'; this was followed by much press comment and correspondence from a number of irate Australians and other visitors and returning residents complaining about unnecessarily rude treatment by immigration officers.[1]

C. GOVERNMENT ACTION IN 1966

Upon the appointment of Mr. Roy Jenkins as Home Secretary in January 1966, the *Sunday Times* (9 January) reported that the new Home Secretary was preparing a massive long-term liberalizing programme, and recalled the outline of needed reforms given in his 1959 Penguin book, *The Labour Case*. These included reform of the immigration laws—which he characterized as 'more suitable to a police state' than to a Britain which is the traditional refuge of the oppressed. 'There is good reason'—added the *Sunday Times*—'for believing that Mr. Jenkins has not changed his views, or modified his reforming zeal.' On 8 February this was confirmed when Mr. Jenkins talked to the press about his view of a Home Secretary's main functions ('. . . as trying to hold a balance between public order and private freedom'). Since the Home Office was responsible for immigration control, it should also be responsible for the positive aspects of the matter. In an article in the *Guardian* (18 February), Cedric Thornberry stressed that, if the Home Office was now to deal even adequately with such spheres of race relations, its general philosophy of government must undergo a radical and rapid metamorphosis.

On 23 May, in his address to the Standing Conference of Voluntary Liaison Committees, the Home Secretary showed indications not only of a positive attitude to integration but of a more flexible attitude to

[1] See Margaret MacIntosh, 'Angry Australians', I.R.R. *Newsletter*, January 1967.

controls than that laid down by the White Paper. It was necessary, he said, to regulate controls so that the intake 'is not put so high as to create a widespread resistance to effective integration policies. Equally it must not be so unreasonably low as to create an embittered sense of apartness in the immigrant community itself. But this will depend, in my view, not only on the numerical decisions but on the way these decisions are administered . . . .'

One provision of the White Paper, that restricting the entry of dependants between the ages of 16 and 18 to cases of hardship only, was reported to have been dropped following a recent but largely unpublicized decision by the Home Secretary (*Northern Echo*, 3 May 1966).[1]

In August the Home Secretary was reported to have made certain other provisions for easing entry procedures. Dependants of Commonwealth citizens already over here would be admitted even if the head of the household had not furnished the authorities with their particulars (new immigrants must, however, still furnish particulars of their dependants to British posts overseas). This marked the end for resident immigrants at least of the I.M.4 system.[2] The C.A.R.D. report to the

[1] In early 1967 it was reliably stated that normally children in the 16–18 age-group would be admitted if coming to join both parents or the only surviving parent. Children would be permitted to join relatives other than parents only in exceptional circumstances (e.g. orphans with no one to look after them in their own country).

[2] The workings of this system (initiated in para. 19 of the White Paper) are difficult to disentangle from press and other reports. On 23 November 1965, the then Home Secretary, Sir Frank Soskice, said that forms had been sent out in October and 569 dependants had been notified on 260 completed forms. The C.A.R.D. evidence to the Wilson Committee gave the following account of its operation: 'This form could be obtained only from the Home Office: no attempt was made to make it available locally. Nor was any attempt made to inform those local official or voluntary agencies likely to be concerned, such as liaison officers appointed by municipal authorities or those paid by the National Committee for Commonwealth Immigrants, immigrant organisations, or liaison committees or other interracial bodies. If the form was applied for in writing, in no case was it sent in under 4 weeks: yet it was possible to collect it in person from the Immigration Department. Even here, a measure of discrimination obtained: English people were allowed to obtain as many forms as they liked for others, while those who, from their appearance, were judged to be Commonwealth citizens, were allowed to take forms only if they themselves wanted to apply. An English member of C.A.R.D. enquired whether local interracial organisations could be supplied with forms to distribute, and was told that this was impossible "because otherwise we should have to give them to Pakistani and Indian organisations, which would make some kind of racket out of them". (This response, quite ludicrous in reference to mere application forms, which could easily have been made obtainable at post offices or police stations, illustrates the pervasive assumption that all Asians are dishonest and corrupt.) Finally, the I.M.4 system was abandoned, just as suddenly as it had been introduced, again without any attempt being made to inform responsible and concerned individuals and bodies of this change of policy.' In mid-1966, a reliable source called the I.M.4 system a brief experiment which did not prove worthwhile. Cmnd Paper 3064 of August 1966 then came into operation.

Wilson Committee cited this as an instance of an official attitude 'which no longer sees the entry of even those limited categories of Commonwealth citizens who are still allowed to come as a right, about which the Government has the duty of informing those citizens who are personally concerned, but as a concession which the Government is regrettably forced to make, and which it must endeavour to contrive is used as little as possible.'

Ways were also being sought to enable High Commissions to elucidate claims when there was doubt about the right of their nationals to be admitted; and to let voluntary associations help look after immigrants temporarily detained at London Airport.[1]

(i) *Revised Instructions to Immigration Officers*

In August 1966 the Home Office published a revised set of Instructions to Immigration Officers (Cmnd 3064). These differed from those originally published in May 1962 (Cmnd 1716) mainly in clarification.

Paragraph 4 on Entry Certificates makes it clear that such a certificate does not guarantee automatic admission but is an indication of qualification. Conditions may nevertheless be imposed.

Visitors are welcomed (paragraph 5) and generally allowed in for an initial period of six months, provided they have adequate means of support for that period.

Students are also welcomed and a concession is made (paragraph 12) to those wishing to finance their studies by paid employment in free time or vacations.

In verification of evidence and documents the Immigration Officer is instructed to base his decision on the whole of the evidence, including anything that may be said by a relative or friend in this country. A would-be immigrant who has been refused admission should not be sent back until he has met a relative or friend in this country who wishes to see him (paragraph 34). It has been noted that the Instructions make no reference to the imposition of conditions save on visitors, students and fiancé(e)s; this has been welcomed as evidence of a change of attitude on the part of the Government.

(ii) *Returning Residents*

The entitlement to readmission of resident Commonwealth citizens is dealt with in paragraphs 35 and 36:

With the sole exception of a person subject to a deportation order, any Commonwealth citizen is entitled to admission if he satisfies the Immigration

[1] In December 1966 I.S.S. (International Social Service) started a six-month study project of the welfare and social needs of immigrants following their arrival at London Airport, at the request of the Home Office. (See *Liaison*, no. 7, April 1967, pp. 16–17.)

Officer that he is ordinarily resident in the United Kingdom or has been so resident at any time during the previous two years.[1] The record of movements in the passport will often show the period of absence from the United Kingdom,[2] and the identification of persons returning after a short absence, e.g. on holiday, will not ordinarily present difficulty. All those who have taken settled employment in the United Kingdom are to be regarded as ordinarily resident here after their first entry and thus entitled to benefit from the relevant provisions. The Immigration Officer should satisfy himself that a Commonwealth citizen who claims to be returning to the United Kingdom after protracted absence has had his permanent home here at some time in the previous two years, bearing in mind that ordinary residence in the United Kingdom is compatible with lengthy absences abroad on business or in the employment of a firm based in the United Kingdom.

If a Commonwealth citizen is not entitled to return because he has not been ordinarily resident in the previous two years, and if he does not qualify to enter the United Kingdom under any other part of these instructions, he can still be admitted if, for example, he has strong family ties here and has previously lived in the United Kingdom for some time. A Commonwealth citizen who had lived most of his life in the United Kingdom and wanted to return here could properly be readmitted after quite a long absence.

These provisions do not refer to the possible imposition of conditions on re-entry envisaged by the White Paper. Nevertheless there is evidence that in a number of cases returning residents have experienced difficulty and delay in regaining admission, although the great majority have experienced no difficulty at all. When difficulty arises, it has been suggested that this is due less to any 'defect' in the existing law or to the attitude of immigration officers than to a need to clarify what is meant by 'ordinarily resident' to both immigrants and immigration officers, and to establish an acceptable form of documentation which any resident immigrant could procure before leaving the country (resident aliens often procure a re-entry visa for this purpose).

(iii) *The 'Working Holiday'*

One of the grievances felt by the 'angry Australians' and others, mostly but not entirely from the 'old' Commonwealth, was that the immigration controls, particularly after February 1965, struck at the traditional institution of the 'working holiday'; this enabled young professionals and others to seek wider experience in their chosen careers, or simply to come here because of special cultural or family ties with

[1] Commonwealth citizens whose stay has been made subject to a time condition are not, in law, ordinarily resident here during the period of the time condition.

[2] Since 1 July 1962 Immigration Officers have stamped the passports of Commonwealth citizens passing through the controls when landing in, or embarking from, the United Kingdom.

Britain. The attitude of such young people was discussed by Margaret MacIntosh:

> Every sensible Australian recognises that Britain has a problem. But each individual Australian traveller feels he is a special case. Very few arrive with the intention of settling here permanently. Most wish to stay one or two years, perhaps, very rarely, more; certainly not their whole lives. Many, although not students in the strictest sense of the word, are seeking wider experience in their chosen fields—for instance, advertising, marketing, publishing, interior decorating—in which up till now this country has offered unlimited opportunities.
>
> These young people I have mentioned are typical of many who arrive, mostly from the 'old dominions', but also from the Caribbean, India, and elsewhere. They are not tourists, they are not students in the strict sense of the word, and they are definitely not permanent immigrants. Some provision should be made for them if Britain is to remain the cultural centre of the Commonwealth. Moreover, the number of people from the 'new' Commonwealth who come into this category will almost certainly increase as their standards of living and education rise. Of course, not all Australians who come to Britain come with such serious intent. The vast proportion are under 25, adventurous, and full of curiosity and the urge to travel. All their lives they have studied English history, English literature; they have sent Christmas cards covered with snow-men and robins, when most of them have never seen snow, and certainly not a robin. They descend on this country with something akin to the emotion felt by an adopted child in search of his origins. They want to see all they have read and heard about since they were children. To finish their practical education. For a thousand reasons. They also hope to work here to eke out their savings, as well as providing a means of getting to know the 'natives'.
>
> If we in Australia are to keep our preference towards Britain and maintain our hitherto strong cultural ties in the face of strong American influence, the more our young people explore each others' countries and get to know each other, the better. This surely is to be encouraged by officialdom, rather than frowned upon, as frequently seems to be the case. (Op. cit.)

On 5 December 1966 the Home Office recognized the institution of the 'working holiday', announcing that any Commonwealth citizen could come to Britain for an extended working holiday provided that he or she could convince the immigration officer on two counts:

1. that his intention is to return home, i.e. that the main purpose of his visit is to have a holiday;
2. that he can support himself even if he fails to find a job.

Immigration officers were instructed to regard letters from parents, relatives, or bankers as evidence of visible means of support. They would not necessarily require the would-be holiday-maker to produce a return ticket. Visitors who had been allowed in for an initial period of three months could apply for an extension. These rules were to apply to all Commonwealth citizens irrespective of race or colour.

(iv) *Continued Complaints*

That all was not yet well at the ports of entry by the winter of 1966–7, despite moves at ministerial level to liberalize procedures, was indicated by further press reports. In an article entitled 'How immigrants meet rough justice at the ports' (*Guardian*, 10 December 1966), Eric Silver gave details of how the machinery had become a 'rejecting device', not because immigration officers are 'racialist ogres' but because they are 'conscientious men required to do an impossible job with inadequate tools'. Registration of births is not compulsory in India and Pakistan, and the officer has to investigate doubtful cases (children around 16) by interrogation and medical tests, usually through interpreters (also employed by the Home Office). The standards, generally applied in medical examinations (inspection of joints, wisdom teeth, and genitals) are designed to check the age of English and American children (and so not necessarily of general application). There is no genuine right of appeal against an immigration officer's decision, though legal devices, like *habeas corpus* or *mandamus*, can sometimes be invoked.

In the case of Habib Khan, who claimed he was 15 and the son of a Pakistani foundry worker living in Bradford, the latter sought a writ of *habeas corpus* after the boy had been held for three days at London Airport. The Home Office decided to oppose the writ on 25 November, but let the boy go 'home' with Mr. Khan, who, with another man, had applied to act as surety (£250 each). On 2 December the Home Office agreed to a fresh inquiry by immigration officers, at which Mr. Khan and the boy would be entitled to bring legal representatives and their own interpreter. This was seen as a major innovation, and one which would, if it became general practice, go a long way towards meeting criticisms of the present screening procedure, though the conclusiveness of the medical tests was still queried. On 7 December the Divisional Court rejected the application for a writ of *habeas corpus*, but Lord Justice Salmon said that though the application had failed it could be regarded as a triumph from a practical point of view; the authorities had been persuaded to set about a thorough investigation. On 16 December the Home Secretary, Mr. Roy Jenkins, decided to allow Habib Khan to stay in Britain unconditionally (during the court hearing fresh evidence of the boy's birth had been produced by his lawyers). This case was hailed as a big break-through by A. R. Cline in the *Spectator* (16 December 1966), but Cedric Thornberry and Anthony Lester issued a warning against being 'over-sanguine' (*Guardian*, 21 December 1966).

Some other young immigrants in this category were less fortunate.

Muhammad Khan was deported back to Karachi after being refused entry on X-ray evidence[1] (*The Times*, 14 December 1966). An Indian girl aged 16 was, however, allowed to stay after several days' detention pending inquiries over her father's citizenship (*Guardian*, 22 December 1966; 23 December 1966). Overcrowding and conditions at the detention suites at London Airport were described by Malcolm Southan (*Sunday Times*, 27 November 1966). In January 1967, two Pakistani boys who had been detained were released after bone X-ray checks; another, aged 11, was sent back to Karachi because of 'a misrepresentation of relationship', which was admitted (*Guardian*, 7 January). An Australian spastic aged 20, who had saved for four years to travel to Britain on his own and work with the British Spastics Society, was at first refused entry at Tilbury because he had not got an employment voucher, but was later allowed in.

In March and April 1967 there was another flurry of complaints and reports of delays and unpleasant incidents experienced by Commonwealth and non-Commonwealth visitors and permanent immigrants alike. The well-publicized incident of the Swedish girl stripped to the waist in mid-March was followed in April by the refusal of entry to a Pakistani boy (allegedly only informally adopted by the man he was joining here) (*Sunday Times*, 16 April; *Guardian*, 18 April); the holding for ninety minutes and medical examination of the 68-year-old wife of the Deputy Prime Minister of Honduras, Mrs. Kathleen Cattouse (*Daily Telegraph*, 22 April); the near-refusal of entry to the brother-in-law of the former Pakistani test cricketer, Mohammed Farooq, here to visit his sick sister (*The Times*, 17 April); and the double-barrelled shot aimed at a Spanish lawyer arriving with £500 and the intention of learning English. After being refused entry and held some days on board ship, he then had most of his money taken by a customs officer on the grounds that only £50 plus £15 could be taken *out* of England (it was refunded three months later) (*The Times*, 25 April). An unexpected one on the credit side was the Home Office's decision to lift the initial ban on an Indian youth who said he was 18 and had come to Britain to marry his 16-year-old fiancée, now in Leicester (*The Times*, 18 April).

Readers of *The Times* (29 March) weighed in with additional evidence, most of it critical ('the always tiresome, and often impertinent, procedure'—'the sneering superciliousness and truculent questioning of these gentlemen'). One correspondent, however, expressed the view that strict frontier control was a lesser evil than the compulsory registration inland practised by many European countries. Earlier, *The Times* (25 March) expressed the view that the complaints were too frequent and convincing to be discounted with an easy mind. Given a continued policy of severe restriction of entry, there would have to be either a

[1] See Bagley, op. cit.

simplification of the mechanism of control or an expansion of facilities.

The entry procedure for Commonwealth immigrants was criticized in the annual report of the National Council for Civil Liberties; the present system was said to be fair neither to immigrants nor to immigration officers, and to have worsened, if anything, during the past year. Women and children arriving at the airport were particularly vulnerable, facing often inadequate interpretation,[1] the humiliation of long interrogations, detentions, and X-ray and medical examinations. Some immigrants were still being refused entry even when in possession of an entry certificate, and the most striking injustices concerned genuine visitors (*Guardian*, 4 April). Later, the N.C.C.L. and C.A.R.D. wrote to the Home Office alleging that immigration officials had been able to obtain information from the Inland Revenue about the families of coloured immigrants (to use for checking dependants' claims about their family relationships); in one case the immigration officer was reported as not satisfied that two Pakistani boys were the father's true sons, because they knew nothing about four other children declared on the latter's income tax returns. Mr. Tony Smythe, general secretary of the N.C.C.L., said he was 'very concerned that private information can be traded between one Government department and another'.

In March 1967, Mr. David Ennals, Under-Secretary of State at the Home Office responsible for immigrants, gave assurances that the Home Office was acting to increase the number of interpreters available at entry points. Later it was reported that two Indian-born men and one man born in Britain of Pakistani parents were being trained as British immigration officers at Heath Row and Dover (*Guardian*, 17 March, 30 March).

(v) *Immigration Officers Defended*

The other side of the immigration officer's life is less frequently reported. As *The Times* (22 May 1967) wrote editorially:

> For several months immigration officers have been under fire, usually for refusing entry to prospective immigrants or for alleged bad manners to immigrants and visitors at ports of entry. . . . There are many other cases where it is beyond all doubt that the would-be immigrant is making a determined bid to defeat the immigration regulations.

The Times was referring to an address given by Mr. Ennals, Under-Secretary, Home Office, at a conference on race relations and the law

[1] In April 1967 there were said to be seven interpreters at ports of entry in Britain (six of them at London Airport) as compared with five in 1966. Main languages were reported to be Urdu and Hindi. It was also stressed that most immigration officers have at least one other language.

in Leeds on 21 May 1967. He stoutly defended immigration officers[1] and criticized agents overseas who tried to make a profit for themselves, and a mockery of British immigration control, by supplying forged passports:

> There are a hundred and one ways of trying to deceive the authorities. Some will pay large sums of money to obtain forged passports. They may pretend to be returning residents. Others will pretend to be relatives of Commonwealth citizens resident in Britain—or try to convince the immigration officer that their relationship is closer than it really is. Others will falsify their age. The would-be evaders not only make life difficult for the immigration officers, it is also grossly unfair to those genuine dependants who may become subject to a searching scrutiny to sort out the genuine from the bogus.

Mr. Ennals quoted three examples of false pretences by intending immigrants:

1. An Indian claimed to be the 63-year-old father of a woman already living here, but the airport medical officer thought he was 'nowhere near' 60 years of age. His 'daughter' said she had two brothers and three sisters; the 'father' said he had only one son and one daughter. The immigration officer then found a letter sent to the Indian by the family, telling him what to say at the airport. It was a 'crib sheet', but he had forgotten what to say when he came up for interview.
2. Two teen-age Pakistani boys, who were met at the airport by a man who claimed to be their father, admitted that they had been coached for five days in Pakistan on what to say at the airport.
3. A Pakistani who arrived with an altered passport claimed to be a returning resident, but it soon became clear that he had never been in Britain before, and was unable to tell a penny from a shilling. He told Mr. Ennals that he had sold his plot of land in Pakistan to pay an agent for his forged passport.

Mr. Ennals went on to say that most of the cases where people were turned back concerned those travelling from India and Pakistan:

> Many of the reports have been garbled and misleading but in almost every case the impression has been given that immigration officers are bureaucratic and unhelpful and that we do not welcome those entitled to come to Britain. This impression is neither correct nor fair to the immigration officer. Wrong impressions endanger our image overseas, and also lead to concern in this country.

He appealed to Commonwealth immigrants to advise relations who might be planning to join them to obtain entry certificates before leaving

[1] As his predecessor, Mr. Maurice Foley, and successive Home Secretaries had done on a number of earlier occasions in this context.

their homes. This would save time and inconvenience at the port of entry and could prevent the misery and waste of money involved in a return trip. Most of those arriving from India and Pakistan did not have entry certificates, yet hardly any holders of entry certificates were refused.

(vi) *Entry Certificates*

The 'entry certificate' scheme to ease entry to Britain for Commonwealth citizens not holding employment vouchers was outlined in the first published set of Instructions to Immigration Officers (Cmnd 1716 of May 1962). The relevant paragraph read as follows:

> . . . administrative arrangements are being made whereby any Commonwealth citizen (other than one who requires a Ministry of Labour voucher) who wishes to be assured that he is unlikely to encounter any difficulty in entering the country may, if he so chooses, apply to the appropriate United Kingdom representative in his own country, or in the country in which he is living, for the issue of an entry certificate. The holder of such a certificate will be refused admission only in the circumstances described in paragraphs 39 to 42 below, or if it is clear that the certificate was obtained by fraud. The fact that a person holds an entry certificate does not of itself exempt him from the imposition of conditions (see, for example, paragraphs 7 and 16) in an appropriate case.[1]

Little has been published about the actual operation and scope of this scheme until recently, but it has in fact been in increasing use from the first imposition of controls: there were 37,810 applications (491 refusals) in the last half of 1962; 59,455 applications (1,095 refusals) in 1963; 76,340 applications (2,162 refusals) in 1964; 86,248 applications (3,694 refusals) in 1965; and 91,179 applications (4,838 refusals) in 1966.[2] From the start Australian and New Zealand visitors and West Indian dependants seem to have made proportionately greater use of the scheme than other nationals; Australia's applications have always constituted the highest single annual total (see below for 1966 table and comments).

At first, despite the qualifications in Cmnd 1716, the entry certificate seems to have been widely regarded as an absolute guarantee of entry. In 1965, however, the White Paper described it as the arrangement under which any Commonwealth citizen seeking admission without a voucher could apply for an entry certificate before leaving home to make 'reasonably sure' of being admitted on arrival. The amended instructions to immigration officers (Cmnd 3064, August 1966) also again qualified the absoluteness of the guarantee. In May 1967 there seemed to be a move in official thinking towards extending, reinforcing,

[1] Paragraphs 39–42 concern refusal on medical, criminal and security grounds, or being the subject of a deportation order.

[2] For detailed statistics of the years 1962–6, see Appendix II.

and encouraging the wider use of the entry certificate system.[1] This was in line with the views of bodies, such as the N.C.C.I., that had been pressing for improvements in the control procedure. It was, however, pointed out that if the system was to function properly, the entry certificate once issued should be honoured; that also the checking should be done before the would-be immigrant left home; that uniform criteria should be applied by investigating officers in all Commonwealth territories; and that the purpose of the certificates should be publicized equally widely throughout the Commonwealth.[2]

Commonwealth Relations Office figures released in early 1967 (see Appendix II) give an indication of the degree to which the entry certificate system was used in 1966 by intending immigrants in different categories and from various Commonwealth countries, also of the number of refusals (though these are not broken down by category of application). It may be noted that, for whatever reasons, applicants in Australia, New Zealand, Cyprus, Malta, and the various West Indian territories made much greater use of the procedure than did those in Canada, India or Pakistan. There were great variations between different countries in the proportion of applicants falling into the various categories, from Australia, and New Zealand, Malta, Cyprus, and Gibraltar, with their high percentage of 'visitors', to Jamaica and the Leeward and Windward Islands, with their high percentage of dependants. The percentage of applications refused also varied considerably between territories, though more detailed analysis and comparison with the overall admissions would be needed to assess the reasons for this variation. In 1966 Jamaica topped the list with 881 refused out of 8,168 applications, followed by Pakistan (838 out of 6,576), the Windward and Leeward Islands (812 out of 3,332), and Cyprus (608 out of 4,719).[3]

(vii) *Deportation*

The deportation provisions of the Commonwealth Immigrants Act (1962) related to both Irish and Commonwealth citizens who had been resident in Britain for less than five years, if convicted of offences punishable with imprisonment (the intention being to deport only the persistent serious criminal, not young offenders or first offenders). The existence of these powers in itself creates a duality of citizenship and makes the

[1] See Mr. David Ennals' speech in Leeds (*The Times*, 22 May) cited above.

[2] Up to 7 March, according to the *Guardian*, the leaflets (I.M.1) with instructions on how to get these certificates had been available only in Canberra. Thereafter, following pressures in Britain, they were distributed throughout the Commonwealth. (*Guardian*, 17 March 1967 and 21 March 1967.)

[3] It is interesting to compare the Cyprus figures with the refusals for Malta (one out of 4,370), and Gibraltar (nil out of 929).

immigrant liable to a double penalty for a single offence. Moreover, the convicted immigrant who is recommended for deportation usually has to await the end of his term of imprisonment before knowing whether the recommendation is to be implemented. The effects of deportation also fall more heavily on the immigrant with a family and on the immigrant whose country of origin is more remote.

In an article on 'Delinquency Among Immigrants',[1] A. E. Bottoms made the following comments on deportation:

> One important difference between immigrants and other offenders is that immigrants may be liable to be deported after conviction. In the case of Commonwealth and Irish immigrants, this possibility only applies for five years after arrival, but aliens may be deported at any time. The deportation order is of some considerable theoretical interest in relation to the theory of deterrence and also because of the double-stage decision-making process involved. . . . Virtually nothing is known about either of these matters in detail. Indeed, astonishingly enough, figures on deportations are published neither in the Criminal Statistics nor in the statistics on the operation of the Commonwealth Immigrants Act. However, they are available upon special application to the Home Office.[2] Perhaps the most interesting feature is the heavy preponderance of the Irish among those actually deported—more than 60 per cent—though perhaps this is partly explained . . . by the fact that deportation to Ireland is an easier and less expensive business than deportation to the West Indies or Asia.

In August 1966 Cedric Thornberry reviewed the way in which deportation powers had been applied since 1962 (*Guardian*, 18 August). Figures recently published, in response to questions in Parliament by Harold Gurden, showed that an average of five Commonwealth citizens were now being deported per week. Since May 1962 there had been 999 deportations (during the same period 232 aliens were deported). The Wilson Committee's terms of reference allowed it to consider procedure, but not the policy underlying deportation. The writer traced the phases of implementation of the deportation provisions since May 1962: the initial spate of recommendations, including the Carmen Bryan case,[3] the courts' retreat from xenophobic ardour after Mr. Henry Brooke urged restraint at Durham in November 1962; and the 10% 'quashing rate' by appeal courts that persisted until September 1964. After Labour came to office, however, the most marked change had been a steep decline in the proportion of recommendations quashed on appeal, from 12% in September 1964 to 5% at the time of writing.

This might suggest, continued the writer, that the lower courts were

[1] *Race*, Vol. VIII, no. 4, 1967.

[2] See Appendix III.

[3] See I.R.R. *Newsletter*, August 1962, pp. 7–9, for details about this early xenophobic period.

being more restrained in their recommendations, but it was also true that, during the twenty months ending in May 1966, the courts had been recommending for deportation at a higher rate than at any time since November 1962. The rate should in fact be falling, not rising, if the intentions of the Act (to deport only the persistent, serious criminals) were being followed. Most of these should have shown up by now, or reached the five-year residence haven, after which deportation did not apply. This revived the old suspicion that the power of deportation might be being used against any Commonwealth citizens convicted of crimes: indeed figures for those deported in the eighteen months before June 1966 showed that no less than 10% were first offenders, while others had been conditionally discharged or otherwise released on conviction. These figures also showed that 63% of those deported were Irish, an absurd use of the power, in the writer's view, seeing that most of them could come back on the next boat.

(viii) *Repatriation*

'Repatriation' was the term used in the White Paper of 1965 (paragraphs 25–26) for the proposed extra power for the Home Secretary to deport Commonwealth citizens, without the recommendation of a court, if they have evaded immigration control.

The term has customarily been used for a process other than deportation. As the writer of the Bow Group pamphlet 'Commonwealth Immigration' (1965) commented:

> There have been recent demands for the offer of a once-for-all basis, of free passages home to all immigrants who wish to return. In fact the National Assistance Board already help, on a discretionary basis, immigrants in real need who wish to leave this country and are unable to afford the fare. 92 people were helped in this way in 1963 and 99 in 1964. It is possible that this scheme should be extended, but there is no evidence to suggest that a large number of immigrants would leave the UK [*sic*] as a result if it were made all-embracing. The implicit suggestion that we are so anxious to get rid of immigrants that we will pay their fares home does no credit to us at all.

(ix) *British Nationality*

Under the British Nationality Act, 1948, with insignificant exceptions, persons who are born, or whose fathers were born, in the U.K. or in a territory which was a colony of the U.K. on 1 January 1949, or at the date of birth if later, or in a U.K. registered ship or aircraft, are citizens of the U.K. and Colonies. Citizenship may also be acquired: by descent (subject to certain requirements) from a paternal grandfather born in the U.K. or Colonies or from a more remote paternal ancestor in the male line; by registration, for citizens of Commonwealth member countries or of the Irish Republic, for minor children, and for women married to citizens of the U.K. and Colonies; in consequence of an adoption order; and by naturalization. The requirements for the grant of a certificate of naturalization include five years' residence in the U.K. or Colonies or five years' Crown service, good character, a sufficient knowledge of English, and the intention to reside in the U.K. or a colony or to remain in Crown service.

A citizen of the U.K. and Colonies does not forfeit his citizenship by acquiring or possessing the nationality or citizenship of another country; nor does a woman who is a citizen of the U.K. and Colonies lose her citizenship by marriage to an alien. Indeed, a citizen cannot be deprived of his citizenship against his will except in very exceptional circumstances (for example, if he has obtained naturalization or registration as a citizen by fraud). Any man or woman who is a citizen is, however, at liberty to renounce citizenship if he or she possesses or acquires the nationality or citizenship of another country.

Citizens of the other independent Commonwealth countries are, in U.K. law, British subjects or Commonwealth citizens. Until the passing of the Commonwealth Immigrants Act 1962, they were free to enter and remain in the U.K. without restrictions of any kind. Similar treatment has been extended to citizens of the Irish Republic, who, in the U.K., are not aliens.[1]

In early 1967 there was some argument as to the status of a particular class of British passport holders in relation to the Commonwealth Immigrants Act of 1962. This was precipitated by the refusal of the Indian Government to allow entry to a hundred-or-so Indians about to be deported from Tanzania, on the grounds that they held British passports. Thereafter, Mr. William Watson, an official of the Canadian High Commission in Dar-es-Salaam (which looks after British interests), issued a statement saying that holders of 'U.K. and Colonies' passports might have lost that status as a result of the independence of the colonial territory from which they derived that status; they would thus not have automatic right of entry into Britain. According to the *Guardian's* Nairobi correspondent, the number of Asians affected by East African pressures and hostilities was likely to rise considerably over the next few years, so that 50,000 or 60,000 might have to leave. Eric Silver added that the position of the Indian deportees hinged on the definition of a U.K. passport, which in the 1962 Act excluded all but

[1] Special transitional arrangements applied to citizens of South Africa, which ceased to be a member of the Commonwealth in May 1961. Under the South Africa Act, 1962, South Africans, unless they were also citizens of the U.K. or some other Commonwealth country, became aliens, but South African citizens who fulfilled certain defined qualifications showing close connexion with the U.K. or a colony by descent, residence or employment could become U.K. citizens by registration if they applied before the end of May 1965.

passports issued by the U.K. Government. *The Times* (3 February) reported that the Commonwealth Office confirmed the gist of the statement made by Mr. Watson. It was apparently the intention of the British Government not to renew, when the many local British passports issued in East Africa to Asians came up for renewal. (The problem of renewal of passports would also affect Kenya-born Europeans.)

In the *Guardian* (4 February), a former British passport official in Kenya, Mr. Donald MacColl, was reported as expressing an opposite view:

> People living in Kenya, Uganda and Tanganyika who did not qualify automatically for local citizenship on independence and derived British nationality from residence there remained citizens of the United Kingdom and Colonies. The passports for which the people were—and are—entitled to apply were issued by the British High Commission as agents of the Government in London. Holders of such passports were exempt from the Commonwealth Immigrants Act. They would only fall within its scope if their passports were issued 'on behalf of the Government of any part of the Commonwealth outside the United Kingdom'; in other words a colonial Government like that of Hong Kong.

Mr. MacColl added that those who qualified automatically for local citizenship on independence were people who had been born there and whose fathers had also been born there. People living there who did not qualify in this way were given the option of registering as local citizens within a two-year period. To do so they had to renounce British citizenship, because the African countries did not acknowledge dual nationality. Under a British Act of 1964, however, people who did renounce it to conform with local laws could reassume British citizenship at any time simply by declaring their loyalty and asking for their passports back. For this reason, Mr. MacColl estimated that there might be as many as 250,000 Asians in the three East African countries who qualified to enter without vouchers. There was, of course, no reason to expect either that they would all come or that they would come in a concentrated wave.

In practice the situation seems to have varied. A handful of Asian immigrants had already entered Britain from East Africa free from control, whereas one Asian from Tanzania was refused entry on 2 January 1967, and then allowed in as a visitor for six months, during which time he hoped to clarify his right to settle in Britain or in India or Pakistan. Later in the year the problem became more acute as the Kenya Government introduced more stringent employment curbs on resident non-citizens. The British Government also admitted that up to 200,000 East African Asians were, if they wished, qualified to enter Britain freely as U.K. citizens.

(x) *A Note on Commonwealth Students*[1]

The admission of overseas students to British universities is a long-established tradition, whose value was recognized in the Robbins Report of 1963. Both the instructions and revised instructions to immigration officers issued in 1962 and 1966 stressed that the Government welcomed Commonwealth citizens coming to this country to follow a course (usual minimum one year) at a university, college, school, or other institution (not a correspondence course), which will occupy all or a substantial part of his time (i.e. not less than fifteen hours a week of organized day-time study).

The revised instructions also contained the following guidance:

> 10. A Commonwealth citizen seeking admission as a student should normally be expected to produce evidence of acceptance for a course of study, beginning shortly, that meets the requirements of the Act (a correspondence course does not meet those requirements) and of ability to meet the cost of the course and of his own maintenance. Little difficulty will then arise unless there are grounds for doubting that his intentions are genuine and realistic, for example where there is an obvious lack of correspondence between the student's previous attainments and the nature of the course he proposes to follow. The Immigration Officer should be on his guard against attempts to use enrolment for a course of study as a means of obtaining admission without a voucher. Attendance at the course must be the student's primary purpose in coming to the United Kingdom; if his primary intention is to work and settle, he must qualify for admission on other grounds.
>
> 11. The entry certificate procedure is particularly appropriate for a student who has not been able to obtain a place in advance. He will have to satisfy the issuing authority that he has had genuine difficulty in making advance arrangements and that he has a reasonable chance of being accepted for the kind of course he wants to follow. Due weight will be given to any evidence the student produces of qualifications he has already obtained, or of sponsorship by his home government or some other educational authority.
>
> 13. An Immigration Officer should be prepared to admit any Commonwealth citizen if satisfied that his principal object in coming to the United Kingdom is to study, even if the requirements of paragraphs 10 to 12 are not completely fulfilled. But, in so far as those requirements are not entirely satisfied, countervailing evidence of the student's *bona fides* should be required.
>
> 16. If a Commonwealth citizen has been accepted for a course of study and there is no reason to doubt his *bona fides*, he should normally be admitted for one year in the first instance and not prohibited from taking employment.[2]

[1] This account is based largely on the British Council's regular publication, *Overseas Students in Britain*, revised edition, London, November 1966.

[2] The one-year period caused anxiety among Commonwealth students, but on 15 December 1965, Mr. George Thomas, Under-Secretary of State at the Home Office, assured a deputation of students' organizations that permission to stay after the first year would be given automatically, provided that students continued the same course. Students who failed would be allowed to stay if the college vouched for them.

But if the Immigration Officer thinks it desirable that the Home Office should later confirm that an intending student has enrolled for a course of studies, or that he is attending the course for which he had enrolled, he should restrict the initial period of stay accordingly and prohibit the student from taking employment in the meantime. In either case, he should explain to the student that he will be allowed to prolong his stay if satisfactory evidence of continuing studies is produced.

There were some early complaints of evasion on this score by Commonwealth citizens who allegedly signed up for fee-paying courses so as to procure documentary evidence of acceptance and then did not turn up at the beginning of term. The detailed statistics about overseas students kept and published annually by the British Council show, however, both that most of those who entered as 'students' were in fact pursuing courses of study, and that the controls of 1962 did not have an adverse effect on the entrance of *bona fide* students.[1]

In 1965/66 there were approximately 71,387 overseas students in full-time courses in Britain. The Council regards as an overseas student one whose age is over 18 and whose permanent place of residence is overseas and who has come to Britain to undertake full-time study, research or training for not less than six months.

There are overseas students in many different types of study: at universities, polytechnics, technical colleges and other colleges of further education; the Inns of Court; colleges of education; in nursing or midwifery; in various types of practical training; at a variety of research establishments and other institutions; at private colleges of music and drama and at schools of English and other subjects.

The figures do not include part-time students, of whom there have for some years been considerable numbers. Many of these came to Britain in order to obtain the same qualifications as full-time students, but found that, either because of lack of qualifications or the means to support themselves, they could not obtain admission to or could not afford to remain on full-time courses; many therefore study either with the aid of correspondence courses or by part-time attendance at evening or other classes, and support themselves by doing a job. The figures also exclude a large number of young people, mainly girls from Western European countries, who come to Britain to learn English and live 'au pair' or take up domestic work.

Of the 71,387 full-time students and trainees, about two-thirds came from other countries of the Commonwealth, in particular from Africa, Asia and the West Indies. The total for 1965/66 compares with 38,500 in 1957/58 and 12,500 in 1950/51.

Overseas students and trainees are to be found in almost every college and at all levels. Many come to Britain to take advantage of educational facilities which are not yet fully developed at home, but the majority are studying or training at or below the level of first degree. Over a quarter of the overseas students in technical and other colleges of further education were qualifying

[1] See Appendix IV.

in the required G.C.E. 'A' and 'O' Level subjects, before proceeding to a degree course in a university or a course of equivalent level in a technical or other college.

At a higher level, there is a continuing steady increase in the number of postgraduate students both from developed and developing countries coming to Britain for study, research or training, within and without the universities. Nearly half the overseas students in British universities in 1965/66 were at postgraduate level.

Of the 71,387 overseas students in Britain in 1965/66, 19,000 were estimated to hold a scholarship or other award, whether from their own government, from a British official source, or from industry, a private trust or an international organisation such as the United Nations. Most of the remainder were either supported by their families or local communities, or by the firms and institutions which accepted them for training. A proportion were self-supporting.

The chief source of awards for students from the developing Commonwealth countries and from a number of foreign countries were their own governments, and funds provided by public boards and corporations; a number were financed by private trusts and commercial undertakings in their own country.

A certain number of scholarships, fellowships and other awards from British Government sources are open to Commonwealth and foreign students mainly at senior academic and professional level. Among these are 500 Commonwealth scholarships awarded mainly for two years to men and women of high intellectual promise who may be expected to make a significant contribution to life in their own countries on their return. Some 550 bursaries are awarded mainly to teachers under the Commonwealth Bursary scheme. (Both schemes arose from the Commonwealth Education Conference in Oxford in 1959.)

There are a number of schemes for technical assistance including the Colombo Plan for South East Asia, the Special Commonwealth African Assistance Plan (SCAAP), Technical Assistance for Countries in Non-Commonwealth Africa (TANCA), the Central Treaty Organisation and a number of other bilateral technical assistance programmes.

The British Council awards scholarships and bursaries in 90 countries for advanced study in Britain. There are Senior Fellowship awards offered by the United Nations Specialised Agencies. More than 900 U.N. Fellows are placed in Britain each year for the whole or part of their Fellowship training under arrangements made by the British Council in conjunction with interested government departments. There are also scholarships and fellowships offered by trusts, learned societies, industrial and professional organisations and by private benefactors. Among the best-known awards provided by trusts are the Rhodes Scholarships. The Confederation of British Industry awards a number of scholarships to enable graduate engineers to gain experience with industrial firms.[1]

[1] *Overseas Students in Britain* (revised edition)—with annual statistical supplements. The issue of increased fees for overseas students became an acute one in early 1967, but space precludes a detailed account of its development, which was in any case widely covered by the daily and weekly press.

In 1965–6, the grand total of students from Commonwealth countries and U.K. dependencies in Britain was 44,411 (as compared with 38,500 for 1957–8 and 12,500 in 1950–51). The number who were admitted as students in 1965 was 8,643 men, 4,540 women and 834 children.

CHAPTER 3

Anti-Discrimination Legislation

Legislation was one of the three prongs of the attack on immigration announced by the Prime Minister, Mr. Harold Wilson, on 9 March 1965. The others (discussed in Chapter 2 and Chapter 4) were intensified controls on immigration and some modest proposals for central co-ordinating integrative activities, coupled with a statement that once in Britain, Commonwealth immigrants should be treated for all purposes as U.K. citizens.

The Race Relations Bill, as published in April 1965, was intended

> to prohibit discrimination on racial grounds in places of public resort; to prevent the enforcement or imposition on racial grounds of restrictions on the transfer of tenancies; to penalise incitement to racial hatred; and to amend section 5 of the Public Order Act 1936.

It got a mixed reception, criticisms being levelled at it on general principles or for its omissions (principally jobs, housing, and religious discrimination), or again because it contained no reference to any conciliation machinery to be used before resort to the courts. *The Times* (8 April) commented editorially: 'Good intentions, bad law'; and the *Observer* called the Bill a 'botched job'. *Tribune* (16 April) thought it 'well-meaning and half-hearted' but deserving of support, while Hamza Alavi in *Peace News* (16 April) found it a token of the Labour Party's 'present defeatist attitude' over racialism in Britain.

The Government was reported to expect the Race Relations Bill to have passed its second reading by mid-May. After expressing the hope that politicians would prior to that date accord it rather fuller discussion, Alan Watkins in the *Spectator* (16 April) commented that the Bill broke new ground with its concern over two different matters—racial discrimination and racial incitement. While the first restricted an owner or manager's economic freedom over admission to theatres, restaurants, and public houses, the second restricted freedom of speech. While few people, he surmised, would object *in principle* to the discrimination provisions (most arguments against them being rather based on their effectiveness), the incitement provisions presented a different situation. Clause 3 of the Bill, in his view, detracted from a principle that had taken over 300 years to establish: namely that where words are concerned, the test of whether they are punishable is not their content or their effect on people's feelings, but their effect on people's behaviour—i.e. the words must tend towards a breach of the peace.

Why was this necessary? asked the writer. Cassandra in the *Daily Mirror* had maintained that it should 'put an end to the Colin Jordans of our time, and those louts who, not so long ago, went about baiting coloured people and assaulting them with iron bars'. But the Notting Hill louts had got four years' imprisonment ('emerging to a total negation of recognition or applause from their quondam peers or their loutish successors in the local corner-boy leadership stakes'—I.R.R. *Newsletter*, Editor), and Mr. Jordan had in fact got a two months' prison sentence under Section 5 of the Public Order Act. Moreover, as Professor Harry Street had pointed out in *Freedom, the Individual and the Law:*

The ruling of the Lord Chief Justice in Jordan's case that the offence is committed if the words are likely to provoke a breach of the peace among the particular audience, even though that audience is an unreasonable one and made up of hooligans whose aim was to prevent the speaker from making an address, confirms the view that the section (i.e. section 5) needs no extension.

The *Spectator* writer concluded by saying that it was disturbing how vague the Home Secretary, Sir Frank Soskice, and his Government colleagues were about the class of people, or the kind of words, against which the incitement provisions might be used. This seemed to place a premium on literacy and skill in the formulation of provocative propaganda, and was likely to inhibit the law discussion necessary before the country could reach a consensus on the inflammatory issue of immigration. In lighter vein, in the same journal, Quoodle (Mr. Iain Macleod) called the Bill a piece of political sky-writing: it did not attack discrimination by landladies, clubs, employers, or trade unions. It was only half a Bill, and that half bad—for the first time the concept of colour would be introduced into the body of British statute law.

Some liberals and advocates of more massive programmes of positive integration also tended to feel that the Bill was part of the prevailing negative and restrictive attitude to immigration; that it had been introduced as an easier alternative to long-term centralized planning, and also one which would be 'a gesture of goodwill (to the immigrant communities), more especially if more unpalatable restrictions on immigration are in the offing', and would promote assimilation or integration by lessening the danger of immigrant communities withdrawing into themselves and becoming militant.

1. BACKGROUND TO THE 1965 RACE RELATIONS BILL

Such legislation had been first announced in the 1964 manifesto of the Labour Party. Party thinking on the matter dates back to 1952[1] when

[1] This section draws heavily on articles by Keith Hindell, 'The Genesis of the Race Relations Bill', *Political Quarterly*, Vol. 36, no. 4, October–December 1965, and Cedric Thornberry, 'Commitment or Withdrawal?', *Race*, Vol. VII, no. 1, July 1965.

the Commonwealth Sub-Committee of the National Executive Committee asked for advice about legislation in this field from the Hon. Mr. Justice Ungoed-Thomas (former solicitor-general) and Dr. Kenneth Little (now Professor of Social Anthropology, University of Edinburgh). Dr. Little gave unequivocal approval to anti-discrimination laws, and suggested machinery such as that of the Fair Employment Practices Commission in the U.S.A. Judge Ungoed-Thomas was less enthusiastic about legislation and came down for a limited criminal sanction.

During the thirteen years of Labour Opposition, it was left to private members to press (unsuccessfully) for anti-discrimination legislation. In 1950 the M.P. for Leyton, Reginald Sorensen, now Lord Sorensen, introduced a 'Colour Bar Bill' which would have made it a criminal offence to discriminate on colour grounds in public places (but did not make any specific reference to Jews).

In 1956 the Member for Eton and Slough, Fenner Brockway, now Lord Brockway, introduced the first of nine annual Bills. It covered discrimination in public places, hiring and dismissal in employment, and racially restrictive covenants and leases. In the later Bills, employment was omitted, but in 1961 a racial incitement clause was added. Though they were not successful, Fenner Brockway's efforts attracted increasingly wide support, and the last four Bills had all-party sponsorship.[1]

A. LABOUR PARTY PROPOSALS

When the Labour Party began to draw up a Bill against racial discrimination and incitement in the summer of 1964, incitement was treated as the main subject by both an N.E.C. sub-committee (which included Sir Frank Soskice, M.P., later Home Secretary) and by a Society of Labour Lawyers' sub-committee, which were preparing drafts.

Both groups proposed stern penalties for incitement to racial hatred, either by extension of the Public Order Act 1936, reserving the right of prosecution to the Attorney-General (Soskice), or by creating a new statutory offence of provoking racial hatred (Society of Labour Lawyers).

Both groups proposed making discrimination in public places a criminal offence, the Society of Labour Lawyers defining public places to include all places of public resort maintained by a public authority.

[1] Sponsors of various Bills included: from the Labour side—Mr. Wedgwood Benn, Mrs. Barbara Castle, Mr. Dingle Foot, Mr. John Stonehouse, Mr. James Griffiths, Mr. Anthony Greenwood, and Mr. Robert Mellish; from the Liberals—Mr. Grimond and Mr. Lubbock; from the Conservatives—Mr. Nigel Fisher, Mr. Julian Critchley, Mr. Patrick Wall, and Sir Godfrey Nicholson.

Neither set of proposals considered including employment, housing, insurance and credit, nor was an administrative law considered.

Later in 1964, a minority group within the Society of Labour Lawyers sub-committee produced alternative proposals calling for an administrative law, which would cover all areas of discrimination. Drawing heavily on United States and Canadian experience with various different types of legislation, the group suggested the creation of a Statutory Commission which would receive complaints, try to get compliance with the law by a process of conciliation, backed by full powers to investigate, to hold hearings, and ultimately to enforce its decisions in the county courts. The Commission should also be able to conduct research inquiries.

These proposals were sent to the law officers of the newly-elected Labour Government. They were also adopted by C.A.R.D. (Anthony Lester, one of the leading members of the S.L.L. sub-committee, was one of the original members of C.A.R.D. and became chairman of its Legal Committee); and by the time the Government's Race Relations Bill was published, a full-scale lobby for a comprehensive administrative law was under way.[1]

In the outcome, the section of the Race Relations Bill dealing with discrimination was amended by the Government itself at the Committee stage[2]—instead of criminal penalties, a Race Relations Board was to be created, and conciliation machinery set up. The Board, however, was not accorded full investigatory powers, and final enforcement powers remained at the discretion of the Attorney-General. Moreover, the scope of the law was not enlarged, either to cover employment and housing, or to apply to religious discrimination.[3]

B. OTHER VIEWPOINTS AND PRESSURES

Professor J. A. G. Griffith wrote in 1959:

A considerable and respectable body of opinion believes that social and personal attitudes to coloured persons and the discrimination which flows from them either are not amenable to legal control at all or ought not to be controlled by law. The arguments of this group are various. It is urged that

[1] See I.R.R. *Newsletter*, February 1965, for article by Cedric Thornberry on 'Law and Race Relations in Britain'. See also *Newsletter*, May–June 1965, pp. 6–7, and I.R.R. *Newsletter* Supplement for May–June 1965 (article by Anthony Lester on 'Racial Discrimination and the Law').

[2] For the debate on the second reading, see Hansard, 711 H.C., cols. 926–1060. At this stage Cedric Thornberry, 'Commitment or Withdrawal?', called the Bill a 'sad, botched-up job reflecting little credit on anyone who has been involved in it'. It was also criticized for inadequacy in a number of fields by a Young Fabian Study Group, *Strangers Within*, pp. 11–13.

[3] The Bill did not in any case apply to Ulster.

public opinion determines these attitudes and that the law ought not to seek to run counter to that opinion; that legislative and administrative intervention would, far from reducing discrimination, tend to increase it by causing further resentment and creating more publicity; that to widen the field of legal intervention too greatly would unduly restrict liberty of thought and speech; that the only effective method is by education.[1]

He cited the Earl of Perth, Conservative Minister of State for Colonial Affairs, and other Government spokesmen, including Mr. R. A. Butler, the then Home Secretary, as taking this view in 1958 and 1959.[2]

There had been little pressure amongst the Conservatives when in Government to support anti-discrimination legislation and the 'freedom of speech and choice' advocates were more vocal and probably more numerous. Once faced with the probability of such legislation, however, the Conservative leadership reacted pragmatically.[3] Before the second reading, the Conservative Party Home Affairs Committee decided almost unanimously that the Bill was 'inept and ineffective' and would be better withdrawn; members were, however, reported uncertain whether to oppose it outright on second reading (thereby courting the risk of being accused of tolerating discrimination), or to challenge it with a reasoned amendment. At the end of the month, a 'reasoned amendment' was tabled in the names of Sir Alec Douglas-Home and Mr. Peter Thorneycroft; it declined to give the Bill a second reading because of the anomalies it would create, because it would introduce heavy penalties when a system of conciliation would be better, and because legislation on race would be likely to create more problems than it solved (*Guardian*, 29 April 1965).

During the debate on 3 May 1965, the Home Secretary, Sir Frank Soskice, anticipating the Opposition amendment, indicated that the Government was ready to listen closely to the arguments in favour of introducing a conciliation process, either before or during the committee stage. From the Opposition benches Mr. Peter Thorneycroft took the Home Secretary up smartly. It was not enough to make a vague offer about conciliation; the 'taint of criminality' must be entirely removed from the discrimination clause, which in any case was too

[1] J. A. G. Griffith, *Coloured Immigrants in Britain*, London, O.U.P. for I.R.R., 1960, p. 173.

[2] The writer himself regarded this attitude as mistaken and the further argument that legislation must not run ahead of public opinion as 'suspect'. He went on to advocate not mere preventive legislation but the establishment of an administrative agency (stressing conciliation) to combat those discriminatory acts that can be controlled by legal action, including house purchase or leases and membership of employers' federations and trade unions.

[3] There seems to have been a widespread feeling among Conservatives that, if there was to be legislation at all, it should extend to the major public spheres of contact and concern—employment and perhaps housing. See Bow Group pamphlet, October 1965, p. 36.

narrow to cover the areas that really mattered—employment and housing. He then went on to attack the part of the Bill dealing with incitement as likely to endanger free speech. The Opposition would tolerate the Bill: (i) if the Home Secretary drastically curtailed Commonwealth immigration; and (ii) if he withheld the measure until he had worked out conciliation procedures. The Solicitor-General, Mr. Dingle Foot, gave a somewhat cryptic explanation about the non-inclusion of religious grounds, and said he was sure that the Bill would cover anti-Semitism as well as colour discrimination. A Tory amendment opposing the second reading was lost by 261 votes to 249.

The *Guardian* (4 May) editorially accorded moderate approval to the Government, but also admitted Mr. Thorneycroft's points on the need to include housing and employment. *The Times* (4 May) welcomed the Home Secretary's flexibility, but foresaw serious difficulties of principle and practice, and suggested that the best course would be to withdraw the present Bill and introduce another containing conciliation measures but shorn of criminal provisions. Thereafter, the Bill was amended (but not extended), and provisions for conciliation introduced.[1]

One prophetic comment on the probable value of the proposed legislation came from Cedric Thornberry:

> The value, in the writer's view, of the proposed legislation would be largely psychological. It would demonstrate that 'authority' is committed to a particular viewpoint and course of action. In the past, authority has been neutral—save in exceptional legal situations, one of which was, in a well-remembered case, highlighted twenty years ago by Sir Learie Constantine. Its neutrality has not been ambiguous—there has been no refusal, to the writer's knowledge, to renew a publican's licence because he operates a colour bar.
>
> But to identify the proposed measure as a piece of window-dressing would be too harsh a judgement. Its value, as has been stressed, would lie in its dramatic effect. It should have been done a long time ago, before patterns of antipathy began to congeal. Now it should be regarded as a first step only. The way prepared, the Government should initiate a programme of research to determine how far existing or imported legal techniques could begin to assist in the diminution of practices which are an affront to any conception of an integrated society. There is much experience in the United States and Canada to be drawn upon. Some may feel that the real test of the Government's good faith lies not in the drama of this legislation; rather in its readiness to examine the appropriateness of more searching legal machinery, and in the priority it accords to investigatory, administrative and other social processes outside the law.[2]

[1] In a long and thoughtful article dealing with the meagre protection hitherto available in Britain to those discriminated against on racial and similar grounds, and the provisions made in the United States and Canada, Jeffrey Jowell criticized the Bill as inadequate and ineffective. ('The Administrative Enforcement of Laws Against Discrimination', *Public Law*, Summer 1965.)

[2] I.R.R. *Newsletter*, February 1965, p. 12.

2. THE RACE RELATIONS ACT 1965

An Act to prohibit discrimination on racial grounds in places of public resort; to prevent the enforcement or imposition on racial grounds of restrictions on the transfer of tenancies; to penalise incitement to racial hatred; and to amend Section 5 of the Public Order Act 1936.

The Race Relations Act is divided into two main parts; (a) Discrimination (in places of public resort and disposal of tenancies), and (b) Public Order, which includes sections on incitement to *racial* hatred and on Public Order without reference to race.

Section 1 on discrimination in places of public resort is to be administered by the Race Relations Board and its local conciliation committees. (Section 5 on the disposal of tenancies is enforceable by the Courts.)

The sections on racial incitement and public order are to be enforced by the police and the ordinary machinery of the Courts.

The sections are set out as follows:

Discrimination	1. Discrimination in places of public resort.
	2. The Race Relations Board and conciliation committees.
	3. Proceedings for enforcement of Section 1 in England and Wales.
	4. Proceedings for enforcement of Section 1 in Scotland.
	5. Discriminatory restrictions on disposal of tenancies.
Public Order	6. Incitement of racial hatred.
	7. Extension of Public Order Act 1936 S.5 to written matter.
Supplemental	8. Short title, commencement and extent.

A. DISCRIMINATION

(i) *Section 1*

Discrimination on grounds of colour, race, or ethnic or national origins is made unlawful in certain areas of public places, viz.:

(a) any hotel, restaurant, café, public house, or other place where food or drink is supplied for consumption of the public;
(b) any theatre, cinema, dance hall, sports ground, swimming pool, or other place of public entertainment or recreation;
(c) public transport (any premises, vehicle, vessel, or aircraft);
(d) any place of public resort maintained by a local authority or other public authority.

A 'hotel' is to be defined in the same way as in the Hotel Proprietors Act, i.e. private residential hotels are excluded, and any place which requires a special contract.

'Discrimination' is defined as: refusal or neglect to afford access to the place in question or any facilities or services available there, in the like manner and on the like terms in and on which such access or services are available to other members of the public.

(ii) *Section 2*

The Race Relations Board is established for 'securing compliance with Section 1 and the resolution of difficulties arising out of it'.

The Board is to set up local conciliation committees which are to receive complaints and undertake the entire conciliation process. If conciliation fails, the local committees are to report the case to the Race Relations Board. If the Board finds that there is a course of conduct which is against the law, and that this conduct is likely to continue, it shall report the case to the Attorney-General.

(iii) *Section 3*

If the Attorney-General agrees with the findings of the Race Relations Board, he can bring injunction proceedings against the proprietor or manager of the place which has been found to discriminate.

Local conciliation committees are required to make periodic reports to the Board, and the Board to make annual reports to the Home Secretary, who will present them in Parliament. (Section 2.)

(iv) *Section 5*

Tenancies: where the consent of the landlord or any other person is required for the disposal of a tenancy, and consent is in fact withheld on grounds of colour, race, or ethnic or national origin, this shall be treated as *unreasonable* withholding of consent in the Courts. Owner-occupiers sharing facilities are excluded.

B. PUBLIC ORDER

(i) *Section 6: Incitement to Racial Hatred*

It will be an offence to publish or distribute written matter, or speak at a public meeting or in public words which are 'threatening, abusive, or insulting', with the intent to stir up hatred against any section of the public distinguished by colour, race, ethnic, or national origin.

Penalties: On summary conviction 6 months in prison, or a fine of up to £200, or both.

On indictment, 2 years or fine of £1,000, or both.

No prosecution without the consent of the Attorney-General.

(ii) *Section 7*

For Section 5 of the Public Order Act 1936 the following is substituted:

It will be an offence to use 'threatening, abusive or insulting words or behaviour at a public meeting, or to distribute or display in public anything which is "threatening, abusive or insulting", with intent to provoke a breach of the peace, or if a breach of the peace is likely to be occasioned'.

C. PROSECUTIONS UNDER THE PUBLIC ORDER SECTIONS

The handful of cases brought under the Act up to the end of April 1967 included: (1) Christopher Bidwell (aged 17) of Notting Hill, found guilty on 18 October 1966 for leaving some pamphlets saying 'Blacks not wanted here' on the front door of Mr. Sydney Bidwell, Labour M.P. for Southall (case quashed on appeal as not constituting 'distribution to the public'); (2) two anti-Vietnam war demonstrators fined at Brighton for 'offensive behaviour likely to cause a breach of the peace' (under the extension of the Public Order Act (1936), Section 5, in the Race Relations Act (Section 7) (see I.R.R. *Newsletter*, November–December 1966, pp. 3–4); (3) Colin Jordan, sentenced to 18 months' imprisonment at Devon Assizes in February 1967 for conspiring to distribute written matter likely to cause racial hatred; Peter Pollard, a young man charged with him, was put on probation for three years.

3. THE RACE RELATIONS BOARD

The Race Relations Board came into existence on 17 February 1966, after weeks of delay, attributed variously to the difficulty of filling the three posts and to official heel-tapping. Its chairman was Mr. Mark Bonham-Carter, publishing executive and former Liberal M.P., and the two other members were the Lord Mayor of Manchester, Mr. B. S. Langton, and Sir Learie Constantine, formerly High Commissioner for Trinidad and Tobago and now in practice as a barrister in London. The former Archbishop of Cape Town, Dr. Joost de Blank, had agreed to serve but stood down in early January after he was appointed as Bishop of Hong Kong. Later Dr. Joost de Blank became Chairman of the London Board.

Once the Board was constituted (with offices at Gaywood House, Great Peter Street, London, S.W.1), a start could be made to operate the Race Relations Act. The Board's first task was to set up local conciliation committees to examine cases of alleged discrimination in public places—but Mr. Bonham-Carter said, after his appointment, that the Board's job would include reviewing its own powers and he could see no obstacle to their being extended. An *Observer* report (20 February 1966) said that it was likely to be allowed to widen its field considerably—possibly to include housing, employment, and credit facilities.

The *Sunday Times* (20 February 1966) forecast a busy time ahead for the Board, with a barrage of complaints alleging discrimination. Four complaints naming public houses had already been received, and most immigrant protest organizations were preparing dossiers. These included C.A.R.D., which was distributing 10,000 complaint forms and several thousand pamphlets entitled 'How to Expose Discrimination'. Many licensed victuallers continued to be less happy about the situation. At Newmarket the national president of the Licensed Victuallers' Defence League attacked the Bill, on the grounds that it took away the right of the publican to refuse to serve a person of another race if he thinks the person 'not desirable' for his premises (*Cambridge News*, 11 January 1966).

The Board's first annual report (published on 26 April 1967, London, H.M.S.O. 437) gave details of its work for the purpose for which it was constituted, that of securing compliance with the provisions of Section 1 of the Race Relations Act and the resolution of difficulties arising out of those provisions.

The Act required the Board to constitute committees, to be known as local conciliation committees, for such areas as it considered necessary. It is these committees which had to deal with complaints under Section 1 of the Act. The Board itself had no express powers to investigate complaints and no powers to undertake conciliation.

A. HEADQUARTERS ACTIVITIES (1966–7)

The Board itself had a headquarters staff consisting of the secretary, the chief conciliation officer, a part-time administrative assistant, and five clerical and typing staff. There was also a part-time legal adviser, and three conciliation officers in the field serving the conciliation committees (such professional staff having been found necessary to undertake detailed investigations and dispose speedily of complaints). To dispel confusion and misapprehension, the Board issued and distributed a pamphlet to explain the Race Relations Act and the Board's functions, what illegal discrimination is, and how complaints are investigated and dealt with. It also produced a printed form of complaint for those who wish to complain of discrimination. Further, a firm of public relations consultants was also engaged to assist with a limited programme to improve public information and communication.

In the research field, the Board sponsored, in collaboration with the N.C.C.I., two investigations. The first (financed by the Joseph Rowntree Memorial Trust) was the survey undertaken by P.E.P. with the aid of Research Services Ltd., to assess the extent of discrimination in Britain in: (a) employment; (b) housing; (c) insurance, credit facilities, and financial services; (d) places of public resort not covered by the Race Relations Act. The second (financed by Marks and Spencer Ltd.) was to examine anti-discrimination legislation in other countries, to assess its effectiveness, and to consider what type of legislation Parliament might consider most suitable should it decide that the Act required amendment or extension. This investigation was undertaken by a small committee consisting of Professor Harry Street, Professor of Law at the University of Manchester (as Chairman), Mr. Geoffrey Howe, Q.C., and Mr. Geoffrey Bindman, the Board's Legal Adviser. This committee was to report in the summer of 1967.

B. THE LOCAL CONCILIATION COMMITTEES

The various conciliation committees were set up only after extensive informal inquiries and discussions on each local situation with a wide range of local officials, individuals, and organizations. Members were appointed on a personal basis, for one year initially; subsequently they were to serve for three-year terms, one-third retiring each year, but eligible for reappointment.

The Act laid upon the local conciliation committees the following duties:

(a) to receive and consider any complaint of discrimination in contravention of Section 1 of this Act which may be made to them (or made to the Board and referred by the Board to them), being a complaint made by or with the authority in writing of the person against whom the discrimination is alleged to have been practised;

(b) to make such inquiries as they think necessary with respect to the facts alleged in any such complaint;

(c) where appropriate, to use their best endeavours by communication with the parties concerned or otherwise to secure a settlement of any difference between them and a satisfactory assurance against further discrimination contrary to the said Section 1 by the party against whom the complaint is made; and

(d) in any case where they are unable to secure such a settlement, or such a settlement and assurance, or it appears to them that any such assurance is not being complied with, to make a report to that effect to the Race Relations Board.

The Committees for the Greater London area and for the North-West[1] were appointed in July 1966, and they had their first meetings on 30 July and 1 August respectively. The West Midlands Committee held

[1] For some press discussion on the North-West Committee's report on the low number of complaints received, see I.R.R. *Newsletter*, January 1967, pp. 3–4.

its first meeting on 1 December, and the Yorkshire Committee met for the first time on 23 January 1967. The latest to be set up was the East Midlands Committee.[1] Whilst one conciliation officer joined the Board's service early in June 1966, no other officers were in the field until December. The local conciliation committees were therefore operating for most of 1966 virtually without professional assistance. Moreover, they were called upon not only to enforce a law which was new in form and substance, but also to operate enforcement machinery for which there were few precedents. It was inevitable in these circumstances that the rate of disposing of complaints should have been slow and that the committees should have proceeded cautiously in the process of gaining experience. There was a marked increase in the disposal rate from January 1967, by which time two of the present three conciliation officers were in the field.

Complaints are received either by the Board or by the committees directly. Where they are received by the Board, they are passed to the committees. Complaints are made either orally or in writing or through a third party with the written consent of the person against whom the alleged discrimination was practised. Complaints can be received in any language, though in fact they are almost invariably made in English. The great majority of complaints have been written ones and almost all of them made by the person who suffered the alleged discrimination.

The general procedure for dealing with complaints, which is broadly divided into two stages, those of investigation and of conciliation, is as follows. First, the conciliation officer interviews the complainant and any witnesses named by him. Then he endeavours to interview the respondent and any other witnesses. The conciliation officer sends reports of his meetings with all parties to the two members of the conciliation committee assigned to supervise the case. When the conciliation officer has completed his investigations, the two members of the committee decide, on the evidence before them, whether there is a *prima facie* case. Clearly, before they do so, they may wish to make further investigations, especially if there is a conflict of evidence. Secondly, if a *prima facie* contravention of the section is found, the committees have a duty to use their best endeavours to secure a settlement by means of conciliation and a satisfactory assurance against further discrimination. But first they notify the respondent of their findings and of his right to dispute it before the full committee. Similarly if they find that there is no *prima facie* contravention, they notify the complainant and advise him of his right to dispute it.

The committees have found that the complainants are usually satisfied if the respondent undertakes not to discriminate in the future. The committees have invariably required a written assurance against further

[1] For membership and headquarters, see pp. 97–8.

discrimination. To facilitate the process of conciliation, the identity of complainants and respondents has not been published unless one of the parties has already given publicity to an incident.

C. CASES INVESTIGATED

Of the 309 complaints received, only eighty-five (mostly relating to public houses) were within the scope of Section 1. Of the remainder ninety-seven related to employment, thirty-seven to housing, and twelve to financial facilities.[1]

All but six of the public house cases came from areas of substantial immigrant settlement, as did eight of the twelve hotel cases.

The Board noted three general types of discrimination. First, there is the overt discrimination of, say, the hotel proprietor who puts a total ban on all coloured people. Secondly, there is the form of discrimination which amounts to segregation, for example, where a publican will serve coloured people only in the public bar, or alternatively, everywhere except in the lounge bar. Thirdly, there is the less open form of discrimination characterized by over-charging coloured customers or keeping them waiting for service in order to discourage them from coming again. Of these types of discrimination, the second has been the most common. The Board is conscious of the fact that the second and third types of discrimination are covered by the definition of discrimination contained within the Act and must therefore be regarded as no less serious than the first. They are certainly no less repugnant. Moreover, it is sometimes complained that immigrants do not sufficiently conform to local customs. But it would clearly be illogical to expect a measure of conformity from any group of people if segregated facilities made it impossible for them to become familiar with the standards to which they were expected to conform.

Despite doubts expressed when the Bill was being debated in Parliament, it has not, in fact, proved difficult to establish whether or not discrimination had taken place in those areas where the law is unambiguous. Where the law is clear, the problems of securing compliance with it have not been difficult; indeed, the mere passage of the law probably decreased the incidence of discrimination. The law unambiguously makes it unlawful to discriminate in public houses, for example. Publicans and others in the trade are aware of the requirements of the law and are also aware that if they do not comply with it, sanctions are provided.

On the other hand, where the law is ambiguous, the problems of enforcement are considerable. Reference is made elsewhere in this report to the doubt as to the status of certain hotels under this section. Of the

[1] For detailed analysis, see p. 96–7.

three cases referred to the Board by local conciliation committees, two have fallen into this category. In both cases, the respondent has simply refused to talk with the conciliation officer concerned or members of the local conciliation committee.

The Board has welcomed the fact that, whilst the licensed trade generally opposed the introduction of the Race Relations Act, both publicans and brewers have co-operated in its enforcement. No complaints against public houses have so far been referred to the Board.

The Report went on to stress the need for independent groups, such as C.A.R.D. and the Indian Workers' Association, if the individual complaint procedure was to work satisfactorily. It accepted the 'testing' method as reasonable but pointed out that if an unnecessarily large group of people were sent to a public house the publican might well be justified in not serving them.

The Board was satisfied that conciliation would have been virtually impossible without the sanctions provided in the Act. It also noted that the machinery for investigation of complaints provided an important safety valve, and that complainants seemed to be accepting the fact that their complaints had been impartially investigated, although the committees had upheld less than half the complaints received.

D. DEFICIENCIES OF THE ACT[1]

(i) The ambiguous wording of Section 1(1), which makes it unlawful 'to practise discrimination' instead of simply 'to discriminate' (i.e. once), while Section 2 (2) imposes an obligation on committees to receive and consider any complaint of discrimination from the person allegedly discriminated against.

(ii) If a single act of discrimination is not settled, the Board has to consider whether there has occurred a 'course of conduct' in contravention of the Act which is likely to continue.

(iii) It is not clear whether the committee has power to proceed (in the public interest) when the complainant wishes to withdraw his complaint.

(iv) Without some evidence of a likelihood of continuance, there is no action which the Committee can take against a discriminator who has refused to give an acceptable assurance against future discrimination.

(v) The Act's limitation to discrimination on the grounds of 'colour, race or ethnic or national origins' may exclude certain groups such as the Jews, the Sikhs, and the Gypsies, which may not be primarily ethnic or racial, but which are so regarded by those who discriminate against them. The position of such groups should be clarified.

(vi) In some cases, persons against whom discrimination has been

[1] As noted by the Board's Report.

alleged have refused to meet representatives of the conciliation committee. This hampers their investigations and could, in certain circumstances, render them impossible. It should be considered whether, with appropriate safeguards, there should be power to compel attendance before the committee, or the disclosure of information to it.

(vii) The Act does not bind the Crown, so that a public authority can only fall within the Act's scope if it is independent of the Crown.

(viii) The Act applies to hotels only within the meaning of the Hotel Proprietors Act 1956 (e.g. possibly not to 'private hotels').

(ix) The provision for confidentiality of communications made to the Board could exclude from evidence an assurance against future discrimination when a later breach is alleged, also communications outside the conciliation process.

(x) The restriction to certain specified 'places of public resort' leads to anomalies, e.g. discrimination by a hairdresser may be unlawful if his premises are inside a hotel but not if they are outside it; one who seeks to buy beer may lawfully be discriminated against in an off-licence but not in a public house; a car-hire service may lawfully discriminate but a regular bus service may not.

(xi) The effectiveness of the sanction of the law could be reduced by the delays inherent in the procedure and the discretion existing at two stages (the Attorney-General and the courts).

E. RECOMMENDATIONS

The Board's Report included the following recommendations:

We believe that racial discrimination exists in this country; not only in places of public resort, but to an even greater extent in employment and housing, and to some extent in financial facilities and certain places of public resort outside the Race Relations Act 1965. We also believe that, although equal treatment in places of public resort is an important indication of an individual's status in society, the effect of discrimination in housing and employment is more painful to the individual and more damaging to society as a whole. We would add that discrimination on grounds of colour, race or national or ethnic origins is so degrading and humiliating an affront to the individual who encounters it that any society which regards itself as civilised should provide a means of redress no matter how rarely it occurs. The Canadians, whose coloured population is relatively small, have laws to deal with the problem of discrimination.

We fully accept that there are substantial differences between the racial situation in the United States and our own. But our own experience of legislation against discrimination is supplemented by what we have learned of such legislation in the United States and Canada. There, despite initial doubts, the law is now regarded as essential to the success of other government policies and is a powerful stimulus to voluntary action. A combination of all these, to ensure equal opportunities for all, is the only sound basis for successful action against discrimination.

Experience shows equally clearly, however, that voluntary effort is insufficient in itself without legislation. Nor should legislation be thought of in terms of coercion. In America, in only a tiny proportion of many thousands of cases, has it proved necessary to invoke the sanction of the law. This is because the process of conciliation is central to this type of legislation.

The role of legislation is as follows:

(1) A law is an unequivocal declaration of public policy.

(2) A law gives support to those who do not wish to discriminate, but who feel compelled to do so by social pressure.

(3) A law gives protection and redress to minority groups.

(4) A law thus provides for the peaceful and orderly adjustment of grievances and the release of tensions.

(5) A law reduces prejudice by discouraging the behaviour in which prejudice finds expression.

For all these reasons, we recommend that the Race Relations Act be extended to cover housing, employment, financial facilities and places of public resort not covered by the present Act; and that the deficiencies referred to in paragraph 38 be rectified. The effect of widespread discrimination has consequences on the whole structure and style of the life of the society in which it takes place, spreading far beyond the individuals who are its victims. We believe there is no more effective way for society to express its disapproval of discrimination, to protect itself from its consequences, or to mobilise opinion and voluntary action against discrimination than through the law.

Analysis of Complaints received up to and including 31 March 1967[1]

Total Received—327

A. *Complaints investigated or under investigation*—89

ESTABLISHMENTS		CONCILIATION AREAS	
Public Houses	54	Northern	—
Hotels	12	Yorkshire	3
Cafés	7	Manchester and District	7
Clubs	11	Liverpool and District	1
Miscellaneous	5	West Midland	17
		East Midland	4
HOW DEALT WITH		Eastern	3
Settled by conciliation	20	Berks., Bucks., and Oxon.	—
Not substantiated	28	Hants., Surrey, and Sussex	1
Referred to Race Relations		Kent	7
Board	1	South Western	2
Under investigation	38	Greater London	41
		Wales and Monmouth	—
		Scotland	3

[1] Appendix III of Race Relations Board Report, 1966–7.

B. *Complaints not investigated as being outside scope of the Act*—238

SUBJECTS		CONCILIATION AREAS	
Employment	101	Northern	1
Publications	24	Yorkshire	19
Housing	37	Manchester and District	41
Shops	7	Liverpool and District	1
Financial facilities	12	West Midland	19
Police	14	East Midland	8
Miscellaneous	43	Eastern	2
		Berks., Bucks., and Oxon.	8
		Hants., Surrey, and Sussex	10
		Kent	10
		South Western	3
		Greater London	111
		Wales and Monmouth	4
		Scotland	1

Conciliation Committees in being on 31 March 1967

A. *Greater London Conciliation Committee*

Headquarters	–	Gaywood House, Great Peter Street, London, S.W.1
Chairman	–	The Right Rev. Joost de Blank
Deputy Chairman	–	Mr. Peter Calvocoressi
Members	–	Mr. Frank Bailey
		Mr. Christopher Brocklebank-Fowler
		Lady Cohen, J.P.
		Mr. Tom Connelly

B. *North-West (Manchester and District) Conciliation Committee*

Headquarters	–	Scottish Life House, Bridge Street, Manchester 3
Chairman	–	Mr. Niel G. C. Pearson
Deputy Chairman	–	Professor Harry Street
Members	–	Miss W. Blackburn
		Dr. S. S. Chatterjee
		Mr. Louis King, J.P.
		Mrs. Betty Luckham
		Mr. A. G. Rose

C. *West Midlands Conciliation Committee*

Headquarters	–	126 Colmore Row, Birmingham 3
Chairman	–	Mr. Oscar Hahn
Deputy Chairman	–	Mr. Nigel T. Cook
Members	–	Mr. L. Adams
		Dr. Farrukh Hashmi
		Mrs. Joan King-Farlow
		Mr. M. P. Ryan
		Mr. Derief Taylor
		Mrs. Margaret Whincup

D. *Yorkshire (East and West Ridings) Conciliation Committee*

Headquarters	–	Yorkshire Insurance Building, 4 South Parade, Leeds 1
Chairman	–	Professor Roy Marshall, J.P.
Members	–	Mr. Eric Butterworth
		Councillor Lewis Corina
		Mr. Ehsan ul Haq
		Mrs. Kathleen I. Hinchcliffe
		Mr. Bernard Lyons, C.B.E., J.P.
		Miss Alice Pickles, J.P.
		Miss M. E. Pinnell

E. *East Midlands Conciliation Committee*

Headquarters	–	Weekday Cross, Nottingham
Chairman	–	Mr. C. Forsyth, J.P.
Members	–	Mr. G. Bromley, J.P.
		Mr. Glyndwr John
		Miss M. F. Robertson
		Mr. C. E. B. Robinson
		Col. G. A. Wharton, M.B.E., T.D., D.L.

4. THE POST-1965 CAMPAIGN TO EXTEND THE RACE RELATIONS ACT

Commenting on the substitution of conciliation for criminality in the Bill, the *Economist* wrote (29 May 1966): 'The Bill, shorn of its criminal aspects as far as discrimination is concerned, could and should now be safely extended to cover all public places, and also the major fields of housing and employment.'

The 1965 Act was in fact vulnerable from the start to criticisms of its scope and procedures, and pressures soon began again from lawyers, politicians, pressure groups, and others to extend the former and strengthen the latter.

The Employment, Housing and Legal and Civil Affairs Panels of the N.C.C.I. examined the desirability of extending the Act to employment, housing, and other fields and recommended that this be done. With the Race Relations Board, as already mentioned, it also commissioned a survey from P.E.P. to ascertain the extent of discrimination. The N.C.C.I. later endorsed the principles of the two private members' Bills introduced in late 1966 (see below).

The Campaign Against Racial Discrimination decided immediately to send to the Race Relations Board all complaints, and particularly those outside the scope of the Act, for propaganda purposes. A 'Complaints and Testing Committee' was formed in May 1966 in order to increase the numbers of complaints to the Board. The 1966 C.A.R.D. Summer Project sent the Board fifty-one complaints of discrimination, almost all outside the scope of the Act, and this was extensively publicized in the national press and the local press in the areas where the Project took place. Following the Project, testing committees were established in Manchester and Leeds, augmenting the work of the London committee.

Other national organizations continued to lobby for amendments to the Act—The Movement for Colonial Freedom, The British Caribbean Association, The National Council for Civil Liberties, and The Friends' Race Relations Committee.

In November 1966, the Fabian Society held a two-day conference in London on 'Policies for Racial Equality', organized by Anthony Lester (then chairman of C.A.R.D.'s Legal Committee).[1] The speakers included Eric Butterworth, sociologist, Department of Extra-Mural Studies, University of Leeds, now at York University; Dipak Nandy, member of N.C.C.I. Panel on Public Relations, member of the C.A.R.D. executive and Field Director of the Summer Project; Bob Hepple, South African lawyer, studying race relations and the law; John Rex, sociologist, co-author of *Race, Community and Conflict: a study of Sparkbrook*, member of the Housing Panel of the N.C.C.I.; Roger Warren Evans, member of the Housing Panel of the N.C.C.I., and the C.A.R.D. Legal Committee; Jocelyn Barrow, vice-chairman of C.A.R.D., member of N.C.C.I. Education Panel; Peter Townsend, sociologist, University of Essex; Jack Jones, assistant executive secretary, T.G.W.U. The Chair was taken at the conference by Mrs. Shirley Williams, Jack Jones, who also spoke, Maurice Orbach, M.P., and Mark Bonham-Carter, chairman of the Race Relations Board. The subjects covered were employment, housing, education, and social welfare.

On 5 December 1966, the Society of Labour Lawyers held a meeting in the House of Commons to discuss the Third Report of its Race Relations Committee. This contained a detailed critique of the Act on the following grounds:

[1] The conference Report was published as a Fabian pamphlet in 1967.

(i) the failure to cover discrimination on religious grounds;

(ii) the restricted definition of 'places of public resort' (not covered are shops, offices, night clubs, holiday camps, and Government offices);

(iii) the Race Relations Board's lack of powers;

(iv) the requirement to show that a 'course of conduct' has taken place contravening the Act (not a single act of discrimination);

(v) the non-provision of individual remedies for the victim of discrimination;

(vi) anomalies and inadequacies in the section dealing with restrictions on the disposal of property;

(vii) the exclusion of areas in which discriminatory practices cause the greatest hardship, such as employment, housing, insurance and credit services.

The report's proposals were summarized as follows:

(i) Foreign experience shows that legislation can be effective in promoting equal opportunities in employment, housing, insurance and credit services, in which discrimination currently exists in this country, provided that a special body is given adequate powers to secure compliance with the law. The effectiveness of such a law would be greatly increased if it were enacted before patterns of discrimination harden in Britain. The vast majority of complaints would probably be settled privately without recourse to formal proceedings.

(ii) Religion should be added to race, colour, and ethnic and national origins as an unlawful ground of discrimination.

(iii) All places of public resort should be covered by the Act, not merely those at present listed in it.

(iv) The Crown, which is not at present bound by the Act, should be bound by it.

(v) Discrimination should be made unlawful in employment, whether by employers, trade unions, Ministry of Labour Employment Exchanges, or private employment agencies.

(vi) Discrimination should be made unlawful in the sale and lease of housing accommodation; in the advertising of the same; and on the part of estate agents.

(vii) Covenants restricting the sale or letting of any interest in land or housing on grounds of race, colour, religion, or ethnic or national origins should be declared void.

(viii) Discrimination in the grant of credit, hire-purchase, and mortgage facilities should be unlawful.

(ix) Discrimination in providing insurance cover should be unlawful.

(x) The powers of the Race Relations Board (whose membership should be enlarged) should be extended; in particular, it should be empowered:

(a) to conduct investigations into and hearings of complaints referred to it by Local Conciliation Committees;
(b) in connexion with such hearings, to subpoena witnesses and require the production before it of relevant documentary and statistical evidence;
(c) to make orders against those in respect of whom complaints had been made and upheld requiring them not to contravene the Act's terms; to take positive steps to uphold the purposes of the Act; and to make money payments to complainants;
(d) pending final determination by the Board, to ensure that alleged discriminators did not take steps which would effectively frustrate any orders which the Board might subsequently make.

(xi) The Society supports the principles of the Race Relations Act (Amendment) Bill, to be introduced in both Houses of Parliament in December. The Bill would give legislative effect to the Society's report.

A. THE RACE RELATIONS ACT (AMENDMENT) BILL

One year after the Race Relations Act (1965) came into effect, Fenner Brockway (now Lord Brockway) was again introducing a special anti-discrimination Bill, this time to amend and extend the existing legislation and, while retaining essentially the civil nature of the procedure, to put teeth into the conciliation procedure by giving the Board powers to subpoena witnesses, take evidence on oath and, in case of disobedience without reasonable cause, to make an order and register it in the Court. This Bill was identical with one introduced in the Commons by Mr. Maurice Orbach, M.P., but Lord Brockway's Bill also included a section on racial incitement and on discrimination by clubs.

In the debate of Mr. Orbach's Bill in the House of Commons on 16 December 1966, Mr. Maurice Foley, Under-Secretary of State for the Home Office, the Minister responsible for co-ordinating immigration policies, stated that a survey was being undertaken by the P.E.P. (Political and Economic Planning) on behalf of the Race Relations Board and the National Committee for Commonwealth Immigrants to establish the extent of discrimination. 'We need more factual information than is now available.' The result of the survey should be known early in 1967. 'If, in the light of the further assessment of the need and the extent of discrimination in this country, we come to the conclusion that existing methods are inadequate, we shall give serious consideration to the need for and the feasibility of strengthening the existing law and administrative machinery,' the Minister declared.

On these assurances Mr. Orbach withdrew his Bill. Three days later Lord Brockway in the House of Lords pressed his Bill to the vote (so that 'members could without party pressures express their own conviction') but was defeated by sixty votes to twenty-three.

On behalf of the Conservative opposition, Mr. Charles Fletcher-Cooke said that they would not resist attempts to outlaw discrimination in employment and housing.

B. DEVELOPMENTS IN 1967

The protagonists of legal sanctions against racial discrimination in employment and those who believe, not in enforcement but in good sense, good intentions, and the use of existing overall provisions and procedures, took up increasingly firm opposing positions in advance of the three events which could bring the issue to the boil. These were the high-level conference on 'Racial Equality in Employment', organized by the National Committee for Commonwealth Immigrants and held in London on 23–24 February,[1] the results of the P.E.P. survey on discrimination in employment (see Appendix V), and, in April, the first annual report from Mr. Mark Bonham-Carter, chairman of the Race Relations Board.

As expected, the conference, and later the two reports, stressed the need for legislation, although some of those attending the conference, particularly representatives of management and organized labour, doubted its wisdom, necessity or efficacy. Meanwhile, the opposition from the two major bodies on both sides of industry, the Confederation of British Industry and the Trades Union Congress, had been consolidating itself.[2] At a meeting of the National Joint Advisory Council of the Ministry of Labour on 25 January, representatives of the T.U.C., C.B.I., and the nationalized industries presented a joint statement opposing the proposed extension of anti-discrimination legislation to employment or denying Government contracts to discriminating firms and offering a declaration of intent. This read as follows:

> We recognise the economic and social advantages of employment policies which will further the integration of people from overseas into the workforce. We are aware of some concern that problems may arise from its increasingly mixed character and we agree that any improper discriminatory practices in employment or engagement will disappear only when integration has been achieved among workpeople regardless of colour, race, ethnic, or national origin.
>
> We draw attention to the successful entry into industry of many thousands of workpeople from overseas. We consider that recruitment practices should be consistent with the orderly integration of the labour force, with equal opportunity for applicants for employment, and with the maintenance of a workforce appropriate to the nature and circumstances of particular undertakings and industries.
>
> We point to the existence of negotiated agreements establishing procedures

[1] See Chapter 5, p. 19.

[2] See *Sunday Times* (8 January) for a review of views held by individual members of the T.U.C. and joint press statement (*Guardian*, 18 January).

for the settlement of grievances and disputes, and expect all those associated together in the operation of industries and services to utilise to the full the methods of voluntary settlement which have been successfully developed over many years. We ask our members on both sides of industry to ensure that joint agreements relating to wages and conditions of employment are enforced for all employees irrespective of their colour, race, or national or ethnic origins.

Accordingly the T.U.C. and the C.B.I. ask their members to examine and subsequently keep under continuous review, the employment policies, practices, and procedures in their industries and services which bear on the full achievement of integration and to eliminate any which militate against it.[1]

This attitude was conditioned by a number of considerations. Both sides of industry are traditionally resistant to legislation in general and regard discrimination as one industrial problem among many to be dealt with by the tried machinery of consultation. Nor did they regard members of the Race Relations Board as sufficiently acquainted with the workings of industry to administer a law against job discrimination. Moreover, they were not convinced that discrimination was increasing, and thought that it could be dealt with by common sense and cajoling rather than threats and creating what they feared might become a coloured privileged class. British Rail's satisfactory integration of many thousands of coloured workers was cited as evidence that legislation was not necessary.

On the other hand, the proponents of legislation pointed out that the existing machinery had not produced adequate results at grass-roots level, where either the shop-steward or the supervisor might share the antipathies of local workers, and where there might not even be a union at all.[2] Moreover, it could not uncover cases of discrimination at the factory gate. Mr. David Winnick, Labour M.P. for Croydon South, accused the T.U.C. and C.B.I. of 'a deplorable act of cowardice' (*Guardian*, 21 January), and the *Sunday Times* (29 January) lashed editorially at humbug and inertia, and praised the fair employment laws of Ontario, Massachusetts, and New York State, with their reliance on conciliation and consent:

. . . Public hearings are rare, court proceedings are almost unknown. But twenty years of experience has shown that the final sanction is vital, both to

[1] As published in the *Sunday Times* (29 January). The joint statement was apparently drafted by a sub-committee and officials. A *Guardian* reporter (26 January) commented on the fact that the issue had received little or no detailed consideration by the principal committees of the C.B.I. or T.U.C. It was perhaps unfortunate that the issue of anti-discrimination legislation coincided with the much wider debate between the T.U.C. and the Government as to whether prices and incomes policy should be voluntary or imposed by Government.

[2] C.A.R.D. continued its documentation of racial discrimination with a memorandum to the Royal Commission on Trade Unions and Employers' Federations in January and a report of forty-three selected cases in April.

deter the discriminator and support the right-minded. It is not a mere negative restraint. Law cannot prohibit prejudice, but it can change conduct, and conduct can affect attitudes. The way people behave affects the way they think and feel. Good law is a moral educative force. The argument should therefore be seen not simply as about the kind of society Britain is but the kind of society we want Britain to become. Inertia about discrimination today—in employment, housing, the provision of credit and insurance services—will mean more than the sum of individual indignities or wasted talents. It will inevitably mean still more injustice and bitterness tomorrow. The Government must see fair employment and housing laws as positive affirmation of the community's faith. Piety is no substitute for policy.

Within the Government the line-up was not rigid, according to several press commentators. Mr. Roy Jenkins, Home Secretary since early 1966, from the start made little secret of his support for stiffer legislation, and in the summer of 1966 the Chancellor of the Exchequer had accepted the principle of a non-discrimination clause in a parliamentary answer.[1] A decision would have to be reached by June 1967 if amendments to the 1965 Act were to be included in the Government programme for the session beginning in October 1967. According to Eric Silver (*Guardian*, 13 January, 24 January), Ministers from the Treasury, the Department of Economic Affairs, and the Ministry of Labour were likely to need a lot of persuasion before committing themselves to another tussle with unions and employers. It was, however, unlikely that nothing would be done. (In late February the Government was reported to have set up an inter-departmental committee to examine the matter.)

This writer saw hope in the fact that the 'battle lines' were not yet firmly fixed, either in Government or in industry. The Government might consider legislating against discrimination in housing (and perhaps insurance and credit) while adopting other methods in the employment field: for instance, a clause denying Government contracts to firms which discriminate.[2] This could be buttressed by a T.U.C.–

[1] For an assessment of the line-up within the Cabinet at mid-winter, see *Observer* (18 December 1966) and *Guardian* (24 January 1967). An interesting development was the intimation in December 1966 from the Conservative front-bench that the Opposition would not resist attempts to outlaw discrimination in housing and employment.

[2] The proposal that the Government should give a lead by barring discriminating firms from contracts, subsidies, etc., was put very forcibly in the C.A.R.D evidence. On a smaller scale this initiative was already being put into effect, or requested, in some areas. The Metropolitan Water Board agreed to obtain such an assurance from contractors; Reading Council set up a sub-committee to consider the suggestion; and Mr. Brian Jones, secretary of Camden Committee for Community Relations (Camden and Lambeth were local authorities that had already taken this step), asked local businesses to sign a pledge that they would employ coloured workers. (*Morning Star*, 3 January; *Willesden Chronicle*, 6 January; *Hampstead News*, 6 January; *Evening Standard*, 26 January.)

C.B.I. declaration of intent. In at least one major union, the T.G.W.U.[1] (later joined by the N.U.G.M.W.), there was influential support for Government action, and some union officials might be prepared to give a more positive lead in demanding legislation against victimization of all kinds (the Royal Commission on trade unions was considering such a proposal). The unions' campaign for the compulsory notification of vacancies could also, if successful, help to give coloured workers a fairer chance.

5. THE POLITICAL AND ECONOMIC PLANNING REPORT AND THE RACE RELATIONS BOARD REPORT

The long-heralded report of the P.E.P. survey on discrimination in employment, housing, and various services was published on 18 April 1967 (see Appendix V), and its findings produced the evidence expected —of widespread discrimination in all fields surveyed. The report was received favourably by the national press, which in general found that the case for some form of extended legislation was strengthened.[2] For instance, the *Guardian* (18 April) commented editorially:

> Perhaps the survey's most significant finding is the undogmatic, often vicarious, nature of discrimination in this country. Coloured workers are commonly turned away by relatively junior staff—gatemen, clerks, secretaries and foremen. Estate agents often discriminate because of what they suppose to be the wishes of their clients. . . . Everyone seems to blame it on somebody else—neighbours, customers, other staff.
>
> Because there is nothing doctrinaire about this kind of discrimination, it should prove particularly responsive to legislative sanctions. Senior management would be less likely to leave decisions to subordinates. Because, motoring apart, we are a law-abiding nation, equality would be more readily accepted as a standard. American experience has produced some striking examples of this sort of public conditioning. Little Rock now has a Negro school superintendent. White unions and management in the segregated South have opened their factory doors to Negroes.

[1] At the end of the N.C.C.I. Conference in February, Mr. Frank Cousins pledged the T.G.W.U. to support such legislation if no other solution could be found. At the opening of the conference the Home Secretary, Mr. Roy Jenkins, had also given a pledge that the Government was ready to extend anti-discrimination legislation in employment if it was shown to be necessary (i.e. if the results of the conference, the findings of the P.E.P. Survey, and the first annual report of the Race Relations Board made a clear case for it).

[2] One 'quality' Sunday paper, the *Observer* (23 April), saw fit to ascertain and reveal the names of the six areas surveyed by Research Services on behalf of P.E.P., both of which organizations had given an undertaking to all those interviewed that under no circumstances would either organization reveal the names of the places where interviews were carried out. Mr. Mark Bonham-Carter deeply deplored the naming: 'it can only make objective enquiries into social problems far more difficult to undertake in the future.' In its editorial the *Observer* called for 'positive discrimination' by local authorities in housing and education.

This time, however, continued the editorial, the legislation, the procedure and the organization must be got right.

The Times (18 April) agreed with Mr. Mark Bonham-Carter (see article in I.R.R. *Newsletter*, April 1967), who had on the day before called for an extension of the Act to cover employment, housing, financial facilities, and 'places of public resort not covered by the Act'. The broader legislation envisaged would be no more than the means of extending the scope of conciliation. It would be particularly valuable in employment. In housing, however,

> it would be essential to exclude the small lodging-house; there must be no invasion of the small landlady's home. Nor could legislation cover the important area of municipal housing, where a determined effort to give positive discrimination in favour of coloured people is required. There may also be some doubts about the effectiveness of legislation for a number of services—motor insurance is a particular example. But the general case for extending the law is overwhelming. This is where liberal opinion should concentrate its efforts—not on seeking to break down the restrictions on immigration. The first challenge for Britain must be to give a fair deal to the coloured people already in the country.

Several later reports, including that of the Race Relations Board itself, published on 27 April (see under Race Relations Board), strongly supported the case for legislation. The nature of the legislation was likely to be influenced by a report to be presented in the summer by the committee which had been studying how it works in other countries (chairman, Professor Harry Street of Manchester University, sponsored by the Race Relations Board, q.v.). The *Guardian* (24 March) reported that they would not recommend one form rather than another, but would set out the alternatives. *The Times* (24 March), however, reported that the United States laws would be the model (including the anti-discrimination clauses in Government contracts).

The widespread view that the Race Relations Board needed enlargement and tougher powers (to subpoena witnesses and to impose penalties) was challenged by Christopher Brocklebank-Fowler in a Bow Group memorandum, 'Race Relations—Legislation and Conciliation' (London, April 1967). While accepting (as in an earlier memorandum, 'Commonwealth Immigration') extension of conciliation-based legislation to employment, housing, and other spheres, he considered that transferring power from the courts to the Board would shorten the administrative process during which conciliation could take place, thus making it less likely. The calls for great powers were largely a reflection of the shortage of local Conciliation Officers; it was preferable that local committees should have sufficient staff to do the job without recourse to legal sanctions.

Towards the end of April, the bandwagon of support for legislation acquired momentum. Mr. Frank Cousins and the T.G.W.U. were joined by Lord Cooper of the National Union of General and Municipal Workers, so that two of the T.U.C.'s three largest unions were now opposed to the T.U.C.'s hitherto firmly-stated belief in voluntarism and traditional procedures for dealing with industrial grievances (reiterated in a long article in its information broadsheet *Labour* of April).[1]

With the Cabinet, Mr. Gunter was variously reported as decided to oppose any extension of legislation (*Sunday Times*, 23 April) and as not expected to oppose it, although sharing the misgivings of industry (*Guardian*, 24 April). This report also said that the T.U.C. and C.B.I. were now believed to have accepted that there would be legislation, but to be focusing their efforts on seeing that it did as little damage as possible to industrial harmony.[2] The Government was reported as ahead of its own back-benchers, but a motion calling for extension of legislation had been signed by over a hundred M.P.s. Sir Cyril Osborne (C., Louth) had tabled a hostile amendment. Conservative views were varied, from Sir George Sinclair and Mr. St. John-Stevas, who wanted extension, to Mr. Ronald Bell, who argued that it would be 'an improper intrusion into the realm of private judgement'.

On 14 May 1967 Nora Beloff, Political Correspondent of the *Observer*, reported that Mr. Roy Jenkins had, at the conference of the London Labour Party the preceding day, publicly committed the Government to extend the Race Relations Act to housing and employment. He said:

> Nobody now believes that we can absorb in this fairly over-crowded island everyone who wants to come. . . . We are regulating immigration—a most difficult and thankless job—with determination, and I hope with humanity. But for those who are already here, and for their descendants, and for those who are allowed to come because they have jobs or families waiting for them, it is essential that they should be treated properly in every way, and given the fullest human rights.
>
> For a Labour Government to fall down on this would be a betrayal without excuse of everything for which the Labour Party has ever stood. If further legislation is necessary to deal with this issue, we should not be frightened of it.[3]

[1] For a critique of voluntary action see *New Society* (16 March 1967).

[2] A proposal that attracted considerable interest was made by Mr. Oscar Hahn, president of the Birmingham Chamber of Commerce, at the February conference on 'Racial Equality in Employment' organized by N.C.C.I. This suggested the setting up of 'fair employment' machinery within industry to deal with complaints prior to their being taken to an independent outside body.

[3] This was confirmed on 26 July, when Mr. Jenkins told the House of Commons that the Act would be extended to cover discrimination on grounds of colour, race, ethnic or national origins (not religion), in employment, housing, insurance and credit facilities. In addition, public places would be given a wider definition than under the present Act; the new legislation would provide the fullest possible opportunity for industry to use its own machinery for conciliation. The new extended legislation was passed in 1968.

CHAPTER 4

Integration

1. DEFINITIONS

'Integration' has for several years been a catch-phrase of local government officials, officers of voluntary associations, the press, and others concerned with the processes of absorbing newcomers in British society. Contrary to popular belief, the term has no strict or generally accepted sociological application. Nor do those who use it so freely necessarily agree upon its meaning, nor realize what complexities, variations, and time-scales may be involved in the overall process.

For instance, evidence from the traditional countries of immigration shows that absorption does not proceed at the same pace in all spheres of association, nor in the same manner for all immigrant groups in the same society, and that it is unlikely to be complete before the second generation, or even later.[1]

An analysis of the various usages of the term 'integration' that are current in Britain suggests that reference is being made not only to two different types of ultimate absorptive process but also to an initial process of accommodation in work, neighbourhood, and outward behaviour through which all immigrants and newcomers pass. Thereafter some immigrant or minority groups, whether by choice or because their socio-cultural background so inclines them, move into either an assimilative phase (total adaptation and acceptance, ultimately fusion) or one of cultural pluralism (conformity in major spheres of association such as economic and civic life, combined with a continuing separate group identity in certain cultural spheres, including religion, family patterns, material culture, and possibly language).

Initially there was, in relation to Commonwealth immigrants, a tendency to assume that Britain was a homogeneous society which ultimately assimilated all newcomers.[2] This may be attributed in part to some traditional but perhaps over-simplified 'melting-pot' views of

[1] An oversimplification *not* accepted by the C.I.A.C. in its definition of 'immigrant children', 2nd Report Cmnd 2266, February 1964, p. 4. 'In this report we use the term "immigrant children" to include both children born overseas and those born in this country to immigrant parents.'

[2] Cf. Judith Henderson in *Coloured Immigrants in Britain*, London, O.U.P. for I.R.R., 1960, p. 114: 'the assumption that—at a national level—we are prepared to accept coloured people as an integral part of British society; that we are thinking in terms of gradual absorption and assimilation of those who wish to make this their permanent home. . . .'

British society, in part to the fact that the first major component of post-war mass immigration from the 'new' Commonwealth was West Indian, i.e. an 'assimilating' group in type[1] if not always in intention.

For years there was also a tendency to equate assimilation with economic absorption or absorbability and to assume that absorption proceeded at the same rate in all spheres of association.[2] That an economic interpretation was inadequate was most clearly stated by Roy Hattersley, Labour M.P. for Sparkbrook, Birmingham. In a Commons speech on 23 March 1965 he admitted that although he had passionately opposed the Bill in 1961 he now suspected that the Labour Party had been wrong to oppose it, not on economic but on social grounds.

'I now believe that there are social as well as economic arguments and I believe that unrestricted immigration can only produce additional problems, additional suffering and additional hardship. . . . I come now to the melancholy view that . . . we must impose a test which tries to analyse which immigrants, as well as having jobs, or special skills, are most likely to be assimilated into our national life.' (This would, he added, favour the English-speaking West Indians as against the Pakistanis.)[3]

Meanwhile, the general interpretation of 'integration' was shifting from 'assimilation' towards 'cultural pluralism'. This could, in turn, be attributed in part to a reappraisal of the real nature of British society (now seen as a heterogeneous, pluralistic entity divided by barriers of

[1] Cf. the admission of a Barbadian anti-assimilationist, Neville Maxwell—*The Power of Negro Action*, London, The Author, 1965—that 'choice [i.e. for West Indians in Britain] does not lie between swallowing everything English in order to become black English men and women—if this metamorphosis is at all possible, not to mention allowable—and rejecting entirely all things English. That part of our culture which is English-orientated—as history would have it—cannot be wished away. . . . Rather, the middle course lies in developing and consciously fostering what is best in our own sub-culture since our original African culture was ruthlessly suppressed and subordinated to the native acquisitiveness of the Metropolitan country.'

[2] This rather superficial and limited interpretation of 'assimilation' was a tacit principle behind the Conservative 'open door' policy but it was also accepted by Labour spokesmen such as the late leader, Hugh Gaitskell (in his speech in the 1961 Second Reading debate on the Commonwealth Immigrants Bill), and George Brown (in a speech against restrictions on immigration on 28 March 1965).

For its application to an earlier post-war immigrant group, the Poles, see Jerzy Zubrzycki, *Polish Immigrants in Britain*, Hague, Nijhoff, 1956.

[3] See Paul Foot, op. cit., pp. 192–4, for a castigation of this 'social' interpretation. A general distinction between economic and social absorption had been recognized earlier by Miss Jennie Lee, who was reported as saying, during a West Midlands Young Socialist Forum, that the influx had been necessary and valuable for the economy but that the Tories had done a 'vile thing' by allowing wave after wave of immigrants to come into the country; they had created not a job problem but a housing and a school problem (*Express and Star*, 23 March 1964).

regionalism, class, education, religion, and so on), in part to the tendency to social and cultural self-segregation shown by the more recent Commonwealth immigrants (Sikhs, Gujaratis, Pakistanis, Cypriots, and others).

The transition from the 'assimilationist' to the 'pluralistic' viewpoint was not yet in evidence when the then Home Secretary, R. A. Butler, moving the second reading of the Commonwealth Immigrants Bill in November 1961, spoke of the increased difficulty of assimilating large self-contained immigrant communities. Thereafter, the C.I.A.C.[1] indicated the shifting of viewpoints in a rather confused manner in its second report. Referring to a 'future multi-racial society' in Britain (by which, according to their own definition, they meant 'non-racial' but possibly pluralistic), the C.I.A.C. nevertheless regarded as a basic aim the assumption that a

> national system of education must aim at producing citizens who can take their place in society properly equipped to exercise rights and perform duties which are the same as those of other citizens. If their parents were brought up in another culture or another tradition, children should be encouraged to respect it, but a national system cannot be expected to perpetuate the different values of immigrant groups.

An adequate knowledge of English was also regarded as advantageous and desirable for adults, and the C.I.A.C. recommended amending the law so that citizens of independent Commonwealth countries resident in the U.K. who wished to register as citizens of the U.K. and Colonies should have to demonstrate a knowledge of English (para. 33).

While rejecting the notion that schools should teach immigrant children to read and write their native languages, the report nevertheless accepted that immigrant children, just because they have their own cultures and backgrounds, can enrich the life of a school. English children could benefit from learning something of the views of English life and English character which are current in other societies, even if these happen to be critical. It might be of value to encourage classes to consider why different communities have developed different customs, and especially to compare them with our own.

Some months before the publication of this report, Sir Archer Hoare, the chairman of Middlesex County Council's Education Committee, had said, with reference to the 8,000 immigrant children attending schools in the area: 'A separate racial community in our midst would be contrary to the English way of life and the only satisfactory long-term solution must be that immigrant pupils, many of whom are drawn from the

[1] Appointed by Mr. Butler as an advisory body, whose terms of reference included the task of examining the arrangements made by local authorities 'to assist (Commonwealth) immigrants to adapt themselves to British habits and customs'.

Commonwealth, should be merged in the general community.' (*Middlesex County Times*, 2 November 1963.) On the other hand, a *Times* report (7 November 1963) from Birmingham suggested that although there was tolerance and mingling at school there seemed to be very little lasting integration thereafter.

From late 1963 onwards the term 'integration', its meaning or meanings were increasingly debated. In an article published on 28 November 1963, *New Society* put forward the view that the overwhelming bulk of immigrants were not being integrated into society, and that large numbers showed no wish to be integrated. 'In other words, we face the risk of permanent voluntary ghettoes, which will be eroded only slowly, if at all, by common education.' But the writer took a more optimistic view of the future of West Indian immigrants ('Given a chance, West Indians—who have largely been brought up to regard themselves as British—are much more likely to mix'). Pakistanis and Indians were regarded as causing most concern, because they showed almost no interest in being integrated.[1]

> Yet at this stage we come to the deepest question of all: is *absolute* integration really desirable? Of course, there must be equality: America's colour problem has shown us the curse of second-class citizenship. There must be a common political and administrative system and no sort of discrimination. But should we seek to iron out all cultural differences? The immigrants may bring cultural riches, which would be lost if dispersed. (Society has not necessarily been a net loser through Jewish isolation from the rest of the community.) And the attempt to force different races into one national mould may lead to intolerance: McCarthyism was one manifestation of it. Perhaps the ability to tolerate and benefit from a diversity of cultures would represent the highest form of national maturity. But this leads into ever-deepening waters: and there are more glaring obstacles to racial harmony to be tackled now.

The 'pluralistic' view gradually gained strength, although it was generally interpreted in terms of pluralistic integration,[2] rather than separate development.[3] Increasingly, too, the distinction between the

[1] Cf. R. H. Desai's study of Gujaratis in Birmingham, *Indian Immigrants in Britain*.

[2] Elspeth Huxley in *Back Street New Worlds*, London, Chatto and Windus, 1964, distinguished three main streams of thought among immigrants: (i) those who want to 'integrate' (assimilate fully); (ii) those who reject integration (self-segregationists); and (iii) the 'half-way housers' in between (pluralistic integrators). See also her article in I.R.R. *Newsletter*, April 1964.

[3] The latter viewpoint was expressed by Mr. Peter Griffiths, Conservative Councillor and from 1964–6 M.P. for Smethwick, whose general policy for immigrants, as expressed in January 1964, was one of 'co-existence' or 'separate development' rather than 'integration'. Another minority interpretation was put by a reader of the *Daily Telegraph* (5 February 1964) who saw it in genetic terms: 'Those who favour mixed racial integration are really acquiescing in national decline. . . .' See also *Sunday Telegraph* editorial on 27 July 1967.

economic and socio-cultural aspects of absorption and the need for positive integratory measures at national level came to be understood and accepted.

The official approach during 1965 was still problem-oriented rather than positive. Part III (on integration) of the White Paper of August 1965 opened with the following paragraph:

> The United Kingdom is already a multi-racial society and Commonwealth immigrants make a most valuable contribution to our economy. Most of them will stay and bring up their families here and there can be no question of allowing any of them to be regarded as second-class citizens. At the same time it must be recognised that the presence in this country of nearly one million immigrants from the Commonwealth with different social and cultural backgrounds raises a number of problems and creates various social tensions in those areas where they have concentrated. If we are to avoid the evil of racial strife and if harmonious relations between the different races who now form our community are to develop, these problems and tensions must be resolved and removed so that individual members of every racial group can mingle freely with all other citizens at school, at work and during their leisure time without any form of discrimination being exercised against them.[1]

Later in the year, however, there was a certain revulsion from the tone and mood of the Smethwick and White Paper era. Controls were now generally accepted but political debate became more moderate and more concerned with integrative action. This trend was facilitated by the modest beginnings of centralized programmes (see below). It gained strength in 1966, particularly after the conduct and results of the General Election in April had shown that coloured immigration was not, or was not to be allowed to be, a major party political issue; the consensus of strictness between the two major parties had effected a political neutralization of the issue, if not a long-term social solution.

The new goal of pluralistic integration and the recognition of social factors in absorption emerged clearly and positively in an address given by the incoming Home Secretary, the Rt. Hon. Roy Jenkins, to a meeting of Voluntary Liaison Committees on 23 May 1966.[2] He said:

> Integration is perhaps rather a loose word. I do not regard it as meaning the loss, by immigrants, of their own national characteristics and culture. I do not think that we need in this country a 'melting-pot', which will turn everybody out in a common mould, as one of a series of carbon copies of someone's misplaced vision of the stereotyped Englishman.
>
> It would be bad enough if that were to happen to the relatively few in this country who happen to have pure Anglo-Saxon blood in their veins. If it were

[1] The precise form of 'integration' envisaged does not emerge clearly from the text, although the importance of social factors is recognized.

[2] It was also accepted by the N.C.C.I. (see 1966 Report, p. 8, para. 1).

to happen to the rest of us, to the Welsh (like myself), to the Scots, to the Irish, to the Jews, to the mid-European, and to still more recent arrivals, it would be little short of a national disaster. It would deprive us of most of the positive advantages of immigration, which, as I shall develop in a moment, I believe to be very great indeed.

I define integration, therefore, not as a flattening process of assimilation but as equal opportunity, accompanied by cultural diversity, in an atmosphere of mutual tolerance. This is the goal. We may fall a little short of its full attainment, as have other communities both in the past and in the present. But if we are to maintain any sort of world reputation for civilized living and social cohesion, we must get far nearer to its achievement than is the case today. Insofar as this is something which can be brought about by Government action, this is now a Home Office responsibility. I welcome this. We have traditionally had the responsibility for the control of admission—of aliens for many years past, and more recently of Commonwealth citizens. I regard this as a distasteful but necessary duty. My instincts are all against the restriction of free movement, whether for work or education or pleasure, from one country to another. Distasteful though it may be, however, it remains a duty.

In present circumstances we are bound, as almost everyone now recognizes, to contain the flow of immigrants within the economic and social capacity of the country to absorb them—the social factor being for the moment, I believe, more restrictive than the economic. . . .

For centuries past this and every other country which has played a part in the mainstream of world events has benefited immensely from its immigrants. Some of them came in much more aggressive ways than those we are discussing today, but at least from the Norman Conquest, to the wave of German and Austrian and Czechoslovak refugees in the thirties, we have been constantly stimulated and jolted out of our natural island lethargy by a whole series of immigrations. Those who came were always made unwelcome by some people, but they have rarely failed to make a contribution out of proportion to their numbers. If anyone doubts this let them look at British business today, and at the phenomenal extent to which the more successful companies have been founded—or rejuvenated—by men whose origin was outside these islands.

But this is not merely a matter of business. Where in the world is there a university which could preserve its fame, or a cultural centre which would keep its eminence, or a metropolis which could hold its drawing power if it were to turn inwards and serve only its own hinterland and its own racial group? To live apart, for a person, a city, a country, is to lead a life of declining intellectual stimulation.

Nor should we under-estimate the special contribution which has been made by the recent immigrants from the West Indies and from India and Pakistan, and from other Commonwealth countries. Some are highly gifted with outstanding talents in a wide variety of human activities. They and many others are making a major contribution to our national welfare and prosperity. They work in our hospitals as doctors and nurses, they build houses and run transport services in our cities. They help to fill the many labour shortages, particularly in urban areas, particularly in vital but undermanned public services which go with a full employment society.

2. GOVERNMENT INITIATIVES AND AGENCIES

For some years during and after the Second World War a small welfare department in the Colonial Office was maintained to deal with the problems of colonial immigrants.[1] This was, however, closed down in 1951 and its duties relinquished to the various governments concerned, as they achieved independence. Until 1965, therefore, for over a decade of large-scale Commonwealth immigration, there was no British Government department or agency directly or solely responsible for immigrant welfare or integration, although representatives of some departments did serve on various voluntary committees (e.g. the Immigrants' Advisory Committee of the London Council of Social Service). Basically, however, the whole matter of integration was left to, and regarded as, the responsibility of the local authorities,[2] the voluntary associations, and possibly the High Commissions.[3]

Questions about Government action on integration began to be asked in Parliament in the early 1950s, but they generally met either with denials that there was a particular problem, or with assertions that existing arrangements were adequate and that the newcomers benefited equally with locals from the welfare services, or again with assurances that the Government was aware of a real problem and was studying it.[4]

A. THE COMMONWEALTH IMMIGRANTS ADVISORY COUNCIL

It was only with the passing of the restrictive and negative Commonwealth Immigrants Act that the Government took even a modest step in the direction of positive integration. This was the appointment of a non-statutory C.I.A.C. whose terms of reference were to advise the Home Secretary (then Mr. R. A. Butler) on any matters which he might

[1] See Hooper (ed.), *Colour in Britain*, pp. 212–3, for an account of the joint wartime Ministry of Labour and Colonial Office Scheme for West Indian workers, with Mr. (now Sir Learie) Constantine as Welfare Officer.

[2] In 1952 a deputation to the Colonial Office was told (what was in fact a projection of the traditional constitutional position) that Commonwealth immigrants were not the responsibility of the Colonial Office while they were in Britain. As British citizens the responsibility was entirely with the local authority where they lived. ('The Dark Million'—1, *The Times*, 18 January 1965.)

[3] The Jamaican-backed British Caribbean Welfare Service was first in the field in 1955. This later became the Migrant Services Division of the High Commission of the West Indies Federation, which did admirable work despite its limited personnel and resources. After the break-up of Federation, the Division also broke up and smaller territorial departments (of which the Jamaican one was again the largest and most active) took over as far as possible the work of reception, welfare, community development, liaison, and information. In recent years similar work was developed by the Indian and Pakistani High Commissions in London and the provinces (for details see Appendix X).

[4] See Paul Foot, op. cit., pp. 129–33, for more detail on this period.

refer to it from time to time affecting the welfare of Commonwealth immigrants in this country and their integration into the community.

Specifically the Council was asked:

(i) to examine the arrangements made by local authorities in whose areas substantial numbers of Commonwealth immigrants have settled to assist immigrants to adapt themselves to British habits and customs, and to report on the adequacy of the efforts made;
(ii) to examine whether the powers of local authorities to deal with matters affecting the welfare of immigrants are sufficient, and whether any further action can usefully be taken by the Government to stimulate action by local authorities; and
(iii) to examine the relationship between action by local offices of Government Departments and local authorities on the one hand, and the efforts of voluntary bodies on the other, in furthering the welfare of immigrants.

It may be noted that these terms of reference still stressed the predominant role of local authorities in the work of welfare and integration.

The C.I.A.C.'s membership, under the chairmanship of Stella, the Dowager Marchioness of Reading, G.B.E., was as follows:

Stella, the Dowager Marchioness of Reading, Sir George Harold Banwell, Mr. Hugh O. M. Bryant, Mr. Adrian Cadbury, Mr. Renee Coussey, Sir George Haynes, Mr. Philip Mason, Miss Marjorie Nicholson, Sir Archibald Nye, Mr. John B. Peile.

During its nearly three years of life the C.I.A.C. took a good deal of evidence and produced four reports containing detailed conclusions and recommendations, in major spheres. The first (Cmnd 2119, July 1963) was concerned with housing; it came out explicitly against specially favourable treatment for immigrants while making certain proposals of general application (hostels, 'patching', home purchase loans, improvement of certain areas). The second report (Cmnd 2266, February 1964) was concerned with education (immigrant children, the aims of the educational system, the teaching of English, teacher-training, and special help for schools with large numbers of immigrant children; text books, flexible dispersal arrangements to avoid *de facto* segregation;[1] the teaching of English to adult immigrants and other forms of adult education, and the need for a wider circulation of advice and information on knowledge and experience already accumulated in various fields by local authorities and organizations). The report ended by recommending the appointment of an advisory officer to fulfil this task (see below). In its third report (Cmnd 2458, September 1964), the Council considered the problems of immigrant school-leavers,

[1] This came shortly after Sir Edward Boyle's Southall-based decision to oppose *de facto* separation in schools.

distinguishing between those who came to Britain when already of school age (i.e. young first-generation immigrants) and those who were born here or came here when quite small. In its further and final report (Cmnd 2796, October 1965), published after its functions had been taken over by the new National Committee for Commonwealth Immigrants (following the White Paper of August 1965), the Council returned again to the question of housing. This report reiterated the first report's view that immigrants must be treated like any other citizens, but contained more detailed proposals for special financial assistance to certain areas, for housing information services and interpreter services to be established, for changes in housing list procedure, and for the encouragement, though not the enforcement, of dispersal.

Over these years, the Council accumulated and rediffused a substantial body of knowledge and expertise which was to provide a valuable basis and a positive climate of opinion for the more centralized work of integration that was to follow. On 23 October 1965, *The Times* paid tribute to the outgoing Council's 'consistently level-headed, practical and undramatic approach' to problems of immigration during a period when public discussion of them had too frequently been 'alarmist, irrational and often downright mischievous'.

B. THE NATIONAL COMMITTEE FOR COMMONWEALTH IMMIGRANTS (1)

The National Committee for Commonwealth Immigrants was formed and its Advisory Officer appointed in April 1964, following the recommendation in the C.I.A.C.'s second report (Cmnd 2266). The Advisory Officer was Miss Nadine Peppard, whose years of experience as Secretary of the Immigrants Advisory Committee of the London Council of Social Service uniquely qualified her for the new post. Its functions had been defined in detail by the C.I.A.C. as follows:

> This officer, as we envisage his role, would be concerned with practical problems arising from the presence of Commonwealth immigrants in Britain. He would make use of the results of research, but not himself be engaged on it. His task would be to bring to the notice of local authorities and voluntary bodies the experiments and methods of work of other bodies and any other relevant information, and he might also suggest new experiments and methods of work in areas where numbers of immigrants had settled. There may well be need for better arrangements to secure liaison between the various Government departments concerned with the welfare of immigrants, but we are clear that an officer doing the sort of work we have in mind ought not himself to be a civil servant. We suggest that he should be appointed by and be responsible to a small voluntary committee. Since there is a need to draw both on specialist knowledge in the matter of race relations, and also on practical experience of

dealing with community problems and with the work of voluntary organisations, we suggest that the Institute of Race Relations and the National Council of Social Service should be among the bodies represented on the guiding committee. As an interim arrangement this committee should in our view be a sub-committee of our Council.

At the outset, the Committee was a small voluntary committee of non-official persons, some nominated by the Commonwealth Immigrants Advisory Council, some by the Institute of Race Relations, and some by the National Council of Social Service, with other members co-opted. Its membership was as follows:

Mr. Philip Mason, C.I.E., O.B.E. (Chairman)
Mr. John B. Peile (Vice-Chairman)
Sir George Haynes, C.B.E.
Miss E. R. Littlejohn, J.P.
Mrs. Hansa Mehta
Mr. George Mitchell, J.P.
Dr. David Pitt
Begum Rashid
Mr. E. J. B. Rose
Miss Joan Vickers, M.B.E., J.P.
Miss Nadine Peppard (Advisory Officer and Secretary to the Committee)

The salary and expenses of the Advisory Officer were covered by a Government grant, but the officer was responsible in matters of policy solely to the National Committee for Commonwealth Immigrants, in whose discretion it lay to interpret the terms of reference.

The Advisory Officer's first year of country-wide work on liaison and co-ordination is described by Paul Foot (op. cit., pp. 221–3).[1] From a hotch-potch of fifteen voluntary liaison committees in April 1964, there was created a coherent network of thirty-one committees, thirteen staffed by full-time officers and financed either by the local authority or the local Council of Social Service. In April 1965, there took place the first centrally organized conference of such local committees.

March 1965 had seen a further step in direct Government involvement in integrative activities. Mr. Maurice Foley, Parliamentary Under-Secretary at the Department of Economic Affairs, became responsible in a personal capacity for co-ordinating Government action and promoting, through the department concerned, the efforts of local authorities and voluntary bodies (see below for further details). This was part of Mr. Wilson's three-pronged plan to deal with immigration problems, the others being stricter controls and the introduction of an

[1] See also 'The Dark Million' 11, *The Times* (29 January 1965).

anti-discrimination and anti-incitement Bill. In mid-June the Department of Education and Science also issued a circular calling on local authorities to make sure that not more than one child in three at schools was an immigrant, to provide more teachers, special English classes, and so on.

In August came the White Paper, with its low ceiling on the annual issue of vouchers and its tighter controls in Part II, and in Part III its proposals for further integrative measures.

C. THE NATIONAL COMMITTEE FOR COMMONWEALTH IMMIGRANTS (2)

After outlining the functions of and conditions for success to be met by local voluntary liaison committees, the White Paper expressed the Government's belief in the 'need for closer co-ordination of effort on a national basis and in particular a need for some tangible evidence of Government support for the existing network of voluntary liaison committees and for the creation of additional committees in other areas where substantial numbers of Commonwealth immigrants have settled'. It continued:

> The Government intend to establish a new National Committee for Commonwealth Immigrants which will be composed of individuals who are able to bring special knowledge and experience to bear on the problems arising from Commonwealth immigration. This will replace the existing National Committee. Its finances and staff will be such that it will be able to expand existing services to the voluntary liaison committees and the regional organisations. The need for a wider sharing of experience has clearly been shown and it is important that the new National Committee should be able to build up a comprehensive body of doctrine which can be flexibly applied to a variety of local situations, extend the range of existing information work, organise conferences of workers in the field, arrange training courses, stimulate research and the examination by experts of particular problems, and generally promote and co-ordinate effort on a national basis.
>
> The Government take the view that the work of the National Committee should not be directly under Government control since its main stimulus must come from the harnessing of voluntary effort, and a degree of autonomy is necessary if the Committee is to remain free from party political influence and other partisan pressures; but the Government propose to maintain close liaison with the work of the Committee and to associate itself fully with the Committee's efforts.
>
> The Government consider it of the first importance that each voluntary liaison committee should be served by a trained, full-time, paid official who should be the direct servant of the committee. As evidence of its wish to give tangible support to the committees, the Government is prepared, in certain circumstances, to make a grant towards the salary of such an official available to each voluntary liaison committee through the National Committee. The

condition will be that the voluntary liaison committee concerned can demonstrate to the satisfaction of the National Committee that the person they propose to employ is fully competent to carry out the particular work which he or she will be called upon to perform. We hope that the local authority concerned will provide adequate office accommodation and secretarial support for the official appointed. In these circumstances, voluntary liaison committees already employing a suitable officer will be eligible to apply for the proposed grant. It will be one of the functions of the National Committee to assist in the recruitment and training of suitable officers where they are not otherwise available to the local committee.

The White Paper went on to pay tribute to the valuable work of the C.I.A.C. since 1962, but considered that its functions could now be included in those of the new Committee.

(i) *Membership*

The full membership of the National Committee was published by the Prime Minister's Office on 17 September:

The Archbishop of Canterbury, Dr. Ramsey (chairman); Sir James Robertson, chairman of the governors of the Commonwealth Institute and formerly Governor-General of Nigeria (deputy-chairman); Mr. Hamza Alavi, vice-chairman, Campaign Against Racial Discrimination; Mrs. Felicity Bolton, secretary, British–Caribbean Association; Dr. Charles Metcalfe Brown, Medical Officer of Health, City of Manchester; Mr. Eric Hawkins, Director of the Language Teaching Centre, Department of Education, York University; Sir George Haynes (later resigned), director, National Council of Social Service; Mr. J. L. Jones, assistant executive secretary, Transport and General Workers' Union; Mr. Philip Mason, director, Institute of Race Relations and chairman of the former National Committee for Commonwealth Immigrants; Dr. David Pitt, chairman, Campaign Against Racial Discrimination and member of the Greater London Council; Dr. Dhani Ram Prem, vice-chairman, Commonwealth Welfare Council for the West Midlands; Mr. E. J. B. Rose, director, Survey of Race Relations in Britain; Professor R. M. Titmuss, Professor of Social Administration, London University; Mr. Dermot de Trafford, managing director, General Hydraulic Power Group Ltd.; Mr. Lewis Waddilove, director of the Joseph Rowntree Memorial Trust and a member of the Milner Holland Committee on London's housing; Miss Dorothy M. Wood, secretary, Nottingham Commonwealth Citizens' Consultative Committee; Sir Lionel Russell, Director of Education, Birmingham.

Added later to the list of members were: Mr. Tassaduq Ahmed, until 1965, president of the National Federation of Pakistani Associations; Mr. F. Dean, Chairman of the Pakistan Society in Manchester; Miss Janet Kydd, Senior Lecturer in Social Science and Adviser to Women

Students, London School of Economics; Mr. W. Kirby Laing of John Laing & Son, Ltd.; Mr. Leslie Scafe (since resigned), now Liaison Officer to the Luton International Council, but prior to his resignation secretary of the West Indian Association in Sheffield; Mr. V. D. Sharma, secretary of the Southall Indian Workers' Association; Mr. G. F. Smith, general secretary of the Amalgamated Society of Woodworkers and chairman of the T.U.C.'s Commonwealth Advisory Committee.

The secretary was and remains Miss Nadine Peppard, advisory officer of the former National Committee for Commonwealth Immigrants.

(ii) *First Steps*

At an inaugural Press conference for the new N.C.C.I., the Archbishop of Canterbury, Dr. Ramsey, was reported as 'politely fencing off' questions aimed at discovering his attitude to the controls section of the White Paper. He stressed that the new committee was charged with the problem of integration irrespective of current policy concerning controls, but intimated that, if the committee found that the work of integration was being hampered by the policy, they would tell the Government so (*The Times*, 28 September). The three immigrant members of the Committee, Mr. Hamza Alavi of C.A.R.D. (later resigned), Dr. David Pitt, G.L.C. member, and Dr. Dhani Prem of Birmingham, elsewhere expressed their view that it was possible to serve on the new N.C.C.I. without supporting that section of the White Paper that dealt with controls (*Daily Sketch*, 18 September 1965; *Guardian*, 23 September1965; *Peace News*, 8 October 1965).

At the first meeting of the Committee, it was agreed that people from outside as well as serving members should be invited to serve on special advisory panels. As ultimately constituted they were concerned with: Children; Community Relations; Education; Employment; Health and Welfare; Housing; Information; Legal and Civil Affairs; Training.[1]

In November it was announced that the Government would increase its grant to the National Committee from £9,000 to £100,000 a year. This would enable the Committee to increase the number of full-time local liaison officers from four to thirty or forty and to treble its headquarters staff.

(iii) *Terms of Reference*

The terms of reference of the National Committee are as follows:

> The National Committee for Commonwealth Immigrants shall be required to promote and co-ordinate on a national basis efforts directed towards the integration of Commonwealth immigrants into the community. In particular the Committee shall be required to:

[1] For details of membership, see N.C.C.I. Report for 1966, Appendix 2.

(*a*) promote and co-ordinate the activities of voluntary liaison committees and advise them on their work;

(*b*) where necessary, assist in the recruitment and training of suitable men or women to serve these committees as full-time officials;

(*c*) provide a central information service;

(*d*) organise conferences, arrange training courses and stimulate research;

(*e*) advise on those questions which are referred to them by Government or which they consider should be brought to the attention of Government.

(iv) *Activities*

Since its first meeting on 15 October 1965, the National Committee has met monthly and covered a wide range of activities. It is an independent body, free from Government control, but it has close links with the Government, in certain matters directly with the Prime Minister and in others with the Home Secretary, to whose department Mr. Maurice Foley, M.P., Minister with Special Responsibility for Immigrants, was transferred in January 1966. Early in January 1967, Mr. Foley moved to the Ministry of Defence and this area of responsibility was taken by Mr. David Ennals, M.P.

After the appointment of the Race Relations Board in February 1967, the two bodies began to work in close co-operation, to ensure that their complementary but distinct roles are fully understood both nationally and locally.[1] The Committee is also in regular touch with all appropriate Government, local government, and voluntary bodies, particularly with the forty-odd voluntary liaison committees which it has encouraged, helped to set up, and co-ordinated all over the country, and which are now organized into a standing committee under its auspices.[2]

Links with immigrant associations have been looser, partly because many are ephemeral or have frequent changes of officers and locale, partly because of the lack of machinery for regular meetings or an overall organizational framework, partly too because of the suspicions or hostile attitudes of some, particularly since the control sections of the White Paper with which the National Committee is sometimes inaccurately and unjustly associated.

In its first annual report, the Committee's work was said to fall into two main categories: the formulation of policy recommendations and the promotion of local voluntary liaison committees, sustained by an advisory service. Education in its widest sense was said to be the essence of the task:

Education in school and out of school, education of adults as well as children, education of newcomers as well as the indigenous population,

[1] See under Race Relations Board (Headquarters Activities), for details of two policy-oriented research investigations sponsored jointly by the two bodies.

[2] See Chapter 8—Voluntary Liaison Committees.

education through conferences, through committee work, through social activities, through the Press, television and radio and, not least, education through legislation: all methods have to be used, all channels of communication discovered. The call for help and information, for talks and discussions, is constant, and both members and staff of the Committee have addressed a large number of organisations all over the country. These have included clubs, groups, professional organisations, schools, training colleges and courses for specialised workers, ministers of religion and many others.

The report continued:

One dilemma is constant: the things which affect immigrants only are few but devastating in their effect. Most of the problems are community problems of deprivation, bad housing and shortage of housing, overcrowded schools, over-strained social services and many other ills of urban life. Immigrants share these problems with the host community, but in a degree intensified by their position—described by Michael Banton as that of 'the archetypal stranger'—and by both the open and the hidden processes of discrimination. The Committee has therefore to steer a somewhat complex course. It is engaged in the work of community relations in the broadest sense and must take care never to build up a separate structure of services, and therefore a separate position, for the immigrant. At the same time, it must do everything possible to reverse the undoubtedly negative trends of today and to ensure that the newcomers and their children become an integral part of the community.

The more specialized work of examining policies and formulating recommendations to be made to the Government, local authorities and other bodies has been carried out mainly through the Committee's special Advisory Panels. The 1966 Report describes their work and we give below a brief outline of the main activities of each.

Education

The Education Panel has looked at three aspects of formal education in the schools: the problem of non-English-speaking children, the broad canvas of teaching for children in a multi-racial society, and assistance to teachers concerned with both these aspects. The Panel now has a sub-committee on teacher-training under the chairmanship of Mr. P. K. C. Millins, Principal, Edge Hill College of Education. The Panel has drawn up a number of documents to assist local education authorities, teacher-training colleges, heads, and teachers. They include a bibliography of materials for use by teachers of non-English-speaking children and adults; a handbook, *Practical Suggestions for Teachers of Immigrant Children,* edited by Mr. Trevor Burgin; and a report by Mr. Alec Dickson of Community Service Volunteers on the help which the C.S.V.'s can give in the schools.

A number of conferences and seminars have been organized, including: three one-day conferences for teachers in the West Midlands; a seminar for about forty educationalists entitled 'Towards a Multi-Racial Society' in July 1966; and a seminar on 'Immigration and the Training of Teachers' in January 1967.

The Panel has also been concerned with developments in adult education, including courses which are a help to good race relations and also the specific problems of the organization of English classes for non-English-speaking adults.

Employment

The Employment Panel under the chairmanship of Mr. D. H. de Trafford has made a number of recommendations to the Committee. These have included an amendment to the Fair Wages Resolution of 1946, seeking to withhold Government contracts from firms which practise racial discrimination; a Declaration of Intent against racial discrimination for endorsement by the T.U.C. and C.B.I. The Panel has nearly completed a book of advice to employers, employees, and trade unions on relations with immigrant employees, and it has discussions with the Ministry of Labour about placement policies in Employment Exchanges.

The outstanding work of the Panel has, however, been the drafting and approval of proposals to extend the Race Relations Act 1965 to employment, housing, insurance and credit, and all places of public resort, and to strengthen the powers of the Race Relations Board under the Act. This work was conducted with representatives of the Legal and Welfare, and Housing Panels.

The Panel was also responsible for proposing and for planning the N.C.C.I.'s major conference on Racial Equality in Employment held in February 1967 (see below, p. 126). Mr. Anthony Lester of the Employment Panel visited the U.S.A. on behalf of the N.C.C.I. in the summer of 1966 in order to organize the North American side of the conference.

Housing

Housing, states the first N.C.C.I. annual report, may well be considered to be the most complex and intractable of all the problems faced by immigrants and by the National Committee in its work. The Housing Panel, under the chairmanship of Mr. Lewis Waddilove, operates on two assumptions: (1) that there is open discrimination in housing, particularly in the private sector, and (2) that even when there is no direct evidence of discrimination, or of any intention to discriminate, most immigrants are in practice excluded from normal housing opportunities and remain at the end of most housing queues.

A series of meetings and studies in 1966 culminated in a report which was discussed with the Rt. Hon. Richard Crossman, the then Minister of Housing, on 3 August 1966. Topics discussed included new towns, housing associations, multiple occupation, and local authority policies. The Panel has also produced for the Minister a report on Areas of Special Need and an examination of policies in relation to immigrants in new towns and in 'twilight' areas of industrial towns.

The Panel has sent a report to the Minister pointing out the dangers of the Birmingham Corporation Act as a model for local authority policy.

Health

The Health Panel, under the chairmanship of Dr. C. Metcalfe Brown, M.D., D.P.H., has been concerned with the social responsibilities of doctors, and has prepared a booklet putting medical facts about immigrants into their social context. The Panel has recommended to the Committee, in accordance with the evidence of the B.M.A. Report (see Chapter 10) that all consideration on health checks should in future move from the premise that state of health should be determined in the country of origin and not on arrival. The Panel has maintained contact with the Ministry of Health and has advised on the kind of literature issued to new arrivals.

Children

The Children's Panel, under the chairmanship of Dr. D. R. Prem, has looked into the needs of children in their homes and children in care. The Panel has concerned itself in particular with the welfare of the pre-school child, and has looked at the provision of registered child-minders, nursery schooling, and playgroups in areas of settlement, and hazards of living in crowded homes. Regarding the problems of children in care, the Panel has recommended discussions with the Home Secretary and the Ministry of Health and with Children's Departments, and the Committee is arranging this.

Community Relations

The Community Race Relations Panel, formed in October 1966 with Miss D. M. Wood as chairman, is basically intended to support and inspire local voluntary liaison committees. The members of the Panel are specially interested in activities for young people, in the availability of premises for clubs and groups and in the possibilities of creating international centres. The Panel's studies of these problems is intended to create a body of expert knowledge of the sort of community activities that are productive and worthwhile.

Training

The Training Panel, under the chairmanship of Miss Janet Kydd, brings together senior people from various bodies who are responsible for training social workers in various fields. Part of the Panel's work consists in stimulating the use of material designed for work in multi-racial communities, in established social work courses; but the Panel is also concerned with direct training in community relations work as it is related to multi-racial areas. This is new work, which requires many different qualities and skills, including 'some administrative ability, courage and skill in the face of discrimination, understanding of people, a grasp of practical needs and practical solutions, a knowledge of group-work techniques, and above all a sensitivity to the interaction of ethnically and culturally different individuals and groups and a knowledge of their cultures and traditions'. (N.C.C.I. Report 1966, p. 19.) In this field, the Panel has organized three seminars for professional workers and voluntary immigrant leaders, and a series of local leadership courses.

Public Relations and Information

The Information Panel, under the chairmanship of Mr. E. J. B. Rose, is concerned not only with the presentation of the work of the N.C.C.I., but with the public image of Commonwealth immigrants, and the whole question of the public education of immigrant and native communities.

Its main project planned is the making of a film, in co-operation with the B.B.C., to provide some insight into the way British society behaves towards newcomers, to make people aware of the harmful effects of their behaviour, and to examine some of its causes.

The Panel has also been concerned with Press treatment of news involving race relations or immigrants, and has asked some local voluntary liaison committees to monitor their local Press so that editorial policies can be compared. To help these committees in their work, the Panel has also circulated a paper to them on Press relations and publicity.

Legal Questions

The Legal and Civil Affairs Panel, under the chairmanship of Mr. Philip Mason, C.I.E., O.B.E., has been concerned with immigration laws and procedure and with relationships between the police force and immigrants.

Soon after the N.C.C.I. was re-formed under the 1965 White Paper, the Archbishop of Canterbury led a deputation to the Prime Minister, in which it was stated that the immigration provisions of the White Paper made the integration tasks of the N.C.C.I. more difficult.

Following the initial policy of the N.C.C.I., the Panel has produced more detailed proposals, criticizing the White Paper for being racially discriminatory and urging that any controls should relate to all immigrants and be based on the economic needs of Britain, and its ability to house and educate people, not directed at Commonwealth immigrants alone. The Panel submitted evidence to Sir Roy Wilson's Committee on Immigration Appeals. This called for some appeal machinery, referred to disparity of treatment between white immigrants and coloured immigrants, to the right of entry of visitors, and to the tone and method of questioning employed by immigration officers. It stressed the need for liaison officers at the airport, who would be empowered to enter into discussion with immigration officers about cases of refusals and be able to present the immigrant's case. It also stressed the need for immigrants to be allowed to meet their families and friends and provide evidence of their assertions. The Panel has also investigated relationships between immigrants and the police, and reported a lack of confidence, and allegations of discriminatory behaviour by the police, in a number of areas. This has been taken up by the Committee, which proposed, among other things, some method of independent review of complaints, and incorporation of special material in police training courses.

Publications

A full list of publications of the N.C.C.I., including special papers, reports, leaflets, and translated publications, is contained in Appendix 4 of the 1966 Report. The N.C.C.I. also publishes *Liaison*, a quarterly magazine for voluntary liaison committees, containing news of central and local activities, and *NCCI Information*, a monthly news-sheet produced in English, Urdu, and Punjabi.

N.C.C.I. Conference on Racial Equality in Industry

In February 1967, the National Committee for Commonwealth Immigrants held a two-day conference on 'Racial Equality in Employment'. The purpose of the conference was to exchange experiences with American and Canadian experts on problems of racial discrimination in employment and the means of promoting equality of opportunity.

The American speakers were: Ben Segal, Director of Liaison, Equal Employment Opportunity Commission, U.S.A.; Joseph L. Rauh, Jr., Civil Rights Lawyer, and General Counsel of U.A.W. (United Automobile Workers' Union); Bayard Rustin, Executive Director, A. Philip Randolph Institute; Norman Nicholson, Vice-President of Kaiser Company, California; Victor Reuther, Director, International Affairs Department, U.A.W.

The Canadian speakers were: Daniel G. Hill, Director, Ontario

Human Rights Commission; George Blackburn, Director, Fair Employment Practices branch, Department of Labour (Canada).

The British speakers included: The Archbishop of Canterbury, the Home Secretary and other members of the Government and Opposition parties, leading industrialists and trade unionists, immigrant leaders, academics, and members of the National Committee.

Altogether there were about 156 participants at the conference, with about thirty-two representatives of management, and about thirteen trade unionists. The T.U.C. refused to take part on a formal basis, but Fred Hayday, chairman of the General Council's international committee, and George Smith, also a member of the General Council, general secretary of the Amalgamated Society of Woodworkers, and a member of the National Committee, attended and put forward views which had been publicized as those of the T.U.C. special (International) committee on the subject. The C.B.I. was represented by Sir Kenneth Allen, K.T., chairman and managing director of W. H. Allen & Sons Ltd., and by Martin Jukes, Q.C., director, General Engineering Employers' Federation.

The subject-matter of the conference centred on the role of Government and, in particular, the effect of 'fair employment practices'-type laws against discrimination. However, Victor Reuther, the U.S. trade union representative, and Norman Nicholson, the U.S. business representative, also discussed voluntary integration programmes which had been initiated by trade unions and business, respectively.

During the speeches of welcome to delegates, the Home Secretary made little secret of his wish for an extension of anti-discrimination legislation and Jack Jones, M.B.E., assistant executive secretary of the T.G.W.U. and chairman of the Trade Union Session of the conference, announced the formation of a special Labour Party N.E.C. Home Affairs Committee to look into the question of extending the 1965 Race Relations Act.

What was interpreted as a near boycott by leaders of major industries and unions of the conference as a whole was, however, countered by the virtual pledges in support of legislation made not only by the Home Secretary, Mr. Roy Jenkins, but also the T.G.W.U. general secretary, Mr. Frank Cousins.

Another interesting development at this conference was a compromise solution which many members of both the pro- and anti-legislation groups considered might provide a useful basis for discussion, put forward by Mr. Oscar Hahn, chairman of Birmingham Chamber of Commerce: machinery administered by fair employment committees within factories employing more than a certain number of workers, with appeal to an outside body only in the event of no solution being found.

After the conference, N.C.C.I. issued the following report:

Four conclusions emerged from the discussions at the conference: (a) that legislation is central to any programme for racial equality; (b) that there is need for further detailed information on the type of legislation which would be acceptable and suitable for this country; (c) that there is need for public knowledge and understanding about the facts of discrimination; (d) that it is impossible to separate employment from housing, education and other areas where race relations are a crucial issue.

D. MAURICE FOLEY

On 9 March 1965, the Prime Minister announced in the House of Commons as part of his three-pronged attack on immigration problems that to speed integration Mr. Maurice Foley, M.P., Parliamentary Under-Secretary at the Department of Economic Affairs, would be responsible in a personal capacity for co-ordinating Government action and promoting, through the departments concerned, the efforts of local authorities and voluntary bodies.

The third prong (on controls) was, of course, looking forward to the July 1965 White Paper, which for the first time imposed an absolute ceiling on the number of Commonwealth workers allowed into Britain. Mr. Foley was therefore appointed to deal with integration at a time when Government policy on immigration was becoming more restrictive. In the Institute of Race Relations *Newsletter*, February 1967, Eric Silver commented: 'Mr. Foley . . . was given the immigration brief as an antidote of conscience to the hard line evolving in the Labour Government after Patrick Gordon Walker's second defeat at Leyton. He was offered the job after protesting at the inadequacies of that policy. . . .'

Maurice Foley was transferred to the Home Office at the beginning of 1966 after Roy Jenkins became Home Secretary. In January 1967 he left the field of race relations and was transferred to the Admiralty. At the same time, David Ennals was appointed to the Home Office post, by now much more part of a system which included the National Committee for Commonwealth Immigrants, the new restrictions on immigration in the White Paper 1965, and the Race Relations Board. Mr. Foley had begun the job before this structure existed, and played a major part in its construction. Eric Silver assessed his work in the following terms:

> His principal contribution was an educational one: the education of Ministers, civil servants, and local authorities in the realities of Britain's racial problems. . . . As a one-man pressure group, inside and outside the Government, he persuaded people in key positions that race relations was not simply the dark side of other problems, that it had to be seen as a whole and had to be attacked in its own right. After persistent lobbying, Ministers and civil

servants in fields like housing, labour and education acknowledged the existence of racial and immigration problems. Through his efforts, there is now a small unit in the Home Office which co-ordinates the work done by different departments towards integrating immigrants[1] and serves as a clearing-house for information.

Away from Westminster, Mr. Foley also convinced a multitude of reluctant local authorities that community problems could not simply be left to the existing machinery devised for other purposes. . . .

Mr. Foley publicly defended the White Paper on Immigration, but he declined to shelter behind the claim that measures were directed at Commonwealth rather than coloured immigrants. It was a matter of race, not because the Government was prejudiced, but because a lot of people in areas where immigrants had settled were. . . . Mr. Foley must share the credit with Labour back-benchers and outside bodies . . . for the abandonment of some of the harsher proposals in the White Paper, such as those broadening the Home Secretary's deportation powers.

E. SPECIAL APPOINTMENTS AND PROVISIONS

Before the reorganization of the National Committee for Commonwealth Immigrants in 1965, and the development of voluntary liaison committees, with regular liaison officers supported by central funds attached to them, it was very much up to the individual local authority, in areas of immigrant settlement, what kind of arrangements to make to aid integration. The result was considerable variety and flexibility.

It was pointed out in 1965 that 'the most useful thing the local authority can do is to appoint a special worker'.[2]

The following are examples of such special appointments which show the diversity of approach.

Birmingham's Liaison Officer for Coloured People was possibly the earliest special appointment in the country. The post was first occupied by Mr. A. Gibbs, a former police officer from York who served in the police in Palestine and East Africa,[3] until 1967, when Mr. P. Hutchinson took over.

[1] See for an instance of the Home Office's 1966 approach to new immigrants the leaflet *Introduction to Britain—A Guide for Commonwealth Immigrants*.

[2] Hooper (ed.), *Colour in Britain*, Ch. 13.

[3] This appointment was mentioned approvingly by the writer of *The Times* series 'The Dark Million' in January 1965. On the other hand, Rex and Moore, writing a year later, expressed some reservations about the aims and approach which this particular officer seemed to be expected to pursue in his task. Co-operation with most local immigrant organizations was avoided because of possible political involvements and contact was, therefore, almost entirely with individuals. The task was seen as 'integration', which was defined as seeing the immigrants (i) got their rights and (ii) conformed.

Some churches have also appointed special workers in certain areas (e.g. the Methodists in Sheffield and the Anglicans in Coventry).

Mr. Eric Irons, J.P., is employed by the Education Committee of Nottingham City Council; he deals with the educational and vocational needs of immigrants, including the organization of courses such as English language classes at various levels (reading, writing, and speech), and special courses for the younger generation to prepare them for entry into technical colleges. Mr. Irons is also the chairman of the Nottingham Commonwealth Citizens Consultative Committee.

Miss Ivy Harrison is employed by the Public Health Department of Westminster City Council. Her work includes personal counselling and conciliation, helping with family problems of immigrants, and public speaking to local groups in order to educate the native English community about the background of immigrants.

Instances of other special workers are: a worker employed by the department of Health and Welfare in Reading; a liaison officer attached to the Health Department in Bradford (which also has two liaison officers working with the local police force); Mrs. Pansy Jeffrey at Kensington Citizens' Police Bureau (financed by the Borough); and a worker attached to the Welfare Department of Islington. The names and addresses of other special workers are listed in Section F of the N.C.C.I. List of Voluntary Liaison Committees, April 1967, pp. 25–27.

Some special workers are immigrants, but there is also a growing number of professional and other qualified immigrants working in local government, not as special workers but dealing with the public as a whole.

Special provisions for immigrants made by radio and television and the press will be discussed in more detail in a forthcoming year book under the heading 'Mass Media'. Here one should, however, just refer briefly to the B.B.C.'s special weekly radio and television transmissions in Hindustani, intended for Indian and Pakistani listeners and containing a mixture of home news, music, entertainment, English lessons, and information and advice on life in Britain (Programme Organizer the late David Gretton).

PART II

MAJOR SPHERES OF ASSOCIATION

CHAPTER 5

Employment[1]

The great majority of recent immigrants from the 'new' Commonwealth countries have come as economically motivated migrants—impelled by the 'push' factors at home of population pressure, unemployment and lack of economic choice, incentives and training facilities, and drawn by the 'pull' factors of full employment, higher wages, wider opportunities, metropolitan amenities, and better social services in Britain.

Employment is in any case one of the major areas of contact and competition between newcomers and the host society. Its importance is further enhanced for economically motivated migrants since it is in this field that they are likely to have the greatest aspirations.

As has already been said, immigration from the Commonwealth to Britain remained free, uncontrolled, and unrecorded in detail until 30 June 1962, when the Commonwealth Immigrants Act came into force. Thus no definitive statistics are available about either the migration as a whole or that section of it which is part of Britain's labour force. It may be stated with reasonable certainty that virtually all the adults in each of the three main ethnic groups—the West Indians, the Indians, and the Pakistanis—are of working age (most of them being in the younger age-groups). This includes the majority of those who have come in as 'dependants'; there is also an unascertained number of children who entered the country in their teens and are already working. These younger immigrants should not properly be classed as 'second generation', although, as will be seen, they tend to be so identified. This is a confusion which can have adverse consequences for members of the 'true' 'second generation', as they enter the labour market.

Not only are a higher proportion of the immigrants of working age, compared with the local population; a considerably higher proportion of them are, as indeed one would expect, 'economically active'. R. B. Davison's analysis of the 1961 10% Census information derived from twenty-eight London boroughs[2] indicated that this is true for males

[1] This chapter was written before the publication of the P.E.P. Report on Racial Discrimination and the first annual report of the Race Relations Board. For the P.E.P. Report scope, methods, and findings, see Appendix V.

[2] R. B. Davison, *Black British*, London, O.U.P. for I.R.R., 1966, pp. 65–68.

from all immigrant groups (88% for Jamaica-born, 76% for Pakistan-born, as opposed to 66% for English-born), and for females born in the West Indies (62% for Jamaica-born, as opposed to 39% for English-born; only 31% of women born in Pakistan were, however, 'economically active').[1]

The difference in the figures for males from the various groups may be explained by the fact that most immigrants are in the younger adult age groups, while among the English there is a higher proportion of retired persons and young adults receiving some form of higher education. The difference between the three female groups cited may be further attributed to differing socio-economic and cultural patterns. More English women stay at home as housewives than do West Indians, who are often the main breadwinners for their children; Pakistani women, on the other hand, rarely go out to work and are not generally brought to England until their husbands are in a position to support them.

1. THE COLOURED IMMIGRANT WORK FORCE

A. NUMBERS

One of the most useful ways to assess the number of immigrant workers is to examine the statistics prepared by the Ministry of Pensions and National Insurance (now the Ministry of Social Security) regarding the number of persons who joined the compulsory national insurance scheme over a certain period. Table 10 below, gives a geographical analysis of new entrants to the labour force in the period 1956–63.

TABLE 10*

Geographical analysis of new entrants to labour force, 1956–1963

(A) COMMONWEALTH

Region	Country total	Regional total
(1) *British Isles*		
Channel Islands	3,651	3,651
(2) *Temperate*		
Australia	46,496	
Canada	21,346	
Cyprus	28,967	
New Zealand	17,946	
Malta	7,095	
Gibraltar	1,927	
	———	123,786

* R. B. Davison, *Black British*, p. 66.

[1] The 10% and 100% 1961 Census statistics are subject to two major limitations. In particular, the 'Indian-born' group (and to a lesser extent the 'Pakistan-born' group), in London as elsewhere, includes up to 100,000 white English persons born in that country; their economic, occupational, residential and social patterns are

(A) COMMONWEALTH (continued)

Region	Country total	Regional total
(3) *Asia*		
Pakistan	67,882	
India	61,777	
Malaysia†	11,327	
Hong Kong	12,236	
Ceylon	5,764	
Aden	3,966	
Persian Gulf States	512	
	———	163,464
(4) *Caribbean*		
West Indian Islands	218,907	
British Guiana	13,936	
British Honduras	241	
	———	233,084
(5) *Africa*		
West Africa	38,210	
East Africa	16,330	
Central Africa‡	3,466	
	———	58,006
(6) *Rest of Commonwealth*	8,464	8,464
	Total Commonwealth	590,455

(B) NON-COMMONWEALTH

Region	Country total	Regional total
(1) *Ireland*	397,047	397,047
(2) *Europe*		
Germany (Federal Republic) ...	67,119	
Italy	66,445	
Spain	37,444	
Switzerland	35,750	
France	25,992	
Hungary...	17,166	
Netherlands	13,598	
Denmark	12,093	
Austria	9,523	
Sweden	7,525	
Rest of Europe	29,480	
	———	322,135

† Malaya, Singapore, Sarawak, North Borneo.
‡ Nyasaland, Southern Rhodesia, Zambia.

likely to conform to those of the English professional, managerial and white-collar groups, thus introducing a large element of uncertainty into any statistical generalizations about Indian immigrants. There is also a considerable bias introduced by under-enumeration, particularly in 'twilight' areas of heavy recent settlement, and in the 10% statistics.

(Table 10—continued)

(B) NON-COMMONWEALTH (continued)

Region	Country total	Regional total
(3) *Africa*		
Union of South Africa	29,688	
Rest of Africa	8,707	
	———	38,395
(4) *America*		
United States of America	16,784	
Rest of America	3,583	
	———	20,367
(5) *Asia* (including Middle and Far East)...	12,386	12,386
Total Non-Commonwealth:		790,330
Total World:		1,380,785

Source: Ministry of Pensions and National Insurance.

According to this Table, 43% of those from overseas who joined the labour force in this period came from the Commonwealth, 29% from the Irish Republic, and 28% were aliens. Of those from the Commonwealth, 163,464 came from Asia, 233,084 from the Caribbean, and 58,006 from Africa. If one adds to this an estimated figure of 30,000 workers from the 'coloured' Commonwealth countries who joined the work force between 1964–66 (exact figures are not available) one might conclude that more than half a million coloured workers from overseas have taken up jobs in Britain in the past decade. There are no figures to show how many of these left the national insurance scheme in this period. One might hazard a guess that two or three out of every 100 workers in Britain are coloured, but this would give a misleading picture because, as we shall see below, they are concentrated in particular industries and regions.

B. DISTRIBUTION BY REGIONS AND OCCUPATIONS

The geographical, occupational and socio-economic distribution of workers in the three major immigrant groups differs considerably. Asian workers are most often found in the North and Midlands, in textiles, steel works, some public services, and the manufacture of some engineering and electrical and chemical goods. West Indians, on the other hand, are mostly concentrated in London and the Midlands in a wide range of industries, including light engineering, food manufacture, clothing and footwear, vehicles and chemicals, in public transport, communications, building, laundries, and the nursing profession.

The economic activities in which the smallest proportion—amounting to a bare handful—of coloured workers are found are agriculture, mining and quarrying, shipbuilding, insurance, banking, and finance.

The Occupation Tables compiled from the 10% sample in the 1961 Census show certain significant differences between the distribution of occupations among all economically active persons in England and Wales and among immigrants.

Table 11 illustrates these differences with reference to certain occupations.

TABLE 11

Occupational Distribution (%): Commonwealth and Irish citizens resident in England and Wales (1961) born in specified countries

(A) MALES

	All Persons	Ireland*	India	Pakistan	Caribbean†
Total Economically active	% 100 (14,649,080)	% 100 (297,180)	% 100 (57,490)	% 100 (13,430)	% 100 (58,070)
Certain Occupations					
Farmers, Foresters, Fishermen	5·1	1·8	1·6	0·4	0·3
Miners and quarrymen	3·1	1·2	0·4	0·1	0·5
Woodworkers	2·7	2·9	0·9	0·5	6·3
Textile workers	1·0	0·4	1·5	8·2	1·1
Construction workers	3·5	6·3	0·7	0·1	1·2
Transport and Communication workers	8·4	7·3	8·2	7·4	11·5
Clerical workers	7·1	5·2	12·7	5·3	3·1
Sales workers	8·0	3·5	6·6	4·3	0·8
Administrators and managers	3·8	1·9	4·7	2·2	0·4
Professional and technical workers	8·0	6·2	18·6	8·6	3·2
Labourers	7·5	20·0	6·7	27·6	24·3
Remaining occupations	41·8	43·3	37·4	35·3	47·3

* Includes Northern Ireland and Irish Republic.

† Includes Guyana, Jamaica, Trinidad and Tobago, and other territories in the British Caribbean.

(TABLE 11—continued)

(B) FEMALES

	All Persons	Ireland	India	Pakistan	Caribbean
Total Economically active	% 100 (7,045,390)	% 100 (152,660)	% 100 (23,630)	% 100 (1,270)	% 100 (31,540)
Certain Occupations					
Textile workers	3·6	1·7	0·5	0	1·8
Clothing workers	5·1	2·5	2·7	0	11·8
Clerical workers	25·9	15·9	39·2	36·2	6·6
Sales workers	12·7	7·8	6·1	7·9	1·0
Professional and technical workers	10·0	20·1	22·3	36·2	22·6
Labourers	1·3	1·8	0·8	0·8	4·3
Remaining occupations	41·4	50·2	28·4	18·9	51·9

Source: General Register Office, *Census 1961: Occupation Tables* (10% sample), H.M.S.O., 1966.

Perhaps the most striking occupational pattern that emerges from this Table is that Pakistani men and Caribbean-born men and women are over-concentrated in labouring jobs. But it is to be observed that (white) men born in Ireland are in much the same position.

Another feature is that persons from the Caribbean seem hardly to be represented in sales work (involving contact with the public); they are also greatly under-represented as clerical workers. On the other hand, the heavy concentration of Caribbean-born women in the professional bracket is not surprising in view of the large number who have gone into nursing.

The figures for those born in India must as usual be considered in the light of the shortcomings of the 10% sample and above all the fact that for England and Wales as a whole, more than 40% of the total actually enumerated were probably white English people (see p. 132, n[1]). This would help to explain the fact that among Indian males there is a higher proportion of clerical workers, administrators and managers, and professional workers than is the case with the population as a whole.

C. SOCIO-ECONOMIC STATUS

Figures from the 10% 1961 Census are available which show the socio-economic grouping of persons born in Jamaica, the rest of the British Caribbean, India, Pakistan, Africa (other than South Africa),

Cyprus, and Malta, who were residing in the six major conurbations (Tyneside, West Yorkshire, S.E. Lancashire, Merseyside, West Midlands, Greater London). When these figures are compared with the socio-economic groupings of the population of England and Wales as a whole the differences are so small, in most instances, that little purpose would be served by showing them here. The only important difference that emerges is that, while 18·3% of male immigrants working in these conurbations were unskilled manual workers, only 9·3% of the overall total of economically active males were classified in this category.

The only detailed analysis of these figures which has been published is that by R. B. Davison[1] in respect of twenty-eight London boroughs. For each separate birthplace the economically active males (aged 15 years and over) were classified into six broad occupational categories, in order of prestige and social class. The table so constructed by R. B. Davison is reproduced as Table 12.

TABLE 12

Occupations of Males (%)

OCCUPATIONAL GROUP	BIRTHPLACES England	Jamaica	Caribbean	India	Pakistan	Poland	Ireland	Cyprus
1. Professional	3	*	1	14	10	7	2	1
2. Employers and managers	9	1	1	10	11	13	3	10
3. Foreman, skilled manual, own account	36	39	33	18	11	34	30	36
4. Non-manual	23	4	10	34	23	17	13	6
5. Personal service; semi-skilled manual, agricultural	15	22	24	13	24	18	20	30
6. Unskilled manual; armed forces and others	14	34	30	10	21	12	31	18
	3,552†	1,389	1,250	1,097	211	1,258	6,143	883

* Below 0·5%. † 1 in 25 sample.

Source: 10% Census analysis.

Table 12 shows that the two West Indian groups, together with the Irish, are found in very low proportions in the highest occupational categories. In the lowest categories there are more West Indians,

[1] R. B. Davison, *Black British*, p. 70.

Pakistanis, and Cypriots than in the top two categories. Proportionately more males born in the Caribbean, Pakistan, Ireland, and Cyprus than those born in England were engaged in unskilled manual occupations. Similarly, proportionately more men born in the Caribbean, Pakistan, Cyprus, Poland, and Ireland than those born in England were working as barmen, maids, cooks, and hairdressers, or were in semi-skilled manual and agricultural occupations. The proportion of men born in all these countries who were foremen, skilled manual workers, and persons working on their own account closely resembles the proportion among the English.

The figures for Indians in the top four occupational categories must once again be interpreted in the light of the limitations outlined earlier. Moreover, the figure of 55% given for Pakistanis in the top four categories, which is higher than that for the Jamaicans, other West Indians, and the Irish, is certainly unreliable in respect of Pakistanis as a whole; very few were included in the Greater London sample, most of them having settled in the North. Here again an unknown number of English people born in what is now Pakistan may be clouding the picture.

D. SOME SPECIFIC STUDIES OF THE DISTRIBUTION OF IMMIGRANT WORKERS

The Census figures can be checked against various other sources of information about immigrant workers. Table 13, below, summarizes the findings of a number of studies and reports, mostly localized, containing information about coloured immigrant workers. These are of varying scope and precision; they include sample surveys, social anthropological field-reports, reports by voluntary organizations, specially commissioned area reports, and so on. The sources of information are also variable: they include employers and a variety of local sources. In assessing the reliability of the results obtained it must be remembered that there is a human tendency for a person to exaggerate the importance of the job that he is doing, so that the proportion of unskilled labour might well be higher than that indicated in the figures. Moreover, the basis of classification of persons as 'skilled' and 'unskilled' is by no means uniform. No summary can do justice to these studies. But they all appear to confirm that:

(a) coloured workers are concentrated in unskilled and semi-skilled manual labour and this tendency is more pronounced among Pakistanis and Indians than among West Indians.

(b) It is relatively rare for West Indians to be engaged in white-collar work and even rarer in the case of Pakistanis and Indians (although there is evidence from other sources that Indian girls are beginning to move into this field).

(c) There are important differences between various areas and industries: for example, in Sheffield Pakistanis are concentrated as labourers in steel works and heavy engineering. In Halifax, on the other hand, although engineering is the second largest industry, very few Pakistanis are employed in it, most of them being labourers and machine-minders in textile factories.

TABLE 13

Summary of selected studies relating to the occupational and/or socio-economic status of coloured immigrants*

Area	Nature of sample or group	Occupational or socio-economic status	
1. England	2,956 interviews among Commonwealth immigrants	(a) *All Commonwealth immigrants*	
		unskilled manual	37%
		skilled	18%
		semi-skilled	11%
		professional and business	9%
		other	25%
		(b) *West Indians*	
		unskilled manual	37%
		semi-skilled	17%
		skilled	19%
		professional and business	2%
		other	25%
		(c) *Indians*	
		unskilled manual	27%
		semi-skilled	12%
		skilled	16%
		professional and business	25%
		other	20%
		(d) *Cypriots*	
		unskilled manual	36%
		semi-skilled	12%
		skilled	21%
		professional and business	23%
		other	8%

* Table 13 was put together by Bob Hepple for his briefing *The Position of Coloured Workers in British Industry*, Report for the Conference on Racial Equality in Employment, N.C.C.I., 1967, on which, in general, this section has drawn very heavily.

(TABLE 13—continued)

Area	Nature of sample or group	Occupation or socio-economic status		
2. England	108 male and 126 female Jamaican immigrants		M	F
			%	%
		unskilled	44	24
		machine operators, etc.	12	24
		semi-skilled	40	36
		clerical	—	2
		others	4	14
			100	100
3. Slough	61 firms employing 872 coloured immigrants	unskilled		34·4%
		semi-skilled		54·1%
		skilled		8·3%
4. Manchester	51 firms employing 735 Negroes (mostly West Africans)	unskilled		55%
		semi-skilled		44%
		skilled		1%
5. Sheffield	3,066 coloured immigrants (West Indians mainly in transport)	labourers		2,002
		factory workers		90
		transport		347
6. Halifax	Pakistanis (900 of all ages)	Mainly unskilled and semi-skilled in textiles		
7. Huddersfield	West Indians (60%), Pakistanis (33%), Punjabi Sikhs and other Indians (7%)	Mainly unskilled and semi-skilled manual labour. West Indians especially in textiles. Indians in foundries and brickworks. Pakistanis especially in textiles.		
8. Nottingham	174 West Indians in 30 firms	(a) *Manual*		
		skilled		16·1%
		semi-skilled		32·8%
		unskilled		47·1%
		(b) *White Collar*		4·0%
9. Smethwick	Mainly Punjabi Sikhs	Mainly in unskilled jobs in foundries. A few craftsmen, bus conductors, and teachers.		

Area	Nature of sample or group	Occupational or socio-economic status	
10. Midlands	100 Indians	factory labourers	47
		assembly line	7
		bus workers	15
		postal workers	12
		clerks, etc.	11
		apprentices	2
		chemists	2
		self-employed	4

Sources:

1. Economist Intelligence Unit, *Studies on Immigration from the Commonwealth. 4. The Employment of Immigrants*, 1961.
2. R. B. Davison, *Black British*, Table 36, p. 74.
3. W. H. Israel, *Colour and Community*, Slough Council of Social Services, 1964.
4. Janet Reid, *Employment of Negroes in Manchester*, *Sociological Review* (NS), Vol. 4, no. 2, December 1956, pp. 119–211.
5. Ruth Slade, I.R.R. *Newsletter*, July 1965 (Supplement).
6. Bryan Hartley, I.R.R. *Newsletter*, February 1965 (Supplement).
7. John Goodall, I.R.R. *Newsletter*, October 1966 (Supplement).
8. F. J. Bayliss and J. B. Coates, *West Indians at Work in Nottingham*, *Race*, Vol. VII, No. 2, 1965, pp. 157–166; Daniel Lawrence, I.R.R. *Newsletter*, June 1966 (Supplement).
9. Roger Bell, I.R.R. *Newsletter*, September 1966 (Supplement).
10. Rashmi Desai, *Indian Immigrants in Britain*, p. 68.

E. THE 'BEAT-THE-BAN' IMMIGRANTS (1961–2)

There was a large influx of immigrants from the Commonwealth to 'beat the ban' in the eighteen-month period (1 January 1961 to 30 June 1962) immediately preceding the passing and coming into operation of the Commonwealth Immigrants Act. It would be useful to have accurate information about the socio-economic status of these 230,000 arrivals (including 98,100 from the West Indies, 42,800 from India, and 50,180 from Pakistan) because this may have made a significant difference to the social status of the immigrant population as reflected in the 1961 Census and in local studies before that date. Since the Act came into operation information has been available from the Ministry of Labour about the occupations of Commonwealth immigrants to whom vouchers are issued for the purpose of taking up jobs (though not all vouchers have been used).

Unfortunately, very little is known about the socio-economic status of those entering the country during the period in which there was this statistical gap. The only research on this matter has been in Huddersfield, where 52% of the male Pakistanis resident there in 1964 had arrived in the period January 1961 to June 1962. A sample taken by Mr. John Goodall revealed that although technically most of these Pakistanis could be described as of the *Zamindar* land-owning class, they came from family holdings so small that they were virtually landless and impoverished. Their educational attainment and literacy levels were generally low and, without exception, on coming to England they went into unskilled and semi-skilled jobs.

As for the West Indians, the total entering in 1961 was 61,600,[1] as compared with 52,700 in 1960. Of this number 28,900 were men, 27,600 women, and 5,100 children, as compared with 29,600, 19,900, and 3,200 respectively in 1960. These show no panic increase of male migration but a continued acceleration of migration by dependent women and children, probably influenced by fears of controls. Since so many of these newcomers were dependants there is no reason to suppose that they radically altered the socio-economic or occupational structure of the existing West Indian settlement.[2] This is a supposition which cannot be extended to the Indian and Pakistani newcomers, few of whom were dependants at this time. There are, however, some reasons for thinking that West Indian migrants of the years immediately preceding the imposition of controls were increasingly drawn from the less skilled occupations and the rural areas.

It has been contended that the majority of arrivals from all new Commonwealth countries in this period were of low socio-economic status, and they would naturally tend to be concentrated in the lowest occupational groups in Britain. It must, however, be admitted that there is no global information available for testing the accuracy of this contention.

F. THE STATUS OF THOSE ENTERING SINCE 1 JULY 1962

After the passing of the Commonwealth Immigrants Act 1962, immigrants coming to Britain to work had to be in possession of a Ministry of Labour employment voucher. These vouchers were in three categories. Category 'A' was for applications by employers who have a specific job, whether skilled or unskilled, to offer a particular immigrant; Category 'B' was for those without a specific job to come to but with certain special qualifications; and Category 'C' was for all others. During 1965 no vouchers in Category 'C' were issued, and after 2 August 1965, this category was discontinued. After that date

[1] Estimates from the West Indies Migrant Services Division, published in Sheila Patterson, *Dark Strangers*, London, Tavistock Press, 1963, Appendix II.

[2] Even less is known about the West Indian arrivals in the first half of 1962, other than that there was a net gain of 31,800.

the list of special qualifications eligible under Category 'B' was also reduced, and limited to doctors, dentists, trained nurses, qualified teachers,[1] graduates in science and technology with a minimum of two years' experience since graduation, and certain professionally qualified non-graduates with similar experiences. This has meant the exclusion of shorthand typists, arts graduates, and building trades craftsmen, who previously qualified under Category 'B'. Malta received 1,000 vouchers a year (reviewed and extended in 1967) and all other Commonwealth countries were allocated 7,500 a year. Not more than 15% of Category 'A' vouchers might go to any one country (apart from Malta). In 1962, 75% of the vouchers issued in respect of the principal 'coloured' Commonwealth countries were in Category 'C' (unskilled—quota). In 1963 this proportion dropped to 63% and in 1964 to 9%. In 1965, as pointed out above, this category was abandoned altogether. Table 14, below, analyses the occupations in respect of which Category 'A' vouchers were issued in 1965 and 1966 in respect of the West Indies, India, and Pakistan.

TABLE 14

Commonwealth Immigrants Act, 1962. Category 'A' Vouchers issued. Occupations as percentage of Vouchers issued.

	WEST INDIES		INDIA		PAKISTAN	
	1965	1966 1st half	1965	1966 1st half	1965	1966 1st half
	%	%	%	%	%	%
Teachers	0·03	0·01	1·13	0	0	0
Nurses	5·30	0·21	1·78	0	0·34	0·67
Doctors*	0·15	0	3·48	0	0·14	0
Other grades and professions	0·34	0	7·36	3·17	0·95	2·67
Draughtsmen, etc. ...	0·89	1·32	9·22	13·29	1·29	0·67
Shorthand Typists ...	0·25	0·66	2·75	1·27	0·29	0
Shop Assistants ...	1·14	0·44	4·45	1·90	3·52	1·33
Waiters and Kitchen staff	31·46	41·32	5·82	2·53	27·00	21·33
Domestic staff ...	6·29	3·96	1·86	1·27	0·88	1·33
Unskilled factory workers	19·28	16·04	26·92	35·45	39·65	44·00
Others	34·86	36·04	35·25	41·15	26·05	28·00
TOTAL	100% (3,242)	100% (455)	100% (1,237)	100% (158)	100% (1,478)	100% (150)

* There was no separate category for doctors in 1966.

Source: Ministry of Labour

[1] See section on Education, pp. 279–84, for a more detailed discussion of the position of immigrant teachers.

From this Table it appears that the bulk of the vouchers in this category were in respect of unskilled occupations and service industries. However, all the Category 'B' vouchers issued in respect of these countries were to persons with skills. When these 'B' vouchers are added to the number of 'A' vouchers issued in respect of skilled jobs, the proportion of skilled persons in the total number of persons granted vouchers is as follows:

1965	–	55%
1966 (first half)	–	76%

This indicates that a large proportion of those entering for work from the 'coloured' Commonwealth possessed skills. If this trend continues the effect might be an increasing polarization, with the bulk of the immigrant population (i.e. those who arrived before 1962) at the bottom end of the jobs scale and most of those entering since 1962 in the top professional and skilled categories.

The bulk of Category 'A' vouchers were thus issued for unskilled jobs and service industries. However, the figures for the issue of Category 'B' vouchers give a different picture. All 'B' vouchers issued were to persons with professional skills and in 1966 the numbers were respectively: India—3,976 (including 667 teachers, 1,511 doctors, 469 science graduates, 922 technology graduates); Pakistan—629 (including 149 teachers, 282 doctors, and 108 science graduates); West Indies—39.

Taking the total of persons with skills or professional qualifications to whom Category 'A' or 'B' vouchers were issued in 1965 and 1966 in these three groups, it emerges that of those entitled to enter Britain recently from the 'coloured' Commonwealth, 55% and 76% respectively had some skills or professional qualifications. In the case of the two Asian groups this suggests that there may be a certain polarization within each group, with the bulk of its membership, those who arrived before 1962, at the lower end of the jobs scale and most of those who have entered since 1962 entitled at least formally to enter the higher professional and skilled levels.[1] This trend is not evident among the West Indians, but their concentration in the Category 'A' lists suggests an element of selection that would put the post-1962 arrivals at least on the same socio-economic and occupational levels as their predecessors.

G. OTHER CHARACTERISTICS OF IMMIGRANT WORK-GROUPS

An account of the general socio-cultural and economic backgrounds of the major immigrant groups has already been given.[2] Here, however, it

[1] In the case of Category 'B' voucher holders there has sometimes been a problem of equivalent qualifications, notably among science and technology graduates and teachers, which could lead to some down-grading.

[2] See pp. 6–11 (above) and earlier in this chapter.

is appropriate to consider briefly those factors that are of particular importance in the sphere of employment, as influencing both the extent and level of the first generation's absorption in the economy and the life chances of their children. These factors include educational background, language, occupational skills and qualifications, employment experience and patterns, and expectations. In most of these there are considerable differences between the three main immigrant groups with which we are mainly concerned.

(i) *West Indians: Educational and Vocational Background*

The majority of West Indian immigrants are Jamaicans[1] and while it is probable that most of them had reached somewhat higher educational standards than the average, they would still be likely to be lower than the average in the U.K. For instance, a survey conducted under the auspices of the University College of the West Indies among persons collecting their passports during a seven-week period in 1961 in Kingston, Jamaica,[2] showed the following levels attained on leaving full-time day school:

Of the *men* interviewed:

4% had no education
16% had grades 1–3
78% had grades 4–6
2% had secondary education
5% had further education

Among the women standards were slightly higher.

In this context language must be regarded as a vocational skill. Although the majority of West Indians speak English as their first and only language, their speech frequently differs significantly from standard English. This can make communication between them and fellow-workers difficult on both sides. Moreover, in some jobs, incomprehensibility can cause risk to life or property. There is an additional drawback of functional illiteracy among those with less education.

As for other vocational skills and qualifications, it is also almost certainly true that most West Indian mass immigrants in Britain are above the British Caribbean average, but below the British average. Information on this subject is, however, patchy and discrepant, but some conclusions may be drawn from a comparison of the degree of industrialization and urbanization, and the number of apprenticeships, technical school and similar places available in Britain and the West Indies respectively.[3] As for the immigrants themselves, the surveys carried out

[1] Educational standards in Barbados and some other islands are higher than in Jamaica.

[2] Reported by R. B. Davison, *West Indian Migrants*, p. 19.

[3] For more details and references see *Dark Strangers*, Penguin, pp. 67–8.

by W. F. Maunder and by the Institute of Social and Economic Research of the University College of the West Indies in collaboration with the Central Bureau of Statistics in Kingston, Jamaica, over the years 1953–5 gave some useful data about the labour history of the migrants leaving for Britain at that time. This included the information that 34% of two groups of emigrants totalling 794 people had left their jobs a year or more before emigrating, while 7% (mainly women) had not worked for three years or more.

Statistics relating to the industrial classification and earnings of this particular group of emigrants showed that, of the males, 23% had come from agriculture and fishing, 31% from manufacturing, 10% from building and construction, 15% from commerce and public utilities, 10% from services, 4% from transport, storage, and communications, and 8% from unclassified occupations. Average earnings ranged between 37s. and 86s. per week, the mean being 57s. Of the women, 8% had come from commerce and public utilities, 23% from services, 8% from unclassified occupations, and 61% from 'manufacturing'. According to the article, this last high proportion was accounted for 'in major part by those whose occupation was defined as "handicraft workers"; the majority in fact were dressmakers and milliners'. Average earnings among the women ranged narrowly between 31s. and 37s., the mean being 35s. per week.

The Department of Labour in Dominica gave the following figures for employment status as claimed by those emigrating to Britain between 1955–1960.[1] Of those in employment, 42% claimed they were unskilled and 34% that they were skilled. The remainder were domestic servants (15%) or in clerical or professional work. Dr. Davison commented that, without some simple trade testing scheme, and allowing for understandable exaggeration for prestige purposes and hopes of future employment, these figures were of very doubtful value as an accurate assessment of real skills.

There is a wide difference of opinion as to the distribution and degree of skills among the West Indian migrants in Britain. This is due mainly to the considerable divergence between the requirements and training opportunities of the two economies, which has resulted in contradictory estimates, according to whether these are based on the migrant's own statement of his skills and former occupation (which in turn may be slightly embellished in the telling), or on the actual work being done in Britain by migrants—or again, on British assessments of their abilities (in which case one must allow for the fact that recent immigrants usually start at the bottom of the work ladder and that local assessments may be somewhat more pejorative than the facts justify).

[1] Reported by R. B. Davison, *West Indian Migrants*, p. 20.

An indication of the divergence between British and Jamaican standards of skill is perhaps afforded by the fact that in 1954 about thirty illiterate migrants claimed to be 'skilled', and another sixty-five in 1955. Over the three-year period, moreover, the number of unskilled migrants from rural areas and of illiterates showed a steady increase, and the Roberts–Mills report anticipated that this trend would continue in later years.

Another source of information about the migrants' skills is based on assessment at the British end. For instance, a memorandum sent to the Trades Union Congress by the Ministry of Labour Staff Association gave the following rough estimate of the division of skills among West Indian work-seekers: skilled—13%; semi-skilled—22%; unskilled—65%. How this estimate was arrived at is not clear, but it seems to have been based on a countrywide consensus of estimates and placing experience drawn from members at local labour exchanges in 1954.

Janet Reid in her study of *Negroes in Industry in Manchester* (unpublished report) found that the 735 coloured workers involved in her survey (just under 15% of the estimated coloured population of Manchester in 1954–5) were distributed in industry as follows: 1% skilled; 44% semi-skilled; 55% unskilled. These figures were, of course, based not on the migrants' own statements but on other people's statements about their status. Other surveys based on migrants' own statements (e.g., *Newcomers in Britain* by Ruth Glass) showed a higher percentage of migrants claiming skilled and non-manual occupations and suggested considerable economic downgrading. On the other hand, R. B. Davison, investigating the occupational claims of applicants for passports at the Jamaican end in 1961, found it a 'somewhat futile exercise' without some simple trade testing scheme, and wrote: 'The great majority of the West Indian migrants are, by British standards, unskilled or semi-skilled workers.' A later survey of immigrants in Croydon industry (carried out for the Institute of Race Relations by Sheila Patterson) found no great evidence of genuine downgrading.[1]

The divergences between self-assessments and estimates by British employers and other agencies emphasize the conflict which frequently exists between the initial expectations of the migrants and their actual placing and work experience in Britain.[2]

[1] A survey conducted among 2,956 Commonwealth and Irish immigrants (main groups: 1,516 Irish, 603 West Indians, 236 Australians, 268 Cypriots, 165 Pakistanis) for the Economist Intelligence Unit in 1961 (Studies on Immigration from the Commonwealth—4) found that the number of immigrants engaged in skilled and semi-skilled work rose after arrival in England.

[2] For more details of first generation West Indian migrants' expectations and attitudes to work see *Dark Strangers*, Penguin, pp. 71–6.

(ii) *Indians: Educational and Vocational Background*

The great majority of Indian immigrants come from two distinct regions of India, the Punjab and Gujarat, both of which are traditional areas of emigration. Most of them are farm workers or craftsmen, whose labour on the family land or in the family business ceased to be necessary. They retain their membership in the extended family and the village-kin group, from whose representatives in Britain they will seek help in finding accommodation and work.

Little detailed information is as yet available about the educational and vocational background of the bulk of Indian immigrants.[1] Certainly few have been in industrial employment in India and many craftsmen may find their crafts not recognized in Britain. Status in India may affect job preference here—for instance, members of some castes might seek lower-paid clerical work rather than industrial work. Language is, however, a serious barrier. The great majority of Gujaratis are literate in Gujarati and may have some acquaintance with written English. Their spoken English is usually poor and difficult for them to improve. The same is true of Punjabis, though slightly more are likely to be illiterate in their own language.

(iii) *Pakistanis: Educational and Vocational Background*

Apart from an educated Pakistani minority, most Pakistani immigrants come from a landless and impoverished rural background. Their educational and literacy levels are lower than those of the Indians (the 1961 literacy figure for Pakistan was 15·3%, the national all-India figure 23%—higher, however, in the Punjab and Gujarat). Their skills are generally thought to be rather lower than those found among Indian immigrants. Few of them speak or write English on their arrival in Britain. There is some evidence that many fulfil their intention of staying five years, earning enough money to buy land or a business and returning home, to be replaced by a son, brother, or other male kinsman, who takes over their house, job, and position in the immigrant community.

H. WORKING PATTERNS

The differences in geographical and occupational distribution of the three main immigrant groups have already been mentioned. There are also great differences in the working patterns of the West Indians on the one side and the two Asian groups on the other. The individualistic English-speaking West Indians are mostly dispersed widely through industry in firms which may operate a low informal quota. It is the

[1] For more details of the minority of professionals, see above, p. 143–4.

practice of most successful employers interviewed to disperse them over their departments and work units, and to integrate them as individuals.

Most members of the two Asian groups are, for a variety of reasons, including traditional industrial ties, the language barrier and the persistence of the extended village-kin group in the migrant situation, employed in industries such as textiles which lend themselves to an ethnic gang system, with English-speaking 'straw bosses' or go-betweens. In consequence, whole departments, usually concerned with the hardest, least skilled, lowest-paid processes, have become virtually segregated in a two-tier labour hierarchy, between whose components there is not and cannot be much communication or sense of working community. The consequences of this are likely to be manifold. Apart from the kind of industrial disputes that occurred at Courtaulds in Preston and Woolfs in Southall,[1] there is little inducement to break through the language barrier, the arrangement is likely to be self-perpetuating, and the particular immigrants are more rigidly typed than the West Indians; thus the younger and second generations could find it even more difficult to be considered for the plum jobs, apprenticeships and traineeships for which the children of skilled or long-term workers are often preferred.

I. INDUSTRIAL ABSORPTION

No overall comparative material is as yet available about the extent to which members of the three major groups have been absorbed in industry. A minority of English-speaking Indians and Pakistanis with acceptable skills have moved out and away from the type of employment just described, and have established themselves as individuals in skilled, white-collar and technical jobs. For the great majority, who only arrived in the years after 1961, it would perhaps be too early to expect much outward dispersal and upward movement.[2]

For the West Indians, who began to arrive in considerable numbers in the 1950s, more evidence is available. It may be useful to summarize the findings of studies of two rather different South London areas, Brixton and Croydon, in the years 1955–8 and 1958–60.[3]

In most cases the reactions of managements, unions, and fellow-workers to coloured workers were conditioned by a complex of factors,

[1] See I.R.R. *Newsletter* Supplements on the Courtaulds dispute (July 1965) and on Woolfs at Southall (January 1967).

[2] The study by Peter Wright gives much more information about the employment of Asian workers in the North and Midlands (*The Employment of Coloured Workers in British Industry*, O.U.P. for I.R.R., 1968). Desai's study of Gujaratis in Birmingham (*Indian Immigrants in Britain*) also has a section on employment.

[3] Patterson, *Dark Strangers*, Tavistock.
Patterson, *Immigrants in Industry*, O.U.P. for I.R.R., 1968.

including: suspicion of an untried labour source; received notions connecting dark pigmentation with low status and low potential; the fact that many coloured workers conformed to the stereotypes and that many who claimed skills failed to meet the craft qualifications; language and cultural differences and difficulties; and at times a chip-on-the-shoulder colour-consciousness among the immigrants.

Nevertheless, in Brixton, and still more in Croydon, it was found that over the years the barriers were not hardening but becoming more permeable and elastic. Utilitarian considerations were prevailing and a *modus vivendi* was being established. Firms that had previously refused to take coloured workers had begun to do so.

Moreover, firms that had threatened prior redundancy for coloured workers in the event of a recession had in fact stuck to 'last in—first out'. Coloured workers with needed skills or good local references were finding the appropriate jobs without much trouble. Informal quotas (between 3 and 10% in most of South London) were being relaxed as immigrant workers became less footloose, joined the unions, and generally conformed to the 'culture' of a particular work-place or industry.

In Croydon, a progressive, expanding, labour-hungry area, the industrial climate was more favourable[1] and there were some West Indian shop stewards and a handful of charge-hands. There was also a fair sprinkling of coloured white-collar workers and some technicians. Even here, however, with the emphasis on skills and suitability rather than colour, the West Indians were not being integrated as fast or completely as the Poles and Anglo-Indians who had preceded them. At that time there were few West Indian school-leavers but a 1966 inquiry showed that a number of private employment agencies were refusing to accept them as clients or were finding it difficult to place them in the many new offices established in Croydon over the last few years.

Thus, although the industrial barriers have creaked back for some coloured migrants, the process does not appear to be going far or fast enough. The next decade will see a crucial race between the hardening of stereotypes about colour and lack of skills and the actual movement of first- and second-generation immigrants out of the worst paid, least attractive jobs into all sections of industry and skill levels.

J. THE YOUNGER AND SECOND GENERATION

It has already been pointed out that the vast majority of younger immigrants already in or just entering the labour market are not true

[1] See also Bayliss, F. J. and Coates, J. B., 'West Indians at Work in Nottingham', *Race*, October 1965.

'second-generation' immigrants. Instead they are young first-generation immigrants, many of whom may only have been in Britain a few years, have not had a full schooling here, may not speak English properly, and are in other important respects not equipped to compete for jobs on an equal basis with local school-leavers.[1]

Meanwhile, they are perpetuating and strengthening the stereotype linking dark colour and lack of skills which has been associated with adult immigrants. Thus, as British-born and British-educated coloured school-leavers begin to come on the labour market they may have an increasingly difficult task to persuade employers that they can meet local standards for skilled and white-collar work. They face other drawbacks. One is the fact that traineeships and apprenticeships are in short supply and usually go to the children of skilled and long-term local workers. Another is that many members of even a true second generation, particularly if their elders have migrated recently or live in areas of heavy ethnic settlement, may not be fully acculturated in British society, or only in a self-segregating or deprived section of it. These children will nevertheless have far greater expectations than their parents, which may be frustrated both by the effects of their home backgrounds and by the hardening of employment barriers against them.

There is also a third group of young people: those born of one immigrant and one local parent (the latter usually being a woman). When the parents are married the family usually remains within the immigrant parent's community, so that the child can be described as second generation.[2] There are, however, many cases in which the child is the abandoned product of casual association by a local woman with a coloured man: in such cases he is likely to grow up within the majority society, but doubly deprived as a visible outsider among other parentless children.

The size of the potential problem was indicated in the 1967 returns from local education authorities to the Department of Education and Science.[3] This gave the following totals for children from the major immigrant groups in primary (and secondary) schools: 73,600 West Indians, 32,100 Indians, 11,900 Pakistanis, 13,900 Cypriots. This was certainly an under-estimate, as the returns came only from schools with ten or more immigrant children. The total has undoubtedly increased since then, as more children of school age have arrived to join their

[1] The C.I.A.C.'s Third Report (Cmnd 2458) deals entirely with the problems of young immigrant school-leavers and work-seekers. See also discussion 9 December 1966, H. C., Hansard, col. 1722.

[2] Reference here is rather to the children of working-class parents. The products of mixed marriages in the professional classes seem more likely to gravitate to the host society.

[3] See Report of Central Advisory Council for Education in *Children and their Primary Schools* (H.M.S.O., 1966), for 1966 figures.

parents, and more children have been born (the birth-rate among adult immigrants is considerably higher than for the general population). A recent estimate of the total number of children born to coloured immigrants in Britain was 200,000.[1]

Another indication of the size of the problem came from the Inner London Education Authority, whose count in mid-1966 showed 2,000 coloured children aged 15 and an increasing number in each age-group below, down to a total of over 6,600 aged 5. By the mid-seventies, it was reported that one in every six school-leavers in Central London would be coloured, with a similar proportion in Birmingham.[2]

The education which these children are receiving will be outlined in the appropriate chapter. Here we may survey briefly some of the evidence available about the qualifications for placing and acceptance of recent coloured school-leavers, the bulk of whom must still be regarded as first-generation immigrants.

In recent years the 'non-discriminatory' rule forbidding the keeping of separate statistics has been relaxed by most education authorities, so that it is increasingly possible to estimate the dimensions of the 'coloured school-leaver problem'. Youth Employment Offices have not, however, been officially permitted to keep such statistics and the Census data do not of course identify the British-born children of immigrants. The 1961 10% Census showed a total of almost 22,000 male Commonwealth immigrants between 15 and 24 years from the coloured Commonwealth countries (including Indian-born) in the working population of the conurbations: of these, 38% were in semi-skilled and unskilled jobs as compared with 22% of British-born youths in the same age-group.

The available material is patchy, inconclusive, and sometimes contradictory. This may to a considerable extent be explained by the fact that it has been collected from two main and very different angles. One approach is from inside the work situation at various levels; the other is from the viewpoint of the immigrants themselves, particularly those claiming to have experienced discrimination.[3] The former approach tends to stress the successful situations and the degree of integration attained; the other inevitably focuses on the experiences of a vocal

[1] Eric Butterworth, 'The School', *New Society*, 16 March 1967, p. 383.

[2] See also Davison, *Black British*, p. 26f., for the high proportion of young children recorded among West Indians in London. The 1961 10% Sample Census showed a total of 33,820 children under 15 (24,450 born in Britain, 9,370 elsewhere) in households with the head or spouse of head born in the West Indies for the six conurbations. Figures for Greater London alone were 24,640 (17,150 born in Britain, 7,490 elsewhere) (Commonwealth Immigrants in the Conurbations—Table B.5). It is hard to relate these totals to those from other sources.

[3] See successive C.A.R.D. reports and third report of the Race Relations Committee, Society for Labour Lawyers, November 1966 (Appendix I).

minority of those who failed to get in or get on, often in a variety and combination of reasons which tend to be presented as straightforward racial discrimination.

There is a fairly general consensus of opinion that it takes longer and is often more difficult to place coloured girls and boys in employment than white youngsters. An *Observer* check of London Youth Employment Offices in the late summer of 1966[1] showed that whereas coloured teenagers could be placed with little difficulty in 'white' areas, white youngsters in 'deprived' areas of heavy immigrant settlement such as Notting Hill, Paddington, and Islington, were almost five times more likely to get skilled jobs than coloured youngsters. In one such London area half the available jobs listed at a busy youth employment office were barred to coloured youngsters, and 'N.C.' for 'No Coloured' (although officially forbidden) was reported to have appeared on the cards of fifty-two firms out of 147, while another twenty-two were said to be unlikely to accept them. Most vacancies for trainee draughtsmen were N.C., as were fourteen out of twenty-seven clerical jobs. Some youth employment offices were said to put green stars (cut in half for Cypriots and Pakistanis in one area) to indicate that an applicant was coloured. Other identifying marks in use were: black star for Borstal, red star for educationally sub-normal, red disc for physically handicapped, yellow disc for deaf or blind. Firms that would employ coloured labour were said to be labelled as such, and there was a tendency to send too many coloured applicants in proportion to white, until they either put on quotas or became 'black firms'.

Similar though less overt resistance to coloured school-leavers was reported by Anne Lapping, after a brief survey of Brixton and Croydon in early 1967 for *New Society*.[2] She also found a widespread reluctance among teachers and youth employment officers on the one side and immigrant teenagers on the other to discuss cases of possible discrimination. This she attributed to the fact that discrimination at present is not dramatic: it does not involve many brilliant school-leavers being turned down for plum jobs, but rather a large number of average and below-average children from secondary modern schools who seem more vulnerable than others to setbacks and rejection. Large firms and publicly controlled establishments were found to be more liberal in policy and practice. Teachers were reported to feel that 'it is more important to give coloured children a feeling of security in school than to give them direct warning about problems they are likely to come up

[1] Colin McGlashan (*Observer*, 25 September 1966).

[2] 'A Hardening Colour Bar?' Pt. 1, 'The Faces' published on 16 March 1967. The other three parts (2. 'The Jobs' by Sheila Patterson; 3. 'The School' by Eric Butterworth; and 4. 'The Law' by a legal correspondent) contain considerable material which has been drawn on elsewhere in this chapter.

against later outside'. The writer went on to discuss the problems of youth employment officers in putting pressure on employers, when private employment agencies would supply white labour without discussion.

The question of preparing coloured children to meet prejudice and discrimination in employment and the outside world (raised in Anne Lapping's article mentioned above) was discussed in 'Racial Integration and Barnardo's', the report of a working party published in 1966. Section XV on 'After-care, Lodgings and Employment' reads as follows:

> Our coloured children are most likely to meet their first serious experience of racial discrimination after they have left the protection of a Branch Home and seek employment and lodgings.
>
> Ideally we would want the children in our care to form such a relationship with a family that the problem of finding lodgings is solved before it arises. However, this cannot always be achieved.
>
> We received evidence which suggests that, in general, lodgings are more difficult to find for coloured children than employment, and it has been suggested that in the absence of strong preference concerning employment the correct sequence for the Welfare Officer helping a coloured school leaver is to find satisfactory lodgings and then to seek employment within easy travelling distance. We accept this view. While it is desirable for Welfare Officers to know all school leavers as well as they can, it is particularly necessary for them to make contact early with coloured children.
>
> We consider that an unnaturally severe strain is placed on any school leaver in our care who has to leave both his school and his Branch Home simultaneously. This strain is not normally imposed on a child in a private family. The difficulties are particularly acute if lodgings present a serious problem, as they do for most coloured children. The problem is also accentuated if a Branch Home is situated in a remote area. Good child care demands that a child should have security and continuity, but our present practice with school leavers can often conflict with this principle.
>
> It is hard for any child to sever contact at the same time with all who have brought him up, his friends, his school, his church, his social activities, and all that is familiar to him, and to adjust to a new kind of life in an adult world of lodgings and employment. A coloured child's first experience of discrimination and prejudice when he seeks lodgings or a job will add to the hardship he is undergoing at this time. We would recommend any practicable measures aimed at helping ease this stress.
>
> One possible way of doing this is that the child should be given the opportunity, during the last school holidays and during week-ends of the last school term, to stay in the lodgings where we hope to place him after he leaves school. Experiments on these lines, which we would like Barnardo's to copy, are already being conducted by the National Children's Home. We should be willing if necessary to pay a retaining fee for the lodgings selected.
>
> We also believe, that, for a child not concerned with examinations, it may help him if he gets experience of doing a job on Saturdays or during school holidays before he looks for a permanent job. This may be of particular value for a coloured child.

The Barnardo's report went on to discuss the problems of placing coloured school-leavers in work:

Some forms of employment are understood still to have very few openings for coloured staff, e.g. police, banks, insurance, accountancy, retail fashion stores, hairdressers, and some other jobs entailing contact with the public. Coloured candidates are also alleged to be at a disadvantage for apprenticeships, training schemes, and promotion. We do not suggest that Welfare Officers should discuss this in such great detail that the school leavers' self-confidence is undermined, unless he expresses interest in a type of employment which the Welfare Officer believes will be difficult for him to obtain. The Welfare Officer should, however, in assessing each case individually, give due weight to these considerations:

(i) whether the child is, in his view, suitable for the work he aims at, even though his colour will be a disadvantage in getting it;
(ii) whether he has sufficient self-confidence to risk being snubbed.

We believe that no child should be advised to take a job below his capabilities; but that on the other hand no sensitive child should be encouraged to risk rebuffs by applying repeatedly for one kind of work, when he will almost certainly have to be content with an alternative.

We were advised by a Youth Employment Officer working in an area with a heavy immigrant population that much of the alleged discrimination against coloured applicants is based, not on colour, but on first generation immigrants' lower average educational standard, their lack of experience of urban life and industry, and poor command of English. Welfare Officers should, if necessary, be prepared to emphasize to potential employers that our coloured children have had the same education and upbringing that our white children have had, and that this excuse for rejecting coloured applicants is not valid in respect of our children. The Youth Employment Officer said that: 'The best way we can help to prepare our children for the life they will have to cope with on leaving our Homes is to emphasize that they are going out into a competitive world where they will be judged on their education and ability.'

Placings of eighty-one coloured boys in employment between 1956 and 1960 and their subsequent progress were also reported. The types of jobs held were:

Merchant Navy or Armed Forces ...	12
Clerical	4
Craft or skilled	18
Catering	10
Miscellaneous unskilled or semi-skilled ...	37

Many of these boys were children of coloured American soldiers or of one Asian parent, none were fully coloured and only four had one West Indian parent (i.e. they are not typical of the present group of coloured Barnardo's boys). The particulars of progress since leaving care were:

Appears satisfactory	35
Known social difficulties in lodgings, work, sex, mental health, etc. (*not* including known delinquency or convictions)	21 (incl. 2 suicides)
Known social difficulties including convictions ...	25 (incl. 1 deceased)
	81

This information was regarded as 'giving grounds for the deepest concern'. Boys in skilled jobs and boys placed from foster homes had in general settled better. The degree of colour could not be correlated with success or failure, nor could the degree of parental contact. Statistical comparisons with information about white children were not made for this early period, when the coloured boys were only a small fraction of the total. The impressions of the Head of the Department formerly dealing with Boys' After-Care were as follows:

(i) Social difficulties are worse for coloured boys than for white ones, although the proportion of white boys who do not settle well and who have convictions is also disturbingly high. A small sample check was taken on this point which showed that 13 out of the 39 coloured boys who were placed in work in 1960 had subsequent convictions compared with 61 out of 256 white boys who left during the same period.
(ii) A few white boys have done outstandingly well. Some have gone to university, or qualified for a profession, or become established in positions of high responsibility. So far, no coloured boy has done this, although some particularly intelligent and ambitious ones still in care are now aiming at Higher Education. Generally speaking, a job is obtainable for a coloured boy but, so far, our coloured boys have seldom been promoted as rapidly or as far as our white boys.
(iii) Congenial lodgings with a sympathetic landlady are of incalculable value to a boy when he leaves our care. Many, including some apparently difficult boys, have settled very well with kind landladies. Others, who seemed to have no behaviour problems when in our care, found it very hard to settle when their lodgings broke down. Mention has been made of the particular relevance of this for coloured boys, who have greater difficulty than white boys in finding lodgings.

The Barnardo's report incurred critical comment on some points from a specialist group of members of the Immigrants Advisory Committee of the London Council of Social Service (I.A.C. [1966] 8). In general, they felt that the tone of the pamphlet was basically pessimistic and did not look forward to a time when differences in colour and origin would be immaterial. They were also disturbed by the use of the word 'half-caste' for 'coloured', found the cover (showing a caricature of a Negro silhouetted on a white background) unsuitable, and were totally opposed to the idea of advising staff to 'prepare a coloured child to meet racial prejudice and come to terms with his colour'. As for the concern expressed about the future of the child who leaves one of their homes at 16, they shared this worry while feeling that it was not particular to 'immigrant children', but so serious a problem as to warrant a fresh look at the provisions of the Welfare State. In conclusion, the group felt that most of the comments in the report could apply equally to European children as to those of non-European descent coming into care, and what was needed was a reassessment of priorities in relation to child welfare and pressures for more services in this field.

Particular difficulties in placing coloured teenagers (and adult immigrants) have also been reported in the case of banks, insurance companies, and the retail trade. Nevertheless, these avenues are not entirely closed, and in the retail trade and catering in particular, reasonable progress has been reported. For several years now certain big stores and catering establishments have also successfully applied a thin-end-of-the-wedge policy by putting selected coloured employees on to selling, waiting at table, and other 'direct contact' jobs. In certain exclusive clubs in St. James', there have been coloured staff for some years now. As for the white-collar work in general, progress has gone somewhat further than in 'face-to-face' jobs. Its extent varies from area to area: in Brixton, for instance, a well-informed local social worker reported as early as 1963 that West Indian girls with the right qualifications experienced little difficulty in getting white-collar jobs,[1] and the same was reported from Paddington.[2] On the more gloomy side were reports in the same booklet of dissatisfaction with placings among West Indian boys in Willesden, and difficulties in Hackney in getting apprenticeships or traineeships. More disquieting were recent reports from areas of old coloured settlement such as Liverpool, where British-born second- and even third-generation teenagers were said to find themselves automatically selected for semi-skilled or unskilled work.[3]

Some more evidence about discrimination in white-collar and professional jobs was published in the late summer of 1966 by C.A.R.D. This was the outcome of an experiment of sending matched white and coloured grammar-school leavers to try for jobs advertised in banks, insurance companies, and similar establishments; a marked difference was noted in the reception accorded to them by the same firms.

Some rather different findings relating not to the grammar-school

[1] In Tesco's new Brixton supermarket, 50% of the staff was reported to be coloured, as a deliberate policy. (*South London Press*, 8 March 1966.)

[2] *Immigrants in London*, N.C.S.S., 1963, pp. 43–5. Most of the information in this paragraph is taken from this report.

[3] *Colour in Britain*, B.B.C., pp. 83–4.

minority but to the secondary-modern majority of coloured school-leavers were reported from Birmingham in 1966, after Westhill College of Education had conducted its second inquiry into the situation of coloured and white teenagers in areas of heavy immigrant settlement, under the heading 'Operation Integration Two'. This received little publicity at the time but its conclusions are of considerable interest. Their sample totalled 381, of whom 55 were West Indian, 47 Asian, and 281 Birmingham-born whites. Nearly all the coloured respondents were first-generation immigrants, but notwithstanding this their work experience seemed good, and more stable than that of the local teenagers. They were less likely to have grammar or technical school education and less likely to be engaged in 'skilled manual' or 'non-manual skilled' work, disparities that might be attributable to their recent arrival. On the other hand, though few immigrants were apprenticed, the proportion was not very different from that among local boys.[1] The report commented:

> Many of the difficulties of coloured immigrants in Birmingham appear to be general to their social class rather than their colour. The figures suggest that they are suffering some of the 'relative deprivations' of the urban working-class youngster in the older neighbourhood. (Though it must be admitted that in some respects, say educational opportunity, they appear to be the 'underprivileged among the underprivileged') . . . If there are few going on to full-time further education, few being apprenticed to trades, few going into the professions, a minority taking up the many options of further education, few using the public library—on all these counts, it can be shown that these are characteristic of a neighbourhood rather than a people of dark skin. May it not be that part of what we thought was colour discrimination was simply an aspect of the structure of social privilege? Practically, this may mean that we see integration as part of a whole problem of social reform and community reconstruction.

Commenting on this conclusion, a contributor to *New Society* special section referred to above wrote:

> This strikes at the heart of the matter. It is not enough to act against job discrimination and to promote fair employment within industry, whether by voluntary or legislative means or both, against an overall background of educational, vocational and other deprivation. The most that such action can achieve for coloured teenagers is equality of under-privilege, or special privileges that will make them a target for bitterness. What is needed is an all-out national programme of reclamation and redeployment to deal with the twilight areas as a whole, to give all their inhabitants, irrespective of colour, equal opportunities, and to integrate them fully.

[1] For all Birmingham school-leavers, however, in 1964–5, the proportion of immigrants entering apprenticeship schemes was said to be 10%, compared with an overall average of 33%. (*Immigration, Race and Politics*, Bow Group Pamphlet, p. 21.)

K. UNEMPLOYMENT

For the last decade or so it has been widely believed that an economic recession could hit coloured immigrant workers harder than the rest of the labour force, through redundancy, thereby making them a greater burden on the welfare state and so increasing local hostility towards them. Conversely, it has been feared that, if redundancy was seen not to affect coloured workers unduly while there was a rise in unemployment among local workers, hostility and tension might also increase.

To what extent are these fears warranted? The evidence so far available does not seem to provide a definitive answer, but it may be briefly summarized here.

(i) *Unemployment before Mid-1962*

From the 10% sample in the 1961 Census, R. B. Davison was able to extract, in relation to persons born in Jamaica, the rest of the West Indies, India, Pakistan, Poland, Ireland, and Cyprus, certain information on employment, 'economically active persons', unemployment, and the categories into which those fell who were not economically active: i.e. those under 15 years, retired persons, housewives, students, and others.[1] These figures made it possible to calculate comparative rates of unemployment between the various birthplace groups in April 1961. In London, for instance, the rate of unemployment was highest among Jamaican-born males, lowest among English-born males (7·4% and 3·2% respectively). In an intermediate position were males born in Cyprus (5·8%), the Irish Republic (4·8%), India (4·4%), and Poland (4·2%). These statistics, and those given by Davison concerning the incidence of female unemployment, are difficult to interpret and do not always agree with local situations as observed by field-workers. Moreover, the usual matters of bias must be taken into account.

Reliable statistics of registered unemployed are kept by the Ministry of Labour through its local employment exchanges. Up to July 1962 a quarterly tally was kept of the number of coloured unemployed, returns being made to headquarters if the number exceeded 100. Tables 15 and 16 below give the total numbers of registered unemployed, the unemployment rate, and the proportion of coloured male and female work-seekers to the total unemployed in the period August 1960 to May 1962.

The number of unemployed varies seasonally and the overall figures for this period showed a rise in 1962, compared with 1961. The coloured unemployed figures, on the other hand, showed a sharp rise over the two years, the really serious increase occurring after November 1961.

[1] Davison, *Black British*, pp. 88–90.

TABLE 15[1]

Total registered unemployed in Great Britain, August 1960 to May 1962

Period	Total (000)	Rate %	Males (000)	Females (000)
August 1960 ...	322	1·4	230	92
November 1960 ...	352	1·6	255	97
February 1961 ...	390	1·7	286	104
May 1961	300	1·3	215	85
August 1961 ...	305	1·4	221	84
November 1961 ...	388	1·7	287	101
February 1962 ...	454	2·0	337	117
May 1962	424	1·9	311	113

(The 'rate %' is the number registered as unemployed expressed as a percentage of the estimated total number of employees.)

TABLE 16[2]

Unemployed coloured immigrants from Commonwealth territories registered for employment at local offices of the Ministry of Labour, August 1960 to May 1962

Date	Total coloured un-employed	Coloured males: Number un-employed	Coloured males: Total % of male un-employed	Coloured females: Number un-employed	Coloured females: Total % of female un-employed
2 August 1960 ...	8,355	5,557	2·4	2,798	3·0
1 November 1960 ...	11,712	7,441	2·9	4,271	4·4
7 February 1961 ...	14,281	9,126	3·2	5,155	5·0
2 May 1961 ...	15,082	9,093	4·2	5,989	7·0
1 August 1961 ...	13,926	8,623	3·9	5,303	6·3
7 November 1961 ...	21,712	14,130	4·9	7,582	7·5
6 February 1962 ...	31,683	22,516	6·7	9,167	7·8
1 May 1962 ...	38,569	27,793	8·9	10,776	9·5

(The figures include those registered as 'temporarily stopped'. They include both claimants and non-claimants of unemployment benefit.)

[1] *Source:* Ministry of Labour, published in Davison, *Black British*, Table 39, p. 82.
[2] Ibid., Table 40, p. 83.

This coincided with the passing of the new restrictions on immigration foretold by the then Home Secretary, Mr. R. A. Butler, at the Conservative Party Conference in November 1961. The rise can to a large extent be associated with the abnormal 'beat-the-ban' influx of new migrants from the 'coloured' Commonwealth (some 230,000 between January 1961 and July 1962), and was therefore politically rather than economically stimulated.

In his book *Commonwealth Immigrants*[1] R. B. Davison, in a detailed analysis of the unemployment figures for the period immediately after the Commonwealth Immigrants Act came into force, shows how the proportion of coloured employment actually fell, or rather rose much less steeply than overall winter unemployment, during the period of generally heavy unemployment between November 1962 and February 1963. This he attributed to the new arrivals' greater geographical and industrial mobility, citing regional statistics to show a rough 'inverse correlation between general unemployment rates and coloured unemployment rates'.

Informants at a number of employment exchanges particularly affected by the influx indicated that placing of the newcomers simply took longer, particularly in the case of women, but that there was little or no trace of a long-term pool of unemployed coloured males. This pattern was characteristic even of an area such as Brixton, which habitually exports most of its resident labour force to work in other parts of London. Neither at this time, nor in an earlier period of mild recession, 1956–8, did a hard core of West Indian unemployed build up. The principal sufferers in the earlier recession had been not those in employment but those seeking work for the first time, and most employers had observed the 'first-in last-out' rule[2] without any conspicuous friction or hostility developing among local workers. This experience seemed to belie the general fears expressed at the beginning of this section about the probable consequences of an economic recession.

Apart from the artificial boost to the unemployment figures in 1961–2[3] it is also clear that the coloured unemployment rate before mid-1962

[1] Chapter III. This also contains an attempt to estimate the incidence of unemployment among coloured workers, which would involve ascertaining the size of the overall coloured working population and its major ethnic components.

[2] See Patterson, *Dark Strangers*, Penguin, pp. 152–3, 126–33.

[3] Ceri Peach showed that before 1962 the number of West Indian immigrants, particularly men, rose and fell with the demand for labour in Britain. It was only in 1961 and the first half of 1962, which saw a decline in the employment index, particularly in 1962, that migration increased under the fear of immigration controls (i.e. political factors in Britain took over from economic ones as determinants of the flow). ('West Indian Migration to Britain: The Economic Factors', *Race*, Vol. VII, no. 1, July 1965, pp. 38–40.)

was higher than that of the overall population.[1] Moreover, as most migrants crowd into areas of labour shortage where the unemployment rate tends to be below that of the national average, local situations could be more serious than the national averages indicate. For example, in Huddersfield in May 1962 coloured men and women made up 45% of the county borough's total number of unemployed. In Nottingham during 1962 West Indian women made up 39% of the total female unemployment figure (as compared with Indian and Pakistani women who made up only 4%). This has been attributed to the reluctance of employers to take them on, and in addition to the fact that unemployed West Indian women made more use of the labour exchanges than did those of other origins.

(ii) *Unemployment after Mid-1962*

After the Commonwealth Immigrants Act came into operation the Ministry of Labour (in February 1963) changed the basis of counting unemployed from the Commonwealth. The count is still taken quarterly, as before, on the first Monday of August, November, May, and February, but the managers of the local employment exchanges included in the inquiry now record the unemployed in territories grouped as below, instead of reporting on the 'coloured' unemployed:

(a) Australia, Canada, and New Zealand
(b) Cyprus, Gibraltar, and Malta
(c) Africa
(d) West Indies
(e) India
(f) Pakistan
(g) Others

It follows, therefore, that the statistics obtained from this new basis cannot be exactly compared with those of the 'coloured' unemployed prepared before July 1962; but it can be reasonably assumed that groups (c) to (g) inclusive consist mainly of 'coloured' persons.

From August 1962 to November 1964 the total of registered unemployed varied very little, except for an unusual increase in February 1963. The number of unemployed males varied between 270,000 and 413,000 and in unemployed females between 91,000 and 141,000 (excluding February 1963). The national percentage of unemployment remained fairly constant at less than 2·5%, apart from the exceptionally high rate of 3·9% in February 1963; in fact, the trend was downward.

The recorded experience of unemployed persons from the Commonwealth can be set against this national background, also showing a

[1] Unfortunately it is not possible to calculate the precise unemployment rate among coloured immigrant workers since there are as yet no reliable figures about the actual number of coloured people at work. (The M.P.N.I. statistics of entrants to the labour force are not useful for this purpose.)

downward trend for both males and females. In August 1962 nearly 7% of the male and 7·5% of the female unemployed were born in the Commonwealth: after that the proportions dropped almost steadily until November 1964, when the proportions were 2% of the males and 3·4% of the females (Table 17).

TABLE 17

Registered Unemployed in Great Britain,[1] *August 1962 to August 1967*

Month	National % unemployed Male and Female	Commonwealth % unemployed Males number (000)	Males As % of national	Females number (000)	Females As % of national
August 1962 ...	2·1	23·6	6·9	9·3	7·5
November 1962...	2·4	21·0	5·1	8·7	6·4
February 1963 ...	3·9	28·1	3·9	8·6	5·5
May 1963 ...	2·4	18·1	4·4	8·3	5·9
August 1963 ...	2·2	13·4	3·6	5·6	4·2
November 1963...	2·1	12·3	3·5	4·8	4·0
February 1964 ...	2·0	12·6	3·6	4·7	4·1
May 1964 ...	1·6	7·5	2·7	3·6	3·9
August 1964 ...	1·6	6·0	2·2	3·0	3·1
November 1964...	1·5	5·1	2·0	3·0	3·4
February 1965 ...	1·6	6·0	2·3	3·3	3·6
May 1965 ...	1·3	4·7	2·1	2·8	3·7
August 1965 ...	1·4	4·9	1·9	2·3	2·9
November 1965...	1·4	4·5	1·9	2·5	3·2
February 1966 ...	1·4	5·5	2·1	2·3	3·2
May 1966 ...	1·2	4·6	2·1	2·1	3·4
August 1966 ...	1·3	5·0	2·0	2·0	2·8
November 1966...	2·3	8·9	2·0	3·0	2·8
February 1967 ...	2·6	13·5	2·8	4·1	3·5
May 1967 ...	2·3	13·0	3·0	4·1	3·8
August 1967 ...	2·4	13·6	3·1	3·9	3·4

Source: Davison, *Black British*, Table 41 (adapted).

A breakdown of the overall figures for Commonwealth unemployment by territories of origin shows that the majority of unemployed come from the 'coloured' Commonwealth. In the absence of reliable figures about the number of people from each group in the work force, however, there can be no definite conclusions about the comparative unemployment rates of the different groups. The high totals for the 'coloured' Commonwealth may only reflect their numerical preponderance in the overall immigration from the Commonwealth.

[1] The count of Commonwealth citizens unemployed does not include boys and girls under 18 years of age, but the national unemployment figure does. Ideally, a comparison should be made between Commonwealth unemployed and adult unemployed.

TABLE 18[1]

Distribution of Commonwealth Unemployed by Territories of Origin (%), *August* 1962 *to August* 1967

(a) Males

Territory of origin (%)

Month	New Zealand, Australia, & Canada	Cyprus, Gibraltar, & Malta	Africa	West Indies	India	Pakistan	Others	Total	Total number of Common-wealth unemployed
August 1962	1	2	7	33	12	41	4	100	23,584
November 1962	1	3	8	36	12	36	4	100	21,044
February 1963	1	4	8	46	11	27	3	100	28,077
May 1963	1	4	9	41	12	29	4	100	18,107
August 1963	1	4	10	32	18	31	4	100	13,380
November 1963	1	5	10	25	17	38	4	100	12,257
February 1964	1	5	10	26	12	42	4	100	12,550
May 1964	2	7	15	32	12	28	5	100	7,469
August 1964	1	7	13	35	12	26	6	100	5,994
November 1964	2	7	15	37	13	21	5	100	5,084
February 1965	1·7	8·1	15·6	38·4	12·3	19·4	4·5	100	5,975
May 1965	1·9	7·1	18·6	38·6	11·8	16·9	5·2	100	4,737
August 1965	1·4	6·1	14·4	41·1	12·3	18·6	6·1	100	4,931
November 1965	2·0	7·3	15·2	41·3	14·3	14·7	5·2	100	4,545
February 1966	1·9	7·1	14·9	45·0	13·4	12·6	5·1	100	5,520
May 1966	2·1	6·5	16·1	42·5	12·9	13·5	6·3	100	4,611
August 1966	1·6	5·6	15·5	41·6	13·8	16·3	5·5	100	4,983
November 1966	1·4	5·6	11·1	42·6	15·6	19·0	4·7	100	8,883
February 1967	1·2	5·9	12·0	42·8	14·9	19·3	3·9	100	13,491
May 1967	1·2	5·6	12·8	42·6	14·9	17·7	5·3	100	13,010
August 1967	1·0	5·6	14·9	38·4	14·9	18·8	6·4	100	13,608

TABLE [illegible] (*continued*)

(*b*) *Females*

Territory of origin (%)

Month		New Zealand, Australia, & Canada	Cyprus, Gibraltar, & Malta	Africa	West Indies	India	Pakistan	Others	Total	Total number of Common-wealth unemployed
August	1962	1	1	6	88	2	1	1	100	9,273
November	1962	1	1	7	88	2	*	1	100	8,681
February	1963	1	1	6	89	2	*	1	100	8,597
May	1963	*	1	6	89	2	*	1	100	8,290
August	1963	1	1	9	84	3	1	2	100	5,636
November	1963	1	1	12	82	3	1	1	100	4,818
February	1964	1	1	11	83	3	*	1	100	4,702
May	1964	1	1	10	82	3	1	2	100	3,589
August	1964	1	1	15	77	4	1	2	100	3,017
November	1964	1	1	15	76	4	1	2	100	3,039
February	1965	1·1	1·3	15·3	76·2	2·9	1·1	2·1	100	3,249
May	1965	0·9	0·9	14·8	76·0	4·3	1·3	1·9	100	2,783
August	1965	1·0	0·7	17·2	72·9	5·0	1·1	2·2	100	2,318
November	1965	1·2	0·7	15·6	71·9	6·4	1·3	2·8	100	2,470
February	1966	1·6	0·7	18·6	68·0	6·9	1·3	2·9	100	2,286
May	1966	1·3	0·6	18·1	72·4	5·6	0·8	1·2	100	2,057
August	1966	1·3	0·9	19·6	69·1	5·8	1·3	2·1	100	1,986
November	1966	1·3	0·9	15·5	70·8	7·4	1·7	2·5	100	2,950
February	1967	0·9	1·4	17·6	71·3	6·2	1·0	1·6	100	4,136
May	1967	0·8	1·3	15·1	72·0	7·3	1·6	2·0	100	4,120
August	1967	0·6	1·5	18·0	67·7	8·1	1·3	2·9	100	3,835

* Less than 0·5%.

[1] Figures up to November 1964 are taken from Davison, *Black British*, Table 42, pp. 87–8; figures after November 1964 were obtained from the (then) Ministry of Labour. (The count of Commonwealth unemployment is taken on the first Monday of each month.)

The 1965–7 unemployment figures could not be analysed in detail owing to lack of time. They are therefore published here for the record, and in the hope that they may prove useful for research workers studying the effects of the 1966–7 'squeeze' on the employment situation of particular groups of immigrant workers. Some figures obtained from information in Nottingham and Coventry up to May 1967 indicated that no unduly adverse effect was experienced in those two cities. The more detailed regional figures kept by the Ministry of Labour do, however, suggest that unemployment increased substantially amongst certain groups of Commonwealth immigrants in particular regions, notably London and South Eastern, Midlands, Yorkshire and Humberside, and North Western. Different ethnic groups, and also male and female workers, were affected to a differing degree in the various areas, but again, in the absence of reliable figures about the actual numbers of people at work in each immigrant group, and also of their exact geographical and industrial distribution, no precise comparisons can be made either between the unemployment rates of immigrants and those of local workers, or between the various immigrant groups during this period of 'squeeze' and mounting unemployment. One must also take into account the fact that an unknown but substantial number of those registered as unemployed (especially women) are likely to have been newly-arrived 'dependants', or young men and women who had just reached the age of 18.

2. EMPLOYMENT POLICIES AND PRACTICES

A. CUSTOMARY BARRIERS

(i) *Craft Barriers and Closed Shops*

Apprenticeships are in short supply and in many skilled crafts traditional barriers still prevail which exclude immigrants as effectively as they exclude most local boys. The Commonwealth Immigrants Advisory Council stated in its third report (Cmnd 2458) that it could find no evidence that immigrant applicants of the right age and with the necessary educational qualifications did not have equal opportunities. It went on to point out, however, that most recent immigrants have arrived in Britain too late in life to be considered for such apprenticeships. The Council recommended that the Minister of Labour should press both sides of industry to make it easier for late entrants to obtain apprenticeships.[1]

[1] In an article 'Training for Immigrants' (*New Society*, 6 April 1967), C. C. Hebron, considering the particular problems facing adult immigrants wishing to acquire skilled and technical qualifications, showed that in practice there were many barriers (educational qualifications, extra fees, language, religion, etc.) that made easy solutions impossible.

Bob Hepple has described the two types of trade union 'closed shop' that also operate, in practice, to exclude immigrant workers from training:[1]

(a) In the 'labour pool' shop the employers and unions form a pool of labour confined to workers accepted by the unions. Coloured workers are excluded not by an overt colour bar, but because the 'pool' is limited to those who have served an accredited apprenticeship which, in turn, is a condition of membership of the union and hence of employment. The union sometimes insists on a fixed proportion of apprentices to fully trained craftsmen, and preference in apprentice-selection is given to the relatives and friends of existing craftsmen. Obviously, the only chance of equality of treatment for coloured workers is here closely bound up with the introduction of a simple system of 'trade-testing' which would make merit rather than nepotism the qualification for training and jobs.

(b) In the 'labour supply' shop, the union is the employer's main or sole source of labour. If the union does not have a positive policy of recruiting coloured workers, or if there is a negative attitude towards the union on the part of the coloured workers themselves, they are not likely to get jobs.

(ii) *Quotas*

So-called 'quotas' or limitations on the number of immigrant workers are widespread in British industry. They usually vary between 3 and 10% and are informal, unwritten, and the product of agreement between management and unions or the long-term labour core.

The origin of the present-day practice may be sought in the collective agreements negotiated between unions, management, and the Ministry of Labour in over forty industries, in relation to the employment of Polish ex-servicemen, East European displaced persons and other European workers.[2] These agreements imposed a normal maximum for 'foreign' labour of 10–15% of the total operatives in specified occupations or in particular establishments. The quota could be increased with the consent of the unions and in practice quotas were not always observed, at least when no suitable British labour was available.

There is evidence that these agreements have been used both for and against coloured Commonwealth immigrants. In one area an attempt was made to apply an agreement so as to exclude Polish and other European workers and make way for coloured British labour. In another, an agreement relating to Europeans was interpreted so as to

[1] Hepple, 'The Position of Coloured Workers in British Industry', p. 28.

[2] For more details of these arrangements and earlier statutory safeguards relating to the employment of alien workers under the Aliens Order 1920, see J. A. Tannahill, *European Volunteer Workers in Britain*, Manchester University Press, 1958, Ch. V.

include Commonwealth immigrants in the 'foreign' category. This led the particular employer to establish a subsidiary non-union company employing only Commonwealth immigrant labour. Apart from these formal agreements, there is evidence of a large number of unwritten shop-floor 'understandings' between management and workers that a quota will be applied.

Where a quota results in a suitably qualified coloured worker being refused employment, this is discriminatory (at least in a technical sense). However, it has been argued that such quotas do have a positive or 'benign' aspect, in that (i) working techniques can be more rapidly communicated if immigrants are spread over the labour force; (ii) there is less chance of friction and rivalry between different groups and absorption is speeded; (iii) the 'character' of the enterprise is not changed—this is important to the employer who does not want to risk losing the bulk of his long-established labour force.

Such low quotas usually cease to be observed with any strictness as absorption proceeds,[1] although employers rarely allow numbers to go up beyond 20 to 30%. Where this does happen, there is a tendency for the labour force to change rapidly, as the establishment acquires the reputation of being a 'coloured shop'.

An alternative policy to the low quota is the 'ethnic gang' system already described.

(iii) *Prior Redundancy Agreements*

The collective agreements relating to quotas for European workers just after 1945 also contained clauses specifying that in the event of a recession they should be made redundant before British workers. In the event, they had become sufficiently well accepted in some industries by the time a recession came for the clause not to be invoked.[2]

In the earlier years of coloured immigration, unwritten 'prior redundancy' agreements were fairly widespread, but they seem to have been invoked with increasing rarity. Instead, the 'first-in, last-out' rule has tended to be observed, particularly in establishments and industries where the unions are strong.

(iv) *Segregated Facilities*

Segregated facilities, or requests for them from local workers, have been noted in a wide variety of industries and establishments over the last decade or so, usually in relation to toilet facilities, but sometimes to canteen arrangements. In general, these situations have arisen at the

[1] There was, however, a recent report of a strike because workers claimed that management had increased the quota. (*Guardian*, 24 February 1967.)

[2] J. A. Tannahill, op. cit., pp. 64–5.

early stages of employment of immigrants and they have been resolved in a number of ways: for instance by firmness or tact on the management side; by special briefing during induction; by union or immigrant group protests.[1]

The persistence of such situations is generally associated with the ethnic work-unit system and with the employment of workers (usually Asians), whose traditional toilet habits incur the disapproval of local workers.

Desai[2] has recorded how these situations traditionally develop. A few white workers complain that Asians are dirtying the lavatories. The management is then persuaded to introduce separate toilets for Asians. In one instance, after Asian workers had voluntarily used their own toilets for a month, white workers were forced to concede that the Asian toilets were cleaner than their own and the practice was discontinued.

In another much-publicized case in Smethwick, the Midland Motor Cylinder Company of Smethwick abandoned its plan for a segregated toilet block for white and Indian workers in one factory, after protests by the Indian High Commission and the Indian Workers' Association. The company, which maintained that the separate facilities at its three other factories were introduced at the Indian workers' own request, agreed to change its new plan with no great resistance; the joint managing director said that, if its Indian employees were now sufficiently Europeanized to use English-type facilities, that was all right with the firm—a few Asiatic-type lavatories might be put in for those who wanted them. Mr. A. S. Jouhl of the I.W.A. said they had nothing against this, provided that Asians were allowed to use the normal toilets if they so wished. Dr. D. R. Prem, deputy chairman of the West Midlands Commonwealth Welfare Council, said he would, in his personal capacity, recommend alterations to the three existing blocks. In his view the matter was an industrial one and should be decided by mutual arrangement with employers and employees; he did not want it to become a political one. Earlier, the A.E.U. national chairman, Mr. Reg Ward, had expressed total opposition to any form of racial discrimination with reference to this case (in November 1964 some A.E.U. workers had threatened to strike if they had to continue sharing facilities with Asians at one of these factories). Later, Mr. Maurice Foley declared that, while recognizing that there were differences of language and religion, 'we should never take measures to perpetuate those differences.'[3]

[1] See Patterson, *Dark Strangers*, Tavistock, pp. 101–25, for instances of this in relation to West Indian and Irish workers.

[2] Desai, *Indian Immigrants in Britain*, p. 85.

[3] I.R.R. *Newsletter*, July 1965, p. 5.

(v) *Upgrading and Promotion Barriers*

The primary barriers faced by immigrant workers are on entry to an industry, firm, work-unit or trade. Later, they come up against secondary barriers at the stage of upgrading or promotion, particularly to positions of direct supervision over local workers. While the latter may be increasingly ready to accept coloured immigrants as fellow-workers, they frequently object to taking orders from them. Indeed, when management promotes such an immigrant to a position of direct authority over local workers and they accept him, this may be taken as an indication of successful industrial assimilation. Such successful promotions are usually carefully planned, the 'pioneer' individuals chosen are likely to be 'better than the locals', and the views of supervisors, shop-stewards and work-groups are canvassed in advance.[1] Where this is not done, there is likely to be resentment, hostility and even threats of strike action. The same can apply for upgrading to more skilled, responsible and better-paid work. The outcome can depend on the attitude of local union officials. If they go along with the workers' pressures, the management may back down; if they enforce high-level policies of non-discrimination, the situation is likely to be accepted.

The process of promotion, usually to the rank of charge-hand, has now begun for West Indians and other coloured workers in quite a number of firms and industries, including the public transport services.[2] In general, the available evidence indicates that they, like other immigrants before them, have to be better than local workers if they are to achieve upgrading and promotion, have to wait longer,[3] and are likely to be put over work-units containing at least some of their own nationals, or to be given responsible jobs which do not involve a direct supervisory function. Moreover, apprentices assigned to immigrant skilled workers may themselves be coloured, not white, boys. There is also some evidence that in establishments where there are a number of 'cushy' jobs, giving higher financial and prestige awards, immigrant workers may find it more difficult to get them.[4]

[1] Hooper (ed.), *Colour in Britain*, pp. 83–4.

[2] A detailed account of this will appear in a forthcoming report on London Transport by Dennis Brooks for the Acton Society Trust. In May 1965 London Transport released figures showing that 29% of male conductors were coloured, but only 7·4% of drivers. There were at that time no coloured inspectors out of nearly 4,500 coloured employees.

[3] On promotion quotas, redundancy, etc., in the West Midlands, see *Immigration, Race and Politics*, Bow Group, pp. 43–5.

[4] The 'colour bar' reported at Euston Station in July 1966 (see I.R.R. July/August *Newsletter*, pp. 5–6) was an instance of this, as Euston passenger guards could earn up to £10 a week more than guards at most other stations, and the staff were reported to be very prestige-minded.

B. INDUSTRIAL TRAINING

Under the Industrial Training Act, 1964, seventeen industrial training boards have so far been established in Britain, covering over nine million employees.[1] The industries covered include many in which immigrants are engaged, such as hotels, catering, textiles (wool),[2] construction, iron and steel, and engineering.

The boards are supposed to encourage systematic training schemes by employers. This is done by raising from employers a levy which is used to pay grants to employers providing training up to an approved standard. An official of the Transport and General Workers' Union recently proposed that grants should be withheld from employers discriminating against coloured workers in respect of training facilities.

A supplementary task of the boards is to set up Government training centres. This has been done in forty skilled trades. There are no published figures about the number of immigrants or coloured workers in these centres. An impression formed at one of them was that about 30% of those being trained there were coloured.

Special efforts are being made by the Ministry of Labour to increase the number of women workers receiving training. In addition, disabled workers, and those with special resettlement problems may be given financial assistance mainly for training in commercial occupations. It is believed that no special attention is given to the training of immigrants.

On the matter of industrial training for overseas nationals, the T.U.C. General Council reported as follows in 1966 (p. 191, item 231):

> In June the Minister of Labour sent further information on arrangements for industrial training prepared by his Ministry in consultation with Industrial Training Boards and the Ministry of Overseas Development. It was intended that the trainees would be nominated by governments in developing countries for practical training or combined academic and practical training for periods up to four years, or for specialised industrial experience for up to six months. The total would not exceed about 500 a year. The Minister for Overseas Development also wrote expressing the hope that the General Council would support the scheme, which would be a useful addition to the country's capacity to provide industrial experience badly needed in many developing countries, especially in the Commonwealth.
>
> The Ministers of Labour and of Overseas Development have been informed that the General Council welcome the scheme as an improvement of the technical assistance facilities so far provided for overseas countries, and it has been suggested that information on the purposes of the scheme and the

[1] See supplement on 'The Industrial Training Act' in *Times Educational Supplement* (17 March 1967).

[2] On 20 September 1966, the Wool Industry Training Board's second annual report contained the information that 9% of all workers in the industry came from overseas.

conditions of training should be given to union representatives in the localities in which trainees will work. The General Council have expressed the hope that some study of industrial relations, including the part played by trade unions, will be included in the programme of all trainees and that they will be brought into contact with the trade union movement.

C. MANAGEMENT

The attitudes and policies of upper and lower management constitute one of the most important factors in the complex process of absorbing immigrant workers in industry. This is because they, in the great majority of cases, whether or not they are co-operating with or checked by organized labour or the settled labour-core, make the major policy decisions; these include hiring and firing, and trying out a new source of labour in a situation of chronic labour shortage. Such a shortage can indeed be said to have constituted an all-important antecedent factor in inducing most employees to consider taking on immigrant labour.

The idea of employing immigrant workers was not until after 1945 a part of British management thinking, other than in specialized occupations and industries, notably the merchant marine, the garment trade, and commerce. The initial reaction to successive post-war groups of immigrants therefore tended to be cautious, even suspicious, but also utilitarian, although there has undoubtedly been a display of prejudice by a minority. On the whole, however, employment practice has been motivated not by personal prejudice, nor even by received stereotypes, but by consideration of a whole complex of factors: chief among them the working ability and general suitability of the immigrants and often the views of the established local labour-core. A fairly general viewpoint is illustrated in the following passage from a speech by Sir Kenneth Allen, chairman of the C.B.I. Labour and Social Affairs Committee, at the opening session of the N.C.C.I. Conference on Racial Equality in Employment on 23 February 1967:

> The attitude of the great majority of employers on the question of selection of personnel is that their major concern must be one of efficiency, bearing in mind that we are engaging human beings and not buying machines. Their constant difficulty has been to obtain enough employees with the skills they need. The colour of a man's skin, his religious beliefs, or his politics are in the main of very little concern to employers when they are faced with the problem of maintaining an adequate labour force.
>
> The employer is not, however, an entirely free agent when engaging employees. He has to take into account the attitudes of his other personnel, and in the case of industries serving the public he will have to take into account the attitudes of his customers. In neither case is he in a position to dictate, and in many cases it would be difficult for him effectively to alter unfavourable attitudes, however much it might be in his own interest to do so.

To achieve the highest efficiency, he not only has to employ individuals but he has to weld them into a co-operative team. It is from this point of view that an employer, when engaging—and when considering promotion—of employees, has to have regard to the attitudes of his other work-people.

Management's generally pragmatic approach is illustrated by the increase over the years in the number of firms that have accepted immigrant labour and the amount of thought given to methods of introducing immigrants to the labour force, to selection, induction and training, to the degree of dispersal, and in general to promoting not only economic but social absorption on and off the shop-floor.

3. THE LABOUR FORCE

The influence of the labour force on immigrant absorption in industry is exerted both through the trade unions at various levels and through the settled labour-core in a working establishment.[1] In general, labour's approach to the employment of immigrants has tended to be more emotional and negative, that of management more pragmatic and positive. This is hardly surprising in view of still prevalent fears of recession and unemployment and memories of the way in which foreign workers have, over the past century and more, appeared to threaten the British workers' security and working conditions, to undercut wages[2] and living conditions, and to weaken industrial organization and action.

Thus, as coloured Commonwealth immigrants have over the last twelve years begun to move into various areas, industries, firms, and occupations, there have been a considerable number of minor (even if widely publicized) explosions, whether from locals, unions, or groups of workers, over their initial entry, which often provided a pretext for protests really concerned with wages, working conditions, and status. Usually these explosions have been quickly stifled, whether by firmness on the part of employers or higher-level union intervention or both. Instances of this are the earlier widespread resistance in public transport services in London and the provinces, the 1962 rebellion of a whole union branch at Alcan in Banbury, and the 1967 strike of 140 women at Metal Closures Ltd., West Bromwich, when a West Indian woman was engaged as a trainee press-operator, allegedly without consultation. At once, an A.E.U. officer came out strongly against the action as a colour bar and the women unanimously decided to return to work.[3]

[1] For the part played by such labour-cores in the absorption of immigrants in Croydon, see S. Patterson, *Immigrants in Industry*, London, O.U.P. for I.R.R., 1968, pp. 243–50.

[2] According to Bow Group report, *Immigration, Race and Politics*, only a few examples of this were found (p. 39).

[3] *Guardian* (24 February 1967).

At a later stage, as we have already mentioned, a *modus vivendi* has usually developed between coloured and white workers, with the work situation becoming one in which the majority of British feel it would be wrong to refuse to work with coloured people, while the majority of West Indians feel that workshop contacts are better than off-the-job relations.

Trade union policies and practice in relation to coloured, and indeed all outside labour, have over the last decade or so been highly ambivalent. This is due to the attempt to reconcile the principles of universal working-class brotherhood and non-discrimination with the fears and antipathies of rank-and-file members. Here it must be remembered that the trade unions' own position is by no means fully secured even today. The total working population is twenty-five and a half million, of whom something under nine million are union members. In general, at national level officials of many individual unions and the Trades Union Congress[1] have expressed their adherence to universal brotherhood and non-discrimination, while at lower levels officials have been more likely to share the attitudes and sometimes the antipathies of local workers. On the other hand, some local unions have, usually through their trades councils, on their own initiative become positively involved in the integration of coloured immigrants (for example in Nottingham, Slough, and Smethwick).[2]

Up to 1965 the T.U.C. tended to soft-pedal any discussion of coloured immigration or colour discrimination among British workers. When it could not be avoided, the T.U.C. took the line that discrimination was not due to colour but to economic fears, and that the solution lay in preventing exploitation, enforcing the 'rate for the job', encouraging the newcomers to join the unions, and in general treating them as exact equals with white workers. In 1955, and again in 1958 (after the Notting Hill and Nottingham disturbances), the T.U.C. conference condemned all forms of discrimination, but the requests of some delegates that the T.U.C. General Council should consider giving some guidance to trade unions and trade unionists generally as to positive steps at local and shop-floor level were not followed up by action.

After the Conservative Government introduced its Commonwealth Immigrants Bill in 1961, the conference stated that the measure was open to serious objections and, while the Bill was not a racial measure in form, it had been interpreted as such in many Commonwealth countries and its operation was bound to weigh against coloured Common-

[1] See Patterson, *Dark Strangers*, Tavistock, pp. 152–68, for a survey of the policies and practice of the T.U.C. and a number of individual unions over the years between 1955 and 1961; Beryl Radin, 'Coloured Workers and British Trade Unions', *Race*, Vol. VIII, no. 2, 1966, for a similar survey between 1958 and 1966.

[2] Radin, op. cit., pp. 172–3.

wealth citizens. In 1964, in a memorandum submitted to the C.I.A.C., the T.U.C. stressed that the problems facing immigrants today in Britain were those which had faced working people for many years, and that immigrants could best serve their own interests by participating actively in the trade union movement.

In 1965, however, the T.U.C. General Council suddenly began to view the situation with alarm. It appeared that there was after all a special and growing problem with immigrants lacking an adequate knowledge of English and of British customs, and settling in large non-integrating communities which constituted an extension of their previous environments. At this time the T.U.C. also accepted the new restrictive Labour Party line as outlined in the 1965 White Paper, although there were some representations to the Home Secretary and Minister of Labour about a 'coherent immigration policy' which would link Commonwealth immigration more closely to job opportunities, labour requirements and the suitability of immigrants to meet these requirements.

At the 1966 T.U.C. Congress, discussion of immigration and discrimination was confined to the approving of a motion from the National Union of Journalists that 'this Congress reaffirms its opposition to all forms of racial discrimination'; this made no mention of the possibility of extending anti-discrimination legislation to cover employment. Nor, in the realm of positive voluntary action, had the T.U.C., up to the end of 1966, issued guidance to members or communication to local trades councils suggesting that local trade union bodies co-operate in the establishment of local liaison committees to aid in integration (as outlined in the 1965 White Paper on Immigration). One member of its General Council, Mr. G. E. Smith, is, however, a member of the National Committee for Commonwealth Immigrants, whose membership is not representative but individual and specialized.

The majority of trade unions seem to mirror the general policies of the T.U.C. in their declarations. Although several national unions have opposed the Labour Party's present position on immigration control, only one trade union, the National Union of Teachers, has set up a committee within its formal structure to deal with some aspect of the issue as it affects the union. Other unions are usually unequivocal in stating opposition to racial discrimination, but are quick to draw attention to the special problems of language, skills, and cultural differences which arise in relation to immigrants. At the same time, the almost universal attitude is that immigrant workers are no different from English workers and ought not to be shown any special consideration or to be allowed any treatment which might savour of 'privilege'. The indications are that most unions not only fail to formulate positive integrative techniques, but positively believe that it would be undesirable to do so.

There are several exceptions. For example, the Nottingham Trades Council (co-ordinating local unions) helped found a local liaison committee to aid integration and paid the cost of a booklet issued by the committee to immigrants, including a section 'Why You Should Join a Trade Union'. The Electrical Trades Union has educational conferences at which questions of immigration and discrimination are discussed. The Bakers' Union, which has many Asian members, has printed handbills with union information in Hindi and Urdu and has encouraged the appointment of coloured shop-stewards. In September 1966, it was reported that the Nelson (Lancs.) branch of the National Union of General and Municipal Workers had appointed its first Pakistani liaison officer to look after the interests of Pakistani workers. The Transport and General Workers' Union has attempted to ensure that every applicant for full-time office with the union is questioned on his views about immigration and integration,[1] and in February 1967 the General Secretary, Mr. Frank Cousins, actually pledged his union to support legislation against racial discrimination in employment if no other solution could be found. This, although it was not an unqualified pledge, went well beyond the official T.U.C. policy, which opposed legislation and supported voluntary action backed by a joint declaration of intent with the employers' organization.

The T.G.W.U., Britain's largest and most variegated union, affords a particularly striking example of polar attitudes on immigration.[2] At top level, particularly in recent years, it has taken an increasingly firm stand against discrimination,[3] and this has been reflected by many officials at lower levels. On the other hand, at local level, a number of its members and even branches have over the last twelve years been amongst the most ready to react against the initial entry of coloured

[1] See also the T.G.W.U. *Record* (January 1966) for a detailed exposé of fiction and fact about coloured workers.

[2] See Patterson, *Dark Strangers*, Tavistock, pp. 154–7.

[3] Cf. the following statement by Mr. J. L. Jones, M.B.E., Assistant Executive Secretary, T.G.W.U., at the opening session of the N.C.C.I. conference on 'Racial Equality in Employment':

Most coloured immigrants are so under-privileged that special efforts are justified to substantially improve their opportunities. This is necessary so that they can catch up and become integrated in our society, as they should. A great deal of education is needed, particularly amongst trade unionists, to treat fellow-workers as equals irrespective of race, colour or creed. Trade unionists should make the cause of equality and non-discrimination their own—it is completely in line with the principles on which our British trade union movement was built. People of goodwill who want to see that coloured men and women are treated fairly and justly should display more courage in the battle for human rights. And our coloured fellow-workers will, I hope, exercise toleration in the knowledge that their struggle is also the struggle of the lowly, the displaced and the under-privileged workers.

workers,[1] and also to tolerate the kind of two-tier labour hierarchy that has built up in establishments employing large numbers of Asians on the ethnic-gang system. This has emerged over recent years in the industrial disputes at Courtaulds factory in Preston, at Greenford and in Woolfs' rubber factory in Southall.[2] In all three there was a weak or non-union tradition, a majority of Asians in certain departments and poor communications between them and union officials or local workers. In at least one case there was also an attempt to use one ethnic group as blacklegs against another, and a lack of sympathy with and full support for the strikers at various levels of the union organization.

One of the oddest cases involving the T.G.W.U. has been the seven-year-long controversy in Manchester over the right of turban-wearing Sikhs to be employed as bus-conductors and drivers.[3] Non-turbaned Sikhs and other coloured workers have been employed for twelve years[4] but for seven years the local Transport Committee and the central bus-men's committee of the T.G.W.U., Manchester branch, have been passing the buck to each other. The basic objection in 1966 appeared to come from the T.G.W.U., which reaffirmed the egalitarian or turban-banning policy that 'the same conditions—including rates of pay, uniform regulations and other regulations relating to the job—shall apply to all men, regardless of colour, race or creed.' The union was reported to be resentful of criticisms that it was guilty of racial discrimination; the dispute was said to be over a principle which, if overruled, left open the floodgates to the demands of religious minorities.[5] The Sikhs themselves were accused of intransigence. In October the City Council reversed, by a majority of seventy-one votes to twenty-three, its previous decision not to permit turbans as part of the uniform, after a highly unruly debate. The Sikhs claimed a moral victory but the battle was still on; the resolution was very carefully phrased and left the decision's implementation to the Transport Committee and the local T.G.W.U. Committee (both of which had consistently opposed it). On

[1] The T.G.W.U.'s Biennial Delegates Conference in 1955 and 1957 reaffirmed belief in the brotherhood of men and condemned discrimination, but called for rational immigration controls and help for the home countries of emigrants.

[2] See I.R.R. *Newsletter* Supplement, January 1967—Southall Part III by Peter Marsh, also article by John Torode, *New Society* (17 June 1965).

[3] See I.R.R. *Newsletters* of September 1966, November/December 1966, March 1967.

[4] According to the *Sunday Telegraph* (22 January 1967), the Transport Department employed men of fifty-one different nationalities.

[5] 'On this point Mr. B. A. Hepple commented that there was nothing novel about making concessions to the religious beliefs of employees. Special provision for Sunday instead of Saturday labour had been made in an Act of 1871 (34 and 35 Vict., c.19) to enable Jews to observe their own Sabbath, and a similar provision is to be found in section 109 of the Factories Act, 1961.' (I.R.R. *Newsletter*, March 1967, p. 107).

4 November 1966, union officials told the Transport Committee that the men would refuse to work with turbaned Sikhs. In early January the Transport Committee decided after all to employ them, but the renewed union threat not to train any turbaned recruits was not immediately tested, since no such applicants had turned up within a fortnight of the decision. In recent months readers' letters to the local Manchester press were generally favourable to the Sikhs' case: participation by turbaned Sikhs in Britain's wars was mentioned, and several correspondents felt that many local busmen were so badly dressed that it would be a relief to see a few smartly-turned-out conductors, turbans and all.

A. TRADE UNION PRACTICES[1]

(i) *Participation of Coloured Workers in Trade Unions*

National trade unions are reluctant to estimate the number of coloured members, on the ground that 'the only colour recognized is that of the union card'. But there seems to be agreement that coloured workers join unions as readily as white workers, if not more so. Many of the industries in which coloured persons are employed, such as construction, woollens, and catering, are those which suffer from weak trade union organization. In these industries immigrant organizations have aided unionization by encouraging coloured immigrants to join their unions. There are coloured shop-stewards in a number of unions. A limited study in various parts of the country for the Survey of Race Relations by Beryl Radin showed that such stewards had been elected by predominantly white sections in fourteen national unions and there are, no doubt, a number of other cases. There are also coloured branch chairmen and secretaries and members of branch committees and other governing bodies. Coloured workers participate in leadership training courses and have been nominated by unions for full-time educational courses.

Beryl Radin reported that 'there would seem to be very few overt obstructions to stop the coloured immigrant from taking part in the activities of his union'. Nevertheless, there are, as we have seen, indications of a lack of communication between trade union leaders and coloured rank and file in several unions. Immigrants are often unfamiliar with trade union conventions and practice, and, in most cases, unions do not bother to explain the established procedures to them. As pointed out earlier, language difficulties and ethnic work-units may widen the gulf between officials and white members, on the one hand, and Asian workers, on the other. Some unions, however, have issued organizing leaflets and other printed matter in various immigrant languages (for example Hindi and Urdu). There are only a few reported

[1] This section is taken almost entirely from Hepple, op. cit., pp. 35–8.

instances in which white members have objected to coloured workers joining the union once they have started work. In one instance there was an objection against transient workers and the branch itself was found to have twenty coloured members in a seventy-five member branch. In other cases, objections to coloured members at branch level have apparently been quashed by the intervention of regional or national officials. In practice, some craft unions exclude immigrants because their qualifications do not satisfy the unions' strict requirements for membership. Only one union—the Amalgamated Engineering Union—is known to have a rule expressly prohibiting racial discrimination (this led to the break-away of its white South African section several years ago).

As far as is known, there has only been one attempt to form a separate union for coloured workers only. This was during the strike at Preston Courtaulds factory in 1965, when members of a predominantly Asian-staffed department went on strike in protest against over-manning. After a white union official had described the strike as 'racial', an official of the Racial Adjustment Action Society called for the setting up of a separate coloured union, but nothing came of this. It is interesting to compare this negative response with the rapid growth at the turn of the century of Jewish trade unions (only one of which—the Jewish Bakers' Union with twenty-eight members, all over the age of 50—exists today). These were, however, not of a specifically racial or religious character, but reflected the absence of unionization in those industries in which Jews were principally engaged. After the 1939–45 War, Polish immigrants also formed several occupational organizations, although these exist in addition to, rather than as an alternative to, British organizations.

(ii) *The System of Collective Bargaining and Coloured Workers*

Collective agreements are usually regarded as being legally unenforceable. However, proposals by the Confederation of British Industries and others have recently been under consideration by the Royal Commission on Trade Unions and Employers' Associations to make them binding in law and not merely in honour. If these proposals were to be adopted without qualifications, provisions in several manning agreements relating to 'foreign' workers would acquire legal effect.

The main provisions of these agreements relate to quotas and redundancy. As described earlier, these were drafted to limit the introduction or promotion of 'foreign' workers such as Poles, Italians, etc., and they have been interpreted both for and against coloured immigrants. Other provisions usually found in these agreements are that (i) wages and conditions of 'foreign' workers 'shall be in accordance with the usual rates paid to British workers'; (ii) 'foreign' workers are to be 'encouraged' or 'obliged' to join the appropriate union. The agreements therefore have a dual character. On the one hand they discriminate against 'foreign' workers; but once these workers meet with the unions' approval their standards of employment are protected. The enforcement of such provisions depends on collective trade union action. As 'foreign' workers are inevitably in the minority in their union, they are not in a position to ensure that the agreements work in their favour. Apart from their frequent application to coloured immigrants, these agreements have probably contributed to the creation of a climate of opinion in which it is considered normal and proper to restrict the entry and promotion of immigrant workers, or to oblige management to dismiss immigrants before local workers.

In this connexion, however, it must be remembered that collective bargaining does not cover the whole industrial field, and that there are many industries in which coloured immigrants are employed which have no agreements on manning.

(iii) *The Role of Union Officials and Shop-Stewards*

Officials and shop-stewards have been found to react to objections by their white members to coloured immigrants in several ways: (i) actively or tacitly supporting the objections; (ii) doing nothing about the situation; (iii) limiting themselves to pronouncements that the objections are 'unofficial'; or (iv) actively attempting to persuade members to withdraw their objections.

Two problems arise out of this. First, national officials often find they cannot act firmly against objections to coloured immigrants, because they do not wish to encroach upon regional or branch autonomy. Secondly, at the branch level white workers are usually in the majority. Branch officials may be reluctant to act against the wishes of the majority for fear of prejudicing their own position as officials. Shop-stewards may decide to 'go along' with a majority rather than be 'carried out' by their members.

(iv) *The Closed Shop and Coloured Workers*

As described earlier, the closed shop operated by some craft unions operates to exclude coloured workers from apprenticeships as much as it excludes many white workers. There is no evidence, apart from this, that the closed shop, as such, is used to exclude coloured workers from jobs. In fact, once coloured workers join their unions objections by white workers to their employment tend to evaporate where there is a closed shop.

B. COLOURED WORKERS AND UNION MEMBERSHIP

It is probably true to say that the great majority of recent Commonwealth immigrant workers are less 'trade-union-minded' than local workers. This is partly because they come from countries where the tradition of trade unionism is younger, weaker, more corrupt or more involved with party-politicking than in Britain; partly because some of them consider that British unions resist or restrict their entry, or do not give them the same support as they do local members;[1] partly again because so many work in weakly-unionized firms and industries, or do not in the early years of migration think of much more than earnings and overtime.

A number of British trade unionists hold the view that coloured immigrants are not trade-union-minded and therefore undermine the solidarity of the British labour movement. Others, however, report that coloured workers present few problems for organization and are at least as receptive to overtures to join the union as are local workers. The situation varies from firm to firm, union to union, and area to area. Immigrant workers usually seem to follow the prevailing trend.[2] Where the union is strong in a firm, they are likely to join—where it is not, they may not think it worthwhile. Few are very active trade unionists, but this applies to most British workers as well.

Immigrants have become shop-stewards in a number of firms and industries up and down the country,[3] and in almost all reported cases of strike action in recent years, particularly in non-segregated work-units, coloured and white workers have come out together with no black-legging. In some cases, indeed, strikes have been called by white workers in protest against alleged discrimination by management against coloured workers.

There are also some indications that coloured members are beginning to take an active role in the organizational work of the unions. Apart from shop-stewards, Beryl Radin was told of some coloured branch chairmen, branch secretaries and members of branch committees or other governing bodies. A few active and interested coloured members have also attended week-end schools and other educational courses. She concluded that, while there are few overt obstructions to stop coloured immigrants from taking an active part in union life, there is a general feeling of uneasiness, an absence of mutual communication and understanding and a major task of information and education still ahead.

4. PUBLIC AGENCIES, SERVICES, AND POLICIES

The main Government employment services are the Ministry of Labour's country-wide network of some 1,000 employment exchanges; and the Youth Employment Service, coming under the Minister of Labour, but operated in most areas through Youth Employment

[1] Cf. Radin, 'Coloured Workers and British Trade Unions', pp. 169–71.
[2] Cf. ibid., p. 167. [3] Ibid., p. 168.

Officers established by local education authorities in accordance with schemes approved by the Minister of Labour.

Employers and employees alike are free to use general or specialized fee-paying private agencies and direct recruitment by advertisement or other methods and, since the Notification of Vacancies Act (1956), employers are no longer compelled to notify Ministry of Labour exchanges about vacancies.

Coloured immigrant workers find work in various ways. In earlier years, the employment exchanges probably played a greater part in job-finding, particularly in the first instance, than they have done latterly.[1] This is because most newcomers either come to jobs or have relations and friends already settled here who can place them at their own work-places. The latter method is most common among Asian immigrants: it has the effect of confining immigrants to particular industries and work-places and of putting the 'go-between' in a powerful position over his fellow countrymen.[2] Such 'go-betweens' are less likely to operate among West Indians, but after the initial period they also tend to look for work on their own, either at the factory gate or through fellow-immigrants.

In 1964 the basic policy of the exchanges was stated by the General Secretary of the Association of Officers of the Ministry of Labour: 'We owe a duty to employers to offer them the best possible selection of applicants within the limits imposed by the employers themselves.' (*Guardian*, 5 June 1964.)

The earliest Ministry ruling on the subject, which operated until 1954, was that exchanges were to refuse any order from employers who put 'unreasonable restrictions' on the kind of worker wanted. Between 1954 and 1964, this was relaxed to allow employment officers to accept 'no coloureds' orders, where they were unable to persuade the employer to change his mind and accept coloured employees.[3] In July 1964, this was tightened up to allow an exchange to withdraw its facilities from an employer who continually discriminated against coloured applicants and to refer the matter to Head Office. In April 1965, a further refinement was introduced by drawing a distinction between those employers who

[1] See Patterson, *Dark Strangers*, Tavistock, p. 131, for the earlier situation as regards West Indians in Brixton; and Davison, *Black British*, p. 78, for a rather different picture. It seems that West Indians in general make more use of the employment exchanges than Asians.

[2] As certain reported cases of bribery and 'protection rackets' run jointly by go-betweens and white supervisors have shown. See I.R.R. *Newsletter* Supplement, P. Marsh, 'Southall, Part III', January 1967.

[3] For an account of the increasingly positive way in which one South London employment exchange handled the placing and absorption of coloured work-seekers between the early 1950s and 1961, see Patterson, *Dark Strangers*, Tavistock, pp. 139–42.

were 'personally prejudiced' and those who were not. In the case of the former, the local employment officers were bound to endeavour to persuade discriminating employers to withdraw 'no coloureds' orders. If this failed, and the matter could not be settled at a higher level, exchange facilities could be withdrawn from the offending employer. In 1966 the distinction between 'personally prejudiced' and other types of discriminating employers was dropped.

The exchanges now consider all the reasons given by an employer for a discriminatory request. These are gone into individually and considered on their merits. Where an employer applies a quota and already employs a reasonable proportion of immigrants, any stipulations designed to maintain his quota are ordinarily regarded as acceptable. Employment officers are, however, required to try to overcome the objections of an employer who appears to be unwilling to employ more than a relatively small number of immigrants. The policy of withdrawing exchange facilities from an employer who practises discrimination is still the ultimate sanction. Up to the end of 1966 this sanction had only been used once.

A. YOUTH EMPLOYMENT OFFICERS

Youth Employment Officers generally share the non-discriminatory approach of the employment exchanges but, like the latter, they are hampered by the fact that if they put too much pressure on employers the latter will simply recruit privately or turn to the fee-charging private agencies.

Their task could, however, be made easier by the passing of the Employment Agencies (Regulation) Bill, 1967. When enacted, it will be unlawful to carry on an agency without a licence, and one of the grounds on which a licence may be refused or revoked will be that an agency is 'improperly conducted'. An applicant for a licence will be obliged to state 'any limitation which the agency places or intends to place upon employers or employees'. The effect of these provisions may be to introduce some sort of limitation on discriminatory job-referrals by private agencies, although this is not clearly spelt out in the Bill.

On 8 December 1966, the (then) Parliamentary Secretary to the Ministry of Labour, Mrs. Shirley Williams, said that, at present, unemployment among immigrant children appeared to be little of a problem, though there were difficulties in certain white-collar and service jobs. The Ministry had recently asked all youth employment offices with more than ten children of immigrant parents on their books (European and Commonwealth) to report on the placing of these children, and there had just been a meeting of thirty youth employment officers and regional officers to get more advice from headquarters. Mrs. Williams went on to quote from a revised circular recently sent by the Central Youth Employment Executive to all youth employment officers:

> Discrimination against persons solely on the grounds of race, colour, creed or sex is contrary to the general policy of the Government and should not be practised or condoned by Y.E.O.s in selecting or putting forward young persons for submission to employment.
>
> In submitting young people for employment, the Y.E.O. should not normally raise the question of an individual's race, colour, or creed with a prospective employer, unless the young person concerned has specifically asked him to do so. However, if the Y.E.O. considers that the placing prospects of a young person would be substantially improved by explaining the position to an employer, for example, to one who had no previous experience of immigrant workers, he may do so on those grounds alone. (*Hansard*, Vol. 737, No. 114, 9 December 1966, col. 1723.)[1]

B. A NOTE ON PRIVATE EMPLOYMENT EXCHANGES

Private employment exchanges, which cater little for manual workers, have been little used by the bulk of unskilled or semi-skilled adult immigrants. Younger and second-generation immigrants with aspirations to the white-collar (and technical) jobs are, however, more likely to need, and seek, their services. There is a growing body of evidence that they encounter discrimination either from the agencies themselves, or, if an agency accepts them, from client firms.[2]

(i) *The Views of Private Employment Agencies*

Take, for instance, the findings of a brief survey of employers' attitudes and policies about the integration of coloured staff in offices, conducted by Julia Gaitskell for the Survey of Race Relations in Croydon in September–December 1966, during which twelve private job agencies were questioned. This was to help build up a picture of the numbers of coloured applicants for white-collar work, and the degree of difficulty experienced in placing them. The agencies' account of the situation relates to the private sector only.

Asked how many coloured applicants they had, the agencies' estimates in September 1966 were as follows:

[1] An earlier discussion of the need for contact between schools and Y.E.O.s was reported in *The Times Educational Supplement* (14 May 1965). See also report of Commons debate (*Hansard*, 9 December 1966, 1715–1725).

[2] See *Strangers Within*, Young Fabian Pamphlet 10, 1965, pp. 30–1; *Observer* (3 May 1964); *Guardian* (29 August 1964); *New Society* (article by Anne Lapping) (16 March 1967).

Agency A	–	5%
B	–	under 10%
C	–	under 10%
D	–	no figure
E	–	under 1%
F	–	under 1%
G	–	under 1%
H	–	under 10%
I	–	under 10%
J	–	variable—0 to 28% per week
K	–	about 25%
L	–	25%+ (highest point summer 1966)

From this one may conclude that, contrary to some suggestions (for example by the Home Secretary), it is common for first-generation immigrants, at least in certain areas, to apply for white-collar jobs.[1] A few of the above agencies mentioned that they had some coloured school-leavers among their summer applicants, but the overwhelming majority of the applicants were first-generation immigrants.

Asked what proportion of firms on books were prepared to accept coloured staff, the following replies were received:

Agency A	–	Well-qualified girls can be placed in London, not in Croydon. (Head of firm mentioned British Council, Shell as O.K.)
B	–	6 out of 500 on books—would tend to send any coloured applicants to these.
C	–	Recently arrived in Croydon—familiar with London quota system—informant said she knew no Croydon firms who would accept right away.
D	–	Now (i.e. September 1966, start of 'freeze') no one will take them.
E	–	About 6 out of about 200 firms dealt with.
F	–	5% estimate.
G	–	3 firms named.
H	–	10% estimate.
I	–	15% maximum—for male technical staff; women harder to place.
J	–	3 out of 1,000 (categoric).
K	–	2% (categoric).
L	–	*c.* 10% estimate (marks firms which accept on employers' cards).

[1] It is of course probable that applicants were registered at several agencies.

With few exceptions, the view of the agency managers and staff interviewed was that in September 1966 it was extremely hard to place coloured applicants. The largest agency, 'J', stated categorically that only three out of 1,000 firms dealt with would accept coloured people on their permanent staff. The highest proportion mentioned (only one agency) was 15% for male technical staff jobs. The agencies with the largest proportion of coloured applicants, 'K' and 'L', estimated that 2% and 10%, respectively, of firms on books would take them. The drop in vacancies following the introduction of S.E.T. and the 'freeze' had, it was said, affected the ability of agencies to place coloured applicants.

Agencies 'J', 'K', and 'L' all mentioned the fact that coloured applicants were a poor commercial prospect for job agencies, who make their money from actual placements. To place coloured applicants meant spending time on fruitless telephone calls, which could have been spent more successfully in placing white applicants.

Quotas were accepted as the normal policy of firms. One interviewee said she had assumed the usual quota to be 10%, but revised her opinion recently down to 5%. 'Spacing' of coloured applicants was mentioned as normal practice in Agency 'K', i.e. when a placement of a coloured person is made, no more coloured candidates are sent to that firm for a period of months. Disturbingly, it seems that a number of firms in Croydon which used to accept coloured staff no longer do so. Agency 'A' wrote: 'It has become more difficult *during the past few years* [our italics] for us to place coloured people in offices.' As example, details of changed policy at five large companies were given.

Agencies did not, however, know the policy of all firms: some coloured candidates might be rejected at interview. One interviewee (L) complained: 'If only you knew one way or the other, it would make things a lot easier.'

C. SOME PUBLIC SERVICES

Information about the employment of coloured immigrants in the transport services has been given earlier in this chapter. Here we may summarize the known position in some other services.

(i) *The Civil Service*

It is generally believed that the record of the Civil Service in employing coloured people according to their qualifications is good compared with that of private industry.

No information is, however, available about the number of coloured immigrants in the Civil Service, nor the levels at which they are employed. According to the Civil Service Commission, applicants include candidates from a number of Commonwealth countries. While race or colour are not regarded as relevant criteria for recruitment to or promotion in the Civil Service, the nationality rule (for permanent appointments) may operate so as to bar some immigrants. This is because the rule requires candidates to be British subjects, British-protected persons, or Irish citizens, and usually at least one of the candidate's parents must be a British subject and the candidate must have resided in the Commonwealth for at least five out of the last eight years preceding his appointment. If he does not qualify under these provisions, the applicant can ask that an exception be made in his case on grounds of his close connexion with a Commonwealth country. There are certain Ministries (for example Defence, Aviation, Public Building and Works and the Cabinet Office) for which the requirements as to place of birth are even more stringent. Similarly, there are special rules relating to the Diplomatic Service. The Civil Service Commissioners interpret 'British' as covering citizens of all Commonwealth countries, even if they are not actually citizens of the U.K. and colonies. This means that all Commonwealth applicants, regardless of colour, who satisfy the detailed conditions set out in the rule, may compete for posts and are considered on equal terms, the best qualified being recommended for the appointment. Promotion takes place according to merit, with due regard to seniority.

The nationalized Bank of England requires its employees to be British by birth and parentage. The Labour Government refused to direct the removal of this restriction in 1965.

(ii) *The Police*

There are no central statistics available about the origin of British subjects recruited into the Police. Recruiting is a matter for each of the large number of local police authorities.

Apart from several special constables, the first coloured policeman in Britain was sworn in as a member of the Coventry police force in March 1966. He had previously been a probationary sub-inspector in the Tanganyika police and arrived in Britain in November 1965. A second coloured policeman, a West Indian, was appointed at Leamington Spa later in 1966. The policy of the Metropolitan Police in 1963 was stated to be that Londoners were 'not yet prepared' for coloured policemen (*Evening Standard*, 8 November 1963). Of twenty-three coloured people who applied to join the Metropolitan Force in 1963 and 1964, seventeen failed to meet physical or educational standards, five were recent arrivals and one was found unsuitable.

Just after P.C. Ralph Ramadhar from Trinidad went on patrol for the first time in Birmingham in January 1967, the Home Secretary,

Mr. Roy Jenkins, gave, in a written reply,[1] details of coloured applicants to join the Metropolitan Police in 1966. Of the thirty-six (all of them men) none was appointed: four of the five summoned for interview failed to attend, and the fifth was rejected as being below the general standard required. Of the thirty-one not called for interview, seventeen were recent arrivals in Britain, seven were of poor education, five were rejected on medical grounds, one was below minimum height and one was above the maximum age limit. Mr. Jenkins described these results as disappointing: 'I attach importance to the recruitment of suitably-qualified coloured policemen and hope that a number will come forward in the future.' (*Guardian*, 8 February 1967.) Later in February 1967, however, the first applicant was accepted.

(iii) *The Armed Forces*

On 28 October 1966, Mr. Gerry Reynolds ordered the withdrawal of all remaining obstacles to the recruitment of suitably qualified coloured soldiers. This followed a disclosure in the *Guardian* of a confidential War Office memorandum of 1964, excluding coloured men from the Foot Guards, the Household Cavalry, the Highland and Lowland Brigades, the Military Police, the Military Prisons Service, the Army Education Corps, the Intelligence Corps, and the Army Physical Training Corps. The Minister wrote to Mr. David Winnick, Labour M.P. for South Croydon, acknowledging that the bar did exist, but saying that most regiments did accept coloured recruits. The number serving was over 2,000 (including 450 N.C.O.s).[2] An army spokesman was reported as saying that there were already coloured soldiers serving in the Brigade of Guards, while the Green Jackets had a Fijian officer. There were also three coloured candidates at Sandhurst.

The *Guardian* (29 November) added that Mr. Reynolds' decision did not affect British subjects born outside the Commonwealth and Ireland. They are excluded from the Navy and the R.A.F. unless the Secretary of State makes a rare exception. They can join the Army, but only as private soldiers. Curiously, until 1953 the Army Act of 1881 discriminated in favour of coloured aliens against white aliens; under Section 95 there could not be more than one alien to every fifty British

[1] Mr. Jenkins also made it clear in an earlier reply to Mr. David Marquand. Labour M.P. for Ashfield, that he was keen to see coloured firemen recruited, Nottingham's Chief Fire Officer, Mr. Frank Hilton, said that the force had one African fireman at present and would gladly accept coloured men who came up to general recruiting standards in education and physique. This sentiment was repeated, somewhat more cautiously, by the county's Chief Fire Officer, who said that the force had no full-time coloured firemen at present. (*Guardian—Journal*, 28 January 1967.)

[2] In 1961 a War Office spokesman had stated that the Army was working on a basis of 2% of coloured men among total recruitments.

subjects in any corps or regiment and they could not rise above the rank of warrant officer or non-commissioned officer. Negroes and other persons of colour, although aliens, were, however, excepted from these provisions, and when enlisted were entitled to all the privileges of a natural-born British subject.

D. THE GOVERNMENT CONTRACTOR

The Employment Panel of the National Committee for Commonwealth Immigrants has proposed that persons contracting with the Government[1] should be required to stipulate that they will not practise or condone discrimination on the ground of race, colour, religion, or ethnic or national origins, in engaging, training, promoting, or discharging any persons in their employment. This proposal was made in February 1966 and was later considered by the Trades Union Congress and the Confederation of British Industries. The Employment Panel has suggested that its proposal could be achieved by an amendment to the Fair Wages Resolution, 1964, of the House of Commons.

This Resolution at present requires contractors to pay the usual wage rates and observe standard conditions of employment established in the particular trade or industry. The Resolution makes it obligatory for civil servants to insert clauses in Government contracts in accordance with its terms. In practice, complaints regarding non-compliance are made to the contracting department or to the Ministry of Labour. The Minister may try to bring about an amicable settlement by conciliation. Failing this, the matter is usually referred to the Industrial Court for decision. The onus of establishing a breach rests on the complainant (invariably a trade union). The decision of the Court has no legal effect, but in practice it has sufficient moral prestige to secure compliance. Should the contractor nevertheless fail to comply with the Court's decision, the contracting department could, no doubt, rely on its common law right to claim rescission of the contract and damages. As far as is known, this has never happened. The real sanction is the loss of future Government contracts.

It is to be noted that the present Resolution does not permit the further administrative sanction of inspection by departmental officers to secure compliance, a provision which has been found to be essential in enforcing anti-discrimination clauses in Government contracts in the U.S.A. The question as to which body—the Industrial Court, the Ministry of Labour or the Race Relations Board—should be responsible for enforcing the anti-discrimination clause, should the Fair Wages Resolution be amended, also remains to be settled.

[1] It has also been urged by a Young Fabian study group that Government business should be withheld from all firms which discriminate (for example banks, insurance, and accountancy firms). (*Strangers Within*, p. 36.)

Apart from the Fair Wages Resolution, Governments have since 1925 used their considerable powers to make grants, loans, guarantees and subsidies as an opportunity to set the pace in regard to fair labour standards. The principles contained in the Resolution have been embodied in statutes which make compliance with these standards a condition for the grant or renewal of a licence or other privilege; in some cases failure to observe recognized terms is made a criminal offence; in others, employees are entitled to complain of non-compliance to the Industrial Court, and the resulting award of the Court thereupon becomes an implied term of their contracts of employment. The main statutes are: Road Traffic Act, 1960, s. 152; Road Haulage Wages Act, 1938, ss. 4–7; Films Act, 1960, s. 47; Civil Aviation Act, 1949, s. 15; Housing Act, 1957, s. 92(3); Television Act, 1954, s. 17; Sugar Act, 1956, s. 24. There are no statutes extending this principle to deal with employers who discriminate.[1]

Some local authorities (including Camden and Lambeth) have passed resolutions requiring employers who contract with the Authority not to discriminate on racial grounds. This is a recent development and it is too early to assess the results of such stipulations.

E. FAIR EMPLOYMENT PRACTICES

It is generally agreed that fair employment practices in industry are desirable as an end, and fairly widely that some positive action towards this is needed. The main difference has been on the means (voluntary, legislative, or both) by which this end should be attained.

There does not at present appear to be any adequate remedy at common law against most forms of employment discrimination. As Chapter 3 (on anti-discrimination legislation) recounts in more detail, a number of attempts have been made by Members of Parliament to secure the enactment of such legislation on this question. A Private Members' Bill introduced in 1956 by Mr. Fenner (now Lord) Brockway included employment discrimination among various types of discrimination which it was sought to outlaw. Several further attempts to legislate were made, but in 1960, as a result of trade union pressure, the provision in regard to employment was dropped from the Brockway Bill. The Labour Government refused to include employment in its Race Relations Act of 1965, apparently on the ground that this measure was basically concerned with 'public order' and it would therefore be inappropriate for it to cover the essentially private relationship of employment. Government spokesmen also said at that time that this was an industrial matter which must be left to the traditional procedures of collective bargaining.

[1] In a parliamentary answer in summer 1966, the Chancellor of the Exchequer accepted the principle of a non-discrimination clause.

Agreements had to be reached by June 1967 if amendments to the 1965 Act were to be included in the Government programme for the session beginning in October 1967. According to Eric Silver (*Guardian*, 13 January 1967, 24 January, 1967), Ministers from the Treasury, the Department of Economic Affairs and the Ministry of Labour were likely to need a lot of persuasion before committing themselves to another tussle with unions and employers. It was, however, unlikely that nothing would be done.

This writer saw hope in the fact that the 'battle lines' were not yet rigid, whether in Government or in industry. The Government might consider legislating against discrimination in housing (and perhaps insurance and credit) while adopting other methods in the employment field: for instance, a clause denying Government contracts to firms which discriminate. This could be buttressed by a T.U.C.–C.B.I declaration of intent. In at least one major union, the T.G.W.U., there was influential support for Government action, and some union officials might be prepared to give a more positive lead in demanding legislation against victimization of all kinds (the Royal Commission on trade unions is considering such a proposal). The unions' campaign for the compulsory notification of vacancies to the Ministry of Labour could also, if successful, help to give coloured workers a fairer chance.

One interesting development was the intimation in December 1966 by Mr. Charles Fletcher Cooke from the Conservative front bench that the Opposition would not resist attempts to outlaw discrimination in housing and employment.

The N.C.C.I. Conference on Racial Equality in Employment in February 1967 was intended to bring together high-level employers, trade union and civil rights workers, and others from the United States and Canada on the one side and from Britain on the other. From the States came Mr. Norman Nicholson, vice-president of Kaiser Industries, Mr. Victor Reuther, director of the International Affairs Department of the United Automobile, Aerospace and Agricultural Implement Workers of America, Mr. Joseph L. Rauh, general counsel to the U.A.W. and top civil rights lawyer, Mr. Bayard Rustin, executive director of the A. Philip Randolph Institute, and Mr. Ben Segal, director of the Office of Liaison of Equal Employment Opportunity Commission in Washington; and from Canada Mr. Daniel G. Hill, director of the Ontario Human Rights Commission, and Mr. George G. Blackburn, director of the Fair Employment Practices branch of the Federal Department of Labour. Their opposite numbers in Britain were for the most part missing (Mr. George Woodcock having refused to attend because he was invited in his own name and not as general secretary of the T.U.C.). The near boycott by leaders of major industries and unions was, however, countered by the virtual pledges in support of legislation made by the Home Secretary, Mr. Roy Jenkins, and the T.G.W.U. general secretary, Mr. Frank Cousins.

Another interesting development at this conference was a compromise solution, which many members of the pro- and anti-legislation groups considered might provide a useful basis for discussion, put forward by Mr. Oscar Hahn, chairman of Birmingham Chamber of Commerce: machinery administered by fair employment committees within factories employing more than a certain number of workers, with appeal to an outside body only in the event of no solution being found.

After the conference, N.C.C.I. issued the following report:

> Four conclusions emerged from the discussions at the conference: (*a*) that legislation is central to any programme for racial equality; (*b*) that there is need for further detailed information on the type of legislation which would be acceptable and suitable for this country; (*c*) that there is need for public knowledge and understanding about the facts of discrimination; (*d*) that it is impossible to separate employment from housing, education and other areas where race relations are a crucial issue.
>
> As a result of the conference, the N.C.C.I. will take the following steps: (i) seek talks with the Home Office, the Ministry of Labour and probably the Ministry of Housing; (ii) make new approaches to the T.U.C. and C.B.I. and individually to the leaders in the trade unions and industrial fields to discuss both the voluntary and legislative approach to the problem; (iii) publish as soon as possible the results of the study of legislation in other countries undertaken jointly with the Race Relations Board (the report of the investigation into the extent of discrimination will be published early in April 1967); (iv) maintain close contact with the United States and Canadian organisations working towards the betterment of race relations.

F. INDUSTRIAL SELECTION SCHEMES AND THE NEW TOWNS

At the end of 1966 there were twenty-one new towns at various stages of expansion in England, Wales and Scotland. Most have attracted industry requiring a large proportion of skilled or semi-skilled labour and there is thus limited scope for unskilled labour. Generally speaking, obtaining housing in a new town depends upon finding employment in it; in those existing new towns directly linked with overspill areas (eight with Greater London; two with Merseyside; and two with the Birmingham conurbation), the basic requirement is that residents are drawn from such areas and, so far as possible, are people in housing need. In some 'older' new towns, large-scale 'immigration' has, however, ceased, new development being largely directed to meeting second-generation needs.

In the London area, there is a special scheme known as the 'Industrial Selection Scheme' under which Londoners in housing need are matched for employment vacancies in the new and expanded towns. The G.L.C. keeps a register for this purpose, on which anyone in housing need is entitled to register an interest. When vacancies occur, selections are made by the G.L.C., in conjunction with the Ministry of Labour through their employment exchanges, from the register, and the names of suitable workers are forwarded to employers for final selection.

On both counts, skills and known housing need, it would appear that the chances of coloured immigrants might be adversely affected, and in fact few immigrants are finding places in new towns. It is known that there are a limited number in Harlow, and possibly in Basildon and Crawley. Nevertheless, a recent examination of applications under the I.S.S. disclosed no significant difference in the final results. By December 1966, however, it was reported that only about one in seven of the London families housed in new towns had been recruited through the I.S.S. Arrangements were, however, being made to increase this number by various schemes, to extend industrial training for unskilled workers in housing need to meet the labour requirements of new town employees, to improve liaison between the various national and local authorities involved and to publicize the possibilities of moving to a new town.

G. OTHER MATTERS CONCERNED WITH EMPLOYMENT AND ECONOMIC ASPECTS OF IMMIGRATION

It has not been possible to cover every aspect of the employment of immigrants and the economic effects of large-scale Commonwealth immigration. These will, it is anticipated, be dealt with in greater detail in forthcoming year books, as the results of contemporary research become available. Meanwhile, readers are referred to two recent major reports:

(1) 'Immigrants and the Social Services' by K. Jones in the *Economic Review* (No. 41, August 1967), which demonstrates that the average immigrant (from the 'New Commonwealth') receives from the social services only about 80% as much as the average member of the whole population, mainly because of the immigrants' age structure. In particular, national insurance and assistance benefits are lower for immigrants —only about £17 8s. a year each, compared with a national average of £31 14s.

(2) 'Immigration: Some Economic Effects', E. J. Mishan and L. Needleman, *Lloyds Bank Review*, July 1966. Here the authors conclude that a large-scale inflow of immigrants into Britain over the next few years would lead to excess demand, i.e. inflationary pressures and a worsening of the balance of payments position. Their argument was queried by Peter Jenner and Brian Cohen in the I.R.R. *Newsletter* (November–December 1966). This was followed by a reply from Lionel Needleman in the *Newsletter* of February 1967.

CHAPTER 6

Housing

1. THE GENERAL SITUATION

The most important single factor in understanding the housing situation for immigrants is the general and very serious housing shortage throughout the country. Five and a half million of the houses in this country are in need of replacement, or 907,000 families in England and Wales, one in every twenty, are sharing their accommodation with other families. Because of this shortage, large numbers of people are competing for limited amounts of accommodation. . . . Within this highly competitive set-up, there are various types of discrimination . . . not only against coloured people, but against all migrant labourers, people with children, and especially people with large families. (Robert Moore in *Colour in Britain*, p. 85.)

For well over a decade studies and reports concerned with Commonwealth immigration to Britain have been stressing that housing is both the greatest problem that confronts the immigrants themselves and the sphere in which the greatest tensions are likely to arise between immigrants and local people.[1] This is still the case, and the major single reason for it is still the one given above by Robert Moore—the overall housing shortage in the labour-hungry urban conurbations, particularly in the private rented sector[2]—often complicated by socio-cultural differences, economic anxieties and various forms of discrimination.

A. PATTERNS OF SETTLEMENT

Recent settlement by 'new Commonwealth' immigrants in Britain has followed a fairly uniform pattern. As monographs and area reports show, the newcomers have gone, not so much to the old peripheral coloured settlements in docklands and ports, but to the more central areas of industrial expansion, labour demand, and housing shortage. Like most newcomers in such areas they have gravitated towards, or been forced into, private sector accommodation, usually 'furnished', in 'zones of transition' or lodging-house areas, such as sections of Brixton and North Kensington in London and Sparkbrook in Birmingham.[3]

[1] 'The immigration problem is 10 per cent prejudice, 30 per cent schooling, and 60 per cent housing.' (Sir Anthony Meyer, Conservative M.P. for Eton and Slough, 1964–6, *Slough Observer*, 23 December 1964.) Thirty-seven out of the 309 complaints received by the Race Relations Board during its first year of activity were concerned with housing.

[2] See Milner Holland Report, p. 227 and *passim*.

[3] For the list of towns of major immigrant settlement in Britain, see above, p. 12–13.

These are areas containing many large formerly middle-class Victorian houses, often on leaseholds nearing their end, which have experienced steady social and structural degeneration since the end of the 1914–18 War. This is the prevailing pattern in the cities of the Midlands and South-East, although in the northern cities there is a greater stock of small, cheap terrace cottages into which immigrants have moved.

It is in such districts that coloured immigrants first settled, and in such districts that the majority still remain, although there is some evidence from more established settlements[1] of movement out, mostly by West Indians but also by some Indian families, to single-family housing in 'better' and less-concentrated areas. This mobile minority of immigrants have gone some way towards solving their own housing and associated neighbourhood problems, and it is not with them that this chapter is primarily concerned.

Some idea of the geographical patterns of immigrant settlement, of the degree of concentration and overcrowding, of household characteristics and amenities, and of mobility can be derived from the 1961 General Census report and the 1961 10% Census report on 'Commonwealth Immigrants in the Conurbations'.

According to the latter report, for instance, 76% of those who (whatever their race and citizenship) gave their birthplace as the British Caribbean, India, Pakistan, British Africa (excluding the Union of South Africa), Cyprus, or Malta were resident in the Greater London area, and represented about 2·4% of the total population (or about 193,000 out of a total immigrant population in the conurbations of 255,000).[2]

The section dealing with households enumerated all those in which the head or the wife of the head was born in one of the specified countries, including children wherever they were born. Most of the households surveyed were of the simpler kind, comprising either one person or a married couple and their children. Nearly half shared a dwelling with some other household and a quarter shared accommodation without the exclusive use of a cooking stove or sink. The average number of persons per room was 1·01, against 0·69 for the conurbations as a whole. There was evidence of overcrowding in London and the West Midlands, where in West Indian households the number of persons per room exceeded 1·5 in more than 40% of the households (the figures

[1] The 1961 Census data, however inaccurate, also indicate that over half of the Commonwealth coloured immigrants in the County of London were dispersed in districts where they formed under 8% of the population.

[2] According to the full Census, there were then nearly 455,000 persons born in these areas living in England and Wales, 308,770 of them being enumerated as resident in the six conurbations. Davison, *Black British*, Ch. III, gives considerable detailed information about the housing situation of different immigrant groups in London in 1961.

for Indian and Pakistani-born residents were less reliable, in view of under-enumeration and the fact that they covered a large number of U.K. subjects (i.e. repatriates rather than immigrants proper). Generally, the percentage of owner-occupiers was high. The difficulty some immigrants have in finding permanent accommodation was reflected in the fact that in the year before the Census 27% had changed their address at least once, compared with 10% for the total population of the conurbations. Their reliance on the private sector was shown by the fact that only 4·5% of Commonwealth households in the six conurbations were council tenants compared with 23% of all households.

The Commonwealth Immigrants Advisory Council reported twice[1] on housing during its three years of life. These reports were based on evidence received from local authorities and other informants, and provide an accurate picture of situations and problems up and down the country as they were seen by officials, voluntary workers, and others who were directly concerned with them at those times. Both reports stressed that the housing problems of immigrants reflect the housing problems of the big cities and must be tackled as a part of the whole, not as a separate problem. Concentration in particular areas and overcrowding were, however, recognized as particularly characteristic of many immigrants, as were the special problems produced by (a) the newcomers' frequent ignorance of local conditions and customs, and (b) discrimination by the local population. The present housing conditions were said to be exerting two principal effects on immigrant-host relations. First, there were general problems of health and disease, due to overcrowding and ignorance of urban conditions; the resulting publicity led to exaggerated stereotyping, frequently expressed in the correspondence columns of local newspapers and racialist fringe groups. Second, the tendency to large-scale concentrated settlement was likely to hamper the development of mutual acceptance between the newcomers and the local population. The general position was described as follows:

> We are convinced that the most acute social problems arise in the large cities and in a few other towns. Some immigrants are satisfactorily housed in private accommodation or in local authority accommodation. But for many who arrive here in advance of their families, accommodation consists of a bed which may even be occupied on a shift system, in a house providing few of the amenities of life. Many families are living in over-crowded premises, generally of the older type. They have gone to these because of the shortage of reasonably priced accommodation. Sometimes they are so concerned to save money that they will not pay the current high rents resulting from this shortage; sometimes they have been able to obtain accommodation only at

[1] First Report (Cmnd 2119, July 1963). Fourth Report (Cmnd 2796, October 1965).

inflated prices or at rents which are so high as to absorb an excessive proportion of their weekly earnings, forcing them to adopt lower standards in other ways. Whatever the reason, the result is often that the established residents, alarmed by the presence of many people of different culture and standards, move away. Many immigrants choose to live close to their own countrymen, but others who would like to move elsewhere find, generally for financial reasons, that they cannot.

B. RESIDENTIAL CONCENTRATION AND 'GHETTOES'

In recent years differing views have been advanced about the actual degree of concentration of Commonwealth immigrants. At one end of the range comes the analysis of Ruth Glass,[1] based on special tabulations from the 1961 Population Census, and statistics derived from the administration of the Commonwealth Immigrants Act since 1962. This indicated that the social, occupational, and geographical distribution of Commonwealth immigrants was rather similar to that of the local population, and that there were hardly any 'coloured ghettoes'. Some other students of immigrant settlement have maintained that this interpretation reflects a two-fold bias in the Census data introduced by (a) the inclusion of up to 100,000 overseas-born British, and (b) a considerable under-enumeration of actual immigrants, particularly Indians and Pakistanis, and others lodging in multi-occupied, overcrowded housing.[2]

Off the academic plane, there has been a widespread tendency by the mass media, local residents and some local authorities to stress and exaggerate the actual extent of overcrowding and multi-occupation, and to speak loosely and misleadingly of 'ghettoes'.[3]

As Kenneth Leech wrote in July 1965:

> The term 'ghetto' is being increasingly used in an inaccurate way in popular writing. A South Bank clergyman told us recently that 'the integration of the immigration population' could only be achieved by 'massive dispersal from the ghettoes'.[4] But what *is* a ghetto? The more irresponsible seem to be

[1] *The Times*, 30 June 1965, 1 July 1965. See also I.R.R. *Newsletter*, December 1965.

[2] See Rex and Moore, op. cit., p. 49 f. Their estimate for the population of Sparkbrook in 1964 shows 44·2% English, the rest immigrant (23% Irish, 26·5% coloured). See also notes by John Goodall and Ceri Peach in I.R.R. *Newsletter*, October and December 1965. It seems likely that the 1966 Census 10% sample survey will suffer from a similar bias. Fortunately, an increasing number of detailed area surveys and reports are becoming available to augment the Census data.

[3] See *Newsletter* for November 1965, pp. 7–8, for other instances of the tendency to talk in terms of 'ghettoes'; also E.I.U. Summary, February 1966, p. 6; Lord Elton in the House of Lords debate, 3 November 1966, col. 702; Colin McGlashan (*Observer*, 12 February 1967).

[4] Nicholas Stacey, 'How the Church Could Survive', *Observer*, 23 May 1965.

using the term to describe any district (however the term 'district' is defined) where there is a sizeable minority of immigrants.[1] Some more informed writers seem to imply that a figure of 20 per cent is a high one, even though such districts are rare. Yet an urban sociologist has recently stressed, on the basis of 1961 Census data, that 'there is no borough in Britain in which more than 11 per cent of the population are coloured immigrants; and there are only 10 with ratios of over 4 per cent'.[2] The same writer continued: 'There are hardly any coloured ghettoes in this country and none in London'.[3] The 1961 Census data showed that there were few Enumeration Districts (E.D.) where Commonwealth immigrants constituted over 15 per cent of the population: Lambeth had 20 such districts, Paddington 13, Kensington 8. But (leaving aside the original notion of enforced residence) a ghetto cannot conceivably be thought of as less than a district where an overwhelming majority of the population is of the same race or nationality.[4] There is no historical justification for using the term 'ghetto' about a district or part of a district in which immigrants constitute only 10–20 per cent of the population.[5]

Kenneth Leech went on to show how the 'ghetto' concept in London evolved during the period of Jewish immigration into East London in the last decades of the nineteenth century. Current evidence showed no such heavy settlements of Indians and Pakistanis in Stepney, although there was a definite and marked concentration of Pakistani males in certain streets, mostly those in which the Jews had first settled. The article concluded:

There is no reason to think that this pattern is typical of patterns of settlement in other parts of London or Britain (Stepney has never been typical at any stage of the pattern of settlement in the country as a whole), but it does mean that a tendency to concentrate in small districts among Pakistanis must be set against the dominant tendency to dispersal among immigrants from the Caribbean. Yet even now it is doubtful if, taking all the factors into account, the figure of 20 per cent has been reached in any E.D. even in this area. In view of its history, the term 'ghetto' would seem a highly inappropriate term to use about such a group as this.

In 1967 Elizabeth Burney castigated, as doubly misleading, the continued description of twilight areas as 'ghettoes':

The coloured population is in the minority in all but the tiniest sections of a very few towns—one or two streets, here and there—and their underprivilege is shared with a very much larger population of white people.[6]

[1] *The Times* ('Dark Million' series—18 January 1965).

[2] Ruth Glass (*The Times*, 1 February 1965).

[3] Ruth Glass, *Newcomers*, p. 41.

[4] See Louis Wirth, *The Ghetto*, Phoenix Books, University of Chicago Press, 1956.

[5] See I.R.R. *Newsletter*, July 1965, pp. 11 and 13.

[6] Elizabeth Burney, for the Survey of Race Relations in Britain, *Housing on Trial*, London, O.U.P. for I.R.R., 1967. In general this chapter draws heavily on this excellent and wide ranging survey.

C. MULTI-OCCUPATION AND OVERCROWDING

Most recent immigrants from the new Commonwealth countries have moved into older, larger houses in the 'less desirable' and deteriorating 'twilight' areas of the big cities. An immigrant who buys one of these houses is likely to let off most rooms to other immigrants in order to meet high mortgage interests and repayments and for gain. These houses (usually Victorian single-family, middle-class houses) were not designed for multi-occupation; the cooking and sanitary facilities are often totally inadequate, and these facilities and the general state of the building are likely to deteriorate still faster as a result.

The housing conditions of immigrants in such areas as London and Birmingham have received particular attention in the Milner Holland Report and elsewhere, and will be described in more detail later. The situations and problems vary considerably, not only as between one area and another, but also according to the particular immigrant group. An instance of such variations was reported by Bedford's Chief Public Health Inspector,[1] in an article discussing the relative degree of integration attained by four recent immigrant groups in the town: Italians, West Indians, Indians, and Pakistanis, in terms of housing standards, family and community organization, and neighbourhood integration. The Italians, the report said, were moving away from multi-occupation towards the single-family type of house, and were well on their way to accepting British ways of life and being accepted. The West Indians were still held back by suspicion and colour-consciousness rather than by problems created by themselves; there were still some difficulties over standards in houses in multi-occupation and occasional complaints over noisy all-night parties. The Indians were well organized and their living conditions had been transformed whenever Indian wives and families had joined them. The Pakistanis were less well educated than the Indians and still presented more problems than the other groups; the vast majority were men living alone in overcrowded, cheap dormitories, which they seemed to prefer to less crowded, more expensive accommodation. At present they needed the greatest assistance but were the most co-operative and willing to co-operate, given the right kind of guidance.

In Sparkbrook, Rex and Moore[2] found that the West Indians, with a male : female ratio of 3 : 2 as early as 1961, were more interested in independent family life than in running lodging-houses, whereas the Indians and Pakistanis were mostly single men, here to earn money quickly, and with a tight-knit kin-village structure which obliged them

[1] E. Avison, 'Immigrants in a Small Borough', I.R.R. *Newsletter*, October 1965. See also Elspeth Huxley, *Back Street New Worlds*, London, Chatto and Windus, 1964, *passim*.

[2] Rex and Moore, op. cit., Ch. 1.

to help their kinsmen and fellow-villagers. Hence the rapid development of multi-occupation, and the lodging-house areas that housed not only fellow-Asians but the mass of newcomers to the city and others (low-paid workers, social deviants, etc.) who could not find accommodation elsewhere.

D. SOCIO-CULTURAL AND ECONOMIC ASPECTS

The variations in settlement patterns, the degree of concentration multi-occupation, and overcrowding, as between different immigrant groups, are obviously conditioned to a considerable extent by such elements as the socio-cultural background of the different groups, their degree of acculturation, and their economic aspirations, whether in Britain or at home. These are discussed in greater detail elsewhere in this book. Here it may simply be pointed out that the great differences between West Indian family patterns and attitudes to women on the one hand, and Asian family patterns and attitudes to women on the other, obviously produce different kinds of housing aspirations as well as household patterns.

The high proportion of owner-occupation found among most immigrant groups[1] (see Table 19) is generally explained in terms of expediency or necessity, at least so far as the coloured immigrant groups are concerned. Undoubtedly, this is true of many, because rented private accommodation is scarce, dear and insecure, because council housing is inaccessible, or simply because old terrace housing is cheap and plentiful (in some parts of the country).

Yet, there is often more to it than that, as experience of the Polish and other displaced exile communities has shown.[2] As Elizabeth Burney discerningly points out,[3] 'there is something of Mr. Biswas in many an immigrant, be he from east or west, who reaches these shores. . . . The goal of owner-occupation is to many immigrants (as indeed to growing numbers of Englishmen) the ultimate symbol of self-sufficiency and success.' This motivation seems to be strongest when the immigrant seeks to acquire a single-family home in a 'good' area, weakest in the lodging-house area, where the operation is a mainly financial one.[4] It is also more likely to be found among West Indian and some Indian

[1] The 1961 Census shows an even higher proportion outside London, in areas where housing is cheapest. See also Burney, pp. 34–5.

[2] Patterson, *Dark Strangers*, Penguin, p. 193.

[3] op. cit., Ch. II, p. 1.

[4] On the contrast between the 'house-proud' look of the owner-occupied home and the tattiness of the lodging-houses, see Burney, op. cit., Ch. II, p. 56. She sees in the immigrants' pride of ownership and home-making instincts a considerable hope for the improvement of the 'decayed' or 'twilight' areas, assuming that local authorities can be positive in their use of improvement grants and generous in the granting of mortgages.

immigrants who have accommodated themselves well to British life and are on the way to being settlers.[1]

There are considerable variations from city to city and district to district in immigrant-host relations in the housing sphere. These depend not only on such factors as the extent of the local housing shortage, the size of the immigrant settlement, and the speed of its build-up, but on a whole complex of historical, socio-economic, and cultural elements on either side. These include such things as traditional local attitudes to outsiders, distinctions of class, culture, and religion, the presence or absence of leaders or sponsors on both sides, political influences, even the attitude of a local newspaper or politician.

Local attitudes (that is to say the attitudes of the settled core of residents, often white-collar or upper artisan class) to immigrant neighbours also vary according to their ethnic origin; but it is by no means the case that one group is consistently preferred. For instance, West Indians may be rated above Pakistanis or Cypriots in one district, but below them in another. This is usually for reasons which are to a considerable extent derived from observation and not merely from second-hand stereotypes,[2] although there is some tendency to generalize from particular unfavourable instances,[3] since relatively few local residents have ever been inside a coloured immigrant's house.

Other reports would seem to confirm what was found in Brixton in the years between 1955 and 1960—that local antipathy to coloured fellow-residents becomes stronger with increasing proximity[4] and is strongest of all among the minority who share a house with them, particularly the statutory tenants in houses bought by immigrants.[5] Most of these sitting tenants are elderly people, often ailing, not very adaptable, and attached to what may have been their homes for many years. This group may be numerically small, and found mainly in London, but their situation has had a considerable influence on the attitudes of local opinion-formers.

In the last two or three years, less has been heard of such cases, although it is not clear whether this should be attributed to the fact that few such statutory tenants now remain (having moved out, died or been

[1] See also Patterson, *Dark Strangers*, Penguin, pp. 172–3.

[2] See Rex and Moore, op. cit., pp. 79–83; and Patterson, *Dark Strangers*, Penguin, pp. 178–83.

[3] For the kinds of complaints made about immigrant neighbours, see *Colour in Britain*, pp. 62–70, and Burney, op. cit., pp. 17–19, 22–3.

[4] Rex and Moore describe the attitudes of some older Sparkbrook owner-occupiers tied to the area by house-ownership, op. cit., pp. 60–68. In Smethwick reactions were often less moderate (see Foot, op. cit., pp. 36–44).

[5] For details of immigrant landlord–local tenant relationships in London (including statutory and uncontrolled tenancies), see the Milner Holland Report *passim*, especially Ch. VII and pp. 188–95 (summarized below on pp. 214–21). For the situation in Brixton up to 1960, see *Dark Strangers*, Penguin, pp. 183–6.

rehoused), or that conditions and relationships have improved in the houses concerned, as a result of the 1964 Rent Act or for other reasons. In any case, the situation of the local people who are uncontrolled, furnished tenants of immigrant or other landlords of lodging-houses has taken its place as a topic of concern.

Neighbourhood attitudes to immigrants are often conditioned by fears of falling-off in property values as well as a general deterioration of the area. The falling-off in house values and general down-grading were usually well under way before the immigrants arrived, but the latter provide a visible scapegoat for anxious local house-owners and visible evidence of the area's down-grading to those who tend to associate colour with low social status and undesirable cultural patterns.[1] What really happens to house values is not definitely established. Some local house-owners may cash in by selling to a coloured immigrant at an inflated price, while others who have held on may later have to sell at a depressed one. In the case of short leaseholds, properties which were virtually unsaleable have sometimes been unloaded at unrealistically high prices on to ill-informed newcomers.[2]

In general, while some local people may lose financially, the immigrant does not generally gain. This applies to both house purchase, where he may have to pay a colour 'premium',[3] and furnished accommodation, where he has usually to pay the high rents generally established among landlords of immigrant lodging-houses. It also applies to the raising of the purchase price, either to take advantage of an immigrant's ignorance of property values, or in a middle-class, middle-income area, in which vendor and agent alike would otherwise be hesitant to sell to a coloured purchaser.

As the great majority of immigrants live in the private sector as owner-occupiers or tenants of immigrant-owned housing, their patterns of settlement, concentration and dispersal depend not only upon where they want to and can afford to buy houses but upon where they are allowed to buy houses.[4] The last point has been a matter primarily of social sanctions, enforced not only by the actual vendor but by the intermediaries,[5] the estate agents, and the building societies, banks, and

[1] In earlier years, their protests sometimes took the tangible form of appeal for lower rating assessments. In a number of places, resident's associations have also been set up (see Foot, op. cit., pp. 210–16, and Burney, op. cit., pp. 212–13, for this sometimes important development).

[2] See Patterson, *Dark Strangers*, Penguin, pp. 171–8, *Colour in Britain*, pp. 62–4, Burney, op. cit., p. 43.

[3] See Burney, op. cit., p. 43.

[4] Colour-bar or similar ethnic provisions in freehold covenants were not illegal until 1968; though their extent was not known, it was not thought to be widespread.

[5] See Burney, Ch. II, pp. 37–49, for the views and activities of some estate agents, conveyancers, building society managers, builders and selling agents for new estates and others in the intermediary category. See also P.E.P. Report, p. 77.

others which can give mortgages.[1] Elizabeth Burney compares the situation of coloured people in the housing market with that of the Victorian working-class—they are thought to lower the tone, and therefore the value, of property. The majority of intermediaries may share these attitudes, or simply be influenced by the profit motive. A minority of agents may be sympathetic, while another minority may actively exploit the situation by selling to coloured people, either the large, old run-down houses conventionally associated with them, or even, it is sometimes alleged, 'block-busting', i.e. selling one house in a street to a coloured family to cause an exodus, then picking up others as they come on the market at low prices.[2]

Building societies are responsible for arranging about three-quarters of all mortgages. Most of them have, as is only to be expected, highly conventional views, not only about the sort of property on which they are prepared to lend, but on the sort of clients to whom they are prepared to make loans (they also have a financial obligation to their depositors). Multi-occupation, older property, particularly if short-lease, and mobile newcomers, especially if single, are not regarded with favour, and where coloured purchasers have been given mortgages, it has sometimes been for lower amounts, or at higher rates, or with some additional conditions, such as a residential qualification, or a year's deposit with the company.

According to Burney, building societies that do lend on equal terms may find themselves so besieged with applications that they impose a quota in order not to be seen as a 'coloured firm'. Most building societies associate coloured settlement with deterioration of property and lowering of property values but some, like many estate agents, have actively helped to perpetuate the vicious circle by steering even upwardly mobile immigrants away from better areas in which it would be possible to disprove the stereotype.[3]

The many immigrant purchasers who cannot get an orthodox building society loan, for whatever reason, look either to the local authority (see below), to the bank or to private sources,[4] including moneylenders. The latter type of loan is usually negotiated by agents or solicitors who specialize in 'coloured' property, and the loans are likely to be short-term and the interest rates from 15% upwards.[5]

The P.E.P. Report, which was designed to assess the extent of discrimination against Commonwealth immigrants in Britain, reported as

[1] The role of local councils in this sphere is discussed below, on p. 209f.

[2] See below, p. 244.

[3] See Report of the Race Relations Board, 1966–7.

[4] Sometimes, the vendor seems to have been the mortgager (at a high interest rate); this happened in Brixton, with some otherwise unsaleable houses.

[5] For some details on such mortgage transactions and the finance companies involved, see *Guardian* (25 January 1967) and *Observer* (29 January 1967).

follows on the situation found in the private sector, both in letting and house-purchase:

Whatever type of housing coloured immigrants seek, they encounter either substantial discrimination or severe handicaps. That the percentage of immigrants who claimed discrimination in private letting is relatively low, compared with the discrimination shown in the same Survey's housing tests, is due to two factors:

(i) the majority of immigrants do not expose themselves to possible discrimination by looking for accommodation on the open market;
(ii) as the situation tests have shown, substantial discrimination can occur without the immigrant who visits an agency or applies to a landlord knowing that it has occurred.

Claims of discrimination were lowest for the Cypriots and highest for the West Indians. The Asian immigrants were particularly prone to seek accommodation only from sources where they knew they would be acceptable (over two-thirds of them had never applied for rented accommodation from a white landlord who was a stranger). Within each of the three coloured groups, the proportion of those people who had exposed themselves to possible discrimination, who claimed actual experience of discrimination, was very similar—between 63 and 67%.

According to the Milner Holland report on housing in London, only 11% of privately-let property is both advertised and does not specifically exclude coloured people. When this section of the private letting market that is notionally open to coloured applicants was tested by the P.E.P. investigators, it was found that two-thirds excluded them in practice. Of sixty advertised properties called on by English, Hungarian, and coloured testers, forty-five resulted in discrimination against the coloured tester—forty cases of refusal and five cases of higher rent. When subsequently interviewed, all landlords admitted that they had discriminated.

The other source of privately-rented property is from accommodation bureaux or estate agents. Situation tests on these sources revealed discrimination in fourteen of the eighteen accommodation bureaux and twenty of the thirty estate agents. Interviews with agents and bureau managers confirmed that the results reflected the general situation and practice. They said, in particular, that 'it was virtually impossible to obtain an unfurnished flat for a Pakistani or West Indian'. The general justification of the discriminatory behaviour was the desire to remain in business. The discrimination was attributed from the agent to the owner and often from the owner to other tenants or neighbours.

In the field of house purchase, similar levels of discrimination were found by situation testing at estate agents. Different estate agents were used but the results were very similar. Of the forty-two estate agents tested for purchasing accommodation, twenty-seven discriminated. As before, follow-up interviews confirmed the discriminatory behaviour and elicited similar types of justification. The two types of discrimination which occurred were that (a) the coloured immigrant was offered fewer addresses or no addresses, and (b) there were significant differences in what he was told about the possibility of his obtaining a mortgage or the type of mortgage he could obtain. Estate agents confirmed that the following were the two main problems in finding houses for immigrants:

(a) Vendors in certain types of area were not prepared to sell to them.
(b) Building societies were loath to give them mortgages. This resulted in many immigrants having to accept mortgages at higher interest rates or initial deposits.

TABLE 19*

Analysis of Property Tenure (%)

(A) HOUSEHOLDS

Tenure	English	Jamaican	Jamaican	Indian	Pakistani	Polish	Irish	Cypriot
Owner-occupiers	13	25	9	16	18	33	8	34
Renting furnished	7	61	75	48	58	18	34	28
Renting unfurnished	53	12	14	26	16	35	40	30
Renting from Council	24	1	1	7	5	13	15	6
Other	3	1	1	3	3	1	3	2
	100	100	100	100	100	100	100	100
Number of households	9,604†	7,597	5,211	2,190	269	3,793	13,914	1,891

* Davison, *Black British*, p. 53, Table 27.
† 1 in 25 sample of English households.

2. (*a*) POLICIES AND TRENDS

To give an overall survey of the housing problem in Britain, of housing legislation, and of measures taken at national and local level to meet the situation, is far beyond the scope of this review.[1] Here an attempt will be made to outline the main housing policies and legislation that affect immigrants, who are particularly vulnerable in localities with

[1] On general policies see *inter alia* The Housing Programme 1965–1970, Cmnd 2838, 1965; D. V. Donnison, *The Government of Housing*, London, Pelican, 1967.

a long-standing, large-scale housing shortage, such as is found in most of Britain's major industrial cities. These are precisely the areas in which workers from outside are needed; nevertheless, no special provisions have been made by the authorities for their housing, other than in a small minority of cases involving sponsored and contract migrants from overseas, and non-resident internal migrants with special skills.

Such ideas as that an expanding and adapting economy needs a flexible national housing policy, that the housing problems of the major conurbations indicate the need for more planned dispersal of industry—in short that jobs and accommodation should be considered and planned in conjunction—are far from being general currency.[1] Housing policy in Britain is still locally-based and locally-oriented, with shortage tending only to strengthen in-group priorities and resentment of outsiders.[2]

A. LAISSEZ-FAIRE AND NON-DIFFERENTIATION AT NATIONAL LEVEL

In the case of coloured Commonwealth immigrants, the housing problem was advanced by Conservative Government spokesmen as a major reason for the introduction of immigration controls in 1962; yet no attempt was made in the Act to relate the volume of immigration to the availability of housing, which is in any case primarily the responsibility of 1,400 local authorities in England and Wales. Instead, controls were related to employment, and the Government endorsed a *laissez-faire* and non-differentiatory approach to immigrant housing, which has in essence been continued by its Labour successor. The keynote of this non-differentiatory thinking was expressed in 1963 by the Commonwealth Immigrants Advisory Council, although it did also recognize the possibility that local authorities could, by the allocation of public housing, help to promote dispersal and in general to influence settlement patterns.

> The housing problems of immigrants reflect the housing problems of the big cities, and must be tackled as part of the whole. . . . We are sure that it would be wrong to propose specially favourable treatment for immigrants. . . .

[1] 'Industry in the West Midlands is the most prosperous in Britain. . . . There are fewer workers . . . than the region's industrialists would like to employ. There are fewer houses than the workers need to live in. . . . There is a crying need for entirely new thought about the lay-out of communities—for a set of answers to the inseparable questions of where to put jobs, where to house people, how to ensure that the people live enjoyably, and how to get them from houses to work. A million and a half people now living in the region, or later to be born there, will need new homes to live in within the next 15 years—even if no more people are attracted into the area by its prosperity.' (*Economist*, 2 March 1966—series of articles on 'Britain's Heartland—the West Midlands'.)

[2] Cf. Margaret Stacey, 'A Fair Deal for Migrant Housing', *Newsletter*, June 1966, pp. 14–17.

We reject any suggestion that houses should be provided especially for immigrants, and while a local authority may choose to put four or five immigrant families within easy reach of each other, we endorse the general view expressed to us that large grouping is undesirable. . . .[1]

In 1965 the Labour Government's White Paper stressed that 'Commonwealth immigrants do not cause the housing shortage. It existed before they began to arrive in large numbers.' It went on to endorse the C.I.A.C.'s view that it would be wrong to give special treatment to immigrants in housing matters:

The sole test for action in the housing field is the quality and nature of housing need without distinctions based on the origin of those in need. The solution must lie in a determined attack on the housing shortage generally and particularly on the shortage of accommodation to rent on reasonable terms. The Government have already announced that a much larger part of the housing programme, in the form of a higher proportion of local authority building, will be devoted to providing rented accommodation for those whose housing need is most acute. This development in policy will itself benefit the immigrant section of the community.

The fact that in the more thickly populated parts of the country it will take many years to overhaul the housing shortage does not mean that no immediate action is possible to relieve the immigrants' housing problems and to assist in their integration into the community. Local housing authorities already have a wide range of powers, which, if judiciously used, can make a major contribution to this end. As time goes on, immigrants will qualify for rehousing by local authorities either by virtue of residential qualifications or through being displaced by slum clearance or other redevelopment. Thus it will become commonplace for Commonwealth immigrants to be rehoused by local authorities in pursuance of their normal statutory responsibilities. This in itself will tend to break up excessive and undesirable concentration.

More immediately, housing associations can play a part in providing accommodation for immigrants and in the process can help to promote their integration. Local authorities will, it is hoped, do their utmost to assist and promote housing associations which have integration as one of their aims.

The main cause of unsatisfactory living conditions among immigrants is the multiple occupation of houses designed for only one family. The limited powers available under the Housing Act 1961 to improve conditions in such houses were somewhat strengthened by the Housing Act 1964. But when this legislation was framed, the gravity of the problem was not fully realised. The Minister of Housing and Local Government is therefore examining the powers with a view to making them more effective. Birmingham City Council is already taking power in local legislation to require registration of houses before multi-occupation begins. The need for legislation to extend similar or additional powers to local authorities is now being considered.[2]

[1] Cmnd 2119 H.M.S.O., July 1963, paras 3 and 9. The C.I.A.C. did nevertheless make certain specialized recommendations, notably on the need for more hostels for single male migrants.

[2] Cmnd 2739 H.M.S.O., paras 34–38.

In its fourth and last Report (Cmnd 2796) in October 1965 the Commonwealth Immigrants Advisory Council made some recommendations for action, which showed that its thinking had moved some way further in the direction of specialized action:

(i) consideration should be given to providing special financial assistance to those local authorities on whose services there are demands greater than normal because of the presence of large numbers of immigrants;
(ii) local authorities should make wider use of their powers to regulate multi-occupation of houses;
(iii) local authorities should consider changes in housing list procedure;
(iv) local authorities should consider making more use of the 'patching' procedure;
(v) local authorities should consider acquiring older-type houses where to do so might relieve the housing shortage;
(vi) housing information services for immigrants should be established;
(vii) an adequate service of interpreters should be established and 'pooling' arrangements between authorities should be considered.

At the end of 1965, the Minister of Housing, Mr. R. Crossman, reaffirmed his total opposition to the idea of providing special housing for immigrants. Applauding Birmingham Corporation's parliamentary Bill to tackle the problems of multi-occupation, he told local authority representatives there:

> The solution is to build the houses to cure overcrowding and remove the slums. If we give you the chance to build the houses in the quantity and quality required, you will be able to settle the problems of the newcomers and established residents according to your own prudence and wisdom.

In 1966 some modest steps were taken towards the goals just outlined and those in the Government White Paper. On 28 February Mr. Crossman named thirty-three local authorities to be given special financial assistance under new amendments to the Housing Subsidies Bill. They included Greater London (all inner Boroughs); Gateshead, Jarrow, West Hartlepool; Bradford, Halifax, Kingston-upon-Hull, Sheffield, Blackburn, Liverpool, Manchester, Oldham, Rochdale, St. Helens, Salford, Stockport, Warrington; Northampton, Birmingham, and Warley. Some, but not all, contain areas of heavy immigrant settlement.

In the same month Mr. Crossman was also reported to be planning a conference of all local housing authorities with high immigrant populations. His answer to the problem was said to be the encouragement of crash programmes so as to disperse segregated areas. In August the Minister received a delegation from the National Committee for

Commonwealth Immigrants.[1] At this meeting problems relating to new towns, housing associations, multiple occupation and local authority housing were discussed and the possibility of a conference was again discussed. This was to pave the way for the issue of a circular from the Minister giving guidance to local authorities and others concerned with housing, on ways by which the special needs of immigrants could be recognized in the formulation of housing policies and procedures. No conference had taken place by the end of 1966, when Mr. Crossman was succeeded as Minister by Mr. Anthony Greenwood, although it was again forecast in the *Observer* of 19 March 1967, and reportedly took place *in camera* in June 1967.

On 22 February 1967 the *Guardian* discerned a 'straw in the wind', in the fact that Mr. James MacColl, M.P. (Labour, Widnes, Lancs.), formerly Chairman of the London Council of Social Services' Immigrants Advisory Committee and 'one of the most underestimated Junior Ministers', had just been given the oversight of immigrant housing in the Ministry.

In late March the *Sunday Times* (26 March) reported that the Ministry of Housing was discussing radical plans to modernize the 'twilight' houses in Britain's cities before they crumble into outright slums: these envisaged a network of big, professional housing associations, financed by a 'national housing bank', and virtually ruling out the private landlord. A survey carried out on behalf of the Town and Country Planning Association gave an idea of the size of the problem, the scope for housing associations, and the cost of renovation as compared with demolition and rehousing (£435m. as compared with £5,110m., even at 1963 prices).

2. (*b*) THE PUBLIC SECTOR—LOCAL AUTHORITIES

The public housing sector is locally based and locally oriented towards 'our own people'. Each of the 1,400 local authorities draws up its own criteria of people in 'housing need' and preference is generally given to people of local origin, particularly in areas of grave, long-term housing shortage. As Elizabeth Burney writes:

> Local authorities . . . are supposed to give houses to all kinds of people who could not make their way in the private market. . . . In London, the Midlands and the North West, where most Commonwealth immigrants live, council houses are much sought after as the only accommodation, other than slum houses, where a working-class family can have the space it needs at a price it can afford.[2]

[1] For N.C.C.I. Housing Panel reports, see below, pp. 244–9.

[2] Burney, op. cit., pp. 59–60.

Devices for ensuring local preference include a residential qualification of varying length, length of time on the housing list, and in some cases the requirement of British nationality.[1] These are included among the other criteria of need, which are balanced up together in a more or less confidential pointing system to decide who will get the meagre number of dwellings that are still available after those who have a claim to rehousing because of slum clearance[2] and redevelopment schemes (and the special allocation for medical and welfare cases). In some cases, there is also reason to believe that, where country of origin is not noted, application and other forms are marked discreetly to indicate origins or colour.

Some local preference by a local authority is inevitable and understandable. In many areas the absolute shortage of housing has caused them to turn a deaf ear to the pleas of successive Governments to give priority to young couples with growing children and at least equal consideration to the families of newly-arrived workers whose labour is needed in the area.[3]

For whatever reasons, few immigrants are housed in council property, in marked contrast to the section of the local population with similar occupational levels.[4] For those who are so housed, there come into

[1] Some recent or current examples are: Greater London, with a five-year residence in most boroughs (one in the particular borough, four elsewhere in Greater London); Smethwick (until it was merged in Warley) (seven years); Wolverhampton, which requires applicants where neither husband nor wife is a native of Great Britain or Northern Ireland to wait twice as long as anyone else before they start counting for points (a post-war rule originally relating to Southern Irish, Poles, and other Europeans—three years, now reduced to two, for such applications); Nottingham, with a five-year waiting-list (though other rules would in theory seem likely to benefit Commonwealth immigrants if they were aware of them); Manchester (two years' residence before application can start to be effective and form asking for all addresses of man and wife since birth); Bristol (six months' waiting for people with three years' residence, otherwise twelve months); Birmingham (five years before any newcomer can go on the register and start acquiring points); Ealing (Conservative and rebel Labour stipulation [proposed but not passed] of a fifteen-year residential qualification for immigrants, compared with five years for British-born residents). See also P.E.P. Report, Part III, for different instances and effects of residential qualifications, and *The Housing of Commonwealth Immigrants*, London, N.C.C.I., 1967, pp. 9–10.

[2] Elizabeth Burney discusses at some length the rehousing of coloured immigrants in slum-clearance schemes and the alternative process of 'deferred demolition' or 'patching' as now employed in Birmingham, Nottingham and Lambeth. Op. cit., p. 64f.

[3] For instance, in the Housing White Paper of 1965, and the Ministry of Housing and Local Government Circular of January 1967. An amendment to the Housing Subsidies Bill of 1966 made special provision for building for the purposes of industrial relocation.

[4] For details of some specific areas, see Elizabeth Burney, op. cit., Chapter IV, and the P.E.P. Report, Part III, *passim*.

operation the subtle gradations of allocation employed by all local authorities to ensure that their books are balanced and their property not rundown. 'Good' families, i.e., quiet, clean, regular-earning families with not too many children, are generally put near other 'good' families in the better and newer estates. 'Bad' families are generally allocated old houses awaiting demolition or shabby inter-war houses. The older properties are also more likely to be larger and cheaper. Many Commonwealth immigrants have large families and not very large incomes, so that they are unlikely to be offered one of the newer, smaller council houses, even before there is any question of colour discrimination. Moreover, the degree of overcrowding and the condition of the public parts of the multi-occupied houses in which many live may not evoke a favourable report from the housing visitor or investigator, on whose sole assessment the allocation is often decided. Beyond that, a tendency is reported among local officials to regard sub-standard or older property as particularly suitable for coloured immigrants, to avoid the alleged risk of trouble in the newer, more suburban estates, and so on.

So far, the main immigrant demand for council houses seems to come from West Indians, immigrants with English wives, and in general the most 'anglicized' newcomers. The scanty evidence about the acceptance of immigrants on 'good' estates suggests that, although there may be an initial outcry, the process is not as difficult as many local authorities fear.[1]

The P.E.P. Report summarized the situation of immigrants in council housing as follows:

> The remaining source of accommodation—council property—could not be tested in the same manner as the other categories of housing. Thus, information on council property is dependent on the immigrant survey and interviews with local authority officials. The main conclusions in this area are:
>
> (i) Very few immigrants are currently housed in council property. This is in marked contrast to the section of the white population with similar occupational levels.
>
> (ii) The present system of council house allocation puts immigrants at a distinct disadvantage. In some cases this is the result of rules that were drawn up before immigrants arrived in substantial numbers. However, we encountered one example of the better housing being denied to immigrants by the deliberate imposition of a residential qualification.
>
> (iii) There is evidence that, where immigrants have been housed, they have been housed mainly in the worst accommodation and this is, at least occasionally, as the result of direct discrimination. Officials stated that this was done in order to allay hostile reactions on the part of white residents.

The types of accommodation currently occupied by the large majority of coloured immigrants will eventually become due for slum clearance or redevelopment, so that council housing will have to be offered. In addition,

[1] See the favourable experience of Local Authority III. (P.E.P. Report, p. 94.)

those who have applied for council housing will eventually come to the top of the list; and the survey of immigrants showed that about one-tenth of the West Indians had gone as far as to put their names on the list. Housing more immigrants in council housing is likely to make immigrants aware of council housing as a possibility and will increase spontaneous demand. This demand will be additionally increased because of the lack of private accommodation that is open to them.

As the demand for council houses grows amongst immigrants, local authorities will find it necessary to formulate more positive long-term aims. For their policies can to a considerable extent influence future settlement patterns and thereby the overall processes of absorption of the various immigrant groups. Authorities can either consolidate incipient coloured quarters by selective clearing and development, by limiting multi-occupation to certain zones, and by rehousing coloured people only in inferior central dwellings.[1] Alternatively, they can adopt a policy of deliberate dispersal, by placing deserving coloured tenants in the 'good' estates, and avoiding over-concentration in all areas.

Up to the present, most local authorities have done little to disperse coloured immigrants out from the central zones of bad housing by means of rehousing. Many have, however, done a good deal to help the immigrants find accommodation and start moving out by means of their mortgage schemes.

Here again, the situation varies greatly from one authority to another. Some give 100% loans freely and with few conditions, while others adopt a conservative approach near to that of the building societies. Attitudes on such matters as the borrower's income, second mortgages, joint ownership, and lodgers vary widely. On the whole, as Elizabeth Burney pointed out, 'local authorities have regarded the granting of mortgages as a social service, and many take the view that it is a useful way of preventing deterioration of older houses. With the emphasis on older, cheaper houses,[2] many of these schemes have been of immense help to immigrants.'[3]

She went on to describe in considerable detail the immense and generous G.L.C. (former L.C.C.) mortgage scheme[4] as the 'one thing which more than anything else has helped the housing of coloured people in Britain'. This involved the lending of nearly £150m. to over 31,000 borrowers during the period March 1963 and July 1965 (when

[1] As in some parts of London, Birmingham, and (or so Ipswich Trades Council claimed in October 1965) in Ipswich (*Evening Star*, 29 October; 3 December).

[2] See Ministry of Housing Circular 24/66.

[3] Burney, op. cit., p. 51. In 1966 over half the coloured owner-occupiers in Lambeth had mortgages from either the G.L.C. or Lambeth Council.

[4] See article by Gillian Stevens, 'Home Loans in London' (*New Society*, 15 July 1965) for the report of a survey in 1964 of comparative opportunities within the Greater London area.

Government sanction for corporation mortgages was suspended). This approach was based on the value of the property rather than the status of the applicant. Immigrants were regarded as on the whole good payers, anxious to become full owners. Coloured immigrants have also benefited out of proportion to their total numbers from the new G.L.C. scheme, started in June 1966,[1] though apparently the G.L.C. has been cautious on the 'valuation gap' and multi-occupation, two matters which affect immigrant buyers more than most others.

Policies adopted by various local authorities included the following, as noted by Burney:[2]

(1) *Manchester*—£11½m. lent to 7,600 applicants between 1955 and 1966. Focus on property, not employment or residential status of borrower. Second mortgages not objected to. Conventional approach and stringent valuation standards nevertheless bear hard on immigrants. Money rarely lent on pre-1914 property.

(2) *Nottingham*—variable-interest rate scheme in operation since January 1965 (with 'squeeze' gap). Loans on older houses. Many applications from coloured people, mainly West Indians, carefully scrutinized and possibility of multi-occupation regarded as virtual disqualification, so that few loans given except on small houses.

(3) *Wolverhampton*—Limited general provisions for mortgages and small and cautious help for immigrants. 'Immigrant' houses subject to annual inspection by the public health department to check that there is no multiple occupation.

(4) *Bedford*—Generous provisions: second mortgages, lodgers and part-owners allowed, subject to council approval. Encouragement of home-ownership thought preferable to giving council housing at the expense of native Bedfordians.

(5) *Bristol*—100% thirty-five-year mortgages available to all immigrants—home ownership regarded as aiding dispersal.

(6) *Birmingham*—A third of loans granted in Handsworth to date have gone to coloured immigrants. Conditions include owner-occupation only. Home ownership said to be of major importance as a factor promoting settlement and integration and neighbourhood rehabilitation.

(7) '*A Yorkshire borough*'—30% of mortgages in 1966 went to immigrants, mainly Pakistanis buying old terraced houses.

Some glimmer of light on the policies of six local housing authorities was also cast by the P.E.P. Report. The relevant conclusions have already been set out on pp. 211–12.

[1] Suspended again on 6 June 1967, when the G.L.C. funds ran out and the Government refused to make more available for the rest of the year.

[2] See also P.E.P. Report, p. 297, for information about the mortgages policies in Areas 1 and 2.

The *Observer* (23 April 1967) alleged that the six areas surveyed by the P.E.P. Report were: (1) Brent; (2) Islington; (3) Keighley; (4) Sheffield; (5) Slough; (6) West Bromwich.

While there were no details of the identification, there were rigorous denials of the details reported in the survey. From Brent came a comment from the housing committee chairman, Alderman Philip Hartley. He described the comments in the report as a 'serious misunderstanding of policy'. A council spokesman spoke of the 'broken pledge' of confidence, but said that the borough had nothing to hide: 'Brent comes out . . . as well as anyone can expect from a report of this kind. . . . There is no racial discrimination practised by either the Council or the officers of this borough. Brent has nothing to be ashamed of.' (*Willesden Chronicle*, 28 April 1967.) Islington and Keighley both firmly maintained that there was no discrimination in the allocation of houses. (*Guardian*, 24 April 1967, 25 April 1967; *Telegraph and Argus*, 25 April 1967; *Islington Gazette*, 28 April 1967.) An Islington Labour councillor, Mrs. Elizabeth Hoodless, who has taken up the matter and inspected the housing files, said that the statement that 'Islington did not rehouse immigrants until recently is clearly inaccurate'.

2. (*c*) SOME SPECIAL AREAS[1]

A. LONDON

(i) *General Problems*

Major sources for the housing situation in London in the early 1960's are the Milner Holland Report (Cmnd 2605), the surveys commissioned by the Committee for the Government Social Survey, and the various reports presented to it by different bodies.[2] Of these one of the most detailed and valuable was the evidence prepared by the Centre for Urban Studies, of which a considerable part was published under the title *London's Housing Needs* by Ruth Glass and John Westergaard.[3] This also contained some material from the Centre's North Kensington Survey, to be published separately. North Kensington, which was among the areas most notorious for 'Rachmanism' in recent years, was also described in vividly impressionistic terms in Pearl Jephcott's book *A Troubled Area.*[4]

[1] These area reports and notes are compiled from past *Newsletter* notes and records. They are thus neither complete, evenly balanced, nor all-embracing; we publish them here as background material which may be of use to inquirers, who are also referred to our series of special area supplements.

[2] Most recent sources are: G.L.C. report in May 1967 on its housing programme; *Our Older Homes*, H.M.S.O., 1966.

[3] Centre for Urban Studies, Report No. 5, University College, London, 1965.

[4] Pearl Jephcott, *A Troubled Area*, London, Faber and Faber, 1964.

In late 1964 the enormity of London's housing problem was underlined by Mrs. Evelyn Denington, Chairman of the G.L.C. housing committee, who said that in Islington alone there was an overspill of 100,000 which the Borough Council could not house. An L.C.C. survey report submitted to the Milner Holland Committee estimated that Greater London needed at least 250,000 more houses, if each family desiring a separate dwelling was to have one. Some form of compulsion might be essential, it was said, if the moving of population out of London was not to be caught up by immigration into London from the provinces and from overseas.

The hardships and stresses that beset London's rented housing were outlined as follows by the Milner Holland Report:

1. The discomfort and inconvenience of obsolete, ill-equipped or ill-maintained property.
2. Housing occupied by several households who share, or altogether lack, basic amenities such as sinks, cookers, lavatories and hot water supply.
3. The unhappiness that can be caused to young families who, for lack of a separate home, 'live in' with relations. The lack of privacy for these households is often more damaging than that suffered by the previous group.
4. Overcrowding, which may occur in any type of property but which is harder to bear where amenities are shared or lacking.
5. Rents which may or may not be reasonable for the property but which are excessive in relation to the tenants' income.
6. The strain imposed by disputes between landlords and tenants, and the more widespread anxieties arising from lack of security of tenure.

Most of these hardships fall into two groups, or complexes, both of which are found in an inner ring of boroughs, mainly north of the river. (a) Obsolete and ill-equipped property covers large areas built to house working-class people during the last century. These areas extend north-eastwards, eastwards and south-eastwards from the centre of London. (b) The sharing of houses (often built originally for households larger and wealthier than those currently occupying them, and ill-adapted for the purpose for which they are now used), overcrowding, excessive rents and the conflicts and anxieties too often arising in these conditions present another complex of problems. This second group of problems is concentrated in smaller, widely scattered areas, mainly spread across the western, northern and eastern parts of inner London. The overcrowding and misuse of subdivided housing found in the western parts of inner London arises principally from the concentration of small households competing for the small units of accommodation available in this part of London. Larger families, who suffer much greater hardships from living in this sort of accommodation, are more often found in subdivided property on the eastern side of inner London.

The Report went on to talk of the paradox of 'squalor in the midst of progress'.

Greater London is one of the wealthiest cities in Europe; unemployment is rare and incomes are rising; population within the built-up area is falling and the number of dwellings is growing; the quality of housing and the general standard of housing conditions are both improving. Yet conditions in *some* neighbourhoods and for *some* people remain bad, and are probably becoming worse; too many people suffer hardships and abuses which should not be tolerated in a civilized community. Although obsolete, ill-equipped and shared dwellings are dwindling, it is in the more fortunate neighbourhoods and among the more fortunate classes of people that they have dwindled most rapidly. Overcrowding is proving a much more intractable problem and this too is being eliminated most rapidly from the neighbourhoods where it is least common. How can such hardships persist in a city which is in many ways so fortunate?

There was no simple cause, and no single remedy, concluded the Committee. One hypothesis which it examined and discarded was that migration to London, particularly from overseas, had created the worst housing conditions and that these could be eliminated by stricter control of immigration:

. . . The numbers of foreign-born people living in London increased by 57% between 1951 and 1961, at which point they were divided in three fairly equal parts according to origin; coming from Ireland, the Commonwealth, and other foreign countries, mainly European. This was a rapid rate of increase, though the total numbers involved are still small by comparison with the experience of many other countries, and the rate of immigration has since been reduced, for the whole country, to a level that in 1964 probably fell below the numbers emigrating from the country. It is clear that recent immigrants are more often found in crowded conditions and in shared houses than native-born Londoners. But immigrants come to London in search of work—and find it, for we have seen no evidence that they are more frequently unemployed or dependent on National Assistance than others in similar occupations. If they did not come, either their places would be taken by migrants from other parts of the country, or a large number of essential jobs would remain unfilled. The plight of the immigrant is the outcome, and too often an extreme example of London's housing difficulties; it is not their cause.

London's housing problems are complicated and deep-rooted, and fundamentally the same as in Charles Booth's day, continued the Report. The main factors aggravating the stresses caused by the shortage of housing in London are:[1]

(i) the rapid growth of employment in London, leading to an exceptionally high proportion of young people and single people and to a high consequent demand for separate accommodation;

[1] Milner Holland Report, p. 205. See also Glass and Westergaard, *London's Housing Needs*, Part I.

(ii) the division of the population of London into more numerous and smaller households, and the consequent increase in demand for housing;
(iii) the accentuation of this demand by the growing numbers of old people who continue to maintain separate households;
(iv) the additional demands caused by the progress of slum clearance, which results in a need to cater for more households than the number of dwellings demolished;
(v) the increasing competition for living space by those with increased wealth caused by higher standards of prosperity, and the consequent upward movement of house prices; and
(vi) the natural demand for higher standards of housing in an era of rapid economic growth and rising prosperity.

The trends of recent years have given fresh urgency to these problems, but the problems themselves are not new. Charles Booth, writing in 1901, said he was 'ready to accept any view, however extreme, of the insufficiency, badness and dearness of the accommodation available for the people in many parts of London. . . . The pressure on housing in London springs from three or four causes. The first two are the natural increase of population, coupled with influx from other places; a third is the need of space for buildings other than dwelling houses, and for the widening of railway lines or of streets; while the fourth follows the requirements of a higher standard of life and health.'

In 1961 the London conurbation, with less than a fifth of the total stock of dwellings, had well over half of all the multi-occupied dwellings in the country. There were, however, only 26,000 dwellings in the whole conurbation which contained four or more households (though there may have been some under-enumeration) but the bulk was concentrated in certain areas and districts within them, thereby posing great problems to the particular local authorities responsible. The principal districts involved were Islington, Kensington, Paddington, Lambeth, Hackney, Willesden, Wandsworth, St. Pancras, Hornsey, Hammersmith and Hampstead. Some of the worst conditions were said to be found in single-room lettings, often occupied by families with children, in old houses with few facilities. This type of letting increased between 1951 and 1961 in thirteen districts and overcrowding increased in the same period in nine districts. Signs of increasing stress were visible in Islington, Kensington, Lambeth, Hackney, Willesden, Hammersmith, Hornsey, and Stoke Newington.

The effect on health of the stresses accentuated by multi-occupation (stresses not inevitable in well-maintained properties but frequent in others) was commented upon by Dr. J. H. Weir, the Medical Officer of Health for Kensington:

. . . the herding together of people, often incompatible, the inconveniences, the lack of space especially for such things as play or pram storage, the inadequate and inconvenient washing, sanitary and food handling facilities, stairs, noise, fetching and carrying distances, and the dirt, dilapidation and depressing appearance consequent upon the neglect of parts used in common, all have their effects. To these must be added the increased liability to home accidents, infections, contagion, risk of fire and mental stress. It is impossible to assess the relative incidence of different types of illness as a result of bad housing. On the other hand, various analyses of applications for rehousing on medical grounds have shown the preponderance of two concomitants of multiple occupation—respiratory illness and psychological or psychosomatic disorders. Examination of statistics given in seven articles on the subject shows that the former group accounts for between 14 and 28%, and the latter between 14 and 31% of applications.[1]

(ii) *Immigrant Landlords and Tenants*

The 1964 Landlord Inquiry showed that half of owner-occupier landlords were born outside Britain, whereas almost all 'extra-mural' and tenant landlords were British born. Among the overseas-born owner-occupier landlords 31% were European-born, 15% were born in the West Indies, Pakistan, India, or West Africa, and 5% were from other Commonwealth countries.

Of overseas-born tenants, three-fifths lived in furnished accommodation, where they constituted a half of all tenants. Newcomers to an area who were not known to a landlord were at a considerable disadvantage in the competition for privately rented property, particularly if, in addition, they had children, and were foreign or coloured.

During the Milner Holland committee's inquiry, a substantial body of evidence emerged about coloured immigrants both as landlords and tenants.[2] According to a Centre for Urban Studies estimate in August 1964 a total of 353,300 immigrants from Asian, African, and Caribbean countries was then living in the Greater London conurbation (or 4% of the total population); of these 194,000 were in the administrative County of London (or 6% of the total population). 47% of the total numbers of such immigrants in Great Britain were estimated to be living in Greater London.

The Milner Holland Report described the general housing difficulties of immigrants as two-fold: first, they have very low priority for public housing, and second they suffer from discrimination by private landlords, including the imposition of a colour tax.[3] These difficulties have led to the widespread purchase of houses: here again the immigrants are often the victims of inexperience, ignorance, and exploitation by self-styled house-agents and loan-providers. A common end result is that the immigrant purchaser finds himself the owner of indifferent or bad property for which he has paid too much, and saddled with

[1] Paper quoted in Milner Holland Report, p. 71.

[2] Milner Holland Report, Ch. 9.

[3] For instance, 27% of landlords in their advertisement survey barred coloured tenants and only 6% said they would welcome them. (Ibid., p. 189.)

liabilities for rates, interest, and repayments, and obligations for repair, far beyond his means. This inevitably leads to high rents and overcrowding, strains and pressures on protected local tenants, who are likely to be bitterly resented; often everything possible is done to persuade them to move, even to the extent of petty persecution, in favour of tenants willing to pay higher rentals.

The Report went on to say that while coloured landlords were mentioned in ninety-nine out of the 790 cases of abuses[1] covered by the survey, a somewhat higher than average proportion of them relating to illegal evictions and improper attempts to get vacant possession, there was no reason to believe that there was an exceptionally high incidence of abuses in property for which coloured landlords were responsible.

In parts of London with a relatively high coloured immigrant population, a large proportion of the cases brought to the notice of Rent Tribunals were clearly likely to relate to persons not of U.K. origin. For instance, the Chairman of the North-West London Rent Tribunal estimated that in the two years prior to 31 March 1964 about 90% of the applicants and also of the landlords involved were Africans, West Indians, Indians, Pakistanis, Cypriots, Italians, Southern Irish, and some Poles, Germans, or Austrians. The cases seemed to fall into four general categories:

Most of these landlords are inexperienced as such and fall into a number of different categories, e.g. those who:

(i) Have purchased a house, usually at an excessive cost, to let in multiple occupation. Their capital is often insufficient for them to carry out necessary repairs or to furnish the rooms properly. They promise tenants that they will have the repairs done and that they will provide better or additional furniture. When these promises are not kept, tenants sometimes apply to the Tribunal.

(ii) Buy a house for family occupation and finding the outgoings high and, having difficulty in keeping up mortgage and hire purchase payments, let one or more rooms to help out. When this accommodation is required for additional members of the family coming from abroad, the tenant, if he hears of this before he is given notice to quit, may apply to the Tribunal to fix a rent in the hope of obtaining some security of tenure.

(iii) Borrow money at a high rate of interest, repayable over a short period, perhaps five years, to purchase a house and then find it necessary to charge an excessive rent to enable them to meet their mortgage payment.

(iv) Being unable to find suitable furnished accommodation, rent an unfurnished house or flat, buy furniture on hire purchase terms and let off rooms to help towards the unfurnished rent and cost of furniture. Sometimes they make little profit, even though the rent they charge for the furnished accommodation may be excessive, because the uncontrolled rent of the unfurnished house is often very high.

[1] For a more detailed account of abuses see ibid., Appendix III.

The Milner Holland Report gave some details of the methods of purchase used by some coloured immigrants, in the form of finance pools among Asians and more modest 'pardners' or 'sou-sou' schemes among West Indians. Normal local sources of financing such as building societies were rarely available to the coloured immigrants or others with no capital and a modest weekly wage purchasing indifferent property.

And, on the occasions when he is, the difficulty remains of bridging the gap between the available mortgage and the purchase price plus the total costs of completion. He is driven to raise money on mortgage at high interest rates; where this is required to fill the 'gap', it will be a second mortgage. These mortgages, and particularly the second mortgage, are often repayable over short periods up to five years; and interest rates from 11% to 15% per annum have been quoted to us. It may be that, the security being indifferent, such rates can be justified; but the cost inflates the difficulties of the purchaser and contributes to many of the troubles we have investigated. A specious advertisement of 'second mortgages at 7%' proves on examination to be a mortgage repayable over 2 to 5 years, by equal monthly instalments, the 7% per annum being calculated over the whole period and added to the original loan capital. Thus an advance of £1,000 on second mortgage 'at 7%' is repayable over 5 years by 60 monthly instalments of £22 10s. 0d., a total of £1,350; the 5-year loan costs £350. The true rate of interest is in fact about 11%.[1] There is no actual mis-statement in the advertisement, but we think it unlikely that the true rate of interest is appreciated at first glance by the coloured immigrant.

The services of mortgage brokers are also sometimes used; and the practices of many operators in this field are not beyond reproach. A number of cases have come to the notice of Citizens' Advice Bureaux in London where survey fees and preliminary charges of all kinds are demanded and paid; when, as often happens, no mortgage results, substantial amounts—occasionally the whole of the sum paid—are never recovered.

Other features of relations between coloured landlords and tenants were noted, especially overcrowding. Census calculations were almost certainly understatements, but the 1963 Tenant Inquiry showed that in the households overcrowded according to the statutory standard half of the heads of households were born outside Great Britain. In a smaller sample in a Paddington area, with overcrowding defined as more than one and a half persons per room, 64% of coloured households were overcrowded compared with 29% for the whole estate. Main reasons for this were the need for economy and the high proportion of children, particularly very young ones.

Repair and cleanliness of premises were also mentioned. There was some truth in the generalization about the shabbiness, dirtiness, and state of disrepair of houses occupied by coloured people, but this applied mainly to the outside of the building and the common parts, while individual rooms were usually clean and well kept. This neglect of the

[1] Calculated on the basis of annual 'rents'.

shared amenities and public ways was the main cause of complaint and unrest among white tenants in buildings shared with coloured people. Noise, late-night parties and other practices that disturbed or annoyed neighbours produced a great deal of friction, whether or not the assertions were generally justifiable.

This chapter of the Report concluded:

> The evidence we have received leads us to five broad conclusions:
>
> (1) The basic nature of the difficulties of coloured immigrants is the same in quality as that of all the newcomers to London without adequate means, arriving at a time when many local authority housing lists are very overcrowded or even closed, and in conditions where they obtain a very low priority for allocation of housing.
> (2) For coloured immigrants these difficulties are accentuated by a marked degree of reluctance to make rented accommodation available to them.
> (3) Their inexperience and their acute need leads them to ill-advised purchases of unsuitable property at high prices, and to involving themselves in expensive mortgages; in these matters they do not receive sufficient reliable professional help and advice, and in a number of respects they are often shamelessly exploited.
> (4) The direct results of the combination of all these factors are overcrowding, the unsatisfactory use of large houses for ill-arranged multi-occupation, and high rent levels.
> (5) Although coloured immigrants are in great demand in London for manning many of its services, they are one of the groups who have the greatest difficulty in securing satisfactory housing accommodation.

(iii) *London's Housing Needs*

In its conclusions, the Milner Holland Report took the view that the 'Sisyphean task' of rehousing Londoners would not be satisfactorily brought about without encouraging private capital back into the housing market for rented flats and houses. By contrast Ruth Glass and John Westergaard came out firmly against this view in their report, stating unequivocally that:

> . . . private landlords cannot be expected to cope with the backlog of housing troubles. . . . Housing must be transformed into a social service. We regard a greatly expanded public housing sector as the only hope for the reduction and eventual solution of London's housing problems.[1]

The latter view was also expressed in the Government's White Paper, *The Housing Programme 1965–70*, which declared in November 1965:

> . . . the experience of recent years has clearly demonstrated that the shortage of rented accommodation will not be overcome by a revival of private landlordism.

[1] Ibid., p. x.

In March 1965 the Greater London Council had given instructions that urgent consideration should be given—in consultation with the thirty-two London borough authorities—to that part of the Milner Holland Report which pointed out that any attempts to improve living conditions in the most densely populated central boroughs could only be carried out by an overall authority for Greater London. On 14 December 1965 the G.L.C. received a report from its Housing Committee which called for an all-out onslaught on London's 'twilight areas', on the lines indicated by the recently announced pioneer agreement between Islington and the G.L.C. to tackle that borough's slum clearance housing and overspill problems in full partnership, 'pooling resources and expertise'. For the new region-wide attack on the twilight zones help would be required from the Minister of Housing: help to raise the enormous capital involved and to grant all the necessary powers to the local authorities. It was, however, made clear that redevelopment would be a long business. Stage 1 would consist of first aid repairs and a determined effort to reduce overcrowding and prevent new people from coming in. To help house the displaced families while their homelands were being rebuilt the committee pointed to such empty 'once-for-all' sites such as Woolwich Arsenal, Croydon and Hendon airports and surplus railway land; the green or undeveloped areas of outer London would also help in the 'rippling out' process for displaced families from the congested areas and part of the overspill would be accommodated in new and expanding towns outside London.

During the debate on this report the chairman and vice-chairman of the Housing Committee, Mrs. Evelyn Denington and Mr. Arthur Wicks, both gave an assurance to Dr. David Pitt, chairman of C.A.R.D., that the G.L.C. never had and never would pass over an area due for 'urban renewal' because it might involve rehousing coloured immigrants who lived there. The G.L.C., it was said, always sought to integrate immigrants 'with the rest of us'; they were regarded as 'just London citizens' and were dealt with like other citizens in their areas. The Housing Committee's chairman added that the Council hoped to expand its programme from something over 5,000 houses a year to 8,000. Mr. David Chalkley (Lab., Lewisham) said that the Council was still short of dwellings (in his estimate, about 300,000 short).

Some weeks earlier Mr. Robert Mellish, Joint Parliamentary Secretary to the Ministry of Housing and Local Government, announcing that the Government would ensure that local councils would be able to secure from the Exchequer enough money to provide some 125,000 new homes during the four-year period 1965–9, had told journalists that there were some 200,000 families more than there were houses in London. This figure was, in the opinion of the *St. Pancras Chronicle* (1 October), expressing a fairly widespread view of the immigration-housing issue:

. . . a scathing indictment of a long succession of post-war planners. Why are all these families in London at all if there are no homes for them? Many of these families have been displaced from their former homes through properties changing ownership and many of them have been on local council housing lists for more than ten years, a truly disgraceful state of affairs. It is surely indisputable that the first claim on such a vital commodity as housing in the Metropolis should have been held by Londoners born and bred. This has not been so. In the disgusting free-for-all in the property market during the post-war years thousands of houses in slum areas have been sold to immigrants at absurdly high prices and are now in multiple occupation, while land speculators and the manipulators of the money market have made it impossible for local authorities in London to buy land for housing. If any politician or local councillor doubts the veracity of this, let him question long-standing residents in such areas as Camden Town, Kentish Town, Islington, Hackney and Stoke Newington where there is a deep-rooted sense of frustration and bitterness—and among the elderly—a deep fear of what the future holds.

Among the new and expanding towns in which part of London's overspill might be accommodated were north Buckinghamshire, Ipswich, Northampton, and Peterborough. It was also proposed to make an overspill town of Barnstaple in North Devon; this aroused considerable local opposition, some of it allegedly because of 'apprehensions about a possible influx of coloured workers into the countryside', but also because of more general objections to the intrusion of urban and industrial development into 'one of the few areas of comparatively unspoilt natural beauty remaining in Britain'. Earlier in the year an L.C.C. plan for an overspill scheme at Mildenhall was suspended when it appeared that the local authorities would not house twenty-five coloured workers employed by a firm interested in moving there from London. The Council was reported to have been strongly swayed by Mr. Trevor Hagger, prospective Conservative candidate for Ipswich, who said that immigrants lived 'ten to a room' and would create 'another Smethwick' at Mildenhall. Two weeks later, however, Mildenhall agreed to take coloured workers 'providing they can be integrated happily' and the expansion scheme controlled.

(iv) *Notes on Some London Boroughs*

Lambeth

The areas named by the G.L.C. Housing Committee's report as the worst for overcrowding and multi-occupation were Paddington, North Kensington, Islington, and Hackney. At the end of 1965 all were reported to be reasonably optimistic about handling their housing problems without taking account of colour. In Westminster, for instance, which includes Paddington, the Housing Committee chairman, Councillor Jack Gillett, was reported as saying that redeveloping an 'immigrant area' would cause complaints and difficulties but could not be side-stepped. A similar view was expressed by Kensington's chairman, Councillor J. E. Baldwin, when commenting upon the 'exaggerated' claims of another borough, Lambeth, whose housing problem (13,500 on the housing list and no building land) was reported as serious but less so than those of the above-mentioned London areas.

By contrast with these areas, Lambeth, for well over a decade the relatively untroubled borough with the no-differentiation, *laissez-faire* approach to its large West Indian immigrant settlement centred on Brixton, began to show apprehension and agitation over the rehousing of coloured immigrants early in 1965. (In a 1964 Lambeth poll concerning neighbourhood complaints in general, the highest proportion (138) had cited 'immigration', in one form or another.)[1]

There were several meetings during the spring and summer of 1965 with Mr. Maurice Foley, Mr. Robert Mellish, and representatives of the G.L.C. and other local authorities. In mid-May a twenty-five-point plan was published by the Labour-controlled Council, parts of which were described by a Conservative Councillor, Mr. Walter Dennis, as 'dynamite'. This plan called for—

> . . . a much enlarged housing programme to deal with the situation, and said that areas of immigrant concentration, when defined by research teams, should be designated as 'areas of special housing need'. Public ownership of such areas was essential, they should be developed comprehensively and not piecemeal, and steps should be taken to prevent further spread of immigrant concentration. Procedure for compulsory acquisition must be speeded up; there should also be a first-aid programme to remedy more serious housing defects. If Lambeth was to avoid race riots, a five-year residential qualification should be maintained before families could apply for council houses 'until progress has been made towards assimilation'. Social workers, some from Commonwealth countries, with special knowledge of immigrants' countries, should also be appointed to the council's welfare departments. (*South London Advertiser*, 13 May 1965.)

In its talks with ministries and the G.L.C. the Lambeth Council had put forward its idea of rehousing a small fixed percentage of coloured families at a time on Council estates (5% was the arbitrary figure put forward as the maximum to maintain a 'level of tolerance' to promote integration);[2] it had also asked the Government to give financial sponsorship for a research project into areas with special immigrant problems. The Government finally decided not to recognize any special housing need linked with the presence of a coloured immigrant population, and also refused help for the survey already commissioned from Research Services Ltd.

[1] See Sharpe in *Colour and the British Electorate*, p. 15.

[2] According to the first 'official' count, forty-nine coloured families were rehoused in Lambeth in 1966.

Lambeth countered with a well-timed and headline-stealing[1] statement entitled 'Immigration from the Commonwealth', issued on 24 November 1965 just before the G.L.C. meeting. In this the Council outlined its housing problem and its need for massive outside help in a situation further complicated by 'the existence of the large and expanding immigrant population' (estimated by the Council at over 30,000 coloured and non-coloured persons).[2]

A particular problem mentioned was the Council's acquisition some years before from the Church Commissioners of freeholds in the Loughborough Park district, including some 200 houses in Geneva and Somerleyton Roads, the most highly concentrated West Indian settlement (six out of every ten residents were said to be coloured).[3] The original intention had been to pull down these houses, rehouse their occupants and rebuild, but this was now said to be impossible. Since the leases were due to expire in June 1966 the Council faced the issue that it must itself become a 'slum landlord of this particular area with its acute social problems'. It could not promise speedily to resolve the bad conditions in Geneva and Somerleyton Roads by rehousing the families living there; but it could and would improve the standard of repair, reduce overcrowding as casual vacancies arose, review exorbitant rents, and reduce the risks of fire. It would also welcome additional powers on the lines of the Birmingham private Bill relating to the registration of multi-occupied dwellings.

This statement, which in effect linked the housing issue with coloured immigration, was condemned by the Lambeth Trades Council as a 'cowardly and despicable action'. The St. John's Inter-Racial Club carried out a house-to-house survey to check the Council's claims of dilapidation and overcrowding. According to this survey, claims of overcrowding were exaggerated; well over half the houses were classified as 'in fair condition', all those classified as poor being owned by absentee

[1] One advance sample from the front page of *The People* (21 November): 'Coloured Slums in Chaos—Official—London S.O.S.—"It's hopeless".'

[2] According to the 1961 Census some 5·6% of the population of 223,763 in the old borough was coloured (4·6% West Indian). The Borough's own sample housing survey in 1966 showed that households with coloured heads constituted 8·7% of the total, concentration mainly in two out of five areas (17% and 10% of total households in each area respectively). That concentration was nowhere very high was indicated by the fact that in January 1967 only one school had more than 50% of West Indian pupils.

[3] For a description of this area and Brixton in general in the years up to 1962, see S. Patterson, *Dark Strangers*, Penguin, *passim*; for an account of the political aspects, especially in the tense pre-election period of 1964, see L. J. Sharpe in *Colour and the British Electorate*, Chapter 2; and for a detailed and discerning report on Lambeth Borough Council's attitude to immigrants and housing up to early 1967 (including the continuing saga of Somerleyton and Geneva Roads) see Elizabeth Burney, op. cit., Ch. V.

landlords. Immigrants were reported to be angry at the statement and alarmed at the Council's decision to charge house-owners for dilapidations after the leaseholds became Council property in June 1966. The G.L.C. and other London boroughs were also reported as annoyed by what they regarded as an attempt to win an unmerited priority by 'hanging from the immigrant hook'.

Meanwhile Lambeth's housing problems and Lambeth's image were not improved by some highly publicized remarks made by Mr. Robert Mellish at the Labour Party Conference in Blackpool in late September 1965. In a speech referring to London's housing problems, he said that, if the conference wanted him to ask Lambeth to give precedence over its own people already on the housing list to coloured people, this would be 'asking Lambeth to create the most grievous racial disturbances we have ever seen in London'. This statement produced both applause and uproarious protests, the latter renewed when Mr. Mellish advised 'those who talk about integration to go to Victoria on a Sunday night and see hundreds of these people coming from the West Indies with no homes here, no jobs, some without friends'.

Mr. Mellish subsequently told the executive committee of the London Labour Party, five members of which had 'strongly dissociated' themselves from the speech, that he regretted the impression his remarks had made and hoped his record in urging London Councils to provide proper housing for immigrants would be taken into account by his critics. The columnist of the *South London Press* pointed out that the charge of racialism levelled against Mr. Mellish concealed the real issue, that of unrestricted immigration, irrespective of skin colour, from, among other sources, Eire with its high birth-rate. 'Can you integrate a quart into a pint pot?' asked the same writer.

As immigrants have moved out from the central areas of settlement, many new streets have gone into multi-occupation in Lambeth as elsewhere. Some are smaller substantial houses, suitable for two-family houses if suitably adapted, but often occupied by three or more. In October 1966 Lambeth introduced a registration scheme for multi-occupied houses in the six central wards of the borough, but the response in the initial months was, not surprisingly, poor. Since 1965 Lambeth has also pushed ahead with decrowding houses in multiple occupation, a policy which was soon followed by reports of increased multi-occupation in Wandsworth, Croydon, and other neighbouring boroughs. Inspection was reportedly confined mainly to the houses financed by Lambeth or G.L.C. mortgages, which forbid tenants.[1]

[1] Elizabeth Burney, op. cit., pp. 128–31, discusses this operation in detail. The Borough also introduced a code of practices for multi-occupied houses in April 1966. In 1966 it was reported that half of the coloured owner-occupiers in Lambeth had mortgages from either the G.L.C. or Lambeth Borough.

Those who remained in the Somerleyton–Geneva Road area at the time of the Council take-over in mid-1966 became direct Council tenants, the Council having agreed to accept as tenants anyone who was in occupancy up to a few weeks before the date. Many rents were substantially reduced and the N.A.B. gave loans to people acquiring furniture for the first time. Some residents disappeared, others were rehoused, or rather 'transferred', often to unimproved short-life houses awaiting redevelopment. Six months later some 150 (over half of them coloured) of the 780 households taken on as tenants had been moved, mostly to similar accommodation within the immediate area. Meanwhile it had been discovered that the physical state of the property was worse than had been anticipated; about a third of the houses in Somerleyton Road were so rotten as to be dangerous.[1]

In March 1967 the Council leader, Alderman Cotton, announced a rate increase and again revived the demand for 'massive assistance' from the government in order to get more land and house its 30,000 immigrants. This was presented as the front page lead story by the *South London Press* (17 March), under the secondary heading 'Council with too many immigrants has bought streets of houses'.

What of the future for Brixton and the West Indian community there? Elizabeth Burney writes:

> In many ways this reflected the wishes of the inhabitants. It would be wrong to give the impression that coloured families all went under protest to the old houses allocated to them, as long as this meant they could remain in the neighbourhood. Officials were often surprised to find how a neighbourhood with such a bad name to the outside world should attract such a strong core of loyalists, of all races. It was after all a very convenient place—handy for many people's work, handy for shopping, especially in the vivid, teeming Brixton market which lay only a few hundred yards off. Many families, too, attached great importance to remaining near their children's schools and, especially retaining rights over one of the rare nursery school places in the immediate neighbourhood. This was said to have been a cause for which several households sacrificed the chance of better accommodation. There is a great deal that is warm, sociable and attractive about central Brixton as its West Indian inhabitants have made it; a great potential for planners to build on if only they knew how. A tenants' association had, for example, been started with the encouragement of the housing department in Geneva-Somerleyton; it got off to a shaky beginning, but at least it was the right sort of idea.
>
> The rebuilding of central Brixton, market, shops and all, is one of the borough council's most cherished plans. Much of the residential property round about it is already in phased redevelopment programmes. Nearly all the houses into which the inhabitants of Geneva-Somerleyton were being

[1] In April 1967 an increasing minority of houses in Somerleyton Road (the worst of the two streets) were empty and barricaded up with boards and bricks.

reshuffled had a 'life' of seven years or less. This could—with emphasis on the conditional—be the justification for the short-term rehousing of coloured families in the Brixton area in houses no one else would accept. A double standard is operated now; whatever happens it must not be allowed to continue to operate when redevelopment takes place. The vitality of the immigrant population of Brixton is one of the area's greatest assets; there is an enormous, scarcely recognized opportunity to use it constructively, in redevelopment which takes full account of social as well as physical needs, and which recognizes the character which the immigrants have stamped on the neighbourhood. To concentrate the West Indians in Brixton slums now, can only be justified if they are given a full share in the new Brixton of the future. To do so would require new, imaginative departures in community planning. The sour American tag says that 'urban renewal means negro removal'. Can Lambeth, on its present record, be trusted to prove this untrue?[1]

Notting Hill and Paddington

Notting Hill gained greater notoriety than Paddington as a result of the racial disturbances of 1958. In many other respects, however, these two joining districts are similar. Both are central reception areas, with a highly transient, ethnically mixed population, little local industry, and virtually no internal social control or sense of local community. Both are overcrowded areas where newcomers come to live because they must, and leave as soon as possible if they have the wherewithal to do so. And both have been foci of anti-social and criminal activities and the scene of operations by speculative property companies which have increased existing frictions between newcomers and local people.

So much background material has now become available about housing and living conditions in these particular areas that it cannot be incorporated here. Readers are referred particularly to the North Kensington Survey conducted by the Centre of Urban Studies (see *London's Housing Needs*) and Pearl Jephcott's study of Notting Hill for the North Kensington Family Study (*A Troubled Area*).[2]

Southall

In Southall (since April 1965 part of the new enlarged borough of Ealing) housing has been a major area of friction for some years. In July 1965 the Conservative minority moved an amendment stipulating a fifteen-year residential qualification for immigrants before they could

[1] Ibid.

[2] See also, *New Society*, 1 August 1964, pp. 144–6, for an article on the housing debates in the House of Commons on 8 and 22 July 1963; and the summary of 'Some Aspects of Rachmanism' in I.R.R. *Newsletter*, September 1963, pp. 7–9; and reports of the work of the Notting Hill Housing Trust, set up in December 1963 by a group of local people, *Guardian*, 23 August 1965, and 'Shelter' in I.R.R. *Newsletter*, February 1967, p. 10.

join the housing list, and a five-year qualification for British-born residents. This was in fact only a gesture since there were very few immigrants on the housing lists. Five Labour councillors also voted for the amendment while one abstained (the amendment was nevertheless defeated). The Labour Party withdrew its Whips from the rebels and, after lengthy bargaining, expelled five of them in early 1966. One was later readmitted without a withdrawal.

In late September Conservatives and the break-away Labour group held a joint meeting with delegates representing residents' associations covering the whole borough, at which priority for 'our own people' was restressed, and also the fact that the restriction was intended to apply to all newcomers, coloured or not.[1]

The atmosphere in Southall was certainly exacerbated by the Southall Residents' Association, founded in 1963 from a nucleus of dissatisfied parents with children at the Beaconsfield Road School. This body had adopted an increasingly militant anti-immigrant attitude as some members who were more concerned with welfare than with racial differences resigned.[2]

On 27 March 1964 the S.R.A.'s chairman, Mr. A. E. Cooney, expressed approval of the British National Party's approach on immigration.[3] Other activities of the Association included a move to introduce a 'no-spitting' bye-law, an agreement with a local estate agent that property bought for sale through the Association should be sold only to white buyers, and complaints to the local M.P. about alleged prostitution and vice in the Northcote Ward. The S.R.A. continued to be active and associated with the B.N.P. throughout 1965, and in early 1966 Mr. Sydney Bidwell, the new and victorious Labour candidate, told a meeting of members that many of his advisers felt that the S.R.A. had fallen into the hands of 'crude racialists'.

The previous Labour M.P., Mr. George Pargiter, who had held the seat since 1950, had for some years advocated residential dispersal of immigrants and on 10 January 1964 had told an S.R.A. meeting that he recognized the need for a complete ban on immigration to Southall. 'As long as we continue to operate as individual states we are entitled to look after our own people; there cannot be this free-for-all any longer.' Explaining this apparent hardening of the line to an Indian Workers' Association meeting in March, Alderman Hopkins (Labour) said:

[1] On the general background see chapter on Southall by David Woolcott in N. Deakin (ed.), *Colour and the British Electorate 1964*. This includes the results of a survey of 200 white households in 1964, which showed that concern about immigration increased with proximity to immigrants.

[2] See Deakin (ed.), *Colour and the British Electorate*, pp. 35–36, and below, p. 254f.

[3] For details see pp. 373–4.

Southall has too many people. It is the duty of the borough council to see that the Indians obey the local laws and regulations which apply to the rest of the community.

The Indians could, however, claim protection in matters like high rents and failure to provide rent books. 'We as a Council will never approve of any racial discrimination.'

In June 1966 the S.R.A. suggested that immigrants be encouraged to disperse away from overcrowded regions by being refused mortgages except in new towns and relatively uncrowded areas.

Other London Boroughs

Lambeth's initial *laissez-faire*, 'Nelson's eye' policy in relation to immigrants afforded a contrast to the special arrangements made by Willesden, another Labour-dominated borough with a large, mainly West Indian settlement of Commonwealth immigrants.[1] Another contrast was in the type of immigrant housing. Much of this consisted of small terraced houses with vacant or part-vacant possession, unlike the large, dilapidated short-lease houses found in Brixton, which appeared to make for a more stable family life than was the norm in the latter type of housing.

Housing was a major source of tension in the solidly Labour South London Borough of Deptford (since April 1965 incorporated in Lewisham). By late 1963 it was reported to have evolved a *cordon sanitaire* policy whereby houses were bought up in a circle round the 'Caribbean quarter' of Childeric Road to let to local Deptfordians.[2]

In Hackney the Borough Council interviewed 500 coloured immigrants in November 1965, the aim being to gather additional information so that services and amenities for the immigrants, and for the benefit of the borough, could be improved. Of the 407 who completed the questionnaire over 40% said that housing was their main problem; only 10% named colour prejudice as their major problem, while 8% mentioned employment. 20% did not complain of any problems at all. The majority (of whom more than four out of five were from the West Indies) had arrived between 1959 and 1962, and 22% had lived at five or more addresses.

In June 1966 C.A.R.D., reporting after a six-month investigation of the effect of the new Rent Act in London, commented on the housing problems of immigrants in Hackney, Islington and elsewhere (*Observer*, 12 June 1966, 19 June 1966).

[1] See (1) Joan Maizels, *The West Indian comes to Willesden*, London, Willesden Borough Council, 1960, (2) Sheila Patterson, *Immigrants in London*, pp. 14–17. Willesden has now been absorbed in the Greater London Borough of Brent.

[2] Alfred Sherman, Deptford, in N. Deakin (ed.), *Colour and the British Electorate*, 1964, pp. 112–13.

Islington was alleged to be 'Area II', one of the six unnamed areas investigated in the P.E.P. Report on racial discrimination published in April 1967. According to the report, investigators claimed to have had 'very great difficulty in gaining access and persuading officers to talk to us', and to have been told by an official that 'until very recently the borough had refused to house any immigrants at all'. The housing committee's chairman, Alderman Bayliss, described the latter quotation as 'absolute nonsense'; the council had been housing immigrants 'for more years than I can think'. A Labour councillor, Mrs. Elizabeth Hoodless, later examined the housing records and said that coloured immigrants had been housed as far back as 1947 (*Observer*, 23 April; *Guardian*, 24 April; *Islington Gazette*, 28 April).

The housing situation in Tower Hamlets, East London,[1] is discussed at length by Elizabeth Burney.[2] She comments:

> Tower Hamlets slums must certainly vie with the worst parts of Glasgow for Britain's housing booby prize and it goes without saying that the immigrant is likely to suffer as much as anybody.

The borough's policy is tough towards the homeless, and one of avoidance in the matter of closing orders and multiple occupation (except in the case of single men—often Pakistanis or Irish—whom it does not have to rehouse). For the housing list it has maintained a five-year residence qualification within the borough itself, unlike most Greater London boroughs.

B. BIRMINGHAM

At the end of 1964 the new Minister of Housing, Mr. Richard Crossman, toured Birmingham's slums and multi-occupied houses, including areas of high immigrant settlement. Afterwards he commented: 'Shocking! I was here in 1937 and little's changed.' Later he said he would give high priority to the consideration of Birmingham Corporation's demand for pre-registration by landlords of multi-occupied houses to stop the spread of 'twilight areas'. At about the same time Mr. Aubrey Jones, then Conservative M.P. for Hall Green, told the Commons that if Britain was to 'break up the ghettoes such as we see in the decaying centre of Birmingham, we have to make housing available to immigrants in larger proportion than their numbers entitle them to. . . . This is the awful difficulty; this is the tragedy, because to do this is to invite resentment from citizens who are natives of these islands. But not to do it perpetuates the problem of the ghetto into the future, causing problems

[1] Formed out of the three metropolitan boroughs of Stepney, Poplar, and Bethnal Green in 1965.

[2] Burney, op. cit., Ch. IV.

of unknown dimensions to our children and grand-children.' (*Birmingham Post*, 18 November.) Commenting on this in a letter to the *Birmingham Post* (23 November), the organizer of the Sparkbrook Association, Mr. Donald Curtis, said that the population of the central areas was still very mixed and immigrants, white and coloured, were in fact finding accommodation in other areas. Only if this ability to move was stopped would ghettoes emerge. Overcrowded lodging-houses caused resentment, but under-occupied large houses, properly converted, could provide a valuable source of extra accommodation.

According to the 1963 Report of Birmingham's Medical Officer of Health, Dr. E. L. M. Millar (published in mid-January 1965), houses in multi-occupation were causing a serious deterioration in housing and living standards, and the present legislation was inadequate to stop 'unscrupulous persons' making 'quick and easy money out of the hardships and sufferings of the homeless' before their properties were identified and made the subject of action under the Housing Act, 1961. At the root of the evil was the shortage of accommodation for newcomers attracted to the city by full employment.[1] Pakistani and Indian landlords (often with Irish and West Indian tenants) were the chief offenders, 950 or 61% of 1,561 houses inspected being owned or managed by them. Of these 950 houses, 83% were overcrowded; 75% lacked sufficient facilities; and 60% were dirty and ill-managed. This ill-management contrasted sharply with the remaining 611 houses, of which only 9% were overcrowded, 8% lacked facilities and 5% were dirty. The report added: 'It is sad to report that 98 per cent of all legal proceedings taken for contravention of legislation governing houses in multiple occupation have had to be taken against Pakistanis and Indians.' A meeting between corporation officials and immigrant representatives had resulted in some improvement. The only real remedy was, however, the provision of thousands of new houses: 'The contribution to that end made in 1963 is pathetically inadequate if considered against a background of 46,500 families on the housing register in a city still offering the attractions of full employment.'

This report evoked answers from, *inter alios*, Mr. J. Joshi, general secretary of the Indian Workers' Association, who cited the colour tax and thought that the selection of houses for inspection showed a colour prejudice; Mr. Bill Dunn, city secretary of the Communist Party, who blamed Birmingham's housing policy, which gave precedence to big business; and Mr. Maurice Ludmer, executive member of the Coordinating Committee against Racial Discrimination (C.C.A.R.D.),

[1] In a report published in December 1965 ('Population Growth and Planning Policy') the West Midlands Social and Political Research Unit at Birmingham University considered the need to steer both population and jobs outside the conurbation, up to a total of 370,000 households by 1986.

who condemned all landlordism and pointed out that the city's immigrant workers were among the worst sufferers from bad housing, bad landlords, and high rents. Dr. D. R. Prem, deputy chairman of the Commonwealth Welfare Council for the West Midlands, said that the problem was not for the Indian community but for the local authority: 'For our part we condemn these landlords who are exploiting others, but we can only tell them they are bringing disgrace to their own country and to the country in which they are living.'

New Society (21 January 1965) commented that there were no quick solutions. Stiff enforcement of overcrowding regulations could only lead to greater homelessness, and the area needed the labour. On the other hand, mismanagement and overcrowding was leading to a swift deterioration in these properties, and also creating more local ill-feeling than any other factor, as a survey in Slough had also shown.[1] The only long-term answer was faster clearance of slum and twilight areas, and a much bigger building programme; meanwhile, immigrant landlords must be forced to spend much more on management and facilities. The 1964 Act had eased the way on this, but there was a shortage of inspecting staff to carry out the work. In Birmingham in 1963, for example, there were only eight public health inspectors, twelve short of the required establishment of twenty.

A different view of the role of Asian landlords in Birmingham was presented by John Rex and Robert Moore, who in 1965 concluded an urban sociological study of Sparkbrook.[2] Admitting the multi-occupation, the overcrowding, and the frequent poor upkeep practised by many immigrant (as by some English) landlords, they pointed out that the coloured landlords were nevertheless providing a vital social service to large families (for example Irish) who would not find accommodation but for them, either in the public or local private sector.[3]

In early 1965 Birmingham took steps to control multi-occupation, with a private Bill to give the Corporation powers to make registration of all multi-occupied houses compulsory, and to make it obligatory to obtain permission for a house to be multi-occupied *before* it is let off in lodgings[4]—thus avoiding lengthy *post-factum* action under the planning legislation of 1961. Robert Moore commented:

The Act is designed to ensure that adequate conversion is effected before

[1] W. H. Israel, *Colour and Community in Slough*, Slough Council of Social Service, 1964.

[2] Rex and Moore, op. cit., qu.v. *passim* for the situation in Birmingham up to late 1965.

[3] Ibid., p. 65; see also earlier interchange between Birmingham Commonwealth Property Owners' Association and Councillor Mrs. M. S. Brown in local press, April 1964.

[4] For a note on the operation of this Act see below, pp. 240–1.

houses are multi-occupied and that standards are maintained—these are desirable and necessary steps, but may adversely affect the overall supply of accommodation (however unsuitable) for immigrants. Property-owning will no longer be economically viable for the immigrant; not only will the short-term returns be too low for the landlord, but the costs of conversion may not be recovered before the lease expires.

Two clauses in the Birmingham Corporation Act are open to criticism; one gives authority for 'the Corporation to refuse to register such a house under the scheme if the person having control of the house or the person intended to be a person managing the house is not a fit and proper person'. This, Birmingham claim, is to allow them to prevent people previously convicted of living off immoral earnings gaining permission for multi-occupation; while such provision is necessary, the record of immigrant landlords may create some generalized feeling against them all as not being 'fit and proper persons'.

The other ambiguous clause grants similar powers of refusal if 'the house is unsuitable and incapable of being made suitable for letting in lodgings, or for occupation by members of more than one family, or *is situated in a locality which renders it unsuitable for such letting or occupation*'. Under this clause two alternative policies are open:

(1) To restrict multi-occupation to the existing central zones, where it is already widespread;
(2) Consciously to spread multi-occupation to areas at present only lightly multi-occupied and relieving the pressure on the inner zones; possibly preventing *any* further multi-occupation in the inner zones.

In so far as it is possible to equate multi-occupation with immigrants, both coloured and Irish (though the Irish fare better in the general housing market), the first alternative policy is likely to create, if not ghettoes, at least immigrant quarters. Birmingham Corporation has evaded every public attempt to establish which alternative they intend to pursue, or on what criteria they will assess an area 'suitable'. Whatever their intentions, there is no doubt that there will be strong pressures to use their powers in the first manner.[1]

The Birmingham Corporation Act was passed in late summer. Criticisms continued from Professor Rex and Mr. Moore, who wrote:

So far from the Council accepting its responsibilities for housing immigrants, it is even holding up re-development in order to avoid them. A few weeks ago a plan to re-develop part of Sparkbrook was rejected by the Council because, according to a member of the Public Works Committee, 'six hundred immigrant families in the area would have had to be re-housed'. So the immigrants will stay where they are in what look like becoming supervised municipal ghettoes.[2]

[1] I.R.R. *Newsletter*, April 1965, pp. 12–13.

[2] *Sunday Times*, 15 August 1965. See also *Birmingham Post* 13 August 1965, 14 August 1965; *Guardian* 27 July 1965, 24 August 1965; *Observer* 31 October 1965; and Rex and Moore, op. cit., pp. 33–34, 227–8.

That the Act's powers were open to serious abuse, unless administered by men of goodwill, was agreed by several Birmingham M.P.s, including Mr. Roy Hattersley (Lab., Sparkbrook). Alderman Harry Watton, leader of Birmingham's Labour Group, also agreed that 'this is legislation that could be abused', but said it was nonsense to talk of ghettoes; the aim was to stop 'this miasma of creeping decay'. The Council was engaging extra health inspectors and would use its new powers rigorously to deal with up to 5,000 multi-occupied houses.

In February 1966 the controlling Labour group on the Council opposed without success a motion by the Labour rank and file to give some immigrants priority points for municipal housing. The mover of the resolution said that with the concentration of West Indian, Irish and other immigrants in some areas there was a very real danger of ghettoes growing up. A year later, however, the Borough Labour Party refused to press for a revision of the housing points scheme or a reduction in the five-year waiting period for immigrants to the city before they could go on the housing register (contrary to the advice of the Minister of Housing, Mr. Anthony Greenwood).[1]

By the end of 1965, it was reported that over 6,000 houses in Birmingham, or some £12m. worth of property, were owned by immigrants.[2] The Corporation was reported to be giving 40% of its mortgages to immigrants (£2,600,000 up to June 1965), but the total amount was a 'drop in the ocean'.[3] The deficiency of dwellings over the number of families living in Birmingham was 31,000, and it was estimated that the shortage would increase to 43,056 by 1971.[4] In 1965 only 1,303 houses were allocated to people on the waiting list.

At the end of 1966 conditions in several areas of multi-occupation were reported very much better than they had been five or six years ago (*Birmingham Post*, 6 December 1966.) In April 1967 the local authority again expressed satisfaction with its measures to improve the 'twilight areas' and the standards of landlords (*Birmingham Post*, 25 April 1967). Mr. Harold Gurden, Conservative M.P. for Selly Oak, was, however, pressing for a full-scale Commons debate on Birmingham's 'mini-Rachmans', most of them immigrants, coloured or white; he wanted to see landlords who were convicted of harassment deported (*Birmingham Evening Mail*, 29 April 1967).

[1] Developments in the matter of immigrant housing in Birmingham over the last few years should also be considered in relation to political aspects and changes: e.g. the anxieties of the Labour Party over their bad performance locally at the general election of 1964; their corresponding relief in 1966; and, even more important, the gaining of control of the City Council by the Conservatives in 1966.

[2] *Birmingham Mail* (8 March 1966).

[3] *Observer* (31 October 1965).

[4] *Guardian* (24 August 1965).

3. RELEVANT LEGISLATION

The Milner Holland Report gives a valuable set of notes about the relevant legislation, under three main heads: (1) legislation relating to the provision of housing by local authorities, housing associations, and housing societies; (2) the general powers enabling local authorities to exercise a measure of control over privately owned housing and to assist with its purchase and improvement; and (3) general landlord and tenant law which applies to privately rented housing.[1]

The first category is mainly concerned with the public sector of housing. Here legislation obliges the local authorities to provide subsidized housing, taking into account the 'housing conditions and housing needs of all members of the community'.[2] A long series of Acts have also given them powers of compulsory purchase and powers to deal with slum clearance and rehousing displaced tenants; provisions for improvement grants for existing buildings; provisions to assist slum clearance and the establishment of a uniform and comprehensive standard of fitness for habitation; higher housing subsidies to certain authorities for specific purposes; the establishment of a fund to enable Exchequer loans to be made to housing associations (Housing Act 1961); and the encouragement of a new kind of housing society (Housing Act 1964).

In the second category, which has so far been of greater immediacy and importance for immigrants, the local authorities have since 1936 had powers in relation to the demolition or closing of houses unfit for habitation and powers to insist on certain standards and to deal with overcrowding.

Post-war legislation introduced and extended powers relating to improvement grants, encouragement of house purchase by means of Council loans, the restriction of overcrowding, and the control of houses let in lodgings. The Housing Act 1961 gave local authorities new and greatly strengthened powers to deal with bad living conditions in houses in multiple occupation, their management, their amenities and the limitation of overcrowding. These powers were still further strengthened by the Housing Act 1964, which provided for compulsory improvement in unsatisfactory areas where at least half the housing has an expectation of life of fifteen years; changes in improvement grants designed to encourage their greater use; and stronger powers to deal with multi-

[1] Milner Holland Report, op. cit., Appendix I. For a summary of the housing powers and duties of local authorities see also J. B. Cullingworth, *Housing and Local Government*, London, Allen and Unwin, 1966. See also Elizabeth Burney, op. cit., Appendix, for a summary of the powers relating to overcrowding, multiple occupation, and slum clearance.

[2] Housing Act 1949, Point I, Section I. Previously the obligation was only to 'the working classes'.

occupation, including registration, and control orders for the worst cases of mismanagement.

In the third category comes legislation providing for rent control for certain classes of unfurnished and furnished dwellings, regulation of landlord-tenant relations and obligations, etc. Certain aspects of this legislation have affected immigrants or immigrant-host relationships in various ways: for example, the rights of the statutory tenant have frequently either not been understood or been ignored. In other cases the immigrant tenant's right to have a rent book, to be given at least four weeks' notice to quit, and to appeal to the Rent Tribunal to have an equitable furnished rent fixed have been ignored by the immigrant landlord.

Since the Milner Holland Report was published some new or strengthened legislation has been passed or proposed. One such law is the Rent Act (1965),[1] which was intended to 'restore the right to retain possession of certain dwellings; to make further provision with respect to security of tenure, rents and premiums; and to restrict evictions without due process of law'. This extended rent control to furnished lettings and generally made the full operation of the cycle of exploitation disclosed now in the national press in 1963 and linked, for extraneous reasons, with the name of Peter (Perec) Rachman,[2] much more difficult. The cycle was essentially a three-phase one: (1) Speculative buying of cheap old property with a number of statutory tenants; (2) removal of the statutory tenants, either by death or departure, sometimes precipitated by unscrupulous 'destatting' operations (moving in new tenants often noisy or otherwise undesirable), to empty rooms, perhaps allowing brothels or drinking clubs to operate in the basements, illegal evictions, cutting off of essential services, and various forms of intimidation (coloured and other immigrants needing furnished accommodation were exploited in this way, and much misery and friction caused to them and the often ageing local statutory tenants);[3] (3) once the houses were

[1] This came into force in December 1965 and the first prosecution, involving alleged intimidation of a coloured tenant by a white landlord in Lambeth, took place in February 1966 (*South London Press*, 18 February 1966).

[2] When the Keeler–Profumo–Ward–Rachman scandals hit the front pages in 1963, Rachman had in fact been dead for eight months, but similar operations were continuing; a number of groups and individuals who had been working to alleviate conditions at last got under hearing and the local Kensington press, long gagged by the threat of a writ, burst into front-page exposures, using material diligently collected for years. Mr. Ben Parkin, Labour M.P. for Paddington, giving a detailed expose of the exploitation cycle in Parliament on 22 July 1963, said: 'This is my moment and I intend to ram it home.'

[3] Mr. Ben Parkin, M.P., stated that Rachman's operations in the late 1950s in Paddington and Notting Hill had greatly contributed to the ill-feeling and racial tension that led to the Notting Hill disturbances of 1958. (For the events of this period see *Newsletters* for June, July, September, and October 1963.)

free of statutory tenants the value of the property would rise and the landlord could either continue to charge his new tenants economic rents or, if the property were in sought-after central areas, convert or sell to developers to convert the houses back into upper-middle and professional dwellings. Before such conversion or sale the whole apparatus of intimidation and eviction would be reactivated against the new tenants who had not even the paper defence of security of tenure.

It was these immigrants and other tenants whom the new Rent Act of 1965 should in theory have protected.[1] Undoubtedly the Act did make the third phase much more difficult, but there are apparently still many tenants who are too ignorant or too frightened to use the machinery of the Act to apply for a reduced rent. In Notting Hill an investigation in 1966 found that since 1962 the number of people occupying some of the old Colville Gardens properties, more recently owned by Davies Investments, which collapsed in early 1967, had been steadily increasing, as well as the income from rents. Thereafter the nine-month-old Notting Hill Neighbourhood Service organized a meeting of tenants, and there was an *en masse* application to the West London Rent Tribunal for security and lowered rents.

After a six-month investigation in London C.A.R.D. came up with a seven-page report in June 1966 containing evidence that the Rent Act was still not biting in parts of London, mainly Islington. Not only was there continued intimidation and harassment[2] but other aspects of 'Rachmanism'—high rents, key money, appalling conditions. In areas such as Hackney, the appeal machinery was jammed because 65% of landlords took cases to appeal (tenants also suffered from lack of legal representation at rent hearings, whereas landlords employed counsel and solicitors). Moreover, the Department was badly understaffed, making it difficult to enforce the Public Health Act.[3]

Use of the new machinery has also been inhibited by the fact that so many landlords are immigrants. As the Liberal Immigration Group commented in its Report on immigration:[4]

[1] I.R.R. *Newsletter*, April 1967, p. 154.

[2] In practice, such harassment has been found very difficult to prove and many cases are unsuccessful. On 25 January 1967 Mr. MacColl, Parliamentary Secretary, told Mr. M. Barnes (Brentford, Chiswick, Lab.) that up to the end of 1966 there were 335 prosecutions for offences under the Rent Act (1965): 203 for harassment and 132 for unlawful eviction. One person was imprisoned and 192 fines were imposed. In April a Birmingham Corporation spokesman said that prosecutions took place at the rate of about one a minute (*Birmingham Evening Mail*, 29 April 1967).

[3] In early June 1966 C.A.R.D. and the Islington Tenants Association held a joint protest march against conditions in several houses owned by a Mrs. G. de Lusignan (*Observer* 12 June, 19 June).

[4] *Current Topics*, Vol. IV, no. 125, July 1965, p. 8.

There is little in it (this Bill) that will affect the status and attitudes of the immigrant landlord and tenant. Most immigrants are suspicious of authority whether it be in the form of landlords, lawyers, or policemen and the landlord/tenant relationship will remain a personal relationship as far as immigrants are concerned, rather than one defined by the law.[1] In Willesden it has been estimated that 90 per cent of the Commonwealth immigrants live either in their own homes or as tenants of immigrant landlords and we have no reason to believe that this does not obtain elsewhere. It seems likely that the power of threat and sanctions and the fear of physical violence will remain more influential than any benefits that this Bill will bring. More information about such things as the effect of threats of eviction would be useful, but unless the immigrant population can be informed of its rights and how to exercise them and persuaded to do so, the Rent Bill does not seem likely to do much to improve their position.

Evidence also became available in 1966 that certain landlords in London were seeking to circumvent the Rent Acts by requiring their tenants to enter into leases in excess of twenty-one years, which would prevent them from applying to the Rent Officer for relief against high rents. The twenty-two-year lease device has apparently been applied in particular to coloured Commonwealth immigrants, who are under great pressures to accept a landlord's term and who are less likely to be aware of the reasons for this long-term lease for accommodation that is usually both bad and expensive.[2]

A. SOME LEGISLATION ON OVERCROWDING AND MULTI-OCCUPATION

'Statutory overcrowding' is defined under the Public Health Act of 1935, which makes it illegal for two people of opposite sexes over the age of 10, not living together as husband and wife, to sleep in the same room. There are also provisions correlating the number of people in a

[1] The accuracy of this prediction has been borne out. In fact even tenants who know about the Act have proved reluctant to go to law, not only for fear of reprisals but general dislike of publicity. The question of the 'family house' in alleged multi-occupation (many 'immigrant' houses fall into this category) has also been a matter of discussion and concern since a High Court ruling in 1966, that a house which was occupied by two branches of the same family—the parents and their son and his wife and children—was not in multiple occupation in the terms of the 1961/64 Housing Acts, gave rise to a number of important issues. The Kensington and Chelsea Council who had required the owner to do certain works under the Act, expressed themselves as being very dissatisfied with the judgment as it would disempower them in many cases of multiple occupation, particularly by what they called 'immigrant families'. Leave to take the case to the House of Lords was refused, the Judge remarking that new legislation was needed if the Council wished to reverse the decision.

[2] See I.R.R. *Newsletter*, January 1967, p. 51.

house with the size of the rooms and the total number of rooms in the house.

The Housing Act (1961) defines a house in multiple occupation as a 'house which, or any part of which, is let in lodgings or occupied by members of more than one family'.[1] This Act set uniform standards of management and gave local authorities their first comprehensive powers to control conditions and numbers in multi-occupied houses. Numbers may be controlled under section 19, whereby the landlord can be directed not to take on new tenants in excess of the stated number; it is not, however, an offence if existing tenants remain.

Local authorities were also given the power under the 1961 Housing Act to set up their own registration schemes for houses in multi-occupation, a power which did not become effective until three years later. They could not, however, refuse registration, so few have bothered to introduce such schemes.

The Public Health Acts (1935 and 1961) also give local authorities the power to take action in the case of any house where conditions constitute a serious threat to health or a 'public nuisance'.

The Town and Country Planning Act (1962) requires planning permission to be given for 'change of use'. The Birmingham Corporation was reported to be using this provision in relation to multi-occupation, on the grounds that it was a 'change of use' for which permission was necessary, and could be refused in areas where it would be 'detrimental to the amenities'.[2]

This approach was strengthened by the Birmingham Corporation Act of 1965, which created compulsory registration of houses let to more than two families or over four lodgers—including those let for the first time. Permission could be refused if the Corporation considered that: the house was unsuitable; multi-occupation would spoil the neighbourhood; the person running the house was unsuitable.

Clearly the last two provisions could be used to confine lodging-house keepers and their tenants to certain areas, thereby helping to create 'ghettoes'. Alternatively, they could be used to create more balanced local communities and to promote dispersal.

During the Birmingham Act's first year of operation 3,000 of the 4,800 houses known to be in multi-occupation were registered; so were fifteen newly-let ones. Permission was refused in sixteen cases: three houses were judged unsuitable and in thirteen cases it was thought that multi-occupation would spoil the neighbourhood. No appeals were made against these decisions.[3]

[1] See p. 239, n. 2, for a discussion of 'family houses in alleged multi-occupation'.

[2] Burney, op. cit., Chapter I, pp. 26–7.

[3] There was, however, said to be a growing tendency for small, non-registerable houses (two families or four lodgers) to be used.

Elizabeth Burney comments that the Corporation's use of its powers seemed to be entirely preventative.[1] Nevertheless she expresses the view that the extension of such powers to every entry (Leeds has them and Manchester has applied) would be a good move, provided that they are used positively, in continuation with improvement grants, to get the best use out of the stock of old large houses.

In November 1966 the N.C.C.I.'s Housing Panel published a statement on the Birmingham Corporation Act, expressing dissatisfaction with it on both social and legal grounds:

> The full implication of this Act cannot be understood if it is looked at in isolation. The crux of the problem is that, given that the points systems operated by local authorities discriminate against newcomers and given the difficulties experienced by immigrants in obtaining mortgages, multiple-occupation is often the only form of housing available to them. The problem of multiple-occupation would therefore be best tackled by opening up other possibilities of housing for immigrants.
>
> In the meantime, however, there is a serious public health problem posed by multiple-occupation as such, and the Panel recognises that local authorities should have powers to deal with it. It is particularly desirable that they should have compulsory powers to establish a register of houses in multiple-occupation. There are, however, serious dangers in allowing local authorities to refuse registration for reasons set out in Section 3 (2) (b) (i) of the Birmingham Corporation Act. As long as it is the case that a large proportion of coloured immigrants are bound to be living in multiple-occupation, refusal of registration on these grounds could lead to racially segregated areas in a city.
>
> The problem which arises here is not in fact one of public health, but of planning. The Panel believes that if local authorities are to be given full *planning* power to refuse registration on grounds of character or amenity of the locality, the individual could be safeguarded by a right of appeal to the Ministry of Housing and Local Government.
>
> As far as other grounds for refusal are concerned, the Panel believes that the only ground on which registration could be refused outright is the unsuitability of the house for multi-occupation. The Council should, however, be under a statutory duty to state its reasons for refusing and appeal should lie to the County Court. The Birmingham Corporation Act does not place the Birmingham Corporation under any such duty. The Panel also believes that, although it would be reasonable to allow conditions to be imposed upon registration as to the qualifications of potential managers of houses subject to appeal to the County Court, it is undesirable that the Council should simply be allowed to refuse registration on the grounds that the manager is not a fit and proper person.

[1] Burney, op. cit., pp. 28–30. Birmingham has been consistent in its tough attitude to lodging-houses and to immigrant landlords. By 1966 up to 98% of alleged action against landlords in the city had been taken against Indian and Pakistani landlords (for details see Burney, op. cit., p. 25).

B. THE RACE RELATIONS ACT (1965)

Section 5 of this Act reads as follows:

(1) In any case where the licence or consent of the landlord or of any other person is required for the disposal to any person of premises comprised in a tenancy, that licence or consent shall be treated as unreasonably withheld if and so far as it is withheld on the ground of colour, race or ethnic or national origins:

Provided that this subsection does not apply to a tenancy of premises forming part of a dwelling-house of which the remainder or part of the remainder is occupied by the person whose licence or consent is required as his own residence if the tenant is entitled in common with that person to the use of any accommodation other than accommodation required for the purposes of access to the premises.

(2) Any covenant, agreement or stipulation which purports to prohibit the disposal of premises comprised in a tenancy to any persons by reference to colour, race or ethnic or national origins shall be construed as prohibiting such disposal except with the consent of the landlord, such consent not to be unreasonably withheld.

(3) In this section 'tenancy' means a tenancy created by a lease or sublease, by an agreement for a lease or sublease or by a tenancy agreement or in pursuance of any enactment; and 'disposal', in relation to premises comprised in a tenancy, includes assignment or assignation of the tenancy and subletting or parting with possession of the premises or any part of the premises.

(4) This section applies to tenancies created before as well as after the passing of this Act.

These provisions do not, as can be seen, cover owner-occupied houses or freehold covenants.

C. EXTENSION OF ANTI-DISCRIMINATION PROVISIONS TO HOUSING

It is widely recognized that the extension of anti-discrimination legislation to housing would be totally inadequate without far-reaching positive measures at national and local level. There has also been much less preparatory public discussion of the precise forms that such legislation might take thereof.

Elizabeth Burney has proposed that a new Bill contain the following provisions:[1]

1. Any covenants restricting the sale or disposal of any interest in land on grounds of race, religion, or nationality should be void.
2. No builder should discriminate in the sale of new houses.
3. No estate agent, or accommodation bureau, or building society should discriminate in their services, or accept discriminatory instructions from vendors.

[1] Burney, op. cit., pp. 447–8.

4. It should be illegal to publish or display any accommodation advertisement stipulating race, nationality or religion (except in the case of lodgings with a family, or in a hotel run for, say, orthodox Jews).
5. No landlord should be permitted to refuse an applicant on grounds of race, nationality or religion, except where he shares the dwelling himself (this would have to be carefully defined in the case of small boarding houses: what in America is called the 'Mrs. Murphy clause').[1]

The above five items should come within the existing conciliation principle of the Race Relations Act 1965. It might also be desirable to include blatant attempts to keep districts 'white' in the criminal 'incitement' clause.

D. THE LOCAL GOVERNMENT ACT (1966)

Clause 11 of Chapter 42 of the Local Government Act (1966) reads as follows:

(1) Subject to the provisions of this section, the Secretary of State may pay to local authorities who in his opinion are required to make special provision in the exercise of any of their functions, in consequence of the presence within their areas of substantial numbers of immigrants from the Commonwealth whose language and customs differ from those of the community, grants of such amounts as he may with the consent of the Treasury determine on account of expenditure of such description (being expenditure in respect of the employment of staff) as he may so determine.
(2) No grant shall be paid under this section in respect of expenditure incurred before 1st April 1967.

[1] Cf. an editorial in *The Tablet* (18 June 1966):

'It would be very high-handed for the Government to say that no one was to let rooms, unless they agree that they shall not have any choice about whom they let them to, that choice shall be called discrimination and punished by law. Some of the most successful of the smaller residential hotels and boarding houses have built up a connexion by personal recommendation, so that the guests live happily together year after year, as people of broadly similar outlook and tastes. This is one of the great alleviations for those who have to live in boarding houses, as their incomes do not allow them to have a flat or a house of their own. What is wanted is the widest variety of such places, and in this variety, of course, there must be the places that will cater for the coloured immigrant. But that is quite different from trying to impose a universal legal obligation which would cut at the root of the private hotel and boarding-house functions.

'The landlady who is unwilling to have coloured lodgers has only to quote Lord Brockway, in his contribution to a book on immigrants, where he explains the entirely different way in which a home is seen by an English person or by a West Indian. He says that to the English person the home is a place into which to retire to be private and quiet: to the West Indian it is a centre to which he has the right to invite his friends, and the conception of a home is meaningless to him unless he can use it as the place in which to give parties. This is perhaps a more sociable view, but those who have to provide the services attendant on such gatherings ought to be free to choose whether they are prepared to do that or not. A great many landladies do not care about students or other young people precisely for this consideration. It is quite natural for the young to be sociable and noisy: it is also quite natural for middle-aged ladies to prefer quiet and gentle elderly lodgers.'

In its report on 'Areas of Special Housing Need' referred to above, the N.C.C.I. Housing Panel welcomed these proposals, while pointing out that their effect would be extremely limited, in that the grants related only to expenditure arising from the employment of special staff.[1]

The general idea that areas with large immigrant populations should be designated as 'areas of special needs' has been criticized on the grounds that it tends to strengthen the stereotype associating the presence of immigrants with the root causes of conditions and special conditions prevailing in a given area, and could lead to such undesirable consequences as segregated housing.[2]

E. ESTATE AGENTS' BILLS

Since 1914 private members' bills, promoted by professionally qualified estate agents and their professional organizations, and aimed at rationalizing the entire profession on ethical lines, have been foundering in Parliament. The latest was the Bill introduced in early 1966 by Mr. Arthur Jones, Conservative M.P. for Northamptonshire South and himself an estate agent. It had Government facilities and three-party support but was killed by dissolution. *New Society* (24 February 1966) and the *Sunday Times* (12 June 1966) forecast that, despite the disappearance of Mr. Jones's Bill, legal action seemed likely in the near future.[3]

4. RECENT RECOMMENDATIONS AND INITIATIVES

A. THE NATIONAL COMMITTEE FOR COMMONWEALTH IMMIGRANTS

In its first annual report the National Committee for Commonwealth Immigrants described housing as the 'most complex and intractable of all the problems faced by immigrants and by the National Committee'.[4] It continued:

> Discussion about the housing of immigrants becomes enmeshed in the network of housing problems affecting the whole community. This is a national problem and the Committee sees the plight of the immigrant pre-

[1] The amount involved was also low: £1½m. spread over the whole country.

[2] Elizabeth Burney, op. cit., p. 243.

[3] See these articles for detailed discussion of current abuses and possible curbs. See also P.E.P. Report, p. 77, and article by Patty Thirlwell, 'The Estate Agent and the Immigrant', in I.R.R. *Newsletter*, January 1966. Instances of individual abuses were reported in the *Tottenham and Edmonton Herald* (17 December 1965) and the *Daily Sketch* (17 June 1966).

[4] N.C.C.I.—Report for 1966, p. 14.

cisely in this context. There is open discrimination in housing, particularly in the private sector. Yet . . . even when there is no direct evidence of discrimination or of any intention to discriminate, the normal processes of administration seem to result in the exclusion from housing opportunities of all but very few immigrants and they remain at the end of most housing queues.

The N.C.C.I. Housing Panel concentrated its work on policy studies and recommendations at national and local level as the only way to achieve any effective easing of the situation. These have included a general background report prepared for discussion with the Minister in August 1966, and published in early 1967,[1] a later report on areas of special housing needs which was sent to the Minister and subsequently published under National Committee sponsorship, and a statement on the Birmingham Corporation Act (see above, pp. 240–241).

Part II of the general report discussed the difficulties faced by Commonwealth immigrants and other newcomers to an area, in getting both private and public housing, and Part III was concerned with proposals for administrative and legislative action that might eliminate or reduce these difficulties.

Part II stated the Panel's view that the Commonwealth (coloured) immigrant faces not only overall housing difficulties arising out of the general housing shortage, and difficulties shared by all newcomers to an area, but also difficulties which differ both in kind and in intensity from those of other groups in the community;[2] these difficulties call for urgent attention, not only for reasons of social justice but because of the danger that the resulting residential patterns will become so entrenched as to determine the social patterns of some British cities for many years to come.

The general housing shortage (aggravated by inadequate standards) is associated with: increases in household formation (due to the increasing numbers of young people seeking separate accommodation and of would-be owner-occupiers); and economic factors, attracting labour to conurbations with serious housing problems.

[1] *The Housing of Commonwealth Immigrants.*

[2] Elizabeth Burney, op. cit., pp. 236–7, also made a series of recommendations aimed at alleviating difficulties falling into the same three categories. Under the heading of 'problems affecting immigrants alone', she included the need for: crash courses to train housing visitors and all others who deal directly with immigrants in the housing selection process; better information about public housing machinery (council mortgages, housing estates, procedures, etc.); on efforts by local authorities to give a lead to public opinion by placing immigrants in houses where they can be seen to have been housed by the council, and generally a positive use of ethnic statistics, a gearing of selection processes in favour of people in genuine housing need, and action linked with other social services.

The difficulties which face all migrants, whether from abroad or from other parts of the United Kingdom, are associated in the main with the housing policies pursued by local authorities. There are three ways of obtaining accommodation from a local authority: (i) through the waiting list; (ii) through displacement in a slum clearance or redevelopment scheme; and (iii) through the special provision made for those in extreme need.

Only in the latter case does initial emergency assistance appear to be unsubjected to any restrictive rules. On the waiting list, the criteria (which vary considerably from authority to authority) are often designed to give weight to the claims of local residents. Residence is either a prerequisite to admission to the waiting list or to the active list, and it is also a heavily weighted factor in assessing the claims of those already on the list.

As for clearance and redevelopment schemes, the N.C.C.I. Housing Panel report suggested that: an authority may deliberately avoid selecting an area with a high proportion of newcomers among its residents, whom it would have a duty to rehouse in other areas; and newcomers may be handicapped by the particular local authority's rehousing policy (e.g. refusal to accept those who have not lived in the scheduled zone since before the initial scheme was made or to accept lodgers, unauthorized sub-tenants in furnished accommodation, single persons, owner-occupiers, etc.).

The special difficulties experienced by recent coloured Commonwealth immigrants are attributable, continued the report, partly to their ignorance about British society, partly to antagonism among the receiving society. If they happen to get public housing, it may on occasion be poorer in quality than that allocated to native applicants. Moreover, because the local authority is often the only available source for a loan to enable them to buy their own house, they are likely to suffer most in times of restriction. In the private sector there are special difficulties in obtaining rented accommodation. Many immigrants therefore resort to purchase, sometimes without adequate information; they may be directed by estate agents to certain streets, and involved in paying high prices and expensive mortgages.

The last part of this report stressed the important role to be played by public and local authorities catering for the housing needs of newcomers in general and immigrants in particular. Although there may be a case for considering whether industrialists and statutory undertakings seeking to recruit newcomers should not play a part in meeting their housing needs,[1] it is the community that stands to gain from the

[1] Cf. Bow Group Pamphlet, *Commonwealth Immigration*, C. Brocklebank-Fowler, C. Bland, and T. Farmer, October 1965, p. 45.

general prosperity brought by higher employment, and therefore the principal responsibility must lie with the local authority.

It may be necessary in certain circumstances to give priority to any newcomers performing essential service functions, to those with special needs, including shift workers and others who must live near their place of employment, and to single men and women workers. Increased mobility of labour is likely to be of crucial importance to the national economy in the next few years, and in this context the new and expanding towns play an important part in providing accommodation for migrants with suitable skills. Meanwhile, failure to provide opportunities to qualify for council housing is forcing immigrants into overcrowded accommodation, which is rapidly deteriorating and thereby causing a loss rather than a gain to the national housing stock.

The N.C.C.I. report made the following recommendations:

1. First, all residential requirements for council accommodation should be subjected to careful scrutiny. We do not suggest that residential qualifications should be abolished altogether. . . . We suggest, however, that local authorities review their current practice and seek to shorten qualifying periods as much as possible. . . .
2. Secondly, we consider that a local authority adopting a slum clearance or redevelopment scheme should, as a matter of general principle, recognise a responsibility to re-house all people resident in the area affected on a specified date, regardless of their legal or contractual status or their length of residence. In cases of difficulty the local authority should not hesitate to use the powers under existing legislation to take over the management of such property. Such measures would do something to reduce the misunderstanding and ignorance which can bring particular hardship to newcomers and immigrants.
3. Thirdly, an important way in which local authorities can help immigrant owner-occupiers is through providing improvement grants. . . .[1]
4. Fourthly, where these and other methods of improvement prove too slow or otherwise unsatisfactory the local authority should give urgent consideration to the possibility of buying and managing houses which are for such purposes. These powers should be more widely used, and the authority must accept the difficulties of managing such property with the consequent responsibility for ultimately re-housing the occupants. . . .
5. Fifthly, the Panel has considered the nature and type of accommodation provided by local authorities for immigrants. The Commonwealth Immigrants Advisory Council, in its 1963 Report (Cmnd 2119) drew attention to the need for hostel accommodation for single men. We would emphasise the need for such accommodation for all single persons, as a major contribution to the solution of immigrant housing problems. Although we are not concerned in this Report with sponsored students, it is clear that hostel accommodation is desirable for a wide range of other students and industrial apprentices. . . .
6. Sixthly, apart from the provision of accommodation and services, local

[1] See advice given by Alderman E. Wistrich, chairman, Camden Committee for Community Relations, in N.C.C.I. Bulletin *Liaison* (No. 3, December 1965).

authorities are in a position to exert influence against racial discrimination in indirect ways. One of these is the insertion of non-discrimination clauses in agreements relating to loans, grants and mortgages entered into by the council in respect of dwellings. . . .

7. Finally we would like to endorse as strongly as possible the recommendation in the report of the Commonwealth Immigrants Advisory Council that means should be sought of publicising the various services provided by the local authority in such a way that all the various immigrant groups become aware of them. . . .

Consideration should also be given to the possibility of collating information on a national basis, from local authorities and the Ministry of Labour about prospects open to immigrants in those parts of the country where both employment and housing opportunities exist, and where pressures are likely to be less acute than in the main conurbations where immigrants now concentrate.

Lastly, the Report's recommendations for action by other bodies, public and private, included the following: concerted social work projects to improve the quality of life in various areas; the creation of local liaison committees; extended action by housing associations; guidance from the Minister of Housing and local government to local authorities; and further legislation in the form of (a) an extension of anti-discrimination legislation to cover housing, and (b) enabling legislation to permit local authorities to deal with areas of special housing need.[1]

The N.C.C.I. Housing Panel's report on *Areas of Special Need*, published in April 1967, had a more detailed focus. Its introduction pointed out that:

(a) the present pattern of immigrant settlement and concentration poses an insoluble problem for certain local authorities which are already overstrained and will find it impossible to alleviate difficulties in all areas of severe housing stress within the foreseeable future. If rapid progress is to be made it can only be with the combined resources of the Central Government and local authorities. Concurrent action is also needed to rehabilitate services such as education, hospitals, child welfare and the maternity services;

(b) local authorities should be empowered to bring such areas under public control as 'areas of special housing need', as the only speedy way to remedy such conditions as: gross overcrowding; high rents for sub-standard accommodation; insanitary conditions of common parts; failure to keep premises habitable because of disrepair; fire risks; lack of play facilities and consequent danger for children;

(c) these areas should be defined in much the same way as Com-

[1] An overnight press round-up of Midland local authorities' reactions to this N.C.C.I. report was made by the *Birmingham Post* (25 April). The general reaction was said to be that many of the policies advocated were already in force; those that were not were regarded as either unnecessary or impractical.

prehensive Development Areas, so that, after definition by the local authority and confirmation by the Ministry of Housing and Local Government the Council could acquire and manage all the houses within the area (this would raise some problems of compensation).

Thereafter the local authority should (i) apply some immediate first aid measures (reduction of overcrowding, reduction of exorbitant rents, carrying out essential repairs, providing acceptable standards of cleaning, lighting and sanitation for the common parts, reduction of fire risks, clearing of vacant sites, and provision of play areas); (ii) redevelop or rehabilitate in accordance with the state of repair and potential amenities of various properties; and (iii) promote active co-operation with local community organizations and local liaison committees, and generally seek to achieve good public relations to ensure that the problems and measures taken to solve them are understood by the public at large.

B. FAIR HOUSING GROUPS

Another approach recently initiated by the N.C.C.I. was concerned with the introduction into Britain of Fair Housing Groups, such as are found in many parts of the U.S. This was included in the experimental work to be done by the National Committee following the granting of £50,000 over a three-year period by the Calouste Gulbenkian to promote schemes directed particularly towards furthering services for children in multi-racial societies and meeting the housing problems of Commonwealth immigrants (*Guardian*, 26 April 1967). Announcing the grant, the Committee's general secretary, Miss Nadine Peppard, explained that the basis of such housing groups was the gathering together of a number of people, some of them influential, who had experience of housing matters.

Among the activities which the housing groups would almost certainly cover were direct assistance to purchasers by accompanying them to view houses and to discussions with owners or estate agents; co-operation with local authorities and reputable estate agents to ensure that would-be purchasers do not meet discrimination; and the provision of an advisory service for immigrants wishing to move.

C. RECOMMENDATIONS OF THE RACE RELATIONS BOARD

The Race Relations Board made the following recommendations on housing, in their first annual report for 1966–7:

Section 5 of the Race Relations Act 1965 makes limited provision against discrimination in housing by prohibiting the refusal on racial grounds of consent to the assignment of a tenancy. It also declares invalid covenants in tenancy agreements or leases which prevent the tenant from disposing of his tenancy or lease to a person of any particular colour, race or ethnic or national origin. These provisions only affect certain situations, in which an existing tenant, with the right to transfer his tenancy, wishes to transfer it to someone to whose race or colour the landlord objects. The section does not deal with covenants which impose similar restrictions on the sale of freehold property, nor does it affect covenants which impose other kinds of discriminatory restriction, such as a covenant brought to our attention which forbade a tenant from entertaining coloured visitors. It has been suggested that such covenants are already invalid, at common law, but the position could be simply clarified by declaring all discriminatory covenants void.

Discriminatory covenants are insignificant compared with the substantial discrimination in new lettings and sales of houses and flats. The P.E.P. evidence in this area is convincing, and it becomes increasingly clear that housing discrimination lies close to the heart of the whole problem of racial inequality. There is, for example, the problem of the prospective tenant who does not get as far as an interview with the landlord, because of the interposition of an estate agent or accommodation bureau, or because he is deterred by a discriminatory advertisement. We now know that both these forms of discrimination are widespread and no measure will be effective to reduce housing discrimination unless they are included in its scope. The harmful effect of discriminatory advertising goes beyond the housing situation itself. It is offensive to the community at large as well as personally humiliating to those against whom it is directed. It seems to us that the law need not intervene where there is a personal relationship going beyond the commercial relationship of landlord and tenant, for example, where some of the facilities are shared between them.

There is evidence that coloured immigrants have been refused mortgages or required to pay higher interest rates than English-born white citizens. It is reasonable for a lender to consider the income of an applicant for a mortgage and his prospect of maintaining it. It is also reasonable, in the case of an immigrant, to consider whether he is permanently established in this country or is likely to return to his country of origin. But these are matters which affect immigrants regardless of race or colour. Moreover, the lender's primary security is not the borrower, but the mortgaged property. Race and colour are as irrelevant in this area as in the others which we have examined.

D. HOUSING ASSOCIATIONS AND HOUSING SOCIETIES

The need for voluntary associations both to lead the way towards statutory action and to supplement it, once available, has been emphasized again and again. These housing associations concerned particularly with immigrants (of which the pioneer was the Aggrey Housing Association in Leeds in the early 1950s) can and do convert overcrowded multi-occupied houses into good flats; they undertake limited building programmes and can act as agents of dispersal. In at least one area, Notting Hill, the Notting Hill Housing Trust seems likely to rehouse more people by the end of 1967 than the whole local Borough (Kensington and Chelsea). In this it is being aided by a national fund-raising body, 'Shelter', formed in the winter of 1966–7, which raised £100,000 in its first three months of existence. 'Shelter' has also helped associations in Birmingham, Liverpool and Glasgow. Another recent London enterprise is the Mulberry Housing Trust, founded unobtrusively in late 1965 by the former Conservative Minister of Housing, Sir Keith Joseph, and working in conjunction with Westminster City Council, which within nine months advanced £300,000 to it. In mid-1966 the Trust had purchased twenty-nine properties (accommodation for eighty-seven families), and it was hoped that within five years the Trust would be owning and managing well over 1,000 dwellings.

The potentialities of Britain's 1,500 housing associations and societies[1] are also being recognized, and promoted, by new Government grants under the Housing Subsidies Act 1967. The effect was to allow the societies to borrow money for house-purchase at $4\frac{3}{8}\%$ instead of 7%. Outside London this could be of great help; inside London the ceiling of £2,000 could limit possibilities.

However effective their work, the associations are basically pioneers and standard-setters. As Robert Moore wrote:

> There is a crucial need for constant educational work at local level among all types of neighbours—often in the face of suspicion, hostility and a lack of desire to understand, and in the face of real social barriers to understanding. No one should imagine that any other group is ever going to conform entirely to their expectations of them, nor that this is even necessary. But, having made these qualifications, there is much scope for neighbourhood associations, housing associations and consultative committees in beginning to meet local needs, in acting as clearing houses for complaints, as lightning conductors for frictions and as organizations through which people meet and begin to understand one another. But none of this will be of any avail if the understanding leads only to a common realization that all face an impossible problem: in other words, such activities can only be fruitful against the background of a large-scale national programme designed to meet, *inter alia*, the general housing shortage.[2]

E. HOSTELS

The number of coloured immigrants in hostels for the homeless may be better known when the results of an inter-departmental survey carried out in early 1967 are published.

[1] About 1,500 in number, of which a few specialize in coloured people's housing.
[2] *Colour in Britain*, B.B.C. Publications, 1961, p. 73.

Hostels for single men, whether immigrants or newcomers to an overcrowded urban area, have been advocated frequently.[1] The provision of hostel accommodation for single immigrants has, however, not been studied very seriously by most local authorities, since the widely reported failure of Bradford to fill the first modern hostel it had built for Pakistani single men: the reasons given were high rents and the immigrants' desire to live together with their own community. Rex and Moore have suggested that there is still room for considerable experiment here, particularly in consultation with immigrant group leaders.[2] Elizabeth Burney, pointing out that Bradford has a large stock of cheap slum houses, deplored the fact that the matter had not been put to test in areas where the housing shortage is greatest.[3]

F. DISPERSAL AND THE NEW TOWNS

Residential dispersal is often seen as the key to ultimate absorption, integration or assimilation of immigrants, particularly in the second generation, when the principle of the local school can create *de facto* segregation of ethnic groups as well as socio-economic classes.

A certain amount of dispersal, or at least resistance to heavy residential concentration can result from the application by employers in an industrial area of the low 'benign quota' in industry (e.g. Croydon by contrast to Southall). Another more premeditated way is to use public housing allocation to promote dispersal. This also applies to the New Towns[4] where, as Elizabeth Burney writes:

> . . . at present looking for a coloured man is like the proverbial needle in a haystack. This is primarily because of the industrial selection process on which New Town (and expanded town) recruitment is based. The intake is notoriously middle-to-upper-working class—semi-skilled and unskilled workers, the categories to which most coloured people belong, are in tiny proportions.[5] If more of the coloured population had their fair share of the better jobs, then dispersal from the inner cities would be facilitated; not only in terms of New Town selection, but also in terms of the generally greater mobility conveyed by better economic opportunities. Little is known of how far their present occupations tie Commonwealth immigrants to their present homes; but common sense suggests the connection is strong.[6]

[1] In late 1965 the then Minister of Housing, Mr. Richard Crossman, rejected the idea of special camps to house immigrants on arrival; he feared they might be taken for concentration camps. (No such scruples appeared to trouble those responsible for the reception arrangements for Polish ex-servicemen and their families, or for displaced persons from the camps, in the years after the war.)

[2] Rex and Moore, op. cit., pp. 261–2.

[3] Burney, op. cit., p. 22.

[4] See C.I.O. Fact Sheet, R.4735/C/8, May 1966 on New Towns.

[5] In 1966 a special 'London Dispersal Group' was set up by Mr. R. Mellish to examine the necessity of bringing unskilled labour to the New Towns.

[6] Burney, op. cit., pp. 246–7.

CHAPTER 7

Education

The educational aspects of Commonwealth immigration have only begun to awake nation-wide attention and concern in recent years. This is primarily because the numbers of immigrant children or British-born children of immigrants have risen sharply and are likely to continue to do so, and because an increasing proportion have been non-English-speaking, as a consequence of the large inflow of Indian and Pakistani immigrants and their dependants that started in 1960–1.[1] In 1967 there were an estimated 200,000 children born in this country of Commonwealth immigrant parents and the Department of Education gave the 1966 figures for four large groups of schoolchildren as follows: 73,605 West Indians, 32,122 Indians, 11,862 Pakistanis, and 13,835 Cypriots. The total of 'immigrant children' represented 2·2% of the total school population. The great majority of those in the older age-groups are still first-generation, not second-generation immigrants.[2]

1. ORGANIZATIONAL ASPECTS

All coloured Commonwealth immigrant groups have tended to settle in areas of labour shortage, most of which also suffer from shortages and deficiencies in housing and the social services, including education. In the latter case, the main problems are too few teachers, inadequate school buildings, and overcrowded classrooms. The extra strain caused by the arrival of an increasing number of immigrant children has been exacerbated in areas where the majority of newcomers were Asians with a mother-tongue other than English.

Such situations and the educational, social and administrative problems involved had for years been the object of discussion and concern among local teachers, local education committees and the educational

[1] For an indication of the earlier position, see E.I.U. Supplement for September 1964, *Immigrant Children in British Schools*.

[2] See p. 150f., above, for a more detailed discussion about the distinction between 'younger first-generation' and 'second-generation' immigrants. As the 1967 N.U.T. report on the education of immigrants pointed out, however, it can be difficult to draw a hard and fast line between the two groups: if the parents of British-born children are forced by hostile pressures, or prefer, to organize themselves into tightly exclusive communities, then the children will present much the same problems as those who were born elsewhere.

press.[1] One of the earliest areas to attract national attention was Southall, where in the years 1960–4 the proportion of immigrant children in the school population rose from 1% to 15% (1,130) by January 1964.[2]

The great majority of these immigrant pupils were non-English-speaking, most of them Sikhs, and teaching difficulties were accentuated by the fact that because of residential concentration they were unevenly distributed. For instance, in 1964–5 Southall's Local Education Authority reported 59 and 58% of immigrants, mainly Asians, respectively, in the Beaconsfield Road Junior Modern and Infants' School. Out of the other eighteen Southall schools, three had between 25 and 35%, another twelve between 10 and 24%, and the remaining three 3%, 2% and 0·9%, respectively.

In the autumn of 1963, increasingly vigorous and highly organized protests from local parents that their children were being held back because the Indian children were getting more than their share of teachers' time, and appeals from the Borough Council, brought the then Conservative Minister of Education, Sir Edward Boyle, down to the area on 15 October. He told Council and parents that segregation in schools seemed to him wrong and dangerous and that integration of the immigrant population should be promoted. He would, however, be glad to see 'the load spread thinner and wider'. As one step in this direction, he later recommended that the population of immigrant (coloured) children in each school should not be allowed to exceed one-third.[3] This was the first official endorsement of the quota or ratio system which was to be championed by some, but not all, L.E.A.s, and enshrined in the Department of Education and Science's logistically orientated Circular, 7/65 of June 1965.[4]

[1] The long list of titles (thirty-seven) recorded under the heading of Education (Adjustment and Integration, Intelligence and Attainment, Language Teaching) in the Institute of Race Relations *Register of Research on Commonwealth Immigrants in Britain* (March 1967) speaks for itself.

[2] Nicholas Deakin (ed.), *Colour and the British Electorate*, pp. 34–5. The Bow Group pamphlet, *Commonwealth Immigration*, in a special study of schools in Southall reported that 19% of primary schoolchildren and 18% of secondary schoolchildren were immigrants (0·9% in the grammar schools).

[3] Shortly after the Southall incident, the Ministry of Education put out a pamphlet, *English for Immigrants*, No. 43, which made the same point again, and gave useful advice on how to teach English; it also included a rather neutral discussion of withdrawal and reception classes. Though much praised at the time, Nicolas Hawkes, *Immigration Children in British Schools*, London, Pall Mall Press for I.R.R., 1966, p. 65, suggests that 'the trend of decisions taken since its publication does not suggest it had much influence'. He commends it for pointing out that *laissez-faire* on the language-barrier creates more difficulties than making effective arrangements to ensure as equal as possible an ultimate status for non-English-speaking pupils.

[4] In Southall, the application of the system meant that children already in schools were left there; new entrants were, however, bussed to reception centres in schools in neighbouring areas for intensive courses, usually lasting one year to eighteen months.

A. THE QUOTA SYSTEM

In its second report, published in February 1964 (Cmnd 2266), the Commonwealth Immigrants Advisory Council discussed, *inter alia*, the problem of numbers:

The number of immigrant children in the wide sense in which we are using the term[1] is going to increase, and, as recent events have shown, the number of immigrant children in particular schools or particular areas may increase very rapidly. . . . There is a good deal of variation from one area to another, but we are satisfied from evidence we have received that educational problems are created by a rapid influx of a large number of immigrant children into particular schools. This is hardly surprising. Children from different backgrounds are, at least at first, going to make heavy demands on the time of their teachers. The presence of a high proportion of immigrant children in one class slows down the general routine of working and hampers the progress of the whole class, especially where the immigrants do not speak or write English fluently. This is clearly in itself undesirable and unfair to all the children in the class. There is a further danger that educational backwardness which, in fact, is due to environment, language or a different culture, may increasingly be supposed to arise from some inherent or genetic inferiority.

But something more than academic progress is involved. Schools want to give their immigrant pupils as good an introduction to life in Britain as possible. The evidence we have received strongly suggests that, if a school has more than a certain percentage of immigrant children among its pupils, the whole character and ethos of the school is altered. Immigrant pupils in such a school will not get as good an introduction to British life as they would get in a normal school, and we think their education in the widest sense must suffer as a result. . . . We were concerned by the evidence we received that there were schools in certain parts of the country containing an extremely high proportion of immigrant children. Moreover, the evidence from one or two areas showed something a good deal more disturbing than a rise in the proportion of immigrant children in certain schools: it showed a tendency towards the creation of predominantly immigrant schools, partly because of the increase in the number of immigrant children in certain neighbourhoods, but also partly because some parents tend to take native-born children away from schools when the proportion of immigrant pupils exceeds a level which suggests to them that the school is becoming an immigrant school. If this trend continues, both the social and educational consequences might be very grave.

. . . The arrival of large numbers of immigrants from the Commonwealth is so recent that the situation is a fluid and changing one. It varies from one

---

Such centres were by 1965 set up in fourteen of Southall's twenty schools. Twenty-one teachers of special classes were recruited at a cost of £50,000, to teach English to those who needed it, and about 500 children were involved. (See N. Hawkes, op. cit., pp. 29–30, 33, 35.)

[1] i.e. to include both children born overseas and those born in this country of immigrant parents.

area to another, and the ways of meeting the problem must also vary; and any suggestions we put forward will need to be examined again in the light of further experience. But we hope all local education authorities will be alive to the advantages of securing that immigrant children are taught alongside native children, and to the dangers of the creation of immigrant schools. We hope they will bear this in mind in planning the locations and catchment areas of their schools. Where special reception classes are required for the teaching of English to new arrivals, local education authorities should consider so locating the classes as to reduce the concentration of immigrant children in particular schools. There are clearly strong arguments against any interference with the general rule giving parents the maximum amount of choice as to their children's school. Arrangements to send children to some alternative school in order to preserve a reasonable balance must be regarded as a last resort, but such arrangements are preferable to *de facto* segregation, which is something to be avoided at all costs.

The idea of the 'benign' quota remained part of central government thinking after the Labour Party came into office in late 1964. The departmental circular to L.E.A.s and other bodies referred to above (7/65) on 'The Education of Immigrants' contained the following recommendations with regard to dispersal:[1]

It is inevitable that, as the proportion of immigrant children in a school or class increases, the problems will become more difficult to solve, and the chances of assimilation more remote. How far any given proportion of immigrant children can be absorbed with benefit to both sides depends on, among other things, the composition of the immigrant group and the number of immigrant children who are proficient in English; the dividing line cannot be precisely defined. Experience suggests, however, that, apart from unusual difficulties (such as a high proportion of non-English speakers), up to a fifth of immigrant children in any group fit in with reasonable ease, but that, if the proportion goes over about one-third either in the school as a whole or in any one class, serious strains arise. It is therefore desirable that the catchment areas of schools should, wherever possible, be arranged to avoid undue concentration of immigrant children. Where this proves impracticable simply because the school serves an area which is occupied largely by immigrants, every effort should be made to disperse the immigrant children round a greater number of schools and to meet such problems of transport as may arise. It is important for the success of such measures that the reasons should be carefully explained beforehand to the parents of both the immigrant and the other children, and their co-operation obtained. *It will be helpful if the parents of non-immigrant children can see that practical measures have been taken to deal with the problem in the schools, and that the progress of their own*

[1] These recommendations were repeated in the White Paper on *Immigration from the Commonwealth* published in August 1965 (paras. 39–42). A special count of immigrant children in state schools was authorized by the Department of Education and Science early in 1966. This would form part of the normal statistical survey made by the Ministry every year, and would provide accurate statistics for policy-makers.

children is not being restricted by the undue preoccupation of the teaching staff with the linguistic and other difficulties of immigrant children.

The circular continued:

Occasions may arise when dispersal measures of this nature are not practicable, or seem in a particular case to involve disadvantages which outweigh the benefits. They should, nevertheless, be given serious consideration, since it is to everyone's disadvantage if the problems within a school are allowed to become so great that they cause a decline in the general standard of education provided.

It is a common experience of authorities that once immigrants have begun to live in an area, they are quickly joined by members of their own families and by fellow-countrymen who wish to settle in the same neighbourhood. It is therefore important that, as soon as there are indications that immigrants are coming in to the area, even though the number of schoolchildren among them may not at first be very great, the authority should decide their policy and make plans for dealing with the rapid and substantial influx of children which may follow. Only if this is done at an early stage, before the problems become acute, will there be a reasonable chance of avoiding by one means or another undue pressure on particular schools. For this purpose, there should be standing arrangements with the local housing and health authorities for any information reaching them about changes in the size or composition of the immigrant population to be passed immediately to the local education authority; such arrangements might, with advantage, be extended to include local liaison and consultative committees where these exist, and the leaders of the immigrant committee themselves, who are likely to be the first to know of new arrivals among their fellow-countrymen.

Bradford and West Bromwich provide two examples of 'purposeful distribution', or the quota system in action. Even before the departmental circular Bradford, with a concentrated immigrant settlement, mainly Pakistani, had imposed a 25% limit in schools, with a lower limit for large primary schools, and still lower proportions for secondary schools. In an ordinary class, the aim was to have not more than 30% of immigrant children (or 15% if they were all non-English-speaking). In 1965 it was reported that three of the city's 150 schools contained over 40% of immigrants, and three more than 20%. The transition to the desired ratio was to be gradual and transport was to be provided (though initially the redirected pupils were either within walking distance of the new school or were considered old enough to travel by bus). The scheme was said to have the full co-operation of parents and teachers.

In Southall and Bradford most of the immigrants are non-English-speaking Asians, and in addition to 'bussing', the authorities have set up reception schools (or classes) to give full-time separate tuition. In West Bromwich, with a coloured school population of only 4%, redistribution has since January 1964 been applied to West Indian as well as Asian children, drawn off mainly from the Beeches Road area (one of heavy concentration). It has also applied mainly to infants, a feature which has attracted some criticism because of the effect of moving such young children up to three miles and the fact that at that early age they can pick up English more easily.

The quota principle met, however, with widespread criticism[1] from educationalists and others[2] and from various immigrant associations on a number of grounds, and was ignored or rejected by many local authorities. A Young Fabian study group commented on the June 1965 circular's 'preoccupation with the counting of heads':

> The Minister has undoubtedly been impressed by the U.S. Civil Rights movement's strong support for a quota system. In this instance the experience of the U.S. is a false analogy, since they are trying to break down long-established patterns of segregation, while here we are endeavouring, or should be, to prevent such patterns forming in the first place. The immigrant concentrations derive from the housing problem. The long-term solution must lie in that direction. The physical moving of schoolchildren, quite apart from its infringement on rights of free choice of school, is tackling the symptom and not the cause. However, as the circular partly suggests, where school catchment areas can be skilfully adjusted *in advance*, to avoid such a gathering of *non-English-speaking* children as would make special language teaching much more difficult, this should be done. Such adjustments should still permit the choice of school to be within walking distance.[3]

In the 1965 Bow Group Pamphlet on *Commonwealth Immigration*,[4] the authors outlined other difficulties:

> There are serious disadvantages to the quota system, most of which were glossed over or ignored in the circular. First of all, it is an educational advantage to have reasonable concentrations of non-English-speaking immigrants in certain schools, so that special classes can be provided on the spot. If immigrant children are spread around neighbourhood schools in small numbers, special classes become harder to arrange. Secondly, the psychological effect on immigrant children who are moved out of their neighbourhood by special transport to a school often a considerable distance away, may be bad. The sensible principle of the neighbourhood school, which is fundamental in English primary education, is overridden.
>
> Finally, the practical administration of such a system is open to abuse.

[1] See, for instance, Nicolas Hawkes, op. cit., pp. 29–34, 64–5. It was, however, approved by the Liberal Immigration Group in its report of July 1965 (pp. 20–21) and by the P.E.S.T. report on *Immigration and the Commonwealth* (p. 22).

[2] There was a protest from the West Indian Standing Conference in London, and from various other immigrant organizations, on the grounds that this was discriminatory if it involved moving English-speaking coloured children, or that there had been no consultation with immigrant representatives.

[3] *Strangers Within*, Young Fabian Pamphlet 10, p. 16.

[4] The pamphlet also gave a detailed account of the operation of the quota system in Southall; for reasons of space this had to be omitted.

Nowhere in the circular does the Department of Education and Science define the term 'immigrant',[1] and it is obvious that the quota can all too easily be based on a colour bar.

The Brent Friendship Council, as a result of the quota circular, asked the Ministry of Education the following questions:

(1) How many schools in the country have more than the recommended number of immigrant children?
(2) How many non-English-speaking children are in the schools?
(3) How many children, classified as immigrant, are there in the total school population?
(4) How many children, classified as immigrant, are there in this country or born overseas?
(5) What is the age-distribution of immigrant children at school?
(6) What objective studies have been made of the 'serious strains' referred to in paragraph 8 of the circular?
(7) What demographic evidence is there concerning the concentration of immigrants in certain neighbourhoods?

The spokesman for the Ministry replied that there were no statistics of this kind,[2] and it is clear that the quota section of the circular has little objective evidence to support it.[2]

B. DISPERSAL—OPPOSITION AND SUPPORT

After the publication of the Ministry circular, a large number of local authorities in fact stated that they were not going to introduce a quota system. These included Wolverhampton,[3] Coventry, Nottingham, Bristol, Leicester, Birmingham and the Inner London Education Authority (I.L.E.A.).[4] In a number of schools with 40 or 50% of immigrant children a quota was not considered necessary and no tensions or local ill-feeling seemed to have arisen. Among the reasons advanced for this easier situation were that some immigrant settlements were less concentrated (the children thus being more widely dispersed in the schools); for instance, Liverpool, Manchester, Sheffield, and Nottingham, by contrast with Bradford, Southall, and Bedford (where most immigrants are Italians), and that certain areas had become used to

[1] The Department has since defined immigrant children as 'children born outside the British Isles who have come here with or to join parents whose country of origin is abroad, and children born in the United Kingdom to such parents who have come here as immigrants during the past ten years'. Children from Northern Ireland and Eire are excluded from this definition.

[2] They have been collected since January 1966.

[3] See *Wolverhampton Express and Star* (25 January 1966) for details and statistics.

[4] Inner London, with more immigrant children than any other authority, rejected it outright, on the grounds that it would be unwise to divorce the child from its home environment or to interfere with parent participation in school activities. *The Teacher* (28 January 1966) reported that the population of immigrant schoolchildren in areas such as Islington, Brixton, and Deptford had reached 50%.

dealing with children from a series of immigrant groups, with numbers increasing gradually and over a longish period. The model for the Minister's circular, on the other hand, was drawn from a rather atypical outer London district (Southall), which had received a single, large, non-English-speaking, culturally alien immigrant group in a period of about three years. The fact that the large numbers of non-English-speaking children entering schools in such areas as Southall could communicate with each other in their own language obviously rendered the educational authority's task more difficult than in areas with mixed ethnic settlements, or with a predominance of English-speaking or at least Creolese-speaking West Indians.

Birmingham's dogged policy of non-dispersal on the grounds of non-discrimination has long been the subject of controversy. In spite of increasing warnings about the development of 'ghetto schools', the Labour group which controlled the city for years until 1966 refused to act. By 1966, with 11,700 immigrant children (of all origins) forming 6·6% of its school population,[1] a situation had been reached in which two primary schools had between 85 and 90% of coloured pupils,[2] another four had over 65%, and sixteen schools, including three secondary, had more than 50%.[3]

[1] *Returns for January 1966*

	Infants		Juniors		Seniors		Total	
	No.	%	No.	%	No.	%	No.	%
Indian	673	1·5	874	1·4	1,131	1·6	2,678	1·5
Pakistani	229	0·5	399	0·7	587	0·8	1,215	0·7
West Indian	2,813	6·4	2,812	4·6	1,946	2·7	7,571	4·3
Other non-Europeans ...	65	0·1	81	0·1	106	0·1	252	0·1
Total ...	3,780	8·6	4,166	6·8	3,770	5·2	11,716	6·6

Children at Special Schools are included in the appropriate groups.
(*Source:* City of Birmingham Education Department)

[2] One example given in the *Guardian* report (11 February 1967) was of Grove Infants School in Handsworth, where, out of 390 children, 36 were English, 3 Pakistani, about 100 Indian, and the rest West Indian. Three of the 40 in the last intake were white, and after a fortnight all 3 left to go to Catholic schools. Another was of Grove Junior School, with just 70 white children among 460 pupils (mostly West Indian) and not an application from a white parent in the last two years. Even here, a new problem loomed, because the more-established West Indians were beginning to move out and more Indians were coming in. One extreme case reported in a secondary school was of a class in which only 6 out of the 32 spoke English and the teacher had to use an English-speaking child as an interpreter.

[3] At the end of 1965 the city's statistician was reported as estimating that in two years' time 10 primary schools at the centre of the city would be attended wholly by coloured children, that 47 of the total of 77 schools in the area would have at least 30%, and that only 4 would have no immigrant children at all. Despite a recommendation for 'dispersal by persuasion' by the Primary Education Sub-committee, the Borough Labour Party nevertheless again rejected a motion favouring dispersal by 96 votes to 78 (*Birmingham Post*, 7 February 1966).

The situation was complicated by the fact that the immigrant settlement is concentrated in the inner ring areas[1] and also that about one-third of local authority primary school places in Birmingham are in 'voluntary' schools run by religious denominations (9,000 Church of England, nearly 16,000 Roman Catholic), for which few West Indian immigrants and hardly any Asians would be eligible, whereas most of the Irish children would use R.C. schools.[2]

Matters were reportedly brought to a head in September 1966,[3] when Mr. T. A. Bloxham, headmaster of Goldern Hillock Road Secondary School in Sparkhill, refused admittance to five or six Asian children on the grounds that they could not speak English. He already had forty children who could neither speak, write, nor read the English language, and 35–40% of his pupils were immigrants; there simply was not the staff to cope with more non-English-speaking children. Similar problems were facing other headmasters in Sparkhill, Sparkbrook, and Small Heath, and some were taking similar steps.

At a teachers' conference in June the feeling had also been expressed that a concentration of 30% was the maximum that any school could cope with and in September pressure for the quota came strongly from *inter alia* the local press, the local N.U.T. branch, the local branch of the National Association of Schoolmasters, and Mr. Roy Hattersley, Labour M.P. for Sparkbrook. The teachers' representative on the local Education Committee said the situation had got out of hand, and the authority's *laissez faire* attitude could only lead to segregated schools. The N.U.T. suggested central reorganization and a reception centre[4] for immigrant children, as a means of ensuring dispersal. This the Education Department rejected. Instead of dispersal it had been spending more money on the structure and appearance of schools with immigrant pupils, providing more clerical and auxiliary non-teaching assistance, more equipment, and paying extra allowances to heads and deputy heads (the N.U.T. was blocking any move to press for special increments

[1] A number of educationalists and others have commented that the best way of avoiding a schools dispersal policy is to facilitate the residential dispersal of immigrants (for example, Eric Butterworth, 'Immigrant Schoolchildren: A Study of Leeds', *Race*, Vol. VIII, no. 3, January 1967, p. 260).

[2] *Economist*, 2 April 1966.

[3] There had been earlier rumblings, as when white parents threatened a boycott of a primary school with 80% of coloured children (*The Times*, 16 November 1965, 4 January 1966).

[4] The local branch of the N.A.S. was pressing for six reception centres, to help dispersal of new entrants, although it agreed with the local Education Department that dispersal of immigrants already established in local schools was not now practicable (*Birmingham Post*, 21 October 1966). This was conceded by the newly-elected President of the Birmingham N.U.T. in early 1967 (*Guardian*, 11 February 1967). See also p. 267, n. 1, below.

for class teachers, though the peripatetic staff[1] who tour schools giving tuition in English to immigrant children receive considerably more pay).

The Borough Labour Party reversed its policy on dispersal in February 1967 by a large majority. The Council, now under Conservative control, nevertheless showed little sign of a definite shift of policy, despite heavy pressure from Mr. Denis Howell, Parliamentary Under-Secretary for Education and Science, in February 1967. There were, however, signs that it might be willing to accept the view that, with immigrants concentrating in particular areas, insistence on the neighbourhood principle would produce even more completely segregated schools. Nevertheless the most that appeared likely to emerge for the next academic year was a start on co-ordination of the children moving from primary to secondary schools in September, while on the primary level all that seemed feasible was a containment policy. An analysis of the immigrant local pupil-ratios in individual schools was also being made by the Education Department, and on this might be based any decision to introduce a measure of dispersal at intake level for 5-year-olds. There was also to be a teacher survey of all Commonwealth immigrant children in Birmingham, with visits to parents and interviews in depth to one in five to discover their views, starting with the West Indians, going on to the Indians, and finishing with the Pakistanis. Meanwhile the N.U.T. had presented more figures to show that dispersal was practical, since the schools with the highest immigrant concentration were surrounded by other schools with very few immigrants, thus the transfer of children from one to the other would present no particular problems. They repeated their warning that unless something were done soon the position would become irreversible, with an increasing number of schools becoming segregated units.

At this stage the only dissent from Birmingham teachers was coming from the local branch of the National Association of Head Teachers. In her presidential address, Miss Myfanwy Edwards said that such dispersal would eventually be decided purely on colour, which the Association believed to be ethically wrong and educationally unsound. The *Guardian* (11 February 1967) reported that in general Birmingham's teachers confirmed that with 25% of immigrants children mixed quite easily; the younger the children the easier were the social adjustments. From 30% upwards, however, the educational problems increased and, as the proportion neared 40%, racial grouping started to be seen in the playgrounds. Even more bluntly, the Midland branch of A.T.E.P.O. stated in a 1966 report that over 20% of immigrant children gave rise to problems immediately. Children started banding together and some got

[1] Numbering 30 in 1966. An increase to 50 was requested for 1967 (*Birmingham Post*, 28 October 1967).

colour conscious, while in secondary schools the educational and social problems expanded.[1]

At national level the N.U.T. continued to hold the view that no predetermined percentage could be on a national scale, but that each local education authority must make a decision that was best suited to the needs of its own area, with reference not only to the newcomers but to all the children affected.[2]

A detailed survey of the wide local variations of practice found in different parts of the country was given in Nicholas Hawkes' book, *Immigrant Children in British Schools*.[3] They included:

(1) The successful 'channelling' policy employed at Spring Grove School in Huddersfield until 1964,[4] when more English had moved from the area and so many Asians arrived that the ratio of three immigrants to two English children was exceeded; so sixty-five secondary children were moved and similar special classes set up in other schools. However courageous and successful, concluded the author, the fact remained that in the end more comprehensive arrangements had to be made.

(2) 'Spreading', 'dispersal' or 'purposeful distribution' (Southall, Bradford, West Bromwich). The writer stressed that redistribution could not in itself be a solution; there was no single 'tolerable' percentage, nor had any official source yet clarified the definition of an 'immigrant child'. The only meaningful ratio would be based not on nationality, colour, or general ability, but on ability in English.[5] Councils should, said the writer, endeavour to foresee crises of concentration in schools and to adjust catchment areas in good time, so that there was no uprooting or wholesale transfer of pupils. They should not be misled by the frequent and heavy emphasis on this point by Government sources into thinking that questions about immigrant children in schools would be answered merely in terms of percentages.

Elsewhere Nicolas Hawkes stressed that it was not so much the overall numbers of immigrants in an area that should be considered but their distribution. Such places as Liverpool and Manchester, with

[1] Much of this account of Birmingham is taken from the E.I.U. monthly summary, February 1967, and the *Guardian*, 11 February 1967.

[2] N.U.T. Report, *The Education of Immigrants*, January 1967, pp. 4–5.

[3] Hawkes, op. cit., pp. 29–34.

[4] Since reported on fully by the headmaster and one of his assistant teachers in the book *Spring Grove*, Trevor Burgin and Patricia Edson, London, O.U.P. for I.R.R., 1967.

[5] Social scientists might question whether socio-cultural factors should be omitted in this calculation. To leave a majority of English-speaking West Indian children in a school with Irish and the remnants of the local population may help to foster or inculcate an English-speaking neighbourhood sub-culture. It is not, however, likely to promote the pupils' integration in the society as a whole.

over 10,000, and Sheffield, with over 5,000, have had a relatively minor problem in schools because of a more even distribution, while Nottingham's problems would have been even more severe but for this benefit of distribution. On the other hand, Bradford and Southall had especially heavy concentrations, although taken overall the former only had just over 4% of immigrants both in schools and in the population as a whole.

Areas with the highest proportions of immigrant children in schools at this time (late 1965) included Southall (19%) and Bedford (17%), mainly Italians, but presenting just as great social and educational difficulties, though they lacked publicity value. In Leeds, seven schools had over 20% and one had at least 50% of immigrants. Figures as high as 50 to 70% could be found in the heavily Cypriot parts of Islington and Haringey. There were many cases of a school's intake changing within a few years, from being almost entirely English to having upwards of three immigrants to one native. Another point for consideration was the ethnic origins of the newcomers. If there was a mixed settlement the language teaching problem was not so difficult as when there was a single ethnic concentration of non-English-speakers with a common tongue. The question of the age at which the children arrived in this country was also important; as a general principle the younger they entered the schools the more easily they would pick up the language.

The Government's renewed emphasis on the dispersal quota in the winter of 1966–7 induced the Education Panel of the N.C.C.I. to endorse the N.U.T.'s view that any decision made should relate to all the children affected and that no predetermined percentage could be applied on a national scale. Where dispersal was decided upon, said the Panel, it should affect children with special educational needs, not children selected on the basis of colour; in certain large urban areas there were numbers of children who, apart from the colour of their skin, were completely identifiable with the native children of these areas. The statement continued:

In view of the pressure apparently being applied to LEAs to comply with the terms of Circular 7/65, the Panel agreed to make the following recommendations to the National Committee at its meeting on March 7th:

In arriving at policies concerning the education of immigrant children, LEAs should apply the following criteria:

1. No single doctrine can govern the wide variety of situations found in the different areas.

2. Only the Local Education Authority can know the special circumstances affecting its own schools and can judge what course to adopt. The essential consideration must be a sensitive regard for the best interests of *all* the children concerned.

3. Where dispersal is not judged the best policy the teachers responsible for teaching children with special educational or linguistic needs must be given

every possible help in the shape of resources and training and smaller classes, to help them to do their work.

Nevertheless, in its school building programme for 1968–9, published on 4 April 1967, the Department of Education and Science expressed the hope that the provision of new primary school places would also help to achieve a more even distribution of immigrant children.

C. RECEPTION

Dispersal, channelling, or *laissez-faire* concentration are different organizational ways of trying to meet the overall set of educational and social problems posed or faced by immigrant children. Whatever the chosen long-term policy, however, there is a need for reception arrangements to promote initial linguistic and social integration.

Here again different policies have been advised and adopted by different bodies and in different areas. Nor are separate reception centres necessarily linked with dispersal policies (or vice versa). For instance West Bromwich, one of the early exponents of dispersal, established a reception centre for intensive English instruction in 1958; but after eighteen months the situation was reassessed by heads of primary schools, who decided that pupils' time, continuity of learning and loyalty to their schools were lost by attending the centre and that more could be achieved in the primary schools themselves. The West Bromwich Director of Education was later reported as saying that reception centres were undesirable on educational grounds; he preferred small group-teaching techniques by which immigrant pupils could be absorbed into the school's main stream.[1]

On the other hand, the N.U.T. report, while leaving dispersal decisions to local authorities, advocated a general period of initiation before full entry to school, to facilitate the 'ascertainment of present and potential capacities . . . [and] of medical matters' and to insulate the newcomers from cultural shock. This could be done in reception centres, separate or attached to a school, or special reception classes, using welfare liaison officers. The reception period should, however, be as short as possible, so as not to encourage isolation, and where possible the transition to normal schooling should be gradual, not abrupt. For locally-born pre-school immigrant children there was, said the N.U.T. report, a very strong case for expanded nursery accommodation and for play-centres, which should also be made available for local children.

A survey of local reception practices in 1965–6[2] showed three basic

[1] *Guardian* (11 February 1967).
[2] Hawkes, op. cit., pp. 34–52.

types of approach: reception classes, withdrawal classes, and reception centres.

As Nicolas Hawkes pointed out, the dilemma facing headmasters and education officers is how to give immigrant children the special intensive language-training that is the key to their integration into the educational system without at the same time giving too much special treatment that will have a socially divisive effect. One solution frequently tried out by individual schools, especially in areas of very high concentration is that of giving courses in English, incorporating useful instruction on urban or British life, in special full-time reception classes with a special teacher. Instances of this system were found in Islington, Southall, and Bedford, of which the former was reported to be the most successful. Southall was using a large number of immigrant teachers (see below) and some classes had risen to thirty instead of the intended twenty members. Bedford had done little to recruit specially-trained teachers, despite its long experience of Italian children (since 1954); meanwhile the situation had been complicated by the recent trebling of its Asian population.

Withdrawal classes consist either of special classes at certain times for the learners or, more commonly, of small groups being withdrawn not necessarily from the same class, to visit the specialist teacher for a certain time. This means a greater degree of social mixing and 'rub-off' of language than under the reception-class system, but less intensive language study and consequent delay in learning enough English to be able to benefit from class instruction.[1]

A combination of staff shortage and an aversion to separate treatment has meant that the withdrawal class is the commonest method of organizing language teaching. Hawkes cited Haringey and Islington (a majority of its specialist teachers), Dudley, Batley, Leicester, Manchester, Ilford, and Smethwick as making use of this system.

Since 1960 Birmingham has evolved a distinctive system, based on intensive part-time teaching, and using a growing team of peripatetic teachers. After September 1963, five schools with a large number of non-English speakers were also made into centre schools with specialist teachers on the staff. Following September 1966, however, when no secondary school places could be found for fifty newly-arrived non-English-speaking children, the Council's secondary education sub-committee declared that, if a similar situation arose again, two special language reception centres for children of secondary school age would

[1] Hawkes, op. cit., pp. 36–38 and 41, for a tentative assessment of these two main approaches and for a suggestion that their relative efficacy should be studied in relation to such factors as the pupil's age and potential ability. Hawkes deplores Circular 7/65's brief reference, which appears to give all its weight to the full-time reception class.

be set up, possibly in school premises but not under the control of any school.[1]

The idea of language reception centres has become increasingly popular. Such a centre may be full-time or half-time, the latter being essentially an extension of the withdrawal class system. Instead of the teacher going to the school, the pupils go to the centrally-placed teacher. London pioneered this idea: Islington and Camberwell have centres for secondary school pupils who attend for half of each day (an arrangement that would not generally be suitable for primary-age pupils because of the distances to be travelled). The effectiveness of this depends on the assessment of needs and co-operation of local head-teachers and staff. Other areas with reception centres are Slough and Bolton, and most recently Halifax, which started in April 1967.

This trend towards special centres has been evolving, as Hawkes commented, despite official Government support for the quite different idea of long-term dispersal. He also noted some moves, which he considered neither necessary nor desirable, towards the adoption of nearly or wholly full-time centres, involving considerable separation from the normal schools, e.g. in Bradford,[2] Walsall, Coventry, and Slough.

Some authorities have found it possible to meet the needs of immigrant children successfully without recourse to special teaching (or to dispersal). Notable among them is Nottingham with 2,250 coloured children—two-thirds West Indian—and nearly 1,000 white immigrant children in a total of 51,500 pupils in February 1965.[3] This policy has been helped by the fact that the immigrant population has so far been distributed reasonably evenly: the highest overall proportion reached in one primary school was 45%, and in a secondary school only 20%. A better staffing ratio, the use of smaller groups, and mixing of pupils so that English is needed as a lingua franca, have produced a situation in which an average of eighteen months (as opposed to Birmingham's two years of withdrawal classes) is required to learn English adequately for normal class purposes.

Other areas with similar 'relaxed' policies are Sheffield, Manchester,

[1] *Guardian* (2 January 1967). In February 1967, Birmingham's Head Teachers' Association called for the immediate introduction of three special education units for non-English-speaking children and a central registering authority for all immigrant children. (*Guardian*, 24 February 1967.)

[2] Bradford could in fact be given as an example of three types of approach: reception classes, reception schools, and reception centres. See T. F. Davies' review of Hawkes' book, *Bradford Telegraph and Argus* (4 March 1966).

[3] For details of Nottingham's experience and methods, see article by George Jackson, Nottingham's Director of Education, in I.R.R. *Newsletter*, February 1966. The January 1967 returns showed a total of 3,886 immigrant pupils out of 52,383 (7·4%). Of the immigrants, 3,000 were 'coloured' (again two-thirds were West Indian), and there were 886 'other immigrants'.

Liverpool, and Cardiff, all helped by a more even distribution, a mixture of nationalities and particular teaching care.

This brief survey of areas and policies shows the considerable range of experience and models available for local education authorities that are only now facing a situation in which increasing numbers of immigrant children are entering their schools.

Such a range of policies differs sharply from an absence of policy, or a belief that working out a policy actively contributes to the problem. A *laissez-faire* approach is, however, likely to cause a lasting deafness to English in some non-English-speaking children and make assessment of the children's abilities difficult, or to lead to down-grading in a streaming system of those who know a little English or, like some West Indians, speak Creolese.[1] There is also the tendency to misuse remedial classes for children who are only linguistically handicapped. In the long run, *laissez-faire*, while ostensibly non-discriminatory, can only promote colour-class identification and *de facto* segregation.

2. EDUCATIONAL ASPECTS

Educational and socio-cultural problems are of course involved in the organizational aspect of integrating immigrant children in British schools. There are, however, certain problems within these two categories that need separate consideration. Under the heading 'educational aspects' may be considered specialist teachers, training, techniques, and materials.

Schools in areas of heavy immigration need an above-average staffing ratio and, at primary level, the help of welfare assistants. In practice, the situation has often been the opposite: these schools have had the largest classes and the least ancillary help. There is also likely to be a problem of overcrowding, with or without immigration.

For schools in such 'areas of educational priority'[2] (whether or not

[1] Some experts believe that the problem of ostensibly English-speaking West Indian children who are in E.S.N. schools and D-streams, so far largely ignored, may be a bigger one even than the needs of non-English-speaking children, on which the main effort has so far been concentrated. Two particular needs indicated in this connexion are: (i) research into the specific remedial needs of the speakers of various West Indian dialects; (ii) the evolution of a satisfactory set of culture-free, non-verbal tests to determine ability accurately, unimpaired by language and other barriers. In the summer of 1967 the Schools Council was reported to have decided to support a centre under Professor J. A. Sinclair at the University of Birmingham to study the pedagogic problems of West Indian children.

[2] The Department of Education and Science did not formally agree to designate such areas, but the announcement of the 1968–9 Major Building Programme in April 1967 mentioned that over £3m. was for the rebuilding of primary schools in thirty-one areas falling within this general description. An estimated £1·7m. worth of this and all other projects was said to fall within the areas with a high immigrant population.

they contain immigrants), the Plowden Report on primary education[1] recommended positively discriminatory treatment in teachers' pay, in building priorities, and in nursery classes for children under 5. For immigrant children specifically, the committee recommended special training for teachers in teaching English and generous staffing for schools with special language problems.[2] The life-long loss, both to all the children in such areas, and to the community as a whole, arising because of inequality of educational opportunity, was, said the report, 'avoidable and in consequence intolerable'.

The need in areas of immigrant settlement has so far been not only for more and better general teachers but for the teaching of English as a second language. Until very recently the number of such specially-trained teachers was small and the training over-indebted to experience abroad, on which almost all the existing materials are still based.[3] Pioneer courses for specialists have been introduced at Furzedown and Edgehill Colleges of Education; one-term, in-service courses combining successful local experience with linguistic training have also been started at London, Edinburgh, and Leeds Universities.[4] In this connexion, however, there is a shortage not only of specialized teachers but of specialized staff to teach them. The in-service courses are considered vitally important for experienced teachers as opposed to young trainees.

Another pioneer course of a somewhat different kind is the Pathway Further Education Centre set up by Ealing Borough in October 1966. This is for young immigrants above the statutory school-leaving age who are unable to join existing courses of further education because of their poor command of English. Ealing Technical College is assisting

[1] A Report of the Central Advisory Council for Education, London, H.M.S.O. 10 January 1967. See also Newsom Report, Ch. III.

[2] According to a communication from the Department of Education and Science in June 1967, the Secretary of State has for several years past (under the power contained in the proviso to Regulation 16(1) of the Schools Regulations, 1959) been prepared to increase the quota of teachers in areas of high immigrant population, if this was needed to improve the staffing arrangements in schools containing large numbers of immigrants. Twenty-one authorities were given additions to their quotas in 1967 and applications for 1968 were currently being considered (the arrangements for 1968 being contained in Circular 1/67). Five authorities have also received extra minor building works allocations for special projects, including language centres, intended to facilitate the teaching of English to immigrant children. Moreover, the Local Authorities Government Act 1966 empowers the Home Secretary to pay grants in respect of the salaries of staff employed by the local authorities specifically to deal with immigrants.

[3] In July 1966 the National Committee for Commonwealth Immigrants published a Bibliography of Teaching Materials (Language Section).

[4] The London course no longer exists. Miss Anne Blatch, who ran it, is now running courses for the I.L.E.A. A more up-to-date list of types of teacher-training available and planned in 1967–8 is given in *Practical Suggestions for Teachers of Immigrant Children*, London, N.C.C.I., 1967, pp. 20–22.

with linguistic specialists and the Centre intends to write its own material and to make it available to other institutions and bodies conducting research. It is in close touch with projects in Leeds, Bradford, Manchester, and London.

In addition to the need for teaching materials (books, apparatus, audio-visual apparatus) related to the British urban background,[1] there is also a need for more work on remedial work in spoken English among those for whom it is the first language (for example, Creolese-speaking West Indians).[2] The National Federation for Educational Research is also working to evolve a satisfactory test of language ability,[3] which A.T.E.P.O. (see below) considers to be as much needed as a culture-free test of general intelligence. Another long-felt need has been for the collection and pooling of information about organizational and classroom procedures and about research at all levels.

Since 1965 there has been increasing activity aimed at meeting these needs for specialized teachers, training, techniques, materials, research, and co-ordination of information.[4] Apart from the organizations mentioned, several specialist projects and new groupings have started work.

March 1965 saw the birth of the very active Association of Teachers of English to Pupils from Overseas (A.T.E.P.O.), a body of teachers and other educationalists in the London area which arose out of an L.C.C. introductory course for specialized teachers but included other interested teachers.[5] Branches were later set up in Birmingham, Bradford, and elsewhere. A.T.E.P.O. was, however, preceded by two years by the pioneering Birmingham association originally known as the Association of Teachers of English as a Second Language; this later adopted the

[1] Birmingham A.T.E.P.O. and the Birmingham Education Department have already produced a series of infant readers (*Living Together*—Books 1–10, D. Brazier and E. Jones, Oxford, Pergamon Press, 1965) in which children from different nations are shown working and playing together in an English primary school. Some teachers have, however, been very critical of the series as a reading scheme.

[2] As was pointed out on p. 268, the linguistic needs of ostensibly English-speaking West Indians have only recently come to be seen as a serious problem. In the past, when West Indian children were the only immigrant pupils, they have usually been overlooked or erroneously treated by down-streaming; more recently, in schools with a large intake of non-English speakers whose difficulties seem much greater, they have also generally been ignored. Latterly, however, there has been increasing understanding of the problem, and Huddersfield has, for instance, given two teachers special responsibility in this field. (See also Burgin and Edson, op. cit., Ch. X, and E. Butterworth, 'The School', *New Society*, 16 March 1967.)

[3] Roger Bell refers to the utility of the Michigan test of aural comprehension, slightly adjusted, for use even with 8-year-olds. (*New Society*, 16 February 1967, p. 247.)

[4] Hawkes points out (op. cit., pp. 62–3) that there is a good deal of expertise available in London in the form of material for teaching English overseas: for example, the British Council, the B.B.C., and the armed forces.

[5] I.R.R. *Newsletter*, September 1966.

same name as the London Association. One of A.T.E.P.O.'s initiatives was to convene a meeting of people from the Association of Teachers in Colleges and Departments of Education (A.T.C.D.E.), the London University Institute of Education, and those colleges which have already planned special courses. Their aim was to define general needs and problems in the improvement of teacher-training. Its conclusions fell under the following headings: (i) problems for child and teacher (cultural background, the social psychology of migration and cultural transition, late arrival, parental influence, remedial linguistic methods, second-language techniques, linguistic assessment); (ii) what is already available; (iii) what needs to be done in both specialized and general training.

In January 1966, the National Committee for Research and Development in Modern Languages established a sub-committee to deal exclusively with English for speakers of other languages. Its first task was to carry out an immediate survey of current research in appropriate fields. The English Teaching Information Centre, which maintains records of research relevant to the general teaching of English as a second language, was to assist this survey, process the data and maintain them as part of the research register. Later in 1966, a new Centre for Information on Language Teaching was set up in London; its Director was Mr. G. E. Perren (c/o British Council, Holborn).

The work of the Education Panel of the National Committee for Commonwealth Immigrants, under the chairmanship of Mr. Eric Hawkins, was concerned with the provision of ideas, advice and information. In 1966 it looked at three aspects of formal education in the schools: the immediate problems of non-English-speaking children, the broad canvas of teaching for children in a multi-racial society; and assistance to teachers concerned with both these aspects. It has already held a number of conferences and seminars for educationists, teachers, and student teachers, and published a bibliography of materials for use by teachers of non-English-speaking children and adults,[1] and a handbook, *Practical Suggestions for Teachers of Immigrant Children* (edited by Trevor Burgin), and a report by Alec Dickson of Community Service Volunteers on the help that such volunteers can give in the schools. A questionnaire was circulated to teacher-training colleges to discover what is being done in the field and the Panel has set up a sub-committee on teacher-training under the chairmanship of Mr. P. K. C. Millins, Principal of Edge Hill College of Education. There have also been a number of talks to adult groups inside and outside the sphere of further education.

[1] See also R. Goldman, *Research and the Teaching of Immigrant Children*, London, N.C.C.I., 1967.

A valuable survey of recently completed but mostly unpublished work in this field was compiled by R. J. Goldman and F. M. Taylor and published in *Educational Research*, June 1966. This has been complemented by the on-going Register of Research (unpublished thesis material and work in progress) compiled by A. Sivanandan and Margaret Scruton for the Institute of Race Relations (second edition, March 1967).

Space precludes a detailed survey of all these research projects, but mention may be made of the most important one: an ambitious three-year English-teaching project started by the Institute of Education at Leeds University in late 1966, under the direction of Professor B. E. Fletcher. The Schools Council has made a £50,000 grant towards that part of it which is aimed at the development of techniques and materials for the teaching of English to Asian and South European immigrant children and the stimulation of development work among teachers in immigrant areas. This is led by June Derrick, who in 1965 carried out a survey of immigrant education for the Schools Council, consisting of: (i) a statistical inquiry into the number and distribution of immigrant children in schools and the provisions that are made by way of teacher supply, provision of materials, etc.; and (ii) a follow-up inquiry in certain areas in greater depth, to study classroom methods, the efficacy of certain arrangements, teacher opinion, etc.

Despite these initiatives, the situation as regards specialist teacher-training and specialist teachers is still regarded as far from satisfactory. Diana Cowan was good enough to contribute the following note after reading over this chapter in draft:

In the vital field of teacher-training, some training colleges have taken the initiative and have started courses on the teaching of English as a second language and have organized lectures and conferences on the backgrounds of immigrant children.

Certain colleges and L.E.A.s have realized the importance of in-service training, but the courses that do exist have usually begun because of the enthusiasm of one or two individuals. There is no overall plan for training in this work and many colleges have still to be persuaded of the importance of training their students to teach in multi-racial schools. In some instances where in-service courses have been organized, head teachers have found it difficult to release members of staff who want to attend. Due to the shortage of teachers this has been an understandable problem, but teachers who have worked in multi-racial schools feel that it is essential that students should be aware of the social and cultural difficulties that immigrant children have to face, and that teachers who are asked to teach English as a second language must be given some basic training in this highly specialized work.

For those specialist teachers already in the schools many problems still exist. Because specialist teachers are comparatively new in primary schools, there are sometimes problems over the status and duties of the language teachers.

Organizational difficulties sometimes arise where children have to come out of their normal classes for intensive language lessons, and the specialist teacher will often have to explain the new methods and the techniques she uses to the head teacher and other members of the staff.

The language teacher needs a great deal of visual apparatus, and as very little of the ready-made material on the market is suitable, she has to make and improvise her own. Many secondary teachers who have not had experience of making what is usually considered to be infant apparatus, have found this a time-consuming task and a strain on their artistic ability. The apparatus that is in the process of being made by Miss June Derrick and her team for the Schools Council Project in the Education of Immigrant Children is eagerly awaited.

There is a feeling of isolation amongst specialist teachers, although the A.T.E.P.O. branches in different parts of the country exist to bring these teachers together. They are limited in the amount of help that they can give. Many teachers feel that there is a need for a central clearing-house where information can be collected and sent out to schools. The A.T.E.P.O. branches organize meetings and seminars in their own areas, but because of the lack of finance, premises, and secretarial help, they are unable to keep their members informed of all the new developments throughout the country.

Experienced teachers are continually being asked for advice by Colleges of Education, students, and practising teachers, and a full-time adviser is needed if these inquirers are to be helped.

With a more co-ordinated system of training and improved communications, the teaching of immigrant children need not be a problem but an educational challenge.

7 May 1967

3. SOCIAL ASPECTS

It has been emphasized that the social and educational aspects and problems involved in the integration of immigrant pupils in the British educational system cannot be entirely separated from one another nor from the organizational aspect. Thus, much in the foregoing sections, including the outline of teacher-training needs and research, relates to the social aspects as well. This section, however, will be primarily concerned with the training and work of general teachers (including materials), the use of immigrant teachers and auxiliary help, the school community, teacher-parent relations, and the home background of the immigrant child.[1]

With the prospect of more specialist teachers, a danger has been noted that the rest of the teaching staff may feel inclined to leave all matters relating to immigrant children to them. The school is also an institution that transmits social values and attitudes, and therefore there are many educational and social problems with which all teachers should be trained to deal, whether or not they actually have immigrant pupils, in the changing, increasingly pluralistic Britain of today.[2] This requires an improvement in the breadth and quality of teacher-training, including an appreciation of social and cultural diversities (and the possibility of utilizing them positively to widen local horizons), a wider tolerance, and an ability to act as social guides and to deal with the prejudices of both local pupils and their parents and the resentments of immigrant parents who see their children conforming increasingly to British patterns.

Teacher-training courses need adaptation and an infusion of the social sciences to meet this challenge, and there is also a need for far more general in-service courses geared to the immigration situation.[3] Here again syllabuses may be traditional and materials such as text-books inadequate, while those that are available are often out-of-date and propagate the outmoded theories and attitudes of colonial times and nineteenth-century pseudo-anthropology.[4]

Within the school community, there are three sets of relationships in which the teacher's influence can be particularly important: those between teacher and immigrant pupils, between immigrant and native pupils, and between teacher and parents (native and immigrant). In the first relationship, problems of communication and discipline are likely to be eased by a knowledge not only of the children's home backgrounds before migration and at present, but of the experiences or expectations of the school which they bring with them.[5]

[1] For a short but detailed general survey of the education of immigrant children, see the final report of the *Labour Women's National Survey into Care of Children*, London, May 1967, Chapter 4.

[2] See *Towards a Multi-Racial Society*, London, N.C.C.I., 1966. For a description of a specific situation in Sparkbrook, Birmingham, see Chapter X by Jennifer Williams in Rex and Moore, op. cit.

[3] The A.T.E.P.O. meeting in March 1966 also dealt with these aspects.

[4] See Stephen Hatch, 'Coloured People in School Textbooks', *Race*, Vol. IV, no. 1, November 1962. The 1966 British Caribbean Association drew up a project for studying the function and content of school textbooks in the context of racial understanding.

[5] See the following: (1) on Punjabi rural schools: A. B. Shaw, I.R.R. *Newsletter*, January 1966, pp. 12–14; (2) on West Indian education: (i) report in I.R.R. *Newsletter* for May 1966, pp. 14–20; (ii) Elsa H. Walters in I.R.R. *Newsletter*, July/August 1966, p. 126; (iii) Audrey Allison in I.R.R. *Newsletter*, November/December 1966, p. 44.

Relationships between the children within the school situation can be influenced, even determined, by teachers. As Oscar Tapper wrote: 'When the adults in a school refuse to countenance any instances of racial intolerance, then it ceases to be a problem.'[1]

This does not necessarily mean that native schoolchildren do not show hostility outside the school, nor that they do not have prejudiced attitudes, derived sometimes from stereotyped thinking and teaching, but above all from the attitudes of their parents and the views current in the neighbourhood.[2] There seems to be a general agreement that very young children are unaffected by ethnic or racial differences; but this may begin to change earlier than is generally believed, given the presence of certain factors such as large numbers, parental fears, neighbourhood resentment, teachers' apathy, ignorance, or repetition of stereotypes. Hostilities are certainly intensified in adolescence, although here again they may be demonstrated more actively outside the school—in the street, the youth club and so on.[3]

In areas of heavy immigration, local parents often feel anxiety and resentment over the possibility of the children's education being held back and impaired because of the presence of large numbers of non-English-speaking or culturally alien newcomers in schools that are in any case likely to be ill-equipped and to have staffing problems. This reaction in Southall sparked off the original one-in-three departmental recommendation in 1963. There are, however, more positive ways of dealing with it—for instance, by improving teaching standards and general atmosphere within the school until even those local parents who move out of the area may ask for their children to stay on, as in Spring Grove, Huddersfield.[4]

Relationships between teachers and immigrant parents differ according to the ethnic groups involved. West Indian parents wish their children to be anglicized and accepted but tend to impose harsh discipline, physical punishments and strict supervision and to be critical of

[1] *Educating the Immigrant: A Sample Survey*, London, University House, East London Papers, Vol. VI, no. 2, December 1963, p. 120.

[2] See *Immigrants in London*, National Council of Social Service, 1963, for a note on this and generally on 'The Young Immigrant and the School', pp. 38–41.

[3] Research into relations between immigrant and English schoolchildren includes the following: (i) Taysin Kawwa: A study of the interaction between native and immigrant children in English schools with special reference to ethnic prejudice. Ph.D. thesis, 'Hostilities of Education', University of London, 1965. (ii) Leo Silberman and Betty Spice, 'Colour and Class in Six Liverpool Schools', Liverpool University, 1950. See also G. Jahoda, T. Veness, and I. Pushkin, 'Awareness of Ethnic Differences in Young Children: Proposals for a British Study', *Race*, Vol. VIII, no. 1, July 1966.

[4] The standards and atmosphere more frequently found were described by Eric Butterworth in 'The School', *New Society* (16 March 1967), and Brian Priestley in *The Times* (24 February 1967).

the more permissive approach to work and leisure in the British school. There is some evidence of excessive job expectations, and children may sometimes be kept on for the extra year in the vague hope of improving their employment chances. Burgin and Edson, however, reported frequent lack of parental interest in their Huddersfield area (*Spring Grove*, p. 22 and p. 92). Jennifer Williams (Rex and Moore, op. cit., pp. 241–2) also noted very little parental contact with the schools, among either English or immigrant parents, in Sparkbrook. There is, however, some evidence that this changes as the immigrants settle down.

In the case of Indian or Pakistani parents, actual communication is difficult because neither parent may speak English (it is in any case often the father who is responsible for such matters as schooling). While Asian parents are likely to encourage learning, most of them resist anglicization over costume, food preferences, and so on (though Jennifer Williams found that most children in Sparkbrook schools abandoned such distinctive practices within a year).[1] There is likely to be still more resistance over religious practices, and, as the children mature, widely differing assumptions about the freedom of children in leisure pursuits, in the choice of jobs and marriage partners, and about the strength of family ties and duties.[2] Asian parents are also likely to encourage the retention of their own language, either actively through lessons, or passively, because the child hears nothing else at home.[3] The teacher and the school may therefore be regarded as the inculcators of undesirable values and the violators of cherished social and religious practices, and become an instrument for the creation of generational tensions.[4] As the N.U.T. Report said:

> It (the school) should not allow itself to become an instrument for the creation of tensions between the child and the parents through seeming to wish to inculcate different attitudes and values that clash with those of the home. The school must therefore inform itself as fully as possible about these matters, and take care that it does not set up unnecessary tensions in the home that would militate against its social and educational intentions. Equally, however, it is of the greatest importance that the parents should be made fully aware of what the school is trying to do, and of the problems that it has to face.

[1] Such resistance is strongest in the case of Indian and Pakistani girls, who face a particularly sharp conflict situation.

[2] Rex and Moore, op. cit., p. 242.

[3] For further discussion of this, see Rosemary Lee, 'The Education of Immigrant Children', *Race*, Vol. 7, no. 2, October 1965, pp. 134–5; Natalie Rein's article in *Venture*, February 1967; Farrukh Hashmi, *The Pakistani Family in Britain*.

[4] See also Rex and Moore, op. cit., pp. 254–7, on generational tensions within immigrant groups and a report on 'The Immigrant Schoolchild and Problems of Adjustment' (C.A.S.E. Conference, January 1963) for an account of how the mental health of Cypriot children suffered as a result of inter-generational conflict.

The problem here is essentially one of communication. This is no new problem, and it is unfortunately true that the links between school and parents generally are strongest where there is least need, that is, with parents who are deeply interested in their children's educational welfare, and whose home itself valuably supplements that formal work of the school. The 'slum' and 'problem' areas of the Newsom Report are precisely those where communication with parents is not only minimal but exists for the most part in terms of hostility. There is a good deal of evidence, however, that the parents of immigrant children have none of this hostility, but are greatly concerned with their children's welfare. There may be suspicion based on ignorance, perhaps even on fear of rebuff, but in many cases the greatest obstacle to full communication is the social traditions of the community, particularly Asian communities where there is a strong tradition of seclusion of the mother. Probably, however, shyness, social self-consciousness and language problems form the major obstacles.

It is in this connexion that liaison and welfare officers of the same race or origin can play an absolutely vital part. There are in this country a considerable number of men and some women, from all the areas from which the immigrants come, with high educational qualifications and in many cases a good knowledge of their adopted country and its customs. Many of them have sought qualified teacher status, but have either been denied it or have run into considerable difficulties over language or different methods and different approaches to teaching from our customary ones . . . there is a good deal of underused ability and in consequence a good deal of frustration and resentment.

On social and educational grounds, we do not believe that immigrants should be employed solely in teaching children of similar origin, as this tends to retard their absorption into normal classes and to prolong and intensify separatist tendencies. Nor is it professionally in accordance with our own concept of qualified status, and our rejection of any notion of a limited and partial qualification.

On the other hand, many of these men and women could play an invaluable part in acting as links between the parents and the school, and in their mutual interpretation. They would find it much easier to gain the confidence of the parents; they would be able to guide the school so that it could respect the views of parents and avoid accidental violation of cherished social or religious practices; and they could explain to the parents the aims and intentions of the school and so seek their support. For instance, the Union has heard of cases where the problems arising over dress, particularly for games, have been entirely overcome through the co-operation of members of the community, for instance religious leaders.

Probably the ideal person for this kind of work is a teacher who is of the same origin as the immigrant community. (In this respect, the tendency for immigrants to congregate into homogeneous communities, though it creates other kinds of difficulties, makes things easier). There are unfortunately not a great number of teachers of this kind, who have overcome linguistic difficulties and difficulties of adjustment to our teaching methods, but where they exist, they can do the greatest service. They are trusted and accepted members of the school community, who can inform and interpret the school and the parents to each other with equal authority, and if they add to these invaluable qualities the energy and enthusiasm of one such teacher in the Midlands, who spends hours of his own free time visiting the parents and persuading them to attend informal and highly successful social functions at the school, then we are getting near the ideal solution.

Unfortunately, however, there are not nearly enough with the qualifications, or with the zeal, of this particular teacher. But there are a good number of well-qualified persons who could be trained fairly easily to do a very good job of this kind. For some, it could be the start of a new and permanent career in itself, analogous with, and possibly part of, the normal school welfare service. For others, it could bring them into close contact with the schools, so that they could familiarise themselves with, and indeed absorb, the atmosphere; they could learn something of the typical approaches to teaching problems, and they could, if necessary, gain a much greater facility in the characteristic vernacular speech patterns and accents of the children, and so overcome the difficulties of communication that create so many difficulties for those who are given the status of, and employed as, qualified teachers. Thus, those with the necessary basic qualifications for qualified status could have an opportunity, while still most usefully employed, of fitting themselves for employment as teachers.[1]

Another kind of tension can arise between some immigrant parents who are less concerned with resistance to anglicization and more concerned with apparent discrimination. This kind of reaction has been noted in certain areas where reception centres or dispersal plans have been introduced, without adequate explanation, so that they may be seen as racially discriminatory.[2]

Yet another important aspect of the relationship between the school and the immigrant home is concerned with the material and spiritual quality of the home environment, which is often such as to hold back immigrant children in their work, impair health, lead to mental stress and generally slow social integration. This was discussed by Natalie Rein, a member of the Comprehensive Schools Committee and the Confederation for the Advancement of State Education, following an investigation of the differing problems of immigrant schoolchildren (Cypriots [Greek and Turkish], Indians and Pakistanis, West Indians, Africans, and a few Italians) in the London area. Environmental problems can include serious overcrowding and noise, often in single-room households, a diet inadequate for the urban British climate, poor hygienic conditions, frequent moves from area to area, the difficulties

[1] *The Education of Immigrants*, pp. 6–7. The report goes on to discuss the administrative and training aspects of such a scheme if generally adopted.

[2] Cf., Coventry Indian Workers' Association's reaction to the City Education Committee's proposal to set up a reception centre. (*Coventry Evening Standard*, 9 February 1967.)

of adjusting from a rural to an urban way of living, unstable or denuded family relationships[1] (among some groups where the mother may be the sole bread-winner), or of parental understanding of schoolwork and activities.[2]

A. IMMIGRANT TEACHERS

In the industrial North, the Midlands, and elsewhere, there is a desperate shortage of teachers, both general and, in areas of heavy immigrant settlement, specialized. This could in theory be eased by recruiting from among the fairly large number of Commonwealth immigrant teachers now in this country (as the Health Service has done in the case of immigrant doctors). The fact that the majority have not been so recruited has given rise to charges or implications of racial discrimination[3] and pleas to recruit more.[4] An extraordinary situation was disclosed in 1966 that, while there were 3,000 immigrants in Britain on vouchers issued to them on the grounds that they were teachers, only 200 were in the classroom.[5]

While resistance and rejections have possibly been influenced by prejudice in a few cases, it has been made clear that the bulk of the rejections were made on good professional grounds, which have not always been explained satisfactorily either to the immigrant teachers involved or to the general public. As the N.U.T. report stresses:

> The Department of Education and Science is anxious not to reject suitable persons who could help in our present teacher shortage. The local education authorities, some of them desperately short of qualified teachers, would not willingly turn away one single teacher whom they believe to be capable of doing the professional job that a teacher is required to do. Equally, the Union and its members individually are most anxious to welcome, and to help, their colleagues from overseas to find suitable employment in this country. The

[1] These are probably most frequently encountered among West Indians, but there is also the situation of the Pakistani adolescent boy living with his father, or in a dormitory of male kinsfolk, and sometimes expected to act as housekeeper. (See Eric Butterworth, *New Society*, 16 March 1967.)

[2] 'The Twilight Children', *Venture*, February 1967. See also Brian Priestley's article on 'second-class children' in Birmingham (*The Times*, 14 February 1967); *Immigrants in London*, pp. 35–38; Simon Yudkin, *The Health and Welfare of the Immigrant Child*, N.C.C.I. pamphlet, 1966 (for a wider discussion of the factors influencing immigrant children).

[3] Cf. a survey by the Sikh Study Circle of Coventry, which claimed that 50% of the Indians on Coventry's buses were university graduates, including at least fifteen teachers (*Coventry Evening Telegraph*, 3 January 1967).

[4] For instance, by Mr. Maurice Foley (*Times Educational Supplement*, 14 May 1965).

[5] Nicolas Hawkes, op. cit., p. 58; *Guardian*, 25 July 1966. See also C.A.R.D. survey of Indian graduates in England (*The Times*, 7 September 1966).

Union is satisfied that there is no racial discrimination in the field of education. On the contrary, we believe that education sets a very good example to the country as a whole.

One initial source of misunderstanding arose because the D.E.S. regulations (Circular 6/59) governing the award of qualified status to teachers from overseas made no reference to their ability in spoken English, their cases being decided purely upon their academic and professional qualifications in their own country. This led to the granting of qualified status[1] to some teachers who had a very limited knowledge of English, and who, on applying to local education authorities, were either rejected or ran into difficulty over probation. This often led to charges of discrimination, and an Addendum was added to the Circular specifying that there should be some competence in English. Ascertainment is, however, difficult and the situation is reported not to have changed greatly, despite consultation between the Ministry of Labour and the D.E.S.

Additional misunderstandings have been caused by the fact that the criteria of acceptability were changed in 1960, on the introduction of the three-year course of teacher-training. This meant that some qualifications that had been acceptable compared with the two-year course ceased to be so. Moreover, in some cases changing standards in the countries of origin have meant that certain qualifications have ceased to be acceptable.

As the N.U.T. report explains, the new requirement for reasonable fluency in English, of a kind that will enable the teacher to communicate with all children, is readily accepted by teachers from countries where English is not normally spoken. It is less easily acceptable to teachers from countries where English is a second language (for example 'new' Commonwealth countries in Asia and Africa). They find that their English is intelligible to educated adults and do not realize that it may not be so to children who may themselves have strong local accents and be resistant even to 'standard' English.

Local education authorities have also found that teachers from some Commonwealth countries have been accustomed to a very different pedagogic tradition, are inclined to be rigid and formal in their approach, and have great difficulty in adjusting themselves to the more informal and child-centred techniques now in wide use in British schools.

The N.U.T. report, however, welcomes the help of all qualified teachers from overseas in a general capacity, notes that their special

[1] A qualified teacher may be employed in that capacity in any maintained school in England and Wales formally, without regard to the age-range of pupils or the subjects taught. There can be no such thing as a qualified teacher with restricted status.

knowledge and experience can be of assistance to colleagues in matters of communication with immigrant pupils and parents, and urges that suitable courses should be provided to help as many as possible to become available for general service. Some with acceptable qualifications may only need English courses, others will need further teacher-training or refresher courses, and perhaps English as well.[1] Others again may seek an alternative in welfare liaison work between the school and the home as a career in itself.

Such English and refresher courses for immigrant teachers have only recently got under way. The 1965 White Paper on Immigration announced that the first full-time course for qualified teachers with little English would start in 1966.[2] Leeds University offered a language laboratory course for Indian and Pakistani graduates,[3] and the Margaret McMillan Training College in Bradford started an intensive course, as did Wolverhampton, Nottingham, and Whitelands College, Putney.[4]

Finance was, however, found to be a problem, for instance by Barking, as the D.E.S. would provide no maintenance for teachers while attending their proposed ten-week course.[5] The City Literary Institute in Holborn began ten-week evening courses in English for qualified graduates and found itself flooded with applications.[6]

An assessment of the results of two courses held at Barking was made by A. H. Dalrymple, Chief Inspector of Schools there.[7] He found them disappointing. All but four of the original number were the subject of unfavourable reports when they went on to teach in schools. Quality of English tended subsequently to decline; there was an unwillingness to continue with further or refresher courses both in English and in other vital subjects; there was a general inability to communicate in class, resulting in loss of discipline; there was a reluctance to act on or to accept criticism for fear of losing face. These results were, he said, confirmed by people with educational experience in India and knowledge of Indian education and conditions. The conclusion reached was that a three months' course was quite inadequate to train these teachers in English and in the theory and practice of English education. Mr. Dalrymple proposed that the English of the would-be teacher should be tested in India by the British High Commission. Unless his spoken

[1] *Guardian* (21 October 1965).

[2] Four-term courses at Whitelands College, Putney, and at West London College. (*Sunday Telegraph*, 5 June 1966.)

[3] *The Times* (17 January 1965).

[4] *Birmingham Post* (28 January 1965); *Nottingham Evening Post* (22 January 1966); *Times Educational Supplement* (4 March 1966).

[5] *Times Educational Supplement* (4 February 1966).

[6] *Daily Telegraph* (6 June 1966).

[7] *Times Educational Supplement* (9 September 1966). In later correspondence his assessment was debated and queried by some readers.

English was satisfactory in accent, intonation, and delivery, and his written English idiomatic and grammatical, he should not be allowed to leave the country on the pretext of becoming a student—many would-be teachers are now coming here primarily to work for a further degree. Those who failed should take a year's course provided by the Government or by the applicant's state, after which he could be tested again. Such a course would be difficult to provide, however, because of the appalling state into which the teaching of English in India had fallen since independence.

Those passing the test would receive a certificate of proficiency in English. When making application in England for a teaching post, they should be subjected to a stiff entrance test in English, plus a searching interview. After passing this, they would be qualified to attend a further course for a mimimum two-year period. After this the immigrant teacher would still be required to attend further classes in English for a probationary period of one year.

In early 1967 the I.L.E.A. experience with ten-week crash courses was also reported as discouraging, and it was said that the courses were to be abandoned. The whole system of training immigrant teachers then came under review. These crash courses had been running for nearly two years; follow-up surveys of seventy-one teachers who completed the course showed that thirty-seven were found to be in teaching posts in the London area. Of these just over half gave 'reasonable satisfaction'. More recent follow-ups indicated that even these standards were not maintained. Faced with the pressure of a class of thirty to forty children, they tended to revert to 'Indian English'. Hopes were expressed that the longer one-year courses running at Whitelands College might produce better results. First 'graduates' were due out in the summer of 1967. There were only twenty of them and the I.L.E.A. wished to see results before planning any expansion. There seems to be no short-term solution to the teacher shortage problem. Lecturers who have been running special courses for immigrant teachers in major cities have been discussing future plans with the Department of Education. A large expansion of the immigrant teacher-training programme is envisaged, but its form is not yet clear.[1]

As for specialized teaching, the N.U.T. report has strongly opposed the introduction of immigrant teachers whose qualifications are otherwise unacceptable, for the specific purpose of teaching immigrant children, who should in any case be encouraged and helped to use English as the normal language of communication in schools. The London Head Teachers' Association, in an earlier memorandum, expressed its opposition to putting a teacher from the same ethnic group in charge

[1] *Sunday Times* (22 January 1967); *Daily Telegraph* (6 February 1967).

of immigrant classes of the same nationality.[1] Nicolas Hawkes noted[2] that

> one of the commonest and most mistaken ideas which have characterised local reactions to immigrant children is that they can be effectively taught only by people speaking their own language. . . . The signs are that immigrant teachers have often been sought out specifically to teach immigrant children.

Apart from initial reassurance to very young children in the first difficult weeks, he found this practice entirely detrimental for a number of reasons: first, the most effective methods of language teaching are based on oral work by the direct method, for which immigrant teachers are no better equipped than British ones; second, most special English classes have a mixture of ethnic and language groups, not just one (where the latter is found, there is a danger that the teacher will lapse into the vernacular and slow progress);[3] third, the element of segregation is underlined in such classes, and the task of preparing the children to rejoin the main stream made very difficult. Segregation does not only affect the children but points up the 'differentness' of the immigrant teachers themselves, whereas recruiting them as general teachers, on the same basis as British candidates, is a contribution to and a measure of integration. Their presence in schools can help to broaden and diversify viewpoints and enrich school life; it also helps greatly to remove the stereotype of linking colour with inferior status.[4]

B. COURSES IN HOME LANGUAGES AND CULTURES

The N.U.T. report considered the suggestion put forward by spokesmen of some immigrant communities that the schools themselves should provide courses in the language and customs of their homelands, so that they might not be alienated from their own background, and possibly from the parents themselves. Conceding that this was a natural enough desire, the N.U.T. report nevertheless commented that in general the schools have neither the staff, the resources nor the time to undertake the language tuition. The report continued:

> Nevertheless, there does seem to be a case for giving some general instruction in the social, cultural, economic and historical background of the guest communities, that might well be very acceptable to the parents of these

[1] *Times Educational Supplement* (15 October 1965).

[2] Hawkes, op. cit., pp. 55–9. He mentions instances in Smethwick, Southall, London, Wolverhampton, Slough, Rochester, and Leicester.

[3] He cites an extreme example of a North London class where a Greek Cypriot teacher in charge of Cypriot children lapsed frequently into Greek, to the active resentment of the Turkish-speaking minority.

[4] Cf. H. E. O. James and C. Tenen, *The Teacher Was Black*, London, Heinemann, 1953 and E. B. Braithwaite, *To Sir, With Love*, London, Bodley Head, 1959.

communities, and might equally be attractive to some children of the host community, and thus might contribute valuably to greater mutual understanding. The Associated Schools Experiment, that has been running for some years with the support of UNESCO in the secondary schools, and has recently been extended to the primary schools, provides an example. Certainly, both the ethos and organisation of the modern primary school, and the lack of prejudice and lively sympathetic curiosity of children in these schools, provide a fertile soil for teaching of this kind. But perhaps the most promising opportunity in this field lies in the Certificate of Secondary Education Examination, above all in the Mode III procedure. Under this procedure, schools can devise their own syllabuses, set and mark their own examinations, and take into account the work done by pupils during the year. A general course along these lines, concerned with the particular countries and cultures represented by the children who themselves, or whose parents, come from them, would be equally valuable as 'pure' education and as an exercise in mutual understanding. We feel, too, that this is a field in which the immigrant communities themselves could play a very useful part, valuable in itself and in the co-operation it would bring about between our education system and the newcomers, to their mutual advantage. Instances of this kind have already occurred in, for instance, Bradford and the West Midlands.

The question of providing native languages is not a new one. It was raised in Bradford and elsewhere by Polish parents in the late 1940s, but as British-born children entered the schools the demand soon fell off, other than as a foreign language to offer in G.C.E. It is believed that some schools still provide such classes, and certainly many Polish second-generation immigrants still speak or wish to speak Polish. This demand has, however, been met since the 1940s by a network of Saturday schools run by the Polish community itself,[1] or by visits to Poland, which have become easier since 1958.

Some educationists feel that, where possible, the demand for such tuition is reasonable and should be met, so long as the teaching of English does not suffer. It has been suggested that such courses might be also of advantage for English pupils, as an alternative to the traditional foreign languages. For this, however, there is no evidence of demand at present. For immigrant children, provided there is sufficient demand and provision of teachers, it is suggested that they could opt out of other foreign-language classes and study their own.[2]

[1] There is increasing evidence that such arrangements are being made by Indian and Pakistani organizations. For Cypriot evening schools in London, see V. George and G. Millerson, 'The Cypriot Community in London', *Race*, Vol. VIII, no. 3, January 1967, pp. 291–2.

[2] Areas in which such demand or arrangements have been recorded include: Punjabi/Hindi in Smethwick (*Times Educational Supplement*, 1 January 1965) and Birmingham and West Bromwich (*Birmingham Mail*, 21 April 1965); Urdu and Arabic in Edinburgh (*Times Educational Supplement*, 7 January 1966); in 1965 Islington appointed a teacher to teach Greek to Cypriot children.

C. EDUCATION—FUNCTION AND AIMS

The ideal role of the school, to quote the N.U.T. report yet again, is to

> play the same part in the education of immigrant children as it does in the education of all children; it must give them the basic skills of communication and manipulation of number, and it must prepare them for the next stage of education, or for initiation into adult society. But this is only the start. Within a community, education at whatever level has much wider implications and responsibilities. It is at one and the same time the instrument for the maintenance of an ordered society and the preservation of its accepted ethos, its principles, explicit and implicit, and for the continuation of its chosen way of life; and yet it must serve as an agency for social change and development.

Behind this lie some deeper questions—which have recently been highlighted for educationists and teachers, as for many others by the large-scale inflow of Commonwealth immigrants. These are questions about the nature of British society today and about the kind of society which it is desirable and feasible to create in the future. All the foregoing discussion in this section, about dispersal, reception, teacher supply and training, curricula, materials, and so on, has been basically a discussion of means towards an implicit end—that of 'integration'. But this term conveys different meanings to different people, and, moreover, there is evidence of a recent shift in thinking about the nature of this goal in official quarters and among some educationists.

At national level the shift has been from a somewhat more assimilationist line to one stressing cultural pluralism. In its second report (Cmnd 2266, 1964) the C.I.A.C. spoke of creating an equal multi-racial society but did not discuss the possibility of a lasting multi-cultural society. Their assumption in relation to education was the following:

> . . . A national system of education must aim at producing citizens who can take their place in society properly equipped to exercise rights and perform duties which are the same as those of other citizens. If their parents were brought up in another culture or another tradition, children should be encouraged to respect it, but a national system cannot be expected to perpetuate the different values of immigrant groups.

Only two years later the new Home Secretary, Mr. Roy Jenkins, defined integration as being, not a flattening process of assimilation, but equal opportunity, accompanied by cultural diversity, in an atmosphere of mutual tolerance.[1] This change of goals may have been influenced to some extent by the fact that after 1960 the majority of immigrants were non-English-speaking, non-Christian and came from tenacious and self-segregating cultures, and also by an increasing awareness that the

[1] I.R.R. *Newsletter*, June 1966, p. 8.

British host society itself may be more pluralistic and less culturally homogeneous than had been previously assumed.

The Home Secretary's definition was accepted and approved by the N.U.T. Its report rejected both segregation on the one hand and obliteration of different cultural and religious differences on the other,[1] and advocated mutual adaptation:

We believe that the social climate of our times would be opposed to any attempt to deprive people of their own typical culture patterns, their own language, and their own social habits, though it may be that any minority, if it is to live in comfort and harmony with the neighbouring majority, may have to accept some modification of habits that conflict with the wishes, and interfere with the comfort, of the majority.

. . . We would assume, therefore, that there would be general agreement that the processes of education should tend for the children, for the parents, and above all for the coming generations, to iron out differences of social behaviour that could create offence to neighbours, but we have no evidence that immigrant communities present a unique problem in this respect. The more important issues lie with questions of religious and cultural patterns. It seems to the Union self-evident that minority groups should not merely be permitted, but should actually be encouraged, to retain their own traditional patterns of behaviour and thought and language, subject to the limitations already mentioned. Indeed, for those who intend to return to their country of origin, this is essential.

It seems to us important, however, that while we should help and encourage the retention of individual cultures, we should also recognise that enrichment of the community will not come until there is not only tolerance, but mutual understanding, and that what appears esoteric may often be a barrier to this. We believe, therefore, that it is an important function of our educational system to help in the mutual interpretation and even interpretation of one culture by another. We should like, therefore, to see our immigrant fellow-citizens made part of our own culture patterns in so far as this is their wish, and indeed encouraged to do so; but the host community should also be prepared to make the effort to gain sympathetic understanding of the different cultures brought into this country.

[1] But see Jennifer Williams in Rex and Moore, op. cit., pp. 237–8, for a different version of the actual role of the school as seen by Sparkbrook teachers. See also Butterworth, *New Society*, 16 March 1967, p. 384, and *Race*, January 1967, pp. 227–8.

PART III
VOLUNTARY ASSOCIATIONS
CHAPTER 8
Non-Governmental Organizations Concerned with Immigrant and Race Relations

1. RESEARCH AND INFORMATION

A. THE INSTITUTE OF RACE RELATIONS

The Institute of Race Relations became an independent body in 1958, but in this new form it continued work which had begun in 1952, when a small group of donors provided funds to start a Department of Race Relations in Chatham House. It was their belief that race relations was a subject that would be of increasing importance in the second half of the twentieth century and that it ought to be studied by a body for whom it was the central concern and the main task.

It was part of the initial conception that the subject should be studied, in so far as possible, objectively and that the Institute should not become a pressure group. The articles of association therefore provide that the Institute as a corporate body shall not express an opinion, although its members and staff may, and indeed sometimes must. The aims of the Institute are to encourage discussion and research and to advise on ways of improving race relations.

The Institute is concerned with race relations everywhere, but in 1952 it was natural for a British body to concentrate on the problems arising from the end of colonial rule, particularly in Africa. But the growing likelihood of racial tension in Britain was foreseen and a collection of cuttings from the British press was begun in 1955; a summary of these cuttings was circulated from 1955 onwards. The first research in Britain was commissioned in 1958. In 1960, the Institute published *Coloured Immigrants in Britain*, which attempted to survey the state of knowledge as it then existed. Today the emphasis is divided between Britain and the rest of the world. The two main research programmes of the Institute are the Survey of Race Relations in Britain (financed by the Nuffield Foundation—for details see below) and the Comparative Study of Race Relations in different regions (financed by the Ford Foundation). The international programme will include books on the growth of race relations in Spanish-speaking America and Brazil, as well as the Caribbean, India, and South-East Asia, and a final volume comparing these developments.

The Institute of Race Relations publishes about ten books a year, through Oxford University Press, a quarterly journal *Race*, and a monthly *Newsletter* with up-to-date information about Britain, and reports from correspondents in Africa, the U.S.A., and South-East Asia, and on current research and action. The Institute has a reference library and a Press cuttings collection. About once a week, meetings are held for members to hear speakers on subjects about race relations in Britain and other parts of the world.

In its work, the subject of 'race relations' is regarded as primarily the study of the relations between groups distinguished by genetic characteristics. But study cannot be fruitfully confined to these narrow limits and inevitably leads to the consideration of other inter-group relationships and of ethnic and other minority groups which may not differ physically from the majority society but whose circumstances can throw light on differences which are more strictly racial. It is a field of study to which many different academic and practical disciplines can contribute.

List of Council Members

Sir Jeremy Raisman, G.C.M.G., G.C.I.E., K.C.S.I. (Vice-President)
Oliver Woods, M.C. (Vice-President)
Leslie Farrer-Brown, C.B.E., J.P. (Chairman)
Michael H. Caine (Honorary Treasurer)
Dr. Robert Birley
Mark Bonham Carter
P. H. A. Brownswigg, C.M.G., D.S.O., O.B.E.
H. R. Finn
Sir Kenneth Grubb, C.M.G., LL.D.
Dr. G. Ainsworth Harrison, D.Phil.
Professor Fernando Henriques, D.Phil.
C. R. Hensman
Professor Hilde T. Himmelweit, Ph.D.
H. V. Hodson
Richard Hornby, M.P.
E. G. Irons, J.P.
Anthony Lester
Dr. H. S. Morris
Dipak Nandy
Professor Roland Oliver, Ph.D.
H. F. Oppenheimer
Sir Ronald Prain, O.B.E.
Professor Margaret Read, C.B.E., Ph.D.
Christopher Rowland, M.P.
Frederick Seebohm
Professor Hugh Tinker

The Institute's monthly *Newsletter* contains the following sections:

1. A unique coverage of the dynamic race relations scene in Britain, dealing with such varying aspects as immigration, legislation, politics, statistics, employment, housing, court cases, health, social integration, the younger generation, education, immigrant organizations and life, etc.
2. Similar coverage (every few months) from correspondents in South Africa, Central Africa, the United States, New Zealand, and South-East Asia. There are also regular reports of current developments in Commonwealth countries, Latin America, Eastern and Western Europe, West Africa, and East Africa.
3. Special series of articles or reports on: migration in Western Europe, immigration statistics, psychology, human biology, education, and housing.
4. Articles on topical issues, profiles, and supplementary reports by experts. Recent contributors have included Bob Hepple, Arnold Mandel, Nathan Shamuyarira, John Lambert, Cedric Thornberry, Roger W. Evans, Derek Ingram, Richard Ogden, Carole Piña, and A. Sivanandan. Supplements include a continuing series of area reports on cities and boroughs in Britain with substantial immigrant settlements: on Pakistanis in London; background reports on other areas such as the High Commission Territory of Swaziland; the new African states of Lesotho (formerly Basutoland) and Botswana (formerly Bechuanaland); Guyana (formerly British Guiana), etc. There are also on-going analyses of immigration statistics.
5. A section entitled *Research and Action*, which contains reports of research in progress or completed; a special series of race relations abstracts; research notes; summaries of relevant articles; news from universities and institutes, and from study groups and organizations concerned with the integration of immigrants and the promotion of good race relations in Britain and elsewhere; and reports of the Institute's five-year Nuffield-sponsored Survey of Race Relations in Britain, which began in the autumn of 1963, and regular news of the work of the National Committee for Commonwealth Immigrants.

The *Newsletter* is valuable topical reading for all individuals and organizations concerned with the academic or practical aspects of race relations all over the world and particularly in Britain, the Commonwealth, and Africa. It is also of great value for reference libraries, social science and other university departments, and is used by a number of high-school groups as a basis for discussions.

Race, the quarterly journal of the Institute of Race Relations, provides valuable contributions to the study of race relations that combine high professional standards with clear and readable language. The reader will find material within his own particular field and also authoritative and intelligible statements from other fields that supplement his work. Articles, contributions to 'Quarterly Forum', and book reviews come from and cover many parts of the world, but with special emphasis on Britain.

The Library is the only one of its kind in Britain covering all aspects of race relations—interpreted widely to include ethnic, linguistic, religious, and related groups—with particular emphasis on Great Britain.

Stock: Books—about 3,000; Pamphlets—about 3,000; Journals—over 200.

Press Cuttings:

(a) Great Britain—comprehensive, classified coverage—from March 1955 to date.

(b) Other countries—cuttings from *The Times*, *Guardian*, *Observer*, and *Sunday Times*—geographical division—from October 1956 to date.

Publications: Coloured Immigrants in Britain: a select bibliography—July 1965.

Commonwealth Immigrants in Britain: a preliminary checklist of research—May 1966.

Register of Research on Commonwealth Immigrants in Britain—March 1967.

Reading Lists—various.

Hours of Opening: Monday to Friday—10 a.m.–1 p.m.; 2 p.m.–6 p.m.

Librarian: A. Sivanandan, B.A., A.L.A.

B. THE SURVEY OF RACE RELATIONS IN BRITAIN

In 1963 the Institute of Race Relations obtained a grant from the Nuffield Foundation to inaugurate a five-year study of the race relations situation in this country. As part of the programme set up with these funds, fifteen major and five minor research projects are being carried out. The results of the first major study were published early in 1967—Professor John Rex and Mr. Robert Moore's study of the Sparkbrook area of Birmingham—*Race, Community and Conflict*. The results of another minor inquiry into the response to immigration in marginal constituencies at the 1964 General Election were published in 1965 (*Colour and the British Electorate 1964*, edited by N. Deakin). Miss E. Burney's study of local authority housing policy, *Housing on Trial*, was published in October 1967. Among other investigations from which the findings are now expected in the near future are: Professor Anthony Richmond's investigation of a West Indian settlement in Bristol; a psychological study of the coloured population of Bute Town, Cardiff; a study of the response of the City Administration of Bradford to Pakistani immigration; and an investigation of crime rates in two police divisions in Birmingham. The final summary report from the Survey is due to be published in 1969.

C. OTHER RESEARCH AND INFORMATION ORGANIZATIONS

It is not possible to list all the academic and para-academic bodies in Britain that are concerned with race relations. Several universities and academic institutions have produced work specifically on race relations in Britain; of these Edinburgh's Department of Social Anthropology, under Professor Kenneth Little, must take pride of place as the pioneer.

Two other units may be mentioned here, although their subject-matter is drawn from outside Britain. One is the Centre for Multi-Racial Studies at the University of Sussex, which was set up in June 1965 for the study of race relations, with particular reference to the Caribbean, West Africa, and Brazil. Its first director is Professor L. F. Henriques, and it is being financed by the Bata Shoe Organisation.

It is proposed to establish a branch of this Centre in Barbados early in 1968, which will also be under the directorship of Professor Henriques and will be run in close co-operation with the University of the West Indies. There will be a resident Warden, Miss Jill Sheppard.

The other unit is the Centre for Research in Collective Psychopathology, which was set up early in 1966 under the sponsorship of the University of Sussex to study group hatreds. Professor Norman Cohn was appointed the Centre's first director, and the two studies based on Britain are concerned with: (i) human destructiveness—a compendium of everything known about the propensity of human beings to torture and kill one another; and (ii) the Nazi exterminations of Jews, Slavs, and others—particularly the absence of a sense of guilt among organizers and executors. The American study is concerned with investigations relating to Negro slavery and its aftermath.

Mention should also be made of the Economist Intelligence Unit, a section of which has for some years concentrated upon the compilation and analysis of statistical information about Commonwealth immigration and immigrants. After 1961 it produced a series of four 'Studies on Immigration from the Commonwealth', and has since produced some occasional papers, forecasts of the growth of the resident coloured population over the next few decades or so, and a regular bulletin up to mid-1967.

An increasing number of research projects have been or are being carried out all over the country. Information on published work is more easily available, but the most complete record of unpublished or on-going research by subject is the biennial Register of Research on Commonwealth Immigrants in Britain, compiled by the Librarian of the Institute of Race Relations, A. Sivanandan, and Margaret Scruton, for the Institute. Increasingly, too, research in various disciplines concerned with race relations in Britain and comparable situations which has been published in learned journals is becoming available through the Institute's new Abstracts Project, the first-fruits of which have already begun to appear in the monthly *Newsletter*.

D. UNIVERSITIES CONFERENCE ON RACE RELATIONS

This conference was held at the London School of Economics on 20–22 April 1966 and co-sponsored by the Royal Anthropological Institute and the Institute of Race Relations.

The following are extracts from the Minutes of Discussion about Future Conferences:

1. At the second session of the morning of Friday, 22 April, the Members of the Conference discussed future procedure.

2. There was general agreement with the idea of holding periodical Conferences on the subject of race relations. It was also agreed that the Royal Anthropological Institute and the Institute of Race Relations should continue to act as co-sponsors and that the British Sociological Association should be invited to join them.

3. It was agreed to leave to the sponsors the responsibility of nominating a committee which would choose a subject and select a list of speakers. There was general agreement that the committee should not be too large and that although it should be inter-disciplinary, members of the committee should not be asked to represent disciplines; nor would it be necessary at every Conference to obtain speakers covering all the disciplines involved. But it was, however, suggested that it would be desirable if a social psychologist and an educationist were included.

4. In discussion the view was advanced that there should be a limited number of plenary sessions after which small panels should discuss more specialist subjects.

The general view of the Conference was finally that the purpose of the Conference was an exchange of ideas between disciplines and that the procedure of panels for separate disciplines would only occasionally arise.

5. It was generally agreed that there was urgent need for more comprehensive methods of disseminating information about research, for sharing information, and for avoiding duplication in library work. The Institute of Race Relations explained that they were hoping to strengthen their library staff in order to make it possible to undertake this work, and it was agreed that this would be the most satisfactory way of undertaking these tasks. It was agreed that the Institute of Race Relations should get in touch with the various Universities and other bodies interested and make suggestions to them about sharing information.

In the meantime, all members of the Conference were asked to tell the Institute of research being done so that it might be included in the monthly *Newsletter*. Members were asked to send notes of research in a brief and compressed form suitable for publication without further cuttings, and volunteers were called for to help with a new project of publishing abstracts of reports in various fields (either in the *Newsletter* or as a new service by the Librarian).

2. WELFARE AND INFORMATION

A. LONDON COUNCIL OF SOCIAL SERVICE: IMMIGRANTS DEPARTMENT

The Department, which is advised by the Immigrants Advisory Committee, works in the Greater London area, providing information and assistance to all bodies interested in the welfare and integration of immigrants from overseas. The Immigrants Advisory Committee has been in existence since 1958: its membership is drawn from the High Commission offices, certain Government departments, local voluntary liaison committees, and other organizations, such as London Transport, the Institute of Race Relations, and the Race Relations Committee of the Society of Friends. The Committee discusses any important questions that arise and makes recommendations on a variety of matters. It has also set up Working Parties and has prepared a number of reports on different subjects. Its secretary until April 1964 was Miss Nadine Peppard; since then Mrs. Mary Dines.

The Department produces a number of books and pamphlets on subjects of current interest, and during the year 1966–7 the following were published:[1]

Teaching English to Adult Foreign Beginners; Notes on Claims to United Kingdom Income Tax Relief in respect of dependants in the West Indies; The Immigrant Child and the Teacher; Cosmopolitan Kensington—

[1] Earlier reports included Sheila Patterson (ed.), *Immigrants in London*, N.C.S.S., 1963, 5s.

the story of an exhibition produced by the girls of Ladbroke School; *Newcomers Guide to London; Commonwealth Children in Britain* (to be published shortly); *Social Workers Groups in Greater London* (a list of social workers available to help local authorities under a mutual aid scheme); list of interpreters and social workers in Greater London with special knowledge of overseas groups; reading lists on Cyprus, India, Pakistan, and the West Indies.

Where there is a need for a broadly-based discussion of special matters of interest, the Department organizes meetings of the bodies concerned, to which representatives of Citizens Advice Bureaux, Councils of Social Service, voluntary liaison committees, and other organizations are invited. During the year 1966–7 three half-day meetings were run on People to People Week, Qualifications for Admission to the United Kingdom and the International Social Service project at London Airport. As a result of the second meeting, the Home Office provided the text of three short papers clarifying some of the regulations that cause difficulties.

The Department also deals with a number of individual inquiries from immigrants who have been referred to them by other agencies, such as Welfare Officers and C.A.B.s. It also supplies information on a variety of subjects to students, especially those in teacher training colleges, and gives advice and information to potential voluntary workers and people wishing to work with others from overseas. The Department co-operates with other voluntary organizations in the London area in matters such as training and informational courses for their workers, and provides speakers for conferences and meetings. It also runs its own conferences—often in co-operation with the Society of Friends—and during 1966–7 ran four on family backgrounds for teachers, social workers, and workers in voluntary organizations, and three on the same subjects for workers in the youth service.

B. VOLUNTARY LIAISON COMMITTEES

The N.C.C.I.'s work fell into two main categories: the formulation of policy recommendations and the promotion of local voluntary liaison committees, sustained by an advisory service. The 1966 Annual Report stated: 'The importance of effort at the local level was recognised from the outset, and the Committee has devoted a great deal of its time and resources to this aspect of the work, both in promoting and advising local committees and in visiting a number of areas for discussions with local authorities and others.'

In a paper[1] on how to set up a V.L.C., Nadine Peppard, General Secretary of the N.C.C.I., has outlined three prerequisites for this:

[1] See Appendix 9.

(a) the sponsorship of the mayor and the interest of the local authority;

(b) a widely representative base, including voluntary and statutory organizations;

(c) full participation by the immigrant community.[1]

She wrote: 'Any suggestions of "welfare of coloured people" in the title of a V.L.C. should be avoided. The keynote should be race relations, harmony, international friendship, interracial activity, integration, etc.'

A later N.C.C.I. paper on the work of the V.L.C.s defined their activities broadly as Information, Welfare, Public Education and Anti-Discrimination work, and emphasized that a V.L.C. should not try to provide special welfare services but to help immigrants to use the existing services. This point about welfare, and anti-discrimination work, are both included in the N.C.C.I. paper on the duties of a liaison officer.[2]

At the end of March 1967, twenty-four V.L.C.s were receiving grants from the N.C.C.I. for liaison officers' salaries, of which twenty-one had appointed liaison officers, and three had advertised posts which would shortly be filled. Thirteen V.L.C.s were negotiating with their local authorities to pay their part of the salary of a liaison officer; nine V.L.C.s had not applied for grants, and six V.L.C.s were themselves in the process of formation. There have been more formed since.

The N.C.C.I.'s March 1967 list of V.L.C.s showed the following (names and addresses of secretaries are not given as these may have changed by the time this Handbook is published. Generally speaking, however, they can be reached c/o the local Borough Council or Council of Social Service):

GREATER LONDON

Bexley Commonwealth Association; *Camden* Committee for Community Relations;* International Association of *Croydon*; *Ealing* International Friendship Council;* *Greenwich*—Committee in process of formation; *Hackney* Citizens Liaison Council;* *Hammersmith* Council for Community Relations; *Haringey* Commonwealth Citizens Committee; *Islington* International Friendship Council; *Kensington and Chelsea* Inter-racial Council; Council for Community Relations in *Lambeth*; *Newham* International Community;* *Southwark* Council for Community Relations; Council of Citizens of *Tower Hamlets*;* *Westminster* Overseas Committee; *Willesden and Brent* Friendship Council.

[1] Such broad-based participation can produce widely differing attitudes in different areas. See, for instance, P. Foot, op. cit., p. 222 f., on a militant phase after late 1964.

[2] See Appendix 9.

CHESHIRE

Crewe International Friendship Council.

LANCASHIRE

Bolton Commonwealth Friendship Council;* *Manchester* Council for Community Relations;* *Rochdale* Council for International Friendship.*

THE MIDLANDS

Birmingham Liaison Committee for Commonwealth Immigrants;* *Leicester* Commonwealth Citizens Consultative Committee;* *Northampton* Council for Community Relations; *Nottingham* Commonwealth Citizens Consultative Committee;* Research and Consultative Group on Overseas People, *Rugby*; *Walsall* Council for Racial Harmony; *Wolverhampton* Council for Racial Harmony.*

NORTH-EAST ENGLAND

Tees-side International Friendship Council.

SOUTHERN ENGLAND

Voluntary Liaison Committee of the *Bristol* Community Council; *Cambridge* and Commonwealth Friendship Council; *Crawley* Committee for Community Relations; *Gloucester* Council for Community Relations;* *Gravesend* International Friendship Council;* *High Wycombe* Overseas People's Consultative Committee; *Luton* International Council; *Oxford* Committee for Racial Integration;* *Slough* International Friendship Council.*

YORKSHIRE

Bradford Consultative Council for Commonwealth Citizens;* *Halifax* and District International Council; *Huddersfield* International Liaison Committee; *Keighley* International Friendship Council;* *Leeds* International Council; *Rotherham* International Friendship Council; *Sheffield* Committee for Community Relations.*

REGIONAL COMMITTEES

Yorkshire Committee for Community Relations, Immigrants Advisory Committee; *London Council of Social Service*; Commonwealth Welfare Council for the *West Midlands*.

AREAS WHERE COMMITTEES ARE IN PROCESS OF FORMATION

Hillingdon; Lewisham; Derby; Coventry; West Bromwich; Newcastle; Bedford; Southampton.

* Denotes committees with grant-aid being paid by, or having been approved by, the National Committee in 1967.

C. SOME INDIVIDUAL ORGANIZATIONS

This survey of some established and energetic Voluntary Liaison Committees and other associations working in the spheres of immigrant welfare and integration is by no means comprehensive.[1] Its purpose is to give an impression of the wide range of work being done, and the selection was mainly influenced by the availability of material and reports. We should be glad to receive such documentation from other organizations, to assist us in the preparation of forthcoming year books; also updating documentation from these organizations.

(i) *The Sparkbrook Association*

The Sparkbrook Association is a Birmingham neighbourhood association that was first formed as a voluntary group in November 1960, to express the grievances of people living in the area about its apparent decline, and to try to do something to improve its amenities. It was initiated by Mrs. Burgess, a Labour Councillor who became the treasurer, under the chairmanship of the Rev. John Reed of Christ Church and with Alderman R. T. Wothers as the secretary. The original committee consisted of doctors, clergy, health workers, teachers, councillors, and representatives of organizations. Its purpose was to tackle the social problems arising from immigration (both white and coloured), the former presenting by no means the least problems. The attention of city and Government departments was drawn to matters which were considered by the Committee to be their responsibility. The Committee realized that much personal social work was urgently required, and as no provision was made for this by the statutory bodies, the Sparkbrook Association was launched in April 1961, for this purpose.

The original membership consisted of people with widely different points of view. To date this is one of the few voluntary organizations that has been examined by sociologists. John Rex and Robert Moore, describing the Association (in *Race, Community, and Conflict*, p. 215), wrote:

> Some were deeply conservative in their notion of what an ideal community should be like and were inclined to focus attention particularly on the moral failings of some of Sparkbrook's residents. Others were more radical and more inclined to demand action by the Council, thus suggesting a political function for the association. Some were business people and some involved in one way or another in social work. Some had lived or worked in the area for many years. Others came from outside, through a general concern with social problems. Some emphasized total community problems, others the problems of family life. One or two from time to time made statements which placed the blame for Sparkbrook's problems on particular ethnic groups.

[1] One notable omission, to be remedied in the next edition, is the Community Centre at Stanley House, Liverpool, now in its twenty-fourth year of operation.

Despite these pulls in different directions, the association started and kept going around the slogan 'Towards a Fuller and Happier Life'. A more vivid description of the aims of the association was conveyed by the Rev. Reed in a short pamphlet about it: 'There are thousands of people here representing some ten differing nationalities. There is much filth, smell, hardship, exploitation but there is also the opportunity to make Sparkbrook an example to the whole world.'

During the first few months of the association's work, an outline was produced listing the problems of the North Sparkbrook area, with suggestions for action. It is worth reproducing in full, both for its descriptive content, and to illustrate the perspective of the association:

N. Sparkbrook Problems and suggested action

Problem	Suggested action
1. *Litter*— paper; food; broken glass.	(a) Education through schools and groups. (b) Publicity. (c) Develop adult responsibility. (d) Litter Act prosecutions. (e) Bigger street bins. (f) More frequent street cleansing. (g) Collection of milk bottles.
2. *Bad Neighbours*— uncivil; uncontrolled children; breaking walls, windows; refuse over next wall; clogging drains.	(a) Visits, education, 'Good Neighbour Campaign'. (b) Where (a) fails, prosecution, and consider some special kind of camp where they can live as families and *work* under good supervision.
3. *Overcrowding*— no baths; insufficient lavatories; bad air.	(a) Inform all landlords of conditions required. (What about landlords who cannot speak English?) (b) Enforce law. (c) Registration and Inspection. (d) New legislation if required.
4. *Overseas Immigrants*— to be integrated and taught hygiene, etc.	(a) Overseas Friends' Committee being formed by the Church. (b) Publicity—leaflets and talks on leaving their own country, on entering England, and Sparkbrook.
5. *Dangerous Pavements*	City Council have been informed and work is now in progress.
6. *Bad Lighting*[1]	Press City Council to reconsider plan under which Sparkbrook waits until 1964–5.

[1] In 1961, lighting was by gas, and Sparkbrook was not due for change until 1964–5. As a result of pressure from the association, the new lighting was in fact installed in the summer of 1963, i.e. two years after the association had begun to complain about it.

7.	*Neglected and Dangerous Houses*	City Council have been informed and improvements are taking place.
8.	*Vandalism*	(a) Police. (b) Better lighting. (c) Better morale.
9.	*Violence*	(a) Police and severe punishment. (b) Better lighting. (c) Better morale.
10.	*Residents Moving Away*	(a) Build up morale and community feeling. (b) Fair treatment, leading to confidence.
11.	*Elderly People Living Alone*	(a) Women's Fellowships and Sons of Rest already exist. (b) Darby and Joan club being planned for Memorial Hall. (Started.) (c) Encourage family responsibility. (d) Organise visits.
12.	*Spiritual Starvation*—giving life without purpose.	Special effort and continuous work by the Churches with co-operation.

Note: Against this background we are to consider whether an establishment like the Birmingham Settlement, Community Centre, etc., would help.

For the consideration of the N. Sparkbrook Committee and local organisations.

(Sgd.) Jack Reed
Vicar of Christ Church.
Chairman.

By October 1961, at first as a result of purely voluntary efforts, and later with gradually increased financial support from the Local Authority, the association had a full-time social worker and by 1963, an Adventure Playground Leader. In January 1965, it had a full-time staff of twelve, in addition to a number of volunteers, and a budget, excluding accommodation costs, of about £4,000. Activities included youth groups, four nursery play-centres, and an Adventure Playground. In the view of Rex and Moore, this has been the most striking success of the association; it has also spread its influence beyond Sparkbrook, whose first Playground Leader was eventually employed by the City Council to do similar work on a city-wide basis. There are also groups for the elderly, and for mothers and babies, meeting at the association's premises. There is a mental health club, and a C.A.B. Representations to the Local Authority and other bodies about local needs continue.[1]

[1] Not all immigrant groups would always agree with the views of the association. For example, Rev. Reed welcomed the Birmingham Corporation Act on compulsory registration of multi-occupied houses, which gives the Council wide powers to refuse permission for multi-occupation, e.g. to preserve the character of an area, or if the landlord is thought unfit to run a lodging-house, and has been strongly criticized for this, on the grounds that such powers could be used to contain, and not spread, immigrant or coloured families' homes. (Rex and Moore, op. cit., pp. 34–5 and p. 227.)

The Association provides a permanent Advice Centre, and much individual case-work is done. Rex and Moore conclude (p. 220): 'The Association has now, while remaining a voluntary body under the control of its own committee, become part of Birmingham's social welfare system.'

(ii) *The Council of Citizens of Tower Hamlets*

Tower Hamlets V.L.C. grew out of a much older voluntary committee dating back to the mid-1930s. Originally organized to counteract the disrupting influence of the Fascists, the Council developed a programme in post-war years that attempted to educate the people of the area—and in particular the younger generations—to understand the beliefs and customs of various nationalities. Through the years, the Council of Citizens has worked under the umbrella of Toynbee Hall, a neighbourhood settlement that came into being towards the end of the nineteenth century.

When the newest immigrants arrived in East London in the 1960s, the basic machinery for working towards integration was therefore already available. In July 1966, the Council of Citizens of East London, together with the Borough of Tower Hamlets and other voluntary and statutory organizations, agreed to set up a Council of Citizens of Tower Hamlets.

These are its aims and objects, as adopted in the Constitution:

To foster understanding and goodwill between immigrant citizens and the community as a whole.

To provide opportunities for people of all nationalities in the Borough of Tower Hamlets to live and work together in friendship.

The Council of Citizens aims to achieve these objects by the following means:

(a) By encouraging among all residents through education and other means, tolerance and respect for each other's difference, customs, beliefs and ways of life.
(b) By educating the community in order to overcome the ignorance from which racial prejudice arises.
(c) By investigating local needs and prompting action to satisfy them.
(d) By encouraging the active participation in the Council's work of statutory and voluntary bodies and interested individuals.
(e) By investigating specific instances of misunderstanding and conflict and trying to effect conciliation.
(f) By arranging and providing for the holding of conferences, exhibitions, meetings, lectures, classes and social functions.
(g) By arranging to print, publish, issue, broadcast and circulate gratuitously or otherwise any reports or periodicals, books, pamphlets, leaflets or other documents or programmes.

This Council of Citizens was recognized by the National Committee for Commonwealth Immigrants as the Liaison Committee for the Borough and both the Archbishop of Canterbury, President of the N.C.C.I., and Earl Attlee, President of the Council of Citizens of East London, joined with the Mayor (Alderman John Orwell, J.P.) and many local statutory and voluntary organizations to inaugurate the new body.

One of the Council of Citizens' most interesting projects began at once: a multi-racial pre-school play group, the premises for which were decorated and manned by a group of volunteers who gave their summer months to do this job. By the end of August there were twenty-six children on the register. In September some of these went to school, but by the end of October there was a strength of thirty on the register of this 'pilot' group, and since then it has often been necessary to refuse applications.

A different type of activity was the survey made of immigrants in trade unions and industry, covering a sample of some 400 firms in East London. The Institute of Race Relations gave a small grant towards this work, and a statistician took charge of the project with five volunteers. The fieldwork was completed at the end of August and the material is to be published.

Another example of the work of the Council of Citizens is the National Health and Welfare Survey, dealing with information available to Commonwealth immigrants in their own languages. This was started in mid-1967 by three volunteers and it was subsequently published by the National Committee for Commonwealth Immigrants.

Conference activity is also important. In autumn 1967 a series of six leadership training seminars for the host and immigration community began with a conference at Toynbee Hall, in co-operation with the liaison committees of Newham and High Wycombe. Teachers' conferences have also been held.

Meanwhile, the East London Council continues its own programme of school-pupils' conference, and of language teaching to Pakistanis.

(iii) *Nottingham Commonwealth Citizens Consultative Committee*

As far back as 1951, the Nottingham Council of Social Service had begun to provide some practical help to West Indian migrants in the town, on a small scale. Ivo de Souza, Welfare Liaison Officer for West Indians at the Colonial Office, urged that a committee be formed to link all those in the city interested in community relations.

In 1954, a voluntary committee was formed, sponsored by the Nottingham Council of Social Service, the Nottingham Council of Churches, and a number of Commonwealth citizens. The committee was broadly based, mostly composed of representatives of voluntary bodies and the churches and including a few representatives from statutory authorities, but the local authority initially took a passive role. However, in 1957 representatives from the Health and Education Committee were appointed. The framework within which the new committee operated was consultative and advisory. In 1956, a full-time secretary was appointed on a three-year grant from the Pilgrim Trust, which had been approached by the Family Welfare Association in London, on behalf of the Nottingham Committee. Miss Dorothy Wood became secretary with the duties of conducting simple research, and helping immigrant citizens in every possible way. She retained the post until 1965. The local authority was the main source of finance between 1960 and 1966 when the National Committee for Commonwealth Immigrants commenced to give considerable help.

The Committee has operated in many fields. Its method has often been to initiate *voluntary* services, which have later been taken over and developed by existing branches of the voluntary social services, by local authority, or by statutory bodies.

1. *Personal Counselling*. The Committee immediately set up a service for this, but in 1960 the Family Welfare Committee of the Nottingham Council of Social Service took over this work, and appointed an additional worker to help the existing staff.

2. *Employment*. An advisory panel of people with industrial experience (both native and Commonwealth) was set up; it established a rota of volunteers available to immigrants every Saturday morning. It also persuaded the local Technical College to provide special classes for West Indian women machinists and encouraged a few local firms to arrange training facilities in their factories. Eventually, the local branch of the Ministry of Labour began to take an increased interest and finally took over the advisory function of the Committee. The Employment Committee still meets, however, to discuss problems of discrimination and to attempt to solve individual cases of difficulty.

3. *Education*. Voluntary English classes were started, but in 1959 the local authority appointed Mr. Eric Irons, J.P., as an Educational Organizer with special reference to the needs of coloured people. The Committee still continues to help the host community to understand the difficulties facing immigrants through the arrangement of conferences, study groups, etc.

4. *Conciliation*. The Committee has always been ready to try to bring about conciliation in cases of friction between neighbours and other discriminatory difficulties, e.g. at public houses.

5. *Social Contacts*. The Committee has taken every opportunity to help with arrangements for joint social activities (host and newcomers) and to enjoy joint cultural events.

6. *Research*. The Committee has arranged for research to be done on

the employment of West Indians (published[1]) and the Indians and Pakistanis in employment (not yet published). It has also stimulated research into the problems of immigrant youth and school-leavers.

7. *A Coloured People's Housing Association* was formed in 1956. By 1967 it owned thirty terrace houses which were let to individual families at reasonable rentals. It has experts in the form of an estate agent and a lawyer who, apart from giving advice on house purchase, undertake conciliation work in matters of discrimination in house purchase, etc.

The White Paper 1965: In the autumn of 1965 the Committee met three times to discuss the White Paper. It was considered paragraph by paragraph and the Committee prepared a reasoned criticism of many of its proposals and of the assumptions underlying the document. These were transmitted through the N.C.C.I. to the Lord President of the Council and also direct to local Members of Parliament. In 1967 the affiliated Commonwealth organizations were as follows:

The Commonwealth Citizens' Association
The Indian Welfare Association
The Indian Association
The Indian Workers' Association
The Pakistan Friends League
The Pakistan Welfare Association
The Sikh Temple (Gurdwara) Managing Committee
The West Indian Students' Association
The Standing Conference of Commonwealth Citizens

1967 Work: The programme for 1967, apart from the activities described above, includes:

(1) An attempt to broaden the horizons of children living in twilight areas by arranging outings to places of interest in the city.

(2) Participation in the Community Welfare Exhibition by the Council of Social Service.

(3) Coach tours for residents in twilight areas to places of interest outside the city.

(4) A week-end of religious services, music, and an exhibition to celebrate the Commonwealth, organized by a Methodist Church in a racially mixed area.

(5) The formation of a Fair Housing Group.

(6) Lectures and discussion meetings with trade union branches, political parties, co-operative guilds, community centres, and women's organizations.

(7) A conference on either employment of Indians or Pakistanis in Nottingham, or on job opportunities for second-generation immigrants.

[1] Bayliss and Coates, 'West Indians at Work in Nottingham', *Race*, Vol. VII, no. 2, October 1965.

(8) Participation in the Human Rights Year Preparatory Committee for Nottingham.

The Committee is considering making a request to an independent organization, e.g. social science department of a university outside Nottingham or management consultants, to evaluate its work.

(iv) *The Westminster Overseas Committee* (*V.L.C.*)

The Westminster Overseas Committee was formally established in January 1966. It grew out of the old-established Paddington Overseas Students and Workers Committee, following the reorganization of London boroughs.

AIMS AND OBJECTS: These have remained the same; they are as follows:

1. To act as a centre for the collection of information and the exchange of experience amongst organizations likely to contribute to the well-being of overseas students and all people from overseas living and working in the area.

2. To take action through joint working parties or by any other means towards bringing all persons mentioned above into closer relationship with the life of the neighbourhood.

3. To keep under review by research and other means the social needs of all the persons mentioned above and to endeavour with their collaboration to find ways of meeting them.

ACTIVITIES AND WORK

1. *Students:* An overseas students' club meets every week. An information leaflet is distributed to students about Westminster social services, libraries, statutory bodies, churches, and leisure facilities, etc. Student trips and outings have been arranged.

2. *Youth Work:* The Paddington Overseas Club has a membership mainly of Caribbean young people. In 1966 a research project was conducted with the members about their aims and ambitions and the results of this have been sent to the committee on immigration and the Youth Services under the chairmanship of Sir John Hunt, set up January 1966 to report mid-1967.

3. *Mothers and Children:* An overseas mothers' club meets, mainly for personal counselling and practical help (this has existed for about eight years). In the evenings C.S.V. volunteers, working with the Westminster Committee keep in touch with working mothers who cannot come to the club. A C.S.V. volunteer also acts as the assistant at a pre-school play group run by the Council for Social Service. During the summer of 1966 a group of students arranged to take parties of children to the park, in the mornings and afternoons, over a period of two weeks. About forty children were involved. A distribution of toys and a children's party were held at Christmas 1966.

4. *Housing:* The Westminster Committee has a £1 share in the Metropolitan Housing Trust, and about six families have been rehoused through this over the last year. The Committee helps such families to move house, find furniture, etc.

5. *Case-work:* A certain amount of follow-up case-work with individual families is done, for example, if they are due to be rehoused by the G.L.C., making sure that this is done.

6. *Press:* The Committee attempts to improve the attitude of the Press in dealing with stories which may involve race or colour, and has succeeded in persuading one local paper not to accept discriminatory advertisements.

7. *Police:* Some work has been done to try and improve communications between the police and local residents, and so improve relationships.

8. *Public Education:* The Committee was hoping to join in organizing a 'People to People' week in November 1967, and in particular to persuade existing organizations (e.g. churches, clubs) to arrange meetings, talks and other activities.

The Committee has compiled a list of Voluntary Help prospects which are *required* in the borough.

The working sub-committee of the Westminster Committee meets every six weeks; it has a roughly 50 : 50 ratio of overseas and native British members.

The Main Committee is composed largely of representatives of organizations, and meets quarterly.

(v) *Oxford Committee for Racial Integration*

The Committee was formed in January 1965 on a purely voluntary basis, although sympathetic local councillors were invited to join immediately.

The Aims and Objects of the Committee are:

1. To uphold the civil rights of immigrant citizens.
2. To encourage understanding and contact between immigrant citizens and the voluntary agencies, statutory bodies and other associations in the City of Oxford in pursuit of the general welfare of the community at large.
3. To promote understanding and goodwill between immigrant citizens and other citizens in Oxford.
4. To combat all forms of discrimination and prejudice founded on racial or religious grounds.

The work of the Committee includes:

1. Organizing of two pre-school play groups, and large scale voluntary coaching of immigrant children at school.
2. Maintaining continuous contact with local authority departments and

public officials about decisions affecting immigrants directly or indirectly, for example the Public Health Department, the Housing Department, the Education Department, the Probation Service, the Children's Department, the Health Visitors and Medical Officer of Health, and the Ministry of Labour Employment Exchange.

3. The Committee has a Press Officer who is on the staff of the local paper, has published a pamphlet for immigrants about Oxford, and is also to publish a pamphlet for the native English community about immigrants and their countries of origin.
4. Fortnightly meetings are held, open to all members, on many different subjects, plus social evenings.
5. Anti-Discrimination work: complaints are forwarded to the Race Relations Board. O.C.R.I. itself conducts negotiations with local employers in the case of any colour-bar, restrictive quotas, or other discriminatory practices. The committee has had several major successes in this field.
6. Immigration: O.C.R.I. handles complaints about refusal of entry or of entry certificates, takes up cases with the Home Office, and has published a leaflet for immigrants about the entry procedures.

O.C.R.I. is affiliated to C.A.R.D.

(vi) *Willesden and Brent Friendship Council*

The Willesden International Friendship Council was first formed after the 1958 disturbances, on the initiative of the local authority, but as a voluntary committee. In 1961 the local authority appointed Mr. Oswald Murray as a full-time liaison officer to serve the W.F.C.

The work of the Council was described as follows by the present Liaison Officer, Mr. Peter Jones:

1. *Conciliation*

The Council tries to iron out disputes or friction between neighbours, or between landlord and tenant. The W. and B.F.C. leaflet describes this in terms of a 'service of reconciliation for households affected by racial friction'. The method used is to send pairs of visitors, one native white British, the other an immigrant, to conciliate with both parties. This has been one of the main activities of the Council from the start.

2. *Social Contacts*

The Council tries to promote social contacts between immigrant and native communities by organizing or sponsoring inter-racial projects, such as a group to do voluntary work among the elderly, a Jazz-Ballet group, which is now being revived, and an international travel club.

3. *Persuasion*

The W. and B.F.C. has tried to persuade landlords not to issue discriminatory advertisements for display in tobacconists, has negotiated with the local press not to use the phrase 'no coloured' in classified advertisement columns, and has from time to time published statements attacking such practices ('racial irritants').

4. *Publications*

A survey of local attitudes was carried out by Joan Maizels after the Council was first set up.

A pamphlet has been written on housing to guide immigrant citizens. Another pamphlet 'issues a warning to those responsible for promoting noisy parties and points out the damage such parties do to the cause of good race relations'.

According to its information leaflet the W. and B.F.C.'s main purpose is 'to assist the merging of the newcomers into the general community, and to devise ways in which they can express their sense of belonging to it. Our law gives them full status as citizens and it is to the benefit of us all that friendship and guidance be extended to them.'

The Council has had its ups and downs as an organization. In 1965, when the Government White Paper on Immigration was published, the Willesden Friendship Council was one of the most outspoken critics; it initially refused to join in the activities of the N.C.C.I. which was formed under Part iii of the White Paper and the Council's Newsletter contained detailed criticism of official Government policies.

The President of the Council is the Mayor of Brent, and the members include the four Brent M.P.s and three local authority representatives. General membership is about equally immigrant and native English.

3. ACTION ORGANIZATIONS AND PRESSURE GROUPS

A. THE BRITISH CARIBBEAN ASSOCIATION

The British Caribbean Association was founded in July 1958 by a group of M.P.s, West Indians, and friends of the West Indies in Britain, with the aims of developing friendship and understanding between 'British subjects of West Indian and United Kingdom origin', and encouraging mutual aid between the two areas.

So far as race relations in Britain are concerned, the B.C.A. has tried to create a good climate of opinion at national level by organizing social and cultural activities and by parliamentary activities and pressures. Its general approach is perhaps characterized by more positive pressure than those of the organizations listed later in this Section. Through its Newsletter, the B.C.A. keeps its members informed about the formation and work of other organizations, reviews major developments in race relations, and gives some news from Caribbean countries.

In March 1966, the parliamentary members of the B.C.A. consisted of twenty-seven Conservatives, five Liberals and sixty-eight Labour members, including several members of the Government. The B.C.A.'s parliamentary activities include the briefing of M.P.s for debates and questions, the holding of meetings for members with M.P.s in the

Houses of Parliament, and deputations to individual ministries about specific problems.

The B.C.A. described itself, in March 1965, as follows:

We are really an association with three main jobs. Firstly, we are a political (though not a party-political) pressure group on matters concerning race relations and the West Indies. Secondly, we are able, by social events and meetings to widen contact, in a limited way, between West Indians and U.K. citizens and to raise issues in these meetings. Thirdly, we can assist personal cases among immigrant West Indians needing advice or limited financial help,

The Parliamentary and political work should probably be mainly concerned, in 1965, with the following:

(a) Pressure on the Government to take all possible steps to help towards reducing racial tensions in this country, and to help assimilate immigrants into the community. The Government has spoken of 'special help' to areas with large concentrations of immigrants, and this is the starting point for our pressure. A deputation has already seen the Under-Secretary of State at the Home Office and asked for the designation of a Minister to co-ordinate the work of all Government Departments in this field, and for a top-level civil servant, with a small department, to assist him.
(b) Pressure to find out what the Government means by its proposal to alter the Commonwealth Immigrants Act, in due course, after consultations with the Commonwealth countries about alternative systems of control. Here our main job is to make sure that the interests of the West Indies, which have suffered most under the Act's working so far, are fully considered. Once again a deputation has already been to see the Commonwealth Relations Office and a report will be given.
(c) Pressure to make sure that the West Indies, particularly the Windwards and Leewards, get financial aid towards their economic development from the new Ministry of Overseas Development.
(d) All possible Parliamentary aid towards formation of the new Eastern Caribbean Federation, and the steps leading up to it.
(e) Careful watch on the proposed new Bill to outlaw racial discrimination in this country.
(f) General work on trade matters and other issues which can help the West Indies by being raised in Parliament.
(g) One very important function is to watch for and to raise publicly any cases of racial discrimination or prejudice where we can get action to counter them; and to press for positive action (for example by the B.B.C.) towards educating people for tolerance.

B. CAMPAIGN AGAINST RACIAL DISCRIMINATION (C.A.R.D.)[1]

C.A.R.D. was formed in December 1964. This was a time of maximum attention to the issues of immigration and racial prejudice in the

[1] Contributed by Julia Gaitskell. This information may be totally out-dated as a result of subsequent 'black militant' take-over bids and personnel shifts.

press and in politics, with Government decisions pending both on immigration control and on racial discrimination and racial incitement. A need was felt for a group which would co-ordinate the views and activities of the different national immigrant communities, so that they could make joint demands, and if necessary organize joint protests.

The first executive committee included: Dr. David Pitt—chairman; Dr. Ranjana Ash and Mrs. Selma James—joint secretaries; Dr. Victor Page—treasurer; Richard Small—press officer; Anthony Lester—chairman of the Legal Committee; Mrs. Frances Ezzreco, Gurmukh Singh and Mrs. Marian Glean.[1]

The National Founding Convention was held in July 1965 in London, at which a constitution was adopted. The Convention was attended by about 250 people, most of them delegates from immigrant and interracial organizations.

(i) *Aims and Objectives*

(1) To struggle for the elimination of all racial discrimination against coloured people in the United Kingdom.

(2) To struggle for the elimination of all forms of discrimination against minority groups in the United Kingdom.

(3) To use all means in our power to combat racial prejudice.

(4) To oppose all forms of discrimination on the entry of Commonwealth citizens into the United Kingdom.

(5) To oppose all legislation that is racially discriminatory or inspired by racial prejudice.

(6)(a) To seek to co-ordinate the work of organisations already in the field, and to act as a clearing-house for information about the fight against discrimination in Britain.

(b) To establish and maintain links with organisations outside the United Kingdom having aims and objects broadly similar to those of C.A.R.D.

(ii) *Structure*

The constitution provides for individual membership and for the affiliation of any group (except political parties) accepting the aims and objects of C.A.R.D. Groups of individual members and affiliates send delegates to an Annual Delegate Convention, which elects the chairman of C.A.R.D., and the members of the National Council—the policy-making body of about forty people. Fifteen members of the National Council are elected on an 'Individuals' list, the rest on an 'Organizations' list, with places for three members each from the main national immigrant groups, Jewish organizations, Arab and African organizations, trade unions, students, interracial organizations. This provision was

[1] Mrs. Glean was in many ways the main inspiration of the organization at the start. She was then Warden of Friends International House, William Penn House, and an active organizer in the Society of Friends. Early in 1965, she left for Paris to take up a job with U.N.E.S.C.O.

intended to prevent the domination of the National Council by any single national group and to encourage the broadest possible representation. The executive committee and the other officers of C.A.R.D. are elected by the National Council. Area Committees may be appointed by the National Council, and such local C.A.R.D. groups have been formed by members in several areas. In March 1967 they existed in Islington, Brent, West Middlesex, Sheffield, Manchester, Leeds, Newcastle-upon-Tyne, and Glasgow. C.A.R.D. affiliates include local interracial groups, which pre-date C.A.R.D., but provide contacts and support for the national organization, for example Oxford Committee for Racial Integration, Leicester Campaign for Racial Equality, the Campaign for Racial Equality in Bradford.

(iii) *The Work of C.A.R.D.*

C.A.R.D. has so far functioned basically as a pressure group to secure changes in Government policies on the following issues:

(1) *Immigration.* C.A.R.D. opposed the 1965 White Paper on the grounds that it was discriminatory against coloured Commonwealth immigrants, and that the powers accorded in it to the immigration officers, and to the Home Secretary, were arbitrary and undemocratic. C.A.R.D. also called for the repeal of the 1962 Commonwealth Immigrants Act. On procedure, C.A.R.D. submitted lengthy evidence to the Wilson Committee on Immigration Appeals, calling for an appeals system and recognition of documentary evidence of right of entry, such as entry certificates. C.A.R.D. also began to handle some individual cases of refusal of entry at London Airport, and on one occasion helped to obtain Home Office revision of a case, by taking it to the High Court (Habib Khan).[1]

(2) *Integration.* C.A.R.D. has placed the main responsibility upon the majority community, to provide equal opportunities on merit for members of national, religious, or racial minorities. C.A.R.D. is highly critical of a purely voluntary policy and has called for laws against discrimination in employment, housing, insurance and credit facilities, and all places of public resort. It maintains that such a law should *not* be a punitive criminal law, but should be administered by a statutory commission, with full investigation powers. The commission would receive complaints, try to end the discrimination by conciliation backed by legal sanctions, including power to hold hearings and, if all else fails, making orders enforceable in the county courts. (See Chapter 3 for background to the extra- and inter-Parliamentary proposals.) C.A.R.D.'s legal proposals were drawn up by the Legal Committee, accepted by the first executive, and by a members' meeting early in 1965.

[1] See I.R.R. *Newsletter*, February 1967, p. 6.

C.A.R.D. opposed the Ministry of Education circular on dispersal of what were called 'immigrant children', on the grounds that this was not the answer to their educational problems, that it was a sop for white parents and intended to be applied to *coloured* children, and that it would make children colour-conscious.

The work of C.A.R.D. can be divided into three broad categories:

(1) *Normal organizational work*, such as providing speakers, holding meetings, canvassing, voter-registration.

(2) *Lobbying*. This includes the production of specialized documents such as the evidence to the Royal Commission on Trade Union and Employers' Organizations; and to the Wilson Committee on Immigration Appeals; personal and written contacts with M.P.s and Ministers; drafting private members' Bills; active participation in the work of other organizations likely to be influential, in particular the specialized Panels of the National Committee for Commonwealth Immigrants, etc.

(3) *Documenting and Publicizing Discrimination* and other kinds of injustice towards immigrants and English-born coloured people.[1] Information about discrimination is obtained by receiving complaints and handling them, by 'testing', and by special projects such as the Summer Project 1966 in which students spent a month working on a variety of activities in three immigrant areas. The Summer Project's aims were described as follows:

(a) to collect actual cases of discrimination and to test firms and agencies for discrimination;

(b) to help establish C.A.R.D. at local level and provide manpower for local C.A.R.D. branches;

(c) to train a core of young people in civil rights work.

(iv) *Future Prospects*

During 1965 and 1966, with some notable exceptions, C.A.R.D.'s work concentrated largely upon trying to obtain changes at Government level. But this alone came increasingly to require that the base of the organization be broadened. The Proposals on Organization of C.A.R.D. accepted by the National Council in January 1967 emphasized the building of local groups and the establishment of contact with more local organizations. Three 'regional organizers' were to be appointed with funds allocated for their expenses, and the aim was to raise enough money for a full-time national organizer. A further Summer Project was proposed with the two aims of contacting and winning over coloured school-leavers, and trying to build local community organizations.

[1] By 31 March 1967, C.A.R.D. had sent a large number of cases to the Race Relations Board, the majority outside the scope of the Race Relations Act. (See C.A.R.D. report, April 1967.)

C.A.R.D. Officers 1965–6: Dr. David Pitt—chairman; Hamza Alavi—vice-chairman; Miss Jocelyn Barrow—general secretary; Dr. Victor Page—treasurer; Anthony Lester—chairman, Legal Committee; Lee Moore—press officer.

C.A.R.D. Officers 1966–7: Dr. David Pitt—chairman; V. D. Sharma—vice-chairman; Miss Jocelyn Barrow—vice-chairman; Miss Julia Gaitskell—general secretary; H. S. Dhillon—treasurer; Anthony Lester—chairman, Legal Committee; Dipak Nandy—field director of project.

Individual Membership 1966–7—c. 2,500.

C. THE NATIONAL COUNCIL FOR CIVIL LIBERTIES (N.C.C.L.)

The National Council for Civil Liberties is concerned with civil liberties and human rights in a range of fields of which race relations are only one; others include freedom of speech and assembly, police conduct, censorship, trade unions and the law, mental health.

The N.C.C.L. has, however, been actively concerned with immigration policies, and with racial discrimination. It strongly opposed the Government White Paper on Immigration 1965, and since then has handled a number of disputed cases, in which arriving immigrants are held up or rejected at London Airport. It is one of the organizations which receives complaints about racial discrimination, and it conducted a detailed inquiry into the racial policies of insurance companies in which, as the 1967 annual report states: 'Some of the replies were more revealing than the companies themselves intended.' The material was used by David Marquand, M.P., in an adjournment debate in January 1967.

N.C.C.L. joined with C.A.R.D. in lobbying for an extension of the 1965 Race Relations Act, and in attempting to achieve reforms of present immigration procedures. It also submitted evidence to the Wilson Committee on Immigration Appeals.

D. CO-ORDINATING COMMITTEE AGAINST RACIAL DISCRIMINATION (C.C.A.R.D.)

C.C.A.R.D. was formed in Birmingham in February 1961 and was originally sponsored by the Birmingham Indian Workers' Association (see below p. 316), the Pakistani Workers' Association, the West Indian Workers' Association and Birmingham University Socialist Union. Twenty-nine other organizations gave their support to a conference called by C.C.A.R.D. The aim of the organization was to combat all forms of racial discrimination. The members of the Committee were: Chairman—Mr. Ludmer; secretary—J. Joshi. The first chairman and secretary to be appointed were respectively V. Yates, M.P., and J. Joshi.

The work of the organization was, at the outset, concerned mainly with combating the campaign to control immigration. During this period, speakers were sent around to rally the support of a number of organizations, trade unions, co-operative guilds, etc., and eleven public meetings were also addressed. A pamphlet putting the case against immigration control was produced and widely circulated. C.C.A.R.D. also organized people to participate in the mass lobbies that took place on immigration.

C.C.A.R.D. has taken up individual cases of discrimination. The very first one was that of the allocation of a council flat to a Pakistani and the threat by white tenants, organized by D. Finney, to refuse to pay their rent. Another type of case has been the allegation of police brutality against immigrants.

C.C.A.R.D. has issued statements on matters which concern the race question and has organized public meetings on questions like the White Paper. It has also held cultural performances, e.g., 'Dog in the Manger', in churches in Birmingham.

During the campaign of the Smethwick Conservatives, C.C.A.R.D. frequently wrote to the press, contacted the Conservative Party nationally, requesting them to take action against the Smethwick Conservative Party and, together with the immigrant organizations in the area, made a general appeal for an anti-Griffiths vote. After the election, a pamphlet was produced, called *Smethwick—Racialism and Integration.*

The most recent activities of the organization were concerned with support for anti-discriminatory legislation. Several publicans' licences were opposed unsuccessfully before the passing of the Act.[1]

E. LEICESTER CAMPAIGN FOR RACIAL EQUALITY

Address: Flat 3, 37 East Avenue, Leicester. (Tel. 77791.)
Secretary, M. Nandy; Chairman, G. Greaves.

The Leicester Campaign for Racial Equality came into existence following a prolonged local fight to remove a colour bar from a public house. Several hundred people were involved in this fight and it seemed clear to the organizers that they would need a permanent body to investigate and take up future cases of racial discrimination. In January 1965, therefore, the Campaign was launched. From the start, it had the support of the two major immigrant organizations in the city—the Indian Workers' Association and the West Indian Sports and Social Club. It has remained an unofficial body, operating now alongside a voluntary liaison committee.

Very early on, it was obvious that the problems which coloured immigrants in the city faced were far more complex than those of

[1] See I.R.R. *Newsletter*, January 1966, p. 5, for an account of C.C.A.R.D.'s testing of possible public house colour bars in Smethwick and West Bromwich by a group of 'freedom drinkers'.

discrimination in public places and the Campaign's work in the first two years of its existence covered a very wide field.

It continued to take up cases of discrimination against coloured people, in public places, housing and employment, and sent cases to the Race Relations Board. A second major field of activity for the Campaign was in keeping up continual pressure on local and national government bodies in the furtherance of its aims. To this end the Campaign organized signature collection, protest marches, a lobby of Parliament in favour of extending the Race Relations Act to housing and employment. Representatives met all the local M.P.s on many issues, and publicized their own views as much as possible, in the local press, national press, and on television and radio.

During the last two periods of electoral registration, the Campaign organized a programme for the registering of immigrant voters. In the General Election, it campaigned for immigrants to use their voting rights and conducted a count on election day to assess their success. About 70% of the immigrants voted. The Campaign also issued statements in elections where race relations questions were at issue, either because of racialist candidates, or as in May 1967, when an Indian stood for election for the Labour Party.

The Campaign has organized language classes in English for Indian women and in Hindi for Health Visitors.

The Campaign has kept up an important function of public education. It holds frequent public meetings, publishes a regular newsletter and often sends its members to speak at the meetings of other organizations.

F. THE STUDENT CONFERENCE ON RACIAL EQUALITY (S.C.O.R.E.)

S.C.O.R.E. began at an informal conference held in Oxford in June 1964 at the invitation of the Oxford University Joint Action Committee Against Racial Intolerance (J.A.C.A.R.I.). This was attended by several university groups, and the meeting was intended originally as a single exchange of information between all those who could be contacted. It was felt that the initiative of the meeting should not be lost, and that a more permanent body, linking student groups working in the field, should be established.

The aims of S.C.O.R.E. were defined as follows: to help student groups working for racial equality by (1) organizing an annual conference; (2) producing a newsletter; (3) co-ordinating activities of groups in individual universities and colleges; and (4) working in close co-operation with other national bodies working in race relations.

S.C.O.R.E. suffered from the difficulty of having no permanent office, and having to maintain contact with student groups whose officers could change each term. Nevertheless, it kept a small secretariat, produced a newsletter and produced a framework within which greater regional and national co-operation and co-ordination can take place. It also maintained a close relationship with C.A.R.D.—for example, the 1965 annual conference included four C.A.R.D. speakers talking about the role of students in race relations in Britain, and out of the discussions at that conference grew the idea of the 1966 C.A.R.D. Summer Project. The 1966 annual conference endorsed a proposal for students to participate in employment-testing on a national scale.

4. IMMIGRANT ORGANIZATIONS

A. WEST INDIAN ORGANIZATIONS

There are a minimum of thirty Caribbean organizations in London, and at least the same number outside London, covering all the main towns in which West Indian migrants have settled. These organizations have, over the years, served a variety of needs in the community, including: (1) organization of social contacts and social functions; (2) organization of practical projects, such as savings clubs and pre-school play-groups; (3) representation of the community to, for example, local authorities about issues which are related to aspects of integration; and (4) provision of a valuable network of communications through which the feelings of the community as a whole upon different issues can be sounded out, and which persists even during periods of passivity through which most voluntary associations inevitably pass from time to time. There is also a handful of extreme leftist or black militant factions and splinter groups which perform a function of negative but sometimes noisy protest.

Nevertheless, compared with immigrant groups that are socially and culturally self-segregating and also more tightly organized on a village-kin-language basis, like the Indians and Pakistanis, internal organization among and within the various West Indian groups, where it exists at all, tends to be loose, fluctuating, weakly-supported and often similar to those of the receiving society. Rex and Moore wrote of West Indians in Birmingham that they had few organizations of their own, most members belonging either to no organizations at all or to those of the host society.[1]

(i) *West Indian Standing Conference in London*

The West Indian Standing Conference was formed in London in 1958 after the Notting Hill disturbances. It provided a structure to link the various West Indian associations, in order to oppose racial discrimination, to develop the resources of the community, and to further the integration of West Indian migrants in Britain.

[1] Rex and Moore, op. cit., pp. 155–63.

The Conference had the support of the Migrant Services Division of the West Indies High Commission until the Federation was dissolved in 1961. Thereafter, the Standing Conference continued holding, on an all-West Indian basis, regular meetings attended by representatives from different groups, including migrants and members of the native British community. The meetings have been a forum for the discussion of all issues affecting West Indians and immigrants generally in Britain. The Standing Conference has also acted as a pressure group dealing with grievances, and in this capacity has sent delegations to Government departments and published reports and pamphlets. It has been in the news for, in particular, its reports about police-immigrant relations, and violence against coloured immigrants.[1]

(ii) *West Indian Standing Conference in Birmingham*

More recently, a West Indian Standing Conference was formed in Birmingham, to co-ordinate West Indian groups in the West Midlands; this has not, however, been active as an organization for some time.

B. INDIAN ORGANIZATIONS

(i) *The Indian Workers' Associations*

At the end of 1966, Indian Workers' Associations were reported as existing in the following cities and towns: Birmingham, Bradford, Coventry, Derby, Gravesend, High Wycombe, Nottingham, Leicester, Leamington Spa, Wolverhampton, Smethwick, Southall, and Southampton.

While there was an overall organization or liaison between at least some of them initially, there is now considerable schism and alienation both between localities and within local organizations (so that in many if not most places there are two I.W.A.s), resulting from a number of factors. Chief among them seem to be: differing attitudes to Indian or rather Punjabi politics;[2] differing attitudes to the Sino-Soviet schism; differing political attitudes generally (while Communists and neo-Communists [whether Moscow or Peking oriented[3]] may dominate

[1] A pamphlet attacking the police in certain areas was published in 1965: Joseph A. Hunte, B.A., *Nigger Hunting in England?*

[2] From published and unpublished material so far available (see Rashmi Desai, *Indian Immigrants in Britain*, for an early stage of the development of the I.W.A. in London and Birmingham, pp. 101–6) the membership would seem to be almost entirely Punjabi and mainly Sikh, despite efforts to extend it to other regional groups.

[3] On the latter, see *Sunday Telegraph* (28 August 1966) on the schism within the Birmingham branch of the I.W.A. In late 1965 Mr. J. Joshi, general secretary, published a pamphlet called *The Victim Speaks*, which said that the N.C.C.I. should be replaced by a genuinely representative body.

some leaderships, there are significant traditionalist and conservative groupings in most organizations); personality differences and clashes between village-kin groups and other factions; and finally, attitudes to British life and politics (e.g. isolationist or integrationist, co-operation with organizations such as N.C.C.I. and C.A.R.D., and support for British political parties). For all these differences and schisms, some I.W.A.s, particularly at critical times, have proved well organized, energetic, and effective, politically if not always industrially.[1]

The Southall I.W.A. has, like Southall generally, been the subject of most detailed study to date. Set up in 1957, it was for six years dominated by two factions, both based on village-kin groups and personalities, built up by peasant caste leaders, one from Hoshiarpur, the other from Jullunder. In 1963 a new faction was organized, based on a new village-kin group, and by 1965 there were two more, one consisting of former untouchables. A sixth faction came into being on a rather different basis, led by a university graduate and experienced politician, who drew his support from the personal prestige which he gained during his term of office as president of the I.W.A., combined with the personal following of a break-away supporter of one of the two original factions.

The situation was further complicated by the involvement of a few individuals with the Punjabi and local Communist Parties, the gaining of personal prestige and a personal following by at least one individual leader who set up as an entrepreneur, the arrival of an increasing number of educated Punjabis, and what seemed to be an exceptional taste for factionalism and schism among the leaders. The wrangling was, however, mainly over personalities and factional advantage than over goals, which is why a single organization could continue to contain traditionalists and Communists, and grow into a wealthy mass organization, with perhaps 3,000 members in Southall itself. In Southall most I.W.A. leaders agreed on the goals of unionization and integration in the British context, while the traditionalists and non-left-wingers were relatively unconcerned about the international causes on which the left-wingers take a stand.

C. PAKISTANI ORGANIZATIONS

In 1966 there were over forty Pakistani organizations in Britain, with an 'umbrella' organization, the National Federation of Pakistani Associations. Almost all were local, in the areas where Pakistanis have settled in numbers (e.g. London, Birmingham, Bradford, Nottingham, Liverpool, Manchester, Glasgow, Newcastle-upon-Tyne). They tended to be based upon a regional (East or West Pakistan) and a village-kin-language basis. Compared with either Indian organizations or West

[1] See Appendix VII on the Woolf's strike at Southall.

Indian groups, the majority were more 'traditional' and home-oriented, and less actively 'integrative' in type (with the exception of such an organization as the Pakistani Caterers' Association in Great Britain).

According to an informant, their activities included some or all of the following:

(1) Fulfilment of a number of welfare functions, e.g. helping immigrants to fill in income tax forms, passport forms, write letters, etc.

(2) Organizing occasional social functions.

(3) Expressing to the Pakistani authorities any grievances or difficulties over such things as the sending of remittances to Pakistan, travel difficulties, customs difficulties, which come within the purview of the Pakistan Government.

(4) Receiving representatives of the Pakistan Government, or other dignitaries.

LIST OF PAKISTANI ASSOCIATIONS (1967)

London

1. National Federation of Pakistani Associations in Great Britain,
   39 Fournier Street,
   London, E.1.
   Tel: BIShopsgate 1493

2. Pakistan Caterers' Association in Great Britain,
   275 Old Brompton Road,
   London, S.W.7.

3. Pakistan Welfare Association,
   39 Fournier Street,
   London, E.1.
   Tel: BIShopsgate 1493

4. Pakistan Friendship Association,
   132 Coventry Road,
   Bedford.

5. Pakistan Workers Association,
   86 Duncombe Street,
   Bletchley (Bucks).

6. Pakistan Welfare and Cultural Association,
   52 Priory Avenue,
   High Wycombe (Bucks).

7. Pakistan Muslim Association,
   64 Dumfries Street,
   Luton (Beds).

8. Pakistan Welfare Association,
   44 West Street,
   Osney, Oxford.
   Tel: Oxford 40522

9. Pakistan Welfare Association,
   393 London Road,
   Reading (Berks).
   Tel: 52614

10. Pakistan Welfare Association,
    47 Copnor Road,
    Portsmouth.

11. Pakistan Welfare Association,
    94 Ranelagh Road,
    Southall,
    Middlesex.

12. Pakistan Society,
    26 Camp Road,
    St. Albans,
    Herts.

13. Pakistan Welfare Association,
    238 Woodbridge Road,
    Ipswich.

Birmingham

1. Pakistan Welfare Association,
   93 Stratford Road,
   Sparkbrook,
   Birmingham 11.
   Tel: VICtoria 3135

2. Pakistan Society,
   261 Goocj Street,
   Birmingham 5.

3. Pakistan Association,
   26 Clause Road,
   Roath,
   Cardiff.
   Tel: Cardiff 30179

4. Pakistan Workers Association,
   28 St. George's Road,
   Coventry.
   Tel: 25429

5. The Pakistan Association,
   11 Melbourne Street,
   Leicester.
   Tel: 59216

6. Pakistan Association,
   114 Cromwell Road,
   Peterborough.

Bradford

7. Pakistan Peoples Association,
   10 Cornwall Road,
   Bradford 1.

8. Pakistan Muslim Society,
   2 Woodthorpe Terrace,
   Huddersfield. (Yorks).

9. Pakistan Association,
   44 West Terrace,
   North Ormesby,
   Middlesbrough.
   Tel: 46822

10. Pakistan Welfare Association,
    145 Peas Hill Road,
    Nottingham.

11. Pakistan Friends League,
    87 Holgate Road,
    The Meadows,
    Nottingham.

12. Pakistan Muslim Association,
    94 Attercliffe Common,
    Sheffield 9.

Liverpool

13. Accrington and District
    Pakistani Friendship Association,
    47 Ranger Street,
    Accrington.

14. Pakistan Association,
    72 Georges Road,
    Bolton.
    Tel: 24568

15. Pakistan Welfare Association,
    14 Flaxman Street,
    Liverpool 7.

16. Pakistan Society,
    Everest Restaurant,
    63 Whitworth Street,
    Manchester 1.
    Tel: CENtral 6268

17. Pakistan Muslim Association,
    25–27 Manchester Street,
    Oldham.
    Tel: MAIn 8869

18. Pakistan Information and Welfare Centre,
    330 Stockport Road,
    Manchester 13.

19. Pakistan Cultural Society,
    6 Shear Brow,
    Blackburn, Lancs.

Glasgow

20. Belfast Pakistani Association,
    6 Clifton Street,
    Belfast 13.
    Tel: 28775

21. Pakistan Social and Cultural Association,
32 Dudhope Crescent Road,
Dundee.

22. Pakistan Association,
8 Clarence Street,
Edinburgh.
Tel: CAL 4204

23. Jamait Ittehad ul Muslamin,
27 Oxford Street,
Glasgow, C.5.
Tel: South 3100

24. Pakistan Social and Cultural Society,
76 South Portland Street,
Glasgow, C.5.

25. Pakistan Association,
29 East Parade,
Newcastle-upon-Tyne 4.

26. Pakistan Muslim Welfare Association,
117 Ramsay Street,
Rochdale.

27. Pakistan Welfare and Social Organisation,
7 Carlisle Street,
Blackburn.

28. Pakistan Welfare Association,
54 Spencer Street,
Burnley.

D. 'COLOURED' ORGANIZATIONS

(i) *The Racial Adjustment Action Society*

The R.A.A.S. alternates between polar phases of highly publicized activities and of extreme secrecy. At the time of writing, it was in one of its secretive phases and would divulge nothing about itself. A look back over its two years of existence, however, afforded some rather uneven and sometimes highly coloured information about its aims, activities, and personnel.

The R.A.A.S. was first brought to general notice by an article about 'Britain's own Malcolm X', Michael de Freitas from Trinidad, in the *Sunday Times* (28 February 1965). Following the descent of Mr. de Freitas and others on the confused scene during the strike at Courtaulds Red Scar Mill, Preston, in May–June 1965,[1] this organization again received publicity in the summer of 1965, in the quality Sunday papers: a further *Sunday Times* article on Mr. de Freitas's activities among London busmen (6 June 1965) and a piece by Colin McGlashan in the *Observer* (4 July 1965). The latter described its claim to represent all coloured immigrant groups,[2] the 'formidable professionalism' of its recruiting drive, and its militant, 'black Muslim' tone. *New Society* (17 June 1965; 24 June 1965) and B.B.C.'s *Panorama* (21 June 1965) presented a more qualified picture of the organization and the man.

Since then, the organization has not developed into the massive black militant organization that was forecast, but it has continued to exist and to publish such journals as *Magnet*. Michael de Freitas's own position in the movement appears to have varied. At one time he was reported as having been forbidden to give interviews; later he was interviewed by the *Daily Mail* (19 May 1966) in his Notting Hill base (in a house that is also the headquarters of the London Free School (secretary, Miss Rosanna Laslett)). In May 1966, the R.A.A.S. was visited by Cassius Clay (Muhammad Ali), and it was reported variously that 'Britain's Black Muslims' had 'taken over' the world champion and that a portion of the champion's takings would go to the funds of the organization. (See *Sunday Times*, 15 May; *Daily Mail*, 16 May, 19 May, *et al.*)

An offshoot of R.A.A.S. called 'Defence' was set up in the summer of 1966 to provide a legal service for any coloured people in trouble with the police. The idea was simply to provide telephone numbers and addresses which people could immediately contact, and reliable solicitors to take up cases. 'Defence' has also worked with other groups interested in police-immigrant relations, such as the National Council of Civil Liberties.

A hand-out published by R.A.A.S. in early 1965 gives an idea of its aims and approach at that time:

BLACK MEN UNITE WE HAVE NOTHING TO LOSE BUT OUR FEARS

R.A.A.S. is an action group, We are calling on all of our Black brothers and sisters to participate in this movement to redress the balance of insecurity, fear and disunity in which we live. We ask of you nothing but discipline and

[1] See I.R.R. *Newsletter* Supplement, July 1965.

[2] In fact, it seems to have begun and continued primarily with a core of professional and white-collar activists from Guyana and Trinidad (whence perhaps its failure to attract massive support from Jamaican workers?).

an end to petty quarrels amongst ourselves. We must make a supreme effort to assert our rights to freedom and our full human dignity.

We all pledge ourselves to:

(1) Guarantee by all means possible the human rights of all coloured people in Britain.

(2) Re-examine the whole question of our identity as Black men.

(3) Protect our religious, social and cultural heritage.

(4) Help promote trades and industries in order to establish and consolidate a strong economic base.

(5) Establish centres for physical, educational, social and cultural activities.

(6) Create co-operative housing projects so that every man's right to decent accommodation can be assured.

(7) Strengthen our links with the Afro-Asian Caribbean peoples in our common fight for the freedom and dignity of man.

CHAPTER 9

The Churches

Like the trade unions, the churches in Britain are often said to have the greatest opportunity of, and responsibility for, helping immigrants to settle and be accepted in Britain—by dispelling ignorance and inculcating tolerance and welcoming attitudes among their British members, by locating and integrating at local level those immigrants who are Christian (mostly West Indians, Anglo-Indians, and some Africans and Asians) and generally by co-operating with other institutions, official and voluntary, to promote the newcomers' well-being and absorption.

1. THE BRITISH COUNCIL OF CHURCHES

A. NATIONAL ATTITUDES AND ACTION

With the exception of a handful of eccentric and ethnocentric individual ministers, all the Churches in Britain have taken a forthright stand against colour discrimination and for active work towards integration. Their attitudes and activities have generally been expressed and co-ordinated by the British Council of Churches (B.C.C.), to which all churches but the Roman Catholic Church belong:

Since 1948 the Council has been exhorting its constituent churches and local Councils of Churches and resolving itself to do everything possible for the welfare of immigrants. First, in 1948, the Executive Committee commended 'overseas students' and 'foreign workers' to the care of the Council and particularly of its Social Responsibility Department, and called for consultations with other interested bodies. In April 1950 the Council itself urged the churches and their congregations 'to take every opportunity of promoting the welfare of non-European workers and students in this country', and recommended that the Government should set up a national advisory panel to co-ordinate all voluntary work on their behalf. In April 1956 the Council called on all local Councils of Churches 'in areas where coloured immigrants are settling' to make increased efforts to ensure their well-being and integration.

In 1958, after the disturbances in Nottingham and Notting Dale, the Executive Committee of the Council issued the following statement:

We are shocked by the evidence of colour prejudice as one of the causes of recent disturbances involving coloured people in Great Britain. Christians will not need to be reminded that in Christ there is neither coloured nor white, but all are one.

The Churches, therefore, through their members have a responsibility to demonstrate their care for people from such areas as the West Indies, and to work for the eradication of attitudes based on fear, self-interest, suspicion or ignorance. To realize this ideal will not be easy in areas of major settlement by coloured people, but it is an effort which Christians are called upon to make.

The Churches could not consent to limitation of immigration on grounds of colour.

We recognize that much has already been done to integrate immigrants into the established community and believe that, with willingness, understanding and perseverance on both sides, the integration which is desirable is also possible.

In these earlier years the West Indians were the major immigrant groups and the Churches' main concern, as the title of a Council pamphlet (published in 1955, and brought up to date in 1958) shows—'Your Neighbour from the West Indies'. This was one of the initiatives of the Consultative Committee on Overseas Coloured Workers set up in 1955 by the Council's Social Responsibility Department and disbanded some years later when its work seemed to have borne sufficient fruit for it to become redundant.

This decision was, however, found to be premature. Tension increased over the period during which the restrictions on Commonwealth immigrants were debated and imposed[1] and in October 1963 a Standing Committee on Migration was set up. Its terms of reference were as follows:

(a) To gather and exchange information on migration with external organizations, including government bodies, both central and local;
(b) To study and consider the basic problems in migration and the contribution which the Churches can make towards their solution.

On 27 April 1965 the Standing Committee presented a statement to the B.C.C. which was approved and published under the title 'Immigrants in Britain'. This contained the following comments, firstly on specialized pastoral and other work, secondly on wider issues:

(1) In specialised ministries, in experiments like that in Notting Hill, and in pastoral work in areas where there are large concentrations of immigrants, very much more is being done than the harsher critics will allow.
(2) The visible results of much sustained and sacrificial work are often disappointingly small.
(3) The total effort is impressive, but in relation to the size of the problem is quite insufficient.

On the wider social, economic, and political questions the Standing Committee submitted the following comments:

[1] The Churches opposed not controls in general, but this particular Bill, on the grounds that it was hurried, improvised, introduced without adequate consultation, and virtually a measure of colour discrimination.

(1) The decision of the present Government to retain the Commonwealth Immigrants Act, the subsequent decision of the Home Secretary to strengthen the controls against evasion of the provisions of the Act, and the general tenor of the debate in the House of Commons on 23rd March 1965, mean that there is now enough common ground for the parties to undertake reasoned discussion. The Churches should welcome such realistic debate, provided that a deliberate effort is made to expose and eradicate the irrational and prejudiced. Any hints of appeal to prejudice, or an approval of discrimination based on colour, however discreetly worded, should be plainly and vigorously condemned by the Churches.

(2) Realistic debate involves the recognition that there is no homogeneous 'coloured immigrant group'. The West Indian is not a Pakistani. The deeply-rooted irrational fear that the immigrant is prospering at the expense of the host community must be exposed. The fact is that the immigrant has contributed substantially to the general economic welfare of Britain. Factual analysis is needed to destroy such dangerous myths.

(3) No generalisation about local situations is everywhere valid, for local reactions have differed according to the size and national composition of the immigrant population, and to the range and quality of local industrial, civic, and religious leadership. But all the evidence we have received testifies to the value of local voluntary committees. These widely representative committees, in which the immigrants play an active part, have in many places notably reduced tensions and promoted mutual understanding. We believe that the importance of these committees should be more fully recognized, and the establishment of others encouraged.

(4) One of the most hopeful fields of local activity is the school, but in areas with a heavy concentration of coloured immigrants there is real danger that the school may become *de facto* 'segregated'. There are some schools where 80% of the children are coloured. L.E.A.s should be encouraged to ensure, as some are already doing, that there is a balance in the composition of the school.

(5) Legislation against racial discrimination—which is inextricably involved in the immigrant problem—is notoriously difficult to draft in a form that does not improperly restrict individual liberty. Legislation will, therefore, be of limited effect. Nevertheless, an Act against racial discrimination, despite its limitations, would be so important as an explicit statement of national attitude that it should be welcomed by the Churches.

(6) Though there is at present need for an expanded labour force in Britain, it is most probable that within a few years the progress of industrial technology will steadily reduce the demand. In the general interest, unrestricted and unregulated immigration is out of the question. The Commonwealth Immigrants Act is an unsatisfactory and negative measure. It should be replaced by regulations that will facilitate planned immigration.

(7) The psychological effect of the present regulations is that the immigrant appears to be trying to get in where he is not really wanted. Planning, where the initiative would be with Government, preferably in consultation with Commonwealth Governments, would see that the immigrant would

plainly appear to come by invitation. The policies of, for example, Australia or Holland could be studied with advantage. Planning might well involve courses of preparatory training in the countries of origin, and possibly, by agreement, quotas based on the industrial needs of Britain. It must certainly involve the provision of adequate housing accommodation for the immigrants.

(8) It is clear that many immigrants are not transients who intend ultimately to return home, but are settlers who will make their home in Britain. There seems to be much confusion of thought about the implications of this development. Should the objective of policy be the eventual assimilation of all immigrant groups, or the integration of culturally distinct but not socially separate communities? The Standing Committee considers that coherent and effective policies cannot be framed until this question has been examined and answered.

(9) These notes comment briefly on very difficult social and economic questions, but the basic question is simply one of human relations. The British Churches, which have condemned so strongly and so rightly racial discrimination abroad, can now very practically 'show their faith by their works'. Part of that service can lie in supporting, against the attacks of prejudice and short-sighted self-interest, the efforts of Parliament, industrialists, trades unions and municipal authorities to ensure that the coloured immigrant does not become a second-class citizen in Britain.

Since that time the Committee has been concerned with such matters as: the Government White Paper of August 1965 (on which it initiated a debate of the British Council of Churches in the following October, welcoming the positive aspects of the Paper, but regretting the level of restrictions imposed); the various reports of the C.I.A.C.; the compilation of a card index of returned missionaries wanting to act as interpreters for Indian and Pakistani immigrants; and the religious teaching of immigrant children belonging to other religions than Christianity. The Committee also keeps in touch with local Councils of Churches to indicate ways in which they can help with the work of integration, with the N.C.C.I. and similar bodies,[1] and with work initiated by the Christian Aid Department of the B.C.C. itself. In early 1967 the Committee (Secretary, Miss Janet Henderson, Christian Aid, 10 Eaton Gate, London, S.W.1) was considering the provision of adequate information for new immigrants about conditions in Britain, and the report of a Bradford study prepared by Eric Butterworth on some aspects of the interaction between Moslems and local people in the city, with special reference to the actual and potential role of the Churches in promoting good race relations. The section on the state of the Churches in the migrant area and the attitudes and morale of ministers and lay officials, was particularly interesting. In a district of concentrated social prob-

[1] Both in Britain and overseas. For instance, the Committee was in regular contact with the Churches' Committee on Migrant Workers in Western Europe.

lems, declining congregations and low funds, immigrants, particularly of an alien religion, could sometimes seem like just one problem among many. Preoccupation with conversion, where it was found, was likely to be regarded as an unfriendly act, and to render ineffective any hopes of communal interaction.

B. ACTION AT LOCAL LEVEL

In November 1966 the Standing Committee on Migration prepared the following list of examples of positive action taken by churches, working singly or inter-denominationally at local level.

(i) *Birmingham*

Both the Anglicans and the Methodists had ministers working full-time amongst immigrants. The Methodist minister himself came from Jamaica, while the Anglican, known as 'The Bishop's Chaplain for Overseas People', was a priest who had served for many years overseas.

In the Sparkbrook/Balsall Heath area of the city the Birmingham Council of Christian Churches, with the backing of Christian Aid, was shortly hoping to appoint a lay person (probably a woman) to work full-time amongst immigrants, in co-operation with the local churches and other organizations (including the Sparkbrook Association, which itself largely owed its existence to the initiative of the local churches).

(ii) *Bradford*

A Methodist minister from Pakistan is working full-time among his fellow-countrymen.

(iii) *Coventry*

Here too there was a full-time Anglican Chaplain for Overseas People, working closely with the Coventry Council of Churches on various projects which the Council sponsored for immigrants (e.g. visiting of newcomers, English classes for Asian women).

(iv) *Glasgow*

A Presbyterian minister from Pakistan is working full-time among his fellow-countrymen.

(v) *London*

In *Brixton* there were two West Indian ministers—one a Baptist, one a Methodist—who had been specially brought over to work amongst West Indians. In *Islington* the Society of Friends was about to establish a 'Neighbourhood House' to further the integration of immigrants into the community (for further information write to the Race Relations

Committee, Friends House, Euston Road, London, N.W.1). In *Notting Hill* a Methodist team ministry set up after the 1958 racial troubles was carrying out effective pastoral and social work amongst immigrants.

(vi) *Sheffield*

There was a Presbyterian deaconess from Jamaica on the staff of a church in a predominantly West Indian area, while for the city as a whole there was a Chaplain and Liaison Officer for Commonwealth Immigrants (the Rev. Harry Brown, 32 Steade Road, Sheffield 7), who was appointed jointly by the Sheffield City Council and the Sheffield Council of Churches.

Other instances are given in the section on the Churches in the B.B.C.'s publication *Colour in Britain* (pp. 185–7). This particularly stressed the value of teamwork.

One recent example of teamwork occurred in mid-June 1966, when a letter was sent to the Home Secretary, signed by eighty-seven out of just over a hundred clergymen of all denominations in most of the major centres of Commonwealth immigrant settlement (including London, Birmingham, Bristol, Bradford, Manchester, Leeds, Liverpool, Coventry, Wolverhampton, Nottingham, Slough, Oxford, Southall, Oldham, Derby, and Cardiff). One of the two Anglican drafters of the letter (the Rev. John Downing and the Rev. Wilfred Wood, a Barbadian) commented:

> In a way, the most encouraging thing was that all these clergymen, who normally cannot agree in a statement of less than one hundred words (the Apostle's Creed) found themselves able to sign a statement of about two thousand!

The letter first asked that the Act be extended to cover racial and religious discrimination in employment, housing, the granting of credit and mortgages, and in insurance. It drew attention to: the startling unawareness of many M.P.s and leading figures of the extent to which racial discrimination is actually practised in the areas mentioned; to the future social dangers of such discrimination, particularly against the second generation; to the present alienation of a great majority of coloured immigrants, in particular the greatest potential for responsible leadership. Proposed as the best method of remedying the situation was the use of conciliation techniques on the North American 'Commission for Human Rights' model. The advantages of this were: (a) that law has an educative effect; (b) that non-prejudiced employers and landlords could use it as an argument; (c) that the system works, only a tiny minority of cases ever going beyond the conciliation or hearing stages. Snags such as the fear that legislation would embitter rather than conciliate, or that it would open the way to organized provocateurs, had been disproved by North American experience. The principle of freedom of association must not and would not be endangered by their proposals, nor was this suggested administrative approach without precedent in the British legal system. The opportunity for action was now at the stage 'where the ordering of our multi-racial society can be shaped'.

C. ASSESSMENT AND POSSIBLE LINES OF ACTION

It is often in their ancillary welfare services (moral welfare, mother and baby homes, children's societies, the provision of hostel accommodation for women or young people) that the churches have come into most direct contact with, and been of most assistance to, the immigrants. These are services that tend, perhaps unjustly, to be overlooked when one is discussing the role of the churches.

Nevertheless, a report prepared by a committee of the London branch of the William Temple Association in August 1966 contained the following assessment of the work of the churches in Britain in relation to immigrants:

> The contribution of particular Christian churches and congregations varies widely. Officially, the churches are closely involved in the work of integration, and the Archbishop of Canterbury in his personal capacity as Chairman of the National Committee for Commonwealth Immigrants. The British Council of Churches has a standing Committee on Migration and related problems. The Methodist and Baptist churches have special national committees dealing specifically with immigration. Individual clergy have played a large part in local committees, and in some cases in the activist organisations. But even in the case of the West Indian immigrants, the churches have not been so successful in easing integration as might have been hoped. Notwithstanding much individual enthusiasm, it was estimated some years ago that 94 per cent of those immigrants in London who used to attend churches in the West Indies had ceased to do so. The West Indies is still basically a church-going society. Britain is not, and therefore the more thoroughly the immigrants integrate into British society, the more likely they are to lose contact with the church. Generally speaking, the free churches have succeeded best in encouraging immigrants to take part in the full worshipping and social life of the church, possibly because their services are less formal and more familiar.
>
> There have been encouraging instances of successful inter-denominational teamwork at local level, where churches have got together to provide immigrants with practical advice, club rooms and so on, or to constitute housing associations. It would be fair to say, however, that the churches have not been conspicuous in the work of social integration.[1]

[1] For an account of the contribution of various churches in the Brixton area and of West Indian reactions, including pentecostal sects, in the years from 1955 to 1960, see *Dark Strangers*, Penguin, pp. 226–33.

Clifford Hill, a Congregational Minister with a large number of coloured people in his North London parish, has outlined a programme of possible lines of action for ministers at the local level.[1] This is not intended as a blue-print, since every area has its own peculiarities and there are great differences between different immigrant settlements, but as a source of possible ideas for ministers, vicars or priests at the local level.

1. *Background Knowledge*

The minister needs to know (a) the background of the immigrants in the area, concentrating particularly on religious interests and customs, attitudes to family life and marriage; (b) their particular needs as immigrants settling in a new world.

2. *Personal Visits*

The minister needs to make personal visits to the immigrants in their homes. Here he can:

(a) answer their questions and explain difficulties, give details about the National Health Scheme, income tax, rates, etc., and any special services for immigrants in the town; or talk to them about the English;

(b) tell them about the activities of the church.

He can also get leading members of his congregation to do visiting.

3. *Removal of Social Tensions*

The minister needs to know about social tensions already existing in the parish, which could lead to a worsening of relations between the residents and the newcomers.

Through, for example, the local Council of Churches (if one exists), he should try to help remove the causes of such tensions.

If there is not already a consultative committee, he should help start one.

4. *Education of Host Community*

The church is an ideal place for combating the ignorance of local residents about immigrants, because it is a meeting point for people from all sections of the community.

At church meetings, lectures can be arranged and films shown. (There are a number of films available about the missionary activities of all denominations in the Commonwealth.)

5. *Combined Projects*

Immigrants and local people must be encouraged to meet, if possible, working on combined projects like community service work and church bazaars. The teenagers can meet through the Sunday school and church youth club.

6. *Flexibility*

There may be a case for rethinking the pattern of church services. Many West Indians are used to more lively hymn singing and a more liturgical form of service.

[1] *Colour in Britain*, B.B.C., pp. 182–5.

7. *Baptisms and Weddings*

Baptisms and weddings are major ceremonies for West Indians, and can be used as jumping-off points for better contact with the people involved.

8. *Special Meetings*

The minister can (a) provide the immigrants—including Hindus and Muslims—with facilities for meeting; (b) organise special meetings which can be used for recreational and informational purposes.

9. *Conclusion*

Basically, the minister needs to go about this not because it is a 'problem'. He needs to approach and get other members of the church to approach West Indians and other Christian immigrants purely and simply as members of the Church who have come from different parts of the world to settle here. The West Indians have no wish to be treated as 'different' in this respect. They should be seen as people with abilities, talents and training from their home Christian background, where they were Sunday School teachers, members of the choir, lay preachers and sidesmen. On this basis they should be invited into the Church to continue where they left off, when they left home. If the minister goes to them with the attitude: 'We are the members of a Christian Church who are seeking to tackle problems in the community, and we want you who are trained as Christians to come in and use your talents alongside us in the work of the Lord Jesus Christ in this community' then there is a real chance of positive results.[1]

The churches are sometimes criticized for refusal to rethink traditional methods of pastoral care. This, of course, has a wider application than just to immigrants. As John M. Crosby writes:

The influx of migrants, rather than creating a new problem, has merely exposed a much deeper failure in the relationships between Church and community. The Church has never come to terms with the Industrial Revolution—for that matter has any traditional institution?

In pre-industrial times, the Church was the centre of the community, but with urbanisation and the constant moving of population, the Church has ceased to be a community and has become an organisation to which people 'come' or 'do not come'! It has little relationship to sociological realities, and its parochial structure is hopelessly irrelevant. Moreover, it is predominantly a middle-class institution, whose culture is an expression of the values of the middle class. It is, I believe, significant that many of the churches which are successfully integrating West Indians into their own congregations are those which are looking radically at their own organisation and are trying to recover the meaning of being a community within the natural structures of contemporary society.

He goes on to describe the concept of the house 'church':

The 'house church' or 'cell' or 'church in the street' is one of those experiments which is being successful in new housing areas and in the inner city

[1] Op. cit., pp. 183–5.

alike. There are new areas where the Church, rather than putting up a building, is starting groups within the street to worship together, to arrange baby-sitting rotas, to visit old people, to discuss common problems. The church building may follow, giving a wider identity to these groups, but it comes from the grass roots and is not imposed from above. This is an attempt to reconstruct the Church (sacraments and all) within peoples' homes. The house church can also be a most effective bridgehead between immigrant and the host community. In his book, Clifford Hill has described the community spirit of the West Indian home, what Sheila Patterson has called 'the cellular household', with its many families sharing a large tenement, and having a very close relationship with each other. This is their community. In Notting Hill, the Methodist Team Ministry is developing a house-church system using these multi-occupied houses as house churches. On Sunday evenings most of the inhabitants of these houses gather together with other members of the church who live nearby, often as many as twenty people squashed into an overheated bedsitter, one sitting on the sink perhaps, and six on the bed. The service itself is informal and depends very much on the group itself. At one house church we would sing hymns only if a particular lady was present. The usual pattern is a bible reading followed by discussion and a period of prayer for particular people in the house or street, or particular issues of concern to those at the meeting. Occasionally, a television programme is used as the 'talking point'.

Then, after the more formal side of the meeting is over, coffee, biscuits, cake (and wine in less non-conformist households) provide the stimulus for exchange of gossip, news and information, often of an extremely secular character. Miss D's roof is leaking and the minister agrees to take it up with the local council. Mrs. P offers a reluctant Mr. C some West Indian home-made wine as a Christmas present. Mr. N is in danger of eviction and the group agree to keep their eyes open for alternative accommodation.

Those who attend these house churches are ordinary West Indians, in no sense the intelligentsia or those who are more likely to be integrated into the community. Many house churches are 'multi-racial' and English people are welcomed. In no way is the spirit of the meeting inhibited as the West Indian is on his home ground.

In conclusion, the writer points out that the house church should not be separate from the wider church community, and in fact most of those who attend house churches were found to attend the church itself on Easter, Christmas and other special occasions.[1]

2. THE WORK OF SOME CHURCHES AND RELIGIOUS BODIES

A. THE ANGLICAN CHURCH

Leaders of the Anglican Church discussed colour problems at the Lambeth Conference of Archbishops in 1958 and, with a greater focus

[1] I.R.R. *Newsletter*, December 1964, pp. 25–7.

on the local situation, at the Convocations of Canterbury and York in January 1959. At that time motions calling for action were modified in favour of motions urging special attention to the problems and the care of the immigrants.[1] In recent years, however, much greater emphasis has been placed on action at various levels, culminating in the agreement of the present Archbishop of Canterbury, Dr. A. M. Ramsey, P.C., D.D., to act in his personal capacity as Chairman of the National Committee for Commonwealth Immigrants, set up in the late summer of 1965. At the inaugural Press conference, the Archbishop stressed that the new committee was charged with the problem of integration irrespective of current policy concerning controls, but intimated that if the committee found that the work of integration was being hampered by the policy, they would tell the Government so.

(i) *The Church of England and Commonwealth Immigrants*

Whilst some recognizable and distinctive work has been done by individual clergymen (for example in Birmingham), and while some dioceses have full- or part-time race relations officers (for instance in Coventry), the Church of England prefers to work at both local level through joint committees or councils with other churches and with public bodies and local authorities. The same arrangement is common at national level; before the Archbishop of Canterbury's link with the present National Committee, the Church had many links (none of them official) with the old Commonwealth Immigrants Advisory Council. In so far as specific church action is needed, the Church prefers to work ecumenically through the British Council of Churches and the World Council of Churches. In so far as public action is required, the Church seeks to help those who are involved and to work through national and local leaders and committees without itself becoming directly involved as a corporate body. Only rarely is it considered helpful for the Church itself to make pronouncements or to take direct and separate action.

As an informant recently wrote: 'The distinctive character of the work of the Church of England in race relations is that it is hard to distinguish it! . . . the problem is that of disentangling the Church of England from the community it exists to serve.'

The help given to those who carry national and local responsibility takes several forms, generally channelled through or initiated by the Board for Social Responsibility of the Church Assembly. In 1960, for instance, under the chairmanship of Sir John Wolfenden, the Board issued a statement on race relations entitled 'Together in Britain' for the guidance of the whole Church. In the same year the Overseas Council issued a factual statement about overseas visitors, including immigrants, under the title 'Your Neighbour'. Both statements included

[1] *Coloured Immigrants in Britain*, pp. 149–51.

lists of organizations concerned with these matters and gave some practical suggestions for Christian Action. A report on 'Our Student Guests' was received by the Church Assembly and fully debated. In May 1962, the Society for the Propagation of the Gospel convened a conference on the integration of West Indian immigrants and a report was produced.

During the debate which led to the passing of the Commonwealth Immigrants Act (1961), the Board for Social Responsibility prepared a 'brief' for the use of M.P.s, peers, and senior civil servants. Similar papers have since then been prepared for debates on the Expiring Laws Continuance Bill (which includes the Commonwealth Immigrants Act), the Race Relations Act and other relevant occasions. These papers are written on the basis of a policy on race relations which is debated twice a year by the Board for Social Responsibility.

Literature of a more general nature is also produced (for instance, *The Responsible Church*, S.P.C.K.), and several special studies have been made with the support of the Board for Social Responsibility: for example, the William Temple Association's report on coloured immigrants in the U.K., which has been published in many forms; and the study of the Pakistan community in Bradford, prepared by Mr. Eric Butterworth for the Central Committee on Migrant Workers in Western Europe.

(ii) *An Example of Church Work at Local Level*

In November 1966 the Rev. P. A. Berry, the Bishop of Coventry's Chaplain for Overseas People, sent us the following note of his work in 1966, under nine headings:

(1) We have had some success in linking with existing youth clubs and encouragement to persuade immigrant young people to attend.

In the school holidays we ran a three-day Holiday Club with an equal number of Indian, West Indian, and English boys and girls, which seemed to be quite successful. In the last few weeks, I have been working to provide a week-day club for young people who are out of work, and this has included a number of immigrants, and as part of the activities of the club we have had English classes. Some of our young people in voluntary service are linking with immigrant teen-age homes and arranging friendly and informal meetings and discussions to help with English. I am also planning, with the Warwickshire Association of Youth Clubs, a residential week-end for some forty teen-agers on the lines of the Holiday Club.

(2) We have two Sikh Temples and a Mosque in Coventry, as well as a New Testament Church of God, which is mainly West Indian. I visit them all and have been asked to preach and to share in discussion groups and bring in members of the host community and students for meetings and discussions.

(3) We have for the past two years held a Service of Friendship for world faiths in the ruins of Coventry Cathedral. One theme of Coventry is the

Ministry of Reconciliation and many members of the immigrant community have taken part.

(4) We have been running a Housing Association for the past two years to help convert old property to answer cases of need, and voluntary help in the conversion has included students and immigrant teen-agers.

(5) We have for the past two years had an informal group of people called Voluntary Welfare Service, linked with the Council of Churches; this group has visited immigrant homes and has been able to make links with the statutory services.

(6) In association with the Education Department, we have arranged a week-end course for teachers of immigrant children about the social background and psychological problems of adjustment.

(7) In association with the Council of Social Service, I arranged a conference on 'The Immigrant Citizen in the Community', which was attended by some 130 representatives of voluntary and statutory bodies.

(8) Earlier in the year I arranged a pastoral 'teach-in' for clergy and ministers on 'The Care of Immigrants in the Community'.

(9) We are linking with the local Indian community in the furnishing of a hostel for first offenders; Indian women are making curtains for the rooms.

This is just a brief summary of some of the projects in which we are engaged, and I hope very shortly a Liaison Committee will be established to co-ordinate the work in which many people are involved.

B. THE ROMAN CATHOLIC CHURCH

The Roman Catholics in Britain have perhaps been more active in work connected with European refugees and students, if only because substantial numbers in these groups are co-religionists. This is, of course, even more applicable in the case of Irish immigrants; of the West Indian and Asian immigrants, however, only those from Trinidad and the former French Caribbean islands, and from Asia the Anglo-Indians afford a sizeable proportion of Roman Catholics.[1]

From the information available, it would appear that the Roman Catholic Church in Britain has experienced the same sort of difficulties in making and maintaining contacts with Catholic immigrants from the Commonwealth as have the Church of England and other denominations.[2] A detailed account of the various activities and church organizations involved was given in two supplements to the I.R.R. *Newsletter* in 1964–5.[3] Among these organizations are the Legion of

[1] For an impression of the work of the R.C. Church among Irish and other immigrants in Sparkbrook, Birmingham, see Rex and Moore, op. cit., pp. 149–53, p. 185.

[2] See Clifford S. Hill, *West Indian Migrants and the London Churches*, O.U.P. for I.R.R., 1963, pp. 25–7.

[3] Dorothy C. Prosser, *The Absorption of Immigrants*, A Brief Survey of the Work of Some Roman Catholic Organisations in Britain, Parts I–II, December 1964–January 1965.

Mary, the Overseas Circles, the Association of Catholic Trade Unionists, the Catholic Housing Aid Society, the Union of Catholic Mothers, the diocesan rescue and adoption societies, the Knights of Saint Columba, the Young Christian Workers, the Family and Social Action group, and the Society of African Missions (particularly in Manchester).

Information and education are promoted by the Sword of the Spirit and also by the Catholic Institute for International Relations (C.I.I.R.), which has increasingly worked in contact with other religious and lay groups concerned with the amelioration of race relations and international understanding. A recent C.I.I.R. publication was *Race and Religion* (1965), a pamphlet aimed at the Catholic layman.

C. THE METHODIST CHURCH

The Methodist Church has for years had a country-wide National Committee for the Care of Immigrants. Its organizing secretary is the Rev. Stanley V. Hollis and its London office (in the Home Mission Department, 1 Centre Buildings, Westminster, S.W.1) acts as a centre for information and advice, co-ordinates the work of branch committees, and organizes regional conferences.

There are also committees at district level in areas where there are immigrants in large numbers. Through these committees action at local level is encouraged, and in a number of cases these local groups have helped in the formation of Liaison Committees. Through these agencies, conferences are arranged, meetings of workers held, investigations made and general help and encouragement given to individual churches.

In the Manchester area, in 1966, a working party carried out a small-scale inquiry into race relations in the area.[1] The chairman of the Bristol district serves on the Voluntary Liaison Committee there, and

[1] This found that many West Indians who regard religion as important do not join any religious body when they come to England. Only ten churches in the district report having ten or more coloured people in the congregation at any one time, and out of 3,200 members of the Church only one hundred are coloured immigrants.

There is clearly a barrier between English Christians and most immigrants, the report states. Neither side knows the other well, and the relationship, or lack of it, is made worse when it is thought that a white Christian fails or refuses to recognize a coloured person whom he has previously met in church. As a result, the coloured person may stop coming. The report adds that these barriers must be broken down, and that a start could be made by meeting in each other's homes. The Church has a duty towards immigrants in helping with their special problems in this fragmented and inhospitable community. Although the Church was the only known quantity for the immigrant on arrival, it has had little success in its work with them.

The report calls for more use of music and congregational response in services, invitations to immigrants to discuss improvements in the way worship is conducted and the appointment of a coloured minister or deaconess in the area. Methodists must also work in the community to ensure that coloured people have equal opportunities in employment, education and housing.

the Rev. Rupert Davies of Didsbury College is the chairman of the Bristol Advisory Committee for Multi-Racial Relationships.

In the Leeds area, the local Methodists are co-operating with the local authorities, with the Councils of Social Service, the Studley Grange Children's Association and other such organizations. The church is also represented on the Yorkshire Committee for Community Relations.

The main Committee itself is sponsoring an experimental project in the Brixton area at Railton Road, where a Youth and Community Centre is being developed under the leadership of the Rev. George F. A. Pottinger. This Centre works closely with the local authorities in a Somerleyton–Geneva Advice Centre, also with the Senior Youth and Community Officer at the King's Cross Training Centre, which last year carried out a 'Neighbourhood Reconnaissance' related to the need for children's work in the area.

There are also the thirteen Methodist International Houses in Britain for foreign students. One of these, Sunnyside in Liverpool, is the pioneer in providing accommodation for married foreign students with families (only one child).

D. THE SOCIETY OF FRIENDS

The Society of Friends has a special Race Relations Committee. Its officers are: chairman—Walter Birmingham; secretary—Douglas Tilbe; assistant secretary—Joan Ralling; student secretary—Roderick Ede.

The aims and work of the Committee are described in its literature as follows:

> The Committee seeks:
>
> (1) To stimulate local action by Friends in the field of race relations.
>
> (2) To influence national policy on aspects of race relations.
>
> (3) To improve race relations in Britain: (a) by working with and for immigrants; (b) by helping overseas students through our student secretary.
>
> (4) To spread knowledge and understanding of the questions involved: by supplying literature and commissioning articles; by providing speakers for local meetings; by arranging conferences and summer schools; by collecting information on race relations projects undertaken by Friends and others in various parts of the country.
>
> With the establishment of the Friends' Peace and International Relations Committee, the overseas work formerly undertaken by the Race Relations Committee has been transferred to the new body, with Leslie A. Smith as one of its secretaries. The Race Relations Committee can thus concentrate on race relations in this country, with all their growing complexity.

Apart from the general work of providing speakers, producing a newsletter, and joining in the lobby against racial discrimination in Britain, the Committee has undertaken some special projects, of which the following are examples:

(1) Islington Project, to establish a community centre with a full-time social worker attached.

(2) A four-day conference on 'Education in Multi-Racial Britain' held in March 1967 in co-operation with the National Committee for Commonwealth Immigrants at Rachel McMillan College of Education.

(3) Three one-day conferences on, respectively, West Indians, Cypriots, and Indians and Pakistanis, in relation to the Youth Service, organized jointly with the Immigrants' Advisory Committee of the London Council of Social Service.

The work done by individual Friends and local meetings cannot be listed here (for instances see the Annual Reports of the Committee). Mention may, however, be made of the initiative and persistence shown by a group of Friends in Brixton in connexion with the Racial Brotherhood organization.[1]

E. OTHER DENOMINATIONS AND RELIGIOUS GROUPINGS

Other Christian denominations have been active in work concerned with race relations and the integration of Commonwealth immigrants in Britain. The Presbyterians and the Congregationalists have relatively few members in the West Indies, but individual ministers and parishes have done positive work.[2] The Baptists start with a greater advantage, since in the West Indies (mainly in Jamaica) they come second to the Anglicans in total membership and their style of worship even in Britain may prove more attractive to many migrants than that of other denominations. The Baptist Union has appointed a West Indian and a Ceylonese minister in London, and in 1961 and 1964 brought over Jamaican ministers to help integrate West Indians in the British churches.[3]

The free churches, and particularly the Baptists in Britain, have, however, had to face not only the drift from the church that characterizes so many migrants from rural areas, particularly in a strange urban industrial setting where the mass of the receiving society has little or nothing to do with the church, but also the pull of the self-segregating Pentecostal groups that flourish and proliferate among a considerable minority of West Indians in Britain.[4]

The Salvation Army and Y.M.C.A. have been active in some areas; in

[1] See *Dark Strangers*, pp. 243–5.

[2] Notably the Rev. Clifford S. Hill, Minister of a North London Congregational church.

[3] See Clement H. L. Gayle, 'A Baptist Minister in Birmingham', I.R.R. *Newsletter*, July/August 1966, for a detailed report of the second visitation.

[4] Ibid., pp. 26–7. See also Malcolm J. C. Calley, *God's People: West Indian Pentecostal Sects in England*, London, O.U.P. for I.R.R., 1965, *passim*; *Dark Strangers*, pp. 302–6, for Pentecostal and other cult groups in Brixton.

April 1967 the National Council of Y.M.C.A.s held a three-day consultation on 'The Y.M.C.A. and the Coloured Immigrant', at which the possibility of doing more work among the second and younger generation of immigrants was discussed.

F. THE COUNCIL OF CHRISTIANS AND JEWS

An organization which merits particular mention is the Council of Christians and Jews, whose objects are 'to combat all forms of religious and racial intolerance. To promote mutual understanding and goodwill between Christians and Jews and to foster co-operation in educational activities and in social and community service.' It has for years been active in educational work towards integration and improved race relations, by means of conferences and meetings at all levels, collaboration with teachers, training colleges, and universities, to initiate classroom methods to help children develop tolerance and understanding, and a wide variety of general and specialized publications.

Since the mid-1950s the Council's Working Group on the Diminution of Prejudice has held annual conferences on various aspects of the subject. The Twelfth Conference, held in January 1967, was on the theme of 'The Promotion of Tolerance and Human Understanding through Educational Techniques'. For the first time the proceedings took the form of a series of practical demonstrations by head teachers, university and other teachers, and school chaplains, of ways in which tolerant attitudes could be fostered by means of school or university programmes and initiatives (in relation to parents, children, staff, education officers, and so on). (Address: 41 Cadogan Gardens, London, S.W.3.)

G. SOME JEWISH GROUPS AND ORGANIZATIONS INTERESTED IN VARIOUS ASPECTS OF RACE RELATIONS:

Central Jewish Lecture Committee of
The Board of Deputies of British Jews,
Woburn House, London, W.C.1.

Anglo-Jewish Association,
Woburn House,
London, W.C.1.

United Synagogue,
Woburn House,
London, W.C.1.

Westminster Synagogue,
Kent House,
London, S.W.7.

Liberal Jewish Synagogue,
28 St. John's Wood Road,
London, N.W.8.

The Association of Reform Synagogues
of Great Britain,
33 Seymour Place,
London, W.1.

The B'nai B'rith,
Tavistock House,
London, W.C.1.

The World Jewish Congress
(British Section),
55 New Cavendish Street,
London, W.1.

The following organizations and units are also among those that have specialized in documentation of anti-Semitic, radical right, and racialist activities:

The Wiener Library,
Institute of Contemporary History,
4 Devonshire Street,
London, W.1.

The Institute of Jewish Affairs,
13 Jacob's Well Mews,
George Street, London, W.1.

H. A NOTE ON PENTECOSTAL SECTS

The minority of West Indians who continue to participate actively in religious life in Britain may be divided into two main groups: the more settled and socially mobile lower-middle or upper-lower class who attend established churches or sects; and the ardent fundamentalist sectarians who set up their own independent pentecostal groups or take over existing local congregations. These sects in Britain, as in the West Indies, represent a passive protest against and rejection of a hostile and rejecting world and offer a compensation and an ultimate reversal of status for the chosen elect.

Beliefs and rituals differ little between the various sects. All are fundamentalist, all place great emphasis on ecstatic experiences, all believe in faith-healing. The main doctrinal division centres around baptism. Members observe taboos on smoking, drinking, swearing, attending the theatre, cinema, gambling, and extra-marital sex. The larger sects exact tithes which may be an actual tenth of the member's income.

Some sects are becoming quite prosperous and are in a position to buy church buildings. Their continuity and influence are, however, undermined by the frequent schisms characteristic of Pentecostal sects, either as a result of doctrinal and other disagreements between sub-groups or because of personal rivalries between individual leaders and would-be leaders.[1]

I. THE WEST INDIAN CHRISTIAN BACKGROUND

TABLE 20

Communicant church membership in the British Caribbean Territories

	Anglican	Baptist	Congregational	Methodist	Presbyterian	Roman Catholic	Other Denominations
Jamaica ...	39,000	29,083	3,350	23,030	13,000	43,000	114,077
British Guiana...	85,329	133	3,500	7,500	784	27,666	12,667
Trinidad and Tobago ...	64,000	13,227	NW	4,500	4,000	100,000	34,358
The Rest ...	116,000	NW	NW	22,900	NW	100,000	32,437
Total ...	304,329	42,443	6,850	57,930	17,784	270,666	193,539

NW means No Work in this area.

The Rest includes Antigua, Barbados, British Honduras, Cayman Isles, Dominica, Grenada, Montserrat, St. Kitts-Nevis-Anguilla, St. Lucia, St. Vincent, Turks and Caicos Isles, Virgin Isles.

The Roman Catholic figures are those for Easter communicants. Where these were not available, an author's estimate has been included.

[1] For a detailed analysis of West Indian Pentecostalists in Britain see M. Calley, op. cit. For accounts of such sects in Brixton and Sparkbrook respectively see *Dark Strangers*, pp. 349–59 and Appendix X, and Rex and Moore, op. cit., pp. 177–190.

TABLE 21[1]

Total Christian community in the British Caribbean Territories

	Anglican	Baptist	Congregational	Methodist	Presbyterian	Roman Catholic	Other Denominations
Jamaica ...	312,000	140,000	12,500	52,770	25,000	126,971	194,024
British Guiana...	129,000	200	18,000	24,200	916	83,000	39,692
Trinidad and Tobago ...	150,000	15,500	NW	15,870	4,000	299,649	60,023
The Rest ...	306,000	NW	NW	62,775	NW	298,880	96,715
Total ...	897,000	155,700	30,500	155,615	29,916	808,500	390,454

NW means No Work in this area.
The Rest includes the same Islands as in Table 20.

[1] Information for Tables 20 and 21 supplied by World Christian Handbook, World Dominion Press, the Society for the Propagation of the Gospel, the Baptist World Alliance, the Commonwealth Missionary Society, the Methodist Missionary Society, the Presbyterian Church of England, the Sword of the Spirit office, and various British Caribbean diocesan authorities. Taken from Clifford S. Hill, op. cit., pp. 3–4, Tables 2 and 3.

PART IV

OTHER ASPECTS

CHAPTER 10

Health

1. LEGISLATION AND PROCEDURE

In 1926 a policy of medical control at ports was agreed by the International Sanitary Conference. On this were based the Port Sanitary Regulations of 1933 in Britain. They authorized Port Medical Officers to examine incoming persons and to exclude those suffering from plague, cholera, smallpox, typhus, and yellow fever. The Commonwealth Immigrants Acts of 1962 went further and specifically excluded persons suffering from mental disorder and all those whose admission to the country would be undesirable for medical reasons. The legislation covering the present procedure for the admission of aliens comes under the Aliens Order, 1953.[1]

Aliens must normally present themselves at a seaport or airport approved by the Secretary of State. There are twenty-one such approved seaports and seventeen approved airports. The immigration officer is entitled to refer any alien to a medical inspector. Generally, he will assess whether or not an alien appears to be in normal health, both physical and mental, and will refer for medical opinion any case in which he is in doubt. Since the benefits of the National Health Service are available free to aliens who fall ill in this country, but not to those who come here with the specific intention of obtaining treatment, he will also refer any alien whom he has reason to suppose has come with the purpose of obtaining free treatment in mind. Lastly, an alien who intends to make his home in this country or to stay for more than a short period will be referred.

It will be seen that the purpose of the examination is two-fold—medical (to minimize the spread of infection) and economic (to prevent a drain on the State health and welfare services of this country). Subject to the facilities at his command the medical officer will make as full an examination as possible and report to the immigration officer, with whom rests the decision whether or not the individual concerned should be admitted.

[1] The following detailed information on procedure is taken from the B.M.A. Report, *Medical Examination of Immigrants*, 1965, paras 65–71, virtually the only systematic country-wide survey of health aspects of immigrants available.

2. COMMONWEALTH CITIZENS

Medical examination of Commonwealth citizens is much more limited.[1] Indeed, until the 1962 Act was passed, Commonwealth citizens were quite free to come and go as they chose, and were not subject to immigration control. Prior to the passage of the Act, when the Bill was before Parliament, the Government gave an undertaking that any control intended in respect of Commonwealth citizens would certainly not be stricter than the control already exercised in respect of aliens.

Under the Commonwealth Immigrants Act, 1962, medical examination is established for the same purpose as for aliens, with the important difference that there is no general power to refuse admission to people ordinarily resident in the United Kingdom, to holders of Ministry of Labour vouchers (i.e. work permits) or to the wives and children under 16 accompanying or joining their husbands or parents. Nor is there any power to admit them subject to conditions. Subject to this, holders of Ministry of Labour vouchers and other Commonwealth citizens who are coming to settle in the United Kingdom will be among those normally examined by the medical inspector when they arrive. If the medical inspector certifies that a person has a serious illness which might endanger the health of others in the United Kingdom, or if he considers that a person is suffering from mental disorder or some serious physical condition which would prevent him from supporting himself and his dependants, he will inform the immigration officer accordingly and the latter will normally refuse admission. Persons suffering from minor physical defects or ailments which do not prevent them from supporting themselves are not likely to be refused admission on health grounds alone.

This is broadly comparable with the Aliens Order, but there are two important exceptions, viz.: The immigration officer will *not* refer the following classes of persons to the medical inspector:

1. Wives or children under 16 years of age of Commonwealth citizens resident in the United Kingdom or of Commonwealth citizens with whom the wife or child enters or seeks to enter the United Kingdom;
2. Persons ordinarily resident in the United Kingdom or who were so resident at any time within the previous two years.

A large proportion of Commonwealth immigrants now entering the country did not therefore until mid-1965 come within the categories that are subject to medical control.[2] For instance, out of 451,231 Common-

[1] See below, p. 347f., for further medical checks proposed by the White Paper.

[2] Annual Report of the Ministry of Health for the year 1964, Cmnd 2688, H.M.S.O., London, 1965. Medical examination of immigrants at ports of entry for 1965: *Commonwealth*—total arrivals, 480,026 (including 46,453 Irish Republic);

wealth immigrants arriving in 1964, 16,929 were medically examined and eight were refused permission to land for medical reasons. The figures for aliens were: 2,429,958 arriving (many short-stay visitors only), 27,832 medically examined and sixty refused permission to land. Where the power to refuse entry on medical grounds was not available, as in the case of dependants, the Government has sought to secure early treatment in the area of settlement. According to the White Paper (Cmnd 2739, 1965) measures had already been taken, in collaboration with port and local health authorities and general practitioners, to secure that an immigrant gets on the list of a family doctor immediately on arrival, is medically examined and has an X-ray if the doctor thinks this advisable.

The White Paper stressed that immigration has not created a serious public health hazard, and that such problems as have arisen in the areas where immigrants have settled have been due in the main to difficulties of adaptation to new conditions, and to disease being contracted after arrival rather than brought in. There have, however, been instances of infectious disease, especially pulmonary tuberculosis, being brought into the country.

The White Paper went on to announce the Government's decision to require home-based medical checks for all immigrants and to extend the powers to make medical inspections at British ports to all immigrants, including dependants:

> It has been decided that in future an immigrant should normally be expected to produce evidence of having undergone a medical test in his own country—both as a wise precaution and because this should reduce the risk of our having to refuse the immigrant entry at our ports. Because of the absence of the necessary legal powers it has not hitherto been possible to bring dependants of Commonwealth immigrants fully within the arrangements for medical inspection at ports. The Government have now decided that an additional power should be taken so that, at the discretion of the immigration authorities, any immigrant, including dependants, may be medically examined at the port of entry and may be required as a condition of entry to this country to report to a Medical Officer of Health with a view to necessary medical treatment being arranged. There will however be no question of refusing entry on medical grounds to entitled dependants and powers will not be taken to do this.
>
> Medical tests abroad will take time to organise in collaboration with the other Governments concerned, and legislation is needed before new conditions can be attached to entry. The necessary preparations will be put in hand, and the new arrangements introduced over a period.

---

total examined, 17,294; reports made, 226; number refused entry on medical grounds, 48. *Aliens*—total arrivals, 2,720,071; total examined, 30,166; reports made, 455; number refused entry on medical grounds, 60.

A year later, the Home Office redefined and issued a new set of 'Instructions to Immigration Officers' (Cmnd 3064, 1966). The section on refusals on medical grounds (para. 39) reads as follows:

The power to refuse admission on medical grounds does not apply to persons entitled to admission as wives, returning residents or children under sixteen. With these exceptions the Immigration Officer should normally arrange with the Medical Inspector for the examination of holders of Ministry of Labour vouchers and other Commonwealth citizens who are coming for settlement in the United Kingdom. Visitors, students and others who intend to remain in the country for six months or more should normally also be referred to the Medical Inspector. Any person, whatever the proposed length of his stay, who mentions health or the prospect of medical treatment as among the reasons for his visit, and any person who does not appear to be in good health or appears mentally or physically abnormal, should also be referred to the Medical Inspector.[1] Any person who produces a medical certificate should be advised to hand it to the Medical Inspector. Where a Medical Inspector certifies that it is undesirable for a person to be admitted for medical reasons or that he is suffering from mental disorder, the Immigration Officer should refuse admission unless there appears to be strong compassionate reasons for not doing so, in which case he should seek instructions from higher authority. Where, exceptionally, no Medical Inspector is available, the Immigration Officer may act on the advice of another duly qualified medical practitioner.

In 1965 the Ministry of Health initiated follow-up measures to promote medical and social care in the area of settlement for those who could not be refused admission and for immigrants in general. A letter was sent on 4 January 1965 to general practitioners setting out arrangements for encouraging immigrants to register promptly and for the G.P.s to arrange for X-ray, wherever desirable. This read as follows:

When they settle in this country, immigrants, both aliens and Commonwealth citizens, are often very unfamiliar with our customs and, in particular, ignorant of the scope and arrangements of the National Health Services. They may at first live under very difficult conditions and some of them in their countries of origin have been particularly subject to the risk of tuberculosis.

The main problem is, therefore, to ensure that at an early date they learn how to use the Health Service and, in particular, for us to secure by voluntary action that those from countries with a high incidence of tuberculosis—particularly from Asia—have a chest X-ray as soon as possible after their arrival in the country. The proposal to secure a chest X-ray in all cases before departure from their country of origin has been very fully explored and not found to be practicable. Nor is routine X-ray of all immigrants at the port of entry a practicable procedure, though it may be possible to arrange for limited numbers to be X-rayed.

[1] These arrangements are without prejudice to any arrangements for the time being in force under public health powers for the medical examination of all passengers from certain countries.

We have therefore been in consultation with the representatives of the medical profession and of the local authorities and the Minister has decided to take the following steps:

(a) At ports of arrival long-stay immigrants, both Commonwealth and alien, who are referred to medical inspectors will be given a hand-out printed in languages which they are likely to understand . . . the aim of which is to encourage them to get on to the list of a medical practitioner in their place of residence so that (if he thinks it desirable) he can arrange for them to go to a mass radiography unit, a chest clinic or a hospital for X-ray.

(b) Long-stay immigrants who are referred to medical inspectors at the ports will also be asked to provide their destination addresses and these will be sent to the Medical Officer of Health of the county or county borough concerned (including also Scotland and Northern Ireland) with a request that he should try to persuade the immigrants to act on the advice they have been given in the hand-out. Medical Officers of Health and local officers of the Ministries of Labour and Pensions and National Insurance will also be supplied with copies of the hand-out in case they come into contact with immigrants who have not received one or apparently lost it.

(c) In the near future it is hoped that arrangements can also be made in respect of those dependants who obtain entry certificates in their country of origin for their names and destination addresses to be entered on a tear-off slip in their passports. This slip will be detached by the immigration authorities and passed to the medical inspectors so that the port medical officer can send the address on to the appropriate Medical Officer of Health in the same way as in the case of holders of Ministry of Labour vouchers.

These procedures should, we hope, help to ensure that long-stay immigrants register with general practitioners at an early stage of their life in this country and do not wait until they fall ill. It should also help to make sure that those for whom it is appropriate have an X-ray at an early stage. We hope that in every case where you think it would be in the interests of the immigrant or his family or associates, you will agree to make the necessary arrangements for X-ray examination.

This circular was followed three months later by a second letter to Medical Officers of Health, encouraging the extension of the tuberculosis preventive services: of the B.C.G. Vaccination Scheme to immigrant school children even outside the normal age-groups, and of chest X-ray of adults and B.C.G. vaccination where appropriate.

3. CONDITIONS OF ENTRY INTO COUNTRIES OF IMMIGRATION

Some form of pre-entry medical examination is found in most countries of immigration. The B.M.A. report of 1965 looked at procedures adopted by the U.S.A., Canada, Australia, New Zealand, the

Netherlands, France, and Switzerland.[1] It found the systems adopted in the United States, Canada, Australia and New Zealand particularly relevant because of these countries' wide experience of immigration and the similarity between their procedures. Members of this working party also looked with particular interest at the experience of the Netherlands, with its immigration from overseas territories and the Caribbean.

In the latter they found no compulsory medical examination for immigrants from overseas Netherlands territories but a comprehensive medical examination in the country of origin for temporary migrant workers. With the exception of Switzerland, where immigrant workers are checked for T.B. and V.D. at a Frontier Service Post, they found two or three factors common to all systems at which they looked:

1. Medical examination has a two-fold purpose—to exclude disease and to prevent sick persons or their dependants becoming a charge on the State.
2. Medical examination is as far as possible conducted in the country of origin.
3. Medical examination is carried out by medical officers of the immigration service for the country concerned, assisted as necessary by local doctors.

The B.M.A. made the following recommendations after its 1965 report:

1. That all persons admitted to this country, other than short stay visitors, should be medically examined before admission.
2. That medical examination of persons wishing to enter the United Kingdom as immigrants should be conducted in the immigrant's country of origin.
3. (i) That every immigrant should undergo a full general medical examination, with special attention to the eyes and skin; (ii) that all immigrants over the age of 12 years should have an X-ray examination of the chest; (iii) that immigrants from certain countries, to be specified from time to time by the U.K. authorities, should have an examination of stool.

[1] *Medical Examination of Immigrants*, pp. 13–23. Its terms of reference were wide—to assemble all the facts relating to the medical examination of immigrants. It met between February and November 1965, and was guided by the following statement:

'To investigate the health problems of immigrants to this country and the possible risk of their bringing in, undetected, diseases which are potentially dangerous to the rest of the community, the B.M.A. Council today agreed to set up a four-man fact-finding Working Party. It will consist of a senior air or seaport medical officer, a chest physician, a radiologist and a medical officer of health.

'In a message the Chairman of the Public Health Committee said that he was "profoundly dissatisfied with the adequacy of the steps taken by the Ministry of Health" to detect immigrants suffering from infectious diseases and the absence of any provision for examining the dependants of immigrants was a grave and continuing risk to the health of the people of this country.

'It was felt that the whole question of the health of immigrants should be reviewed urgently by the Association and it would be the purpose of the Working Party to assemble all the facts.

'A Working Party of this size will be able to deal with the matter with the urgency that is necessary. Its members will be free to take evidence from any source they wish including people of all views.'

4. That any immigrant found to be suffering from any of the diseases or conditions listed in paragraphs 133 and 134[1] in an active or infectious form be excluded for as long as he or she continues in that condition; and that any immigrant who is suffering from any other disease which, in the opinion of the examining doctor, would constitute a risk to the health of others should, at the discretion of the U.K. authorities, be excluded.
5. That any system adopted should utilize the services of Government medical officers from this country, and, through them, of local doctors approved for the purpose by the Government of the United Kingdom.
6. That the advice on medical arrangements for long term immigrants given by the Ministry of Health in their circular letter of 22 April, 1965, be implemented with vigour.

The report also recorded the fact that between 1956 and 1964 the Representative Body of the Association had passed no fewer than eighteen resolutions urging the adoption of some form of medical examination, particularly a chest X-ray, before entry.

The Health Panel of the National Committee for Commonwealth Immigrants, chaired by Dr. C. Metcalf Brown, who had also been Chairman of the B.M.A. Working Party, later recommended that all consideration of health checks should in future move from the premise that state of health should be determined in the country of origin and not on arrival.

4. IMMIGRANTS AND PUBLIC HEALTH

The health of immigrants has been considered from two main viewpoints in various studies on the subject: (a) the introduction, reintroduction, or increasing the incidence of diseases into Britain, which are prevalent in the countries of origin of immigrants (the subject of requests for health checks, etc., in the above), and (b) the susceptibility of immigrant groups to illnesses which they may contract after their arrival here, many of which may also be common to native-born people living in similar social or working conditions.

Both approaches, and particularly the first, have sometimes led on to considerations of comparative standards of general health and rates of susceptibility to disease, and proneness to certain diseases and of possible risks to the health of the local population (sometimes couched in objective medical terms, at others in emotionally-charged anti-immigration campaigns).

The B.M.A. Report mentioned earlier in this chapter was concerned

[1] Tuberculosis, V.D., Yaws, Trachoma, Keratoconjunctivitis, Leprosy, Smallpox, Cholera, Typhus, Plague, Yellow Fever, Typhoid and paratyphoid fever, Dysentery, Parasitic infections of the gastro-intestinal tract. Mental disorders, Epilepsy, Malignant diseases, Drug addiction, Alcoholism.

primarily with diseases which might be introduced to Britain by immigrants, and in particular, diseases which might be easily communicated to other members of the public. It had this to say about the scope of the public health aspect of Commonwealth immigration:

> The problem which faces us . . . is one of concentration of immigrants in a limited number of urban areas. Although this exacerbates the difficulty of housing and education, in some ways it facilitates the provision of follow-up medical supervision in the area of residence. . . .

The Report added that it is useful to know the whereabouts of particular immigrant groups because many of the countries from which they come have their own endemic diseases and infestations, and also nutritional problems which could produce a lower resistance and a higher susceptibility to infection. Apart from communicability of disease, the Report referred briefly to some other public health problems posed by immigration: overcrowding, insanitary conditions of living, overstraining of the N.H.S. (especially the maternity services).[1]

5. SOME SPECIFIC DISEASES

A. TUBERCULOSIS

The incidence of T.B. over the country as a whole has fallen in recent years. New notifications of respiratory T.B. in England and Wales were: in 1959, 24,408; in 1963, 16,343; in 1964, 15,019 (provisional); in 1965, 13,552; in 1966, 12,372.

Deaths from all forms of T.B. have also fallen: 1961, 3,334; 1962, 3,088; 1963, 2,960; 1964, 2,484; 1965, 2,234; 1966, 2,199.

The overall incidence among immigrants is, however, much higher than that among the native-born population.

In two cities, Birmingham and Bradford, the rate of new notifications of all forms of T.B. remained roughly stationary between 1959 and 1964, largely because of the much higher rates of T.B. among Indian and Pakistani immigrants (but not West Indians). The figures for Birmingham were: 1959—793 cases, of which 113 were not born in Great Britain or Ireland, and 1964—742, of which 229 were not born in Great Britain or Ireland. In Bradford total notifications in 1959 were 285, of which ninety-two were born in Asia, and in 1964, 338 notifications, 200 of which were Asians, mainly Pakistanis.[2] In Smethwick, however, although immigrants contributed 46·8% of new T.B. cases, the total numbers fell between 1954 and 1964 from 192 to seventy-nine cases.

[1] See C.I.B.A. report on 'Immigration—Medical and Social Aspects', 1966, in a paper on 'Public Health Aspects of Migration', by K. Schwartz, and for the often controversial discussion that followed.

[2] British Tuberculosis Association Survey, 1966.

The incidence of T.B. among different immigrant groups varies. The B.M.A. Report listed the Birmingham notification figures for 1960–62 by country of origin, and the rates per 1,000 for each group.

TABLE 22

City of Birmingham, 1961 Census Population: mean annual tuberculosis notifications for 1960–62, and notification rates per 1,000 per year, by place of birth for each group

	Males			Females		
Place of Birth	Population	Mean no. of cases per yr.	Rate per 1,000 per yr.	Population	Mean no. of cases per yr.	Rate per 1,000 per yr.
England	463,648	309·7	0·67	501,570	196·3	0·39
Wales	11,232	7·3	0·65	10,328	3·3	0·32
Scotland	7,081	9·3	1·3	6,058	3·7	0·60
Ireland	32,667	69·0	2·1	26,294	35·0	1·3
Rest of Europe ...	4,296	5·0	1·2	4,125	3·3	0·8
British Caribbean	9,534	12·3	1·3	6,764	11·7	1·7
India	3,077	14·0	4·5	1,724	7·3	4·2
Pakistan/Ceylon	5,189	94·7	18·2	242	2·0	8·3
Aden	674	3·3	4·9	626 (Aden and Rest of Asia)	—	—
Rest of Asia ...	1,168	3·0	2·6			
Africa	931	2·3	2·5	629	0·3	0·5
Rest of World ...	1,668	0·7	0·4	1,295	0·3	0·5
Not stated and visitors	3,459	11·0	3·2	2,908	7·0	2·4
	544,624	541·7	0·99	562,563	270·3	0·48

Whole city: population 1,107,187; mean number of cases per year, 812·0; rate per 1,000 per year, 0·73.

The Rates per 1,000 are calculated on the basis of the 1961 Census figures, i.e. the Pakistani rate may be unduly high because of probable large-scale under-enumeration.

Source: B.M.A. Report 1965.

The British Tuberculosis Association carried out a national survey in 1965, of 3,806 notifications. The analysis showed that

rates of tuberculosis notifications were larger for those born in Ireland, the rest of Europe, the British Caribbean area, and Africa than for those born in Great Britain. But they were not more than four times as large. However, for those born in India and Pakistan the rates of tuberculosis notifications were considerably larger than for persons born in Britain—twelve times as large for those born in India, and twenty-six times as large for those born in

Pakistan. There was a higher proportion of non-respiratory T.B. among immigrants from India and Pakistan compared with those born in Britain. . . . The rate (of respiratory T.B.) for Indian immigrants was nine times, and for Pakistan twenty-two times that for British-born patients.[1]

Many smaller-scale studies have been conducted into the incidence of T.B. among various immigrant groups:

(i) *West Indians*

A study in Birmingham in 1956–7 found a low incidence of T.B. (see also Table 22); while one in London in 1957–61 suggested a lower prevalence of T.B. among West Indians than among British-born. A Birmingham study in 1964, however, found a prevalence 2–4 times that of the British-born. This might represent a real change in the incidence of T.B. among West Indians.

(ii) *Chinese*

A study in 1961 reported a high incidence of T.B. among Chinese from Hong Kong working in the catering trade in Soho, London, perhaps twelve times as high as British-born working in the same trade, and thirty times as high as the general population of south-west London.

(iii) *Cypriots*

A study in 1963 reported a high incidence of T.B. among Cypriots in London.[2]

On the general question of the extent to which tuberculosis was being imported into the country, the B.M.A. Report commented:

It is known that many immigrants come from some areas in Asia where there is a higher incidence of TB than exists in this country.[3] On the other hand, many who come from the rural areas of Pakistan, for example, have an absence of natural immunity and those of them who are exposed to infection are likely to contract the disease in an acute form. Some immigrants may, at the time of entry, have the disease in a latent form. In these cases lesions may break down under conditions of life in this country after arrival, and thus the disease is reactivated. It has been estimated, however, that somewhere between 40 per cent and 50 per cent of those male Pakistani immigrants who are ultimately found to have tuberculosis, within twelve months of immigration, would have been detected had they been X-rayed prior to entry.[4]

[1] British Tuberculosis Association Survey, 1966.

[2] Source for these studies: *Tubercle*, London, 1964, pp. 45, 279.

[3] Ireland has low rates in the rural areas, as has the British Caribbean. Asian levels are much higher than in Britain (C.I.B.A., pp. 59–60).

[4] D. K. Stevenson, 'Tuberculosis in Pakistanis in Bradford', *British Medical Journal*, 1962, 1, 1382–6.

It has been estimated that about half the cases of T.B. among immigrants are contracted after arrival in Britain. The B.M.A. Report also mentions an absence of family life, malnutrition, poor housing conditions, and urban life generally as contributory causes of poor health among immigrants, including the contraction of T.B.

B. VENEREAL DISEASES

It is traditional, as R. R. Willcox recently pointed out,[1] to blame venereal diseases, especially syphilis, on the neighbours. Hence such colloquial terms as the 'English', the 'French', the 'Spanish' disease, depending upon the nationality of the speaker.

Venereal diseases in Britain reached peak figures in 1945–6, at the end of World War II. By the mid-fifties, partly because of the availability of rapid and effective treatment with penicillin, partly because of more settled social conditions, the numbers of cases (particularly of syphilis, but also of gonorrhoea) had fallen steeply. After the low point of 1957, however, there was a rise in incidence: new cases of infectious syphilis were nearly twice what they were in 1957, while new cases of gonorrhoea had doubled since 1954, and in 1964 were at about 80% of the 1945–6 peak.

This recrudescence was (particularly among teen-agers) a world-wide phenomenon; it has occurred in the U.S.A., and a large number of European countries, including those without significant immigration. The contribution of immigrants to the current situation should therefore be critically examined.

Statistics on the incidence of venereal diseases among different immigrant groups and the U.K.-born population are available from the studies of the *British Co-Operative Clinical Group*. (Corresponding to 81–93% of all the cases treated in clinics in England and Wales.) The tables below are taken from the C.I.B.A. report, pp. 65, 66, and 67.

TABLE 23

Country of origin of patients with venereal disease, given as a percentage of the total number of patients attending clinics in England and Wales, 1964

	Primary and secondary syphilis		Gonorrhoea	
	Male	Female	Male	Female
West Indians	5·9	9·7	22·5	8·6
Other immigrants* ...	33·5	11·3	27·1	8·8
United Kingdom ...	60·6	79·0	50·4	82·6

* 'Other immigrants' include immigrants from Asia, Mediterranean, Eire, Europe, Africa, and elsewhere.

[1] C.I.B.A. Report, 'Immigration—Medical and Social Aspects'; see the chapter on 'Venereal Diseases and Immigrants' *passim* for a detailed account and statistics.

TABLE 24

Estimated numbers of cases of gonorrhoea in West Indian, other immigrants, and U.K.-born males (England and Wales)

	1952	1955	1958	1960	1961	1962	1963	1964
West Indians	465	845	5,375	6,788	8,059	8,017	7,029	6,536
Other immigrants*	4,234	3,759	5,488	6,654	7,527	7,847	7,950	7,873
U.K.-born	10,811	9,475	11,535	13,176	13,933	12,465	12,916	14,641
Total	15,510	14,079	22,398	26,398	29,519	28,329	27,895	29,050

TABLE 25

Estimated number of female patients with gonorrhoea in immigrants and others (England and Wales)

	1952	1955	1958	1960	1961	1962	1963	1964
West Indians	18	41	324	565	744	832	856	741
Other immigrants*	172	241	296	651	622	682	946	758
United Kingdom	3,395	3,484	4,869	5,936	6,222	5,595	6,352	7,116
Total	3,585	3,766	5,489	7,152	7,588	7,109	8,154	8,615

* 'Other immigrants' include immigrants from Asia, Mediterranean, Eire, Europe, Africa, and elsewhere.

At the time of the C.I.B.A. Report West Indians of both sexes were calculated to have a gonorrhoea rate more than nineteen times as high as those of the same age groups in the home population. The West Indians were by far the largest single immigrant group, their numbers rising from an estimated 3% of overall infections in 1952 to a peak of 28·3% in 1961, but declining after that to 22·5% in 1964. The rise since then has been checked, but the figures for those born in the U.K. contrive to show a rise, albeit less pronounced. Among immigrants other than West Indians, particularly Asians, there has also been a continued rise. The figures for U.K.-born females have, however, risen considerably, thereby increasing the local problem of gonorrhoea in both sexes (regardless of immigration).

The B.M.A. Report commented on the medical and social aspects of venereal diseases:

> We understand that it is the experience of venereologists in charge of clinics, that gonorrhoea and syphilis amongst male immigrants are most frequently contracted after arrival and often through the agency of white prostitutes.

This is a social as well as a medical problem, and one which medical examination prior to entry will not solve.

From this it is apparent that syphilis is not as much of a problem amongst immigrants as gonorrhoea. In any case we have been informed that infectious syphilis has not, up to now been much of a problem in this country. It is true that it is now increasing amongst the population at large, and it appears that in some instances this is being passed on to immigrants by prostitutes.

From the point of view of reducing the incidence of venereal disease, we do not consider that medical examination of immigrants to exclude cases of disease is as important as measures to improve contact tracing and to provide better social circumstances and readily available facilities for diagnosis and treatment. We have referred already to the desirability of admitting immigrants in family groups, so far as possible, and to the continuing need for good after-care. Nevertheless, it is only sensible that when a prospective immigrant who is suffering from venereal disease in an active form seeks admission to this country, he or she should be excluded until treatment has been given and a cure has been effected.

Yaws. We feel that persons suffering from this disease should not be admitted whilst the disease, which is so readily susceptible to a single dose of penicillin, remains active. This would, in practice, probably produce no appreciable delay in a prospective immigrant's entry into this country.

C. SMALLPOX AND LEPROSY

These traditionally abhorrent diseases have both been utilized in the political debate over immigration.[1] The B.M.A. in its report recommended that all persons, immigrant or not, should, coming from an infected local area or endemic area, who are not in possession of a satisfactory certificate of vaccination, be refused permission to land.

A similar provision should apply to the other international quarantinable diseases, viz. plague, cholera, yellow fever, typhus.

On leprosy the Report took an unemotional stand:

At the end of 1963, the Leprosy Register maintained by the Ministry of Health showed that there were 291 cases outstanding in England and Wales of whom 168 were classified as quiescent.[2] Corresponding figures for 1964

[1] Smallpox among Pakistanis came into the news in early 1962, at the height of the debate on the Commonwealth Immigrants Act. See above, p. 20; also I.R.R. *Newsletter*, November 1963; Eric Butterworth, 'The 1962 Smallpox Outbreak and the British Press', *Race*, Vol. VII, no. 4, April 1966. Leprosy figures have been asked for in Parliament from time to time and in addition the Prime Minister, Mr. Harold Wilson, in November 1964, used the phrase 'Parliamentary leper' in connexion with the campaign of the victorious Smethwick Tory, Mr. Peter Griffiths, thereby earning a rebuke from several medical correspondents who objected to this lay perpetuation of an unjust and outmoded stereotype.

[2] Annual Report of the Chief Medical Officer to the Ministry of Health, 1963, H.M.S.O., London.

were 340 and 159.[1] More up-to-date figures were given by the Minister of Health in a written answer to a Parliamentary Question on 19th July 1965, when he said that there were 336 cases in England and Wales at 5th July 1965, an increase of 106 compared with 31st December 1960.

The great majority of cases of leprosy existing in this country are under adequate control and treatment and only a very few constitute a potential health hazard. There is, however, some evidence that those suffering from the disease attempt to conceal it, and in the early ineffective stages it is difficult to recognize. As the disease may have taken ten years or more to declare itself, it is difficult to guess at the future size of the problem. All in all, we feel that whilst recognizing that much public reaction to the subject is emotionally generated, it would be a mistake to dismiss the risk altogether. Further, a medical examination which detected the presence of the disease would be in the patient's own interest. We consider that the general medical examination of the patient should include a thorough examination of the skin and that entry should be refused where the disease is found in an active and infectious form. Where the disease is of long-standing and in a quiescent state, we see no reason why the patient should not be admitted, subject to appropriate medical surveillance at least for some time.

6. SUSCEPTIBILITY TO DISEASE—ENVIRONMENTAL FACTORS

Immigrants may be susceptible to illness for a number of different, mainly environmental, reasons, some of which are shared by certain elements among the native-born population:

(1) Change of location in itself involves a greater exposure to disease.

(2) Change of diet and climate can lead to nutritional disorders.

(3) Housing conditions may be poorer than among the general population.

(4) Working conditions may be poorer than in the general population.

(5) Immigrants may be subject to greater stresses than the native-born, and in the first years probably lack the compensating factor of family life and security.

Such factors are contributory causes of illnesses such as T.B., venereal diseases, rickets, and anaemia, and a condition akin to eczema in children. The Plowden Report commented, with regard to the health of immigrant children:

> Although some immigrant children are at first upset by the English climate, they are usually well nourished and clothed. When their health is poor, this is usually due to complaints which were common among working-class people before the last war.

[1] Annual Report of the Chief Medical Officer to the Ministry of Health, 1964, H.M.S.O., London.

A condition which is *not* acquired in Britain, but imported, is infestation by worms. Most types are not transmittable in Britain; hookworm, however, can be transmitted. Dr. B. Gans (Greenwich District Hospital, London), in the C.I.B.A. Report, stated: 'Among children recently arrived from the West Indies, worm infestation is not uncommon. . . . I doubt if they (these types of worm infestation) constitute an important paediatric or public health problem. . . .'[1]

A. CLIMATE AND DIET

Life in a cold climate may require a different diet to maintain health. Dr. Simon Yudkin (Whittington Hospital, Highgate, London), in a paper 'The Health and Welfare of the Immigrant Child', pointed out the necessity for immigrant children to take vitamin D to prevent rickets. This disease has reappeared in Britain after its disappearance for about ten years. Dr. Gans reported that West Indian mothers traditionally do not offer a balanced diet to their babies until well into the second year; until then children are fed milk and carbohydrate weaning foods, which contain practically no iron, so West Indian babies are frequently anaemic. This too carries the danger of rickets. Some local authorities have taken action and produced educational material about the nutritional requirements of children. The Slough Health Centre, for example, had pamphlets printed in Urdu, Hindi, and Punjabi. The reappearance of rickets has also been reported from Scotland and elsewhere with reference to Pakistani and other Asian children.

Poor housing and multi-occupation are a contributory cause of health hazards among immigrants and others in the same circumstances. For example, it is not easy to arrange home confinements, and there is a greater risk of home accidents, especially from oil-heaters. A report published by the Slough Council of Social Service states:

> The use of such oil heaters will continue wherever overcrowding is experienced, because: (a) individual electricity meters rarely are provided and it would be difficult for tenants and landlords to agree on the cost of heating by electric fires; (b) gas supplies are often not piped to individual rooms, with coin meters; (c) it is difficult for several tenants to maintain and account for supplies of coal in limited storage space; (d) oil heaters are portable and reasonably economical when operated with care, according to instructions. . . .

The Consumer Council has published a leaflet in Urdu and Punjabi about the care needed in operating oil fires, and pointing out that it is an offence to leave a child under 12 alone in a room with an unguarded fire or heater. A number of fires have been caused by oil heaters not conforming to British standards.

[1] 'Immigration—Medical and Social Aspects', p. 87.

Working conditions may cause some diseases, or higher incidence of diseases, among immigrant groups. For example, the studies of T.B. among Chinese, and among Cypriots, referred to above, were both related to workers in the catering trade, in which T.B. rates are higher than in the general population. Similarly, work in the mills, in areas like Bradford, may contribute to the high incidence of T.B. among Pakistani immigrants there.

CHAPTER 11

Crime and Enforcement

1. DELINQUENCY AMONG IMMIGRANTS

Reports about crime and immigrants suffer from similar handicaps to those concerned with immigration and health. National origin may not be the most useful, and is certainly not the only, basis for analysing such statistics as there are: comparisons with the overall crime-rate are likely to be less meaningful than comparisons with similar socio-economic, age, residential, or other groups among the native-born population.

In the case of crime, no conclusions can be drawn about the criminal tendencies of various national groups. Crime rates for the countries of origin, and for immigrant groups in Britain, differ completely: in some cases the home-country rates are much lower, in others higher than the available figures suggest for immigrants resident in Britain. There is also the problem that little specialized research on delinquency among immigrants has been published,[1] and that no single set of figures of convictions and prisoners, broken down by country of origin, can on its own be relied on as a statement of 'the truth about crime among immigrants'. Discussion about crime levels among immigrant groups can become emotionally charged, and statistics are frequently used in a wrong or distorted context to make sweeping political points.[2] As Terence Morris wrote in 1964:

> It was most unfortunate that, immediately prior to one of the vital stages of the discussion of the Commonwealth Immigrants Bill, an article in *The Times* anticipated the publication of the material in this book in such a way as to suggest that coloured immigrants from overseas were responsible for a significant proportion of the increase in violent crime.[3] The effect,

[1] John Lambert has carried out a study, as part of the Survey of Race Relations, with assistance from the Centre of Urban and Regional Studies, Birmingham University, on crime rates and police attitudes towards immigrants, in a Birmingham police district which covers areas with high concentrations of Commonwealth and Irish immigrants. See article in *Sunday Times*, 30 July 1967, on preliminary findings.

[2] The bulk of the following section, including Tables 26 and 27, is drawn from an article by A. E. Bottoms, Research Officer at the Institute of Criminology, University of Cambridge, on 'Delinquency among Immigrants', *Race*, Vol. VIII, no. 4, April 1967.

[3] Similar references to this material were made more recently by Mr. Norman Pannell, M.P. (Hansard, 27 November, col. 396) and in the *Sunday Telegraph* 29 December 1963).

though hardly deliberate, was almost certainly unfortunate. It assisted in hardening the stereotypes of the racially prejudiced, who welcomed with enthusiasm any attempt to stem the flow of coloured people into this country, and who were already scraping the bottom of the barrel for rationalisations in the form of arguments about housing and health.[1]

A. IRISH IMMIGRANTS

Bottoms concluded that, even allowing for the fact that many Irish are in the younger adult age groups, Irish immigrants are on the whole over-represented in the crime figures, compared with the overall population, particularly in the case of robbery statistics.

Nevertheless, he warned readers that this conclusion must be qualified by looking at the unemployment rates among Irish immigrants (higher than for native-born) and such factors as their social class, and the type of urban neighbourhood in which they live, etc. The apparently high incidence of Irish crime in England poses important problems in crime causation, especially when compared with the very low rates of crime in Ireland itself. Suggestions for further research into this include examination of the impact of urban environment upon former rural immigrants, and the consequences of the removal of the external controls of the Church and the family, when an immigrant comes to Britain from Ireland.

TABLE 26

Violent crime in London, 1950–1960

Offenders (of both sexes) convicted of indictable crimes of violence in the Metropolitan Police District in 1950, 1957 and 1960, classified by place of birth and type of violence committed. *Source: Crimes of Violence* by F. H. McClintock assisted by N. Howard Avison *et al.* (1963).

1950	U.K.	Eire	Common-wealth	Others	Total
1. Sex offences	30	6	1	1	38
2. Attacks on police ...	141	12	4	4	161
3. Domestic disputes ...	255	29	29	13	326
4. Fights in pubs.	128	24	6	1	159
5. Attacks in streets ...	178	16	14	—	208
Total	732	87	54	19	892
Total minus domestic disputes	477	58	25	6	566
% full total	82·1	9·7	6·1	2·1	100·0
% minus domestic disputes...	84·3	10·2	4·4	1·1	100·0

[1] T. Morris, 'Crimes of Violence' (in a review of the book of the same title by F. H. McClintock, London, MacMillan, 1963, I.R.R. *Newsletter*, February 1964).

1957	U.K.	Eire	Common-wealth	Others	Total
1. Sex offences	46	3	2	2	53
2. Attacks on police ...	157	40	12	6	215
3. Domestic disputes ...	296	63	79	21	459
4. Fights in pubs.... ...	184	53	33	7	277
5. Attacks in streets ...	268	40	39	7	354
Total	951	199	165	43	1,358
Total minus domestic disputes	655	136	86	22	899
% full total	70·0	14·7	12·2	3·1	100·0
% minus domestic disputes	72·9	15·1	9·6	2·4	100·0

1960*	U.K.	Eire	Common-wealth	Others	Total
1. Sex offences	100	—	8	—	108
2. Attacks on police ...	180	36	40	12	268
3. Domestic disputes ...	360	88	140	16	604
4. Fights in pubs.... ...	284	52	4	16	356
5. Attacks in streets ...	352	44	40	16	452
Total	1,276	220	232	60	1,788
Total minus domestic disputes	916	132	92	44	1,184
% full total	71·4	12·3	13·0	3·3	100·0
% minus domestic disputes	77·4	11·1	7·8	3·7	100·0

1961 Census (Males)					
L.C.C. area	83·5	4·4	6·8	4·7	100·0 (0·6 not stated)
Greater London area ...	89·0	3·1	4·2	3·3	100·0 (0·4 not stated)

* Estimate based on a 50 per cent sample of cases in the first half of the year.

Bottoms added that, if the Irish were grouped together with other foreign-born offenders in this study, it could be shown (i) there was a significant difference between the pattern of robbery-types of offenders born within and without the U.K., and that this difference existed in both 1950 and 1957; (ii) that there was no significant difference in the distribution of types of robbery between the two years when the two groups of those born within and without the U.K. were analysed separately; and that (iii) the *overall* distribution of types had changed significantly between 1950 and 1957, so that it could be deduced that the increase in proportion of the foreign-born had significantly affected the overall distribution of robbery-types. (For these and other statistical calculations the writer acknowledged his debt to Mr. Timothy Jones.)

B. 'NEW' COMMONWEALTH IMMIGRANTS

The available figures show that the incidence of crime among 'new' Commonwealth immigrants is not excessive. An examination of Table 26 shows that, if domestic disputes are excluded, the proportion of crimes of violence committed by Commonwealth immigrants fell between 1957 and 1960, and that, even in 1957, it was only one and a half times as great as the norm for the general population in the Metropolitan police district[1] (the L.C.C. area). An examination of Table 27 indicates that where Commonwealth immigrants are involved in crime, it is in crimes against the person and not in crimes against property.[2]

TABLE 27

Immigrants appearing at Bradford Court, 1965

Offenders (of both sexes), aged over 17 appearing at Bradford City Magistrates' Court between 30 June and 28 August 1965, who were dealt with in No. 1 Court (where the great majority of non-motoring cases are heard), classified by nationality. *Source:* unpublished data collected by Court observation by Mr. A. K. Bottomley of Cambridge, and made available by Mr. Bottomley and the Clerk to the Justices, Bradford, to the writer.

(a) Indictable Cases

Nationality	Group A* (Violence against person)		Group B* (Larceny, etc.)		Group C* (Breaking offences)		Total	
	No.	%	No.	%	No.	%	No.	%
Great Britain ...	12	53·1	121	89·7	39	92·9	172	86·9
Pakistan/India ...	5	23·8	8	5·9	—	—	13	6·6
Ireland (all parts) ...	—	—	5	3·7	3	7·1	8	4·0
West Indies ...	3	14·3	—	—	—	—	3	1·5
Other immigrants ...	1	4·8	1	0·7	—	—	2	1·0
Total	21	100·0	135	100·0	42	100·0	198	100·0

* Only persons in certain offence categories were included. So: *Group A excludes* homicide, robbery with violence (but not simple robbery), and sex offences except rape and assault with intent to rape, and *includes* possessing offensive weapons; *Group B includes* larceny, taking and driving away, all indictable fraudulent offences, and receiving; *Group C excludes* sacrilege and possessing housebreaking implements by night.

[1] Bottoms commented: 'In the light of all this, it can be seen how totally without foundation is the assertion by Norman Pannell, M.P., in a recent book (*Immigration —What is the Answer?*) that it would appear from Mr. McClintock's book that

(b) Non-Indictable 'Public Order' Offences

Nationality	Drunk and Disorderly		Breach of Peace, Wilful Damage, etc.		Total	
	No.	%	No.	%	No.	%
Great Britain ...	66	74·2	26	56·5	92	68·2
Pakistan/India ...	1	1·1	4	8·7	5	3·7
Ireland (all parts) ...	10	11·2	15	32·6	25	18·5
West Indies	—	—	—	—	—	—
Other immigrants ...	12	13·5	1	2·2	13	9·6
Total...	89	100·0	46	100·0	135	100·0

(c) Overall Population, Bradford

Percentages of place of birth of male persons resident in Bradford County Borough at the time of the 1961 census:

	%
Great Britain	90·6
Ireland (all parts)	1·6
Commonwealth	4·0
Foreign countries	3·2
Birthplace not stated	0·6
Total...	100·0

Two categories of crime in which Commonwealth immigrants are very much over-represented in proportion to their numbers in the London Metropolitan area are crimes involving prostitution and possession of drugs. In the year 1962–3 Commonwealth immigrants were responsible for 43·4% of convictions in the Metropolitan area for living

immigrants are guilty of at least six times as many crimes of violence, in relation to their numbers, as the indigenous population.' It should be added that the co-author of this book, Fenner Brockway, does not give a résumé of the available statistics in his attempt to refute allegations of criminality, but falls back upon the deportation returns as an indication of the incidence of crime (158 West Indians, 4 Indians and 6 Pakistanis as compared with 378 Irish, 26 Maltese, 13 Cypriots and 10 Canadians for the two and a half years from July 1964) (p. 99). Norman Pannell correctly points out that only immigrants with less than five years' residence are liable for deportation if convicted of a serious crime, so that this is not an adequate indication of overall crime incidence (p. 31).

[2] A similar picture was presented for Birmingham in 1962 and 1963 by the authors of a Bow Group pamphlet, *Immigration, Race and Politics—A Birmingham View*, published in March 1966. This also mentioned high rates for possessing drugs (mostly West Indians possessing marijuana or *cannabis indica*) and high rates among the Irish for crimes against property.

on immoral earnings[1] and 60·3% of all convictions for possession of drugs (though this proportion may well have declined recently in view of the rapid increase of drug-taking among the English). Social factors which may be partly responsible for this include the greater frequentation of prostitutes by an immigrant population with a high proportion of single men, and the customary taking of marijuana (but not 'hard' drugs) by some West African and Caribbean groups. Since both appetites can be commercialized, it is possible that the figures represent to some extent an organized minority of professional criminals in these fields.

A. E. Bottoms concluded:

> On the available evidence there is then no general immigrant crime problem in Britain, at least relative to other criminal problems. The Irish rates tend to be relatively high, but do not seem to have changed much over the years. There are many social factors which might explain the high rates if systematically examined. . . . As for Commonwealth immigrants,[2] they seem to be almost remarkably crime-free except in relation to violent offences, and even here the threat of the group to the society at large is diminished by the high incidence of domestic violence [which can] turn a moderate domestic quarrel into an indictable offence.

C. JUVENILE DELINQUENCY

As the number of younger and second generation immigrants grows, this will be a subject of increasing importance and urgency on which continuing research is needed. American experience is that crime rates for the second generation of immigrants are almost universally higher than for the first, however high or low that may have been in relation to other groups, including the majority society. A second American conclusion is that groups actively seeking assimilation are likely to show higher crime rates than self-segregating groups, indicating a possible resort to delinquency as a rebellion against failure to achieve adequate acceptance.

In Britain, some of the known social conditions in which children of immigrants live give cause for concern: e.g. the growing number of coloured children in care of the local authorities;[3] the splitting up of

[1] Source—Home Secretary in the Commons in July 1963 (quoted by Pannell, op. cit., pp. 29–30). This was out of a total of 182 convictions for possession of drugs, of which 79 were of Commonwealth citizens (including 20 Maltese and 8 Cypriots), 22 of Irish. The figures for drug convictions over the same twelve months were 607, of whom 372 were from the Commonwealth.

[2] He also deplored the lack of differentiation between the four main groups of new Commonwealth immigrants, West Indians, Indians, Pakistanis, and West Africans, as well as the Cypriots and Maltese (all of whom make different kinds of response to the host society).

[3] See Katrin Fitzherbert, *West Indian Children in London*, Bell, London, 1967.

parents, or of brothers and sisters, due to immigration by stages,[1] poor housing condition and inadequate nursery schooling, and so on. The existence of hostility and discrimination towards coloured people and the awareness of this passed on from parents to their children could also be pointers to a possible problem of delinquency. In view of the generally low rates of crime among Commonwealth immigrants, however, second generation rates may not be dramatically higher, at least among West Indian immigrants.

2. IMMIGRANTS AND THE POLICE

A. RECRUITMENT OF COLOURED POLICEMEN

The issue of recruitment of coloured police can be seen both as one aspect of the employment sphere with reference to the special role of the policeman, to placing coloured immigrants in jobs involving contact with the public, and also authority over members of the public, and also as an aspect of police-immigrant relationships.

The recruitment of coloured police has been seen as one step to improving police-immigrant relationships, both by the Home Office and by various West Indian organizations. In February 1966, the then Home Secretary, Mr. Jenkins, in reply to a question at a Press conference, said that he would like to see more coloured policemen in Britain if suitable applicants came forward. He thought this might do something to bridge the gap between coloured immigrants and the police.

The response of the Police Federation was that any move to establish a more direct contact between the police and the coloured immigrant communities was welcome: 'A useful purpose is served by recognising that tensions do exist. . . . Mr. Jenkins believes that this move will foster better race relations; we do not disagree with him.' It pointed out that recruitment was the responsibility of the Chief Constable in each area.

In March 1966 the Chief Constable of Coventry, who was also President of the Association of Chief Police Officers in 1966, went on record in favour of recruitment of coloured police officers, not for special work among immigrants[2] but for ordinary police duties (Bradford had earlier appointed some coloured 'police-immigrant liaison' officers). In the same month Coventry became the first town to recruit a coloured police officer, a former officer of the Tanzanian police, Mohamed Daar, who had come to Britain from East Africa in November 1965. In July 1966, Birmingham accepted two coloured

[1] There is also the problem of generational clashes between old-country norms and culture patterns and those acquired by the second generation in Britain. (See Patterson, *Immigrants in London*, pp. 34–5).

[2] This proposal has sometimes been made in earlier years, but was rejected on the grounds that Britain is not an apartheid state, with separate 'racial' police forces to deal only with their own groups.

police officer recruits, a Trinidadian and a Pakistani (both subsequently had racialist slogans painted near their homes).

In October 1966, Mr. Jenkins said in his speech at Goldsmiths Hall that he wanted 'far more coloured magistrates, police, fire and ambulance men'. In December 1966, the first coloured school-leaver joined the police cadets—in Bath. London appointed its first coloured cadet early in 1967. Earlier statements had expressed the view that the time was not yet ripe and that appointments should be made from second-generation or longer-settled immigrants.

In a written reply to a question in Parliament in April 1967, the following minimum figures were given for coloured staff in the police, prison service, fire service, and probation service in England and Wales:

Police, 6; Prison Service, 34; Fire Brigades, 9; Probation Service, 9.

The following information was also given in April 1967 about coloured applicants to the Metropolitan Police, for 1966:

36 coloured people applied; none were appointed. 5 were offered interviews, but 4 failed to attend, and the one who did so was said to be not up to standard. Of those not offered an interview, 17 were recent arrivals[1] to Britain, 7 had had a poor education, 5 were rejected on medical grounds, 1 was rejected because he did not attain the required height (5ft 8in) and 1 was rejected because he was over the age limit (30 years old).

A number of coloured J.P.s have been appointed since the beginning of 1966, in London and several other towns. Eric Irons was the first in Nottingham in 1962 and Mrs. Crabbe the last in London in 1967.

B. POLICE–IMMIGRANT RELATIONS

No serious or systematic inquiry into police–immigrant relations as a whole in Britain has been carried out[2] and inevitably it is the cases of actual bad relations or complaints that are most widely reported and publicized.[3]

[1] This is not a reason for rejection in all forces; e.g. Coventry's first coloured policeman, Mohamed Daar, appointed in March 1966, had come to Britain in November 1965.

[2] But see Michael Banton, *The Policeman in the Community*, for an analysis of the policeman's general role. See also *Police—A Social Study*, Church Information Office, April 1967.

[3] For instance, when C.A.R.D. in April 1967 published a report giving a selection of forty-three complaints of discrimination which were thought to stand up to examination, most press reports concentrated on the five complaints against the police. See also the wide coverage given to the somewhat sensationally-titled W.I.S.C. pamphlet by Joseph A. Hunte, *Nigger Hunting in England?*, concentrating on the complaints section but not on the moderate general comments (e.g. on West Indian attitudes to the police at home) and the positive suggestions for improvement. For police reactions to the charges, see I.R.R. *Newsletter*, June 1966, p. 11.

The Campaign Against Racial Discrimination, the West Indian Standing Conference (London), the National Council for Civil Liberties (see also their 1963 pamphlet, *Civil Liberties and the Police*, especially p. 6), Willesden and Brent International Friendship Council, Islington C.A.R.D. branch, Manchester C.A.R.D. branch, have all received a number of complaints from coloured immigrants against members of the police.[1] The complaints did not always allege racial bias or claim that no other groups receive poor treatment, although in certain cases racial abuse played a large part, indicating racial bias in treatment.

Complaints and allegations have covered the following points:

(1) Lack of protection, or failure to take action, against assaults on coloured people, or attacks on their property, either by racialist groups (e.g. in Leamington Spa in the summer and autumn of 1966, or in Southall when there was a series of window-breaking attacks), or by apparently non-political groups picking upon coloured people and attacking them either for purposes of theft, or simply in order to beat them up (e.g. in the Belsize Park and King's Cross area in the autumn and winter of 1965 and 1966). In some of these cases, representations to the local police, sometimes through Scotland Yard (in London) by the local community, or by the High Commissions concerned, could have led to redistribution or an increase in police patrolling in the affected areas. (In Leamington Spa in the autumn of 1966, local Indian shopkeepers were reported to be arming themselves with shotguns to warn off potential window-breakers, because the attacks had continued over such a long period.)

(2) Bias in making arrests, or in failing to make arrests (e.g. a case was reported from Willesden in which a West Indian asked the police to do something to prevent his Irish neighbour from parking his car in front of the West Indian's home, and was told that nothing could be done. When he parked his own car in front of the Irish man's house, he was arrested and fined for obstruction).

(3) Police brutality on or off police premises, sometimes followed by arrest and prosecution for assault on the police. The use of force where this was not normal, or warranted, e.g. the alleged use of dogs to a group of West Indians in South London following a private party, one of the cases described in West Indian Standing Conference report, *Nigger Hunting in England* by Joseph Hunte.

(4) Victimization over a period of time, and racial abuse.

[1] Over recent years, relations between police and the public as a whole have been the subject of debate and inquiry, including the Royal Commission on the Police (report published in 1962), to which over fifty individuals and organizations reported. See also Derrick Sington's article on 'Police and Immigrants' (*New Society*, 24 February 1966).

(5) Attempts to persuade people to drop cases, either against other members of the public, or against the police.

(6) 'Framing' of people, in particular by drug-planting.

Individual cases which have been reported to the organizations above, have been taken up from time to time—either by means of publicity and public discussion or by formal police inquiry. The Campaign Against Racial Discrimination has a 'Law and Order' sub-committee, to which delegates from other organizations are invited, and which is attempting to collect evidence and co-ordinate policy on these matters. C.A.R.D. has called for the setting up of a 'civilian review board' to investigate complaints about police conduct. So far, however, complaints have generally been dealt with on a piecemeal basis, by those submitting them, and by the particular police forces against whom the complaints have been made. In the case, however, of the pamphlet by Joseph Hunte, Chief Superintendent J. R. Norman, at that time police liaison officer for coloured immigrants in London, commented: 'Speaking in broad terms, I would have thought relations between police and immigrants were improving. We are getting used to each other.' He added that Scotland Yard had supplied some statistics for Joe Hunte's report. The allegations made in the report were denied by the Metropolitan Police.

In July 1965, in answer to a question by Mr. Paul Rose, M.P., about the training and educational measures employed by the Metropolitan Police to promote a greater understanding of the problems of immigrant communities, with a view to securing better relations between the police and all sections of the public, Sir Frank Soskice pointed out that the Commissioner of Police of the Metropolis had made special arrangements to promote greater understanding of the problems of immigrant communities. These arrangements included a series of talks given last year by a member of the Staff of the High Commissioner for Jamaica to the teaching staff of the two metropolitan police training schools, and the inclusion of this subject in the regular talks on current affairs given at schools. The attendance at one of the training schools of numbers of overseas students from all parts of the Commonwealth, was, Sir Frank maintained, also helping greatly to promote understanding. Furthermore the Chief Superintendent had been given special responsibility for liaison between the Metropolitan Police and representatives of coloured immigrants and was active in promoting closer contacts.

At the end of 1966 the National Committee for Commonwealth Immigrants reported:

> Reports from various parts of the country indicate that in some areas there is a lack of confidence between police and immigrants and allegations are made from time to time of police discrimination, inadequate protection for

immigrants and prejudiced behaviour. The Committee has recommended a number of positive measures designed to restore confidence and to assist both police and immigrants. On the basis of studies made, the Committee has discussed with the Home Secretary the possibility of establishing an independent means of investigating complaints, the recruitment of more coloured policemen, the establishment of an exchange scheme with Commonwealth forces at all levels, and methods for closer liaison and incorporation of appropriate material in police training courses. Although agreement was not reached on all these matters, the discussions have produced useful results, particularly on the question of training. There is to be an increasing use of outside speakers on the subject of race and community relations at police training courses and the Committee hopes to assist in this most important field throughout 1967.

CHAPTER 12

Extremist, Racialist, and Fringe Organizations[1]

1. THE POST-FASCIST AND NEO-NAZI GROUPINGS

The policies, practices, and in many cases the leading personnel of the insignificant post-Fascist, neo-Fascist and neo-Nazi groupings in Britain today can be traced back to the far larger and more menacing movement of the inter-war years. Then the movement achieved its strength against a background of mass unemployment and widespread disillusionment with the traditional political parties and capitalism and Communism alike. The theme was a 'Greater Britain' and the scapegoat was, increasingly, international Communism and international Jewry. Today, such influence as the various splinter-groups have achieved, apart from their appeal to a handful of individuals of idiosyncratic or aberrant psychological make-up, may perhaps be attributed to such factors as lowered national status and prestige, producing a climate of 'post-imperial blues', the aimlessness of the affluence-oriented society and the shadow of nuclear warfare. The theme for the post-Fascist and neo-Nazi leaders remains a 'Greater Britain', although different methods of achieving it are advocated. A new scapegoat has been added, that of the Negro or coloured immigrant, who provides a day-to-day reminder of lost glories overseas and present problems at home, and who is a competitor for housing, jobs, and women.

A. THE UNION MOVEMENT

Still officially led by Sir Oswald Mosley, a sophisticated political veteran of seventy, this was formed in London on 7 February 1948 and is the political successor of his pre-war British Union of Fascists. It has dropped or modified many of its pre-war policies and ideas, and, unlike the neo-Nazi groups, the Union Movement has discarded the narrow Fascist or National-Socialist nationalism of pre-1939 days and favours union with Europe,[2] with Africa protected from Soviet intervention by

[1] In early 1967 the available hard information about the various tiny 'black racialist' and 'black power' groups was insufficient to allow of an accurate coverage and evaluation here. This was despite regular appearance by some of their members at Speakers' Corner, Hyde Park, and despite earlier inflated coverage of one group, the Racial Adjustment Action Society and its colourful leader, Michael de Freitas (otherwise Michael X or Michael Abdul Malik) by some sections of the national press.

[2] Unlike the B.N.P. and the N.S.M. (see below).

a new African Monroe doctrine and subdivided into separate black and white states, the latter only being involved in a European-African economy (this is a 'wind of change' modification of Mosley's earlier, post-war plan for the pooling of African colonies to provide a source of raw materials for Europe). In internal policies the Union Movement has discarded the idea of the one-party state and the corporate state; instead it advocates a creed of 'European Socialism', a combination of syndicalism and private enterprise designed to appeal to the 'small man'.

Officially, anti-Semitism has been dropped but there is still a good deal of latent, residual anti-Semitic feeling which emerges in private discussion or under heckling. The 'colour problem' has taken the place of the 'Jewish problem' and the Movement has concentrated on areas, such as North Kensington (of Notting Hill disturbances fame), with large coloured settlements. Here Sir Oswald Mosley stood as parliamentary candidate in 1959, losing his deposit for the first time in his political career. (At Shoreditch and Finsbury in 1966 he got 4·6% of the poll—1,126 votes.) The Movement's official policy on immigration is that all immigrants should have their fares paid home and that British policy should be changed to see that they have good jobs and fair wages there, at least in so far as the West Indies are concerned. Sir Oswald himself believes that race crossing is undesirable on genetic grounds, but denies that he has ever accepted Nazi racialist doctrines. Colour prejudice emerges more strongly amongst members of the Union Movement rank-and-file, but it is likely that the more bigoted anti-Semites and racialists have been skimmed off or gravitated to one of the neo-Nazi groupings.

The Union Movement had about a thousand members at the beginning of 1961. Like the B.U.F., it has long revolved around its leader, Mosley, who, despite his virtual eclipse in 1939, was always a man of far greater personal, intellectual, and political calibre than anyone else in the three groups. His son Max plays an active part, but the effective leader, propagandist and organizer is Jeffrey Hamm, a minor B.U.F. member in Harrow before the war who, after detention under Defence Regulation 18B, joined the Royal Tank Corps. After the war, he founded the British League of Ex-Servicemen, which ran regular open-air meetings in the East End, notably at Ridley Road. The Movement's publication is the bi-weekly *Action*; its symbol is a lightning flash in a circle. Five U.M. candidates stood (unsuccessfully) in the 1967 G.L.C. elections.

B. THE BRITISH NATIONAL PARTY

Like the British National Socialist Movement, which it ejected in April 1962, the B.N.P. is more directly inspired by German Fascism and Aryan and Nordic racialism, whereas Mosleyism drew its main initial strength from Italian Fascism and acquired its anti-Semitic, pro-Nazi orientations only after a year or so of life.

The B.N.P. stands for the synthesis of patriotism and socialism, is attempting to achieve success by legal, political means, and is careful to avoid infringements of law and order at its public meetings. One or two members have recently been expelled for disregarding this policy. It was founded by a 35-year-old industrial chemist and journalist, John Bean of Thornton Heath. Since 1959, its president has been 49-year-old Andrew Fountaine, a wealthy Norfolk landowner who fought for Franco in Spain, rose from ordinary seaman to lieutenant-commander in the Navy during the War and subsequently entered politics as a far-right, anti-Communist Conservative. After Central Office refused to endorse him as candidate for Chorley, Lancashire, in 1950, he formed his own party, the National Front, in 1953, but lost his deposit when standing as a 'National' candidate in Norfolk South-West in 1959.

John Bean, who has described himself as the 'British Goebbels', started his political career some thirteen years ago, like Colin Jordan and John Tyndall, in the League of Empire Loyalists; this was founded in 1954 by A. K. Chesterton, the former editor of the B.U.F.'s *Action*, who represented the super-patriotic rather than the Nazi stand in pre-war Fascism and National Socialism. By June 1958 Bean and Tyndall had led a dissatisfied group of members out to form the National Labour Party, with headquarters in Thornton Heath, Croydon. This group was active in Notting Hill during the disturbances in September 1958. It moved to Arnold Leese's[1] House at 74 Princedale Road, Notting Hill, where Colin Jordan's White Defence League (slogan—'Keep Britain White'; publication—*Black and White News*) was established in November 1958. In 1960 the N.L.P. merged with the White Defence League to form the British National Party (symbol—the 'sun-wheel' cross of Arminius, who defeated the Roman Legions in the Teutoberger Forest in A.D. 9; publication—*Combat*). Apart from its activities in Britain, the B.N.P. began to extend its links with Nordic-minded groups of similar political beliefs belonging to a 'North European Ring' and located in Stockholm, Reykjavik, Bodo (Norway), Brussels, Copen-

[1] Arnold Spencer Leese—born 1877, a retired veterinary surgeon of 'Nordic' appearance with service in India and Africa. He led the small, Nazi-modelled, racialist, anti-Semitic 'Imperial Fascists' from 1929 to 1940 and was never linked with Mosley, whom he dismissed as a 'kosher Fascist'. Before the war, he was sentenced to six months' imprisonment on charges of 'inciting a public mischief' against His Majesty's subjects of the Jewish faith (by allegations that they indulged in ritual murder). Detained under Defence Regulations 18B between 1940 and 1943, he celebrated V.E. Day with a book arguing that with the defeat of Hitler, the Jews and Freemasons had won a battle but not necessarily the war. He died in 1956, leaving a young friend, Colin Jordan, to continue the political campaign.

hagen, Greece, Pietermaritzburg, Birmingham, Alabama and Arlington, Virginia (publication—*The Northern European*, edited by Colin Jordan).

The Jordan–Bean merger was prompted, according to Bean's account after the break-up, by the fact that Mrs. Leese, Arnold Leese's widow, had leased to Jordan the house in Princedale Road, which had since the early 1950s been the site of the Britons' Publishing Society.[1]

By early 1962 Fountaine and Bean, according to their own statements to the press, had decided that Jordan's activities were compromising their hopes of winning wider support and perhaps attracting Union Movement supporters. Bean told a *Daily Mail* reporter that Jordan had a 'Fuehrer obsession' and was a 'Hitler-loving rebel': 'All Jordan ever wanted to be was to be a disciple of Hitler. By aping the jackboots, uniforms, customs and ideology of Germany in the thirties he was doing us more harm than good.' (10 August 1962.) Noyes Thomas of the *News of the World* (9 September 1962) quoted Fountaine as saying: 'Jordan was like an in-growing toenail. Now he's out we are a lot more comfortable. We gained a lot by his expulsion.' The gain was expressed in terms of an accession of twenty to thirty new members weekly (membership was not disclosed but was estimated at about 500 in mid-1962). The B.N.P.'s ejection of Jordan and his supporters has, however, had one adverse consequence, since Jordan's new organization remained in the conveniently situated house in North Kensington.

John Bean remained national leader until 1966. He stood as parliamentary candidate for Southall in the 1964 and 1966 elections, getting 9·1% and 7·4%, respectively, of the vote. In the autumn of 1966, he resigned from the leadership, reportedly to leave himself free for manœuvre in the amalgamation discussions between the B.N.P. and the League of Empire Loyalists. He retained editorship of the Party's monthly publication, *Combat*, and the confidence of the tough activist group within the Party led by Ron Tear. Philip Maxwell-Eden became the new leader.[2]

C. THE NATIONAL SOCIALIST MOVEMENT[3]

Until 1964, as the British National Socialist Movement, this was the third, smallest, and most extreme of the post-Fascist or neo-Nazi organizations in contemporary Britain. Unlike the Union Movement and the British National Party, it had no pretensions to be a respectable, non-violent political party putting up candidates at elections.

[1] George Thayer, *The British Political Fringe*, London, Blond, 1965, pp. 96–105.

[2] The early part of the account given above of Post-Fascist and Neo-Nazi groupings generally, and of the Union Movement and the British National Party in particular, has been taken mainly from the I.R.R. *Newsletter* Supplement, October 1962.

[3] See I.R.R. *Newsletter* Supplement, November 1962.

Its aims were set out in a pamphlet by its leader, entitled *Britain Reborn*. After a somewhat impassioned introduction describing Britain in the 'twilight of decadance' (*sic*), held in the grip of Jewish 'kings of chain-store, hire-purchase and take-over', facing 'racial ruination', debauched by Democracy, the writer outlined his programme for making Britain great again by introducing 'a British form of the great National Socialist world creed of rejuvenation'. The programme provided for:

(1) the liberation of Britain from Jewish control;[1]

(2) the protection and improvement of the 'Aryan, predominantly Nordic blood', which is the only basis of Britain's past and future greatness. Only Aryans can be members of the nation and citizens of the State; non-Aryans will have their naturalization revoked and future naturalizations will be granted only to Aryans. All non-Aryans will be gradually deported, all sexual relations with Aryans prohibited, and all existing mixed marriages dissolved. Measures will be taken to improve the British stock and to prevent the reproduction of inferior stock;

(3) the establishment of a National Socialist authoritarian form of government, and Parliament will become an advisory body with a membership on an occupational basis. The monarchy to be preserved in its existing titular form;

(4) national unity;

(5) the retention of nuclear weapons and the maintenance of adequate defence forces; conscription to be reinstituted; American control of British forces to be terminated;

(6) folk Socialism and the rejection of both Capitalism and Communism and the class warfare, fomented by the Jews, on which they are both based; corporate organization of industry and guild organization of trades, professions and other occupations;

(7) farming to be encouraged, and thereby 'a wholesome national community based on blood and soil';

(8) all religious beliefs and practices that do not conflict with the racial and national deeds of National Socialism to be allowed and protected;

(9) the 'encouragement and expansion of our native Aryan culture . . . and the eradication and exclusion of all detrimental alien influences';

(10) radical reform of the educational system to make it an effective

[1] A broadsheet entitled 'Hitler Was Right' included the following passage: 'Democracy means Jewish Control, National Decline, Racial Ruin. Hitler raised Germany from the depths of Democracy. He sought the friendship of Britain in creating a new Europe based on national unity, social justice, racial betterment and defence against Communism; but the Jews forced Britain to declare war on their behalf. Hitler fell, but National Socialism lives on, and is today the only force which can save our nation and race from ruination, and build a new and greater Britain for the British.'

instrument for social harmony, national unity and National Socialist good citizenship; free and compulsory state schooling, the exclusion of 'class' differences and inclusion in the curriculum of a positive and thorough training to inculcate knowledge and pride of race and nation; a compulsory National Socialist Youth Movement, culminating in a period of national service, comprising first labour service and secondly service with the armed forces;

(11) the withdrawal of Britain from the multi-racial Commonwealth and the establishment of a new and close association of Britain, the White Dominions and the other British areas of white settlement. In Africa a separation of the races into White and Black States;

(12) promotion throughout the Aryan world of the National Socialist revolution against Democracy and Communism and the National Socialist New Order of the White man based on race; opposition to all schemes of union which overrule, deny and seek to cancel by mixture the distinctions of race, including the European Common Market[1] and the United Nations Organization.

Behind the B.N.S.M. (motto—'For Race and Nation'; bulletin—*The National Socialist*; activist group—'The Spearhead') was Colin Jordan (44), a former public school boy who served with the Fleet Air Arm, R.A.F. and Army during World War II and later took a history degree at Cambridge, where he was secretary of the University Nationalist Club. By profession a schoolteacher, he taught at a secondary modern school until he was dismissed by the Coventry education authority.

Jordan has been active in this type of movement for about fifteen years. He came early under the influence of the ideas of Arnold Leese, whose widow owns the Princedale Road house and founded the Birmingham Nationalist Club in the early 1950s. By 1956 he was Midlands organizer of the League of Empire Loyalists; John Bean was then the League's Northern organizer, becoming London secretary in 1957. By 1958 they seemed to have found the League too tame for them; without side-stepping into the Mosley ranks, both Jordan and Bean formed, respectively, the White Defence League and the National Labour Party, which were to merge in 1960 as the British National Party.

In early 1962, Jordan was rejected as national organizer in favour of Bean, but with a minority of members, including the Spearhead élite, remained in possession of the house in Princedale Road, where he inaugurated his own National Socialist Movement. Membership in 1967 was estimated at between thirty and fifty. Activities were circumscribed later in the year when Jordan, John Tyndall, the national organizer, Roland Kerr-Ritchie (research officer) and Dennis Pirie,

[1] Unlike Mosley's Union Movement, which favours entry, the British National Party also opposes the Common Market.

were all sentenced to short terms of imprisonment under the Public Order Act.

In 1964 the process of fission was continued when John Tyndall and Dennis Pirie split away from Jordan to form the Greater Britain Movement (see below).

Colin Jordan continued his activities, now aided by his wife Françoise (niece of Christian Dior), an enthusiastic Nazi whom he had married in true 'Aryan' style in black leather attire and with blood-mingling. Following a series of synagogue burnings in the winter of 1964–5, several young Nazis were arrested and made statements alleging contacts with both of them. The organization was reported to have gone down by the end of 1966.[1] The *National Socialist* had not appeared for some time, membership was less than 200 and Colin Jordan was in jail for offences against the Race Relations Act. His wife Françoise was also in prison in Nice, convicted of distributing racialist literature.

D. THE GREATER BRITAIN MOVEMENT

A large proportion of Jordan's membership went with John Tyndall when he split away from the N.S.M. in 1964. His organization is rabidly anti-democratic, anti-Semitic, anti-colour, and racialist (their official programme advocates measures to 'prevent procreation on the part of all those who have hereditary defects, etc.'). It is much better organized than the N.S.M., issues a regular magazine called *Spearhead*, and has held well-publicized, provocative meetings in the East End. At the end of 1966, Tyndall was serving a six-month sentence for being in possession of weapons.

E. THE KU KLUX KLAN

A minute off-shoot of the American Ku Klux Klan appeared in June 1965,[2] when it held a meeting where newspapermen outnumbered sympathizers. Before and after, however, fiery crosses were dumped at the houses of various immigrants in the Midlands and London and 'death sentences' were pronounced on various people. The Home Secretary announced that, if the Grand Imperial Wizard of the American Ku Klux Klan, Mr. Robert Shelton, fulfilled his stated intention of coming to England, he would be refused leave to land. Seven people were found guilty of cross-burning at Rugby and another man was sentenced to eighteen months' jail for planting fiery crosses in Leicester.

[1] *Jacob's Letter*, December 1966.

[2] The *Wiener Library Bulletin*, Autumn 1965, Vol. XIX, no. 4, New Series, no. 1, gave an account of sporadic K.K.K. activity in Britain since 1956.

Thereafter activity declined as the autumn drew on. The Union Movement, the B.N.P., and the N.S.M. all disclaimed any connexion with the K.K.K., and the U.M. and N.S.M. said that any members who took part in Klan meetings or activities would be expelled. Nonetheless, the *Sunday Mirror* (13 November 1966) published a photograph of Robert Rolf, together with Colin Jordan, giving Fascist salutes at Leamington; Robert Rolf was a member of the group sent to prison for burning Ku Klux Klan crosses.

2. ANTI-IMMIGRANT ORGANIZATIONS

These groupings were originally local protest organizations which arose in the specific climate of the West Midlands of the pre-Smethwick years. They were 'grass-roots' lower middle-class, 'little England', pressure groups, not linked in philosophy or in personnel with the London-based neo-Nazi and post-Fascist fringe movement. Their leaders were often local politicians, Conservative, or occasionally Labour, for the most part untainted by earlier Fascist or Nazi associations. In the words of Paul Foot, such men could

> command a very much higher degree of respect and attention than the official neo-Fascist parties. . . . The plain fact is that the Immigration Control Associations which arose in Birmingham and the surrounding area in 1960 and 1961, by means of their concentration on a single issue, their ability to move freely among members of established political parties and their dissociation from nominal Fascism, had a greater impact on British politics than any of the extremist right-wing parties could have done.[1]

The most powerful of the three West Midlands groups was the Birmingham Immigration Control Association, started as a committee in October 1960 by an engineer, Mr. Albert Mucklow, an estate duty consultant, Mr. John Sanders, a Mr. Harry Jones, and a Conservative city councillor, Mr. Charles Collett, who had for several years campaigned against uncontrolled immigration. In 1961 the Association fell a prey to factionalism, over the issue of putting up independent candidates or supporting the Conservatives. Mr. Tom Jones, formerly a Labour Party member, was voted out and formed his own group, the Vigilant Immigration Control Association, based in Handsworth. Harry Jones also broke with Sanders, and set up the British Immigration Control Association, which was soon joined by Donald Finney and his Smethwick branch, who found Jones more forceful than Sanders. Sanders' organization stuck to Birmingham, while Harry Jones' new organization moved into Wolverhampton, West Bromwich, and Smeth-

[1] Paul Foot, op. cit., p. 209.

wick. In the latter, Don Finney's branch was to work very hard for the return of Mr. Peter Griffiths in the general election of 1964.[1]

All three anti-immigrant associations[2] then unleashed a protest campaign of postcards, meetings, and signatures (e.g. Sir Cyril Osborne's nation-wide petition in favour of immigration control) aimed mainly at the Conservative Party and the local Conservative M.P.s. Particular targets were Mr. Aubrey Jones (then M.P. for Hall Green) and Sir Edward Boyle (Handsworth). Of the thirty-nine resolutions calling for immigration control submitted to the Conservative Party conference of 1961, five came from the Midlands, and Mr. John Sanders, with his close business and political contacts with local party leaders, could reportedly assume a good deal of responsibility for the prevailing climate of opinion in Birmingham.

The British Association and the Vigilant Association did not continue after the Commonwealth Immigrants Act, although Don Finney kept his Smethwick branch going for a time. He and other individuals continued active in the anti-immigration movement, his next initiative being the English Rights Association, of which he was chairman (aim—fighting to 'stop the continued degrading of our race'). In late 1966 this was reported to be affiliated to the Southall Residents' Association[3] and the London and Home Counties Tenants' Association, and in touch with the Patriotic Party, whose chairman was Major A. R. Braybrook.[4] One of Mr. Finney's earlier supporters, the 'colour-bar youth club' organizer, Mr. Ken Bunch, was also reported to be connected with an organization called the Argus Britons' Rights Association (chairman: Tom Jones, formerly of B.I.C.A.), and to be a member of the Racial Preservation Society, Midlands Division (of which more below).

The Birmingham Association initially closed down but started up again in the summer of 1964. It is said to have assisted local Perry Barr Conservatives in their eve-of-election anti-immigration leaflet campaign,[5] having been specifically refused permission to work in Sparkbrook for the Conservatives there.[6]

[1] For more details of Mr. Finney's later Council activities after 1961, and their probable effect on the Smethwick situation, see N. Deakin (ed.), op. cit., p. 80f. In the 1966 general election Mr. Finney, deprived of the Conservative umbrella, announced that his English Rights Association would support, not Mr. Peter Griffiths, with whom he expressed disillusionment, but Alderman George Hawkins, Conservative candidate for West Bromwich. Alderman Hawkins, after conditionally accepting, was instructed to decline this support and did so.

[2] For fuller details of the work of these groups, see Foot, op. cit., pp. 195–220.

[3] See Foot, op. cit., pp. 210–16.

[4] *Wiener Library Bulletin*, Autumn 1966, Vol. XX, no. 4, pp. 8–9. See also Thayer, op. cit., p. 61 n.

[5] Deakin (ed.), op. cit., pp. 160 and 162.

[6] Foot, op. cit., p. 203.

B.I.C.A.'s general line was a straightforward opposition to all future immigration from Afro-Asian countries. After the election it streamlined its organization and began to form links with like-minded groups and individuals inside and outside the Midlands and to coalesce into a new kind of national 'racial preservation' movement which has provided an umbrella for quite a number of right-wing extremists, although again it does not appear to be entirely immune from factionalism.

3. THE 'NEW LOOK' RACIAL PRESERVATION SOCIETIES

These have consistently aimed at 'peaceful separation' and 'human repatriation' of coloured immigrants. The rise of the Midlands and Sussex Racial Preservation Societies is documented in a report by a study group of the Manchester University Liberal Society published in 1966.[1] The Midlands Division was formed out of the A.B.R.A., while the Sussex Society was started in June 1965 by Mr. James J. Doyle, an antique dealer of Lewes Crescent, Brighton. A common factor was that the first vice-chairman of both organizations, as of the London (Southall) Division, was Raymond Bamford, a wealthy activist who writes articles on religio-racial themes (e.g. the 'race soul'), has opened a bookshop in Edinburgh to sell 'good conservative literature', travels widely abroad, and is reportedly the 'chaplain' of the National Youth Movement of the British National Party. Recently he seems to have moved away from official association with the R.P.S.

The Racial Preservation Society does not appear to lack funds and claims several thousand members, in the Midlands, Sussex and London, including a number of clergymen and other professional people; this helps to convey an impression of outward respectability. It has published and distributed widely and freely, five issues of a paper variously entitled the *Southern News*, the *British Independent*, the *Midland News*. Copies of this have been referred to Sir Elwyn Jones, the Attorney-General, for possible action under the Race Relations Act, so far without action being taken.[2] A more recent publication is the *New Nation*, officially a students' magazine, edited by J. Macintyre, photographer of the *Midland News* and a committee member of the original B.I.C.A.

The R.P.S. was thrown into some disarray in November 1966 when the chairman of the Sussex Division, Mr. James Doyle, was charged

[1] See also I.R.R. *Newsletter* (March 1966), pp. 9–10, for a note on the activities, publications and connexions of the Sussex Racial Preservation Society by David Spector. A Manchester branch of the R.P.S. was set up just before the 1966 General Election, and has reportedly been co-operating with the Union Movement in the area.

[2] *Daily Mail* (22 February 1966); *The Times* (6 March 1967).

with receiving and subsequently sentenced to three years' imprisonment. Some officers of the Sussex Division thereupon appear to have linked up with the Southall Branch (Mr. Robin Beauclair, chairman, Miss Gracie Woods, secretary) in a new organization called the Society for the Protection of All Races (S.P.A.R.), which was presented as the legitimate successor to the R.P.S., in a canvass of R.P.S. members. In Issue No. 5 of the R.P.S. *Southern News*, this was indignantly refuted by Thomas Jones and J. Grenville-Stuart on behalf of the R.P.S.

Despite this set-back, the new 'racial preservation' movement does show a continuing trend towards more centralized co-ordination, greater professionalism, and better financing. Other trends have been towards the propagation of a 'scientific racialism' and links with right-wing extremist groups outside Britain (e.g. West Germany, South Africa, and the Scandinavian states).

4. THE NATIONAL FRONT

For some months in late 1966 there were reports of merger negotiations between various right-wing extremist organizations and splinter-groups, aimed at setting up a respectable and viable political party. The initial discussions apparently took place between the B.N.P. and John Tyndall's Greater Britain Movement. Then the Racial Preservation Society entered the scene, but negotiations were complicated by the leadership crisis within the R.P.S. and the long-established, well-publicized League of Empire Loyalists[1] came into the picture.

Reportedly involved in the negotiations were: A. K. Chesterton, a founder-member of the B.U.F. in 1932, editor of *Action* till 1938, editor of the right-wing journal *Truth* after the war, and since 1953 editor of *Candour*, which in 1954 became the official journal of the newly-founded League of Empire Loyalists; Austen Brooks, son of Colin Brooks, a former editor of *Truth*, full-time organizer of the League of Empire Loyalists and initiator of many of the Tory-baiting and other stunts that characterized the League's activities in the 1950s; and 'Judge' Simmons, according to *Jacob's Letter* (No. 1, December 1966), a former Colonial Service judge, now on the editorial board of *Candour* and allegedly playing an increasingly important part behind the scenes in the B.N.P. since he joined it in early 1966.

On 7 February 1966, representatives of the League of Empire Loyalists and the British National Party signed Articles of Association to bring into being a merger known as the National Front. This organization, like its constituent parts, officially eschews violent and

[1] For fuller documentation about this organization, see Thayer, op. cit., Chapter 5 and *passim*, but note incorrect allegation that the League was involved in the 1958–9 Notting Hill riots (which led to a libel action, see *The Times*, 1 November 1967).

non-constitutional procedures. Its first trial of strength came in the Greater London Council elections of April 1967. In the event, however, the unprecedented swing to the Conservatives overwhelmed all minority party candidates of whatever political leanings, and its three candidates got little support, although direct comparisons with 1964 are not possible in most cases.

The 'objectives'[1] of the new National Front are as follows:

(1) To replace what is now known as 'The Commonwealth' by a modern British world system which, while ensuring the sovereign independence of each nation, would work for the closest co-operation between the United Kingdom, Australia, New Zealand, Canada and Rhodesia, and in which, if they so desired, the Republics of South Africa and Ireland would each occupy an honoured place.

(2) To permit the association with this new world system of approved Afro-Asian countries on terms acceptable to its foundation members.

(3) To achieve for the system adequate economic and agricultural self-sufficiency to make possible the creation of the financial and military strength needed to guarantee its freedom both from Communist domination and from coercion by the power of the international money-lending houses and their financial and political agencies.

(4) To seek within non-Communist Europe and elsewhere suitable alliances which would replace involvement in treaty organizations destructive of national sovereignty, and would resist hostile interference by the United Nations and similar organizations.

(5) To give unremitting support to British and other European communities overseas in their maintenance of civilization in lands threatened with a reversion to barbarism.

(6) To review financial 'overseas aid' and other gifts by Britain where there is neither strategical nor political compensation therefor.

(7) To establish in the United Kingdom a Government sufficiently strong and courageous to eradicate the present malaise of liberal internationalism and to imbue the people with a pride in Great Britain's past and faith in her future once the realm has been restored to spiritual health and sanity.

(8) To preserve our British native stock in the United Kingdom, to prevent interracial strife such as is seen in the United States of America, and to eradicate race-hatred, by terminating non-white immigration, with humane and orderly repatriation of non-white immigrants (and their dependants) who have entered since the passing of the British Nationality Act, 1948.

(9) To ensure that just profits, salaries and wages, founded on a fair partnership between employers and employees, are guaranteed by maintaining the principle of private enterprise within a framework of national guidance, wherein employees would be genuinely represented in all matters pertaining to hours, wages and working conditions. Consumer interests would also be represented to ensure protection from monopolistic and other malpractices.

(10) To prevent misuse of the land of Britain.

[1] *Patterns of Prejudice*, Vol. 1, no. 2, March/April 1967, published by the Institute of Jewish Affairs.

(11) To encourage home-ownership to give the people a personal stake in their country.

(12) To create a national movement to give guidance for the healthy mental and physical development of British youth.

(13) To adopt all measures necessary to combat crime and to protect police and prison officers in the execution of their duty, and to reverse the tendency to give more consideration to the criminal than to his victims.

An interesting sidelight on the attitudes of some activists in the movement, during the period when the R.P.S. was still involved, is afforded by the following letter in the *Kentish Gazette* of 10 January 1967:

To the Editor,

The British National Party, the League of Empire Loyalists and several individuals of the Race Preservation Society have merged to form The National Front—the largest Right Wing group in Britain.

The policy of The National Front is the same as the old B.N.P.

Its main points are:

1. The end of all non-European immigration into Britain and the return of those coloured immigrants already here to their respective countries, in a humane manner, in order to prevent the racial chaos which is now occurring all over the U.S.A.

2. The replacement of the Coloured Commonwealth with a union of Britain and the White Dominions.

3. The ending of overseas aid except where it clearly benefits Britain.

4. The establishment of a strong National Government which will restore honour, pride and greatness to this country.

Leadership of the Party and, in fact, membership as a whole consists of war veterans and ex-servicemen and women. This is not a membership requirement but it follows that those who were old enough to care about Britain in the past, care about Britain in the present and about its future.

What is a membership requirement is, that, applicants are of natural British/European descent, through both parents.

Our intention is to become the Government in order to carry out our policy.

(Sgd.) Gerald Rowe,
(Kent Area Organiser)
The National Front,
19 St. John's Lane, Canterbury

Underneath the Editor commented acidly:

War veterans and ex-servicemen and women who 'care for Britain' may also recall—with a nasty taste in their mouth—that their main enemy was a nation led by a party which also demanded certain racial characteristics of its members.

In addition to personality clashes, the rival pulls of respectability and the desire for more violent action have always been a potential source of discord and schism within these extremist groups, and it was reported that a parallel organization, to be known as the National Action Group, was being formed to accommodate the more activist element, probably under the leadership of Ron Tear of the B.N.P. Later, however, the National Action Group was dropped and Ron Tear was put in charge of the East London branch of the National Front, which had by now been joined by the B.N.P.

5. ANTI-FASCIST ORGANIZATIONS

Inevitably, the neo-Nazi and post-Fascist movements led to the rise of anti-Fascist organizations, as had been the case in the 1930s. Once again, although the coloured immigrant had become the main official target of at least some of the new extremist groupings, the major component of the purely anti-Fascist movements has been made up of London Jewish veterans and activists. An account of the various groupings and their differing approaches is given in George Thayer's *The British Political Fringe*, Chapter 5. The rise and decline of the Yellow Star Movement from its inception in July 1962 has also been documented in detail by Geoffrey Ashe.[1] Within it there grew up a hard-core militant faction called the 62 Group, which was, according to Thayer,[2] an exact imitation of the war-time 43 Group. This has survived,[3] as has the North and East London Anti-Fascist Committee, also (like the Y.S.M.) started by the Rev. Bill Sargent of Dalston and a few Jewish members of the old L.C.C., and specializing in more moderate but effective anti-Fascist techniques aimed at denying all good speaking sites in an area to neo-Fascist groups.

[1] I.R.R. *Newsletter*, April 1964, May 1964.
[2] Thayer, op. cit., p. 88 f.
[3] See article by Malcolm Southarn (*Sunday Times*, 19 February 1967).

APPENDIXES

I – IV *Statistical*

V – X *Other*

TABLE A

Classification according to purpose of journey of Commonwealth citizens subject to control under the Act admitted to the United Kingdom: 1 January to 31 December 1966, with totals for 1965

Territory that issued passport	Visitors for three months or less (1)	Visitors for more than three months (2)	Students (3)	Holders of Ministry of Labour vouchers (4)	Dependants accompanying or coming to join the head of the household (5)	Persons coming for settlement not included elsewhere (6)	Diplomats and officials (and their dependants) (7)	Passengers in transit (8)	Persons joining crews of ships or aircraft (9)	Persons returning to the U.K. from temporary absence abroad (10)	Total (11)
Aden	705	28	121	21	80	21	5	60	—	646	1,687
Australia	46,564	12,512	552	165	1,098	272	706	2,960	79	17,490	82,398
Barbados	702	54	325	193	895	35	5	46	18	751	3,024
Botswana*, Lesotho† and Swaziland ...	252	23	59	2	46	4	17	41	—	119	563
Canada	102,087	2,300	687	76	1,475	271	1,025	14,532	379	12,658	135,490
Ceylon	1,812	131	572	140	329	52	102	302	27	1,963	5,430
Cyprus	4,452	113	373	80	587	118	88	166	11	2,691	8,679
Gambia	112	14	27	—	19	1	7	43	1	67	291
Ghana	2,708	82	579	9	508	18	297	585	18	1,323	6,127
Gibraltar	1,463	27	61	8	53	9	7	90	8	521	2,247
Guyana‡	1,133	92	368	18	551	54	10	111	5	1,700	4,042
Hong Kong	1,641	76	681	106	951	46	3	109	45	2,984	6,642
India	16,000	370	1,182	2,433	13,357	918	1,049	5,858	1,144	11,158	53,469
Jamaica	2,548	108	499	237	6,622	218	100	215	6	6,463	17,016
Kenya	1,143	48	423	6	460	54	92	269	6	1,020	3,521
Leeward and Windward Islands ...	516	58	212	146	1,493	136	17	26	7	616	3,227
Malawi	117	8	78	1	9	1	40	59	—	55	368
Malaysia and Singapore	2,271	200	1,410	59	332	36	115	181	3	2,769	7,376
Malta	3,902	100	99	651	302	87	41	546	152	2,582	8,462
Mauritius	1,724	67	747	88	476	31	14	154	—	1,625	4,926
New Zealand ...	11,868	4,420	185	79	323	104	155	677	26	6,360	24,197
Nigeria	3,173	95	1,113	49	1,257	56	209	718	203	1,791	8,664
Pakistan	6,161	94	791	721	9,319	205	366	1,709	288	12,597	32,251
Sierra Leone ...	846	41	229	4	98	9	125	137	28	373	1,890
Southern Rhodesia ...	1,467	82	100	11	56	30	5	177	1	721	2,650
Tanzania	831	21	415	5	91	8	52	228	1	649	2,301
Trinidad and Tobago	1,987	163	802	34	317	39	66	210	6	2,068	5,692
Uganda	722	31	357	5	115	10	89	253	—	465	2,047
Zambia	384	36	162	—	18	22	83	182	—	95	982
All other territories ...	3,186	153	622	114	789	113	93	284	14	1,715	7,083
TOTAL	222,477	21,547	13,831	5,461	42,026	2,978	4,983	30,928	2,476	96,035	442,742
Total for 1965 ...	*210,937*	*19,808*	*14,017*	*12,880*	*41,214*	*2,968*	*4,259*	*32,187*	*1,949*	*93,354*	*433,573*

* Formerly Bechuanaland. † Formerly Basutoland. ‡ Formerly British Guiana.

Source: Commonwealth Immigrants Act 1962, Statistics 1966.

Notes on the Classification in Table A

Each incoming passenger is classified in one of the categories below according to the assessment of the immigration officer who examined him.

(1) *Visitors coming for three months or less*. In addition to tourists, this category includes business visitors and all other types of short-term visitor (including their dependants) not shown elsewhere.

(2) *Visitors coming for longer than three months*. Included under this head are all those (including dependants) who are likely to remain in the United Kingdom for more than three months (but are not coming for permanent settlement) and who do not hold Ministry of Labour vouchers or fall into the category of 'students'.

(3) *Students*. Included in this category is any person admitted to the United Kingdom for the purpose of undertaking a course of study, as defined in paragraphs 9–16 of the Instructions to Immigration Officers (Cmnd 3064). A dependant who accompanies a student is not included in category (2).

(4) *Holders of Ministry of Labour vouchers*. This category includes all holders of vouchers, including some who may not be proposing to settle in the United Kingdom, but does not include persons coming to take the types of employment for which vouchers are not required (see paragraph 21 of Cmnd 3064).

(5) *Dependants*. This category is limited to dependants accompanying, or coming to join, the head of the family with the intention of settling in the United Kingdom. It includes, for example, dependants who accompany a voucher-holder and dependants admitted to join a person already working in the United Kingdom. Dependants not coming for permanent residence are normally classified as visitors in category (1) or (2). Dependants of diplomats and officials are put in category (7).

(6) *Persons coming for settlement not included elsewhere*. Examples are persons coming to marry and settle in the United Kingdom, and persons of independent means coming to the United Kingdom for retirement.

(7) *Diplomats and officials*. This category includes those persons who are exempt from immigration control under section 17 of the act.

(8) *Passengers in transit*. Persons passing through the United Kingdom in transit, including those proceeding to the Channel Islands, the Isle of Man or the Irish Republic, are shown in this category. (No record is made of persons who land for only a few hours before proceeding on the same ship or aircraft.)

(9) *Persons joining crews of ships and aircraft*. This category includes only persons who arrive as passengers but are under contract to join ships or aircraft in the United Kingdom and are to leave as members of the crew.

(10) *Persons returning from temporary absence abroad*. This classification includes students and long-term visitors returning to the United Kingdom from temporary absence. It also includes all persons ordinarily resident in the United Kingdom returning from absence abroad.

TABLE B

Numbers of men, women and children among persons admitted as long-term visitors, students, Ministry of Labour voucher holders, dependants and other persons coming for settlement: 1 January to 31 December 1966, with totals for 1965

Territory that issued passport	Long-term visitors			Students			Holders of Ministry of Labour vouchers		Dependants			Other persons coming for settlement		
	Men	Women	Children	Men	Women	Children	Men	Women	Men	Women	Children	Men	Women	Children
Aden	8	11	9	107	7	7	19	2	1	40	39	12	7	2
Australia	3,986	8,039	487	360	148	44	124	41	43	581	474	119	102	51
Barbados	15	29	10	101	216	8	84	100	11	109	775	9	19	7
Botswana,* Lesotho† and Swaziland ...	14	9	—	42	15	2	1	1	—	16	30	1	3	—
Canada	789	1,157	354	420	201	66	44	32	66	720	689	133	78	60
Ceylon	56	60	15	359	206	7	98	42	21	170	138	26	18	8
Cyprus	50	47	16	247	117	9	40	40	39	255	293	31	40	47
Gambia	7	3	4	20	5	2	—	—	—	13	6	1	—	—
Ghana	54	22	6	433	113	33	8	1	8	323	177	8	10	—
Gibraltar	12	12	3	35	10	16	4	4	1	27	25	3	5	1
Guyana‡	31	49	12	117	242	9	9	9	17	137	397	17	20	17
Hong Kong	33	29	14	379	233	69	87	19	16	427	508	14	9	23
India	234	118	18	955	175	52	2,100	333	856	4,887	7,614	391	288	239
Jamaica	38	56	14	146	346	7	138	99	71	647	5,904	48	84	86
Kenya	21	20	7	299	92	32	6	—	13	130	317	32	8	14
Leeward and Windward Islands ...	12	35	11	76	128	8	94	52	12	176	1,305	16	28	92
Malawi	6	1	1	58	20	—	1	—	—	6	3	—	1	—
Malaysia and Singapore	85	89	26	813	550	47	32	27	11	186	135	11	20	5
Malta	38	59	3	56	34	9	533	118	6	129	167	39	32	16
Mauritius	20	29	18	530	215	2	74	14	15	193	268	12	11	8
New Zealand	1,472	2,786	162	125	47	13	60	19	14	182	127	52	37	15
Nigeria	71	18	6	829	258	26	46	3	13	941	303	10	30	16
Pakistan	62	21	11	709	65	17	671	50	165	2,944	6,210	83	47	75
Sierra Leone	19	17	5	148	78	3	2	2	3	45	50	5	3	1
Southern Rhodesia	27	51	4	48	50	2	8	3	2	21	33	17	8	5
Tanzania	12	9	—	269	123	23	2	3	4	38	49	4	2	2
Trinidad and Tobago	52	81	30	178	605	19	11	23	12	71	234	12	17	10
Uganda	22	5	4	235	112	10	5	—	4	31	80	5	4	1
Zambia	26	5	5	116	45	1	—	—	—	9	9	5	5	12
All other territories	73	59	21	381	189	52	64	50	26	138	625	46	37	30
TOTALS	7,345	12,926	1,276	8,591	4,645	595	4,365	1,096	1,450	13,592	26,984	1,162	973	843
Total for 1965	*6,848*	*11,157*	*1,803*	*8,643*	*4,540*	*834*	*9,710*	*3,170*	*1,485*	*14,992*	*24,737*	*1,092*	*1,316*	*560*

* Formerly Bechuanaland. † Formerly Basutoland. ‡ Formerly British Guiana. Note: 'Children' means persons under 16.

Source: Commonwealth Immigrants Act 1962, Statistics 1966.

TABLE C

Ministry of Labour Vouchers

Applications received and vouchers issued between 1 January 1966 and 30 December 1966, with totals for 1965

Territory which Issued Passport	Category A		Category B		Categories A and B	
	Applications Received	Vouchers Issued	Applications Received	Vouchers Issued	Applications Received	Vouchers Issued
Aden	80	19	1	—	81	19
Australia	192	8	423	224	615	232
Bahamas	1	—	1	—	2	—
Barbados	352	294	2	1	354	295
Bermuda	5	—	—	—	5	—
Botswana,* Lesotho† and Swaziland	2	—	1	1	3	1
British Honduras	1	—	1	—	2	—
Canada	183	11	259	146	442	157
Ceylon	158	16	326	156	484	172
Cyprus	674	134	14	3	688	137
Fiji	28	6	11	6	39	12
Gambia	1	2	—	—	1	2
Ghana	47	4	7	5	54	9
Gibraltar	39	10	13	6	52	16
Guyana‡	153	19	17	8	170	27
Hong Kong	638	121	33	21	671	142
India	2,153	306	8,613	3,976	10,766	4,282
Jamaica	1,039	283	27	11	1,066	294
Kenya	24	6	12	4	36	10
Leeward and Windward Islands:						
Antigua	36	23	1	1	37	24
Dominica	178	52	2	1	180	53
Grenada	284	65	2	—	286	65
Montserrat	14	19	—	—	14	19
St. Kitts	42	24	1	—	43	24
St. Lucia...	118	33	—	—	118	33
St. Vincent	104	84	—	—	104	84
Malawi	2	—	1	1	3	1
Malaysia	75	20	41	28	116	48
Malta	889	795	11	11	900	806
Mauritius	337	84	16	7	353	91
New Zealand	78	4	145	91	223	95
Nigeria	120	15	44	23	164	38
Pakistan	3,464	301	2,177	629	5,641	930
Rhodesia	47	2	23	16	70	18
St. Helena	47	13	—	—	47	13
Seychelles	97	47	—	—	97	47
Sierra Leone	6	1	1	1	7	2
Singapore	56	4	34	19	90	23
Tanzania	25	4	12	6	37	10
Tonga	—	1	—	—	—	1
Trinidad and Tobago ...	179	37	20	17	199	54
Uganda	17	2	2	2	19	4
Zambia	3	1	1	—	4	1
Others	31	5	24	4	55	9
TOTAL	12,019	2,875	12,319	5,425	24,338	8,300
Total for 1965 ...	*18,674*	*8,644*	*8,988*	*7,402*	*34,813* (Includes Category C 7,151)	*16,046*

Applications made in 1966 for which Vouchers will not be issued§

Category A	Category B	A and B
5,659	3,498	9,157

* Formerly Bechuanaland.
† Formerly Basutoland.
‡ Formerly British Guiana.
§ Either because a voucher is not required or because the conditions for issue are not satisfied.
Source: Commonwealth Immigrants Act 1962, Statistics 1966.

APPENDIX II. ENTRY CERTIFICATES ISSUED, 1962–7

Entry Certificates Issued 1962

Territories	Visitors	Students	Relatives and Depen- dants	Others	Total	Refused
Aden...	101	91	9	102	303	—
Australia	5,500	196	407	203	6,306	1
Antigua	19	13	51	17	100	1
Barbados	116	184	332	100	732	35
Basutoland ...	6	24	4	—	34	—
Bechuanaland ...	2	3	—	1	6	—
British Guiana ...	207	272	481	182	1,042	84
Canada	351	240	165	227	983	3
Ceylon	120	160	96	32	408	—
Cyprus	685	277	282	112	1,356	32
Gambia	12	32	13	2	59	—
Ghana	338	414	220	56	1,028	5
Gibraltar	212	32	10	7	261	—
Grenada	6	15	133	32	186	3
Hong Kong ...	300	377	101	179	957	1
India	887	876	1,120	502	3,385	124
Jamaica	746	228	3,436	756	5,166	42
Kenya	196	366	121	74	607	14
Leeward and Windward Islands	83	100	568	172	923	10
Malaysia (components of) ...	139	313	61	199	712	—
Malta	384	72	126	134	716	1
Mauritius	58	110	55	20	243	—
New Zealand ...	3,226	174	227	134	3,761	—
Nigeria	617	1,727	990	239	3,573	128
Pakistan	747	392	493	423	2,055	6
Rhodesia and Nyasaland ...	34	59	5	54	152	—
Sierra Leone ...	190	152	63	21	426	—
Swaziland	—	—	—	—	—	—
Tanganyika	12	171	6	25	214	—
Trinidad	592	436	247	141	1,416	2
Uganda	70	233	34	18	355	—
Zanzibar	3	35	3	3	44	—
Others	49	68	54	75	246	3
Total	16,002	7,825	9,780	4,210	37,369	492

Entry Certificates Issued 1963

Territories	Visitors	Students	Relatives and Dependants	Others	Total	Refused
Aden	260	188	28	207	683	—
Australia	9,360	246	348	203	10,157	—
Barbados	348	324	538	243	1,453	5
Basutoland, etc. ...	8	57	7	3	75	—
British Guiana ...	571	280	785	318	1,954	95
Canada	442	245	280	270	1,237	8
Ceylon	152	195	176	54	577	5
Cyprus	258	273	374	277	1,182	4
Ghana	735	646	399	122	1,902	32
Gibraltar	225	20	14	9	268	5
Hong Kong ...	655	419	236	547	1,857	—
India	1,198	671	1,818	634	4,321	261
Jamaica	1,366	236	4,833	2,063	8,498	83
Kenya	356	598	261	115	1,330	44
Malta	1,086	68	296	270	1,720	4
Malaysia	219	509	162	317	1,207	3
Mauritius	51	104	129	27	311	5
New Zealand ...	4,919	125	181	105	5,330	—
Nigeria	1,555	1,894	1,859	283	5,591	291
Pakistan	360	452	1,322	1,104	3,238	192
Rhodesia	37	41	14	86	178	—
Sierra Leone ...	400	130	115	66	711	6
Tanganyika ...	17	234	17	27	295	—
Trinidad and Tobago	1,216	537	270	204	2,227	8
Uganda	170	340	50	84	644	3
Zanzibar	31	62	4	2	99	—
Others	463	287	1,081	579	2,410	41
Total	26,458	9,181	15,597	8,219	59,455	1,095

Entry Certificates Issued 1964

Territories	Visitors	Students	Relatives and Dependants	Others	Total	Refused
Aden	235	114	29	363	741	29
Australia	11,734	239	169	257	12,399	—
Barbados	398	372	753	309	1,832	86
Basutoland, etc. ...	2	61	2	15	80	—
British Guiana ...	716	565	895	441	2,617	221
Canada	361	271	295	378	1,305	6
Ceylon	59	271	230	103	663	3
Cyprus	1,078	250	539	247	2,114	11
Ghana	958	669	359	68	2,054	43
Gibraltar	238	24	17	3	282	—
Hong Kong ...	1,399	967	779	1,264	4,409	3
India	1,102	737	2,009	1,439	5,287	410
Jamaica	1,335	470	7,423	2,919	12,147	141
Kenya	356	477	232	134	1,199	98
Leeward and Windward Isles	241	193	1,915	645	2,994	98
Malawi	—	—	—	—	—	—
Malaysia	479	1,040	224	343	2,086	1
Malta	1,423	132	296	316	2,167	3
Mauritius	29	211	218	48	506	1
New Zealand ...	5,157	163	216	88	5,624	—
Nigeria	1,749	2,943	1,999	571	7,262	163
Pakistan	284	469	1,511	774	3,038	132
Sierra Leone ...	484	207	61	103	855	35
Southern Rhodesia	38	48	9	78	173	—
Tanzania	32	364	39	38	473	53
Trinidad and Tobago	814	744	471	292	2,321	12
Uganda	212	405	79	99	795	13
Zambia	1	3	—	1	5	—
Others	268	265	130	249	912	—
Total	31,182	12,674	20,899	11,585	76,340	2,162

Entry Certificates Issued 1965

Territories	Visitors	Students	Relatives and Dependants	Others	Total	Refused
Aden	376	171	93	434	1,074	114
Australia	14,969	283	295	433	15,980	5
Barbados	471	483	863	388	2,205	157
Basutoland, etc. ...	18	45	4	3	70	—
British Guiana ...	814	507	557	399	2,277	133
Canada	657	361	377	584	1,979	14
Ceylon	585	450	384	138	1,557	7
Cyprus	2,217	390	706	287	3,600	288
Gambia	48	44	21	14	127	2
Ghana	1,522	714	432	113	2,781	25
Gibraltar	587	83	24	16	710	—
Hong Kong ...	878	786	866	1,016	3,546	28
India	690	615	1,795	1,425	4,525	310
Jamaica	667	432	7,440	1,678	10,217	586
Kenya	400	513	115	78	1,106	149
Leeward and Windward Isles ...	288	243	2,303	609	3,443	527
Malawi	2	20	1	—	23	—
Malaysia	680	1,611	213	334	2,838	10
Malta	1,798	158	268	521	2,745	—
Mauritius	610	472	359	77	1,518	9
New Zealand ...	6,122	170	330	211	6,833	1
Nigeria	2,062	1,459	1,704	667	5,892	813
Pakistan	487	607	2,389	1,327	4,810	386
Sierra Leone ...	501	384	72	228	1,185	45
Southern Rhodesia	40	61	18	53	172	—
Tanzania	40	483	78	24	625	32
Trinidad and Tobago	1,126	826	352	320	2,624	46
Uganda	265	438	53	140	896	4
Zambia	26	26	6	9	67	2
Others	287	237	76	223	823	1
Total	39,233	13,072	22,194	11,749	86,248	3,694

Entry Certificates Issued in 1966

Territories	Visitors	Students	Relatives and Dependants	Others	Total	Refused
Australia	13,755	510	888	830	17,983	1
Barbados	544	400	827	436	2,207	225
Botswana	3	82	1	—	86	—
Canada	797	366	391	787	2,341	2
Ceylon	918	734	351	421	2,424	18
Cyprus	3,428	458	568	265	4,719	608
Gambia	59	51	25	16	151	—
Ghana	1,225	571	526	543	2,865	38
Gibraltar	828	80	7	14	929	—
Guyana	776	521	478	775	2,550	201
Hong Kong ...	869	943	1,096	1,002	3,910	21
India	627	579	1,267	1,334	3,807	482
Jamaica	494	459	6,456	759	8,168	881
Kenya	139	594	98	66	897	67
Leeward and Windward Isles...	329	357	2,142	504	3,332	812
Malawi	7	20	4	—	31	—
Malaysia	998	2,005	338	306	3,647	12
Malta	3,233	182	224	731	4,370	1
Mauritius	1,236	937	331	109	2,613	6
New Zealand ...	5,806	124	364	285	6,579	1
Nigeria	1,634	1,358	1,084	685	4,761	470
Pakistan	823	736	3,451	1,566	6,576	838
Sierra Leone ...	528	253	25	223	1,029	21
Rhodesia	46	72	22	84	224	—
Tanzania	95	494	84	34	707	4
Trinidad and Tobago	1,094	986	243	243	2,566	121
Uganda	270	450	45	83	848	7
Zambia	10	18	3	7	38	—
Others	273	254	91	203	821	1
Total	42,844	14,594	21,430	12,311	91,179	4,838

APPENDIX III

NUMBER OF DEPORTATION ORDERS, 1962–7

Number of deportation orders made under the Commonwealth Immigrants Act 1962, by nationality and year

	1962 (from 1.7.62)	1963	1964	1965	1966	1967 (to 31.5.67)
Irish Republic ...	95	152	140	161	171	77
West Indies:						
Barbados ...	4	2	3	—	2	—
Guyana	8	9	9	5	8	1
Jamaica	19	32	36	40	25	6
Leeward and Windward Islands	5	6	13	8	6	2
Trinidad and Tobago	2	7	6	6	4	1
Turk and Caicos Islands	—	—	1	—	—	—
Aden	1	1	—	—	—	—
Australia	2	2	2	—	4	3
Canada	1	8	1	—	3	1
Ceylon	—	1	—	—	—	—
Cyprus	1	9	3	10	5	3
Fiji	—	—	1	—	—	—
Gambia	—	1	2	—	—	—
Gibraltar	—	1	—	1	1	—
Hong Kong ...	2	2	—	—	—	—
India	1	2	1	2	3	4
Kenya	—	1	—	—	1	—
Malta	4	12	10	5	5	3
Mauritius	1	—	—	3	—	—
New Zealand ...	2	1	—	1	—	—
Nigeria	2	—	2	5	3	1
Pakistan	—	5	1	8	11	5
Sierra Leone ...	—	3	—	1	—	—
S. Rhodesia ...	—	—	1	—	—	—
Tanzania	—	—	1	—	—	—
Others	—	—	—	—	1	—
Total	150	257	233	256	253	107

Source: Home Office.

APPENDIX IV. NUMBER OF STUDENTS, 1959–66

Comparative approximate totals for countries having the largest number of students

	Nigeria	India	Jamaica	France	Malaysia*	Germany	Guyana	U.S.A.	Trinidad and Tobago	Pakistan	Ghana	Hong Kong	Kenya	Barbados	Iran	Iraq
1959–60	6,000	3,510	1,940	1,775	2,280	1,830	630	1,120	1,100	1,570	1,840	1,550	1,030	670	950	1,165
1960–61	6,800	3,400	2,980	1,990	2,296	2,010	765	1,270	1,370	1,245	3,793	1,580	1,272	1,080	1,110	1,660
1961–62	7,836	3,496	3,151	1,993	2,560	2,015	869	1,346	1,622	1,470	3,348	1,559	1,592	1,247	1,435	1,910
1962–63	8,954	4,281	4,083	1,876	2,729	1,889	1,329	1,428	1,858	1,711	1,885	1,619	1,532	1,210	1,657	2,120
1963–64	8,630	4,129	3,841	2,052	3,144	1,813	1,318	1,611	1,844	1,924	1,991	1,715	1,593	1,248	1,451	1,813
1964–65	8,067	4,343	4,092	2,589	3,271	2,436	1,452	1,944	1,931	2,285	1,949	1,429	1,672	1,469	1,457	1,638
1965–66†	6,522	4,529	3,930	3,130	2,830	2,281	2,273	2,174	2,154	2,127	2,071	2,001	1,823	1,664	1,611	1,540

* Figures for Singapore, which became independent in 1964, are excluded throughout.
† See Table A.

Source: Overseas Students in Britain, British Council Handbook, November 1966, Table K, p. 48.

APPENDIX V

POLITICAL AND ECONOMIC PLANNING (P.E.P.) SURVEY ON RACIAL DISCRIMINATION

This is an abridged version of the P.E.P. survey which was made at the request of the National Committee for Commonwealth Immigrants and the Race Relations Board and was financed by a grant from the Joseph Rowntree Memorial Trust. The survey was undertaken by Research Services Limited. P.E.P. and Research Services had the benefit of advice from an Advisory Committee, whose members are listed below:

Mr. Mark Bonham-Carter (Chairman),
Chairman, Race Relations Board

Mr. Nicholas Deakin, Assistant Director,
Survey of Race Relations in Britain

Professor C. A. Moser, C.B.E.,
Professor of Social Statistics, University of London

Mr. Dipak Nandy,
Lecturer, University of Kent

Miss Nadine Peppard, General Secretary,
National Committee for Commonwealth Immigrants

Professor John Rex, Professor of Social Theory and Institutions,
Durham University

Mr. E. J. B. Rose, Director,
Survey of Race Relations in Britain

Professor R. M. Titmuss, C.B.E., Professor of Social Administration,
University of London

Mr. D. H. de Trafford, C.B.E., Chairman, Employment Panel,
National Committee for Commonwealth Immigrants

Mr. L. E. Waddilove, O.B.E., Director, Joseph Rowntree Memorial Trust,
Chairman, Housing Panel,
National Committee for Commonwealth Immigrants

1. Background

This report presents the findings of a series of related studies in the area of racial discrimination.[1] The objective of the studies was to assess the extent of discrimination against Commonwealth immigrants in Britain. The area of study had to be closely defined to complete the work in the time allotted. Thus, the objectives were limited to particular priority areas.

The first priority was those areas of potential discrimination which are not covered by legislation. These areas included: (i) employment; (ii) housing, including private rental, purchase and public rental; (iii) credit facilities, insurance and personal services.

The second priority was that, when interviewing immigrants, the sample was restricted to four groups—those from the West Indies, India, Pakistan and Cyprus—selected in six areas of England.

2. Methods

In each area, and for most aspects of potential discrimination studied, three methods of inquiry were used. The methods were: (i) personal interviewing with immigrants; (ii) personal interviewing with people in a position to discriminate; (iii) 'situation tests' where the conditions of potential discrimination were reproduced. Whenever possible all three methods were employed.

(i) *Personal interviewing with immigrants*

Interviews were conducted with 974 immigrants. The interviews were conducted by people in the same group (Indians by Indians, Cypriots by Cypriots, etc.) using a questionnaire translated into the appropriate first language. Pilot work had confirmed the evidence from the United States that this procedure was necessary. The interview was introduced as a study of how people were settling in Britain. Thus, the interview began with questions on their arrival and expectations on arrival. After the initial questions, the interview was designed to examine, for each field covered:

(a) the extent to which immigrants felt they were discriminated against as a group;
(b) the extent to which these feelings were based on personal experience which had been interpreted as discriminatory, or on second-hand experience;
(c) the evidence which the informant had for concluding that the experience was one of racial or colour discrimination.

The sampling method differed from that commonly employed in social surveys. Any study of immigrants has to overcome severe sampling problems because of the absence of reliable information on the numbers and location of immigrants. All people working in the field of race relations learn that the standard sources of information (e.g. Census or Electoral Registers) are not

[1] By 'discrimination' is meant a practice or policy which affects members of minority groups differently because of colour or country of origin, in ways that are either of significance to them personally or of significance socially.

reliable or complete in their data on immigrants. Thus the sampling was carried out as follows:

(a) Six areas were selected in conjunction with the advisory committee. The areas were selected to represent local and regional differences, different densities and different compositions of immigrants. The selection of the areas also avoided those areas which have been intensively surveyed in previous studies of race relations. The effect of this consideration was to exclude many areas which are most well known to the public as areas of high density or a high level of racial tension.[1]

(b) Within the six areas the population sampled was male heads of households who were of the four groups under study.

(c) Within each of the six areas the two wards estimated to have the highest density of immigrant population were selected.

(d) In each of the wards a street-by-street count was carried out to identify addresses where immigrants lived. This work was carried out by white British interviewers. Their task was to ascertain the addresses and record the nationality of the immigrant occupants so that the appropriate interviewer could be sent subsequently.

(e) For each of five areas 200 randomly selected addresses were issued. In the sixth area only a small number of addresses were found and 50 were issued. With supplementary issues, 1,163 addresses were issued and 974 interviews completed.

(f) Within each address all male heads of households were listed and one selected according to special procedures to ensure a random selection.

(ii) *Personal interviews with people in a position to discriminate*

In the main fields covered, such as employment, housing and certain services, interviews were carried out among the people who came into contact with immigrants in an official capacity, or people whose roles enable them to comment upon the nature and incidence of discrimination. The main areas of interviewing were:

Employment: National and local employers; national and local trade union officials; the staffs of employment exchanges and private employment bureaux.

Housing: Estate agents; accommodation bureaux; building societies; local authority officers.

Services: Bank managers, insurance companies.

The method of sampling differed according to circumstances. For example, the selection of national employers was purposive, to ensure that nationalised industries as well as private corporations, service industries as well as manufacturing industries were included. Similarly, the trade unions were selected

[1] Area I was in the South, with a mixed industrial character and established West Indian settlement. Area II was similar, except that it also had a significant Cypriot community. Area III, also in the South, was modern, light industrial in character, and had a recent mixed settlement of West Indians, Pakistanis, and Indians. Area IV, in the North, was one of traditional heavy industry, with a recent settlement of Pakistanis. Area V was similar, but also had a West Indian group. Area VI was a mixed industrial area in the Midlands, with an established settlement of West Indians and Indians.

according to their coverage of occupations that immigrants tend to enter. However, where standard sampling methods were applicable—such as with estate agents or employment bureaux—standard sampling methods were employed.

All interviews were conducted by special interviewers employed by Research Services Limited. They are either social science graduates or experienced industrial market research interviewers. In each area they worked under an executive responsible for briefing, allocation of informants, and general supervision.

(iii) *Situation testing*
In certain of the fields situation testing was carried out. The main objective of the situation testing was to provide an independent reference and check on the information reported by the immigrants and the people in a position to discriminate. All situation tests were conducted with teams of three testers. Each test-team consisted of a coloured immigrant, a white alien and a white Englishman. Such testers would independently apply for accommodation at landlords or estate agencies, employment at an employment bureau, or a car at a car hire firm. The occupational role and the requirements were controlled (where they were slightly varied it was always in favour of the coloured immigrant).

Also, in the field of employment, certain situation tests were carried out after the survey of immigrants. Firms where discrimination had been claimed had testers apply for the same type of occupation as had been applied for by the informants who claimed discrimination.

3. Discussion on Method

A three-pronged approach was used because a combination and comparison of the three sets of evidence provides a powerful tool for assessing the nature and extent of discrimination in each of the fields studied.

The overall summary (pages 5–6) is based on the combined evidence. In other sections the results for the individual fields are presented in terms of the various methods used. In reading the detailed information for each method, the limitations for each method should be borne in mind.

(i) *Survey of immigrants*
The assessment of the incidence of discrimination by interviewing immigrants themselves has to take into account the following influences:

(a) The situation where discrimination takes place may be such that it is impossible for the immigrant to know that it occurred. If a person is told a flat has been taken, a job is filled or that to hire a car will cost £12, the immigrant will not be aware of discrimination unless he has information that the flat is still vacant, the job remains to be filled and that the normal price to a native of similar driving experience is £10. In other situations, such as local authority housing, the complexity of the system makes certain knowledge impossible. Such factors will tend to minimise the level of discrimination reported.

(b) The reverse of the above is where the lack of incontrovertible evidence of discrimination leads to claims that are imaginary. In the event this problem did not prove to be very large. The incidence of 'you just know' or 'you can always tell' as a justification of reporting an incident as discriminatory was very small, and such cases constituted a low percentage of the claimed experiences of discrimination.

(c) Figures on the experience of discrimination based on all immigrants have to be evaluated in terms of a background where (for any particular field) a large proportion of immigrants will not have exposed themselves to the possibility of discrimination.

(ii) *Surveys of people in a position to discriminate*

(a) Interviews with people in a position to discriminate were not expected to produce a clear and unbiased estimate of discrimination. For reasons given below, the discrimination reported may be regarded as a minimum. However, apart from presenting the point of view of the people against whom claims of discrimination are made by immigrants, substantial information on discriminatory procedures was obtained.

(b) In the interviews a number of reasons for wishing to conceal the situation were found. Many revealed that whatever personal feelings may be, they believed that all people *should* be treated the same. This might be termed the 'sorry, no coloureds' syndrome. Also, many people in employment and housing were aware that legislation was being discussed. Most felt that such legislation would complicate their lives and were aware that a published report on the incidence of discrimination might have some impact on such a possibility.

(iii) *Situation testing*

The 'situation testing' provides the hardest evidence, in that the variables could be controlled and almost all parts could be supervised and independently verified. However, the level of discrimination shown by the tests indicates the level that would occur if coloured immigrants applied for housing and services on the same basis as the white population. As many coloured immigrants control their exposure to situations that might prove discriminatory, the actual level reported by the immigrant population is lower.

SUMMARY

4. General

The study has revealed substantial discrimination against coloured immigrants in the main aspects studied—employment, housing and the provision of services. The differential treatment and experiences of coloured immigrants as against other minority groups (such as Cypriots and Hungarians) leave no doubt that the discrimination is largely based on colour.

The West Indians, Pakistanis and Indians studied find discrimination the most disappointing feature of life in Britain. In contrast, the number of Cypriots experiencing discrimination is small and their disappointment is largely centred on such items as climate, food or the cost of living. Of the three coloured groups the experiences of the West Indians have been the worst. To a considerable extent this is due to their higher expectations on arrival and their greater desire to participate in a British pattern of life. This has caused them greater exposure to rejection and rebuff, and therefore to having a greater feeling that discrimination occurs in the various areas of life. One of the striking features of the life pattern of many of the Asian immigrants is the manner in which they organise their lives so that they have the minimum exposure to situations that may result in discrimination.

In the survey immigrants were found not to be hyper-sensitive about their colour or over-ready to claim discrimination or a colour bar. The detailed examination of discrimination in the main body of the report shows:

(i) immigrants tend to make claims of discrimination only when there is at least strong circumstantial evidence and usually unequivocal evidence of discrimination;

(ii) that the extent of claims of discrimination by immigrants is less than might be expected from independent evidence of the degree to which discrimination actually occurs.

The latter point is mainly attributable to the extent to which occasions that might lead to discrimination are avoided, or to the extent that discrimination is not overt.

5. Employment

Discrimination in employment is the biggest single criticism in immigrants' spontaneous criticism of life in Britain, and it is the area in which the greatest number of individual claims of discrimination were made. Of all immigrants interviewed, 36 per cent claimed discrimination and provided verbal evidence to this effect. Detailed examination of this evidence shows that in over a third of the cases the fact of discrimination was obvious: the reasons for not employing them being phrased as: 'No black bastards wanted'; 'No vacancy and why don't you go back to your own country'; 'We don't want any more Indians'.

In other cases the verbal evidence was more circumstantial. The claimed incidence of discrimination was highest for West Indians (45 per cent) and lowest for Cypriots (6 per cent).

Although the claims of discrimination were necessarily verbal recollections, there is no reason to dispute the veracity of their claims. Firms against which claims had been made were listed and 40 were selected. When an Englishman, a Hungarian and a person of the appropriate coloured group subsequently applied for the same type of job as had the original claimant, the number of cases of discrimination were:

Number of cases where no job available	10
Number of cases where employment possible	30
Discrimination against English tester	—
Discrimination against Hungarian tester	13
Discrimination against coloured tester	27

All the testers applied with a work-history of comparable experience and qualifications.

The tests also revealed, what had been indicated by the immigrants, that people in relatively low levels in a company's hierarchy play a very important role in the discrimination in employment. Such people as receptionists, personnel clerks, secretaries and gate-keepers were frequently the people who operated a filter system and turned immigrant applicants away.

Although among employers only four explicitly stated that it was company policy not to employ any coloured staff, the general attitude of employers was that coloured immigrants will be employed only: (i) if the labour shortage becomes too acute; (ii) for particular menial tasks. Obviously, the two factors are often inter-related, and there is general relief if neither occurs through sufficient white labour being available.

The reasons given to justify the attitude against employing immigrants mostly fall into one of three broad categories: (i) that the existing staff will not like it; (ii) that customers will not like it; (iii) that the immigrants are under-skilled, indolent or unlikely to stay with the company.

The question of customers not liking it is naturally more prevalent among service industries. Of the 60 retailers in the sample of local employers, 3 stated they would not employ coloured assistants at all, 14 stated they would not do so on the counter, and 3 stated they would not do so on particular counters (fresh food, corsetry, etc.).

The claim that immigrants were too mobile and under-skilled was common in most industries. These comments may be contrasted with some of the findings of the survey:

(i) Almost half the immigrants had been in their present occupation for over three years.

(ii) The higher the qualifications of the immigrant the more frequently was discrimination claimed. The percentage of people in each group claiming discrimination is:

English trade qualification	70 per cent
English school-leaving qualification (G.C.E. etc.)	44 per cent
No qualifications	36 per cent

Claims of discrimination were similarly high among people with formal qualifications obtained before coming to Britain. These and other results contained in the main body of the report indicate that it is those immigrants with the highest qualifications and general ability (language ability, familiarity with British life and customs, etc.) who experience most discrimination. This point was reinforced by the evidence of the owners and managers of employment bureaux, all of whom claimed that the majority of employers would not accept coloured office staff, even when properly qualified. Some of their estimates were that 90 per cent of their clients would not accept coloured office staff.

In discussing the employment of immigrants, employers frequently mentioned opposition from white employees. In some cases this was met by having unofficial quotas so that the number of immigrants was kept below a particular level in any one department. The difficult introductory period was also frequently mentioned by employers with coloured labour. Of these a number reported that after a while hostility diminished or ceased.

Both in terms of recruitment policy and the effects of employing immigrants, there was a considerable difference in the evidence of senior employers and trade unionists, who were speaking on a national level, and the local managers or trade union officials in the six areas. Whereas the national representative of large employers or unions tended to say that there were no major problems and to stress the existence of equal opportunity, the people at local level raised many examples of discrimination and stressed the problems of employing immigrants. In addition to resistance to initial recruitment, there were demands for such things as separate canteen and toilet facilities, and rejection by a majority of employers of the possibility of promotion for coloured workers, because of the resentment they expected from their white staff.

6. Housing

Whatever type of housing coloured immigrants seek, they encounter either substantial discrimination or severe handicaps. That the percentage of immigrants who claimed discrimination in private letting is relatively low compared with the discrimination shown in our housing tests, is due to two factors:

(i) the majority of immigrants do not expose themselves to possible discrimination by looking for accommodation on the open market;

(ii) as the situation tests have shown, substantial discrimination can occur without the immigrant who visits an agency or applies to a landlord knowing that it has occurred.

Claims of discrimination were lowest for the Cypriots and highest for the West Indians. The Asian immigrants were particularly prone to seek accommodation only from sources where they knew they would be acceptable (over two-thirds of them had never applied for rented accommodation from a white landlord who was a stranger). Within each of the three coloured groups, the proportion of those people who had exposed themselves to possible discrimination, who claimed actual experience of discrimination, was very similar —between 63 and 67 per cent.

According to the Milner-Holland report on housing in London, only 11 per cent of privately-let property is both advertised and does not specifically exclude coloured people. When this section of the private letting market that is notionally open to coloured applicants was tested, it was found that two-thirds excluded them in practice. Of 60 advertised properties called on by English, Hungarian and coloured testers, 45 resulted in discrimination against the coloured tester—40 cases of refusal and 5 cases of higher rent. When subsequently interviewed, all landlords admitted that they had discriminated.

The other source of privately-rented property is from accommodation bureaux or estate agents. Situation tests on these sources revealed discrimination in 14 of the 18 accommodation bureaux and 20 of the 30 estate agents. Interviews with agents and bureau managers, confirmed that the results reflected the general situation and practice. They said, in particular, that 'it was virtually impossible to obtain an unfurnished flat for a Pakistani or West Indian'. The general justification of the discriminatory behaviour was the desire to remain in business. The discrimination was attributed from the agent to the owner and often from the owner to other tenants or neighbours.

In the field of house purchase, similar levels of discrimination were found by situation testing at estate agents. Different estate agents were used but the results were very similar. Of the 42 estate agents tested for purchasing accommodation, 27 discriminated. As before, follow-up interviews confirmed the discriminatory behaviour and elicited similar types of justification. The two types of discrimination which occurred were that (a) the coloured immigrant was offered less addresses or no addresses, and (b) there were significant differences in what he was told about the possibility of his obtaining a mortgage or the type of mortgage he could obtain. Estate agents confirmed that these were the two main problems in finding houses for immigrants:

(a) Vendors in certain types of area were not prepared to sell to them.

(b) Building societies were loath to give them mortgages. This results in many immigrants having to accept mortgages at higher interest rates or initial deposits.

The remaining source of accommodation—council property—could not be tested in the same manner as the other categories of housing. Thus, information on council property is dependent on the immigrant survey and interviews with local authority officials. The main conclusions in this area are:

(i) Very few immigrants are currently housed in council property. This is in marked contrast to the section of the white population with similar occupational levels.

(ii) The present system of council house allocations put immigrants at a distinct disadvantage. In some cases this is the result of rules that were drawn up before immigrants arrived in substantial numbers. However, we encountered one example of the better housing being denied to immigrants by the deliberate imposition of a residential qualification.

(iii) There is evidence that, where immigrants have been housed, they have been housed mainly in the worst accommodation and this is, at least occasionally, as the result of direct discrimination. Officials stated that this was done in order to allay hostile reactions on the part of white residents.

The types of accommodation currently occupied by the large majority of coloured immigrants will eventually become due for slum clearance or redevelopment, so that council housing will have to be offered. In addition, those who have applied for council housing will eventually come to the top of the list; and the survey of immigrants showed that about one-tenth of the West Indians had gone as far as to put their names on the list. Housing more immigrants in council housing is likely to make immigrants aware of council housing as a possibility and will increase spontaneous demand. This demand will be additionally increased because of the lack of private accommodation that is open to them.

7. Motor Insurance and Car Hire

Within the fields covered, other than employment and housing, it was discrimination in motor insurance which was having the greatest impact on coloured immigrants. Fifty-eight per cent of those immigrants who had tried to obtain motor insurance claimed personal experience of discrimination. In seventeen out of twenty tests with insurance companies the coloured immigrant experienced discrimination (either being refused insurance altogether or quoted a higher premium) compared with the matched white alien and English testers. This discrimination in car insurance was also reflected by differential terms in car hire.

8. General Conclusion

The inquiry has shown that there is, without any doubt, substantial discrimination in Britain against coloured immigrants in employment, in housing and in the provision of certain services such as motor insurance.

The Survey summary concluded with the following observations:

This is the situation which exists now. It exists when, in both employment and housing, many immigrants are following ways of life which do not bring them into contact with potential discrimination. There were some suggestions from people in a position to discriminate that time would reduce discrimination; familiarity would reduce hostility and make immigrants more acceptable.

Such optimism is not borne out by the findings of the research, which show two main trends:

(i) As immigrants become more accustomed to English ways of life, as they acquire higher expectations and higher qualifications, so they experience more personal direct discrimination. This is apparent in the local differences between areas with established communities as opposed to new communities. It is reflected in the experiences of school-leavers who are the children of immigrants. Their numbers will increase.

(ii) Awareness of discrimination, prejudice and hostility tends to make immigrants withdraw into their own closed communities.

(Supplement to Institute of Race Relations *Newsletter*, April 1967)

APPENDIX VI

(From Institute of Race Relations *Newsletter*, April 1966, pp. 2–10.)

THE 1966 GENERAL ELECTION

by NICHOLAS DEAKIN

I would forecast that in at least 12 constituencies there will be full-blooded Smethwick-type campaigns at the next General Election and in a similar number of others a strong line will be taken somewhat to the right of official party policy. . . . No industrial constituency will be able to duck the issue, because if the candidates prevaricate the electorate will force them to take up clear positions. At the same time feeling is rising in suburban and rural areas. . . .

(Mr. Peter Griffiths—*Sheffield Telegraph*, 16 July 1965)

The former Member for Smethwick and others (like the present writer) who argued from the effects of the immigration issue in the 1964 Election that in 1966 there would be a corresponding fluctuation in the results, at least in those seats directly affected by migration, were wrong. Putting it at its simplest, the overall swing to Labour in such seats was 3·8%, compared with 2·6% for the country as a whole. Of the 17 Conservative-held seats among the 50 in the *Economist* list of constituencies affected by immigration 13 were captured by Labour. More important, in the West Midlands, the area most commonly singled out as one in which Labour's electoral progress would be jeopardised by the issue, Labour made two gains—both in seats in which the question of immigration had been crucial in 1964—and achieved a swing of 3·7% in their favour. Finally, although the question of immigration was raised in a few places by candidates taking a 'strong' line (to employ Mr. Griffiths' definition) there is no evidence that candidates using it did any better or worse than their party colleagues. Mr. Griffiths himself, who opened his campaign with the pronouncement that immigration remained the most important issue in his constituency and that it would be hypocritical to pretend otherwise, later opted to focus on housing and crime (in particular the necessity for severer penalties) but saw his 1964 majority of 1,774 become one of 3,490 for his Labour opponent, the actor Mr. Andrew Faulds, a swing of 7·7% against him.

Under the circumstances it is hardly surprising that the significance of the issue of immigration in British politics is now being written off altogether—'we have buried the race issue', said Mr. Brian Walden (the Labour Member for Birmingham, All Saints) on election night, and several of his colleagues, including Mr. Faulds, have echoed his views since then. More flatly, Gallup has pronounced as follows: 'Swing (in seats affected) well above national average. . . . Immigration not an election issue'.

But before joining Mr. Walden at the funeral it might be worth taking a closer look at the background to the political neutralising of a social issue which undoubtedly still arouses a good deal of feeling both in the areas that have received migration and (a fact that is still too easily forgotten in the present debate) among the migrants themselves.

SENSE AND SENSATIONALISM IN THE PRESS

It is possible to single out a number of separate factors working towards this neutralisation: it may be convenient to start with one of the less important. This was the volume of attention paid to the whole question of the immigration issue and its likely consequences by the press. Harsh words have been said—and will no doubt continue to be said—about the standard of press coverage given to the issue, but at least there is no doubt that after the last election the notion that immigration as a social issue with political overtones was taboo as a subject finally disappeared. The opening of the 1966 campaign brought reporters in large numbers to the West Midlands, and in particular to Smethwick; it also saw the beginning of a complete series on the political implication of the issue, by David Loshak of the *Daily Telegraph*. Mr. Loshak's constituency reports were restrained and on the whole sensible: taken together, they pointed to the general conclusion that the immigration issue was not going to be of great importance—a conclusion that the sub-editors responsible for his stories found it increasingly hard to accept. His opening piece, indicating that 'in perhaps only a dozen divisions, for local reasons, is (the) reaction strong enough to disturb traditional voting patterns' was headlined 'Racial issue factor in 50 divisions': a later piece about Willesden East concluding that Liberal intervention might lose Mr. Reg Freeson (Labour) the seat, and that such a defeat 'is in danger of being misinterpreted as a defeat for his stand on immigration' earned the headline 'Race problem puts Labour in danger'. (25/3)

Other stories were less sensible, if more straightforwardly presented; e.g. those by Mr. Loshak's colleague John Petty (17/3), and a sadly sub-standard piece by James Cameron (*Standard* 22/3). But taken together, the journalists did ensure that any candidate with a mind to raise the issue was bound to have to cope with awkward questions from reporters and publicity for the answers. One particular episode illustrates the point clearly. In February 1966 Mr. Donald Finney, Mr. Griffiths' ally in the crucial period leading up to the 1964 campaign (totally neglected by the press, with one honourable exception), announced to the *Guardian's* correspondent that he was disillusioned with his former leader and that he and his supporters in the 'English Rights Group' that he has set up would support Alderman George Hawkins, the Conservative candidate for West Bromwich, in the forthcoming campaign. This announcement provoked a flood of stories and interviews both of Mr. Finney and Alderman Hawkins; the upshot was that Alderman Hawkins, who had at first conditionally accepted the offered support, was instructed to decline it, and did so. As John Mackintosh put it in the *New Statesman*, 'Finney is furious with the press for hounding him out of the political mainstream. He has lost his most powerful weapon: the respectable umbrella of the Conservative Party' (25/3). . . . And indeed Finney showed his rage in no uncertain terms to those who approached him thereafter.

A CONSENSUS OF STRINGENCY

But by far the most important factor in determining the degree to which the issue emerged, and one from which a series of other secondary consequences flow, was the convergence of the policies of the two major parties. Enough has been written about the Government's White Paper of August 1965 to make it unnecessary to remind the reader of more than the basic facts: that the chief proposals in the White Paper were a reduction of the intake of workers from the Commonwealth to 8,500 per annum and a number of further restrictions on dependants, coupled with certain proposals for integration of migrants in this country, that it provoked bitter opposition both from certain Members and nearly all immigrant organizations, and that it was overwhelmingly popular in the country at large—Gallup found 88% of the population in favour and 5% opposed. The draftsman responsible for the Labour manifesto (widely presumed to be Mr. Peter Shore, Mr. Wilson's P.P.S. and Member for multi-racial Stepney) evidently thought so as well; the manifesto merely stated that 'we shall continue realistic controls, flexibly administered', adding that there would be an 'imaginative and determined programme to ensure racial equality'. Events were to justify this view that the lily needed no gilding: even in the Midlands Gallup polls taken during the election showed that the electorate did not see much difference between the two parties when it came to the handling of the immigration question. In other words, Labour's vulnerable flank, the widespread view that they would be likely to be 'soft' on immigration for doctrinaire reasons, had been effectively shielded by the White Paper.

The Conservative Party made great play during the 1964 Election campaign with the argument (of which Sir Alec Douglas-Home in particular made full use) that they were the party that had introduced immigration restriction in 1962 against Labour opposition: they also had to contend with the accusation made by the less scrupulous of their Labour opponents that the immigrants had 'come in under the Tories'. On this occasion it was thought necessary to put forward a programme in which even more stringent restrictions on immigration were a central feature: this came as something of a surprise to many observers, who had supposed that the Government's policy represented a *ne plus ultra* in this direction. The essence of the new proposal was that new entrants would be admitted on a probationary basis, to be reviewed at the end of two or so years to determine whether they could then become (in Mr. Heath's rather unfortunate phrase) 'permanent immigrants'. They would also have to register the number of dependants they wished to bring with them. This policy, Mr. Peter Thorneycroft (then Shadow Home Secretary) explained in a party political broadcast, would have two advantages:

> We should know for the first time the size of the problem of dependants waiting to come in; we should be able to check more easily who is a dependant, and in the case of new immigrants we should be able to give priority among the small number we admit to those with few dependants.

However, any encouragement that this new line may have given to the more extreme elements in the Conservative Party was sharply checked both by the party chairman, Mr. Du Cann, and Mr. Heath. The latter, questioned on television by Robin Day, said:

This is absolutely plain and clear, the Conservative Party will have nothing whatever to do with any kind of racial discrimination at all. And if I find any candidate is doing this I shall certainly not condone it; I shall condemn it.

Thus the combined efforts of the two major parties, described in a *Times* leader (22/3) as 'the door-banging of the manifestos', was to establish a consensus on the immigration issue, in which the Liberal Party could perhaps be described as a sleeping partner, and which not even the efforts of that experienced lobbyist and letter-writer Lord Elton could disturb. Nor did the divergence of views between the parties on the Rhodesian issue 'spill over' to any significant degree into discussion of immigration.

EXTREMISTS IN THE COLD

It must be conceded straight away that the new bipartisanship had one important by-effect: by cutting away their ground for manœuvre it minimised the importance of the extremist groups that in several cases had made surprising progress in 1964. These groups may be roughly divided into two categories—the ostensibly non-political pressure-groups and the minor political parties. The first can be disposed of briefly. The Birmingham Immigration Control Association had played a considerable part in the campaign in the Birmingham area in 1964, particularly in relation to Dr. Wyndham Davies' unexpected win at Perry Barr. But on this occasion the Association had clearly been caught napping by the announcement of the Election: a half-hearted attempt was made to arrange a 'Voter's Veto' and to circulate literature to supporters, but these activities made no discernable impact. Similarly the Racial Preservation Society, whose Newsletter under its various titles had achieved a wide circulation (see March 1966 *Newsletter*), made some attempt to influence the electorate by distributing literature in selected constituencies, together with a special leaflet defending the Society's conception of racial purity, but the effect seems to have been negligible.

One of the minor parties standing on this issue also needs only a brief reference. The Union Movement put up no candidates at the Election of 1964; on this occasion they had four—Jeffrey Hamm at Birmingham, Handsworth, F. T. Hamley at Manchester, Ardwick, D. H. Harmston at Islington South-West and Sir Oswald Mosley himself at Shoreditch and Finsbury. All four did badly; Sir Oswald's own vote (1,126—4·6% of the poll) must now finally destroy his pretensions to being the only national figure capable of attracting votes by force of personality among the extremist groups. The British National Party is a more serious proposition; its leaders are not handicapped, as Mosley is, by association with pre-war Fascism and they have shed the dogmas of anti-Semitism in order to focus more clearly on the colour issue. But their Smethwick candidate, Roy Stanley, did very badly (perhaps because there is very little scope for an extremist in the Smethwick situation, with most of his appeal already pre-empted—as D. H. Davies found when standing as a 'stop immigration independent' two years ago): Mr. G. Rowe in Deptford failed to consolidate all the support gathered in the very amateurish campaign which the independent Mr. Atkins ran on a similar platform two years ago, running 480 votes behind him for a total of 1,906 (7·1%). Only the

B.N.P.'s star performer, their general secretary Mr. John Bean, succeeded in making any real impact (in Southall) and his vote descended from 3,410 (9·1%) in 1964 to 2,768 (7·4%) on this occasion.

Similarly, the founder and leader of the New Liberal Party, Mr. A. E. Lomas, whose platform contained in its immigration plank perhaps the most striking over-simplification of the election ('Stop immigration, thus overcrowding. THIS WILL SOLVE THE HOUSING PROBLEM') lost almost half his 1964 support, polling only 1,127 votes, compared with 2,053 last time. Of the gaggle of independents who made some mention of the issue, perhaps only Dr. Brown of the National Democrat Party, who stood at Ipswich, is worth a comment—he polled 769 votes. It is perhaps worth adding that the performance of all these candidates, minor party and independent alike, was put in the shade by that of Mr. P. Downey, standing under emotional circumstances at Nelson and Colne, on the issue of capital punishment. He polled 5,117 votes (13·7%) and saved his deposit—a very rare achievement for an independent candidate standing against both major parties.

AND THE IMMIGRANTS THEMSELVES?

Although the electoral damage done by the minor parties was minimised by the position adopted by the major parties, one might have expected there to be a countervailing factor in the resentment aroused among the immigrants, particularly against the Labour Party. In the event, this resentment, although it undoubtedly existed, does not seem to have had much political significance. No organisation yet speaks for the immigrants as a whole; CARD'S attempts to fill the vacuum have met with only partial success—while the R.A.A.S. is a successful sick joke at the expense of the British press. As far as individual ethnic groups are concerned, the fragmentation of the West Indian community in this country makes it difficult to generalise about the West Indian reaction: the Standing Conference of West Indian Organisations perhaps comes closest to providing a source of organised opinion, in London at least. Standing Conference, however, confined itself to cautious attempts to persuade West Indians to participate in the election, at least to the extent of voting: similar attempts were made by other immigrant organisations in various parts of the country to raise the low rate of registration and encourage voting, often in an attempt to dramatise the possession of equal citizenship and its attendant rights. But these moves were non-partisan and on a limited scale—there was no sign of the protest candidatures that had been threatened in more than one place after the White Paper.

In the Midlands, however, a coalition of the Indian Workers' Association, the Standing Conference (Birmingham section) and the Pakistani Welfare Association took the opportunity provided by the Prime Minister's visit to Birmingham Rag Market to issue a statement deploring the change of front by the Labour Party on the immigration issue. They followed this up with a statement advising their members in the Birmingham marginal seats of Sparkbrook (estimated number of immigrant electors 3,300) and All Saints (4,000) to abstain from voting as a protest. Those concerned were at pains to explain that their statement, which aroused a good deal of controversy and some dissent from other immigrant organisations, was directed not against the Labour Party but against the two individual Members concerned, Messrs. Walden and Hattersley, and their views. An extension of this policy (unofficially described as 'vote Labour against Fascists and abstain elsewhere') led to support being given to Mr. Foley in West Bromwich and Mr. Faulds in Smethwick—the latter may have gained as much as 1,500 votes in this way. Local circumstances also led independently to a vigorous campaign being conducted within the local Indian community in Southall on behalf of Mr. Syd Bidwell, the Labour candidate.

The results of these various initiatives within the immigrant community are difficult to evaluate, particularly since in some areas a significant proportion of the migrant vote may have gone to the Conservatives. It is clear, however, that the abstention campaign did not hurt either Mr. Hattersley (who had a swing of 8·6% in his favour) or Mr. Walden (7·7%).

A final possibility, that of intervention by a candidate from the anti-Government Radical Alliance in a seat affected by the issue, was canvassed at the outset of the campaign but never materialised. Mr. Hattersley, who was most frequently named as the target for such a candidature, professed indifference at the possibility: in view of the dismal performance of the only Radical Alliance candidate who did stand (Miss Pat Arrowsmith at Fulham), he was probably justified in electoral terms.

NO 'DEVIANTS' AFTER ALL

Despite this general background of press vigilance, an agreed view uniting the major parties and the comparative ineffectiveness of the extremist parties and most of the immigrant organisations, special circumstances in individual constituencies might have been expected to produce a few deviant campaigns or 'strong' campaigns, in Mr. Griffiths' terms. In the end, not even one such campaign materialised, largely because of the firm handling of the situation by Conservative Central Office. Alderman Hawkins' position in West Bromwich has already been outlined: after Finney's withdrawal he had a number of statements about the need for a complete ban on migration to the town and dispersal of those already present; these tended towards an extreme position but came within the latitude provided for Conservatives by Mr. Heath's statement that to advocate different or stronger controls was not racialism. Miss Maddin in Southall also advocated a complete stop on immigration to the town, but her case was deployed with restraint. Two London Conservative candidates showed signs of introducing the issue into their campaigns. Mr. Giles in Deptford, facing like Miss Maddin an opponent from the B.N.P., felt it necessary to state in his election address:

> My views on this controversial subject have been widely publicised in the local and national press. For years I gave warning that unchecked immigration could create friction. For the sake of everyone, including those immigrants who have been here a number of years, I advocated the enforcement of strict controls.

Mr. Douglas Wilson, fighting to retain the marginal seat of Lambeth Norwood, went further. His election address called, in a bold headline, for

'No More Immigrants in Lambeth', and one particular passage, later distributed as a duplicated sheet, said that 'unless something is done, the people of Lambeth, who have paid their rates, taxes and national insurance stamps for years, will find the facilities to which these payments entitle them swamped by newcomers who have hardly contributed a penny'. This leaflet was promptly dispatched by Mr. Wilson's opponents to the Conservative Party leadership and almost equally promptly withdrawn—probably to the relief of the candidate, who was manifestly wary in his dealings with reporters over the incident. Apart from this episode and the extremist candidatures in Islington, the issue broke surface in a confused incident in Greenwich, when a Labour canvasser was alleged to have told an elector that the Conservatives would 'flood the country with blacks'. The allegation was strongly denied and the incident petered out.

One Midland seat, Wolverhampton North East, briefly gained attention after the attractions of West Bromwich as the most likely locale for a sensational result began to fade. The attention was not so much of a result of the General Election campaign as of the candidature of Mr. Joe Holland, a local builder, at the local elections. Standing on an overtly racialist platform, Mr. Holland—who had previously won a Council seat as an independent with tacit Conservative support—came a close third in his ward with 1,175 votes. A series of accusations and counter-accusations between the General Election candidates about whether the Conservative Mr. Geoffrey Wright, was prepared to make a play for these votes (he had gone as far as to advocate a five-year standstill) culminated in the issuing of a writ by Mrs. Short, the defending Labour Member. The uncertainty produced by these events lasted until 10.07 p.m. on election night, when Wolverhampton North East, the second seat to declare, gave Mrs. Short a greatly increased majority (the swing in her favour was 5·9%) and disposed of the possibility of any surprise defeats in the Black Country.

A number of other Conservative candidates for seats not affected by immigration—notably Sir Gerald Nabarro, seeking (successfully) to return to the Commons at Worcestershire South—felt it necessary to make controversial statements on the issue, but the firm line taken by Central Office prevented them from taking the matter further. Labour candidates were more inclined to stick to the letter of the manifesto: a questionnaire circulated to 537 Labour candidates by the *Daily Express* produced 344 replies in favour of the Government's policy and only 22 supporting without qualification 'a relaxation of the Immigration Act'.

NON-ISSUE OR ACCEPTED ISSUE?

The course of events during the election campaign accordingly bore out the general view among informed observers that the political heat had gone out of the issue in comparison with earlier years, and this view was reinforced by the polls taken during the campaign, both in the Midlands and nationally. National Opinion Polls found that only one person in twelve ranked the issue as the most important facing the country; one-third put it last in significance in a list of seven (*The Times*, 24/3). In the Midlands, immigration invariably lagged behind housing, and in Perry Barr, a seat largely won on an immigration scare in 1964, it was ranked behind roads. (*Birmingham Evening Mail*, 25/3).

These conclusions were also reached on an impressionistic level by direct observation of events during the campaign compared with their equivalents of two years before. One example may perhaps suffice. On the eve of polling in 1964 Mr. Marcus Lipton, the Labour Member for Brixton, addressed a packed meeting in Lambeth Town Hall. He had had the disagreeable experience of being rung up and told that he had been sentenced to death by the Brixton S.S., but even allowing for this his handling of the audience was not very happy. He was vigorously heckled by members of one of the neo-Fascist splinter groups and was manifestly unhappy under fire. At question time he fumbled when questioned about immigration and had to be rescued by the chairman—a particularly humiliating experience for a seasoned performer who specialises himself in Question Time at the House. Worst of all, he spoke like a man uncertain of his position and of the repercussions of the issue on his political future. On the eve of polling in 1966 Mr. Lipton addressed another crowded meeting in the same building. His confident, knockabout political turn was delivered with total command of the audience—only a few feeble Conservative hecklers attempted to hold up his progress and they were swept aside with practised skill. Immigration came up only once, when Mr. Lipton, as an aside during a passage on planning, castigated the Conservative Government for failing to plan for the concentration of population in the South-East. Apart from one anguished Conservative cry of 'Not true' this thrust went totally unremarked. The contrast was complete.

Granted a decline, for whatever reason, in the tensions previously present, what are the prospects for the future? Optimists are pointing to the time factor as a solution in itself—familiarity breeding acceptance; cynics are already suggesting that we are all racialists now. Without going as far as this, it is legitimate to take the view that the politicians have abandoned (temporarily, one hopes) their role of leading and educating public opinion in favour of a series of belated adjustments to it. It should be added that this willingness to come to terms with both the legitimate anxieties and the prejudices of the population at large extends right across the political spectrum—degrees of inclination to right and left as indicators of virtue on this issue are obsolescent. Of course, it would be wrong to neglect the other side of the balance sheet: the passing of a Race Relations Act, however inadequate, and the greatly increased support given to an expanded National Committee for Commonwealth Immigrants. If these admittedly limited achievements were possible during a period of tension, it seems at first sight legitimate to hope that a good deal more can be accomplished now that the atmosphere is calmer.

The rock on which these hopes may split is one of the politicians' own construction: the effect of the retreat in the face of public opinion may be to limit permanently the extent to which progress in integration can be made. The crucial miscalculation, it seems to some of us, has been to suppose that stringent controls ('realistic' controls, in the jargon of the manifestos) would quieten fears rather than legitimise and perpetuate them. A secondary error was to suppose that somehow the confidence of the immigrants could be maintained during the retreat: the ludicrous avowals by both parties that immigrants are to be treated exactly the same as other citizens, presumably even while they are turned away, deported or suffered to enter on ticket-of-leave, are presumably made with this intention. They cannot be convincing, even to those that made them—much less to the immigrants.

The net result, then, is that we are at least secure against political exploitation of the issue of the extremists, and this is a clear gain. But it is necessary to be clear about how this has been achieved: we have assimilated the racialists, not the immigrants. Under the circumstances, perhaps the most interesting facet of the Election, considered from the point of view of future race relations, was the reaction of the immigrants themselves in the face of this new solidarity in the host community. No clear picture emerges. A section, perhaps the largest, opted out—disillusioned, or more often not involved or interested. Another section voted *en bloc* for their special interest, as they defined it, in local circumstances. But a third element voted as individuals—individual trades unionists, parents, tenants or landlords; they felt, as Dr. Prem put it, that 'the election is not a referendum on immigration but covers many important national issues'. Asked about how the West Indians in his constituency would vote, one London candidate replied 'on the issues'. If this kind of involvement can be maintained and increased, particularly in the much-vaunted new generation now beginning to emerge from the schools, we may yet be luckier than we deserve.

APPENDIX VII

BRITISH VOTERS AND THE IMMIGRATION ISSUE

Attitudes on the part of the native Briton towards coloured immigrants have been investigated with some regularity since the issue of immigration first became publicly visible as a result of the disturbances in Nottingham and Notting Dale in 1958. Both the Gallup Poll and National Opinion Polls have examined attitudes in some depth and studied the reactions of electors towards the proposals made by successive governments in their attempts to deal with the question of immigration. However, most of these investigations have examined attitudes towards immigration in isolation; the danger is that the reactions obtained from respondents in different situations may not have equivalent weight—one would expect the saliency of the issue to differ for different respondents according to their exposure to the realities of the issue.

In the course of the General Election campaign of March 1966 the Gallup Poll administered a questionnaire to a sample of nearly 6,000 voters. In the course of this operation respondents were asked to select the issue which struck them as 'the most urgent facing the country at the present time'. The answers to this question, which were classified in eleven categories, offered a useful opportunity of testing the relative importance spontaneously assigned to the immigration issue by voters; further examination of the data also reveals the degree of importance attached to the issue in relation to exposure to the problem. Another factor that sets this investigation apart from most earlier ones is the very large size of the sample. This means that a considerable amount of detailed analysis is possible and that the comparatively small differences in the proportions of those expressing concern about issues can be regarded as significant. We are very grateful to the Gallup Poll for giving permission for unpublished material to be reproduced here.

ECONOMIC SITUATION AND HOUSING RATED MUCH MORE URGENT

In the first table respondents to the question requiring the selection of an issue as the most urgent facing the country are broken down by voting intention, area of residence, social class, age and some further occupational, residential and other characteristics. For comparative purposes five issues, apart from that of immigration, have been selected. These are: the economic situation (selection of which might be said to be a crude index of political awareness and involvement in the election, since this issue was generally agreed to be the most important); education (an issue that affects most ordinary citizens but is not usually thought of as a political one, in the party sense); housing (concern over which has often been equated with concern about immigration); labour relations (which might in some circumstances be an index of right-wing inclination); and the Commonwealth (which, under the circumstances of March 1966, was equivalent to concern about the Rhodesia issue).

The first point to note is that, in the sample as a whole, only 5 per cent of those questioned selected immigration as the most urgent problem facing the country. This compares with the choice of the economic situation by nearly half the sample and of housing by 15 per cent. Only education among the issues selected causes less concern than the question of immigration. It should be stressed at this point that the mere selection of the issue as the most urgent does not necessarily imply prejudice on the part of the respondent. However, the present Government's policy on the immigration issue has been the subject of substantial agreement by both major parties and, according to an enquiry carried out in August 1965, by 87 per cent of the adult population. To express concern at this point with the Government's policy is presumably to reject that policy; a position that would be likely to be adopted only by a few liberal critics (who would be likely to select other issues as having higher priority), and by those who feel that immigration should be stopped altogether. It is therefore arguable that most of the 5 per cent selecting this issue disapprove of the Government's policy and do so because they feel that it is insufficiently stringent.

PARTY MEMBERSHIP AND CONCERN

Turning to the different groups within the sample, we find that there is no difference between supporters of the two major parties. Both those intending to vote Conservative and those intending to vote Labour correspond exactly with the sample as a whole in the extent to which they select the immigration issue. However, Liberal supporters seem significantly less concerned. Marked differences begin to appear when area of residence is considered. The first group to show a stronger propensity to select the issue are those residing in marginally held Labour seats. These were defined by Gallup as seats that would fall to the Conservatives with a swing of up to 2·3 per cent and have also been affected by immigration; interest in the issue was therefore to be expected. The incidence of selection rises further in those areas that have been defined as 'colour problem districts'. There are fifty of these constituencies; they were selected by A. J. Allen and Associates, the market research firm, on the basis of the electoral importance of the immigration issue and included most of those with a substantial immigrant population (although this doesn't necessarily mean that all cities in which the issue is a sensitive one were included). Both the Midlands and the Greater London conurbation area also showed a higher level of concern, but by far the highest incidence of selection in any specific group of the sample is among those resident in Birmingham—11 per cent of these selected the issue.

Other less spectacular distinctions also appear. Women seem less concerned than men, and those in the higher class categories (as defined in market research terms) less than the lower; the young and the old seem slightly less concerned. Wives of manual workers are very much less concerned, but manual workers are more concerned. These workers support Labour in the proportion of three to one; in view of the fact that Labour supporters as a whole display no more than average concern, this would seem to imply either that the level of concern of Labour voters is diluted by a dose of middle-class supporters who think the issue less important, or that manual workers feeling more concern vote Conservative. This view receives some support from the fact that concern is apparently lower among trades unionists (who are more likely to support Labour) than among workers generally, and would be in line with McKenzie and Silver's tentative findings on the Conservative supporters in the working class.[1]

HOUSING AND IMMIGRATION ISSUES ASSOCIATED?

Some relationship does appear to exist between concern about housing and concern about immigration. Both rise in the colour problem areas and in Birmingham; both are very low in upper-class respondents and among those who own houses. However, the group that expressed most concern about housing (women manual workers) also expressed least concern about immigration. In general, where special reasons exist for anxiety about housing (particularly among those renting from private landlords) the issue will emerge independently of immigration, as one would expect. Concern about education was uniformly low, except for the 35/44 age group, who will have young children. Concern about the Commonwealth appears to some extent in London and to a greater degree among upper-class respondents. It does not appear to be related to feeling on the immigration issue.

CHARACTERISTICS OF THE RESPONDENTS BY BIRTH-PLACE

It has also been possible to obtain certain information about those answering the questionnaire as a whole. Sixty-one of these were born in the Commonwealth, 149 in Ireland and 63 in other countries abroad.[2] Although these numbers are comparatively small and any conclusions must be subject to very cautious interpretation, it is interesting to compare these respondents with the whole sample.

Those born in the Commonwealth are a small group and may include some natives of Old Commonwealth countries. In terms of geographical distribution, the Commonwealth-born respondents match fairly accurately the profile obtained of immigrants from the New Commonwealth at the 1961 Census, although it must be noted that the Gallup sample is not strictly comparable, since it is drawn from the Electoral Register, which is of course confined to adults. The balance between the sexes is almost precisely the same; the class division, insofar as comparisons can be made, is similar although rather larger numbers of the Gallup sample are to be found in the lower categories. The Gallup sample also contains a rather

[1] In Richard Rose (ed.), *Studies in British Politics* (Macmillan, 1966), pp. 21–34.

[2] Detailed analysis of the 63 foreign-born respondents is not included—they do not form a group of sufficient homogeneity to justify such analysis. It may be worth recording that, in general terms, they are older than the Commonwealth-born group (more than half are over 75), of higher socio-economic status, inclined to support the Conservative Party and to own their own housing. About a quarter live in areas affected by immigration from the Commonwealth.

larger proportion of manual workers than the 10 per cent sample data on employment in the 1961 Census would lead one to expect. Other characteristics are generally in line with information from other sources; the very small proportion in council housing and the comparatively large number of car-owners and house-owners (by coincidence precisely the same as in the whole sample) are both predictable. The fact that only just under a third live in the areas defined as 'colour problem district' reflects the basis on which the districts were selected rather than on the credibility of the sample. The information that a considerable number of the Commonwealth-born live in safe Conservative seats is less surprising than it might seem; several Conservative-held constituencies (Leicester S.W., Moss Side, Wolverhampton S.W., Walsall S., Birmingham (Edgbaston)) contain areas of substantial immigrant settlement.

The most interesting piece of information to be obtained from this section, however, is that the majority of the Commonwealth-born intended to vote Conservative, subject to the proviso that only slightly over half of them thought it likely that they would vote. This runs contrary to the generally accepted view that Commonwealth immigrants support the Labour Party. Although some observers have detected an increasing tendency on the part of Asian immigrants to support the Conservative Party, most people would find it hard to agree that many West Indians would express a serious intention to vote Conservative—and, even allowing for the possible presence of some Old Commonwealth citizens, the West Indians are likely to be in the majority in the sample. Certainly the contrast between the Commonwealth-born and the Irish, who live up to their reputation of supporting the Labour Party, is very striking. But in the absence of further data one can only speculate: perhaps along the lines that an expressed intention to vote for the Conservative Party, perceived as the party of those who have arrived socially and are financially secure, may be seen as a claim for acceptance and even respect—without the necessity for action to substantiate the claim.

N.D.

(Supplement to Institute of Race Relations *Newsletter*, March 1967)

GALLUP I

Selection of Problem as 'Most Urgent Facing the Country at the Present Time'

Characteristics	*Problem chosen* % Immigration	% Economy	% Education	% Housing	% Labour Relations	% C'wealth Relations	No.
Whole sample	5	44	4	15	6	8	5,978
Men	6	54	4	13	8	9	2,760
Women	4	36	4	17	5	8	3,210
Voting intention							
Con.	5	53	3	12	7	10	2,273
Lab.	5	39	5	18	6	7	2,887
Lib.	3	50	3	11	8	9	388
D/K	3	29	3	15	4	7	432
Resident in							
Safe Con. seat	4	49	4	14	6	9	2,514
Safe Lab. seat	5	40	4	16	7	8	2,934
Marginal Lab.	7	44	5	23	6	11	378*
Con.	5	46	5	16	5	9	1,620*
'Colour problem' areas	8	39	2	22	4	6	532
Midlands	7	45	3	14	8	9	1,098
All Borough/ Conurbation	7	41	3	20	5	7	2,300
Greater London Conurbation	7	42	3	20	6	10	1,205
Birmingham	11	37	2	21	3	3	293
Social Class							
Upper	3	62	3	4	6	12	150
Middle	4	57	4	10	6	10	1,381
Working	5	42	4	17	6	8	3,937
V. poor	6	24	3	17	5	7	506
Age							
Under 35	4	43	4	21	5	7	1,354
35–44	5	46	6	15	5	8	1,230
45–64	5	49	3	15	8	9	2,219
65	4	34	3	9	7	9	1,115
Own car	5	52	4	12	6	10	2,701
Selected Work Characteristics							
Employed on manual work	7	45	4	18	7	8	1,883
Woman manual worker	4	28	3	26	3	4	416
Wife of manual worker	3	31	4	18	4	6	1,219
Trades Union member	6	47	5	19	8	8	1,514
Type of House Tenure							
House owner	4	51	4	11	7	9	2,839
Rent from Council	5	39	4	17	6	7	1,583
Rent from private landlord	6	38	2	23	5	8	1,229

* unweighted

GALLUP II

Characteristics of Respondents

	Commonwealth-born (N=61)	Irish-born (N=149)	Whole Sample (N=5,978)
	%	%	%
Male	59·0	53·7	46·2
Female	41·0	46·3	53·8
Voting intention			
March 1966			
Lab.	27·8	65·8	48·0
Con.	47·6	25·5	37·8
Lib.	3·3	4·7	6·4
Other	—	—	0·6
D/K	21·3	4·0	7·2
Will certainly vote	57·4	75·8	80·9
Resident in			
Safe Con. seat	42·6	38·3	42·1
Safe Lab. seat	41·0	51·7	49·1
Marginal	16·4	9·4	7·7
(All) Borough or conurbation	67·2	61·7	38·5
Greater London conurbation	31·1	28·1	20·2
Birmingham	13·1	9·4	4·9
'Colour problem' areas	29·5	16·8	8·9
Social class			
Upper	3·3	—	2·5
Middle	21·3	16·1	23·1
Working	67·2	75·2	65·9
V. poor	8·2	8·7	8·5
Age			
Under 35	27·8	32·8	22·6
35–44	41·0	24·2	20·6
45–64	27·9	28·9	38·2
65	3·3	14·1	18·6
Own car	41·0	26·2	45·2
Telephone	24·6	17·4	27·2
Selected Work Characteristics			
Employed on manual work	42·6	50·3	31·4
Trades Union member	26·2	34·2	25·3
Type of House Tenure			
House owner	47·5	28·2	47·5
Rent from Council	13·1	34·2	26·5
Rent from private landlord	27·9	26·2	20·6

NOTES—GALLUP I AND II

Not all figures for samples add up under each category to the precise total.

A marginal Labour seat was defined as one vulnerable to a swing of up to 2·3 per cent to Conservative, and affected by the immigration issue.

A marginal Conservative seat was defined as one vulnerable to a swing of up to 4·4 per cent.

Safe seats are those not vulnerable to such swings in either direction.

APPENDIX VIII

AREA REPORT—SOUTHALL

Part III*

by Peter Marsh†

WHAT WENT WRONG AT WOOLF'S?

The six week strike (or five week lock-out, as it is more accurately known) of rubber workers at Woolf's Solar Works, Southall, ended on Monday in almost complete victory for the union and the strikers. (*Paul Foot in* Tribune *14/1/1966*)

The Indian workers whose six week strike at a Middlesex rubber factory ended on Monday start their return to work with their industrial complaints unresolved. (*News item in the* Daily Telegraph *12/1/1966*)

A year ago Punjabi Sikhs were to be seen patrolling outside the gates of R. Woolf and Company (Rubber) Ltd., a small rubber factory which stands on the boundary between Southall and Hayes, Middlesex. For over six weeks—from 30 November 1965 to 12 January 1966—nearly 600 workers, the vast majority of whom had migrated from the Hoshiapur and Jullundur districts of the Punjab, maintained a strike at Woolf's factory, which gained the admiration of hundreds of thousands of trade unionists up and down the country because of its solidarity in face of the bitter hostility of the management. Nevertheless, the general public remained confused about the reasons for and aims of this strike. Because the majority of the strikers were Punjabi Sikhs, many of the national newspapers, including the *Daily Mail* and the *Guardian*, laid special emphasis on the racial aspect of the situation; thus what was a conflict between employer and employees about pay, conditions and trade union membership, became a garbled story of dignified, turbanned Sikhs at war with their employer and their Pakistani neighbours.

What is the situation today at Woolf's? Unquestionably the union as an

* Southall Part I (by I.R.R.) was published as a supplement in March 1966 and gave a general background report of the area. Southall Part II (by Dewitt John) was concerned with the 1966 elections and the Sikhvote, and appeared as a supplement in April 1966. Copies of both are still available.

† Peter Marsh began university work at Ruskin College, Oxford, at the age of 27, where he studied political science and sociology between 1961–3. He then went to Trinity College, Cambridge, as a mature student, 1963–5, after which he spent a year doing post-graduate work at the new University of Essex, where he concentrated on problems of minority groups. He is now Publicity Director for the Joint Palestine Appeal.

organised force inside the factory has been smashed. At the beginning of the strike in November 1965, there were four shop-stewards: Atwal Singh, S. S. Khera, Ajmir Singh and a university-trained Convenor, N. S. Hundal. At the end of the strike only Khera and Atwal Singh were prepared to return to the factory. Shortly after the resumption of work in January, Atwal Singh returned to India because a brother had been killed in the India–Pakistan fighting. The sole remaining shop-steward carried on alone until June, when he became ill; on his return to the factory, in early August, he was told that his old job was not available. He was offered an alternative, which meant a smaller pay packet and less pleasant conditions. He refused to go back on this basis and the Southall branch of the T.G.W.U. is still pressing his case for victimisation pay.

Thus today there is not one shop-steward inside the factory, the large body of inarticulate Punjabi workers remain leaderless and impotent, and in the present economic situation unwilling to take any further initiative.

A MATTER OF TRADE UNIONISM, NOT RACE

The point that was lost by many of the journalists reporting this strike by exotic-looking figures living in the greyness of a London industrial suburb was that it was basically a labour dispute, complicated by the fact that the overwhelming majority of the strikers were Punjabis, and that in addition it also involved the small Pakistani community in Southall. Before the dispute in 1965, the firm of Woolf's employed about 800 workers; the unskilled work in the factory was done by Punjabis, Pakistanis, West Indians, a small group of local women and a handful of Irishmen. The nature of the work at Woolf's, which makes rubber accessories of the motor car industry, is unpleasant, dirty and laborious and, although after the Second World War the management was able to use demobilised Polish labour for a few years, they ran into difficulties thereafter. In the early 1950s the growing inflow of Punjabis to Britain was tapped by a personnel officer who had worked with Sikhs during his military service; this provided another more lasting solution to labour problems at the factory.

The firm of Woolf's had moved into Southall in the early 1930s. At that time it was able to employ people from the idle coalfields of South Wales and County Durham. The firm's attitude towards trade union organisation can best be expressed in the words of one of its directors: 'This is a family firm. We don't need a union.' As a well-known local trade unionist said: 'Woolf's has always been regarded as a black spot. In the thirties its labour force was made up of people desperate for a job.' In 1940 a union branch was formed inside the factory by the General and Municipal Workers' Union, but it petered out during the War. When Mr. Gwilym Evans, a staunch trade unionist and one of the organisers of the 1940 branch, returned to the firm after 1945 after demobilisation, the firm preferred to pay him for the statutory six months without letting him back into the factory.

In 1960 a serious attempt was made to organise the Indians through the efforts of two local trade unionists, Mr. Len Choulerton of the A.E.U. and the local district officer of the T.G.W.U. responsible for General Workers,

Mr. Danny Evans. The firm completely ignored correspondence with the T.G.W.U. and, although over 300 workers were paid-up members in the factory, the firm's refusal to confer recognition led to the break-up of the union.

At this time the unskilled workers were working a 45-hour week and being paid a minimum rate of four shillings per hour. The T.G.W.U. called in the Ministry of Labour to mediate, but the firm pursued its policy of refusing recognition. The Punjabis were unwilling to strike, the membership began to lapse and the organisation faded away.

WOOLF'S WORKERS ORGANISE SUCCESSFULLY

More than three years went by before another attempt—and this time a successful one—was made to organise Punjabis at Woolf's. The decisive factor in 1964 was the intervention of the Indian Workers' Association (Southall), an organisation which hitherto had concentrated its energies on cultural and welfare objectives. For years the I.W.A.'s leaders had been fed with a continuous stream of complaints about bribery at the firm, tales of poor conditions and exploitation of Indian workers. The leadership of the I.W.A. was composed of men of different political views, Communists, Socialists and traditionalists, but all were united in the belief that the Indian workers at Woolf's should be unionised and should not stand outside the British trade union movement. In 1963 there was a conjunction of factors which led to the successful assault on this anti-union citadel. Five members of the I.W.A. executive were working on the shop floor and the then president of the I.W.A., Mr. Sardul Singh Gill, was a young, energetic, experienced political leader.

Some members of the I.W.A. executive were also in close touch with the local Communist Party branch and the party played some part in encouraging the Indians to organise, and in providing trade union contacts who might be able to help them. The most important advice given to the Indians was that organisation of the workers at Woolf's had to be launched from outside the factory. Previous experience with the company had shown clearly that the employers did not want a union, and were likely to use all the power at their disposal to destroy a new one. One factor which was crucial to the creation of a union at the factory was that of an educated and experienced leadership, and by 1963 this was no longer a problem.

A deputation of the Indian community's leaders went to the district officer, Mr. Danny Evans, explained the position to him and asked for enrolment forms. For weeks local trade unionists and members of the I.W.A. executive campaigned on the doorstep after working-hours to convince Punjabi workers of the need for union organisation. Despite the conditions at the factory, it was a difficult task to rouse many of the workers. Many had experienced the fiasco of 1960 and believed that the management was too wily to be overcome, while others feared possible intimidation from the management; there was, however, a third category of people who had a vested interest in the perpetuation of the existing state of affairs.

These men were members of a bribery ring at the factory. The existence of bribery is simply explained. The great majority of Punjabis who came to Southall were peasants who came from an environment where the passing of 'gifts' to the civil service bureaucracy is customary. Many of the immigrants were quite unable to speak intelligible English. The first step in their new life was to seek out fellow Punjabis who could advise them to get accommodation and jobs. Many paid up to £20 for an introduction to 'someone' at the factory. The higher echelons of management at Woolf's have always been against such procedures but were powerless to act because the Indians themselves sanctioned the system. This was the situation ten years ago, although today, as a result of managerial intervention and possibly of a change in Indian attitudes, bribery in the factory is almost non-existent. Once a man had got into the factory there was then the question of passing 'gifts' to get on to the better-paid jobs, or those jobs where one could work long hours of overtime. Some unscrupulous foremen were quite happy to fall in with the Indians' requests.

A strong union was a threat to such practices—hence the cold response of some Indians to the idea of a union. The natural conservatism of many of the workers was another unfavourable factor. In 1963 the Punjabis were by far the largest ethnic group in the factory—a source of both strength and weakness. Large numbers meant in practice ethnic solidarity, but small groups of Pakistanis, West Indians and English women held aloof. The Punjabis had taken the initiative and it was therefore considered by the other groups to be an 'Indians' Union'.

PROTRACTED CAMPAIGN AND CAPITULATION—1964

After weeks of campaigning for members, a meeting was finally called by the Southall branch of the T.G.W.U. and a list of 452 members with their up-to-date contributions handed over to union officials. The management was approached by letter giving details of the union membership. The firm began to pursue their old tactics of vacillation and dilatoriness. The Ministry of Labour was called in to use its good offices to bring the two sides together. The firm remained reluctant to recognise the union. It sent its personnel officer to see the president of the I.W.A., Mr. Gill, to dissuade him from supporting the idea of a union. Mr. Gill was told that the firm was paying good wages, conditions could be improved and a union was, therefore, unnecessary. Mr. Gill for his part was determined that there should be a union. On 20 January 1964, Danny Evans on behalf of his union wrote to the management; there was no reply. On 30 January another letter was sent, this time by 'recorded delivery'. On 6 February a letter was sent by the Chief Industrial Relations Officer of the Ministry of Labour to the firm. On 7 February the firm wrote to Mr. Evans: 'In reply to your letter of 30th January we are not aware that any of our employees are members of your union and we cannot therefore suggest that any good purpose would be served by the meeting you suggest.'

The next step taken by the workers' leaders was to call a general meeting on 22 February 1964, to hear union officials and plan the next stage of the campaign. The firm's resistance crumbled and a formal agreement was signed with the T.G.W.U. in April 1964 granting the union official recognition, an event which was the outcome of many years of struggle at the factory. The signing of an agreement in April was a great victory for all workers at Woolf's, but unfortunately it was only a victory in a campaign that had yet to be decisively won.

From April onwards there were a series of stoppages, 'go-slow' tactics and one-day strikes. The Punjabis were showing their strength and the firm its inability to come to terms with the new situation. In October–November 1964, there was a 20-day stoppage at the factory, which ended with the firm capitulating and the workers going back to work with their demands met.

What had official recognition meant for the workers at Woolf's? The working week was reduced from 45 to 42 hours and the basic rate of pay was increased by sixpence an hour. But the firm still refused to allow a union officer on the shop floor to inspect working conditions. The shop-stewards were being warned by Mr. Evans against what he regarded as hasty action and he had advised against the 20-day stoppage. The Punjabis had, however, won a significant victory by pressing hard with their new-found strength.

THE TEN MEN

Between May and August 1965, the management sacked ten men, including a shop-steward. The management maintained that the men were 'undesirables', but from the shop floor this seemed to be a campaign waged to weed out militants. Moreover, a procedural agreement had been signed between the firm and the union about the procedure to be adopted in dismissing workers, and this was interpreted by most of the Punjabis to mean that the management no longer had a right of dismissal. As Mr. Evans told me: 'The Indians thought because of union recognition the management had no right of dismissal.' It was one thing to draw up an agreement which itemised the logical process of dispute but quite another to ensure that its clauses would be interpreted in a flexible manner.

The cases of the ten men were taken up by the union, but weeks turned into months without a clear sign of what had been decided by the management and the union. 'Go-slow' tactics were adopted in the factory and many union members began to withhold their contributions. A situation which might have been cooled through decisive action was allowed to simmer and finally boil over.

It was the suspension of these ten men and not the suspension of Mukhtiar Singh that created the climate which produced the explosion on 30 November 1965, when the night shift walked out, followed by the day shift. In the ultimatum drawn up by the shop-stewards on 30 November for presentation to the management, there is no mention of Mukhtiar Singh, the man singled out by the Press as the *cause célèbre*. The truth is that Mukhtiar Singh was known by his workmates as an unreliable figure who had been involved in various altercations with the management. The shop-stewards recognised that, if they were to call out their fellow workers, they would have to find some other grievances on which to base the stoppage. This they did when they called for a closed shop and an increase in pay for Lister truck drivers.

The shop-stewards' action was dictated by their hearts rather than their reason. The time was not opportune for a strike. Woolf's produce accessories for the motor car industry and their trade is at its slackest period before Christmas. Mr. Fred Howell, the new district officer responsible for Woolf's, was in favour of a stoppage to cover the period of suspension imposed on Mukhtiar Singh. The stoppage was intended as a warning to the management. The shop-stewards nevertheless drew up their ultimatum without the knowledge of the district officer and made demands which had to be withdrawn at his insistence. Mr. Howell was well aware of the past history at the factory and promised the Convenor his support, but the support of a sympathetic district official is not the same as 'official support' from the union, which can only be sanctioned by the regional secretary. 'Official support' means in practice strike benefit and this was never given to the strikers during the strike or subsequently. At the beginning of the stoppage most of the Punjabis were lapsed members of the union and even the Convenor was technically out of the union because of non-payment of dues. Union inactivity over the ten men had undermined the men's faith in the union and they had remonstrated by withholding their dues.

THE STRIKE WAS NEVER OFFICIAL

From the beginning of the strike most of the men on the shop floor seem to have been under the impression that they would get 'official support' from the union. When the day shift arrived at the factory gates on the morning of 1 December, a steward told them that the stoppage would be given 'official support' within a few days. From the beginning of the stoppage Mr. Howell, by word of mouth and practical example, did everything he could to have the stoppage put on an official basis. An emergency meeting of the National Joint Industrial Council of the Rubber Industry recommended that the firm take back all the strikers pending negotiation about the outstanding grievance—the case of Mukhtiar Singh. The firm refused to accept the formula for resumption of work. They were willing to take back all the men on their terms—that is on the basis of re-employment, which would mean that they could eliminate men whom they regarded as trouble-makers.

For six weeks the great majority of the strikers fought on under the impression that they would be given 'official support'. The stewards and the district officer had miscalculated about two important points: (a) the truculence of the management; and (b) the reaction of the regional secretary of the T.G.W.U., Mr. Bert Fry, the only man who had the status and authority to sanction strike pay. Mr. Fry, however, refused to sanction strike benefit, on the grounds that most of the strikers were no longer members of the union. Union officials at local level were for sustaining the strike by the payment of benefits. At regional level the attitude was different and this gap was never bridged throughout the strike.

Another important factor which militated against the success of the strike was what appears to have been a conflict between the industrial and administrative wings of the union, personified in the opposing views of Mr. Bert Fry and Mr. Bert Ray, respectively Regional Secretary and National Officer.

At one point during the strike Mr. Ray made a statement in Southall in which he said he was ready to give the stoppage 'official support'. If this phrase 'official support' is to be interpreted as meaning financial aid for the strikers, Mr. Ray had neither the authority to promise such support nor the power to provide it. Mr. Fry insists that he was in favour throughout the dispute of 'industrial support', which apparently means enlisting the aid of union members in firms dealing with Woolf's to support the strikers by refusing to handle goods. The fact is that these terminological distinctions, which would sorely try experienced English trade unionists, mean little or nothing to the Punjabis.

Notwithstanding all the difficulties already mentioned, the strikers were also contending with some 'fifth column' activity. During the six-week-long stoppage, there were various occasions when lorries crossed the picket lines. While the pickets were telling the drivers that the strike was official—management representatives were handing the drivers pieces of paper with the name of an official at regional headquarters and a prepared question, and insisting that the stoppage was unofficial. We asked Mr. Bert Ray about these slips of paper and the official concerned. 'The management had somehow cottoned on to the fact that there was a distinction between "industrial support" and "official support". How they did that we do not know and this has caused us some concern about the leakage of information. . . .' The official concerned could only give one answer to the particular question and that was that it was not an 'official strike' but that it was receiving 'industrial support'.

For six weeks 500 men fought on despite the lack of 'official support', which they thought would come. They were sustained by their community, in money and goods. After the strike had ended, the union recommended that a lump sum should be paid to the strikers who were in benefit at the time of the strike, i.e. those who were paid up. Up to Christmas 1966, to our knowledge, not a single penny had been paid out. No doubt reasons can be produced for this delay, but to the man on the shop floor, whether he is English or Indian, it means false hopes and broken promises.

SOME LESSONS OF THE WOOLF'S DISPUTE

One lesson that emerged from the Woolf's dispute was that of the poor communication between union officials and their members. This is an inherent fault in all large organisations, but in this case it was accentuated by the fact that the overwhelming majority of strikers were not articulate in English or in the subtleties of trade union practice. The T.G.W.U. in recent months has been involved in strikes at Preston, Greenford and Southall in which Asian workers were predominant. Is it not time for the policy-makers of this great union to recognise that they have special responsibilities towards their Asian members? Many of them need preferential or at least specialised treatment. One way to guarantee it would be to have an officer in the union with particular responsibilities for the education and training of Asian trade unionists who live in our midst.

In contrast to the T.G.W.U. the small Bakers' Union, which has many Indian and Pakistani members in the Southall district, has gone to the length of printing handbills with union information in Urdu and Hindi, and perhaps as a result, has a far better record in labour relations than its more powerful brother. For a union of its size and resources, the T.G.W.U. seems to be doing very little to integrate its Asian members, although in the late 1940s it gave a lead to other trade unions by a massive recruitment drive among Polish ex-servicemen and the appointment of a full-time organising secretary of Polish branches (needed at that time because most Poles were still in separate camps and hostels).

(Supplement to Institute of Race Relations *Newsletter*, January 1967.)

APPENDIX IX

NOTES FOR GUIDANCE ON THE FORMATION OF A VOLUNTARY LIAISON COMMITTEE

The main prerequisites for such a committee are:

(i) The sponsorship of the mayor and the interest of the local authority.

(ii) Full participation by the whole community, both host and immigrant.

(iii) A widely representative basis, non-political and non-sectarian, and embracing both voluntary and statutory organizations.

1. First Steps

The sponsoring body for a committee of this kind might be a Council of Social Service, a group of individuals, or the local authority itself. In any case, the initial procedure and the final structure of the committee would be much the same.

As a first step, it is advisable to gain the interest of a number of councillors and other leading citizens and organizations in the town or borough. Then a public meeting should be called, preferably by the mayor, to put the idea to them. It should be emphasized at every stage that this is *not a committee to serve the interests of one section of the community, but a committee to promote racial harmony. It is therefore beneficial to all.*

2. Representation

In addition to the Mayor, Leader of the Council, Town Clerk, and other local authority representatives (both members and officers), such as the Housing Manager, Medical Officer of Health, Public Relations Officer, etc., representatives from a wide variety of organizations should be invited to the public meeting. The following list serves for example and is not necessarily comprehensive:

Political Organizations

All parties represented.

Professional Organizations, Service Organizations, Social Clubs, etc.

Rotary; Inner Wheel; Round Table; Toc H; British Legion; Trades Council; Chamber of Commerce; Townswomen's Guild; Women's Co-operative Guild; Working Men's Clubs; Youth organizations of all kinds; International, Commonwealth, and immigrant associations of all kinds.

Social Service

VOLUNTARY	STATUTORY
Council of Social Service	Probation Service
Council of Churches	Children's Department
Citizens' Advice Bureau	Welfare Officer
Family Welfare Association	Youth Organizer
Moral Welfare	Manager of Employment Exchange
W.V.S.	National Assistance Board
	The Police

In addition, all denominations of the Church should be invited and co-operation should also be sought from anyone with community interests: local doctors, magistrates, solicitors, large local firms, etc. Real interest is not of course forthcoming from every organization, but an effort should be made to keep representation broadly based. In addition, enthusiastic individuals are a great asset, whether they represent an organization or not.

There may already be immigrant associations in the area which can be approached for representation, but if not, the office of the appropriate High Commissions may be able to supply some names, as also may the National Committee for Commonwealth Immigrants.

3. CONSTITUTION

An Executive Committee should be elected from among members of the proposed committee and it can then draw up its constitution. This should ensure adequate local authority as well as voluntary representation. Allowance should also be made for co-options as the work proceeds. A model constitution which may act as a useful guide is available from the National Committee for Commonwealth Immigrants.

The committee's terms of reference should be wide, covering all possible ways of working towards racial integration. No set plan can be drawn up at the outset as this work is essentially empirical. Useful lines of inquiry are: assessment of the number and nationalities of coloured people in the area, housing problems, social activities, informal language tuition, participation of immigrants in the civic life of the town, employment problems, reduction of racial tension where it exists.

4. TITLE

The title of the committee should combine a clear definition of its liaison function with an indication of its all-embracing nature. There may be local reasons for differences of emphasis and these are reflected in the two titles increasingly considered to be the most appropriate: (*Name of Town*) *Commonwealth Citizens' Committee*, and (*Name of Town*) *Council for Community Relations*. (*Name of Town*) *International Friendship Council* is also popular, and (*Name of Town*) *Liaison Committee* might be considered too. At all events, any suggestions of 'Welfare' should be avoided, as should reference to colour.

5. FINANCE

In the Government White Paper, *Immigration from the Commonwealth* (Cmnd 2739, Part III, *Integration*), Government funds were made available through the National Committee for Commonwealth Immigrants for the employment of a full-time official for the committee, the local authority being expected to assist with premises and secretariat.

A grant of £1,500 per annum towards the salary of a full-time official is available. Further details of the procedure for obtaining grant-aid can be obtained from the National Committee for Commonwealth Immigrants.

The General Secretary to the National Committee for Commonwealth

Immigrants, Miss Nadine Peppard, will be glad to assist with further information and advice.

April 1967

National Committee for Commonwealth Immigrants,
6 Tilney Street, London, W.1.
(Tel.: Mayfair 8901)

THE DUTIES OF A LIAISON OFFICER

Paragraph 75 of Cmnd 2739, *Immigration from the Commonwealth*, states: 'The Government consider it of the first importance that each voluntary liaison committee should be served by a trained, full-time, paid official who should be the direct servant of the committee. As evidence of its wish to give tangible support to the committees, the Government is prepared, in certain circumstances, to make a grant towards the salary of such an official available to each voluntary liaison committee through the National Committee. The condition will be that the voluntary liaison committee concerned can demonstrate to the satisfaction of the National Committee that the person they propose to employ is fully competent to carry out the particular work which he or she will be called upon to perform. We hope that the local authority concerned will provide adequate office accommodation and secretarial support for the official appointed. In these circumstances, voluntary liaison committees already employing a suitable officer will be eligible to apply for the proposed grant. It will be one of the functions of the National Committee to assist in the recruitment and training of suitable officers where they are not otherwise available to the local committee.'

It is important that the stress should not be on welfare or individual casework, but rather on liaison between the immigrant and every section of the host community, with regard to social services, both statutory and voluntary leisure activities and full participation in the life of the town or city. In order to achieve this, the liaison officer needs the full backing and co-operation of the local authority.

In addition, several cities and towns have appointed officers with specific welfare duties, some to Public Health Departments, some to Education Departments, or some to the Town Clerk's Departments (of Information). The Local Authority, of course, is responsible for paying the salaries of these officers.

The duties of a liaison officer can therefore be defined as follows:

1. To promote and assist in programme of public education for positive and harmonious relationships within the community.
2. To be the focal point for inquiries of any kind from the host community in connexion with problems or relationships in general with immigrants.
3. To work in full co-operation with Central and Local Government Departments (e.g. Ministry of Labour, National Assistance Board, Health, Education and Children's Departments, Probation Service, etc.) and the Commonwealth High Commission offices.
4. To participate in the activities of immigrant organizations and give help where required.

5. To assist the immigrant to use existing social services and facilities, and where necessary to form a link between the two.
6. To be available to social workers, officials of all kinds, etc., as an adviser on special aspects of immigrant problems.
7. To participate in the widest possible range of social activities designed to draw immigrants and host community together.
8. To take advantage of opportunities (e.g. at national conferences) to meet liaison officers and workers from other areas, to increase his/her knowledge and understanding of the problems, and the way in which these are being tackled in other areas.
9. To take appropriate action against discrimination wherever it occurs.
10. To act as secretary to the Committee.
11. To be responsible for the organization of the Committee's office.

It is clear from the above that the job of liaison officer is an exacting one, calling for energy and initiative and the willingness to give far more than the usual working hours. It is essential that the officer should regularly attend a wide variety of evening and week-end meetings, and social activities, and become a familiar figure in the city, in whom both immigrants and host community can have confidence when difficulties arise. This is a job which cannot be done in the confines of an office or of regular office hours.

(These notes were prepared in early 1967 by the National Committee for Commonwealth Immigrants.)

APPENDIX X

THE HIGH COMMISSIONS

1. Indian High Commission

The High Commission of India maintains contact with the Indian community in the United Kingdom through its Consular Department in London and its three Regional Offices in Birmingham, Liverpool, and Glasgow (each under the charge of an Assistant Commissioner).

In view of the large increase of Indian nationals in this country during recent years, the High Commission has decided to appoint three Welfare Officers to undertake fieldwork as an experimental measure. Two of the three have been appointed, one in London, one in Birmingham.

The offices of the Consular Department and the Assistant Commissioners are situated at the following places:

First Secretary (Consular)
High Commission of India
India House,
Aldwych, London W.C.2
Telephone: TEMple Bar 8484

Assistant Commissioner
High Commission of India
86 New Street, Birmingham 2
Telephone: MIDland 0366

Assistant Commissioner
High Commission of India
146 North Street, Glasgow C.3
Telephone: CENtral 2801

Assistant Commissioner
High Commission of India
4 Rodney Street, Liverpool
Telephone: ROYal 6630

The welfare of the student community is looked after by the Education Department:

Education Department
High Commission of India
India House, London W.C.2
Telephone: TEMple Bar 8484

2. The High Commission of Pakistan

The Labour Division of the High Commission, headed by the Labour Attaché, is responsible for work among Pakistani nationals living in Britain. There are six liaison officers: two for London; one for Birmingham, the

Midlands and S. Wales; one for Bradford and the North-East; one for Liverpool, the North-West and N. Wales; and one for Scotland, the North of England and N. Ireland. Their addresses are as follows:

The Labour Division
39 Lowndes Square, London S.W.1
Telephone: BELgravia 2044

Victoria Building
5 Corporation Street, Birmingham 2
Telephone: MIDland 5391

Refuge Buildings, Second Floor
9 Sunbridge Road, Bradford, Yorkshire
Telephone: Bradford 25348

Fowler Buildings
7 Victoria Street, Liverpool 2
Telephone: CENtral 2025

58 Royal Exchange Square
Glasgow C.1

There is also a Pakistani Government representative in Leeds. His office is at:

CMA House
3rd Floor
King Street, Leeds 1
Telephone : 36439

The Labour Attaché and liaison officers are active in five main spheres:

1. They assist trade unions, employers, social workers, employment exchanges, health and education authorities who are dealing with Pakistanis and want to know more about their background.
   (For instance a liaison officer may be asked what food should be provided in a factory canteen used by Pakistanis; or, again, hospitals with Pakistani patients may get in touch with the High Commission about dietary sheets.)
2. They advise and assist the immigrant, who, for example, might be having trouble with getting a job or is in some personal difficulty.
3. They give talks and lectures to schools, societies, or groups who want to know more about Pakistan and Pakistanis. The Press Attaché at the High Commission in London can also provide films and literature on Pakistan.
4. They encourage and support, where possible, the formation of local Pakistani associations.
5. They aim at fostering goodwill between the immigrant and host communities; this involves general liaison work with voluntary and statutory organizations.

3. The High Commission of Jamaica

The Welfare Division of the Jamaican High Commission is active in three spheres:

(i) Reception of Immigrants

At the port of disembarkation (usually Southampton and London Airport) members of staff of the division are present to help newly arrived immigrants. This usually means providing information about trains and travel facilities; advice with baggage problems; customs declarations, etc.

(ii) Information and Advice

General advice and information is given to immigrants to help them adapt to their new environment. This is largely to get them acquainted with the agencies and services such as the National Health Service, labour exchanges, housing authorities, and welfare services generally, to which they have recourse in times of need.

The Welfare Division is an important link between Jamaicans and the various voluntary and statutory social services in the country. Thus teachers, probation officers, children's officers, and hospital matrons, for example, frequently find it helpful to discuss problems affecting Jamaicans with officers of the division.

(iii) Social Integration

A most important activity of the Welfare Division is to help to stimulate understanding and acceptance for West Indians who have come to this country. This is done in three main ways:

(a) Through effective liaison with all bodies concerned with immigrants—local authorities, welfare departments, the police, consultative committees, etc.
(b) Through positive practical action for aiding integration in the areas of housing, education, or employment.
(c) Through close contact with the many West Indian community associations in the country. Members of the commission staff frequently attend their meetings, which provide a valuable opportunity for disseminating information amongst immigrants to help them to adjust to the accepted customs of their street or neighbourhood. For example, many associations have frequently discussed, and on their own initiative, circularized members about complaints from the host community, and suggested action which could be taken to reduce friction between neighbours.

Much of this work for social integration is undertaken by three Regional Welfare Officers:

The Northern Regional Welfare Officer:
Falkner House
Falkner Street, Manchester 1

The Midlands Regional Welfare Officer:
38A Paradise Street, Birmingham
Telephone: MIDland 1691

(The Midlands Region Welfare Officer now deals only with the Midlands.) London, South-East and South-West Region of England and Wales are covered by the third Regional Welfare Officer. He operates from the main offices of the Welfare Division:

32 Bruton Street, London W.1
Telephone: GROsvenor 3871

4. The High Commission for Trinidad and Tobago

The consular services of the High Commission are available to all nationals of Trinidad and Tobago resident in this country. The High Commission has one office:

Office of the High Commissioner for Trinidad and Tobago
51 South Audley Street, London W.1
Telephone: HYDe Park 2601

Assistance of all kinds is offered to Trinidad and Tobago nationals by this office.

1. Issue of passports and Emergency Certificates.
2. Information on the Immigration and Visa Regulations of Trinidad and Tobago.
3. Welfare officers, probation officers, etc., from the host community receive the co-operation of the High Commission whenever they are involved with someone from Trinidad and Tobago and request assistance.
4. An officer of the High Commission visits nationals in prisons and attends at Magistrate Court hearings.
5. The repatriation of sick and destitute nationals.

The Information Section of the High Commission provides lecturers to address conferences, schools, women's groups, etc.

Books and pamphlets on Trinidad and Tobago as well as documentary films can be obtained from the High Commission.

5. Commission in the United Kingdom for East Caribbean Governments

Address: 10 Haymarket, London S.W.1
Telephone WHItehall 7902.

The Commission represents the governments of the following islands of the Caribbean:

Antigua, Barbados, Dominica, Grenada, Montserrat, St. Kitts-Nevis-Anguilla, St. Lucia.

The main functions of the Welfare Division are as follows:

(a) Reception.
Meeting and advising new arrivals at the port of entry.
(b) Passports.
(c) Location of individuals.
Tracing persons on behalf of relatives residing in the West Indies. Queries about dependent relatives in the West Indies.
(d) Children and Young Persons.
(i) Liaison with children's departments about children in care. (ii) Advice to probation officers, schools, etc. (iii) Adoption queries. (iv) Matters relating to children coming from the West Indies to the United Kingdom.
(e) Sponsored sc emes (concerning the recruitment of workers).
(f) General.
Industrial, matrimonial and accommodation problems, unmarried mothers, sick and destitute persons, deceased persons' estates, prison and hospital visiting where necessary, repatriations and deportations, etc.

The Commission is represented on many of the committees concerned with the problems of immigrants in the United Kingdom.

6. The Guyana High Commission

Prior to 26 May 1966, there was a British Guiana Commission in London dealing mainly with students, nurses, and Government officers on training courses and channelling trade and other inquiries to Guyana. Subsequently, the status was raised to that of a High Commission for Guyana in the U.K. on the attainment of independence.

The High Commissioner is Sir Lionel Luckhoo, C.B.E., Q.C., who is also High Commissioner for Barbados. In addition to a head of Chancery who is responsible for the general organization and work of the High Commission, as well as the students, nurses, and welfare sections, there are two Second Secretaries and a Third Secretary responsible for trade, industry, economics, finance, protocol, consular, and information matters.

The address of the High Commission is 28 Cockspur Street, London, S.W.1, but the Students, Nurses, and Welfare Sections are situated at 229 High Street, Kensington, London, W.8.

BIBLIOGRAPHY

Bibliographies

Goldman, R. J., *and* Taylor, F. M., *Coloured Immigrant Children: a survey of research studies and literature on their educational problems and potential —in Britain*, in *Educational Research*, Vol. 8, no. 3, June 1966

Grayshon, M. C., *and* Houghton, V. P., *Initial Bibliography of Immigration and Race*, Nottingham, Institute of Education, University of Nottingham, February 1966

Great Britain, Warren Spring Laboratory, *Register of Research in the Human Sciences, 1959/61, 1960/63, 1962/65*, London, H.M.S.O.

Joint Conference on Research in Race Relations in Britain, London, 27 March 1961, *Report*, in *Race*, Vol. 3, no. 1, November 1961

Leeds, University, Institute of Education, *Teaching of English to Immigrant Children: a booklist*, Leeds, Institute of Education, 1966

National Book League, *English for Immigrant Children*, selected by J. C. Young, *and others*, for the London Association of Teachers of English to Pupils from Overseas, London, N.B.L., 1967

National Committee for Commonwealth Immigrants, *A Bibliography of Teaching Materials: section on language*, London, N.C.C.I., July 1966

Richmond, A. H., *Britain*, in *International Social Science Bulletin*, Vol. 10, no. 3, 1958

Sivanandan, A., *compiler*, *Coloured Immigrants in Britain: a select bibliography*, London, Institute of Race Relations, 1967

——, *Race Relations and Education: a reading list*, London, Institute of Race Relations, 1967

—— *and* Scruton, M., *compilers*, Register of Research on Commonwealth Immigrants in Britain, London, Institute of Race Relations, Library, March 1967

General

Banton, M., *The Coloured Quarter*, London, Cape, 1955

——, *White and Coloured: the behaviour of British people towards coloured immigrants*, London, Cape, 1959

Beetham, D., *Immigrant School-leavers and the Youth Employment Service in Birmingham*, London, Institute of Race Relations, 1968 (Special Series)

British Medical Association, *Medical Examination of Immigrants: report of the working party*, London, B.M.A., 1965

Brocklebank-Fowler, C., Bland, C., *and* Farmer, T., *Commonwealth Immigration*, London, Bow Publications, October 1965

Burgin, T. *and* Edson, P., *Spring Grove: the education of immigrant children*, London, Oxford University Press, for I.R.R., 1967

Burney, E., *Housing on Trial: a study of immigrants and local government*, London, Oxford University Press, for I.R.R., 1967

Butterworth, E., *Immigrants in West Yorkshire*, London, Institute of Race Relations, 1967 (Special Series)

Calley, M. J. C., *God's People: West Indian Pentecostal sects in England*, London, Oxford University Press, for I.R.R., 1965

Campaign Against Racial Discrimination, *Memorandum of Evidence presented to the Royal Commission on Trade Unions and Employers' Associations*, London, C.A.R.D., 1966

Chater, A., *Race Relations in Britain*, London, Lawrence & Wishart, 1966

Church Assembly, Board for Social Responsibility, *Together in Britain: a Christian handbook on race relations*, London, Church Information Office, 1960

Ciba Foundation, Symposium on Immigration, Medical and Social Aspects, London, December 1965, *Immigration, Medical and Social Aspects*, edited by G. E. W. Wolstenholme and M. O'Connor, London, Churchill, 1966

Collins, S., *Coloured Minorities in Britain: studies in British race relations based on African, West Indian, and Asiatic immigrants*, London, Lutterworth, 1957

Conference on Racial Equality in Employment, London, February 1967, *Report*, London. N.C.C.I., 1967

Conservative Commonwealth Council Conference, London, 1965, *Commonwealth Migration*, prepared by P. Wall, M. Chandler, J. Moorhouse, J. Russell, and T. Zinkin

Coxon, T., *Second Class Citizens*, London, Independent Labour Party, 1965

'The Dark Million', in *The Times*, 18–29 January 1965

Davison, R. B., *Black British: immigrants to England*, London, Oxford University Press, for I.R.R., 1966

——, *Commonwealth Immigrants*, London, Oxford University Press, for I.R.R., 1964

——, *West Indian Migrants: social and economic facts of migration from the West Indies*, London, Oxford University Press, for I.R.R., 1962

Deakin, N. (ed.), *Colour and the British Electorate, 1964: six case studies*, London, Pall Mall Press, for I.R.R., 1965

Derrick, J., *Teaching English to Immigrants*, London, Longmans, 1966

Desai, R., *Indian Immigrants in Britain*, London, Oxford University Press, for I.R.R., 1963

Dr. Barnardo's Homes, *Racial Integration and Barnardo's: report of a working party*, Hertford, D.B.H., 1966

Downes, D. M., *The Delinquent Solution: a study in sub-cultural theory*, London, Routledge & Kegan Paul, 1966

Economist Intelligence Unit, *Immigrant Children in British Schools*, London, E.I.U., September 1964

——, *Studies on Immigration from the Commonwealth:*
1: Basic Statistics
2: The Immigrant Communities
3: Social Integration and Housing
4: The Employment of Immigrants
5: The Effect of the Commonwealth Immigrants Act, 1962
London, E.I.U., 1961–63

Egginton, J., *They Seek a Living*, London, Hutchinson, 1957

Elton, G., *1st Baron Elton of Headington, The Unarmed Invasion: a survey of Afro-Asian immigration*, London, Geoffrey Bles, 1965

Evans, P. C. *and* Le Page, R. B., *The Education of West Indian Immigrant Children*, London, N.C.C.I., 1967

FitzHerbert, K., *West Indian Children in London*, London, G. Bell, 1967

Foot, P., *Immigration and Race in British Politics*, Harmondsworth, Penguin Books, 1965

Glass, R. *and* Pollins, H., *Newcomers: the West Indian in London*, London, Allen & Unwin, for Centre for Urban Studies, 1960

Glass, R. *and* Westergaard, J., *London's Housing Needs: statement of evidence to the Committee on Housing in Greater London*, London, Centre for Urban Studies, 1965

Goldman, R. J., *Research and the Teaching of Immigrant Children*, London, N.C.C.I., 1967

Goudie, J., *and others*, *Strangers Within*, London, Fabian Society, November 1965

Great Britain, Acts and Bills, Race Relations Act 1965, London, H.M.S.O., 1965

——, Race Relations Act 1965 (amendment) Bill, London, H.M.S.O., June 1966

Great Britain, Committee on Housing in Greater London, *Report*, London, H.M.S.O., 1965

Great Britain, Commonwealth Immigrants Advisory Council:
Report, July 1963
Second Report, February 1964
Third Report, September 1964
Fourth Report, October 1965
London, H.M.S.O.

Great Britain, General Register Office, *Commonwealth Immigrants in the Conurbations*, London, H.M.S.O., 1965

Great Britain, Home Office, *Admission of Commonwealth Citizens to the United Kingdom*, London, H.M.S.O., February 1967

——, Commonwealth Immigrants Act 1962: control of immigration statistics 1962/63–1966, London, H.M.S.O., 1962–67

——, Committee on Immigration Appeals, *Report*, London, H.M.S.O., August 1967

Great Britain, Ministry of Education, *English for Immigrants*, London, H.M.S.O., 1963

Great Britain, Ministry of Labour, Commonwealth Immigrants Act 1962: notice to prospective employers, London, H.M.S.O., 1962

Great Britain, Oversea Migration Board, *Reports 1954–61*, London, H.M.S.O., 1954–61. Subsequent issues entitled 'Statistics'.

Great Britain, Prime Minister, *Immigration from the Commonwealth*, London, H.M.S.O., August 1965

Griffiths, P., *A Question of Colour*, London, Leslie Frewin, 1966

Grigg, M., *The White Question*, London, Secker & Warburg, 1967

Hall, S., *The Young Englanders*, London, N.C.C.I., 1967

Hashmi, F., *The Pakistani Family in Britain* (2nd ed.), London, N.C.C.I., 1967

Hawkes, N., *Immigrant Children in British Schools*, London, Pall Mall Press, for I.R.R., 1966

Heineman, B. W., *The Politics of the Powerless: a study of the Campaign Against Racial Discrimination*, London, Oxford University Press, for I.R.R., forthcoming

Hepple, B., *The Position of Coloured Workers in British Industry*, London, N.C.C.I., 1967

Hill, C. S., *Black and White in Harmony: from a London minister's notebook*, London, Hodder & Stoughton, 1958

——, *How Colour Prejudiced is Britain?*, Gollancz, 1965

Hiro, D., *The Indian Family in Britain*, London, N.C.C.I., 1967

Hooper, R., *editor*, *Colour in Britain*, London, B.B.C., 1965

Huxley, E., *Back Street New Worlds: a look at immigrants in Britain*, London, Chatto & Windus, 1964

International Social Service, *Immigrants at London Airport and their Settlement in the Community*, London, I.S.S., June, 1967

Isis, *Race Prejudice: Smethwick*. *Issue of* 21 November 1964, No. 1477

Israel, W. H., *Colour and Community: a study of coloured immigrants and race relations in an industrial town*, Slough, Council of Social Service, 1964

James, H. E. O. *and* Tenen, C., *The Teacher was Black*, London, Heinemann, 1953

Jephcott, P., *A Troubled Area: notes on Notting Hill*, London, Faber, 1964

Lenton, J., *and others*, *Immigration, Race and Politics: a Birmingham view*, written by J. Lenton, N. Budgen, K. Clarke, London, Bow Publications, March 1966

Lester, A. *and* Deakin, N., *editors*, *Policies for Racial Equality*, London, Fabian Society, July 1967

Little, K. L., *Negroes in Britain: a study of racial relations in English Society*, London, Kegan Paul, 1947

London Council of Social Service, *Commonwealth Children in Britain*, London, National Council of Social Service, 1967

——, Immigrants Advisory Committee, *East Pakistanis in London: report of survey*, by Mrs. Mariyam Harris, London, L.C.S.S., 1967

McClintock, F. H., *Crimes of Violence*, London, Macmillan, 1963

McCowan, A., *Coloured Peoples in Britain*, London, Bow Group, 1952

Manchester University Liberal Society, Study Group, *Anti-immigrants organizations*, London, Union of Liberal Students, 1966

Marsh, P., *The Anatomy of a Strike: unions, employers, and Punjabi workers in a Southall factory*, London, Institute of Race Relations, 1967 (Special Series)

Maxwell, N., *The Power of Negro Action*, London, The Author, 1965

Milson, F., *Operation Integration: an enquiry into the experiences of West Indians living in Birmingham with particular reference to children and young people*, Birmingham, Westhill Training College, 1961

——, *Operation Integration Two: the coloured teenager in Birmingham, an enquiry conducted in 1966*, Birmingham, Westhill College of Education, September 1966

National Committee for Commonwealth Immigrants, *Areas of Special Housing Need*, London, N.C.C.I., May 1967

——, *Practical Suggestions for Teachers of Immigrant Children*, London, N.C.C.I., 1967

——, *The Second Generation: report of a conference at St. Edmund Hall, Oxford. 18–20 March 1966*, London, N.C.C.I., 1966

——, *Towards a Multi-racial Society*, London, N.C.C.I., 1967

National Union of Students, *Integration and the Student: memorandum to the Government Committee on Integration*, London, N.U.S., 1965

National Union of Teachers, *The N.U.T. view on the Education of Immigrants*, London, N.U.T., January 1967

Pannell, N. *and* Brockway, F., *Immigration: what is the answer? Two opposing views*, London, Routledge & Kegan Paul, 1965

Patterson, S., *editor*, *Immigrants in London: report of a study group set up by the London Council of Social Service*, London, National Council of Social Service, for L.C.S.S., 1964

——, *Dark Strangers: a sociological study of a recent West Indian migrant group in Brixton, South London*, London, Tavistock Publications, 1963,

——, *Immigrants in Industry*, London, Oxford University Press, for I.R.R., 1968.

Plebs, *Immigration. Issue of* December 1965

Political and Economic Planning *and* Research Services Ltd., *Racial Discrimination*, London, P.E.P., April 1967

Power, J., *Immigrants in school: a survey of administrative policies*, London, Councils and Education Press, 1967

Pressure for Economic and Social Toryism (P.E.S.T.), *Immigration and the Commonwealth*, London, Conservative Political Centre, 1965

Rex, J. *and* Moore, R., *Race, Community and Conflict: a study of Sparkbrook*, London, Oxford University Press, for I.R.R., 1967

Richmond, A. H., *Colour Prejudice in Britain: a study of West Indian Workers in Liverpool, 1942–51*, London, Routledge, 1954

——, The Colour Problem (new edition), London, Penguin Books, 1965

Ruck, S. K., *editor*, *The West Indian comes to England: a report prepared for the Trustees of the London Parochial Charities by the Family Welfare Association*, London, Routledge, 1960

Schools Council, *English for the Children of Immigrants*, London, H.M.S.O. 1967

Senior, C. *and* Manley, D., *A Report on Jamaican Migration to Great Britain to the Jamaica Executive Council*, Kingston (Jamaica) Govt. Printer, 1955

Silberman, L. *and* Spice, B., *Colour and Class in Six Liverpool Schools*, Liverpool, Liverpool University Press, for Social Science Department, University of Liverpool, June 1950

Singh, A. K., *Indian Students in Britain: a survey*, London, Asia Publishing House, 1964

Stephens, L., *Employment of Coloured Workers in the Birmingham Area*, London, Institute of Personnel Management, 1956

Tajfel, H. *and* Dawson, J. L., *editors*, *Disappointed Guests: essays by African,*

Asian and West Indian students, London, Oxford University Press, for I.R.R., 1965

Unesco, *The Positive Contribution by Immigrants*, Paris, U.N.E.S.C.O., 1955

Watson, A. R., *West Indian Workers in Britain*, London, Hodder & Stoughton, 1942

West Indian Standing Conference, London Region, *The Unsquare Deal: London's bus colour bar*, London, W.I.S.C., July 1967

Wickenden, J., *Colour in Britain*, London, Oxford University Press, for I.R.R., 1958

William Temple Association, *Coloured Immigrants in the United Kingdom*, London, N.C.C.I., 1967

Wright, P., *The Employment of Coloured Workers in British Industry*, Oxford University Press for I.R.R., forthcoming

Yudkin, S., *The Health and Welfare of the Immigrant Child*, London, N.C.C.I., 1965

——, *0–5: a report on the care of pre-school children*, London, National Society of Children's Nurseries, June 1967

INDEX